The Measure of All Minds

Are psychometric tests valid for a new reality of artificial intelligence systems, technology-enhanced humans, and hybrids yet to come? Are the Turing Test, the ubiquitous CAPTCHAs, and the various animal cognition tests the best alternatives? In this fascinating and provocative book, José Hernández-Orallo formulates major scientific questions, integrates the most significant research developments, and offers a vision of the universal evaluation of cognition.

By replacing the dominant anthropocentric stance with a universal perspective where living organisms are considered as a special case, long-standing questions in the evaluation of behavior can be addressed in a wider landscape. Can we derive task difficulty intrinsically? Is a universal g factor – a common general component for all abilities – theoretically possible? Using algorithmic information theory as a foundation, the book elaborates on the evaluation of perceptual, developmental, social, verbal and collective features and critically analyzes what the future of intelligence might look like.

JOSÉ HERNÁNDEZ-ORALLO is Professor of Information Systems and Computation at the Technical University of Valencia. He has published four books and more than a hundred articles and papers in artificial intelligence, machine learning, data mining, cognitive science, and information systems. His work in the area of machine intelligence evaluation has been covered by both scientific and popular outlets including The Economist and New Scientist. He pioneered the application of algorithmic information theory to the development of artificial intelligence tests.

The Measure of All Minds

Evaluating Natural and Artificial Intelligence

José Hernández-Orallo

CAMBRIDGE
UNIVERSITY PRESS

CAMBRIDGE
UNIVERSITY PRESS

Shaftesbury Road, Cambridge CB2 8EA, United Kingdom

One Liberty Plaza, 20th Floor, New York, NY 10006, USA

477 Williamstown Road, Port Melbourne, VIC 3207, Australia

314–321, 3rd Floor, Plot 3, Splendor Forum, Jasola District Centre, New Delhi – 110025, India

103 Penang Road, #05–06/07, Visioncrest Commercial, Singapore 238467

Cambridge University Press is part of Cambridge University Press & Assessment,
a department of the University of Cambridge.

We share the University's mission to contribute to society through the pursuit of
education, learning and research at the highest international levels of excellence.

www.cambridge.org
Information on this title: www.cambridge.org/9781107153011

First published 2017
First paperback edition 2024

A catalogue record for this publication is available from the British Library

Library of Congress Cataloging-in-Publication data
Names: Hernández-Orallo, José, author.
Title: The measure of all minds : evaluating natural and artificial intelligence /
José Hernández-Orallo.
Description: Cambridge, United Kingdom ; New York, NY : Cambridge University Press,
2017. I Includes bibliographical references and index.
Identifiers: LCCN 2016028921 I ISBN 9781107153011 (hardback : alk. paper)
Subjects: I MESH: Mental Processes – physiology I Artificial Intelligence – trends I
Man-Machine Systems I Social Skills I Evaluation Studies as Topic
Classification: LCC R855.3 I NLM WL 26.5 I DDC 616.8900285–dc23
LC record available at https://lccn.loc.gov/2016028921

ISBN   978-1-107-15301-1   Hardback

Contents

List of Panels   *page* ix

Preface   xi

PART I   A LONG-PONDERED OUTFIT

1   **Extended Nature**   3

1.1   Face the Diversity   3

1.2   The Machine Kingdom   7

1.3   The Space of Behavioural Features   11

1.4   Psychometric Profiles and Intelligence   17

1.5   An Opportune Venture   20

1.6   Formulating the Quest   24

2   **Mind the Step: Scala Universalis**   27

2.1   Taxonomies, Measurements and Definitions   27

2.2   Paradigms of Behavioural Measurement   30

2.3   Accuracy, Specialisation and Calibration   35

2.4   The Difficulties of Universal Scales   40

2.5   Factors: Subjective or Relative?   44

2.6   The Relevance of Algorithmic Information   48

2.7   Driven by Refutation   52

PART II   THE EVALUATION DISCORDANCE

3   **The Evaluation of Human Behaviour**   59

3.1   Telling *Idiots Savants* Apart   59

3.2   The Assessment of Personality   62

3.3   The Assessment of Cognitive Abilities   65

3.4   Intelligence, IQ and the *g Factor*   68

3.5	The Testing Bazaar	73
3.6	Item Response Theory	77
3.7	Discrimination and Adaptive Tests	82
3.8	Population Relativity	86
4	**The Evaluation of Non-human Natural Behaviour**	**93**
4.1	The Biological Role of Behavioural Features	93
4.2	The Study of Animal Behaviour	98
4.3	Measurement in Animal Behaviour Research	102
4.4	More Systematic Animal Evaluation	106
4.5	The Far-Reaching Roots of Cognitive Life	111
5	**The Evaluation of Artificial Intelligence**	**117**
5.1	Baring Intelligence: The AI Effect	117
5.2	Horses for Courses	119
5.3	The Mythical Human-Level Machine Intelligence	126
5.4	Telling Computers and Humans Apart Automatically	132
5.5	Task-Oriented Evaluation	135
5.6	Characterising General-Purpose AI Systems	141
5.7	Towards a Feature-Oriented Evaluation	146
6	**The Boundaries against a Unified Evaluation**	**152**
6.1	The Fragmented Evaluation of Behaviour	152
6.2	Tools for the Boundaries	155
6.3	IQ Tests Are Not for Machines	161
6.4	Cross-Discipline Unification or Refoundation?	168
	PART III THE ALGORITHMIC CONFLUENCE	
7	**Intelligence and Algorithmic Information Theory**	**175**
7.1	Information and Algorithms	175
7.2	Simplicity in Cognition: Ants and Bits	181
7.3	Induction and Compression	184
7.4	Intelligence Tests from AIT: The C-test	191
7.5	What Do IQ Tests Really Measure?	198
8	**Cognitive Tasks and Difficulty**	**201**
8.1	Interpreting Tasks and Instances	201
8.2	Tasks as Stochastic Interactive Machines	206
8.3	Trials, Solutions and Policies	209
8.4	The Elusiveness of Difficulty	213
8.5	Difficulty as an Intrinsic Property	215
8.6	Algorithmic Notions of Policy Acquisition Effort	221

8.7   Task Difficulty as Policy Search   224
8.8   Task Instance Difficulty   229

9   From Tasks to Tests   234
9.1   Agent Characteristic Curves   234
9.2   Sampling Task Items Effectively   238
9.3   Item Choice by Difficulty   246
9.4   Revisiting Discriminating Power and IRT   250
9.5   Scrutinising Item Pool Design   256

10   The Arrangement of Abilities   259
10.1   Facing the Task Continuum   259
10.2   Nonalgorithmic Models of Cognitive Abilities   262
10.3   Task Composition: Pureness and Breadth   267
10.4   Task Similarity: Information and Difficulty   273
10.5   From Tasks to Abilities   275

11   General Intelligence   283
11.1   Ars Generalis Ultima: Optimal Agents   283
11.2   Considering All Tasks   287
11.3   Task Diversity from a Universal Distribution?   290
11.4   Ensuring Diversity: Considering All Policies   297
11.5   Is There a Universal *g* Factor?   301
11.6   What Makes *g* Stronger?   304

PART IV   THE SOCIETY OF MINDS

12   Cognitive Development and Potential   313
12.1   Early Sensorimotor Representations   313
12.2   Cognitive Development Evaluation   317
12.3   Different Aids to Cumulative Acquisition   322
12.4   The Conceptual Landscape   326
12.5   The Dynamics of Behavioural Features   330
12.6   The Power of Being Universal   333
12.7   Estimating Potential Abilities   335

13   Identifying Social Skills   341
13.1   What Is Distinctive about Social Contexts?   341
13.2   Multi-agent Test Beds   348
13.3   Social Tasks: Competition and Co-operation   352
13.4   Populating Tasks   359
13.5   Assessing Policy Acquisition in Social Contexts   364

14   Communication Abilities   370
    14.1   The Role of Communication   370
    14.2   What Are Verbal Abilities?   373
    14.3   Assessing Language Development   379
    14.4   Languages: Created to Be Learnt   382
    14.5   How Much Does Language Facilitate Cognition?   388

15   Evaluating Collective and Hybrid Systems   392
    15.1   Characterising Collective Tasks   392
    15.2   Crowds and Teams   398
    15.3   Analysis of Collective Psychometric Profiles   403
    15.4   Mustering a Hybrid   410

        PART V   THE KINGDOM OF ENDS

16   Universal Tests   417
    16.1   One Test for All?   417
    16.2   Choosing the Right Interface   420
    16.3   Resolution Range: Test Adaptation   424
    16.4   Unorthodox Universal Assessment   429
    16.5   Desiderata for Universal Tests   435

17   Rooting for Ratiocentrism   438
    17.1   Personhood   438
    17.2   Assessing Moral Agency and Patiency   446
    17.3   The Directions of Cognitive Modification   449
    17.4   Agents of Risk: The Role of Evaluation   453
    17.5   Superintelligence   456
    17.6   Demography, Democracy and Intelligence   461

18   Exploitation and Exploration   467
    18.1   New Grounds   467
    18.2   The Impact of Universal Psychometrics   471
    18.3   Coping with Demands   474
    18.4   A Short Distance Ahead, Plenty to Be Done   477

        References   483
        Index   541

Colour plates are to be found between pages 176 and 177

Panels

1.1	New to science	*page* 5
1.2	The physical Church-Turing thesis	8
1.3	Some questions for universal psychometrics	25
2.1	Measuring instruments: white-box or black-box?	33
2.2	Cortical neurons for several animals	42
2.3	Ayumu the chimp acing a spatial memory test	49
2.4	The 'artificial flight' analogy	54
3.1	Smart dogs on a normal scale	61
3.2	The Big Five	63
3.3	The Flynn effect and the negative Flynn effect	88
4.1	Innate versus acquired: a matter of degree	97
4.2	Aesop's clever crow	99
4.3	Cognition without neurons	113
5.1	The big switch: the AI homunculus	121
5.2	Superhuman: be the best at something	124
5.3	Turing's imitation game	128
5.4	What is *Beyond the Turing test*?	131
5.5	Matching pennies: an adversarial imitation game	133
5.6	Caught by the adversarial CAPTCHA	134
5.7	The exploration-exploitation dilemma	145
6.1	Machine Intelligence Quotient (MIQ)	156
6.2	Are pigeons more intelligent than humans?	160
6.3	Is a 960-line Perl program more intelligent than humans?	162
7.1	Non-universal descriptional complexity	177
7.2	A universal (but informal) descriptional complexity	178
7.3	Loaded dice and Solomonoff's prediction	186
7.4	The 'intuitive' continuation of Thurstone letter series	193
7.5	Generating test items using AIT	194

8.1	The relative numerousness task	202
8.2	General requirements on cognitive tasks	207
8.3	Gaming the relative numerousness task	212
8.4	Levin's universal search for tasks and policies	225
8.5	Instance difficulty for the multiplication task	230
9.1	A single-agent elementary cellular automaton	241
9.2	An agent policy language	242
9.3	The psychometrician's sieves	248
9.4	The easiest hard problem	252
10.1	The Analytical Language of John Wilkins	268
10.2	Cutting Galton's round cake on scientific principles	276
11.1	AIXI and other theoretical AI agents	285
11.2	The universal library and the no-free-lunch theorems	289
11.3	Spearman's Law of Diminishing Returns (SLODR)	305
12.1	The body culture: measuring *embodiment*	315
12.2	A biased tabula rasa: the "child programme"	324
12.3	A conjecture about universal machines	335
13.1	Is intelligence social?	343
13.2	The Darwin-Wallace distribution	361
14.1	Language learnability: Chomsky against the empiricists	382
14.2	Universality and human language uniqueness	384
14.3	Creating and evolving the Robotish language	387
14.4	Occam, Epicurus and language	390
15.1	Vox populi or vox expertorunt	398
15.2	Crowd IQ through majority voting	399
15.3	The c factor: evidence of a universal g?	402
15.4	Women: IQ and social sensitivity	404
16.1	Situated testing versus artificial apparatus	422
16.2	The falsifying power of universal tests	425
16.3	Liking 'curly fries' to look more intelligent	432
17.1	Probably cognitive capability and animal personhood	441
17.2	No robots in the "Society for the Liberation of Robots"	449
17.3	Intelligence explosion?	457
17.4	"It's the demography, stupid"	462
17.5	Anti-monopoly laws for intelligence	465
18.1	Jobs: skills matter more than tasks	476

Preface

The quintessence of intelligence is one of the big questions still beyond our understanding. In the past, science has unravelled many other previously puzzling questions through measurement, a fundamental tool for the identification, comparison and classification of natural phenomena. Not surprisingly, a very significant portion of our still scant knowledge about what intelligence is – and what it is not – comes from this measurement effort. For more than a century, psychometrics, comparative psychology and other disciplines have developed a rich collection of measurement instruments for quantifying various behavioural properties in the animal kingdom, prominently placing humans as a yardstick.

Beyond the enormous landscape of behaviours in the animal kingdom, there is yet another gigantic space to be explored: the machine kingdom. A plethora of new types of 'creatures' is emerging: robots, animats, chatbots, digital assistants, social bots, automated avatars and artificial life forms, to name a few, including hybrids and collectives, such as machine-enhanced humans, cyborgs, artificial swarms, human computation systems and crowd computing platforms. These systems display behaviours and capabilities as peculiar as their developers and constituents can contrive. Universal psychometrics presents itself as a new area dealing with the measurement of behavioural features in the machine kingdom, which comprises any interactive system, biological, artificial or hybrid, individual or collective.

The focus on an enlarged set of subjects generates plenty of new questions and opportunities. Are IQ tests valid for arbitrary machines? Can we devise universal cognitive tests? Can we have a formal definition of intelligence solely based on computational principles? Can the structure of cognitive abilities and empirical latent factors, including the dominant g factor, be extrapolated beyond biological creatures? Can this be studied theoretically? How should artificial personalities be measured? Do we need intelligence to evaluate intelligence universally? The classical paradigms used to evaluate natural and artificial systems have not been able to answer (or even formulate) these questions precisely. Also, customary evaluation tools are gamed by these new kinds of systems.

Recently, however, there has been a significant progress in a principled approach to the evaluation of behaviour based on information theory and computation. The anthropocentric stance is replaced by a universal perspective where life forms are considered as particular cases. Classical tools in human psychometrics, comparative psychology and animal cognition are not jettisoned but rethought for a wider landscape and substantiated on algorithmic grounds.

This book provides a comprehensive account of the concepts, terminology, theory and tools that should compose a unified framework for the universal evaluation of behavioural features. The exposition does not avoid some notions that are less consolidated, such as the arrangement of the space of abilities, the evaluation of personality or the process of ability development. The ideas that do not work are openly criticised, to aid the understanding of the many scattered scientific contributions that have recently appeared in different areas. In fact, some of these theories only make real sense – or no sense at all – when they are put together.

Many of the current conundrums in the evaluation of natural intelligence derive from the empirical evaluation of 'populations' (human groups, age ranges, species, etc.). The consideration of any conceivable behaviour (natural or artificial) and any imaginable 'machine population' provides a falsifiability criterion for any general claim, theory or test about behavioural features. The machine kingdom also brings a myriad of subjects to evaluate, with fewer experimentation constraints than those posed by humans and other animals. The theoretical underpinning on computation and information theory leads to several key formalisations, such as the concepts of task difficulty and policy-general intelligence. These new grounds illuminate blatant questions such as what human intelligence tests really measure.

Artificial intelligence can also benefit from the distinction between task-oriented evaluation and feature-oriented evaluation, jointly with a less anthropocentric methodology for the development and assessment of general-purpose agents. If properly overhauled, many tools from psychometrics can enter the scene of artificial intelligence evaluation, such as item response theory and adaptive testing. Similarly, the experience in the design of interfaces from animal evaluation can be crucial beyond natural intelligence.

Psychometrics, comparative psychology and artificial intelligence evaluation usually speak different languages. A great effort has been made to render this book accessible and valuable for researchers and students in all these areas and, extensively, to any interested reader outside these disciplines. As a result of the integration of different areas, some paradigms will be challenged and some hypotheses will be refuted. The outcome for the future is an integration of well-founded principles for the evaluation of behaviour in humans, non-human animals and all other machines.

BOOK STRUCTURE

The book is organised in five parts.

Part I presents and frames the goals. Chapter 1 describes the diversity of behaviours resulting from a surge in the types of computers, robots, enhanced humans, hybrid systems and collectives thereof, with various types of communication. How can these systems be analysed and, ultimately, measured? This chapter specifies the conceptual characterisation of the so-called machine kingdom and the space of behavioural features, defines the scientific inquiry as a universal generalisation of psychometrics and enumerates the questions that are addressed during the rest of the book. Chapter 2 delineates the methodological principles to answer these questions, some fundamental concepts of measurement theory, the motivation for using the theoretical tools from computation and algorithmic information theory and the strengthened refutation power of those theoretical and empirical results over an enlarged set of subjects.

Part II provides the necessary background from the three areas universal psychometrics is built upon: human psychometrics, comparative (animal) cognition and artificial intelligence (AI); their existing links; and the barriers against a unified approach. The purpose of these chapters is not to give a comprehensive review (for which many specialised textbooks are available) but to focus on the concepts and tools that may be required or questioned during the book. Chapter 3 gives an account of psychometrics, IQ tests, the g factor, item response theory and adaptive testing in general and out-of-the-norm populations. Chapter 4 portrays a very particular view of the evaluation of non-human biological behaviour, ranging from apes, in many ways comparable to humans, to the detection of the so-called minimal cognition in bacteria, plants and extraterrestrial life. Chapter 5 analyses the chaotic state of AI evaluation, with disparate approaches ranging from Turing's imitation game to robotic competitions and the unsuccessful attempts so far towards a feature-oriented evaluation. Chapter 6 confronts the three previous chapters. What is common and distinctive in the different approaches to the evaluation of intelligence and other behavioural features?

Part III presents the foundations for universal psychometrics based on computation and algorithmic information theory (AIT). Chapter 7 introduces AIT and shows how it pervades cognition. AIT can be used to generate test items that look very much the same as those that appear in some IQ tests, unveiling what these tests really are. Chapter 8 defines cognitive tasks in a universal way. Many different notions of difficulty are described, and a general difficulty function is formalised and derived from Levin's universal search. Chapter 9 elaborates agent characteristic curves from this new concept of difficulty. Tests must be constructed through an effective sampling over a range of difficulties, analysing the role of discriminating power in non-adaptive and adaptive tests. Chapter 10 tackles a controversial issue: how analytical notions of task similarity can be used to define what abilities are and to arrange the space of abilities from specific to general. Chapter 11 interprets general intelligence as the result of considering all tasks and, alternatively, in terms of whether a universal g factor exists.

Part IV delves into the significance of intelligence and other behavioural features in environments that harbour other systems, competing, co-operating or enhancing the subject's abilities. Chapter 12 investigates how cognitive development can be evaluated, from early perception to more conceptual abstraction. In the context of universal machines, such as humans and computers, potential features must be carefully understood in a probabilistic way. Chapter 13 deals with social skills, covering both competition and co-operation of humans, non-human animals and multi-agent systems in artificial intelligence. The Darwin-Wallace distribution is introduced as a way of characterising agent-populated environments. Chapter 14 is devoted to communication, which is key in knowledge exchange and development and in co-ordinating social organisations and collectives. Chapter 15 analyses the evaluation of groups and hybrids. How do the abilities of collective or symbiotic systems depend on the abilities of their members and their organisation? A recurrent question emerges all throughout this part: how crucial and distinctive are developmental, social, verbal and collective skills and drives?

Finally, Part V discusses what lies ahead. Chapter 16 considers what a universal cognitive test might look like. Test adaptation and interface customisation are key to evaluating a subject for which we lack any previous information. Chapter 17 has a more speculative character, arguing that measurement must play a crucial role in appraising the cognitive systems that the future may bring. Chapter 18 closes the book with the implications and the lessons learnt from universal psychometrics, and the way in which it can have a significant impact.

Shaded panels are spread throughout the book to introduce stand-alone concepts and questions, and keynote boxes spotlight the most important ideas. The highlights at the end of each chapter capture its take-away messages and the essential bits for subsequent chapters. This is meant as a checklist for those readers from diverse backgrounds who defer or skim through a chapter and wonder whether they are nevertheless ready to undertake the next one, especially in more technical parts of the book.

ACKNOWLEDGEMENTS

From the range of behavioural features that characterise us, we all experience a decisive struggle between our shortcomings and the way to overcome them. The people I relied on – my extended mind – tipped the scales for this book.

First and foremost, paraphrasing Stanisław Lem's *The Futurological Congress, I never would have* written this book *if it had not been for Professor* David L. Dowe, *who gave me clearly to understand that this was expected of me.* Most of the motivation, essence and even style of this book are the consequence of more than a decade of joint intellectual ventures. He always asked the ingenious questions. I just played Sancho.

The anYnt project turned from fancy into milestone for many of the key concepts and test models that pervade the book. I am most grateful to all the members of the project: David L. Dowe, again, Sergio España, Javier Insa and, most especially, Mariví Hernández-Lloreda.

Many people have contributed with valuable comments and corrections to the book drafts, insightful conversations, providing help with graphical material or answering some technical questions. Thanks to Sam S. Adams, Stuart Armstrong, Frank Bergmann, Harold Boley, Miles Brundage, Angelo Cangelosi, Nader Chmait, Douglas K. Detterman, David L. Dowe, Cèsar Ferri, Peter Flach, Arthur Franz, David J. Gunkel, Thomas Hendrey, M. Victoria Hernández-Lloreda, Enrique Hernández-Orallo, Bill Hibbard, Katja Hofmann, Frank Jäkel, Wendy Johnson, Michal Kosinski, Meelis Kull, Jan Leike, Leonid A. Levin, Miquel Llorente, Fernando Martínez-Plumed, Alexey Melkikh, Elena Messina, Carlos Monserrat, Shane Mueller, Stephen Muggleton, Adolfo Plasencia, Huw Price, Ricardo B. C. Prudêncio, M. José Ramírez-Quintana, John Rust, Ute Schmid, Aaron Sloman, Albert Soler, Robert Sparrow, David Stillwell, Claes Strannegård, Jared P. Taglialatela, Jan Arne Telle, Andrés Terrasa, Kristinn R. Thórisson and Susana Urbina.

I owe special gratitude to Lauren Cowles, Adam Kratoska, the anonymous reviewers and the rest of the team at Cambridge University Press for their guidance, invaluable feedback and professionalism throughout the entire book process.

Above all, my warmest thanks go to Neus, Enric and Jaume, who responded so generously to the new glutton in the family. I hope they – and everyone else – appreciate that, regardless of the wrongs of this book, writing it was the right thing to do.

Part I

A Long-Pondered Outfit

1

Extended Nature

Instead of fruitless attempts to divide the world into things with and
things without the essence of mind, or consciousness, we should
examine the many detailed similarities and differences between systems.
– Aaron Sloman,
The Structure of the Space of Possible Minds (1984)

A PHENOMENAL DISPLAY is taking shape before our eyes. A variety
of new behaviours present themselves embodied as computers, robots,
enhanced humans, hybrids and collectives with sundry types of integration and
communication. Can all possible behaviours, extant or extinct, actual or conceivable, natural or artificial, be embraced by the *machine kingdom*, the set of
all computable interactive systems? What is the essence of each of these systems, how do they usually react and what are they able to do? The understanding
and measurement of these behavioural features is not only a fascinating scientific challenge but an earnest need for society. It is needed for devising policies
in all areas of life, from labour to leisure, and for the assessment of the effective progress and safety of the engineering disciplines behind this surge. What
theory and tools do we have for this scrutiny? We only have some scattered
pieces of the puzzle, and some of them do not match. It is time to integrate, sort
and systematise these bits in the widest perspective. For this purpose, we must
set a common conceptual ground upon which we can formulate old and new
questions properly.

1.1 FACE THE DIVERSITY

Many biologists view our current time as a period of massive extinction. With
the exception of some global catastrophes, this century will wash away more
species than any other in history: millions, if not billions, of species.

3

The rate of this Anthropocene extinction is around 100 times the natural rate. Not yet tantamount in magnitude and diversity, but accelerating at a far greater rate, there is an opposite explosion of new creatures.

This massive explosion is about a different kind of breed. We call them computers, and they are all around us. They are constantly equipped with new types of communication and organisation, new bodies and interfaces and apparently whimsical ways of hybridisation. We have seen the rise of dustbots, digital pets, video game bots, robot swarms, online assistants, roboroaches, machine-animal herds, chatbots, machine translators, *animats*, algorithmic artists, crowdsourcing platforms and driverless cars. The contraptions are blending and pervading everything, leading to incipient cyborgs, enhanced – or atrophied – humans, human-assisted computers and emergent entities in social networks. Everyone can carry a chess master in her pocket device.

The physical capabilities and the external look of these artefacts are usually misleading about what they do and, most especially, about what they are able to do from a cognitive point of view. Endow a computer with facial expression and we will consider it more capable than what it really is. We will even empathise with it, as we do with dolls and puppets. In the opposite direction, however, one of the reasons behind the success of digital social networks, virtual worlds, online games and other *artificial ecosystems* is that they mostly rely on what their users do and say, on how they behave, on what they are capable of, and not on what they look like physically. This is a liberation experience for many people, who – perhaps for the first time in their lives – can be judged for what they really are.

The analysis of two interactive systems that differ on their physical capabilities and appearance is hampered by many confounding factors, if not simply thwarted by prejudices. Great effort has been put into the areas dealing with the evaluation of human behaviour to make testing procedures, such as exams, as independent as possible from physical traits and any other extraneous factors. Similarly, the evaluation of behavioural features in animals is performed with interfaces that try to isolate or discount all these confounding effects. Of course, this is not always easy or even possible, but the effort pays off when it is. Ultimately, the most elegant way of expressing the same idea was introduced by Alan Turing, with his famous imitation game, the Turing test: machines should be judged by what they do through a teletype communication.

We must then look at all this with the utmost neutrality, from an aseptic, unprejudiced standpoint. Panel 1.1 exemplifies the appropriate attitude when we observe a new organism.

When we make the effort of removing all the physical differences and look at each artefact or organism in a purely behavioural way, we get a much better

> **Panel 1.1**
> **New to science**
>
> "There is a label on a cage that states simply, 'This machine is new to science'. Inside the cage there sits a small dustbot. It has bad temper. No bad-tempered dustbot has ever been found. Nothing is known about it. It has no name. For the mechanist it presents an immediate challenge. What has made it unique? How does it differ from the other dustbots already known and described?"
>
> The preceding paragraph is adapted from Morris's 'The Naked Ape' (1967), where 'machine' replaces 'animal', 'dustbot' replaces 'squirrel', 'bad temper' replaces 'black feet' and 'mechanist' replaces 'zoologist'.
>
> This paragraph represents the kind of unprejudiced standpoint about what the real *subject* of study is. Of course, this standpoint does not ensure a scientifically rigorous account, nor does it make the analysis any easier, but it sets a non-anthropocentric perspective.

understanding of what an organism truly is. Only with this perspective can we say that, for instance, a group of bacteria and a herd of sheep behave in a *social* way, despite the enormous physical differences between them and between their environments.

What are the organisms we need to scrutinise? The systems that are responsible for the new behaviours can be categorised into several groups:

- Computers: this refers to any type of computational behaviour, including any artefact that is designed with some kind of artificial intelligence (AI). We particularly emphasise those systems featuring machine learning, natural language processing, social interaction, complex perception and cognitive development (Russell and Norvig, 2009; Cangelosi and Schlesinger, 2015). AI systems that are responsive to situations they were not programmed for are becoming more versatile and relevant in our daily lives, doing or taking less mechanical, more cognitive jobs. Artificial general intelligence (AGI) is aiming at more ambitious goals such as open-domain question answering systems, developmental robotics and compositional learning.
- Cognitively enhanced organisms: here we refer to living organisms, such as "cyborg rats" with computer-controlled electrodes implanted in their brains (Yu et al., 2016), or more customary cyborgs, such as a deaf person with a cochlear implant. We also include humans whose cognitive abilities are altered by the use of any "tool of the mind" (Carr, 2011), such as a pen and paper, regarded in Plato's Phaedrus as "an elixir of memory and wisdom"

first, but a cause of atrophy afterwards. Actually, the notions of "extended mind" (Clark and Chalmers, 1998; Menary, 2010) or "natural-born cyborg" (Clark, 2004) make this concept very broad: every modern human is a cyborg. What we are envisaging is how humans can enhance their cognitive abilities by the use of technology (Cohen, 2013) or counteract age-related decay and mental disabilities in general through cognitive prosthesis (Hampson et al., 2012; Berger et al., 2012). For instance, how is our memory affected when we have access to the Internet? Are certain abilities being atrophied by the 'Google effect' (Sparrow et al., 2011)? Is technology making us 'stupid' and 'shallow' (Carr, 2008, 2011)?

- Biologically enhanced computers: there is no need for science fiction to see humans working for machines. This is already happening in several forms. Technically, 'human computation' (Von Ahn, 2005, 2009) "is simply computation that is carried out by humans" (Law and Von Ahn, 2011), seen as part of a more general problem a computer cannot solve efficiently. In practice, we see bots, some of them malicious, that rely on humans to recognise some difficult speech bits, to break authentication schemes (such as CAPTCHAs) or simply to be supervised. On one hand, this creates new questions about what cognitive abilities a computer can have with a bounded number of questions or interactions with a 'Human Oracle' (Shahaf and Amir, 2007). On the other hand, making a computer depend on people also creates availability and reliability problems. Humans make mistakes all the time.
- (Hybrid) collectives: any of the preceding groups can be structured in many different ways, including swarms or collectives combining humans, other animals and computers. A blind human with a guide dog is a traditional example. Actually, every hybrid can be seen as a collective, leading to new ways of co-operation, competition, communication and delegation. Video games and virtual worlds are playgrounds where the line between humans and computers is more blurred, and bots are evaluated by traits such as believability or enjoyability (Hingston, 2012). Online social networks are a good example of new types of interaction that might require some specific cognitive abilities or even change personality. Closely related, crowdsourcing is a paradigm whereby complex tasks are partitioned (by humans or computers) into smaller tasks that can be solved by humans or computers (Quinn and Bederson, 2011). A final integration stage can be a committee consensus (Kamar et al., 2012), but many other possibilities exist ("Crowds guiding AIs" and "AIs guiding crowds", Kittur et al., 2013).
- Minimal or rare cognition: many rare types of cognition are indeed new to science. Recent research in many different areas has been able to recognise new types of cognition in plants (Calvo-Garzón and Keijzer, 2011), bacteria (Van Duijn et al., 2006) and even forests at very different spatiotemporal

scales. Minimal cognition is also created and explored in virtual environments, with theoretical cognitive models (Beer and Williams, 2015) or artificial life organisms (Beer, 2015) that are endowed with minimal abilities to adapt to changes.

The emergence of so many new artefacts and systems requires a full re-examination of what behavioural features are and how they are measured. The first thing in this endeavour must be a more precise characterisation of the set of subjects to be analysed, beyond the traditional boundaries (humans, non-human animals and computers).

1.2 THE MACHINE KINGDOM

No matter how wild and diverse life may be, it is constrained by the rules of evolution and natural selection. Some behaviours are extremely unlikely, because the existence of organisms displaying them would require an improbable sequence of mutations and selections according to their odds of success and reproduction. The extant and even the extinct organisms are the "lucky ones", but one can consider "the set of all possible people allowed by our DNA" (Dawkins, 2000) or, still more generally, the set of all possible organisms (or genomes), the "Library of Mendel" (Dennett, 1995).

From a behavioural point of view, and before the discovery of DNA and the advent of computers, we have also been interested in systems that are not strictly living organisms: herds, social communities, symbiotic systems, etc., as well as mythical beasts, fictional characters and all "imaginary beings" (Borges, 1957). How can we characterise all behaviours displayed by all possible *interactive* systems? To answer this question we need to look at the principles of computation, as described in Panel 1.2.

There seems to be general agreement that the behaviour of a slug or a sponge can be simulated by a computer with arbitrary precision. By the evolutionary continuum, it is possible, in theory, to do the same with a mammal and, ultimately, with the human brain. The nuances appear when we discuss whether the resources and knowledge to do this will ever be available.

Under this view, all possible biological organisms and computers are machines, with extant ones being a subset. We can now give a definition of the whole set.

> **Keynote 1.1.** The **machine kingdom** is the set of all interactive systems taking inputs and producing outputs, possibly asynchronously, through interfaces, bodies, sensors and actuators, etc.

Panel 1.2
The physical Church-Turing thesis

The notion of a Turing machine, as defined by Alan Turing in 1936 (Turing, 1936, 1937), is still one of the most elegant models of computation. Turing showed that some problems are not decidable, i.e., there is no computable process that can answer them, such as the *halting problem*, the problem of determining whether an arbitrary Turing machine stops for an arbitrary input. Turing also introduced the notion of *universal* Turing machine (UTM), a Turing machine that can simulate any other Turing machine. Current computers are actually *resource-bounded* universal Turing machines, capable of *virtually* emulating other devices and implementing different programming languages, most of which are *universal*, also referred to as *Turing-complete*.

Alan Turing also postulated – and Alonzo Church in different terms – that any function that is effectively calculable is computable by a Turing machine. This is known as the Church-Turing thesis. One variant of the Church-Turing thesis, which goes beyond functions to interactive systems, is the *physical* Church-Turing thesis, stating that "every finitely realizable physical system can be perfectly simulated by a universal model computing machine operating by finite means" (Deutsch, 1985, p. 99).

A mechanistic view of the human mind is a consequence of this thesis – every physical process in the universe, including those happening in every living thing, would be computable with finite resources (finite storage space and computational steps). We widen this view with machines that may be non-deterministic, such as probabilistic Turing machines, with a source of randomness (possibly through analog components or sensors), or non-functional, such as interactive Turing machines (or other computational models of interaction; Goldin et al., 2006), as many everyday computers.

Unless explicitly stated otherwise, we will restrict the attention to resource-bounded machines. The same algorithm running in a faster computer is, in terms of the machine kingdom, a different machine. We will generically refer to the elements of the machine kingdom as agents or subjects, especially when confronted with an environment, a task or a test. Figure 1.1 shows a simplistic Euler diagram where animals and humans are placed inside the machine kingdom.

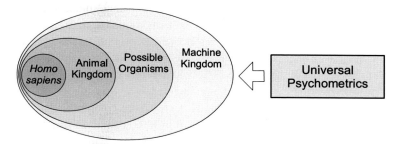

Figure 1.1. The machine kingdom embracing the animal kingdom. Though not explicitly shown on the Euler diagram, other living things, hybrids and collectives also belong to the machine kingdom.

There are several reasons why we make this move to a machinery scenario. The first reason is the avoidance of any kind of anthropocentrism or biocentrism. The second reason is that we want to make it more explicit that classical boundaries between the natural and artificial domains vanish. The third reason is that we want a more formal foundation for our analysis of subjects, their properties and abilities. For example, we can define distributions over the elements of the machine kingdom, which can take the role *populations* play for natural organisms.

The view represented by the machine kingdom is familiar in some disciplines. Artificial life is an area that bridges life produced in a virtual environment with the one produced in a physical environment. Artificial life goes beyond the constraints of the life on Earth (gaiacentrism) but also beyond the constraints of all organic life (biocentrism), by considering any possible organism. One significant feature of artificial life is that the environment is not considered as a separate entity from the organism. The identification of the subject in the environment and the channels of interaction are crucial. During most of this book, we will assume that the organism is well delimited. In Chapter 16, however, we will explore the notion of universal test, which requires the identification of the subject in the environment, and we will discuss the relevance of an appropriate interface.

Bio-inspired robotics is also an area halfway between the natural and the artificial, initially focusing on morphological and locomotive mechanisms but recently paying more attention to behaviours, closer to cognitive robotics and developmental robotics. In fact, some animal behaviours are emulated by artificial systems, known as *animats* (Wilson, 1991; Webb, 2009; Williams and Beer, 2010).

Cognitive science deals with the analysis of perception, attention, memory, learning, knowledge, emotion, reasoning and language in humans, other animals and computer models. Basically, cognitive science studies the "Space of Possible Minds" (Sloman, 1984), with the term "mind" seemingly setting a preference for a very small, and not well defined, subset of the machine kingdom. In fact, the essence of mind was usually analysed at a more philosophical level with related but different concepts, such as materialism, determinism, free will, creativity, unpredictability and, ultimately, consciousness.

In general, the use of the term "mind" is now more comprehensive, as for Dennett's (1996), Goertzel's (2006) and Hall's (2007) "Kinds of Minds", Yudkowsky's "Mind Design Space" (2008) or Yampolskiy's "Universe of Minds" (2015a, p. 35), the latter also being used as a way of resuscitating the old (theistic) body-mind dualism (see, e.g., Carter, 2007, p. 12).

Following Sloman, we will not look for a qualitative essence of mind (or, more interestingly, person, whose characterisation will be seen in Chapter 17) but for a range of behavioural features that characterise all the elements in the machine kingdom. In fact, trying to avoid the use of the word 'mind' and its connotations, Sloman suggests the "space of possible 'behaving systems', to coin a neutral phrase" (Sloman, 1984), which is much closer, if not equal, to what we are referring to by the 'machine kingdom' here. Actually, some definitions of theoretical cognitive science just refer to "information processing systems" (Simon, 1980). In the end, our fixation on the behaviour of all interactive systems derives from our interest in the *measurement* of what systems do.

Once we have defined our *Cosmos*, in which humans are nothing more than a pale dot, what are we going to do with these *billions and billions* of machines? Our goal is to measure and classify them in terms of their behavioural features. This is what we call *universal psychometrics*.

Keynote 1.2. Universal psychometrics is the analysis and development of measurement tools for the evaluation of *behavioural features* in the *machine kingdom*, including *cognitive abilities* and *personality traits*.

The use of the term *behavioural* feature instead of the more usual *psychological* or *mental* feature emphasises the general scope of the machine kingdom. Similarly to human psychometrics, universal psychometrics also covers attitudes, interests, beliefs and knowledge evaluation. In addition, while the term *cognitive development* is not explicitly included, universal psychometrics should also deal with the evolution of systems as a result of learning, education or other changes in the environment.

Do we have appropriate tools for the evaluation of these features for the diversity of systems in the machine kingdom? We can knock on several doors here. Human psychometrics is the paramount discipline when we think of psychological measurement in general, and intelligence in particular. Much of what we know scientifically about cognitive abilities in humans originates from what psychometric research has done during more than a century. Countless test batteries are available for different groups and abilities. Intelligence quotient (IQ) tests are just one type of these tests, arguably the most popular and controversial. Can we use some of these psychometric tests for the variety of systems in the machine kingdom? This question will be addressed in more detail in Chapter 6, but we can anticipate that many psychometric tests are designed for some particular human populations, and their use in other populations is disputable.

Some of the new artefacts (e.g., animats) are closer to animals (or swarms) than humans. Comparative psychology is the discipline that has been concerned with the evaluation of the cognitive abilities of a range of species in the animal kingdom. Many hurdles had to be overcome, such as how to perform tests without the use of language, how to make animals focus on a task and how to choose the right interface and rewards. This encompassing effort gives comparative psychology more flexibility for the evaluation of all these new systems. We will reuse some of these ideas and techniques, but we will also see that many tests are focused on very specific animal traits and lack the breadth and depth of psychometric tests.

And what about artificial intelligence? Do we find tools in artificial intelligence to evaluate its artefacts? Turing's imitation game has deservedly become very popular, but it is not really the way artificial intelligence evaluates its systems. In practice, artificial intelligence uses specialised tests for each particular task. Chess-playing computers are evaluated with completely different tools than self-driving cars. Indeed, there is no general methodology for AI evaluation, with many different competitions and benchmarks being developed in the past decades. In the end, AI evaluation tools are task oriented rather than feature oriented.

The limited integration between these disciplines suggests a full overhaul of their principles and tools, much beyond a naive generalisation of human psychometrics. In particular, we must start with a re-examination of what features are to be measured.

1.3 THE SPACE OF BEHAVIOURAL FEATURES

Imagine for a moment there were an art to answer every solvable question, a procedure to unravel every intelligible mystery of the universe. Imagine you were given an *Ars Generalis*, the universal key that opens all locks.

Figure 1.2. Different variants of Llull's Ars Magna. The set of attributes ('principia') varies in number, from 16 (Ars Demonstrativa) to 9 (Ars Brevis or Ars Generalis Ultima). [Courtesy of the *Biblioteca Virtual de Patrimonio Bibliográfico*, Spanish Ministry of Education, Culture and Sport.]

Among all the possible doors to be opened, there is one you should eventually open, the one who hides the most coveted enigma, the Ars Generalis itself.

Ramon Llull, the thirteenth-century Majorcan philosopher, pursued a general art to "know every natural thing" (Llull, 1295, VII, 87). Through several versions of his Ars Magna he introduced a series of universal principles, represented on concentric spheres, as shown in Figure 1.2, which every non-divine creature should have in some finite amount, ultimately explaining "all forms of thought" (Jaulent, 2010).

Despite the naivety to modern eyes, Llull's quest is remarkable for his time, mostly because the Ars Generalis was designed with the purpose of being methodical, *mechanic*. Indeed, the Ars Generalis has been recognised as one of the most influential ideas in the history of computation and artificial intelligence (Fidora and Sierra, 2011). The most extraordinary feature, though, was that every creature had a set of principles or properties that made it distinctive. The identification of a precise set of properties, and their contribution to the Ars Generalis – what we would call intelligence nowadays – was one of the greatest difficulties Llull had to face.

Even before Llull, humans have been able to characterise other cognitive systems, including humans and many other animals, also using abstract properties. The more descriptive and predictive the properties and the more accurate their assessment can be the better.

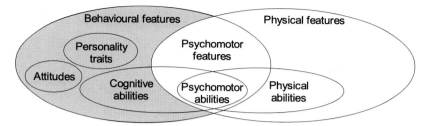

Figure 1.3. The space of features.

From a scientific stance, finding abstract attributes that best describe the behaviour of an entity is one of the key questions of behavioural sciences. Ethology helps us understand animal behaviour, putting more emphasis on the biological and evolutionary perspectives, with varying degrees of abstraction. Early cybernetics was seen as a "theory of machines", analysing all "ways of behaving" (Ashby, 1956), but usually remained at the concrete level rather than capturing abstract aspects of behaviour. Instead of specific models, comparative psychology, psychometrics and, by extension, universal psychometrics try to find general properties of behaviour.

> **Keynote 1.3.** A **behavioural feature** is an abstract property, characteristic or construct about the elements of the machine kingdom that can be inferred by observation and interaction.

Figure 1.3 shows the space of behavioural features as opposed to the space of physical features, with an area of overlap covering psychomotor features. The figure only shows some subcategories, but the space of behavioural features can be subcategorised in many different ways according to abilities, personality traits, attitudes, beliefs, knowledge and emotional states.

The evaluation of attitudes, interests, beliefs and knowledge is usually part of human psychometrics and will be so considered in universal psychometrics. Attitudes and interests are still partially sensitive to the *state* of the system, determined by beliefs, knowledge, goals and emotions. An individual can reconsider their attitudes towards objects or groups of subjects (e.g., after reading a book, one can develop a positive attitude towards homosexual people and a poor attitude towards religious people). This instability does not mean that we cannot find correlations between attitudes (e.g., political views tend to organise around clusters), but it makes the characterisation more difficult and volatile.

To characterise the elements in the machine kingdom we will mostly focus on those behavioural features that are most stable: personality traits and cognitive abilities. Of course, they can still be dramatically affected by development, pathologies or accidents. *Personality traits*, in particular, represent "consistent patterns of behavior, especially expressive or stylistic behavior" (Barenbaum and Winter, 2008).

Keynote 1.4. A **personality trait** is a behavioural feature of an interactive system in the machine kingdom that captures a facet of its character or temperament, describing what the system tends to do (i.e., how it usually reacts to situations).

Personality traits may or may not have a monotonic relation to any notion of quality or performance. For instance, very low and very high values of *openness* may be considered worse than an average value. Also, depending on the goals, a particular personality trait such as being extroverted might be beneficial or not, or even neutral.

Since personality traits are not so strongly linked to the resources leading to maximum performance, they are easier to modify by emulating other agents. This is a common-day phenomenon, from casual imitation to professional actors. It is also one of the first issues in the analysis and re-creation of artificial personalities, in social networks or in robotic pets, leading to a burgeoning area known as "personality computing" (Vinciarelli and Mohammadi, 2014).

Cognitive abilities, on the other hand, are properties that describe what subjects are able to do. They are distinctive from personality traits and other behavioural features in that abilities must be linked to actual performance (Kline, 2000). Particular abilities can be qualitative (such as being able to count to ten or not) or, more commonly, quantitative (such as the number of digits that can be recalled from a series). The more difficult a task instance is the higher the ability has to be to solve it. Cognitive abilities are usually *gradient* features, i.e., the more the better.

Since cognitive abilities are linked to performance in a task, we need to clarify what a cognitive task is. Many tasks, especially those situated tasks where the subject is immersed in a real environment, require both physical and cognitive skills, as outlined in Figure 1.3. For instance, sports require psychomotor abilities, strength and fitness. Excluding these abilities would rule out many tasks where perception and cognition are crucial, such as playing a musical instrument or driving a car. Instead, we will consider cognitive tasks as *performance tasks* that are "not essentially dependent on any *particular* sensory or motor system" (Jensen, 1998, p. 52).

> **Keynote 1.5.** A **cognitive task** is an interactive series of stimuli that allows for different observable behaviours on the subject. It is cognitive as far as *performance* is involved, and its interface can be changed or virtualised without affecting the essence of the process.

Using the notion of cognitive task we can now give the following definition.

> **Keynote 1.6.** A **cognitive ability** is a gradient property of an interactive system in the machine kingdom that allows the system to perform well in a class of cognitive tasks.

A quantitative measurement of an ability is influenced by the breadth and difficulty of the class of tasks a subject is able to do. Nonetheless, a misleading result about a class of tasks (e.g., mathematical ability) might be produced by a subject being capable of solving very difficult tasks of one particular kind (e.g., solving systems of equations) but failing at easy ones of a different kind (e.g., calculating the area of a square). In this case it is perhaps better to refer to *attainment* rather than a real ability. But how can we precisely identify what a cognitive ability is and distinguish it from more specific attainment? Are there infinitely many abilities, as many as sets – or distributions – of tasks? How can we find the right set of abilities? We will briefly overview early attempts failing at finding a representative set of abilities.

For instance, cognitive abilities in humans could be traced to the organ that produces them, the brain, in the very same way that we can trace a physical ability, such as the speed of a runner, to the physical characteristics of her bones and muscles. Juan Huarte (1575) tried to find the link between the brain and the space of abilities. He identified three "rational powers" ('memory', 'understanding' and 'imagination'), based on Aristotle's and Galen's four humours and corresponding elemental qualities. These powers were innate and determined by the size and configuration of the brain. Strongly influenced by Huarte, Franz Gall introduced phrenology, the theory that some parts of the brain could be responsible for some mental functions, which, in turn, had an important influence for Paul Broca and some early brain anatomists, evolutionists, anthropologists and psychometricians. However, Gall went far beyond scientific evidence, by linking abilities and personality traits with the shape of the

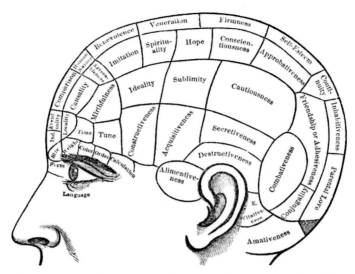

Figure 1.4. Location of human 'faculties' according to phrenology (Fowler and Fowler, 1859, p. 10). [Courtesy of U.S. National Library of Medicine.]

brain. Figure 1.4 shows a fabricated decomposition of the brain and its alleged functionalities according to phrenology, which is now considered a pseudo-science. Since some parts of the brain have been shown to have specialised functions, the view of the brain (and its behaviour) as a conglomerate of sep-arate associated aspects or mental faculties – the old 'faculty psychology' – has suffered periodic revivals, such as Fodor's "modularity thesis", posited in 1983, or Minsky's "society of minds", published in 1988. This view, however, has to be taken very carefully, and balanced with the evidence of a high degree of plasticity in the brain.

One very special case of a postulated behavioural feature is conscious-ness, also with enormous efforts to locate it somewhere, or everywhere, in the brain. There have been several proposals to measure it in different ways (Brazdău and Mihai, 2011; Arrabales et al., 2010). But is it a cognitive abil-ity? The answer hinges upon whether it is really a property of the subjects in the machine kingdom that makes them succeed in some tasks. If this were the case, consciousness could even be considered a quantitative (Baum, 2004, p. 362) rather than a qualitative property, or even a multidimensional feature. The key issue, however, is whether consciousness is predictive for future perfor-mance and, most especially, whether it can be isolated from other behavioural features. Like any other postulated ability, we will need to keep a very sceptical stance.

The failures of Llull, Huarte, Gall and many others should alert us to how easy it is to assign a set of arbitrary abilities to spurious physical or behavioural phenomena. These theories are not always easy to be falsified, and the controversy is still vivid today for any set of abilities, including those that are obtained by rigorous empirical methods in psychometrics. In fact, in the past two or three decades there has been a revival for the identification of more and more 'talents', 'gifts' or 'intelligences'. Similarly, we should also critically scrutinise any monolithic view of the space of cognitive abilities, where intelligence is chosen as the only possible ability. The following section interprets these two extremes, and some theories in between, with the special role of intelligence in them.

1.4 PSYCHOMETRIC PROFILES AND INTELLIGENCE

Most living creatures on Earth are highly specialised to a particular habitat. Even those that display a wide geographical range have very strict constraints on climate, food, predators, etc. But, certainly, while some of them struggle to escape extinction, others seem to flourish. For instance, do cockroaches rule the world? Or the Antarctic krill? The truth is that no species can be said to be more successful or predominant overall, not even by counting the number of individuals or their total biomass.

The machine kingdom is no different. A plethora of devices, applications and algorithms have been devised and selected to operate in many different environments, some of them real and some of them virtual. Do smartphones rule the world? Or are the omnipresent Wallace multipliers (1964) taking it over within millions of microprocessors?

Adaptation is usually performed through specialisation. Ethological evidence shows that very complex behaviours can be completely driven by *instinct*, a kind of innate inclination for some behaviours, such as birds building their nests or moths being drawn to light. Computer science and artificial intelligence have developed many particular systems that are able to solve important but specialised problems, such as opening a bank account, vacuuming the carpet, finding us a partner, playing chess against us or driving our cars.

The natural world has exceptions to this innate behaviour rule; some organisms are able to *learn*. Some species adapt in one generation, by learning from the environment. Others adapt in very few generations, without significant genetic variations, through cultural adaptation, one of the most remarkable traits of the *Homo sapiens*. Some AI systems are also able to adapt to other tasks, by configuring or tuning their behaviour through the use of training data, or in a more elaborate autonomous mental development.

If systems may perform well by innate (programmed) behaviour or by acquired (learnt) behaviour, should we evaluate whether subjects are able to do some tasks or whether they are able to *learn* to do some tasks? In the latter case, does it make sense to evaluate whether a system can learn a single task instance or a wide range of tasks? Is this not tantamount to evaluating intelligence?

The space of abilities must be something more structured than all sets of tasks. What we are truly aiming at is a *representative* set of behavioural features, such that the elements in the machine kingdom can be characterised with them. This view is known as the "geographic metaphor" (Cianciolo and Sternberg, 2008). Unlike Llull's Ars Magna, phrenology and many other attempts in the past, psychometrics was the first discipline to *scientifically* address this representative set of behavioural features, with the empirical analysis of test results over human populations. Many different models of the intellect were developed by Thorndike, Cattell, Horn, Carroll, Guilford and many others, as we will see in Chapter 3. Some of them only included cognitive abilities, others were conceived for personality traits and a few considered both kinds of features. With them, we may say that an individual is very good at verbal tasks but weak at visual processing. Similarly, for personality, we may say that the individual is very impulsive, but not very co-operative. In a nutshell, according to some of these psychometric models and the associated test batteries, we can derive a *profile* that characterises any human being. By generalising these ideas to the machine kingdom, we may locate any system in the space of behavioural features.

> **Keynote 1.7.** A **psychometric profile**, given a set of behavioural features, is the set of measured values for a particular subject.

Attempts at defining a set of behavioural features for some kind of general profile for the machine kingdom have been increasingly more frequent. The PerMIS workshops on the performance metrics for intelligence systems, and the associated white papers, aimed at a "vector of intelligence", composed of "intellifactors" (Meystel, 2000b). Unfortunately, the idea never fully materialised. Warwick (2000) proposed the so-called hypersphere or rosette of intelligence, including as many "subjective" dimensions as needed. Masum and Christensen (2003) talked about the "task space" in the context of "task breadth", a concept that will appear in subsequent chapters in this book, but no actual set of broad

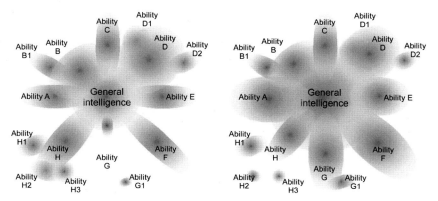

Figure 1.5. Two individuals in the machine kingdom with different figurative profiles of their cognitive abilities.

abilities was given. From an astrobiological point of view, Herzing (2014) presented a set of dimensions to characterise all forms of life, with a combination of both behavioural (external) and physical (internal) traits.

Havel (2013) discussed his own "profile of intelligence" in "a certain abstract multi-dimensional super space", known as the intelligence space (IS), such that for each individual or group "there exists just one representing point in IS, whose coordinates determine the extent of involvement of particular abilities". The questions of how many dimensions there are and their dependencies are left open, as well as how and whether comparisons should be made. Many of these proposals resemble the theory of "multiple intelligences" (Gardner, 1983), which we will briefly discuss in the next chapter.

These attempts show how difficult it is to find a way to assign appropriate psychometric profiles to the elements in the machine kingdom. One of the few things for which there seems to be some consensus in the area of human psychometrics is that *general intelligence* plays a central role in the space of cognitive abilities. One common view is that, even admitting infinitely many specific facets, such as 'being good at chess' or 'translating Chinese text into English', there is a small set of more general components, with general intelligence on top of them. This view considers that general intelligence pervades all other abilities; when general intelligence is high all the other abilities are also enhanced. This hierarchical conception of the space of cognitive abilities (as shown in Figure 1.5) deviates from a multidimensional perspective, with orthogonal and flat dimensions.

Is this view of general intelligence as a central cognitive ability taken for granted, even *definitional*? Certainly not; the centrality of general intelligence in the machine kingdom is just a hypothesis. Despite its having strong supporting evidence for humans, it is an open question whether this can hold universally. Indeed, we should be prepared to admit that Llull was not only wrong in his selection of principles but he (and we) might be wrong too in the interpretation that there is an *ars generalis*, an art that could solve all solvable problems.

This is also why we have not presented any definition of intelligence yet, apart from some informal accounts. There are many definitions of intelligence (see, e.g., Sternberg, 2000; Legg and Hutter, 2007a) and all of them take a particular stance. In the tradition of psychometrics, we will do without a definition of intelligence for the moment. This does not mean that we take Jensen's position that "it is best simply to get rid of the term 'intelligence' ..., the ill-fated word from our scientific vocabulary" (Jensen, 1998, p. 49). Instead, the concept will be refined during the book, ultimately aiming at a formal, computational and measurable definition.

1.5 AN OPPORTUNE VENTURE

In previous sections, we have pondered several arguments about the need for new concepts and tools that give a response to new systems and phenomena. We have also set up a universe of discourse for this challenge: the machine kingdom and the space of features, coupled by psychometric profiles. But has this been explored before? Has it already been achieved? If not, why are there more chances for success at this moment? Or, simply, how can this book contribute?

Let us start with some previous attempts. We have seen already that Sloman defined a set of 'behaving systems'. In the very same paper, 'The Structure of the Space of Possible Minds' (Sloman, 1984), he also made a call to analyse this structure. His "aim for now [was] not to do it – that's a long term project – but to describe the task" (Sloman, 1984). Unfortunately, the task has not been undertaken since.

We can identify some reasons for this. First, Sloman's challenge was too ambitious, as it encouraged the construction of systems and not just their evaluation: "we can begin to account for different abilities found in human beings and other animals, as well as constructing machines which display such abilities" (Sloman, 1984). This is more in the perspective of cognitive science, where machine models are built to understand how humans or other animals work. Second, the tools were perhaps not ready, as acknowledged by Sloman himself: "there is still a lot more to be done to discover precisely what sorts of computational and representational mechanisms are capable of accounting for what sorts of abilities" (Sloman, 1984). Third, despite the focus on 'behaving systems', Sloman did not explicitly support a behavioural *evaluation* of these abilities through black-box tests, measuring what the system does. In fact, he has recently advocated for an exclusively white-box approach, inspecting how things are done (Sloman, 2014b). The fourth reason was motivation. The need for evaluating the abstract behavioural properties of machines, especially in a black-box way, was still a science fiction theme, such as Asimov's "robopsychology" (Asimov, 1950). This study of robot personalities was not an imperative at all. In 1984, Internet, as we know it, did not even exist.

Sloman has recently sharpened his position by claiming that black-box approaches will never give us absolute certainty about properties of machines (Sloman, 2014b). His argument refers to, but is not based on, Rice's theorem, which states the impossibility of having an effective procedure to determine a property of machines in general, using either (or both) black-box and white-box approaches. Sloman's position (personal communication, 2015) is not that any experimental black-box observation of a natural or artificial system is "futile" – which would make empirical sciences useless for those uncountable situations where the box cannot be opened – but that black-box tests have the limitations of inductive inference.

A common approach that has led to predictive and explanatory insight in artificial intelligence, cognitive science and many other sciences is a combination of black-box and white-box approaches. Newell and Simon encouraged the construction of machines and programs, "as a way of discovering new phenomena and analyzing phenomena we already know about" (Newell and Simon, 1976). Another example of a very ambitious programme is Yampolskiy's 'intellectology' (possibly inheriting from Bibel's term 'Intellectics', Bibel, 1980), which "will study and classify [the] design space of intelligent agents, work on establishing limits to intelligence (minimum sufficient for general intelligence and maximum subject to physical limits), contribute to consistent measurement of intelligence across intelligent agents, look at recursive self-improving systems, design new intelligences (making AI a sub-field of intellectology) and evaluate capacity for understanding higher level intelligences by lower level ones" (Yampolskiy, 2015a, p. 35). Despite this diversity of goals, some of them are shared with universal psychometrics.

It is important to clarify the goals and the constraints for the analysis of the machine kingdom. If the goal is to understand the diversity and make a taxonomy of all these systems, then both white-box and black-box approaches are useful. If the goal is to evaluate in a fair way two or more intelligent systems of different nature, architecture and algorithms, independently of how they implement their behaviour, then black-box testing is the way to go. In this regard, the demanding scenarios we have discussed in the previous sections require measurement instruments that are black-box.

Keynote 1.8. Black-box approach: A major aspiration of universal psychometrics is to design measurement tools that work when the only information we have available is the behaviour of a previously unknown system.

As a result, the question here is not whether black-box approaches are futile – the evidence in natural and artificial intelligence evaluation has shown that they are not – or even whether they are worse or better than white-box approaches. The question is how accurate we can be with black-box tests and whether they can shape the space of behavioural features.

Despite this convergence in the recognition of the challenges and the possible directions, the problem we are facing might be badly formulated. One could argue that the theory of computation has already analysed the kinds of machines and the kinds of problems they can solve. This is true, and we also have a well-established taxonomy of machines, ranging from Turing machines to finite state automata. Computational complexity theory distinguishes several problem classes such as **P**, **NP** and **PSPACE** (see, e.g., Arora and Barak, 2009). Of course, the theory of computation will be fundamental for universal psychometrics, as chemistry is to biology, but it does not give us a characterisation of the behaviour of a complex cognitive system. Moving to other disciplines, one could argue too that biology, ethology, (evolutionary) psychology, comparative cognition and even psychiatry have been charting the space of life behaviours, but, unfortunately, they are not meant to extend their analysis to machines. All these disciplines are not the solution, but are instruments for the solution.

It seems then that the problem is worth being undertaken and it has not been solved yet but, why is this the right moment? We will enumerate several reasons for this:

- *Virtualisation of interactions*: as we have discussed, there is a dramatic increase in the number of situations where interaction takes place in artificial scenarios, such as digital social networks, virtual worlds, video games or crowdsourcing, and systems and individuals appear anonymously – black-box – with no knowledge whatsoever of their characteristics.
- *More general and adaptive AI systems*: the widespread use of machine learning techniques from areas such as reinforcement learning, deep learning or

autonomous mental development shows that many AI systems are not programmed to do things, but trained to do things.

- *Renewed interest in AI evaluation*: the rise of AI benchmarks and competitions has been formidable. The problem of machine evaluation is taking the agenda of AI and science in general (You, 2015; Marcus et al., 2016). This is an explicit realisation of the relevance of measurement to incentivise progress in AI (Brundage, 2016), if not a foundational issue to properly characterise the requirements of general AI systems.

- *The need for full detachment from anthropocentrism in the study of behaviour*: as new cross-species studies and tests, such as the Primate Cognition Test Battery (Herrmann et al., 2007), are developed in comparative cognition, the *Homo sapiens* is put in its place, but a void is created. What is to be put instead as the measure of all things?

- *Reinvention of the wheel*: the limited interdisciplinarity and integration between AI, comparative cognition and psychometrics, despite the efforts of cognitive science, has led to many concepts and ideas being bad versions of the original. For instance, the debates about whether there are many 'intelligences' or just one, and whether intelligence is subjective, objective or just an ill-defined concept, re-appear in some disciplines again and again.

- *New theoretical developments*: The evaluation of artificial systems (e.g., through the Turing test or specific tests) and natural organisms (e.g., using psychometric tests) has been strongly anthropocentric and disconnected from the theories of computation and information. New measurement proposals based on algorithmic information theory have been introduced in the past 20 years, but are not well known yet, are too technical or mix positive and negative results. Putting some order will finally unfold their full potential.

- *Inconsistencies from a wider landscape*: Some theories and results make sense within their disciplines. But would they stand if put together? The machine kingdom gives us a stronger refutation power, in the Popperian sense. For instance, the arrangement of abilities may hold for some subsets of the machine kingdom, but not for others. Some tests are meaningful for one population, but useless for others.

- *A more pressing need to analyse AI risks and ethics*: A crucial aspect to determine the risk of a technology is a proper measurement of its capabilities. This must be present in the analysis of more robust or ethical artificial intelligence (Bostrom, 2014; Russell et al., 2015; Hibbard, 2015b) and the impact of AI in the job market depending on the abilities involved (Levy and Murnane, 2012; Frey and Osborne, 2013).

- *A renewed debate about the "future of psychometrics"*: The "pathologies" of psychometrics (Barrett, 2004; Michell, 2008; Humphry, 2011; Sijtsma, 2012; Conway and Kovacs, 2015), in terms of validity, measurement units and foundations, give rein to alternative theories with controversial support (Waterhouse, 2006; Murphy, 2006).
- *Superintelligence is closer – pundits forewarn*: Steven Pinker says ironically that "human-level AI is still the standard 15-to-25 years away, just as it always has been" (Brockman, 2015). In addition, the term 'superintelligence' transmits a very monolithic view of intelligence. Instead, we should talk about superabilities and ask whether those can be measured beyond the human level.
- *An overarching perspective about "the future of intelligence"*: several events and initiatives are analysing how intelligence (both natural and artificial) will develop in the following decades, individually and collectively as a "global brain" (Bernstein et al., 2012).

This list establishes an unprecedented opportunity, for which we need to set some priorities. Instead of asking whether universal psychometrics is possible, it is better to talk about how far we can reach and where to start. This is configured by the questions we raise next.

1.6 FORMULATING THE QUEST

The statement of a more general problem, as represented by universal psychometrics, leads to new questions, challenges and opportunities. Panel 1.3 highlights those questions that are deemed most relevant, thereby receiving more coverage in this book.

Throughout the book, we will find some positive results about these and other questions. We will also fail to answer some of them properly. In both cases, but especially in the second case, we will discuss some attempts that are postulated as solutions, but do not work in practice or are merely inconsistent. We will identify what the flaws are. Some paradigms and formulations look elegant and enticing, but fail under a deeper scrutiny. This is our version of Thomas Huxley's great 'tragedy' of science: an ugly system in the machine kingdom will unceremoniously slay a beautiful theory.

During this necessarily cross-disciplinary book we will overhaul (and eventually define and formalise) many concepts and tools, such as cognitive task, test validity, interface, adaptive test, difficulty function, agent characteristic

---

Panel 1.3
Some questions for universal psychometrics

The list of *ignoramuses* for universal psychometrics follows:

1. How can behavioural features be measured in the machine kingdom? [2, 6–16, 18]
2. How universal and adaptive can a behavioural test be? [3.7, 9.5, 16]
3. Are IQ tests valid for any machine and what do they measure? [6.3, 7.5]
4. How can abilities be identified, through task breadth or similarity? [10]
5. Is intelligence one or many, objective or subjective? [7, 11]
6. Can we formalise task difficulty without particular populations? [8]
7. Is there a common component for all abilities, a *universal g* factor? [11.5]
8. Can general intelligence be independent of the task distribution? [11]
9. Will scales fully range from minimal cognition to supercapacities? [2, 9]
10. Can intelligence be defined solely with computational principles? [8, 11]
11. Should collectives and hybrids be evaluated unlike their individuals? [15]
12. Is intelligence useful for adaptive testing and self-assessment? [16.4]
13. Can social abilities be measured through *situated* tests? [13]
14. What kind of ability can capture communication and language skills? [14]
15. How can *potential* abilities be measured and how do they develop? [12.5, 12.7]
16. Can any universal machine and human become arbitrarily intelligent? [12.6, 17.3]
17. How can cognitive abilities and personality traits develop in general? [12.2, 12.5]
18. Are behavioural features sufficient to characterise personhood? [17.1, 17.2]
19. What are the limits and consequences of supercapacities? [17.4, 17.6]
20. Can human, animal and AI evaluation benefit from an integration? [6, 18]

Some of the preceding questions may look too idealistic, or resist a precise formulation. The goal of this list is to set the directions for the rest of the book. The numbers in superscripts on the right show the chapters and sections in the book where the questions are addressed. These indications do not suggest that these chapters or sections should be read in isolation.

---

curve, universal test, test administration, task distribution, to name a few. These definitions are not simply instrumental to approaching the questions, but they are also meant to serve as a common conceptualisation with intrinsic explanatory value. Our ultimate goal is to lay new foundations and explain some phenomena with them. It is too soon to tell how far we will reach with the questions and the definitions, but we have inexorably set the course.

CHAPTER HIGHLIGHTS

- New kinds of systems to be evaluated and characterised including computers, cognitively enhanced natural organisms, biologically enhanced computers, collectives and other cognitive systems (Section 1.1).
- The machine kingdom covering all interactive systems (Figure 1.1, Keynote 1.1) under the physical Church-Turing thesis (Panel 1.2).
- The space of behavioural features including personality traits and cognitive abilities (Keynotes 1.3, 1.4, 1.6, Figure 1.3).
- Universal psychometrics measuring all systems in the machine kingdom in terms of their behavioural features (Keynote 1.2), inferring psychometric profiles with a black-box approach (Keynotes 1.7, 1.8).
- A series of challenges, opportunities and open questions (Sections 1.5, 1.6, Panel 1.3).

2

Mind the Step: Scala Universalis

> Each new machine that is built is an experiment. Actually constructing
> the machine poses a question to nature; and we listen for the answer by
> observing the machine in operation and analyzing it by all analytical
> and measurement means available.
> – Allen Newell and Herbert A. Simon,
> *Computer Science as Empirical Inquiry* (1976)

T HE FIRST chapter discussed why universal psychometrics is needed, what
it should address and why this is a good opportunity. In this chapter we
discuss how all this can be achieved. We need to analyse how behaviours are
to be classified and how behavioural features can be defined and measured.
For this purpose, we need to determine the nature of these behavioural features
and what the role of measurement is. In fact, we will see that there is a choice
between two main kinds of measurement, *pragmatic* and *representational*, with
very different explanatory power, applicability and accuracy of measurement.
The methodology to analyse the space of behavioural features also depends on
this choice, as also do the theoretical and experimental tools.

2.1 TAXONOMIES, MEASUREMENTS AND DEFINITIONS

The *scala naturae*, the great chain of being, was the predominant theory for the
classification of organisms from Antiquity to the Middle Ages. Despite its limitations, Aristotle's *History of Animals* was the embryo of all subsequent taxonomies of living things, including Linnaeus's *Systema Naturae*, the father of
modern biological taxonomy, and had a strong influence in early evolutionists,
such as Lamarck, Blumenbach or even Darwin. Blumenbach viewed *scala naturae* as a basis "to order the natural bodies according to their greatest and most

manifold affinity, to bring together the similar ones, and to remove from each other the dissimilar ones" (Blumenbach, 1790, pp. 8–9 cited in Mayr, 1982, p. 201). The principle of similarity could appear in terms of a self-evident affinity, such as the similarities between parrots and pigeons, or through analogy, such as the similarities between seals and penguins. In the end, the use of different concepts of similarity would lead to different taxonomies. Actually, many taxonomies use several features at a time, and taxonomists may have heated debates about which feature is most relevant. It is only very recently that species can also be classified through phylogenetic analysis using DNA information. However, the very notion of species is still linked to the ability of interbreeding and producing fertile offspring and not about a rupture in the DNA continuum. But more conspicuously, a difference of one single nucleobase between two individuals – rendering almost identical genotypes – may enable or disable a series of important genes, leading to very different phenotypes.

The case of biological taxonomies is an excellent starting point for our discussion. We have defined the machine kingdom as a generalisation of the animal kingdom, and it can be seen as a superset of all living beings. From biology we have learnt how complex it is to define a taxonomy that is universally accepted, even when the main mechanisms have been unravelled, such as why the individuals exist (natural selection), and their evolutionary history can be traced back (through fossil records or DNA analysis). In both natural and artificial systems it is easy to realise – as any programmer knows well – that *information distances* in the genotype (program) are difficult to translate to *similarities* of the phenotype (traits), and vice versa. Anyhow, we see that to work out any taxonomy, we require the establishment of a set of relevant traits and the construction of similarity criteria using them.

Similarities can originate from observations with the naked eye or from more complex observation procedures, based on measurement instruments or protocols. The result of a measurement is a quantity or a quality of an individual, which can then be used to a better understanding of the single individual or, for taxonomists, to an ascription to a group, family or domain. The goal of a measurement is to reduce our uncertainty about an object, so that we can predict some of its behaviour according to the measurement and the theories about the magnitude, the object and its category (e.g., if a piece of metal is too hot, it will melt or shine or conduct electricity).

The dilemma in science, and measurement in particular, is not a choice between quantitative and qualitative, but between objective and subjective. For instance, Linnaeus was the first to classify humans among the apes in his *Systema Naturae*. This was a qualitative move that was revolutionary for the time. Since then, the organisation of the ape family, for instance, has changed many

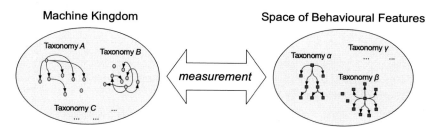

Figure 2.1. Measurements connect the machine kingdom and the space of behavioural features. Elements in the machine kingdom and elements in the space of behavioural features can be organised in taxonomies.

times. Actually, recent phylogenetic analysis comparing DNA has grouped humans, chimpanzees and bonobos closer together than the rest of the apes.

The properties that are observed or measured change or evolve with time jointly with the taxonomy itself. This means that the effort for constructing a taxonomy over the individuals is paralleled with the effort of organising a taxonomy over the properties of the individuals. In psychometrics, for instance, theories of intelligence are hierarchical taxonomies over the set of cognitive abilities. This duality is better realised when we see that measurements link properties with individuals. In the case of universal psychometrics, measures, in the form of tests, link the machine kingdom with the space of behavioural features, as shown in Figure 2.1.

But what happens when new artificial entities can be created at will? Can we always create an element that breaks any taxonomy? In this case, the parallelism with biological taxonomies is insufficient. Language taxonomies illustrate this with interesting particularities. Namely, the similarity criteria and measured magnitudes to compare natural languages are not directly extensible to artificial languages, which do not follow the same underlying theory (and constraints) as natural languages. For instance, the regularity of the invented language Esperanto, and the way its vocabulary was compiled is at odds with the rest. Many language taxonomies today still relegate artificial languages to a special family of languages, the constructed languages, without properly integrating them into the rest of the taxonomy.

The language domain also shows that some features are easy to define and measure, while others are much more problematic (e.g., mutual intelligibility). Is it always the case that a good definition ensures a good measurement procedure and vice versa? The answer is no, and we can find some examples. The speed of light has a very precise definition, but it is not easy to measure. Consumer satisfaction is difficult to define in a formal way, but it can be measured in practice. How can we measure a concept for which we do not have a definition?

Psychological measurement relies on the actual construction of tests:

> **Keynote 2.1.** A **behavioural test** is a measurement tool that can capture occurrences of behaviour.

In fact "all psychological tests of any kind measure nothing more or less than samples of behaviour" (Urbina, 2011), in the same way that physical instruments measure samples of physical phenomena. Therefore, we know what the test, the instrument, records, but what does it measure? This is what we explore next.

2.2 PARADIGMS OF BEHAVIOURAL MEASUREMENT

Measurement in the social sciences is said to be more difficult than measurement in other scientific disciplines (Hand, 2004, p. 163), such as in *metrology*. This difficulty of measurement in psychology has been compensated by a strenuous effort in rigour. Many tools of modern measurement theory were developed for psychological measurement by Galton, Pearson and Spearman before becoming tools in mainstream statistics. Statistics plays an important role in measurement because of the notion of replicability, which is usually achieved by repetition and aggregation. In the end, measurement is only useful if it is consistent.

> **Keynote 2.2.** The goal of **measurement** is the consistent "assignment of numbers to represent the magnitude of attributes of a system we are studying or which we wish to describe" (Hand, 2004, p. 3).

The crucial part is again the "attributes of a system", so we need to know both the universe of attributes and the universe of systems. Hand's definition is standard, but the relevance of the term 'magnitude' has to be clarified. Not all measurements are of quantitative things. We can measure binary responses (present or absent, right or wrong) or multi-valued. When they are repeated and aggregated over a series of trials we actually measure a frequency, or probability, which becomes a number.

One feature of measurement theory in the physical sciences that is generally overlooked in the social sciences is the *unit* of measurement. Without a proper

Table 2.1. Kinds of measurement according to the type of the attribute, whether they have a zero and what kinds of relations they preserve (Stevens, 1946)

Kind	Zero?	Preserves relations?	Example
Nominal	No	No	The four states of matter
Ordinal	No	No	Educational level
Numerical			
Interval	Arbitrary	Interval differences	Temperature in °C
Ratio	Absolute	Ratio proportions	Temperature in K

unit of measurement, we can have an ordinal appraisal, but not a fully fledged quantitative account of the phenomenon. A magnitude without a unit lacks a meaningful additive structure. Table 2.1 shows several types of measurement, with only 'ratio' being additive.

There are two main approaches to derive a scale in testing: *normed-referenced* and *criterion-referenced* measurement (Glaser, 1963). Normed-referenced measurement derives the scores of an item or test according to the results of a population. In intelligence quotient (IQ) tests, for instance, the score is normalised to have a mean (and median) of 100 and a standard deviation of 15. The *unit*, albeit never recognised as such, would be mapped to 1/15 of the standard deviation. That means that two IQ measurements of, let us say, 135 and 105 differ in 30 units, twice the standard deviation. This lack of a proper (or non-normative) notion of measurement unit has been particularly highlighted by Kline and Michell (Kline, 1998; Michell, 2000, 2008), but it is generally acknowledged in some way or another in psychometrics. For instance, David J. Bartholomew says that general intelligence or, more precisely, the *g* factor, is not measurable in the proper sense, but just "weakly measurable", "at the ordinal level" (Bartholomew, 2004, p. 145). If properties are analysed in a quantitative way, without first clarifying whether the properties are actually quantitative, measurement in psychology can even be stigmatised as a "pathology of science" (Michell, 2000, 2008).

Criterion-referenced measurement, in contrast, derives the scale from a series of levels that are achieved when a series of skills and competencies – the criteria – are met by the subject. A spatial analogy test can give absolute scores or grades depending on how many figures appear in the items. A subject that is able to solve most of the analogies involving two objects but very few of those involving three objects would have a score around two. This scale would be continuous and absolute and would not depend on any population.

Similarly, a different, ordinal, scale may be established according to the kind of the relations involved in the analogy.

Some attributes can be measured *directly*, but others must be measured *indirectly*. For instance, we can measure the length of a stick directly and the distance to a storm indirectly, by the delay of thunder. It is important, especially in the case of attributes that are measured indirectly, to distinguish between the manifest or observable variables (e.g., the symptoms) and the latent variables (e.g., the pathologies). The use of the observable variables instead of the variables of interest may be motivated by the inaccessibility of the latter or may just be a practical issue.

Be it direct or indirect, the crucial distinction about measurement is whether it is *representational* or *pragmatic*:

> **Keynote 2.3.** In **representational measurement** we have a precise concept or *definition* of what is measured. When the feature, or construct, being measured is not fully conceptualised or defined, but still useful, we say it is non-representational or **pragmatic**.

Thermometers perform a representational measurement. By contrast, we might measure the 'tenderness' of a loaf of bread with a spring scale. This measure can be a good predictor of the sales of a particular type of bread. However, the concept of 'tenderness' has not been fully understood.

IQ tests are pragmatic measures of an indicator, known as IQ. It is pragmatic because IQ is a very good predictor of many aspects in human life. "IQ is useful, but stating exactly (in representational terms) how it relates to intelligence is impossible at least in part because there is no clear definition of intelligence" (Hand, 2004, p. 59). Of course, one can define intelligence as what is measured by the IQ tests (Boring, 1923; Van Der Maas et al., 2014). This is what Gould (1981) refers to as the fallacy of the *reification* of intelligence.

In the first chapter we distinguished behavioural features from physical ones. Measurement instruments that only rely on behaviour are consistent with the history of psychometrics and comparative cognition and with the philosophical views that machine intelligence could be determined through tests of perceptible behaviour, first expressed by Ayer, and later Turing with the introduction of the imitation game. As we introduced in Section 1.5, this does not preclude the existence of two kinds of measurement instruments for behavioural features: black-box (e.g., IQ tests) and white-box (e.g., brain size). For instance, in Panel 2.1 we show several approaches of each for human intelligence.

Panel 2.1
Measuring instruments: white-box or black-box?

Are larger brains more intelligent? Are faster brains more intelligent? Are greyer brains more intelligent? These questions have motivated sundry measurement instruments in psychology. Some of these instruments are white-box approaches and do not test the behaviour of the subject at all. However, they are still able to report some moderate correlation with IQ values. The following table enumerates several measurement instruments, whether they are black-box (BB) and the correlation with IQ (or related tests and indicators, depending on the study).

Instrument	BB	Cor	Source
Total brain volume	No	0.42	(Betjemann et al., 2010)
Frontal lobe volume (MRI)	No	0.41	(Thompson et al., 2001)
Grey matter volume (MRI)	No	0.37	(Narr et al., 2007)
Simple reaction time	Yes	−0.49	(Deary et al., 2001)
Response time with 4 choices	Yes	−0.51	(Deary et al., 2001)
Arithmetic (WAIS)	Yes	0.68	(Deary, 2000a)
Thurstone Letter Series	Yes	0.52	(Stankov, 2000)

The preceding list shows a very diverse range of instruments to choose from if we want a rough approximation of IQ for humans. The interesting – and provocative – question, from the perspective of this book, is which of them, if any, is still useful and meaningful for arbitrary machines.

Psychological assessment has traditionally been performed with a black-box approach, which comprises simple observation but also the most common and systematic approach through the use of tests. A non-behavioural white-box approach can perform an indirect measurement of a cognitive ability through the measurement of some physical traits. For instance, brain size (or more precisely the encephalisation quotient, normalised by body mass) has been proposed as an indirect instrument for intelligence evaluation in mammals. Actually, in humans, there is a significant correlation of brain size with IQ results, as shown in Panel 6.1. Accurate white-box approaches used to be invasive, such as physical brain exploration, using the number or density of neurons, the proportion of grey and white matter, or the degree of demyelination.

White-box measurement is increasingly more popular as precise noninvasive neuroimaging becomes more widespread. These techniques are being used to predict *future* reading skills, working memory capacity, response to depression or dyslexia treatments. In fact, "neuromarkers often provide better predictions (neuroprognosis), alone or in combination with other measures, than traditional behavioral measures" (Gabrieli et al., 2015). Examples are reported for the prediction of future mathematical ability in children of 6–16 years of age and second-grade reading abilities for kindergarteners.

Computers seem perfect subjects for white-box measurement. In fact, the introductory quote of the chapter by Newell and Simon advocates for computer science as an experimental science, but continues with a vindication of white-box approaches: "neither machines nor programs are black boxes: they are artifacts that have been designed, both hardware and software, and we can open them up and look inside. We can relate their structure to their behavior and draw many lessons from a single experiment. We don't have to build 100 copies of, say, a theorem prover, to demonstrate statistically that it has not overcome" (Newell and Simon, 1976).

Despite the encouraging results and prospects of white-box approaches for both natural beings and artificial systems, there are important reasons why we should focus on black-box evaluation, mostly using tests as instruments. First, white-box approaches are not as powerful as they may seem. AI artefacts of today are much more complex than systems of the 1970s. In consequence, the correspondence between program and behaviour is difficult to trace, with similar behaviours corresponding to very different programs and vice versa. In fact, any attempt to do some kind of phylogenetic analysis, i.e., a 'phyloalgorithmic' analysis, to understand and classify AI systems, will hardly be consistent with their behaviour. The main problem, though, is that, instead of a fully fledged specification, many AI systems of today start with some basic principles and require a training or development stage to solve a task. For instance, the area of developmental robotics starts with robots that learn from the interaction with the world. Likewise, many adaptive systems are tuned by the use of a huge amount of training data. As a result, the behaviour of the system and its functionality has to be evaluated. For instance, Mnih et al. (2015) present a deep reinforcement learning system that is able to learn to play 49 Atari 2600 video games. Even if the algorithm is well understood and explained, it is basically unpredictable how the system is going to behave for each of the 49 games. An experimental (black-box) evaluation is not only necessary, but also the yardstick used to assess the quality of the system.

It can be argued that things would be different if the training process could lead to some kind of inspectable and intelligible knowledge, as in some symbolic approaches to machine learning (Gulwani et al., 2015). However, for any complex problem it is not clear that even with complete access and understanding of all the learnt rules, the analysis could lead to an accurate prediction of its performance. Similarly, for humans, even if, e.g., a non-invasive scan detects that a child's brain has a high potential of mathematically abilities, at some point we need to check whether the child *actually* has the ability, with a traditional behavioural test.

A second, more important, reason for a black-box evaluation is that we want to measure and compare elements in the machine kingdom with different architectures and mechanisms. This can only be possible if we have measurement instruments that are not specialised for the inner workings of a given organism, but can cover a wide range. This does not mean that we need to define a test for all, a universal test, as we will discuss in Chapter 16, but that the tests are based on properties that can go across different types of organisms.

A third, practical reason is that, in many situations, especially in virtual environments, we do not have access to the code of the system. We may not even know whether the behaviour comes from a human or a computer.

White-box approaches (and hybrid tests) can still be a very powerful source of insight for universal psychometrics, but a subject-independent measurement must ultimately be about how the system works as a black-box, through behavioural tests.

2.3 ACCURACY, SPECIALISATION AND CALIBRATION

Whatever kind of measurement instrument we use, it must be accurate. In measurement theory, accuracy is usually analysed under two indicators: validity and reliability.

> **Keynote 2.4.** The **validity** of a measurement is the agreement with what is purportedly measured. When we do not have a good model or definition of what is being measured, validity is interpreted as the degree in which the measurement leads to useful predictions or understanding about the object that has been measured.

The first interpretation of validity (accordance with the true concept) is sometimes known as *face validity* and is related to representational measurement, whereas the second type is known as *predictive validity*, more related to pragmatic measurement. Tests of response time are examples of instruments with

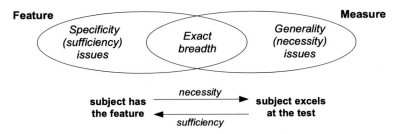

Figure 2.2. Generality and specificity issues affecting validity.

face validity, because it is clear what is being measured (and its units). Face validity can be undermined by systematic errors. For instance, if a response time test is performed using a device or computer connected through a network, the connection delay will create a systematic error – a bias – and the measurement will be higher than it should be.

Many other psychological measurements rely on predictive validity, such as IQ tests. IQ has been shown to correlate with and predict many behaviours and outcomes in human lives, such as academic success, non-religiosity and health.

Poor validity, especially when related to a representational measurement, may have two sources: a measure is too general (it includes some features that are not part of the notion to be measured) or it is too specific (it does not account for all the features the notion is thought to encompass). In other words, the measure should account for all, but not more, of the concept features it tries to represent. We refer to these two issues of validity as the *generality* and the *specificity* of the measure, which can determine the *sufficiency* and the *necessity* of a test, respectively. Figure 2.2 represents specificity and generality, which can happen simultaneously.

The other leg of accuracy is reliability:

Keynote 2.5. The **reliability** (or precision) of a measurement refers to low variability of multiple measurements.

Poor reliability may be caused by the operator, external (confounding) factors, stochastic processes and memory effects (how previous items affect the result of subsequent items), among other things. Basically, unreliability depends on nonsystematic errors, i.e., the variance of the results. The idea that two administrations of the same test over the same object should give the same result is known as test-retest reliability. A common procedure is to repeat the test for the same individual and check whether the correlation of results is high. Many IQ tests have a test-retest reliability higher than 0.95.

Assume that we have a theoretical notion of a behavioural feature Ψ for any subject or agent π as the overall performance for a set M of problems, tasks or items (each with a response or result R) under a certain probability distribution p. We could then give a representational definition of the feature as the following weighted sum (note the use of the symbol $\triangleq$ for definitions):

$$\Psi(\pi, M, p) \triangleq \sum_{\mu \in M} p(\mu) \cdot R(\pi, \mu) \qquad (2.1)$$

If M is finite, a common choice for p is a uniform distribution, and the expression simplifies to $\frac{1}{|M|} \sum_{\pi \in M} R(\pi, \mu)$. This just defines a behavioural feature as the performance over a set of items or situations. For instance, let us consider the ability of performing additions within a time limit of 10 seconds defined by a set of tasks M that comprises all additions of two natural numbers, and let p be a distribution over M, such as a composite geometric distribution over pairs of numbers giving more probability to small numbers. We also need to define how numbers are represented and presented. More importantly, we need to determine how we score right answers, wrong answers and empty answers, so that item results are commensurate (on the same magnitude range). In this case, we could assume a classical pen and paper test with $R(\pi, \mu) \triangleq 1$ if the addition is correct and 0 otherwise.

Usually, Eq. 2.1 specifies the feature, but the way an actual test is administered may be different. For a given feature ψ, the administration of a non-adaptive test can be defined as

$$\hat{\psi}(\pi, M', w) \triangleq \sum_{\mu \in M'} w(\mu) \cdot R(\pi, \mu) \qquad (2.2)$$

where $M' \subset M$ has been sampled from M (using the distribution p or not) and w is a weighting function. For instance, if we design an addition test for humans, instead of using p, we can just create the set M' to have 5 sums of two digits, 5 sums of three digits, 5 sums of four digits and 5 sums of five digits, to have an appropriate range of items of different difficulty. We exclude very easy sums (one digit) because they are not expected to be discriminative for humans in the same way we exclude very large sums because humans cannot usually do them in less than 10 seconds. Given this finite set M' we can calculate w in such a way that the sample weighting is in consonance with the original distribution.

In this example we see that the accuracy of the test may be affected by many characteristics of the test, including R, M' and w. For instance, a bad choice of

w may affect validity in a significant way. Reliability would be clearly affected by the use of a sample M' of just 25 items. We could increase the reliability of the test by including more items, as the variance between tests would be reduced. Logically, there must be a compromise between the reliability of a test and the time that is required to have a good measurement. The ratio of these two things is referred to as *efficiency*. Adding more items is not the only way of increasing reliability. A better sampling choice could increase reliability if we ensure that more diverse items are generated or we use a better estimation of difficulty (e.g., the sum $1111 + 2222$ is very easy).

The aggregation in Eqs. 2.1 and 2.2 assumes that the values of R are commensurate across different items in M. Otherwise, the whole sum would be imbalanced and the use of p or w would be pointless, as one item might give a magnitude many times higher than another, or might have anomalous measurements. This is related to a more general problem of how several manifest variables originating from a test are aggregated. For instance, there are alternative aggregations other than average-case performance, such as best-case performance or worst-case performance, or the use of a median. The choice depends on what we want to measure, and Eq. 2.1 could also be defined in a different way. For instance, if we are concerned with measuring a person's steadiness when performing additions, then a worst-case performance aggregation or a higher penalty for errors would be more meaningful. This is just a brief illustration of the many subtleties of finding an appropriate definition Ψ and deriving an actual implementation of a test that leads to a valid and reliable measurement $\hat{\psi}$.

A common source of error in behavioural measurement emanates from subjects that can see (or foresee) some of the evaluation apparatus. This is a general problem in measurement, as *the thing being measured is affected by the measurement procedure*. Measurement 'interference' can make some subjects improve because they know they are being evaluated (the Hawthorne effect) while others may show worse results (get nervous, suspicious or defiant). However, the most treacherous source of error is the knowledge of the subject (or its designer) about the measurement:

Keynote 2.6. The **evaluation specialisation** is the preparation or modification of the evaluee to excel in a test, leading to a measurement error. This phenomenon is known by different names, such as 'measurement overfitting', 'teaching to the test', Goodhart's law or Campbell's law, depending on the discipline and the context.

Many consider this a reliability issue, especially when this knowledge is acquired by repeated testing (sometimes known as the 'memory effect') and detectable by a test-retest approach (Hand, 2004, p. 139). However, on many occasions, specialisation errors are more systematic than non-systematic, and they can be considered a validity issue, especially for AI systems. For instance, if the system has some information, training or familiarity with the test, the result will probably be better, creating a systematic bias.

The evaluation specialisation problem will be recurrent in the rest of the book. It clearly happens for animals and humans, but it is with computers that the effect reaches its most radical effects. The systems can be specialised for the feature (Eq. 2.1) or for the test (Eq. 2.2). It is very easy to construct a system that performs well for addition problems if we are told beforehand that the system is going to be evaluated for that skill only. Of course that does not make the result invalid per se, as the machine is indeed able to perform additions. The problem appears if the skill was meant to be used as an indirect indicator of another ability. In fact, before the advent of computers, mastery in arithmetic was considered to be a good indicator of intelligence. Now that a pocket calculator does better than any of us, we cannot longer associate basic arithmetic skills with the intelligence of an arbitrary machine. If some IQ tests still feature arithmetic tasks, it is because that indirect measurement works for humans.

Evaluation specialisation can happen for a skill or a particular test. If M' or w in Eq. 2.2 are publicly known, then it is easy to rote-learn (or to hardwire a system) such that the test is gamed completely. This is an example of a failure of face validity that originates from a bad definition of the test or a bad administration, since the test no longer measures the skill. Indeed, it is not surprising that many IQ tests are not public, because otherwise the subjects would prepare and specialise for them, in the very same way as exams are not disclosed until they are taken.

Another term that is usually associated with measurement accuracy is calibration. Calibration tries to avoid systematic errors, such as overestimation and underestimation. It can also involve an adjustment of the scale, since a measurement can systematically overestimate on a range of values and systematically underestimate on a different range, even if the *global* bias is zero. However, this natural meaning of calibration is usually replaced by a different notion in psychological measurement. David Hand explains the difference very well: "note that the word 'calibration' here is used in a sense slightly different from, say, calibrating a weighting scale. In the latter case, 'calibration' might mean adjusting the baseline so that the machine is accurate. In the present case, 'calibration' is effectively producing a different scale for each distinct norm group" (Hand, 2004, p. 155). In other words, *norm-based* psychological measurement calibrates a measurement instrument for a particular population and is very different to a physical calibration, for which instruments can be more accurate in a narrow range, but they are calibrated against the full universal scale.

This has profound consequences when we apply a measurement instrument, a test, to a different population. What if we apply an IQ test to a chimpanzee? Even if we adapt the interface, the results will be wrong and misleading (in this case, an underestimation is the most likely result of the process). More conspicuously, we do not need to move between species to see this problem. What if we apply a verbal test for children to an adult? Or an IQ test for adults to an adult human who has grown up without contact with any civilisation? What about mentally disabled people?

While all this has set enormous difficulties to psychological testing in the past, the calibration problem is in principle solvable, as we have the notion of the 'population' we want the test to be calibrated for. However, when we incorporate machines into the landscape, the notion of population evaporates. What is a machine population? The consequences are appalling:

Keynote 2.7. Calibration for the whole machine kingdom population: It is unclear what reference subpopulation or machine distribution to choose to universally calibrate a behavioural test.

This is, as we already discussed in the previous chapter, one of the main motivations for this book and, by extension, for universal psychometrics.

2.4 THE DIFFICULTIES OF UNIVERSAL SCALES

In physics, the relevance of Kelvin "absolute thermometric scale" does not really lie on whether there is an absolute zero but rather that the scale is quantitative, universal and one-dimensional. This is more extraordinary as we realise how complex the notion of temperature is, linked to entropy and other key concepts in physics. Other fundamental physical phenomena have more dimensions. Waves are measured by frequency, amplitude and velocity. In the context of cognitive evaluation, are cognitive abilities quantitative, universal and one-dimensional? Can we universally talk about any element in the machine kingdom, as having more or less of each ability?

For instance, memory is a behavioural feature. Indeed, many cognitive tasks cannot be solved without memory. Does it make sense to say that one subject has better memory than another, with a one-dimensional scale? In technical terms, one can argue that we need to be more specific, as there is short-term memory, long-term memory, working memory, sensory memory, etc. That is all very well, but even if we are more specific, does it make sense to measure, e.g., short-term memory, on a one-dimensional scale? The answer hinges upon whether we are doing a representational measurement with a precise definition of memory. As the answer is usually negative for cognitive abilities – with exceptions such as response and reaction time – the issue is solved pragmatically with a construct. This construct is *assumed* to be quantitative and one-dimensional, and the results of one or more tests are associated with the constructed magnitude. But this pragmatic solution does not mean that the related original feature is necessarily monolithic or that the derived scale really corresponds to the *unit* of the original feature. Actually, if we are talking about memory, we should measure it in bits, as we do with computers, and not by some aggregated score or, worse, by a position statistic given by the test results within a particular human population.

One paradigmatic case of a pragmatic one-dimensional measurement is again the IQ, for which a *calibrated* scale is derived for an adult human population, with the mean and standard deviation set on 100 and 15, respectively. With the complexity and subtleties of a concept such as intelligence, it seems clear that one single constructed magnitude loses information about the original feature, but it is useful (predictive and/or explanatory) for many purposes. In fact, some information is lost on purpose, as IQ usually aggregates many tests covering a range of abilities. This is an example of a multidimensional construct being reduced to a one-dimensional construct and scale, with a unit that derives from a distribution.

Is this obsession for one-dimensional scales a revival of the *scala naturae*? For instance, Panel 2.2 shows a scale of mammals according to their cerebral cortex size (the unit is the number of neurons). This scale is especially reassuring for humans, as we appear at one edge.

The fundamental problem when we consider the full animal kingdom and, ultimately, the machine kingdom is how a universal scale can be meaningful for every possible subject, like the thermometric scale. A universal scale does not necessarily mean that we require an absolute zero, but that we need some units or reference points for a proper mapping to that scale. In other words, even if we say that the intelligence of a rat is, let us say, 10 units, and that of a human is 100 units, and decide to use these two kinds of subjects as yardsticks, we still need some mechanism to extrapolate between these two points, below 10 and most especially above 100. This would be similar to setting 0 degrees Celsius on freezing water and 100 degrees Celsius on boiling water, without knowing what a degree represents. Unfortunately, for the machine kingdom, we cannot

---

Panel 2.2
Cortical neurons for several animals

What does the number of cortical neurons say?

Animal	Million neurons	Source
Mouse	14	Herculano-Houzel et al. (2015)
Dog	160	Roth and Dicke (2013)
Cat	300	Roth and Dicke (2013)
Pig	307	Herculano-Houzel et al. (2015)
Capuchin monkeys	720	Roth and Dicke (2013)
Horse	1,200	Roth and Dicke (2013)
African elephant	5,593	Herculano-Houzel et al. (2015)
Bottlenose dolphin	5,800	Roth and Dicke (2013)
Chimpanzee	6,200	Roth and Dicke (2013)
Whales	10,500	Roth and Dicke (2013)
Human	16,300	Herculano-Houzel et al. (2015)

This and other scales are predictive of performance in problem-solving tasks, especially if corrected by body size (Benson-Amram et al., 2016). This does not mean, however, that we can understand this scale as an intelligence scale or make statements such as humans being three times more intelligent than elephants.

---

derive the unit by taking some data and assuming a normal distribution, as done with IQ results, because we do not have a reference population any more.

We may criticise the use of the scale shown in Panel 2.2 for many reasons, but there is one compelling argument in its favour: neurons are responsible for cognitive behaviour, so the number of neurons sets a maximum capacity of the brain. The kinds of neurons each organism has and how they are organised are perhaps more important, but their number is still useful as a rough approximation of maximum capacity. This is even more meaningful when we realise that a cognitive ability must necessarily be linked to the capacity of an organism, to its *cognitive resources*. Any scale about cognitive abilities reflects that they are gradient features, i.e., a higher magnitude means higher capability. However, this does not necessarily mean that more difficult, or challenging, situations can be solved. A system can consistently score better than another independently of the difficulty of the items, just by solving more exercises (e.g., being more steady). However, it is still intuitive to expect that people with high cognitive abilities are able to solve difficult problems. In fact, steadiness will ultimately have a stronger effect on complex tasks, involving more elements where a mistake can be made, than on simple tasks, involving fewer elements.

> **Keynote 2.8. Ability and difficulty are complementary** and will affect performance. The *steadiness* of the system will also contribute to performance, especially as the tasks become more difficult. Consequently, evaluating cognitive abilities without the concept of difficulty is, at best, questionable.

All this is not new for psychometrics: item response theory, as we will see in the following chapter, sees ability (referred to as proficiency) and difficulty as complementary. However, in item response theory, it is customary to derive difficulty from experimental data using a subject population. Can we do the same without a population?

A difficulty function that is not derived from a population must be based on some definitory characteristics of the problems the ability is expected to solve. For instance, in an addition problem, difficulty can be properly linked to the resources needed to compute each particular item, which of course depend on the two numbers involved. Even for a relatively well understood problem like addition, the difficulty function is not straightforward (why is $1111 + 2222$ much easier for humans than $7892 + 2359$?). However, despite the obstacles, an absolute difficulty function depending on the nature of the problem and not on the subjects should be pursued.

If an absolute difficulty is defined, the scale for cognitive abilities can be set to go from zero difficulty to maximum or infinite difficulty. Indeed, this is true for some *physical* abilities too. For instance, high jumpers are evaluated by the difficulty of the jump, which is directly related to its height. In general, this approach addresses the unit of scale from the very beginning, with difficulty functions associated with many different units: bits, seconds, centimetres, number of items, etc.

As a consequence of the importance of difficulty, we should not give the same value and weight to easy instances as to difficult ones, as for the definition (Eq. 2.1) or measurement (Eq. 2.2) of cognitive abilities. This will force us to reunderstand these equations in terms of difficulty in the following chapters. For personality traits, there is no connection with difficulty, thereby needing a different approach.

2.5 FACTORS: SUBJECTIVE OR RELATIVE?

In addition to the scale and units of each behavioural feature, in the previous chapter we anticipated that the identification of cognitive abilities could be one of the major questions for universal psychometrics. How many cognitive abilities are there? How do they relate to each other? Again, the answer to these questions depends on the population of interest. For humans, these questions have been analysed for decades by psychometrics, using tests comprising different tasks. The results from the tests, the manifest variables, are then analysed very thoroughly using latent factor analysis. The extracted latent factors are finally incarnated or reified as abilities. To identify a unique set of factors, factor analysis makes several assumptions, such as conditional independence of the manifest variables (each of them can solely be explained by the latent variables, without the use of all the other manifest variables), and conventions, such as setting latent variables to have unit variance and zero mean. Unlike the apparently similar principal component analysis (PCA), factor analysis relies on a model that makes inferences about the underlying factors or latent variables for the general population, despite the fact that the data are just taken from a sample of subjects and task items (for a thorough discussion see Bartholomew, 2004, chap. 7).

However, when we set the machine kingdom as the universe of interest, we can no longer work in the same way. First, all the findings using factor analysis for the human population may hold or not beyond humans. For instance, if the analogical reasoning ability is highly correlated with the inductive reasoning ability in humans, is it necessarily the case for other animals, or for an arbitrarily constructed machine? If a single subject scores very well on ability *A* but very poorly on ability *B*, is it sufficient evidence to consider *A* and *B* as different abilities? Certainly not, as the correlations are relative to the chosen population. One single subject would not alter a large population significantly. But things would be radically different if we replicated that subject millions of times. Without a clear reference population in the machine kingdom, we will need to analyse the relations between abilities in a different way. But how?

One possible approach is to define a distribution over the machine kingdom and use it to derive a sample with which factor analysis can be used. This approach, however, hinges upon a reasonable choice of a distribution for the machine kingdom, which includes all possible interactive machines, most of them doing nothing of interest. A different approach relies on a representational measurement. We need to formulate theories that explain, and eventually prove, that some abilities must be linked to other abilities. In other words, theories that say that – under some assumptions about the system – if a system is able to solve problems of kind A of difficulty h_A then it necessarily must solve problems of kind B of difficulty h_B. It may be the case that for two abilities we cannot show that one implies the other, but we can at least show that there is a relation that can be expressed as a similarity function.

On top of all the previous research questions we have the problem of locating the role of intelligence among all the other abilities. There seems to be an agreement that if intelligence is a cognitive ability it must be a special one. But as soon as we scratch the surface, the disagreement appears. Is it an amalgamation of many other cognitive abilities? Or is it a core ability that contaminates all the others? Can we have cognitive abilities that are unrelated to intelligence? Again, these questions have been approached with tools such as factor analysis. Charles Spearman, who developed the basics of factor analysis for this purpose more than a century ago, postulated (Spearman, 1904, 1927) that there was a single main factor:

Keynote 2.9. The *g* **factor** is a single factor that accounts for a large proportion of the human variability in performance on all intellectual tasks and, most especially, on IQ tests.

General factors can be found in other domains and may even become everyday concepts. Following the "sports analogy", Flynn (2007, p. 6) says that "we have all said of someone that they have athletic ability and meant that they seem to excel at all sports not just at one, so they have [a high] athletic *g* score". So it should not be controversial to associate the *g* factor with a general cognitive ability or even with general intelligence. What is not universally accepted is to understand that there is a common cause or essence for the phenomenon (Van Der Maas et al., 2006; Conway and Kovacs, 2015).

A more important source of disagreement is how to accommodate all other cognitive abilities. Thurstone (1938) replied with his *several* primary mental abilities, which we will see in the following chapter (Table 3.1). The discussion between a multi-dimensional or one-dimensional view of intelligence found a way out in the so-called hierarchical approaches, such as Carroll's three-stratum theory (Carroll, 1993), where the *g* factor is placed at the top, primary abilities at an intermediate layer and secondary abilities at the bottom layer (Figure 3.2). We will analyse this and other *theories* of intelligence in the next chapter.

A multi-dimensional or hierarchical view of the space of abilities is very different to the so-called theory of multiple intelligences (MI) (Gardner, 1983) and other theories that introduce new 'intelligences', such as the emotional intelligence (EI) theory (Salovey and Mayer, 1990), or very peculiar effects between abilities, such as the Mozart effect (ME) (Rauscher et al., 1993). Until evidence is found in favour of any of these theories, the statements of their relevance must always be cautious (Goleman, 1996; Murphy, 2006). For instance, the view that every child has a hidden talent at which she can excel is comforting for parents, but is against scientific evidence. Waterhouse (2006) stated that the "MI theory has no validating data, that the ME theory has more negative than positive findings, and that EI theory lacks a unitary empirically supported construct".

At this point, it is too soon to discuss whether all intellectual abilities are correlated with the g factor or there are abilities that are not correlated at all (for a discussion, see, e.g., Alliger, 1988). It is also too soon to determine what hierarchical organisation is best and what abilities are just reformulations of other abilities or constructs with absolutely no predictive or explanatory power at all. The crucial question for universal psychometrics is whether all the correlations between intellectual abilities are a contingent or a necessary finding. In other words, must all intellectual abilities be correlated? However, since the notion of correlation is population-dependent, for the machine kingdom we should reformulate the question: is there a general ability such that for every system that has a certain degree in that general ability, the system must necessarily have a certain degree in other intellectual abilities? In other words, is there an *ars generalis*?

But how can we find evidence about the set of abilities and their relationships for the entire machine kingdom? Kevin Warwick claimed that, in his book (Warwick, 2000, p. 3), "the intelligence of humans [would] be directly compared with that of animals, insects and robots". However, later in his book, he stated that "comparing the intelligence of individuals in different species is therefore almost meaningless, except of undertaking specific tasks" (Warwick, 2000, p. 201). His proposal is actually a caricature of the multiple intelligence theory, a "theory of subjective intelligence", where the term 'subjective' is not understood as 'relative' but simply as individual, particular and arbitrary. He disdains psychometric research by stating that "IQ tests do not truly measure intelligence" (Warwick, 2000, p. 85). But it is not just a problem of IQ, he claims, but plainly that "it is not possible to compare two individuals and categorically state that one has a higher intelligence than the other" (Warwick, 2000, p. 70). Then he proposes a hypersphere or rosette where every possible ability can be considered, including "smell abilities" (Warwick, 2000, p. 160) or "telepathy" (Warwick, 2000, p. 145). As there is always a task for which an individual can excel, all individual rosettes would be equally good (Warwick, 2000, p. 139). In the end, the conclusion of Warwick's book is then that "it is perhaps impossible to achieve an objective test of intelligence. Each test of intelligence would need to be different for each species, for each collective group within a species, and ultimately for each individual within a species" (Warwick, 2000, p. 209).

Universal psychometrics must be at stark contrast with the methodology of Warwick's book and its conclusions. However, he does highlight the dangers of postulating theories that are not falsifiable and are not accompanied by some theoretical and experimental support. Going beyond humans paves the way of postulating illusory theories, and this has happened in artificial intelligence since its inception.

Another reason why we highlight these theories is that we cannot consider *every* possible ability, as defined by every possible task, or a sampling on them. We need to derive abstract abilities that are representative for wide groups of tasks. David Hand puts it this way: "any test which purports to measure general intelligence, rather than merely one of the subtypes which have been postulated, must include within it components which assess the different types of cognitive processing. This may not be easy to achieve. Certainly, the notion that one can sample from the space of possible cognitive functions, in the same way as one can sample from the space of people who will be given the test when validating it, is difficult to defend" (Hand, 2004, p. 161).

This discussion is closely related to the choice of M and p in Eq. 2.1, for intelligence and for any other ability. The idea of choosing M as the set of all possible tasks and p as a way to sample from it in a 'balanced' way seems attractive. It has several pitfalls, though:

- It would be very surprising if by choosing tasks randomly one could cover the right relevance of abilities such as abstract reasoning, planning, inductive reasoning or verbal abilities.
- If p does not take difficulty into account the aggregation will be spoiled from the very start, as very easy tasks could dominate the distribution.
- Treating every possible problem as equally likely, something that is associated with the so-called no-free-lunch theorems (Wolpert and Macready, 1995), leads to the impossibility of the very concept of intelligence (Edmonds, 2009). This will be challenged in Chapter 7.
- It would not make sense to use tasks where intelligence is useless. One should test on problems that are solvable by *learning*, such that each task triggers a change in behaviour.

Summing up, what we are discussing here is that any distribution over all tasks that does not recognise their cognitive structure (in terms of task difficulty or similarity) may be unsatisfactory for defining and testing intelligence and ultimately unable to identify a general or central component, such as g. The interest in one general component is not motivated by an oversimplification of intelligence as a single number, but rather because the g factor has been found to be the best predictor of performance for any arbitrary cognitive task. This interest is reinforced by research showing that the *g* factor may also be present in non-human animals (Matzel and Kolata, 2010; Reader et al., 2011) and human collectives (Woolley et al., 2010). The existence of a general intelligence component beyond humans and non-human animals is an open question we will investigate in this book.

2.6 THE RELEVANCE OF ALGORITHMIC INFORMATION

As we have already realised, the extension of the universe of systems that are to be measured creates serious difficulties about how to define measurement instruments, their scale and their relation. Things even become more challenging when we consider the desiderata for such instruments: a "scientific measure of intelligence . . . should be . . . non-Boolean, factorial, non-anthropocentric, computational and meaningful" (Hernández-Orallo, 2000a). The first two desiderata summarise the need for a universal quantitative scale and a multidimensional perspective, respectively. But what about reconciling the last three? Why and how should intelligence measurement be non-anthropocentric, computational and meaningful? Let us start with the last one, that the measure must be meaningful. As we cannot identify populations, we need a representational measure based on face validity, instead of a pragmatic one based on predictive validity. For instance, many of the traits for which IQ scores are predictive and explanatory in humans, such as academic success, fertility and health, are meaningless for computers.

If physical phenomena use physical theories to devise good measurement instruments, cognitive phenomena, which are linked to information processing, should be grounded on computation and information theory. Choosing tasks that are defined in *computational* terms is the way of making them meaningful. This also makes them *non-anthropocentric*, as the instruments are not an extrapolation of human intelligence tests but derived from first principles. In addition, as the measurement tools are representational, a computational analysis of the tasks and the abilities defined from them can shed light on their (*factorial*) relationships. Finally, once the abilities and the tasks measuring them are realised in computational terms, we can also derive the difficulty functions and a gradual, *non-Boolean*, scale from it.

The construction of tasks that account for some ability in a computational way does not mean that these tasks are completely different from those already found in psychometric tests. In fact, there is no prima-facie reason to exclude many of the tasks that have been used in psychometrics and animal cognition. The informal accounts of a task or its difficulty can be formalised in

---

Panel 2.3
Ayumu the chimp acing a spatial memory test

Spatial working memory can be measured in many different ways. One particular task was chosen by Inoue and Matsuzawa (2007) to evaluate the spatial working memory of chimpanzees. During the task, Ayumu and other chimpanzees were shown consecutive numbers from 1 to n placed on randomly chosen cells on a 5 × 8 board. The numbers were visible for exactly some limited *exposition time* after which they disappeared (but the cells remained highlighted). Then the subject had to select the cells in the correct order, from 1 to n. See Figure 2.3 (top).

The use of Arabic numerals makes this task appear suspiciously *anthropocentric*. Other symbols could have been used instead, provided the subject is previously trained about their order, as happened with the chimpanzees. This did not seem to be a limitation for them, as young chimpanzees were able to accomplish the task with sequences of up to nine numbers and exposition times of just 650, 430 and even 210 milliseconds, in which time humans can barely recognise the numbers.

---

computational terms. For instance, to start with a simple case, Panel 2.3 discusses a task that was used to evaluate spatial memory.

This test is an example of a representational measurement, as it is clear that to remember the sequence, the subject must have to possess some short-term memory. Nonetheless, there are many other confounding factors, such as the ability of recognising patterns, the ability of locating objects in two dimensions, the psychomotor ability to press on the squares and the ability to memorise and use an order of nine elements. For instance, suppose we change the panel to a 6 × 6 board and highlight half of the cells (18) while the others are kept off. After a short exposition time, the subject has to press on the cells that were highlighted, in any order. This modified task is also a spatial working memory task. What can we say about the relation of these two tasks theoretically? Will any subject scoring well on one also do well on the other? One requires order and the other does not. One requires the location of 7 squares (out of 40), while the other requires the location of 18 (out of 36). Of course, we can construct a machine that excels (better than humans and chimpanzees) on one but not on the other.

This is not, though, the right question. The question is whether there are non-specialised systems that can *learn* one task without being able to learn the other. We would require a computational model of a learning machine and also a

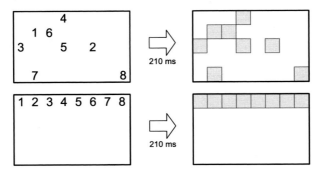

Figure 2.3. Top left: a panel shown for 210 ms. Top right: Once the numbers have disappeared, Ayumu had to use his memory to press on the squares following the order that was set by the numbers. The panels on the bottom show a different instance.

model of what concepts are required for each task (e.g., the first task requires the concept of order while the second does not). Also, the notion of difficulty should be generalised for the two tasks. What is the difficulty of 9 locations that must be remembered in a given order compared with the difficulty of 18 locations that must be remembered without any particular order? If set in some convenient mathematical terms, the problem can be studied computationally. Actually, this is not very far away from the programme that Simon and Kotovsky started in the 1960s with letter series tasks (Simon and Kotovsky, 1963).

This task example can be defined in terms of information processing and it can be addressed with current computer technology, using a camera, a computer vision system, a character recognition program and a simple storage and retrieval system. However, do we have any computer nowadays that can be trained – not programmed – to solve these tests, as Ayumu was trained? The answer is that this is now starting to become possible, as illustrated by some examples such as Spaun, a massive neural model brain (Eliasmith et al., 2012), or the deep reinforcement learning system playing Atari games (Mnih et al., 2015). What we are actually measuring with these systems is the ability of learning new tasks. Actually, this is the most important conclusion from the study with these chimpanzees (Inoue and Matsuzawa, 2007): they are able to learn an alphabet, recognise an order in it and use all this information to select a sequence on a spatial panel.

By a careful analysis of the requirements of many tasks, we may be able to find a set of tasks to measure the feature we are interested in. Any other confounding factors from the task should be eliminated (e.g., we should try to remove order and spatial abilities if we just want to evaluate memory). But what if the elimination of all confounding factors is not possible (either in the task or in the interface)? One possible approach is to use several tasks that have different confounding factors with the desire that they will cancel. A better approach is to use other tests that measure these factors independently so that they can be discounted. Actually, these other tests can be used to ensure that the subject has some necessary abilities that are required for other subsequent tasks. While all this requires painstaking care and dissection of the possible processes involved to solve each task, there seems to be no way around it if we aim at a representational measurement. This is not new for psychometrics, comparative cognition and cognitive research in general. The difference is that for the machine kingdom this is now *necessary* and has to be done more carefully.

As a result, the analysis of requirements and the interactions between tasks must be tackled with more powerful and general theoretical tools, from computation and information theory. Their integration, algorithmic information theory (AIT), will be fundamental. AIT will be properly explained in Chapter 7, but we can get a rough idea by comparing the top and bottom panels in Figure 2.3. Imagine we would code the patterns using a programming language. It is likely that the length of the *shortest algorithm* (program) for the top pattern (its Kolmogorov complexity) would be higher than the length of the shortest algorithm for the bottom pattern. As a result, we infer that the instance on the top requires more *information*. As this task is about memory, we see the top instance as more difficult.

There are several reasons for the relevance of AIT:

- AIT links computation with information and provides a series of concepts and tools to understand key notions such as pattern, random data and transformation effort.
- Difficulty functions will be grounded on variants of Levin's universal search, arranged by program size and computational steps.
- There are important connections between AIT and inductive inference, which ultimately lead to a better understanding of what learning is.
- Some theoretical learning agents based on AIT, under some conditions, are shown to be optimal for all learnable problems. This means that general agents are possible.
- The concept of universal distribution – a notion derived from AIT – is a useful approach upon which one can formalise the distribution of problems and tasks (the p in Eq. 2.1) and even the distribution of agents in the machine kingdom (mostly from a social perspective).

These reasons will be better understood in Chapter 7, where the first two items are seen as *procedural*, linked to the computational resources that are required by the subjects to perform a procedure, while the last three are related to *epistemological* questions about what tasks and abilities represent. In due time, we will also discuss some of the limitations of AIT, such as its incomputability and the choice of a reference machine.

2.7 DRIVEN BY REFUTATION

In the previous sections of this chapter we have identified the extent in which old and new tools can be useful. Before entering the parts of the book where we scrutinise many different theories based on these tools, we need a scientific methodology to appraise them. In particular, we can figure out new tasks, refurbish old ones, derive new abilities, group them into families and fabricate taxonomies. How do we know they are correct? A theoretical analysis can be very helpful, but there are invalid routes that we may not be able to detect easily in a theoretical way.

It is precisely what looks like a limitation that we need to reverse. If the goal is confirmation, a wider space is an inconvenience, but if the goal is refutation, then a wider space is an advantage. Any finding or proposal we may stake as universal may not hold for humans, or may not hold for some non-human animals, or may not hold for some particular kind of machine.

> **Keynote 2.10.** The machine kingdom is a **vast source for refutation**. Any task, ability, test or theory of intelligence must stand the scrutiny of all the possible elements in the machine kingdom.

Our course is then set as a long-term exploration of constructs, tools and theories, many of which will be soon falsified theoretically, with some particular machine models, or experimentally, with actual AI systems, humans or non-human animals. For instance, if we devise a test that purportedly evaluates intelligence for which a dull machine scores equal or better than humans, then we can conclude that the test does not work, and it can be rejected as a universal test for the machine kingdom. In fact, we will show quite a few examples of this in the following chapters.

This is not a surprise, as science must be guided by refutation. If our theories are falsifiable, we are free to explore any possible trajectory, any route. For good or for bad, our understanding of intelligence in general is still so scant that many hypotheses are consistent with the few principles behind the current paradigm, which we may also be tempted to break.

In the rest of this book we will see a few theories for which strenuous efforts have been made elsewhere to accumulate confirming evidence. This is exactly the opposite of what we should do. We must always look for refutation examples – even if they slay a beautiful theory. But it is the epic failures from which we can learn the most. As a result, we will analyse those theories that are shown to be problematic, thereby filling the book with more negative than positive results. Showing what does not work (and why) is one of the duties of a book such as this.

For instance, the task in Panel 2.3 was designed to evaluate spatial working memory. Through experimentation, however, we see that working memory can be masked in subjects with eidetic imagery, such as the chimpanzee, excelling at this problem. In this case, a chimpanzee is not required for refuting this task as a spatial working memory. A computer would also scan the image, store it and then would have infinite time to work with it. Of course it requires memory, but the amount of working memory that a human requires to solve the problem (in the order of hundreds of bits at most) has nothing to do with the memory that the eidetic imagery or the photograph use. Actually, an enhanced human with a camera would do the same. In the end, trying to evaluate 'working' memory is against our principle of evaluating behaviour. Working memory seems to indicate how the problem is to be solved, through the use of some intermediate memory for concept combination, assumed to be different from general short and long term memories. As we see, it is relatively easy to find pitfalls for a measuring instrument when it is aimed at a wide range of subjects.

There are many other sources of information and refutation that do not originate from measuring. Three other processes are closely related to the measuring of a behavioural feature: its definition, its understanding and its construction. One might think that had we a definition of intelligence, for instance, it would automatically translate into testing instruments and accurate measurement. But this is not true. Also, we can have some understanding of a concept without a proper definition and vice versa. Similarly, we can construct something without properly understanding it – by copying it piece by piece, or neuron by neuron – or without having appropriate measurement mechanisms, etc. We can see how this happens with the classical 'flying' simile for intelligence (see Panel 2.4).

Cognition is far more complex than flying, but we can figure out that we may require many measurement instruments (of abilities, traits or, simply, tasks). With them, we will be able to derive constructs, determine their relationships and arrange them in a meaningful way. This is what psychological measurement

Panel 2.4
The 'artificial flight' analogy

The classical 'artificial flight' analogy (see, e.g., Ford and Hayes, 1998; Russell and Norvig, 2009) compares flying with intelligence. Do we have a measuring instrument to determine the degree of flying?

We do have many flight instruments, such as altimeters, airspeed meters, chronometers or vertical and horizontal speed indicators. Does it mean that we lack a conceptual definition of flying? The truth is that the concept of flying is not that straightforward. It relies on constraints such as the object not being supported by anything other than the air that surrounds it and the lift, propulsion or buoyancy being self-generated. A pole vaulter, a ball or a meteorite do not fly. But this still gives freedom to the ways a balloon, a plane or a bird fly, which are very different.

Flying is a good example of a concept with very convoluted relationships between its definition, understanding, measurement and construction. Intelligence, and behavioural features in general, are not simpler.

has done, but since we are aiming at a larger and more diverse set of subjects, we need a new methodological perspective.

All the combinations between definition, understanding, measurement and construction are worth being pursued. We have argued that measurement is crucial for the other three processes but, overall, progress in any of the four processes benefits the other three. Psychology and comparative cognition have mostly focused on measurement and understanding, artificial intelligence has paid attention to construction, whereas cognitive science – and philosophy – has concentrated on the definition and understanding.

In the three chapters that follow we will give an overview of which shores these different disciplines have reached independently for humans, non-human animals and AI systems, respectively. They will be the basis for a first attempt at unification immediately afterwards.

CHAPTER HIGHLIGHTS

- Two main kinds of measurement: representational and pragmatic (Keynote 2.3). Representational measurement distinguishing between the distribution that defines the feature (Eq. 2.1) and the distribution or sample that is used in a test administration (Eq. 2.2).
- Validity and reliability as the two main components of measurement accuracy (Keynotes 2.4, 2.5). Evaluation specialisation (overfitting) as one important cause of lack of validity (Keynote 2.6).
- Scales (calibration) and factors (such as g) not 'subjective' but 'relative' to a population. An overhaul needed for the machine kingdom, because populations are arbitrary (Keynotes 2.7, 2.9).
- AIT crucial for a representational measurement and for the notion of difficulty (Section 2.6). Difficulty inherent to cognitive abilities (Keynote 2.8).
- Great refutation power of the machine kingdom (Keynote 2.10). A valid test for one group possibly invalid for a different group.

Part II

The Evaluation Discordance

3

The Evaluation of Human Behaviour

> In order to know whether a child has the intelligence of his age, whether
> he is retarded, or advanced, and how much, we need to possess a precise
> and truly scientific method.
>
> – Alfred Binet,
> *Les idées modernes sur les enfants* (1909)

MUCH OF WHAT we know about intelligence has originated from psychometrics. Other psychological traits, such as human personality, have also been the object of study of psychometrics. In this chapter, we will look back at the roots of psychometrics and its current development for the evaluation of personality and cognitive abilities. About the question of one or many 'intelligences', we will overview how several models arrange abilities in a hierarchical way. Intelligence quotient (IQ) tests will be discussed, as well as the meaning and existence of the *g* factor. We will cover the major developments in item response theory and adaptive tests, as they will prove key for the rest of the book. Finally, we will briefly touch on some of the heated debates, such as the nature versus nurture dilemma, the analysis of group differences, the Flynn effect and the way variously gifted and disabled people affect psychometric theory and testing.

3.1 TELLING *IDIOTS SAVANTS* APART

The oldest accounts of formal systematic psychological testing are said to have originated in China about three millennia ago. The assessment of candidates for public service officers comprised the 'six skills', the 'six conducts' and the 'six virtues' (Rust and Golombok, 2009). At the beginning of the seventh century CE, an "essentially open competitive examination took place annually or every three years, [with gradually] adjusted examinations [that] were based on general learning rather than specific or technical knowledge" (Teng, 1943). These procedures were borrowed for Western academic and civil recruiting during the seventeenth and eighteenth centuries.

Recruiting was just one of the motivations behind the birth of modern psychological testing. During the second half of the nineteenth century psychological testing was further elaborated as a tool to understand and improve children's mental development and education, to detect the intellectually ill or disabled and to ascertain how the principles of evolution, adaptation and individual differences emerged in the realm of psychological traits. Some of these motivations yielded psychometric methods that are *functionality-oriented*, for practical problems, such as a selection for a job. Others lead to more *trait-oriented* psychometric methods, for which tests are correct if they consistently identify some psychological trait with both explanatory and predictive power across a range of situations.

Nowadays, psychological assessment is widespread; we do tests at school, to get a licence or to apply for a job. During its early days and well into the twentieth century, psychometrics had to struggle against the view that measurement in the social sciences was ill-conceived. To make things worse, psychoanalysis had given a bad reputation to the use of non-observable *latent* phenomena in psychology, and the early association of psychometrics with eugenics and racial supremacy would be a stigma for years to come. As a reaction to all this, psychometrics took a very rigorous approach to the construction of tests and the analysis of results. Most early psychometricians made significant contributions to statistics.

One way of looking at the discipline is as a sequence of fierce clashes between opposed views. The two 'fathers' of psychometrics, Francis Galton and Alfred Binet, could not have started from more radically different perspectives.

Francis Galton came from a Victorian family of great intellect – Charles Darwin was his half-cousin, both grandsons of Erasmus Darwin. Strongly influenced by his half-cousin's theory of natural selection, he collected evidence that members of eminent families were more likely to become eminent. He was most concerned that talented lineages could have their breed overwhelmed by the idiots and the imbeciles, which would be a catastrophe for the nation. As a remedy, he created a new discipline, 'eugenics', and advocated for measures that would foster the birth rate of the most able, creative individuals. His views about women, races, countries, history and many other topics were fiercely at odds with some political sensibilities at the time (and, of course, nowadays). One example can be seen in Panel 3.1.

Panel 3.1
Smart dogs on a normal scale

Galton analysed "mental power" as a "natural ability" of human populations. He looked at the "deviation from an average", considering a normal distribution. This can be considered the first attempt of scaling a cognitive ability relative to a population. Lower-case letters (from lowest 'g' to highest 'a') were used for grading those groups below average and upper-case letters (from lowest 'A' to highest 'G') for groups above average. Idiots would be located inside the class 'f' or below and geniuses in 'F' or above.

As an example of Galton's unbridled statements, he wrote: "I presume the class F of dogs, and others of the more intelligent sort of animals, is nearly commensurate with the f of the human race, in respect to memory and powers of reason. Certainly the class G of such animals is far superior to the g of humankind" (Galton, 1869, p. 36).

Despite perhaps being offensive in expression, Galton challenged the *scala naturae* with an early view of universal psychometrics.

In addition to his statistical contributions, Galton focused on tests of simple cognitive processes, such as psychological sensitivity to colours and blindfolded "weight discrimination". He also experimented with the 'digit span' task (recalling a sequence of numbers). He saw that the speed of perception (reaction time and sensory discrimination) was related to intelligence, an issue that would later become a recurrent issue in psychometrics (Boake, 2002). He was also interested in personality ('character'). Although, initially, he did not go much beyond his prejudices (Galton, 1883), he soon introduced some of the basic ideas of modern personality measurement, such as the lexical hypothesis (Galton, 1884), which states that major character traits are represented by major words in (any) language. Despite the relevance he assigned to inheritance, and his understanding that the perception speed was difficult to improve, he coined the expression "nature versus nurture" and was most interested in the study of twins.

In the realm of abilities, he considered 'mental power' as a general ability. He did not believe that able people were good at only some kinds of tasks, but rather that they could develop well in any other profession: "people lay too much stress on apparent specialities, thinking overrashly that, because a man is devoted to some particular pursuit, he could not possibly have succeeded in anything else" (Galton, 1869).

Alfred Binet was concerned about the other extreme of the population: the "idiots", "imbeciles" or "feebleminded" – categories for the mentally disabled that were very vague at that time. Binet's programme was centred on education, which had become compulsory in 1882 in France. This universal extension of education posed enormous difficulties to teachers, as they were not used to children with mental disabilities. Binet's goal was to identify those children that were only mildly impaired. He considered that these abnormal children were treatable, by grouping them in a special class or a special school.

During the first years of the twentieth century, he developed a series of tasks and tests to tell these 'idiots' apart. Jointly with his collaborator Théodore Simon, he completed the first version of the Binet-Simon test in 1905. The test included questions of different levels of difficulty and types, such as definitions of abstract terms and concrete objects or resemblances. Verbal knowledge and good judgment were fundamental in these tests. Typical questions were of the following sort: "In what way are a fly, an ant, a butterfly, and a flea alike?" or "When one breaks something belonging to another what must one do?" (Boake, 2002). Henry H. Goddard translated the test into English and distributed it in the United States in 1908, soon becoming widespread in schools and even for immigrants at Ellis Island. Mass testing became common a few years later, in the context of military recruiting. Vast amounts of psychometric data were obtained from millions of recruits since the early "Army Alpha" was established in 1917 – currently the Armed Services Vocational Aptitude Battery (ASVAB).

Two important ideas emerged in the early days of psychometrics. The first one was the notion of a test, instead of an interview or the evaluation by observation. The use of test questionnaires facilitates a more objective evaluation and the systematic collection of very useful data from many individuals. Instead of *situated* tasks, these tests were composed of abstract objective tasks. In other words, many of the tests to evaluate the adequacy of a candidate soldier did not feature real situations he had to face in duty, but a 'questionnaire'.

The second was the distinction between typical (conduct) behaviour tests (personality, motivation, values, integrity, etc.) and (maximum) performance tests (general capacities, specific competences, knowledge, etc.). The categories seen in Keynotes 1.3, 1.4 and 1.6 and Figure 1.3) are in accordance with this distinction. Let us first focus on conduct traits, personality in particular.

3.2 THE ASSESSMENT OF PERSONALITY

Lawrence Pervin described personality traits as "those structural and dynamic properties of an individual as they reflect themselves in characteristic responses to situations" (Pervin, 1970, p. 2). This makes up a characterisation of

---

Panel 3.2
The Big Five

The Five-Factor (or Big Five) model (Costa and McCrae, 2005) comprises Extraversion (E), Agreeableness (A), Conscientiousness (C), Neuroticism (N) and Openness to experience (O). The factors were identified by analysing the terms that people use when describing temperament using natural language (John et al., 2008).

The Big Five model, according to Costa and McCrae (1992), "is supported in four ways: (i) the five traits have high stability and are identified using different assessment techniques (e.g., both self-report questionnaires and peer ratings); (ii) the five traits are compatible with a wide variety of psychological theories including psychoanalytic, psychometric and folk-psychological; (iii) the five traits occur in many different cultures; and (iv) the five traits have a biological basis. There is good evidence for points i, ii, and iii, and point iv, although debatable, is not essential to the model".

---

individuals, which allow people to identify other people and predict their behaviour. Personality is usually associated with a set of qualities that make one person distinct from another.

Modern psychology and psychometrics talk about traits that can be measured and can exist in a higher or lower degree, an approach known as 'trait theory'. In psychometrics, several aspects are considered, such as temperament, motivation, values, attitudes and beliefs (Rust and Golombok, 2009). One recurrent question is to determine how many personality traits there are. Cattell et al. (1970) proposed 16 personality factors (16PF), whereas Wiggins and Eysenck identified the "Big Two" (Wiggins, 1973; Eysenck et al., 1985), extraversion and neuroticism (emotional instability). Cattell himself had anticipated that a way to reconcile these different views was to propose a hierarchical view, where his 16 factors could be grouped into five primary factors (Cattell, 1946). An evolution of this proposal led to the Five-Factor model, described in Panel 3.2.

This model (sometimes enriched with Dominance and Activity, and occasionally with more traits) is nowadays the most common taxonomy, although some other models are also used. For instance, there is a multi-layer hierarchical view of personality traits, which even advocates for a 'General Factor of Personality' (GFP), involving, Woodley and Bell (2011) say, "a combination of higher levels of cooperativeness and lower levels of contentiousness". The GFP would appear to be related to notions such as social intelligence or

How Accurately Can You Describe Yourself?

Describe yourself as you generally are now, not as you wish to be in the future. Describe yourself as you honestly see yourself, in relation to other people you know of the same sex as you are, and roughly your same age. So that you can describe yourself in an honest manner, your responses will be kept in absolute confidence. Indicate for each statement whether it is Very Inaccurate (VI), Moderately Inaccurate (MI), Neither Accurate Nor Inaccurate (NN), Moderately Accurate (MA), or Very Accurate (VA), as a description of you.

	VI	MI	NN	MA	VA	
1. Am the life of the party	○	○	○	○	○	(E+)
2. Feel little concern for others	○	○	○	○	○	(A−)
3. Am always prepared	○	○	○	○	○	(C+)
4. Get stressed out easily	○	○	○	○	○	(N−)
5. Have a rich vocabulary	○	○	○	○	○	(O+)
6. Don't talk a lot	○	○	○	○	○	(E−)
7. Am interested in people	○	○	○	○	○	(A+)
8. Leave my belongings around	○	○	○	○	○	(C−)
9. Am relaxed most of the time	○	○	○	○	○	(N+)
10. Have difficulty understanding abstract ideas	○	○	○	○	○	(O−)

Figure 3.1. Excerpt of ten items from a Five-Factor personality test using the international personality item pool (Goldberg et al., 2006). The letters in parentheses in the last column (not shown to the subjects) indicate the factor: (E) Extraversion, (A) Agreeableness, (C) Conscientiousness, (N) Neuroticism and (O) Openness to experience. In the original source, N was referred to as "emotional stability" and O as "intellect/imagination". For items with a + sign, the responses add values from 1 ("VI") to 5 ("VA"). For items with a − sign, the values are reversed (from 5 to 1).

even emotional intelligence. Despite the many advocates of GFP (Just, 2011; Veselka et al., 2012), there are also its detractors (Revelle and Wilt, 2013).

How are personality traits evaluated? *Situated* testing may be common for animals and children, but for adult humans there is a more practical alternative: the use of questionnaires. The questions can even be answered by another person (e.g., a boss, a peer or an acquaintance). In this case, however, the accuracy will highly depend on how well the person knows or likes the evaluee. As a result, the most common approach is the use of self-evaluation questionnaires (John et al., 2008). Figure 3.1 shows some examples of these questions.

Naturally, a self-evaluation questionnaire has important implications on the reliability and validity of the tests, as the subjects can cheat and distort the result. This is especially cumbersome for integrity testing (i.e., to measure honesty and ethical behaviour) and other attitudes and values. Many confounding factors may appear, as there is a relation between personality and cognitive abilities at the trait level, but also during the very measurement process (e.g., subjects with low levels of intelligence may find cheating more difficult). Still, there are some ways of evaluating sincerity.

An alternative to these self-report tests is represented by the so-called projective tests, which are free-response tests based on recording the reaction or interpretation towards ambiguous or meaningless stimuli. The most famous such test is the 'Rorschach test', which shows several inkblots that have to be interpreted by the subject. Similarly, the 'thematic apperception test' uses ambiguous pictures that have to be described. Other projective tests may include exercises where subjects have to draw a picture, to complete a sentence freely, to arrange pictures, etc. In general, there are important concerns about the validity and reliability of projective tests, and many consider them to be mostly pseudoscience. Finally, psychophysiological approaches (such as heart rate, skin conductance, brain activity) can be combined with either self-report or projective tests to detect cheating or to measure the reaction in front of some stimuli.

Overall, none of the approaches to personality testing developed so far is completely reliable (see Rust and Golombok, 2009, chap. 9). Also, validity is linked to the set of traits actually representing the concepts that their factor name (e.g., extraversion) and its definition may indicate.

3.3 THE ASSESSMENT OF COGNITIVE ABILITIES

When looking at the performance tests, which are more properly cognitive and leading to gradient measurement, a crucial differentiation was made between cognitive abilities and attainment. An *idiot savant* could memorise Tolstoy's *War and Peace* verbatim or could excel at a very specialised and routine task after days or years of practice, but struggle at learning new tasks. This established an important distinction between knowledgeable and intelligent subjects, between encyclopaedism and discernment. Cianciolo and Sternberg (2008, Figure 2.1) describe a "continuum of mental tests", from those that "measure what a person can do intellectually without the benefit of specific training or education" (abilities) and those that "measure the effects of a systematic program of instruction or training" (attainment). This distinction is fundamental and should not be confused with the question of whether intelligence and other cognitive abilities can be improved by education, training or general culture, or by other kinds of "gymnastic of the mind", as Binet advocated (Binet, 1909). We will address this question later on in this chapter.

> **Keynote 3.1. Distinction between attainment and abilities**: The spectrum of features that depend on performance tasks has been analysed in terms of concrete, specific instructible skills and knowledge (attainment), and abstract, general inherent capacities (abilities).

How were the early psychometricians able to make the distinction? They transformed an early opposition of 'concrete' versus 'abstract' tasks into a related (but different) distinction: culture-bound versus culture-fair tests (Eysenck, 2007, pp. 18–21). For instance, the question "Guernica was painted by . . ." is culture-bound, while the question "A hand is to an arm as a foot is to a . . ." is culture-fair. Both, of course, require knowledge of natural language (which is of course culture), but the first one requires specific encyclopaedic knowledge, whereas the second does not go beyond common knowledge. As knowledge began to be removed from the tasks, they became more abstract.

Still, the number of possible abstract tasks is still infinite. Should we give scores for all of them separately? Charles Spearman, heavily influenced by Binet, began to be fascinated by a phenomenon that repeatedly appeared in the test results. The more cognitive and culture-fair the tests were the more he found that the results of different tests correlated, something known as the "positive manifold":

Keynote 3.2. Positive manifold: Given a set of cognitive tests, the results for a population of individuals are positively correlated, i.e., those subjects obtaining good (respectively poor) results on some tests tend to do well (respectively poorly) on others.

Spearman pioneered (a simplified) factor analysis to analyse this phenomenon. Given a tetrad of observed variables a, b, c and d, he built a correlation matrix with all correlations ρ_{xy} between a variable x and y. He observed that $\rho_{ab} \times \rho_{cd}$ was generally roughly equal to $\rho_{ac} \times \rho_{bd}$. From there, he was able to identify a *latent factor*, which he called g, and calculate the saturation of every variable. The square root of the saturation of each observable variable was the correlation with g, the *loading* of the variable. In fact, he found that this happened for tests of very different kinds, something that is known as "indifference of the indicator" (Spearman, 1927).

Since then, factor analysis (FA) has evolved considerably and has been (and still is) the most important tool in psychometrics. Basically, factor analysis can be applied to observable or manifest variables to determine a (minimal) set of latent or hidden factors. However, the application of FA is not easy. Also, it is usually confused with the apparently similar principal component analysis (PCA), a data reduction technique. For instance, it is important to clarify that a latent factor is not the 'cause' of the observation. It may be an emergent unobserved variable, as in the "mutualism model" and others (Van Der Maas et al., 2014; Conway and Kovacs, 2015).

Table 3.1. Thurstone's primary mental abilities "in order of the proportion of individual difference explained" according to Schaie (2010). The second column shows the way they are usually measured.

Ability	Measurement
Verbal	Multiple-choice recognition vocabulary tests
Spatial orientation	Perception of spatial relationships
Inductive reasoning	Letter series completion
Number ability	Sums for addition problems
Word fluency	Recall of words according to a lexical rule
Associative memory	Recall paired associates or list learning
Perceptual speed	Letter cancel, simple stimuli or number comparison

The use of factor analysis has helped to put some order in the analysis of tests, items and abilities, but the understanding of all the relations and constructs is still far from clear. This has led to a high diversity of models and theories of intelligence, depending on how many basic abilities or factors are recognised and how they are structured.

In Spearman's two-factor theory of intelligence (Spearman, 1904), the results of particular tests depend on a general factor (g), common in all tests, and some specific 'factors' or specificities (s), due to the unique abilities in each. More properly, this is a one-factor model, as the specificities are not really considered. Many multiple factor theories reacted against this extremely simplified view, such as Kelley's model (1928) and Thurstone's theory of primary mental abilities (1938). As mentioned in Section 2.5 Thurstone identified seven *primary* abilities, which are shown in Table 3.1. Like Thurstone, J. P. Guilford was against the idea of a general factor. In fact, his structure of intellect comprised between 120 and 180 abilities (Guilford, 1956, 1967, 1982). However, each ability was actually a combination of a content (figural, symbolic, semantic or behavioural), a cognitive product (units, classes, relations, systems, transformations, or implications) and a mental operation (cognition, memory, divergent production, convergent production or evaluation).

The hierarchical theories were introduced as a way to reconcile lumpers and splitters, with their opposed views between one common factor and more than a hundred factors. Vernon (1950) and Burt (1949) pioneered these new models, but it was Cattell and Horn's hierarchical structure (Horn and Cattell, 1967) which was most successful. One relevant innovation of this model is the division of g into *fluid* (gf) and *crystallised* (gc) intelligence. Fluid intelligence represents the ability of abstract reasoning and solving new problems, without

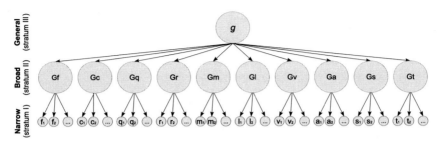

Figure 3.2. Cattell-Horn-Carroll three-stratum model, featuring *g* on the top (third) level, with ten broad abilities at the second level: Fluid Intelligence (Gf), Crystallised Intelligence (Gc), Quantitative Reasoning (Gq), Reading and Writing Ability (Gr), Short-Term Memory (Gm), Long-Term Storage and Retrieval (Gl), Visual Processing (Gv), Auditory Processing (Ga), Processing Speed (Gs) and Decision/Reaction Time/Speed (Gt). The bottom (first) level can include many more 'narrow' abilities or types of tasks.

the need of previously acquired knowledge. Crystallised intelligence represents the ability of using previous knowledge in the context of a new problem. This distinction is not the same as culture-fair and culture-bound; crystallised intelligence is not a mere retrieval of facts from memory but their application to a problem.

Cattell and Horn's model was replaced by the three-stratum theory of intelligence, proposed by Carroll (1993), which is now frequently known as the Cattell-Horn-Carroll theory (Keith and Reynolds, 2010). Figure 3.2 shows the abilities in this theory.

There are many other hierarchies, all of them elaborating a particular conceptual theory from the experimental data. Despite the differences, most are based on the use of factor analysis and related techniques and place a central factor *g* in the middle or top of the arrangement. A notable exception is Gardner's theory of multiple intelligences (Gardner, 1983), which has received strong criticisms because of its little empirical evidence (Waterhouse, 2006), as we discussed in the previous chapter. Another non-psychometric approach is Sternberg's triarchic theory, which distinguishes three kinds of intelligence: analytic, creative and practical (Sternberg, 1985, 1997).

3.4 INTELLIGENCE, IQ AND THE *g* FACTOR

The location of the *g* factor at the top or the centre of many models of intelligence, jointly with its association with the term *general intelligence* may suggest that we can happily equate *g* with intelligence. This is occasionally done for the sake of exposition in the analysis of group differences, since "intelligence typically has been defined as Spearman's *g* ... and has been assessed using IQ tests, which are believed to be good measures of *g*" (Cianciolo and Sternberg, 2008, p. 110). However, a general exchangeability of all these terms (even by reification) is not only inaccurate but also misleading. An IQ score is a weighted aggregate of the result of the set of tasks that compose an IQ test, very much like the schema of Eq. 2.2. The *g* factor, on the contrary, is not any aggregation of results. It is a construct, a latent variable, that determines a high degree of the *variability* in the results of cognitive tasks for a human population. But it is a valid measure as well since, by assuming some distribution parameters for the scale, a *g score* can be obtained for each individual.

The *g* factor has several "advantages over IQ" since "in constructing an index like IQ we are therefore open to criticism [that] the result we get depends on the subjective selection of items. ... But the factor method enables us to assess the uncertainty generated by the fact that we have used only some of the possible items" (Bartholomew, 2004, p. 52). In other words, if we change the number or weight of some types of tasks in an IQ test (e.g., more verbal tasks), this will have an important effect on the IQ score, as it is an aggregation that follows the schema of Eq. 2.2. However, the change will have a more limited effect on the *g* score, as the redundant task items are usually coalesced.

> **Keynote 3.3. IQ score versus *g* score**: IQ scores strongly depend on the composition of tasks in an IQ test, whereas *g* scores are less dependent.

The emergence of *g* from factor analysis has been replicated by numerous experiments (Jensen, 1998; Sternberg, 2000). Despite the evidence, the *g* factor is still a source of controversy, and some argue that *g* simply does not exist or that it is the result of an emergent consequence rather than a cause (see Detterman, 1982; Bartholomew, 2004, for some of the views in favour and against).

The statement that a single dominant factor (*g*) exists is different from the statement of the *positive manifold*, which is less controversial. There have been some theories tying to explain the positive manifold without *g*. An extreme view is to consider abilities independent, showing 'zero correlation' (Alliger, 1988) so that the positive manifold would just appear because the tasks do not represent pure abilities. Lacking convincing experimental results, evidence against *g* has been sought elsewhere, such as the *evolutionary diversity hypothesis*. This hypothesis states that to ensure higher adaptability of the species, the *Homo sapiens* brain unevenly distributes its capacity into different abilities, so that at least some of the members of the group can survive when environments change. A related idea is the hypothesis of *specialisation of roles in the tribe*. This would mean that some of us are born with the abilities to be the shaman of the tribe whilst others would be well suited as hunters, but none can be said to be more intelligent than the other.

It is important to clarify that the existence of a *g* factor does not preclude the existence of a diversity of abilities. In fact, the following passage from Spearman has been used frequently as his acknowledgement of the specialisation-of-roles hypothesis, or the "genius-at-something" view: "every normal man, woman, and child is ... a genius at something....] It remains to discover at what" (Spearman, 1925). However, this is qualified as follows: "this must be a most difficult matter, owing to the very fact that it occurs in only a minute proportion of all possible abilities. It certainly cannot be detected by any of the testing procedures at present in current usage. But these procedures are capable, I believe, of vast improvement" (Spearman, 1925). The point is that independence is rare and only for very specific tasks. In other words, it is very hard to find general cognitive tasks that are not contaminated by *g*. Intelligent people are usually good at most cognitive tasks.

For the majority advocating for *g* (Hand, 2004), its understanding or explanation is the controversial issue. There has been an important amount of work to connect it to the results of some elementary cognitive tasks and mental chronometry, as pioneered by Galton. For instance, 'simple reaction time', which measures how quickly a subject reacts to a stimulus (a light or a sound) has some correlation with *g* (Jensen, 1980, 1993, 1998). If we slightly modify the task such that the subject has to make a decision (e.g., pressing the appropriate button after a yellow or blue light), known as 'choice reaction time', this correlation increases (Deary et al., 2001). Some other variations, such as "inspection time", can show even higher correlations. This led to the hypothesis that *g* was linked to some kind of "mental speed" or "information processing speed" (Deary, 2000b, p. 271). Further than that, reaction time (RT) tasks and other *elementary cognitive tasks* were suggested as a way to find a *measurement unit* for intelligence, to express it as a ratio scale measurement, with a zero point and additive units, instead of an ordinal measure. Whilst the idea can be traced back to Thurstone (1937), the most explicit suggestion was made by Jensen: "one of the attractive features of RT with respect to *g* theory is that ordinal measures of *g* are correlated with measures of RT, which may afford the possibility of measuring *g* on a ratio scale" (Jensen, 2000b).

This information-processing approach (Sternberg, 1977) also led to the analysis of working memory, using tasks such as 'digit span', already introduced by Binet. The correlations of tasks involving working memory with *g* have been

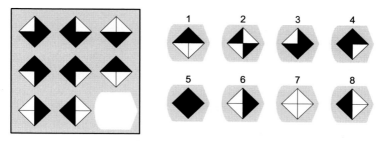

Figure 3.3. A Raven's Progressive Matrices item. The subject must choose one of the eight numbered options to complete the 3×3 matrix. [Re-creation inspired by the original matrices (which are copyrighted).]

replicated many times (Nisbett et al., 2012). In this case, however, it is not so simple to develop a unit or ratio scale from the tasks (Engle et al., 1999). Brain scanning techniques (Deary and Caryl, 1997) have been used to see whether intelligence, speed and *g* can be traced to some characteristics or areas of the brain.

Although most general cognitive tasks correlate with *g* (Jensen, 1998, p. 35), some show higher correlation than others. This poses the question of whether there are some representative tasks for *g*, or even for general intelligence. If this were the case, it would have important practical and theoretical implications. On the practical side, one single task would suffice to measure general intelligence. On the theoretical side, the analysis of these tasks would provide insights about what general intelligence is.

Actually, these tasks exist, some of them showing a very strong correlation with *g*. Analogical and inductive inference problems are among those with highest correlations. For instance, series completion problems (either using numbers or letters) have been common in intelligence testing (we will see one particular example, Thurstone letter series completion problems in Panel 7.4). Other very popular tasks with high *g* loading are Raven's Progressive Matrices (RPM), developed in the 1930s by Raven, Spearman's student, which built upon Spearman's "matrix relations" task. The most common presentation of the RPM task (Raven et al., 1992) is shown in a 3 × 3 cell grid of figures (see Figure 3.3). Tests composed of Raven's Progressive Matrices can reach a correlation of about 0.80 with *g* (Jensen, 1998, p. 38).

There is no generally accepted explanation of why these tasks have such a strong correlation with *g*, but the relevance of analogical and inductive inference suggests a preponderance of *learning* over other cognitive processes. Because of this high correlation, many tests feature Raven's matrices, or some other inductive or analogical inference problems. However, for higher reliability, and to appraise other factors at the second level of the hierarchical models, the so-called IQ tests are used, which integrate a wider variety of tasks.

The acronym IQ comes from Intelligence Quotient, a term coined by William Stern (1912) as the ratio of mental age (introduced by Binet) to chronological age (multiplied by 100). From here, the modern conception of IQ scores as a normalised and standardised value was introduced at Stanford University by Lewis Terman as a way to adapt the Binet-Simon test for adults in the United States (which would be known as Stanford-Binet test). Since then, the Stanford-Binet test has been very influential for other tests (e.g., the Army Alpha), and it has also evolved over a century to the present day. The Stanford-Binet Intelligence Scales, Fifth Edition (Roid, 2003), is aimed at all ages. The latest version has a balance between verbal and nonverbal abilities, organised into 15 subtests: vocabulary, comprehension, absurdities, verbal relations, quantitative reasoning, number series, equation building, pattern analysis, copying, matrices, paper folding and cutting, bead memory, memory for sentences, memory for digits and memory for objects. The reliabilities of the tests are around 0.90.

In 1939 David Wechsler built a test specifically devised for adults, the Wechsler Adult Intelligence Scale (WAIS). A version for children followed in 1949, the Wechsler Intelligence Scale for Children (WISC). Several other versions have appeared since then. WAIS-IV (Wechsler, 2008) consists of ten core and five supplemental subsets for people between 16 and 90 years of age. WAIS-IV removed the verbal/performance categories from earlier versions and now presents four indices:

- Verbal Comprehension Index (VCI), which comprises the core subtests: similarities (verbal reasoning), vocabulary and information (acquiring and retrieving general factual knowledge) as well as a supplemental subtest, comprehension (social conventions).
- Perceptual Reasoning Index (PRI), which comprises the core subtests: block design (visual problem solving), matrix reasoning (fluid inductive and spatial reasoning) and visual puzzles (abstract spatial reasoning) as well as two supplemental subtests, picture completion (visual perceptions) and figure weights (quantities and analogies).
- Working Memory Index (WMI), which comprises the core subtests: digit span (mental focus and rote learning) and arithmetic as well as one supplemental subtest, letter-number sequencing.
- Processing Speed Index (PSI), which comprises the core subtests: symbol search (visual scanning and discrimination) and coding (visual-motor speed, memory and co-ordination) as well as one supplemental subtest, cancellation (perceptual speed).

From them, two broader scores can also be derived: the Full Scale IQ (FSIQ), which combines VCI, PRI, WMI and PSI, and the General Ability Index (GAI), which only considers VCI and PRI.

There are many other intelligence tests, most of them providing IQ scores (see Urbina, 2011). Despite the high reliability and validity results for many of the aforementioned IQ tests, psychometricians are reluctant to say that any of these tests measure intelligence. It is more accurate to say that they measure IQ, which can then be interpreted or related to other phenomena or variables.

3.5 THE TESTING BAZAAR

IQ tests are only one particular kind of psychometric test. Many other tests exist for cognitive abilities and personality. In fact, it is quite common that new tests are created for a particular purpose by combining other tests or their items. How is this done? How can we be sure of a good outcome? In this section we will briefly overview the offer of tests, how they are selected and how their results are interpreted depending on the underlying testing theory.

The first thing is to decide what kind of test is required for what is to be measured. For instance, many options are available for testing personality. The NEO Personality Inventory and the NEO Five-Factor Inventory (McCrae and Costa, 2010) are self-report tests that use 240 and 60 questions, respectively, to determine the "Big Five" personality traits. Similarly, the Minnesota Multiphasic Personality Inventory (MMPI) is also a self-report test that covers personality and psychopathology (Ben-Porath, 2012).

If the goal is to measure the appropriateness for college, several options have been developed in many countries. The most well known are the ACT and SAT college entrance exams. Their origins can be traced back to the psychological tests for college freshmen of the American Council on Education, ACE (Thurstone and Thurstone, 1947), which comprised six tests arranged in two groups, *quantitative*, including arithmetical reasoning, number series and figure analogies tasks; and *linguistic*, including same-opposite, completion and verbal analogies tasks. Figure 3.4 shows an item from the figure analogies task.

ACT covers four skill areas: English, mathematics, reading and science. SAT assesses reading, writing and mathematics skills. Progressively, the percentage of tasks evaluating attainment over abilities has been increasing. For instance, Figure 3.5 shows some examples of the word analogies task found in early versions of SAT, but dropped since the 2005 version.

Other cognitive tests can be more dependent on the application of specialised knowledge, i.e., a crystallised use of knowledge and experience. For instance, the Bennett Mechanical Comprehension Test (BMCT) evaluates everyday

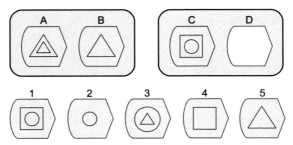

Figure 3.4.   Figure analogies task from the 1942 edition of the psychological test for college freshmen of the American Council on Education, ACE. [Redrawn following (Evans, 1965).]

reasoning on a series of domains about the physical world, aimed at the evaluation of applicants for technical positions (e.g., electricians and mechanics). The BMCT comprises 68 items such as the ones shown in Figure 3.6.

Once the kind of test (or mixture thereof) is chosen the next thing is to build or get a test. Developing a new test involves an important effort as many aspects have to be taken into account (see, e.g., Downing and Haladyna, 2006, for a comprehensive guide). Alternatively, there are many existing tests from several catalogues. We have to bear in mind that most tests are copyrighted and not publicly available, in part to protect the reliability and validity of the results, as evaluees could have access to the items and their solutions. Some tests have been applied massively in exactly the same way for several decades, so their results can be used to compare the evolution of IQ and educational attainment of a population or a whole country. Disclosing the tests would be the end of it.

As a result, tests are usually purchased (even for scientific purposes) from general or specialised publishers, which include instructions and, in many cases, a limited number of authorised copies for administration. Recently, nonetheless, there have been several proposals to contribute with libraries of items and tools to develop new tests. The international personality item pool (Goldberg et al., 2006) is an open collection of self-report personality questions, such as those shown in Figure 3.1, with instructions about how to combine them to build different kinds of personality tests. Similarly, the Psychology Experiment Building Language (PEBL) and test battery (Mueller and Piper,

carpenter : wood   mason : _____
    sun : planet   earth : _____
teacher : chalk   soldier : _____

Figure 3.5.   Example of a word analogies item in the SAT college entrance exam. [Adapted from (Turney, 2011).]

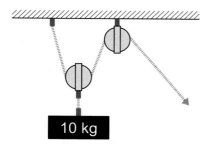

Approximately, how much force is
needed to lift the weight?

a) 10 kg   b) 5 kg   c) 1 kg   d) 20 kg

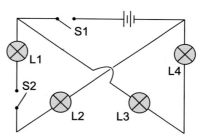

If switch S1 is closed and switch S2
is open, which lights will turn on?

a) L1 & L2   b) All   c) L3 & L4   d) None

Figure 3.6.   Two BMCT items. [Re-creation following (Klenk et al., 2011).]

2014) provides open-source software to develop new cognitive tests, with about
60 tests already implemented. Other platforms, such as Concerto (Scalise and
Allen, 2015), allow users to create online adaptive tests.

Tests, purchased or not, are measurement instruments and, as such, require
scaling and calibration. In some cases, the unit of measurement is clear, such
as seconds for reaction time. Many other tests are a combination of item results
and the magnitude of the measurement is not necessarily meaningful. For
instance, if one subject is correct on 10 items and another is correct on 20 items,
does the second one possess double the ability or trait of the first one? Instead,
as we saw in Section 2.2, scores are usually scaled, through criterion-referenced
standardisation or norm-referenced procedures.

One particular case is normalisation, which is a kind of transformation that
makes transformed scores follow a normal distribution. IQ tests are usually
normalised to have a mean of 100 and a standard deviation of 15 (still 16 for
the Stanford-Binet test). With this, and using the cumulative density function
of the normal distribution, we can infer that an IQ score of 130 implies that the
subject is above 98.9 per cent (approximately) of the adult population.

Once a test is administered and we get a score, can we trust its accuracy?
In Section 2.3 we introduced the two components of accuracy for any measurement instrument: validity and reliability. Validity has been understood in
many different ways (see, e.g., AERA, APA & NCME, 1999; Borsboom et al.,
2004), but one popular conception is that "a test is valid if it measures what it
is supposed to be measuring" (Kelley, 1927). Still, in psychometrics, there are
many other interpretations, beyond face and predictive validity seen in the previous chapter, such as construct validity, content validity, concurrent validity
and differential validity (see, e.g., Wainer, 2000, p. 194).

Independently of the particular interpretation, the notion of validity has been put into question in terms of the opposition between the traits that are specific (functionality-oriented, attainment) and general (explanatory, abilities). The focus on task-oriented testing was aligned to the use of "competencies" or "achievements" instead of general skills in educational assessment, which became popular in the 1970s and 1980s. With this view, only functionality-oriented tests would be valid (McClelland, 1973). This restrictive view of test validity, however, has had strong counter-reactions. For instance, Barrett and Depinet (1991) argue that "intellectual ability and aptitude tests predicted occupational success even when the aptitude test was an avionics battery not specifically designed for general use".

A common source of validity issues is bias, as we saw in the previous chapter. This can be cultural bias, when associated with language, customs, etc., and may manifest itself as an interface bias. For instance, Scheuneman argued that some tests were advantageous to East-Asian children because of the use of artificial letters and symbolic forms, with which these children are more familiar (Scheuneman, 1979).

The other component of accuracy, reliability, is usually understood in psychometrics as stability of the measure for the same subject for different administrations. As we also introduced in the previous chapter, a typical measure of reliability is the correlation (usually Pearson correlation) between the results of a series of subjects for two different administrations. Depending on how the administrations are performed, the notion of reliability is slightly different. 'Test-retest' reliability can be affected by the subjects being familiar after the first administration. To avoid this phenomenon, 'parallel-form' reliability performs two tests in parallel and 'split-half' reliability splits the items into two sets (but the reliability of the whole test requires some statistical corrections from the correlation, such as the Spearman-Brown formula).

Several theories of measurement have been developed in psychometrics in the past century. Two major families (Borsboom, 2005) dominate the theory and practice in psychometrics: classical test theory (CTT), also known as true score theory, and item response theory (IRT) (Embretson and Reise, 2000; De Ayala, 2009). CTT is built upon the concept of "true score", seen as the expected value of the observed score. Consequently, the goal is set on reducing the error, so that the psychological trait is actually what the test measures. IRT, on the other hand, considers that what we measure or observe is determined by one or more latent traits or variables.

The schema of CTT is usually represented as $X = T + E$, where X is the observed score, T is the true score and E is the error. CTT assumes that (1) all errors are random and normally distributed, (2) errors are uncorrelated with the observed score and (3) measurements for the same subject are independent (Rust and Golombok, 2009). CTT has been mainly criticised for confounding the theoretical attributes with the raw values given by the instruments and for the assumption of the same error for all subjects (Borsboom, 2005). Despite its shortcomings, CTT is still very common in psychological practice, especially for personality traits. IRT, on the other hand, relies on more complex models and tools, and some of them hinge on stronger assumptions than CTT. In the end, IRT is a special case of the latent variable approach, which is a general well-founded approach to measurement (Hand, 2004, chap. 3). In what follows, we will focus on IRT not only because of its conceptual superiority, but also because it will better abide the leap to universal psychometrics in this book.

3.6 ITEM RESPONSE THEORY

Because of the nature of IRT and the level of detail that we require, this section will be more technical. It is worth the effort as several notions we will see here reappear (properly adapted or overhauled) in other parts of the book. Keynotes throughout the section try to emphasise those essential bits, which will be summarised in the highlights at the end of the chapter.

One key difference between CTT and IRT is that CTT usually focuses on tests while IRT puts more emphasis on *items* – each of the exercises, problems or questions that compose a test. Another important difference is the relevance that difficulty has for IRT. Indeed, the origins of IRT can be traced back to Thurstone, who identified 'difficulty' as a crucial notion in psychometrics:

> **Keynote 3.4. Proficiency as maximum achievable difficulty**: "The ability of an individual subject to perform a specified kind of task is the difficulty E at which the probability is 1/2 that he will do that task" (Thurstone, 1937, p. 249).

This, in turn, is related to the earlier concepts of *width*, as the percentage of correctly solved tasks (for a range of tasks) at a level of difficulty, and *altitude*, as the highest difficulty a subject can reach, given a minimum width threshold (Thorndike et al., 1927). An aggregate performance result, called the *area*, can also be derived from these two concepts. IRT develops these concepts in a rather elaborate way.

Most IRT models are based on the idea that each underlying trait ranges on a dimension with two sides: "the position that each item occupies on this dimension is termed that item's *difficulty* (usually denoted b); the position

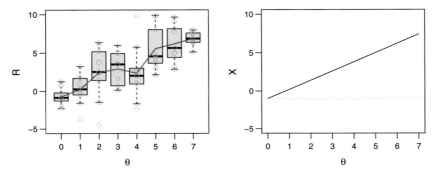

Figure 3.7. Left: Responses (*R*) for a non-binary item grouped by subject's proficiencies. The whisker boxes show the dispersion (quartiles and median) for each value of proficiency θ and the solid lines connect the expected values (the means). Right: Item characteristic curve using a linear model for a continuous score item with parameter $z = -1$ and $\lambda = 1.2$, which approximates the data of the left plot. The dotted line shows the zero-proficiency expected result.

of each examinee on this dimension is that examinee's *proficiency* (usually denoted θ)" (Wainer, 2000, p. 62). This translates to the so-called item characteristic curves and the person characteristic curves (Embretson and McCollam, 2000), respectively, which we will use several times in the rest of the book. We plot a non-observable (latent) variable (either θ or b) on the *x*-axis and an observable variable on the *y*-axis (the performance, or 'response').

Many metrics and tools in IRT are said to be *population-independent* or, more precisely, *distribution-independent*. The expected response for a given proficiency (or a given difficulty) is independent of how many subjects we have for that proficiency (or how many items we have for that difficulty). This will prove crucial for universal psychometrics, as we will discuss in Chapter 9.

Figure 3.7 (left) shows the results for a group of subjects with the same item, where the subjects have been grouped by proficiency θ. The higher the proficiency, the higher the expected response. We also see the dispersion of responses for each proficiency. In Figure 3.7 (right) we see an example of a linear item characteristic curve, assuming a linear model (Mellenbergh, 1994; Ferrando, 2009), which is common for continuous responses. The model defines $X(\theta)$ as the expected performance (response) for an arbitrary examinee of proficiency θ, as follows:

$$X(\theta) \triangleq z + \lambda\theta \qquad (3.1)$$

where z is the intercept (zero-proficiency expected result) and λ is the slope.

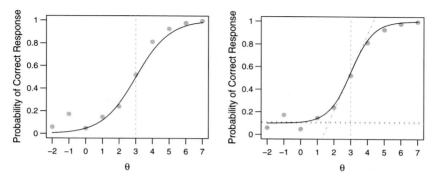

Figure 3.8. Left: item characteristic curve using a 1PL (Rasch's) model with parameter difficulty $b = 3$. The model tries to fit the empirical results for the item (small grey circles). Right: item characteristic curve using a 3PL model with discrimination $a = 1.5$ (dash-dotted), item location $b = 3$ (dashed) and chance $c = 0.1$ (dotted). We also show the zero-proficiency expected result $p(\theta) = z$ (here at 0.11 also dotted). The model seems to fit the grey circles better now.

Not all continuous score items (e.g., a task giving points) fit a linear model, especially if they are bounded. Also, many tests rephrase the items or set a threshold of performance such that the response, defined as correct ('1') if above the threshold and incorrect ('0') otherwise, becomes binary. Nevertheless, most tasks are binary originally (e.g., an answer being right or wrong). In all these cases, the expected value of the response $\mathbb{E}[R|\theta]$ can be understood as the probability of a correct response. Now, a logistic model is more appropriate than a linear one. By denoting the answer of an item j by x_j, this probability is defined as

$$p_j(\theta) \triangleq \mathbb{P}(x_j = 1|\theta) \tag{3.2}$$

We will omit the subindex when dealing with just one item. The first and simplest item response model for binary responses is Rasch's one-parameter model (1-PL) (Rasch, 1960), defined as follows:

$$p(\theta) \triangleq \frac{1}{1 + e^{-(\theta-b)}} \tag{3.3}$$

These *item response functions* can be plotted as *item characteristic curves*. Figure 3.8 (left) shows Rasch's one-parameter model, with parameter $b = 3$. The models, and the corresponding item characteristic curves, do not show $\sigma^2 = \text{Var}[R|\theta]$. In the non-binary case, the variance depends on the actual distribution of responses (e.g., Figure 3.7 (left)) while for the binary case, the (Bernoulli) variance would be simply $p(\theta)(1 - p(\theta))$, which is maximum for

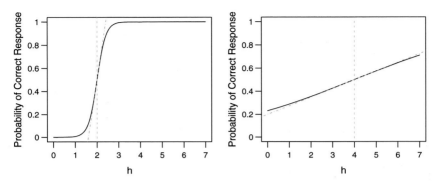

Figure 3.9. Two 2PL item characteristic curves. Left: difficulty $b = 2$ and discrimination $a = 5$. Right: difficulty $b = 4$ and discrimination $a = 0.3$. The item on the left is highly discriminative around $b = 2$ but not very useful to discriminate far from that region. In contrast, the item on the right is barely discriminative everywhere. The result will mostly depend on the steadiness of the examinees, or other factors, and not so much on their proficiency.

the steepest part of the curve, the most uncertain (and informative) part (exactly $\theta = 3$ on Figure 3.8 (left)).

Rasch's model makes the strong assumption that given two different items $j = 1$ and $j = 2$ with the same difficulty b, then for any individual with a given proficiency the probability of giving a correct response to $j = 1$ will be the same as the probability of giving a correct response to $j = 2$. This means that the slope of the sigmoid function is the same for all items. The 1PL model assigns unit slope at $\theta = b$ to all curves. This model only requires the determination of one parameter, difficulty.

Several extensions have been proposed to Rasch's one-parameter model. The two-parameter model (2PL) incorporates a new parameter a to allow for different slopes:

$$p(\theta) = \frac{1}{1 + e^{-a(\theta - b)}} \tag{3.4}$$

Figure 3.9 shows two items with different slopes. The 2PL model is usually seen as the model that most closely corresponds to a view of difficulty estimation per item as a normally distributed random variable H with mean b and standard deviation σ (the measurement error for the item). By difficulty estimation we mean, for instance, that several experts could assign a value of difficulty, looking at the item description. This estimation for the item difficulty

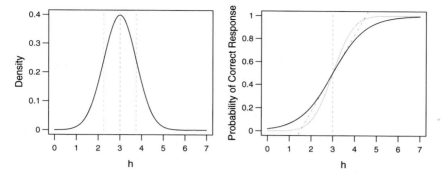

Figure 3.10. Left: a normal distribution showing the difficulty probability with mean $b = 3$ and standard deviation $\sigma = 0.75$. Right: item characteristic curve corresponding to this distribution as a cumulative distribution with the same parameters (in solid grey) and a logistic 2PL model (in solid black) with discrimination $a = 1/\sigma$.

would have cumulative distribution

$$\mathbb{P}(H \leq h) = \Phi\left(\frac{h-b}{\sigma}\right) \tag{3.5}$$

using the error function Φ. This cumulative function of difficulty is dually translated into the probability of correct response in terms of proficiency, $p(\theta)$. Although the corresponding normal model could be used today, the computational limitations when IRT was introduced prompted the approximation seen in Eq. 3.4 using a logistic function with $a = 1/\sigma$. Figure 3.10 shows an example of the normal distribution on the left and its cumulative distribution jointly with the approximate 2PL model on the right, with $b = 3$ and $\sigma = 0.75$ ($a = 1.33$).

Finally, the three-parameter model (3PL) (see, e.g., Lord et al., 1968) adds a parameter to account for those cases for which the subject can get correct responses by accident or by random guess:

$$p(\theta) = c + \frac{1-c}{1 + e^{-a(\theta-b)}} \tag{3.6}$$

In the three-parameter (3PL) model, c is the *chance*, *guessing* or asymptotic minimum (the value obtained by *random* guess, as in multiple choice items), b is the *difficulty* or item location (now the value of θ leading to a probability half way between c and 1, i.e., $\frac{1+c}{2}$) and a is the *discrimination* (as before, the maximum slope of the curve). The zero-proficiency expected result is given when $\theta = 0$, which is exactly $z = c + \frac{1-c}{1+e^{ab}}$. Figure 3.8 (right) shows an example of a 3PL item characteristic curve.

One caveat about these models is the choice of the scale of proficiency. Had we multiplied proficiency by two, we could have found new parameters a and b such that all curves would give the same expected response. This means that we have infinitely many monotonic transformations of proficiency. Even if we "scale proficiency so that θ has a mean of zero and a standard deviation of 1 in some reference" (Wainer, 2000, p. 68), item models and curves are still uncomparable, as they are derived from different populations. The so-claimed 'population-independence' of IRT then crumbles, unless some of the parameters are derived for each of the ordinal categories in a criterion-referenced scale (Janssen et al., 2000).

3.7 DISCRIMINATION AND ADAPTIVE TESTS

In this section we will see how the models seen in the previous section can be used for adaptive tests. First, we need to understand the parameters that characterise each item. The interpretation of the parameters b as difficulty and c as chance seems relatively straightforward, but the discrimination parameter a is less intuitive. As Ferrando (2012) points out: "the term 'discriminating power' is rather imprecise. In a broad sense, it refers to the degree to which a score varies with trait level, as well as the effectiveness of this score to distinguish between respondents with a high trait level and respondents with a low trait level". Basically, a curve with a very high slope for a value of θ is highly discriminating in this proficiency region, but the curve will be almost flat when we are far from θ and unable to discriminate two subjects that are both below or above this region, as we see in Figure 3.9. Conversely, for a low slope, a wide range of proficiencies are covered but the result of the item will not be so informative as for a higher slope. As we saw previously, a can be seen as $1/\sigma$, where σ is the standard deviation of the difficulty that is experienced for the item. If all subjects above proficiency b solve it correctly and all subjects below proficiency b solve it incorrectly, we could say that the item difficulty perception (or the difficulty estimation error) would be normally distributed on b with zero variance, which would correspond to an infinite discrimination (a step function). Thus,

> **Keynote 3.5. Discrimination and uncertainty**: Discrimination can be interpreted as the inverse of the variance of the observed difficulty.

This is but just one interpretation of the notion of discrimination.

In classical test theory and classical test development (Downing and Haladyna, 2006), the discriminating power of an item is usually understood as a correlation of the item with the series of items (the whole task or sample of items in the test). In other words, it is not only whether the item separates the subjects, but rather whether it also separates the subjects in the right way, i.e., that the item is *representative* of the trait. One classical definition in the area of classical item analysis (Livingston, 2006) relies on the idea that the test measures some proficiency θ and we have the results for many items and subjects. With this view, an item is discriminating if the subjects that solve the item successfully are mostly of high proficiency while the subjects that do not solve the item successfully are mostly of low proficiency. Any appropriate statistical index and metric that formalises this idea can be used to measure this, usually under the name 'discrimination index'. One particularly simple choice is the upper-lower index $2\frac{(n_{high}-n_{low})}{n}$, where n_{high} is the number of successful answers from the high group and n_{low} is the number of wrong answers from the low group. If the proficiency measured by the test is quantitative, *high* and *low* can be taken as the first and last quantile, respectively (quartiles are a common choice).

Another discrimination indicator is the ϕ-coefficient, which is a normalisation of the chi-square statistic that boils down to a binary version of the Pearson correlation coefficient, the point-biserial correlation (Richardson and Stalnaker, 1933), but other correlation coefficients can be used (Livingston, 2006).

Independently of the particular metric for the discrimination index, the value is usually between -1 and 1, where negative values mean that the item is so confusing that high-proficiency subjects do it wrong and low-proficiency subjects do it right. Low positive values denote poor discrimination. If the discriminating power is 1, this means that one single item is sufficient to tell between two proficiencies above and below the difficulty of the item, if there is no variance in the measurement. Items whose discriminating power are close to 1 are of most interest to psychometricians, since a reliable test can be built with very few of these items.

One of the goals of discrimination metrics is to discard bad items and to keep the good ones in a *pool* of items. The arrangement of a pool of items and their characterisation using item response models enables a suitable selection of those items that could better fit a subject or population and make the testing procedure more efficient. In this process, the curve parameters have to be estimated, depending on the model. This is almost always done empirically, by applying the item to a *population* of subjects whose proficiency we already know. Of course, there is a certain circularity here; the proficiency of subjects is usually determined by tests, too. Several solutions may be deployed here: the application of a pretesting procedure or the use of informal assessments of

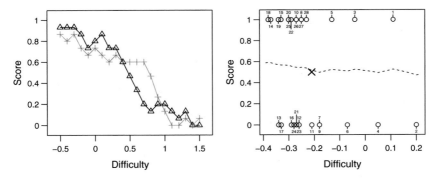

Figure 3.11. Left: *person characteristic curves* for two different subjects after a non-adaptive test with 315 items and a uniform range of difficulties from −0.5 to 1.5. Each point shows an aggregation (the average) of the response of all the items of the same difficulty (in 21 bins of 0.1 width each). Right: Results for an adaptive test with 28 items (data from Weiss, 2011, Figure 8) with an estimated proficiency −0.21, shown as a cross. Each point (shown as a small circle) represents the response of a single item and the adjacent number indicates the order in which it was administered.

either the proficiency of subjects or the difficulty of tasks, with possibly further refinements or iterations of the process.

Once we have a pool of items with their associated parameters, we can finally make a selection of items to perform a test for a particular subject. From the results we can calculate an estimate of the proficiency $\hat{\theta}$. Figure 3.11 (left) shows the results by difficulty (a person characteristic curve) for a traditional test that is administered to two different subjects. Given a curve, we can attempt many approaches to determine the proficiency of both subjects. For instance, we can calculate the point of the curve such that the score equals 0.5. This may yield more than two values, as the curves are not monotonic. A different approach could be to calculate the area under the curve in a given difficulty range, which would correspond to an expected value, assuming all items and difficulties have the same probability. In the figure, both curves have roughly the same area, but different shapes.

Statistical estimation, such as a Bayesian approach or a maximum likelihood method can be used to determine proficiency. First, we know that for a subject of proficiency θ and a set of $j = 1 \ldots m$ items, we have that the probability of one particular combination of results $\mathbf{x}$ of the 2^n possible combinations for these items is its *likelihood*,

$$\mathbb{P}(\mathbf{x}|\theta) = \prod_{x_j=1} p_j(\theta) \cdot \prod_{x_j=0}(1 - p_j(\theta)) = \prod_{x_j=1} \mathbb{P}(x_j = 1|\theta) \cdot \prod_{x_j=0} \mathbb{P}(x_j = 0|\theta)$$

$$(3.7)$$

according to the definition of p_j in Eq. 3.2. The preceding expression means that if we have three items, the probability that a subject of proficiency θ answers items 1 and 2 correctly and item 3 incorrectly, i.e., $\mathbf{x} = (1, 1, 0)$, is given by the product of the curves for items 1 and 2 and the complementary of item 3. Eq. 3.7 assumes independence of responses when conditioned by the same proficiency.

If we observe one particular set of responses, from Bayes' theorem,

$$\mathbb{P}(\theta|\mathbf{x}) = \frac{\mathbb{P}(\mathbf{x}|\theta)\mathbb{P}(\theta)}{\mathbb{P}(\mathbf{x})} \propto \mathbb{P}(\mathbf{x}|\theta)\mathbb{P}(\theta) \tag{3.8}$$

i.e., the probability that a subject has a proficiency θ given a series of results $\mathbf{x}$ is proportional to the conditional probabilities of the results given that proficiency multiplied by the a priori proficiency probability. The value θ that maximises Eq. 3.8 is the estimated proficiency. If we have any knowledge or plausible assumption about $\mathbb{P}(\theta)$ we can incorporate it when estimating θ. In fact, as the logistic models are continuous and have an easy derivative, this allows for several estimation methods. The maximum likelihood estimation (MLE) further simplifies Eq. 3.8 by assuming that $\mathbb{P}(\theta)$ is uniform, namely that, a priori, all proficiencies are equally likely.

Keynote 3.6. The **area under the person characteristic curve** is the average of the response vector, i.e., $\bar{\mathbf{x}}$, if we choose (or weight) items with a uniform distribution of difficulties.

The methods for the estimation of proficiency, such as MLE, usually provide an estimation of its standard error $\hat{\theta} + \varepsilon$ (e.g., if using MLE, the variance of the likelihood). This is the particular (and simple) notion of test reliability in IRT. It is dual to the interpretation of item characteristic curves expressed as a difficulty estimate following a normal distribution by Eq. 3.5 (also Figure 3.10 (left)). Here, for person characteristic curves we would consider a complement of the cumulative normal distribution to get a decreasing curve fitting the values of Figure 3.11 (left), whose slope would be (dually) related to the standard error of the proficiency estimate.

IRT is very frequently applied in the context of (Computerised) Adaptive Testing (CAT) (Wainer, 2000; Weiss, 2011). Unlike non-adaptive tests where a batch of items is fixed or selected before the test, in adaptive testing, the results of previous items are used to choose more or less difficult items to approach the region of proficiency of the subject. The goal is to choose the most informative item at every step, using, e.g., an item information function, which is derived from the probability of correct response of the items, $p(\theta)$. If this is achieved, adaptive tests become much more efficient than non-adaptive ones.

However, the application of adaptive testing is more laborious, as it requires "(1) to characterize the variation among items in a useful way. (2) determine efficient rules for selecting items to administer to an examinee. (3) arrive at scores on a common scale, even though different examinees have been administered different items" (Wainer, 2000, p. 62). The use of different items for each subject is not really a problem if the item parameters are well estimated. Indeed, there is less risk that the subject overspecialises or gets good scores by focusing on the easy problems (the evaluation specialisation problem, Keynote 2.6). Also, with adaptive tests the subjects are challenged but not overwhelmed, so there are positive effects on efficiency, but also on accuracy.

In an adaptive test, the first item may depend on a priori knowledge about the subject's proficiency. If nothing is known, an item of medium difficulty could be chosen as a start. Some randomness for the first choice may also be desirable to prevent all tests from starting with the same item (as this could lead to subjects being used to or knowledgeable of this).

The use of an adaptive test mostly provides points around the subject's proficiency level. This can be seen in Figure 3.11 (right). Conspicuously, a binned average or even a smoothing does not portray the clean picture of the left plot, as outer parts of the difficulty range are usually missing. In an adaptive test, the procedure rarely uses low difficulties, where the subject is usually correct, and high difficulties, where the subject is usually incorrect. With this, the error of the proficiency estimation can be reduced very quickly. The average result of the presented items is of no use at all in adaptive testing, as more proficient subjects will take more difficult items. If the test is well designed, the expected number of items that are solved correctly will be about the same as the number of items that are solved incorrectly.

For more information about IRT, its extension to numerical and non-binary categorical responses, its application to criterion-referenced measurement and their use in adaptive tests, the interested reader can refer to several good sources (Wainer, 2000; Embretson and Reise, 2000; Janssen et al., 2000; De Ayala, 2009). We will revisit the role of difficulty (derived in a different way in Chapter 8) and the notions of discriminating power, adaptive testing, item characteristic curve and, most especially, the person characteristic curves in Chapter 9.

3.8 POPULATION RELATIVITY

Galton (1869) introduced the expression 'nature versus nurture', which he interpreted in the following way: "man is so educable an animal that it is difficult to distinguish between that part of his character which has been acquired through education and circumstance, and that which was in the original grain of his constitution" (Galton, 1883, p. 128). Galton was a firm advocate of the heritability of mental abilities and – to a lesser extent – character, but it was also a matter of common sense that the full potentiality could only be achieved with a suitable environment:

Today it is generally agreed that both nature and nurture play a role. Consequently, the *question* is then usually rephrased as follows:

Keynote 3.7. Nature versus nurture: For a behavioural feature (a personality trait or cognitive ability), which proportion of its variability across individuals *in a population* is genetic as opposed to environmental?

The most common approach to study the question has been the assessment of some people with related genetic substrate in different environments and vice versa, such as familial studies with twins and adopted children. If we study twins in different contexts, most of the variability will be explained by the environment; if we only study adopted children in the same family, most of the variability will be explained by the genetic substrate. To talk about a 'proportion' we need to assume how frequent these situations are, i.e., any derived proportion is relative to an *assumption* of the distribution of individuals and the distribution of environments. For example, does the society being studied have universal access to a good education or very unequal access? Any number such as 60 per cent nature versus 40 per cent nurture (for any feature, such as g) has to be understood in the context of a particular population in a particular society at a particular time. For instance, we can say that a personality trait such as extraversion is more (or less) malleable than neuroticism, but this highly depends on the population (e.g., women or men) and the environment (e.g., a totalitarian theocratic society or an open society). Under this perspective of relativity, it is easy to understand the long-running controversy about the 'educability of intelligence', i.e., the sometimes contradictory evidence about the effectiveness of a "gymnastic of the mind" (Binet, 1909). Likewise, behavioural genetics (Plomin and Asbury, 2005; Plomin et al., 2013; Plomin and Deary, 2015) must carefully interpret the high predictability of many behavioural features from genetic information.

One common way out of the dilemma between nature and nurture is to consider that different ability levels may require different educational environments to reach their *potential* maximum, which is determined by the genetic substrate. This is basically Binet's view, with the acknowledgement that even with perfect

---

Panel 3.3
The Flynn effect and the negative Flynn effect

In 1936 Edward A. Rundquist analysed the IQ scores of a historical series of cohorts evaluated every year. He realised that average IQ improved year after year (Rundquist, 1936; Williams, 2013; Thompson, 2013). However, this effect did not get widespread awareness until Flynn performed a series of analysis of several test batteries, such as Wechsler's and Raven's, for several decades. The increase in IQ scores was so significant during the twentieth century, at about "a rate of 0.30 points per year ever since 1947" (Flynn, 2007), that the variation may even be considered a 'confounding variable', posing serious questions to most theories of intelligence.

Several possible explanations of the Flynn effect have been proposed, in terms of better nutrition, health, education, increased exposure to testing, heterosis, exposure to more lively, light and visual environments, family size and child rearing practices (Williams, 2013). Despite all these explanations, the fact is still puzzling: if IQ tests say something about intelligence, "were we getting that much smarter or were our ancestors mentally retarded?" (Flynn, 2013). Flynn's careful examination attributes the effect to human thinking increasingly relying on more "abstract" or "scientific" concepts (Flynn, 2007).

At the end of the twentieth century the Flynn effect started to slow down, stopped or even reversed in some developed countries (Lynn and Harvey, 2008; Dutton and Lynn, 2013). A stabilisation is consistent with a view that nurture quality has reached a maximum. However, a decay is more difficult to take. Several explanations have been proposed, including a higher level of immigration of people with lower IQs and the negative correlation between intelligence and fertility rate.

---

individualised diagnosis and prognosis, some individuals will get farther than others, as happens with the gymnastics of the body.

This view is consistent with the so-called Flynn effect, described in Panel 3.3. It seems that IQ scores increase in many countries and stabilise when an appropriate level of quality of nurture (including health, nutrition and education) is achieved.

The negative Flynn effect has revived the interest in eugenics, a term also coined by Galton. Indeed, Galton performed some example calculation of how quickly two different trait proportions in a population could be altered if one group put off their marriages until middle age and reduce their offspring.

Despite almost being a taboo term because of its devastating use in the twentieth century, 'mild' eugenic policies are being currently applied in immigration, population control and assisted reproduction in many countries. Indeed, several sociopolitical factors and some (inconclusive) evidence about genetic deterioration (not only for the negative Flynn effect but also in other traits) in modern populations (Lynn, 1996) has renovated the interest in eugenics (Lynn, 2001).

In the discussion about nature and nurture, the topic that has dominated the attention of psychometrics in the past century is group differences. Differences (in averages but also in variability) have been found in many different groups according to sex, ethnicity, social class, culture, etc. (e.g., Gould, 1981; Herrnstein and Murray, 1994; Jensen, 1998; Loehlin, 2000; Bartholomew, 2004; Cianciolo and Sternberg, 2008; Nisbett et al., 2012). How much of their variability is related to nature or nurture? Or is it due to a bias problem in the tests? As a consequence of a purported suspicion of bias against some ethnicities, some court cases have banned IQ tests for educational remedial diagnosis in many US states (Rust and Golombok, 2009), which, unfortunately, has not necessarily led to better opportunities for these ethnicities. For universal psychometrics in the rest of this book, we will pay attention to other criticisms about bias, such as whether tests are anthropocentric or simply culture-bound. More conspicuously, many findings in behavioural research might be based on very narrow human subpopulations in the Western world. If this were the case, there would be no "*a priori* grounds for claiming that a particular behavioural phenomenon is universal based on sampling from a single subpopulation" (Henrich et al., 2010).

In particular, there are many out-of-the-norm subpopulations for which these 'human-universal' theories may fail. For instance, hyperthymesia is a particular kind of a savant syndrome (Treffert, 2009), a condition of an individual that shows extraordinary specific abilities without a corresponding high level in general intelligence (in many cases, indeed, these syndromes are associated with low levels in IQ tests). These individuals clearly introduce some disruptive data for some theories of intelligence, the g factor and the validity of some tests (e.g., subjects with hyperthymesia are expected to feature excellent performance on the digit span task).

But a savant syndrome is just one possible condition associated with mental disabilities. What happens if a monolithic IQ scale is used? In 1921, the American Association on Mental Retardation – now American Association on Intellectual and Developmental Disabilities – published the following criteria: moron (IQ 50–75), imbecile (IQ 25–50) and idiot (IQ < 25). The categories were revised in 1961 to borderline, mild, moderate, severe and profound, and since then the cutoffs have become more ambiguous (Detterman et al., 2000). Nonetheless, IQ tests are still the most common approach to diagnosing mental retardation. Instead of IQ tests, some specialised tests focus on more elementary cognitive tasks, such as simple and choice reaction time, recognition tasks or stimulus discrimination. For instance, Detterman's Cognitive Abilities Test (CAT), can be more appropriate for a finer assessment of intellectually disabled people.

Like mental impairment, giftedness can also be detected using IQ tests, although there is no clear consensus on a threshold to consider an individual gifted (Callahan and Hertberg-Davis, 2012). In fact, there is also some criticism against giftedness being limited to IQ tests, arguing that the subindicators of these tests should be analysed in the context of hierarchical or triarchic models of intellect. In a similar vein, there is a position that giftedness should be linked to extraordinary performance in relevant spheres of human activity (Tannenbaum, 1986). This latter view is close to Gardner's model of multiple intelligences (Gardner, 1983). With this view, individuals with some savant syndromes could be impaired and gifted at the same time.

One of the areas of agreement about giftedness and impairment is that the earlier the diagnosis is made the better. Many IQ tests have variants for children and are used for the detection of educational needs. For instance, the Wechsler Preschool and Primary Scale of Intelligence, Version III (WPPSI-III) is aimed at children roughly between 2 and 7 years old. For very small children, the test includes basic vocabulary and knowledge about the world, use of pictures, building blocks, etc. Tasks for older children include more complex verbal comprehension and perceptual classification items. The Wechsler Intelligence Scale for Children, version IV (WISC-IV) is a related test, devised for children between 6 and 16 year of age. Because of the older age, the subtests in WISC are more similar to those of WAIS. Still, future diagnosis may be radically different. As we mentioned in Chapter 2, there has been a significant advance in the prediction of future abilities and mental pathologies for very small children using neuromarkers and brain scanning (Gabrieli et al., 2015).

A very different case is the evaluation of individuals with some kind of perception impairment, such as deaf and blind people. As many cognitive and personality tests are mostly visual, they do not need any adaptation for the deaf or hearing impaired, although some items may be biased against them. The issue is significantly different for the visually impaired (Bradley-Johnson and Morgan, 2008). Most tests require an important adaptation, in particular those about cognitive abilities, which typically include items that are thought to be presented visually (e.g., Raven's matrices) or aimed at measuring "visual processing".

It is important to clarify that visually-impaired people can still have high perceptual reasoning abilities, including *spatial* abilities, in the sense that they can reason about spatial phenomena and location with the appropriate presentation of the information. In practice, some tests (such as the verbal WAIS or WISC) are accommodated (Burns, 1998), whilst others are specifically designed for impaired people (such as the Blind Learning Aptitude Test or the Cognitive Test for the Blind). We will discuss the relevance of the interface in cognitive testing in Chapter 16.

Overall, the complications in the analysis of individuals or groups that are out of the norm of adult humans is more symptomatic of the difficulties and controversies surrounding psychometrics and psychological testing. Also, the lack of a continuum in methodologies and theories between this chapter and the following one is very illustrative of the difficulties of psychometric research at the lowest edge of cognition in the *Homo sapiens*. Actually, out-of-the-norm cases are an extremely valuable source of evidence to better understand how behavioural features should be measured beyond humans. They are also a powerful refutation tool, whenever an individual consistently obtains very different results on two tests theorised to measure the same construct.

Nevertheless, when compared to the difficulties with special cases, we can really acknowledge the results, progress and applicability of psychometrics for the bulk of the population and see the success and widespread use of psychometrics. In the end, after a century of history, this discipline is able to provide tests and tools that measure human cognitive abilities and personality with more than reasonable accuracy.

CHAPTER HIGHLIGHTS

- The "Big Five" as representative personality traits (Panel 3.2).
- Distinction between abilities and attainment relying on culture fairness (Keynote 3.1), with the positive manifold suggesting a general factor for abilities (Keynote 3.2).
- Cattell-Horn-Carroll hierarchical model as a compromise between g and multiple abilities (Figure 3.2).
- IQ scores more dependent on test composition than g scores (Keynote 3.3).
- The principle of proficiency as maximum achievable difficulty (Keynote 3.4) turned into parametric models in IRT (Section 3.6).
- Different interpretations and indexes for discrimination and its use for adaptive testing (Keynote 3.5, Section 3.7).
- Person characteristic curves as an insightful way of representing a person's responses in terms of difficulty (Figure 3.11, Keynote 3.6).
- Most findings in human psychometrics strongly dependent on the (sub)population, defined as a combination of nature and nurture (Keynote 3.7) and changing with time (Flynn effect) (Section 3.8, Panel 3.3).

4 | The Evaluation of Non-human Natural Behaviour

As investigators get smarter and invent new methods of investigation
animals get smarter also.
— Thomas J. Bouchard Jr,
Genes, Evolution and Intelligence (2014)

T HE TRADITIONAL DISTINCTION between humans and all the *other living beings* is symptomatic of the relevance of the *Homo sapiens*. However,
this relevance led in the past to an anthropocentric stance, which has been,
and still is, highly pernicious for many disciplines, such as biology. Comparative cognition and evolutionary psychology take a different perspective, with
humans being the norm rather than the exception. The evaluation of behaviour
is a fundamental tool in these disciplines, but the methodology and principles
differ from human psychometrics. Is animal cognition so different from human
cognition to justify a completely different evaluation methodology? And what
about other living organisms, such as swarms and plants? Actually, when we
move around the tree of life we find some awkward cases of adaptation, with an
arguably minimal cognition ranging from the very small (bacteria) to the very
big (ecosystems). Ultimately, we can further extend our cure for anthropocentrism to gaiacentrism as well, by thinking about extraterrestrial life. How are
behavioural features evaluated in this highly diverse range of organisms?

4.1 THE BIOLOGICAL ROLE OF BEHAVIOURAL FEATURES

Juan Huarte developed Galen's purported view that the "rational powers" of
men and other animals just differ in their degree: "Galen said that the difference which is found between man and brute beast is the selfe same which is

93

found between a fool and a wise man; which is nought else than in respect of the more and the less. This (truly) is not to be doubted, that brute beasts enjoy memorie and imagination, and another power which resembles understanding, as the Ape is very like a man, and that his soule takes use of the composition of the braine, it is a matter apparant" (Huarte, 1575, pp. 29–30). However, this "apparent" gradation was only taken seriously when it was seen in the context of the theory of evolution, three centuries later, epitomised by Charles Darwin's famous statement: "the mental powers of the higher animals do not differ in kind, though greatly in degree, from the corresponding powers of man" (Darwin, 1871, chap. XVIII). Even under an evolutionary perspective, this view was (and is still) not shared universally. Alfred Russel Wallace, co-discoverer of natural selection, believed that some other kind of "power" or intervention was required for the origin of life, higher animals and consciousness. Wallace was strongly influenced by a dualistic view of the mind based on spiritualism, which led him to deny that his own natural selection theory could accommodate the evolution of "moral and intellectual faculties" (Wallace, 1870).

The overwhelming scientific evidence has supported Darwin's over Wallace's views. However, in practice, some behavioural features, despite their gradual transition in one generation, are better understood, analysed and classified in terms of quality, and not degree, in the same way we do for physical traits: we usually consider a human hand and a particular fish fin as qualitatively different, when not simply unique to one species. Nevertheless, only in a practical, methodological or even philosophical sense should we accept a discussion (even if we disagree) about a purported "Darwin's mistake", a "discontinuity" or a "missing link" (Penn et al., 2008). For instance, Lloyd Morgan and Edward Thorndike differed about whether associative learning in non-human animals and humans was comparable (Thorndike, 1911, p. 126), with Thorndike recognising that "only a small part of human association is at all comparable to [animal association]" (Thorndike, 1911, p. 127). Still, this is perfectly compatible with the evidence that "nowhere more truly than in his mental capacities is man a part of nature" (Thorndike, 1911, p. 294).

The really interesting question is not whether the most distinctive trait of humans, among the apes, is their nakedness or their use of language but why some animals display different ranges and degrees of behavioural features, and what environmental pressures led to them, in the very same way that other physical traits developed. In brief, what is the role of behavioural features in evolutionary terms? For instance, Darwin covered a wide range of behavioural features, including both personality traits and cognitive abilities, when referring to animals: "all have the same senses, intuitions, and sensations, similar passions, affections, and emotions, even the more complex ones, such as jealousy, suspicion, emulation, gratitude, and magnanimity; they practise deceit and are revengeful; they are sometimes susceptible to ridicule, and even have a sense of humour; they feel wonder and curiosity; they possess the same faculties of imitation, attention, deliberation, choice, memory, imagination, the association of ideas, and reason, though in very different degrees. The individuals of the same species graduate in intellect from absolute imbecility to high excellence. They are also liable to insanity, though far less often than in the case of man" (Darwin, 1871, chap. III).

From this variety of behavioural features, some can be beneficial for some environments but deadly in others. Indeed, the notion of a 'more advanced' trait does not make sense, as many traits appear and disappear along the evolutionary history depending on environmental changes. This is more conspicuous for personality traits than cognitive abilities, but it is also easy to see that some cognitive abilities may become useless for some environments (e.g., visual abilities for blind mole rats). Only general intelligence, seen as an inheritable behavioural feature (Bouchard, 2014), can make the point as a 'more advanced' trait at least partially, as we will discuss later on.

In addition, the evidence of convergent evolution, not in behaviours, but in cognitive abilities, is not only against the view of a *scala naturae* – even in a metaphorical sense – but also against the idea that once a "good" ability is createed, it is never lost (Shettleworth, 2013, p. 8). For instance, crows, chimpanzees, orangutans and humans use tools in the wild, even if their most recent common ancestor most probably did not. More interestingly, bonobos do not use tools very much, even if it might be the case that the most recent common ancestor of extant great apes did. This is exactly the same as with physical abilities, such as flying. Flying seems a fantastic ability in the animal world, independently developed for insects, bats and birds, but some species in these groups have lost the ability to fly as the result of natural selection.

Natural selection just dictates that any trait, either physical or behavioural, that is favoured by the environment will prevail. But how are behaviours created in the first place? Every life form exhibits some kind of interaction and development in an environment. Even a motionless prokaryote interacts with its environment displaying a range of behaviours, and undergoes chemical reactions that affect its body and future behaviour. Some particular bodies are able to succeed in some particular environments, and the same happens with some particular behaviours. Bodies and behaviours are the result of mutations and selection pressures. This is the way that species *adapt* to changes in their environment. Have all behaviours been developed in this way since evolution started a few billion years ago?

The answer is no. There is a different mechanism by which new behaviours are created. For instance, an ant finds the route to a particular source of food and repeats that behaviour day after day, until the environment changes. Indeed, new findings of food elsewhere will cause the ant to change its behaviour hundreds of times during its life. Note that this adaptation, during the life of an organism, is of course not exclusive to behaviours, but also to physical traits. An animal, e.g., a human tourist, will soon generate some skin melanin after basking in the sun during her first day of holidays. But we know that Lamarck was wrong and none of these acquired traits will be inherited. However, to complete the picture, some of the behaviours can be learnt from other individuals and persist, *culturally*.

We have reached one crucial point in our discussion, the distinction between those behavioural features that are *innate* and those that are *acquired*. On one hand we would have those behaviours that all members of a species would display, independently of the environment. For instance, fish swim in the opposite direction of a predator. On the other hand, we would have those behaviours that are produced after the interaction of the individual with its environment. For instance, a monkey will not eat a particular fruit again if it caused gastric distress the first time.

It is true that a species can display some complex behaviours shared by all the conspecifics systematically, which are hence seen as innate. Shettleworth (2013, p. 11) says that this kind of species is "not exceptionally intelligent in general". Each of these behaviours has been the result of what is referred to as adaptive specialisation:

Keynote 4.1. Evolutionary adaptive specialisation, in the context of behavioural features, is the display of new behaviours by a species as the result of natural selection of those more fitted to the species's environment.

The accumulation of a great range of behaviours is usually associated with a certain "modularity" of animal cognition (Shettleworth, 2013, p. 10), i.e., the existence of independent parts (e.g., in the brain) that account for different specialised innate behaviours. For example, one part of a fish's brain would code the policy that makes it swim away from predators and another part would code the policy that makes it look for food in warmer waters. These behaviours would ultimately be coded in different parts of the DNA before being manifest in the brain, the phenotype. This modularity would mirror what happens with physical traits too, in the very same way that a chiselling beak and a red crest

---

Panel 4.1
Innate versus acquired: a matter of degree

"Attempting to classify behavior as learned as opposed to innate is meaningless" and "nothing in behavior or cognition is either wholly learned or entirely innate" (Shettleworth, 2013, p. 13) are very strong statements, but accurate in general. For instance, fully learnt behaviour would be reduced to an animal learning something over a tabula rasa, with no innate construct, representation or bias at all about the world. On the other hand, entirely innate behaviour in animals would reduce behaviour to reflexes.

The issue must be understood as the percentage of variability in a *population* due to genes versus environment. This is what we did with the nature versus nurture debate seen in Section 3.8. As a result, unless we are more precise about the origin of a particular behaviour it is more accurate to talk about a *predisposition* (Shettleworth, 2010b, p. 13).

---

are different features of a woodpecker. In contrast, acquired behaviours would be memorised in the brain but, unlike innate behaviours, the exact part of the brain where they may end up may be more variable, especially in brains with more plasticity.

This view is oversimplistic, though. First, most animals combine instinctive behaviours with acquired behaviours, including humans. Second, many innate behaviours are altered or improved by experience. A baby shark, with an innate predator behaviour, will improve after some experience. However, if instinctive and acquired behaviours are intertwined, where are the adjustments recorded in the brain? In the 'predator' module or somewhere else? Actually, any crisp distinction between innate and acquired traits, and even an opposition between modularity and plasticity, needs to be put into question. Panel 4.1 discusses this issue.

With the understanding of predispositions to behaviours, individual adaptation through learning is no longer seen as the inhibition of instinctive behaviours that are replaced by new, acquired behaviours, but the development or refinement of behaviours due to environment change. The question about intelligence is then reframed as the ability of creating or refining previous behaviours over some existing predispositions. This is in accordance with a developmental perspective of cognition, as we will see in Chapter 12.

Finally, the idea that cognitive abilities are developed in species that face a more diverse range of environments has to be put into question as well. Many apes are struggling for survival, as they live in rather particular habitats, while other, usually considered less intelligent animals, like cockroaches, can adapt to a *diverse range of environments*. Even if we were able to restrict to cognitive environments without the contamination of physical factors (something that we will discuss in some other chapters in this book), it is not clear either what we mean by environment diversity. Consequently, definitions of intelligence such as "the built-in flexibility that allows individual organisms to adjust their behaviour to relatively rapidly changing environments" (Stenhouse, 1974, p. 61) are problematic. It seems that the only way to link environment diversity with intelligence in a minimally consistent way is with the view of *biodiversity* (Hortal et al., 2009).

> **Keynote 4.2. Intelligence and biodiversity**: Cognitive abilities are linked to survival when an organism competes and co-operates with individuals of the same and other species, by modelling and anticipating their behaviours.

This boils down to social environments, as we will explore in Chapter 13.

4.2 THE STUDY OF ANIMAL BEHAVIOUR

The complex role of cognition in evolution seen in the previous section has always encouraged research on animal behaviour. Ethology, behavioural ecology, comparative psychology and the more recent term of comparative cognition have been joining forces to unveil how animals behave. Ethology and behavioural ecology have focused on what animals usually do, mostly in their natural situations, such as foraging, mating, predating or parenting. Comparative psychology and cognition have put the emphasis on how these behaviours work and what their 'causal mechanism' is (in Tinberger's terminology, 1963), i.e., on "the study of cognitive processes in all species of animals, humans included" (Shettleworth, 2013, p. 1). This has usually been performed in controlled situated experiments, with the goal of confirming or refuting some previous hypotheses about the cognition of one or more species, trying to determine what animals tend to do or are able to do.

As an example of a situated experiment, we can go back to the sixth century BCE, as shown in Panel 4.2.

The fable of the crow and the pitcher sets a situated problem, which some animals will be able to solve and some others not. This can be seen as a cognitive task. However, let us bear in mind that, as a situated problem, physical traits are also relevant. The main interest of the experiment is not to determine the degree

---

Panel 4.2
Aesop's clever crow

Aesop's fables are a famous collection of tales from ancient Greece, most of them representing anthropomorphic animals having various personalities and cognitive abilities. In *The Crow and the Pitcher*, a thirsty crow, unable to fit its head into a narrow long pitcher, is able to make the water rise by throwing pebbles in.

Only recently has this particular fable caught attention from scientists as a challenging mental riddle, reframed as an experiment to analyse the use of casual tools, plans, perseverance, insight and complex cognition about the physical world. Surprisingly, as if augured by the fable, corvids are among the very few animals that are actually able to solve this problem (Bird and Emery, 2009; Jelbert et al., 2014), jointly with great apes (Hanus et al., 2011) on similar tasks. This is more striking as many humans are unable to solve the riddle.

---

of success of the crow according to the dimensions of the pitcher, the water level, etc., but to answer questions about the cognitive processes involved. In fact, if the crow is not able to solve the task, we can infer almost nothing about these processes.

In general, the main problem is the interpretation of the experiment, since very different conclusions can be obtained depending on the particular stance of the investigator. For instance, George Romanés had a more anthropomorphic, or mentalistic, stance. He interpreted actions in terms of "desires", "emotions" and "ratiocination", as we would infer from a human (Romanés, 1885). Edward Thorndike, on the contrary, had a behaviouristic position, rejecting any introspective interpretation (Thorndike, 1911). Many other opposed interpretations followed in the past century, and many observations that *indicated* intelligence were later on explained by 'killjoys' in terms of non-intelligent processes (Shettleworth, 2010a; Biemans, 2012).

But how can we choose between mentalistic, behaviouristic and other plausible interpretations? Lloyd Morgan proposed the following rule:

Keynote 4.3. Lloyd Morgan's Canon: "In no case is an animal activity to be interpreted in terms of higher psychological processes if it can be fairly interpreted in terms of processes which stand lower in the scale of psychological evolution and development" (Morgan, 1903, p. 59).

This is but Occam's razor applied to the interpretation of animal behaviour experiments. For instance, if an observation can be explained by Pavlovian conditioning, which is a simple mechanism that is shared by many species, we should not look for other more complicated explanations.

Edward Thorndike was, for instance, very strict in his interpretations. First, he described that, in many cases, animals use trial and error in a 'situated search', i.e., a *physical search*: "The process involved in the learning was evidently a process of selection. The animal is confronted by a state of affairs or, as we may call it, a 'situation'. He reacts in the way that he is moved by his innate nature or previous training to do, by a number of acts. These acts include the particular act that is appropriate and he succeeds" (Thorndike, 1911, p. 244). The interpretation is then very Spartan: "here we have the simplest and at the same time the most widespread sort of intellect or learning in the world. There is no reasoning, no process of inference or comparison; there is no thinking about things, no putting two and two together; there are no ideas – the animal does not think of the box or of the food or of the act he is to perform. He simply comes after the learning to feel like doing a certain thing under certain circumstances which before the learning he did not feel like doing" (Thorndike, 1911, p. 245). This contrasts with a *mental search*, i.e., an 'intellectual search', as performed by humans. Thorndike explains the difference: "human beings are accustomed to think of intellect as the power of having and controlling ideas and of ability to learn as synonymous with ability to have ideas. But learning by having ideas is really one of the rare and isolated events in nature. There may be a few scattered ideas possessed by the higher animals, but the common form of intelligence with them, their habitual method of learning, is not by the acquisition of ideas, but by the selection of impulses". These two types of search have to be added up to *evolutionary search*:

> **Keynote 4.4. Kinds of search**: It is not easy to tell how an animal has come to solve a task, by evolutionary, physical or mental search.

Apart from the interpretation of the experiments, the real question is to determine the kind of processes that are to be studied and which tasks or situations are used as the basis for the experiments. Many books on comparative cognition are illustrative of the many kinds of processes that have been investigated. For instance, Wasserman and Zentall (2006) distinguish ten parts in their book,

Table 4.1. Areas of animal cognition research according to the table of contents of Wasserman and Zentall's book (2006).

perception and illusion
attention and search
memory processes
spatial cognition
timing and counting
conceptualisation and categorisation
pattern learning
tool fabrications and use
problem solving and behavioural flexibility
social cognition processes

as shown in Table 4.1. Another common classification distinguishes three main domains: *physical cognition*, *social cognition* (Tomasello and Call, 1997; Shettleworth, 2010b) and *basic processes* (or fundamental mechanisms).

Many questions and experiments can be formulated for any of these areas and domains. For instance, given two possible hypotheses, e.g., chickens do or do not imitate behaviour, the researcher must devise an experiment for which only the two hypotheses are plausible so that the outcome can falsify one of the hypotheses. Finding such an experiment is not easy. Many times, experiments only provide indications in favour of one hypothesis, but are not able to reject the other. This is more likely the more dependencies the task has with the species, its environment, the interface, etc. This, in fact, is very common, as many of the tasks are situated and generally less abstract than the psychometric tasks we saw in the previous chapter. For instance, if a chimpanzee can use a stick to access some ants, does it mean that chimpanzees are capable of general tool use, or only those tools that can represent some kind of extension of their limbs? If the animal is not tested with other tool-using situations, it is very difficult to tell.

Some experiments are extremely sophisticated and laborious. For instance, in the past decades there are numerous experiences of chimpanzees and other apes brought up in human environments (Gardner and Gardner, 1969; Terrace, 1987; Savage-Rumbaugh and Lewin, 1994; Segerdahl, 2012; Rumbaugh, 2014). This is anecdotal evidence that is hardly reproducible, but nonetheless very useful to demonstrate the *potential* capabilities with a very rich environment and development programme.

A further intricacy for the study of animal cognition is that the same result for two different species (or even individuals of the same species) can be produced by very different processes. For instance, spatial orientation is a kind of ability whose processes are usually considered modular, with particular mechanisms depending on the species. Animals can orientate in many different ways: using landmarks (a tree, a rock) or using path integration ("dead reckoning"). Actually, ants, pigeons and apes locate and remember food very differently. Some of them can even take advantage of specialised sensors (e.g., the Earth's magnetic field).

A final question is the range of species that are compared. Early experiments focused on dogs, cats and rats (Thorndike, 1911; Skinner, 1938; Watson, 1967) with limited species comparison. This has changed in the last few decades, with apes, monkeys and humans – for comparison – becoming very popular. Despite the improvement, this new focus on apes was accused of "chimpocentrism" (Beck, 1982). Today, experiments cover a much wider range of the animal kingdom: mammals (cetaceans, elephants, etc.), other vertebrates (birds, fish) and invertebrates (bees, ants, cephalopods, etc.). More importantly, an increasing percentage of the studies are multispecies (Shettleworth, 2009).

4.3 MEASUREMENT IN ANIMAL BEHAVIOUR RESEARCH

Today, there is an important collection of results about the behaviour of many species, comprising the three main domains of animal cognition mentioned earlier: basic processes, physical cognition and social cognition. However, are these "experimental explorations" (Wasserman and Zentall, 2006) leading to measurement tools and test batteries that can be used systematically? The answer to this question requires a more careful analysis of what has been done and how.

The study of animal behaviour has been dominated by qualitative questions, in terms of presence or absence of a trait, e.g., "whether other species have abstract same/different categorization" or "whether animals have abstract numerical or social concepts" (Shettleworth, 2013, p. 47). The answers are usually referred to the whole species, even when only a few individuals have shown the trait (e.g., "bonobos are able to use a complex language but cannot ask questions", instead of "Kanzi the bonobo is able to use lexigrams but never asked a question with them"). Clearly, the situation is different from that of psychological tests designed for humans, and psychometrics in particular. In fact, we have to prise the appropriate research out of the literature in the area of animal behaviour, to find concepts such as normative scales, item difficulty, or test reliability and validity. This is not due to a lack of rigour, but to different scientific goals and, most especially, to the additional complications that animal research entails in terms of experimentation procedures, population size and diversity.

In the context of universal psychometrics, we would like to see whether there are quantitative, rather than qualitative, measurements that allow us to put different animals – including different individuals of the same species – on the same scale. This aspiration was already expressed, very explicitly, by Francis Galton, as we saw in Panel 3.1, and by Edward Thorndike, who figured out "a program of tasks to" (Thorndike et al., 1927, p. 340–341) sort animals by their purported intelligence: "earthworms, crabs, fishes, frogs, turtles, rats, cats, dogs, monkeys, chimpanzees" and, finally, humans of several intellectual classes, "locating zero difficulty by experiment". He suggested that "the difficulty of the intellectual task which the earthworm's intellect can master is so near zero difficulty that a level slightly below it may safely be accepted as an approximate absolute zero of intellectual difficulty, sufficiently close for all purposes, theoretical or practical".

The preceding "program" can be considered simplistic from a modern perspective – mostly because of a monolithic intelligence scale, still too much resembling a *scala naturae* – but sets a quantitative, measurement approach, based on general behavioural features, instead of a taxonomy of animals according to the behaviours they do and do not display. But where are the difficulties for such a programme, in a renewed non-monolithic way?

The main difficulty is test administration. This starts with getting the animal motivated to solve a task or inducing it to display some behaviour. Because language cannot be used to give instructions or indications to an animal, the use of rewards and punishment is commonplace in animal cognition research. Thorndike himself warned about the troubles of finding the good rewards, or "satisfiers" (Thorndike, 1911, p. 245). It is important to clarify that the use of rewards and punishments does not imply that some training (or learning), or any change of behaviour in time, takes place. We can use food to examine animal perception abilities, or to analyse trajectories, with no intention of modifying animal behaviour other than the particular measurement. In fact, for some studies we may prefer to avoid even the slightest degree of habituation, using just one and only one trial per animal. In these cases, the term 'bait' or Thorndike's 'satisfier' capture this idea better than 'reward', which is usually associated with some kind of cognitive postprocessing after it is given.

Of course, rewards and punishments can be used to alter behaviour intentionally, a phenomenon that was formulated as the "law of effect" by Thorndike (1911, p. 244). This effect is stronger the higher the number of times the process is repeated, an associated phenomenon that is known as the "law of exercise", today expressed around the general concepts of "reinforcement" and "conditioning":

Keynote 4.5. Conditioning: Animals have a predisposition in favour, neutral or against a range of stimuli. These predispositions can be used as unconditional stimuli (in classical conditioning) or as rewards and penalties (in operant conditioning) to make the animal display some other predisposed behaviours or, by repeated trials, to alter – or *condition* – its behaviours, including the very change of their disposition towards the stimuli.

If the predispositions of an animal before an experiment are not well known, the result of the experiment may be completely biased. For instance, animals react differently to food in a dangerous situation depending on how hungry they are. This uncertainty about the state of an animal leads to very strict protocols in animal research (about feeding times, habits, etc.). Researchers must first ensure that an animal is sufficiently motivated to make a cognitive effort (if that is needed) to solve the task. This is not different from humans, especially small children.

Closely related to rewards and penalties is the choice of a right interface. The majority of studies use a visual interface, which is adapted to the animal's characteristics, based on the knowledge of the animal (e.g., colour blindness, contrast, vision range). Vision, however, is not the most important or developed sense in many animals. The reason for the dominance of visual interfaces in animal behaviour experiments is presumably partly anthropocentric. For instance, the results of an elementary discrimination task can be much better if the olfactory system is used instead of the vision system, as has been shown in rats (Slotnick, 2001). Similarly, only a few animals are said to pass the 'mirror test', i.e., to recognise themselves in the mirror, and so are believed to have a more fully fledged notion of 'self'. However, dogs (and many other animals) can recognise themselves by their odours, where they have been, their territory, etc.

Apart from rewards and stimuli, there are other caveats. Animals may like to cheat and get the rewards by other means or may want to 'communicate' something to the tester. This issue is not different, in principle, to the administration error that happens in human evaluation, but for non-human animals the choice of the interface plays a more critical role:

Keynote 4.6. Administration error due to inappropriate interface: Any cognitive evaluation may underestimate or overestimate measurements if the interface, including the framing of actions and observations, rewards and punishments, the context of the administration and the subject's metacognition and intentions about the measuring process, are not well chosen and understood.

Underestimation is far more common than overestimation, due to the inability to frame the task with an appropriate administration interface. This phenomenon is opposite to the overestimation phenomenon that is usual when *interpreting* results of animal evaluation, which motivated Morgan's Canon. Of course, both phenomena do not compensate each other and vastly compromise test reliability and validity.

It can be argued that the specialisation of some perception mechanisms is so manifest in many animals that the actual measurement will never reach the potential measurement (test potential), because the interface can never be optimised for the subject (an issue we will discuss in the most general case in Section 16.2 in Chapter 16). This criticism usually neglects the neuroplasticity of the brain of many animals. For instance, in a remarkable experiment with originally colour-blind mice, to which human colour receptors were introduced, "mice apparently acquired an added dimension of sensory experience, implying that the mammalian brain has the innate ability to extract information from novel and qualitatively different types of visual input" (Jacobs and Nathans, 2009). This suggests that perception systems are general enough to a change of interface (provided it happens soon in development or is trained adequately), very much the same as humans can chat by writing instead of speaking.

The ultimate goal of a fair interface is to prevent any limitation that is not purely cognitive or is not related to the trait that is to be measured. In animals (but also with small children and people with disabilities), it is difficult, but not impossible, to frame an experiment to reduce contamination from the physical components of the task and the subject. Only if this is achieved, can we talk about a fair comparison of two different subjects for the same task. One possible way of doing this, at least for some animals, is to reduce the interface to some sensors and actuators. The animal must be first trained to use the actuators regularly in relation to the perception device (a light, a sound, a pictogram, etc.). This may take weeks, or even months, of training. Once this first stage is accomplished, a new cognitive test can be performed with more reliability and validity, using the perception device and the actuators. Many tasks have been framed in this way, using, e.g., sound signals and levers with rats. Today,

Figure 4.1. Some of the chick pens designed by Edward Thorndike were con-figured as mazes of progressive 'difficulty', according to the number of 'possible avenues'. These were used to analyse the spatial capability of the chicks more systematically. [Adapted from (Thorndike, 1911, Figure 15, p. 61).]

computer screens, joysticks and buttons are becoming popular for animals too. For instance, the relative numerousness task with cetaceans, as we will see in Chapter 8 (Panel 8.1 and Figure 8.1), can replace boards with computer screens.

4.4 MORE SYSTEMATIC ANIMAL EVALUATION

The same *testing apparatus* (including rewards, actuators and an arrangement for stimuli) can be used to perform a series of tasks for the same species, so that the apparatus can be validated in more general terms, independently from a particular task. This goes in the direction of making experiments more systematic with a species or, at least, with a particular group of animals (in a zoo, an aquarium or a sanctuary). Edward Thorndike was the first to devise the first testing apparatus for the study of fish, chicks, dogs and cats. Actually, he became famous for his puzzle boxes, but he also devised special fish bowls and chick pens. For instance, for chicks, he used pens configured as mazes (Thorndike, 1911, p. 61). Once he realised that the setting was useful and discriminative for the chicks, in terms of the time the chicks took to get out of pens with different arrangements, he started to devise the characteristics of the pens more systematically. For instance, Figure 4.1 shows the disposition of three of the simplest pens (mazes) used in some of his experiments. He also explored steps, platforms, strings to pull, etc.

Since then, a large number and variety of apparatus have been devised for the analysis of animal behaviour. However, many apparatus are not sufficiently abstract to be used for a wide range of tasks and, especially, for a wide range of species. For instance, radial arm mazes (see Figure 4.2 (left)) were introduced by Olton and Samuelson (1976) for the study of spatial memory in rats.

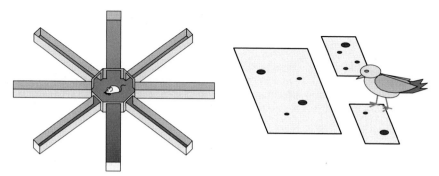

Figure 4.2. Left: an eight-arm maze, used for the study of spatial memory in rats. Right: an interface for a number matching task used for birds. [Right figure adapted from (Koehler, 1941).]

In principle, they can be adapted to other species, including humans (Mandolesi et al., 2009). However, the farther we go from the psychomotor and physical characteristics of the animal that originated the apparatus, the more difficult the comparison is. For instance, how can this apparatus be adapted for dolphins? Would the results be comparable? Probably not, as dolphins and rats have very different psychomotor and location systems. Because of all this, *when the species makes it possible*, more and more tests nowadays are designed with the use of some standard representation (instead of actual objects). For instance, Koehler (1941) introduced a number matching task for birds using a representation (see Figure 4.2 (right)). Nowadays, computerised apparatus are becoming common for some animals, such as the one for Ayumu the chimpanzee shown in Figure 2.3, because the interface can be adapted using different sensors and actuators, with the animal not being embedded (or embodied) in the testing apparatus.

As any artificial apparatus may entail lack of motivation or proficiency, it is very important to validate the interface by the use of control exercises. These can be defined in such a way that a reference response can only be obtained if and only if the animal is dexterous with the interface and motivated by the reward. Next, the evaluator can start with the particular task she is interested in with different degrees of difficulty. For instance, Fragaszy et al. (2009) study chimpanzees and capuchins using a joystick to navigate a cursor inside a maze that is shown on a screen. Mazes are presented in an order of increasing number of forks.

Apart from a fair interface design, the construction of a quantitative comparison across several species is admittedly a very difficult problem, but there

Figure 4.3. Left: an example of an odd-one-out problem, such as those used with pigeons by Zentall et al. (1974, 1980). The animal must choose the figure that looks different from the other three. Right: a more difficult one where one object differs in size. [Freely adapted from (Thomas, 1996).]

are at least two possible (compatible) approaches. The first one is to devise more abstract tasks, as independent of any animal as possible. Tasks should be devised to measure a particular behavioural feature in general. Then, the effort is made to adapt the task to several animals in the fairest possible way. For instance, the odd-one-out exercises were designed to test the ability to recognise similarities in a geometric domain, *in an abstract way* (Zentall et al., 1974, 1980). Figure 4.3 shows two items. Whilst originally used for pigeons, they have also been applied to other species, including humans (with more difficult items), as a paradigmatic example of a culture-fair test (Dehaene et al., 2006).

This task, despite being abstract, still involves many processes. For instance, it depends on elementary visual abilities to recognise shapes. If these abilities are not present, then the other abilities to be measured (learning abstract relations) will never be displayed. As a result, when a particular individual or group performs poorly, the ultimate reason is unclear. For animals, unlike humans, the existence of several elementary perception abilities cannot be taken for granted. On many occasions, this problem can be solved by checking that those processes that are necessary for the task (but not evaluated) are present in the animal (e.g., by a previous control task about discriminating circles and crosses).

The second approach to get quantitative comparisons is the use of *batteries* of tasks. The use of several tasks enables a systematic evaluation of behavioural features rather than of particular tasks. For a systematic testing, it should be irrelevant whether two animals solve the task in very different ways, using very different cognitive mechanisms, and brain modules. We can even compare a single animal with a swarm.

How can such a systematic testing be done in practice? As we saw in the previous chapter, the administration of test batteries with a good number of tasks and a large subject population has been common in humans, but it is prohibitively expensive for most animal species. Nonetheless, we see that incipient – and titanic – efforts have been performed in this direction for animals too. Let us analyse a few systematic approaches for the two main types of behavioural features we care most about in this book: personality traits and cognitive abilities.

As we have seen with Aesop's *The Crow and the Pitcher*, animals have always been used as ideals for human virtues and defects and for many personality traits. Following this tradition, it is not surprising that the *scientific* analysis of personality and temperament in animals has received significant attention in animal cognition research. Risk aversion, self-control, aggressiveness, etc., are useful predictors about how an animal behaves in a range of artificial tasks and real situations. In particular, some of these personality traits can have a strong effect in the evaluation of cognitive abilities. For instance, pigeons are afraid of change and of new things (neophobia), and this may have an effect on their learning abilities (Seferta et al., 2001).

But how is personality evaluated? For instance, personality traits in dogs (Svartberg and Forkman, 2002) have been analysed using the "Dog Mentality Assessment" (DMA) test, composed of 10 separate subtests with 33 behavioural variables such as whether the animal co-operates, greets, shows interest in play, follows or grabs things, shows aggression during play or from sudden appearance, etc. The subtests are outdoors, with several 'stations' arranged along a path in a wooded area. Judges give scores to the dogs by observation. Using factor analysis, Svartberg and Forkman (2002) identified five major traits: "Playfulness", "Curiosity/Fearlessness", "Chase-proneness", "Sociability" and "Aggressiveness".

In many other studies, the personality of the animals is judged with a questionnaire that is filled in by a group of human 'raters', using forms such as the so-called Chimpanzee Personality Questionnaire (CPQ). For instance, in a recent study with chimpanzees, "raters were instructed to base their judgments on their general impressions of the chimpanzees" (Úbeda and Llorente, 2014). The analysis of personality or temperament traits can also be done without third-person reports, using real tasks. For instance, self-control is evaluated on both chimpanzees and small children (aged 3 and 6) in (Herrmann et al., 2015). Finally, different approaches can be combined. Gosling and John (1999) used an extended Five-Factor Model to develop "the landscape of animal personality", by reviewing 19 studies of personality factors in twelve nonhuman species. The analysis showed that Extraversion, Neuroticism and Agreeableness appear in most animals, followed by Openness. A separate Conscientiousness dimension happens only for chimpanzees, and the Dominance and the Activity dimensions had limited experimental support.

Cognitive abilities for animals have also been analysed with task batteries for various purposes. For instance, in rodents, we find a battery for temperament, personality and cognitive evaluation that includes "open field activity, light-dark exploration, rotarod, prepulse inhibition (PPI), acoustic startle habituation, conditioned fear, Morris water maze, and hot plate" (McIlwain et al.,

2001) and another battery that includes "Y-maze, Morris water maze, circular platform, visible platform, passive avoidance, and active avoidance" (Deacon et al., 2002). Only one task is common between both batteries, despite the use of rodents in both cases. This also happens in narrow domains; for instance, in a special issue on numerical cognition in animals, featuring 16 studies involving mammals, birds, fish and invertebrates (Agrillo and Beran, 2013), no common battery is used either, and species comparison can only be done in a qualitative way.

However, there are a few cases where the same battery is used repeatedly for the same or different species. For instance, a small battery to evaluate fundamental cognition mechanisms (abstract categories, such as distinguishing "same" from "different", linked to visual recognition) was introduced by Cook et al. (1997) for pigeons. Later, with variations, the battery was applied to other animals, such as rhesus macaques and capuchin monkeys with a quantitative comparison (see, e.g., Shettleworth, 2010b, sec. 6.5.4).

A more illustrative example of the same comprehensive battery used for several species can be found in (Herrmann et al., 2007). The same exercises (the Primate Cognition Test Battery) were used for three species of apes (chimpanzees, orangutans and small human children) and later on with other primates (Schmitt et al., 2012). The interfaces are different, with different apparatus and rewards for each species. The battery includes 25 items of the physical and social domains, including scales about space, quantities, causality, social learning, communication and theory of mind. Similar batteries have been used in related research (Herrmann et al., 2010; Herrmann and Call, 2012). Indeed, Herrmann and Call (2012) make a call for the advancement of the field using "test batteries that can be administered to a large number of individuals of multiple species", capturing "cognitive, motivational and temperament dimensions".

Unfortunately, these studies are still the exception rather than the rule. Thornton et al. (2014) "suggest that future work should adopt lessons from psychometric research, where tests are designed to target specific cognitive processes and test outcomes can be clearly evaluated on the basis of correctness, giving quantitative scores of individual performance".

This opens up new avenues of research. First, by the quantification of the cognitive differences between individuals, researchers can analyse their influence on Darwinian fitness and their heritability, shedding some light on the so-far obscure area of how behavioural features evolve. Second, abilities can be arranged following a "cognitive taxonomy", or even a "natural history of cognition" (Rowe and Healy, 2014). Third, researchers can analyse whether some findings in humans are also found in other species, such as positive manifolds and primary factors, including the g factor.

Keynote 4.7. Psychometric approach in animal behaviour research: The use of a more systematic testing using batteries over larger animal populations renders new intra- and inter-species findings such as the *g* factor beyond humans.

None of these avenues is completely new, especially the last one. Indeed, the study of general intelligence in animals was endeavoured by Robert Thorndike (Edward's son), who designed an experiment to study the general intelligence of rats (Thorndike, 1935). He found a general factor capturing 2/3 of the common factor variance. This value was also found, but in a lower degree, in further studies (Anderson, 1993; Crinella and Yu, 1995), strongly supported by others (Plomin, 2001; Matzel and Kolata, 2010), and, after an impressive comprehensive analysis in (Reader et al., 2011), reunderstood with the statement that a general factor has appeared at least four times as a "convergent evolution in capuchins, baboons, macaques and great apes", with more *g*-loaded cognitive abilities being more inheritable in primates (Woodley et al., 2015).

Nonetheless, this general factor has been put into question for other species (e.g., Herrmann and Call, 2012). This equivocal evidence is explained by Thornton and Lukas (2012) as the result of small sample sizes, with a lack of genetic and environmental variability precluding the finding of general factors. Bouchard (2014), in an extensive literature review of the *g* factor in mice, birds, dogs, primates and even across taxa concludes that positive findings of a *g* factor are widespread and also posits that this can be explained as a result of convergent evolution. Fernandes et al. (2014) has found similar results for interspecies general factors (G, to distinguish it from intra-species *g*). In the end, the upshot of the discussion is that modularity and "general biological intelligence" (Bouchard, 2014) must coexist as parts of the explanation of animal cognitive behaviours.

4.5 THE FAR-REACHING ROOTS OF COGNITIVE LIFE

At the end of the previous chapter we discussed the cognitive measurement of out-of-the-norm human beings. Are there out-of-the-norm specimens for behavioural features in the whole tree of life? We could argue that this question does not make sense, as cognition only applies for some complex forms of life, basically a subset of the animal kingdom. Any other kingdom or domain in any classical or phylogenetic taxonomy would not really display any behaviour that we could consider cognitive in any way.

Again, this is a rather anthropocentric perspective, which has been put into question by the discovery of complex adaptive behaviours in many organisms or suborganisms that were assumed to have a very simple interaction with the environment, such as plants, fungi, immune systems, bacteria, genomes and metabolic systems (Trewavas, 2005). This has raised questions about what cognition is, how *minimal* it can be, and even whether all life is cognitive in some way.

The most interesting implication of looking at unconventional cognition is that, for some relatively simple organisms, it seems possible to understand their behaviour (and even replicate it). If this is the case, we would be able to relate the behavioural (black-box) evaluation with a more structuralist (white-box) evaluation. This would create many opportunities for a perspective that would be neither mentalistic or behaviouristic but in alignment with the "cognitive revolution" and one of its core ideas: "the mental world can be grounded in the physical world by the concepts of information, computation, and feedback" (Pinker, 2003).

To understand how behavioural features originate, we should look at concepts such as 'embodied cognition' (Varela et al., 1992; Chemero, 2011) and 'minimal cognition' (Beer, 2003; Beer and Williams, 2015). More remarkably, the capability of a system to self-organise and maintain its organisation, embodied but constituting a bounded entity in an environment – known as 'autopoiesis' (Maturana and Varela, 1980; Beer, 2004, 2015) – would be claimed to be crucial, if not definitory, for life. In the end, since "Maturana and Varela…hold that all autopoietic systems are inherently 'cognitive'" (Van Duijn et al., 2006), all kinds of life would be cognitive.

This is all very well, but does it mean that we can measure cognition for any living organism in a meaningful way? This is exactly what Edward Thorndike claimed. However, he put earthworms at the absolute zero (Thorndike et al., 1927, p. 340–341). Nowadays, as earthworms have been found to exhibit a very complex behaviour and presumably non-zero cognitive abilities, we would need to look for another absolute zero. And this is not easy, as we can see in Panel 4.3.

The research on bacteria is especially noteworthy because the behaviour of some of them is beginning to be reasonably well understood, since their genetic analysis is relatively easy compared to other life forms. Despite this relative genomic simplicity, some bacteria are capable of remarkable behaviours, e.g., "the E. coli bacterium is capable of traversing gradients of attractant or repellant chemicals in its environment. This behavior involves many of the components it needs to qualify for traditional definitions of cognition i.e., perception, memory, and action" (Van Duijn et al., 2006). Also, there is a reasonably

---

Panel 4.3
Cognition without neurons

Very different kinds of living beings outside the animal kingdom have been found to show some complex behaviours, featuring adaptation, memory, pattern recognition abilities and even anticipation. Among these organisms we find many plants, slime moulds, fungi or bacteria, or subsystems such as the immune, the urothelium and the metabolic systems, or even the genome (Nakagaki et al., 2000; Trewavas, 2005; Birder et al., 2010). Despite their diversity, these systems have one thing in common: what they lack, a neural system. This is why they are usually referred to as non-neural organisms (Ginsburg and Jablonka, 2009).

For plants, for instance, the findings go beyond classical conditioning (Haney, 1969) to more complex behaviours (Applewhite, 1975) – sometimes disputed (Sanberg, 1976). The evidence that some of them, such as the slime moulds, can even solve mazes and other complex problems optimally (Nakagaki et al., 2000) has even led to the use of the term 'intelligence' to describe their capacity.

---

good understanding of how bacteria, in a colony, *communicate* through signal transduction proteins. Between 10^9 and 10^{12} bacteria can co-ordinate to process information in what is called a "super-brain", with a computational power able to "solve optimization problems that are beyond what human beings can solve" (Ben-Jacob, 2009).

In fact, different species of bacteria have been compared by using a *genetically based* "bacterial IQ", a white-box indicator based on "the total number of signalling proteins encoded in a given genome" (Galperin, 2005). Independently of the adequacy of these terms for bacteria (or others such as "mathematical skills", Ben-Jacob, 2009), behaviours are understood in a very minimalistic way, as the interaction of phenotype and genotype. Also, behavioural research in bacteria is more manageable, in many ways, than for animals (ant colonies, bee swarms and other animal flocks; see, e.g., Strassmann et al., 1997).

Plants are also interesting because of their time scale and the kinds of stimuli they react to (light, chemical components, plagues) and their actions (growth of root, branches and leaves). Some of their reactions and adaptations happen so slowly that we are not able to perceive them unless long-term careful observation is used. Also, "the concept of the individual, to which intelligence and behaviour are intimately linked, cannot usefully be applied to plants" (Firn, 2004). Plants aggregate other organisms, hybridate and form genets and ramets

(Harper et al., 1977). Nevertheless, Anthony Trewavas has been able to identify problem-solving abilities and adaptation in plants and has derived a 'rosette' of intelligence, a kind of rudimentary factor analysis using traits such as "flexibility in leaf weight:area, speed of new leaf production, sensitivity to shade, flexible operation of photosynthesis, stomatal sensitivity (closing and opening speed after perturbation) and abscission sensitivity" (Trewavas, 2005). These traits are arguably *phytocentric* and thereby cannot be used to compare to other living systems.

Finally, similar things happen on a larger scale, not only in time, but in space. For instance, forests can be said to adapt to the environment in a scale of tens, hundreds or even thousands of years, using their effect on the soil as a kind of memory. Note that, despite the time scale, this is not performed as an evolutionary adaptation, but as a living collective.

Keynote 4.8. Adaptation and resolution: The non evolutionary adaptation of a living system can take place at very different spatiotemporal scales and at the level of individuals or collectives.

The diversity of resolutions will set important challenges about how to evaluate all these living systems, as we will see in Chapter 16.

Despite all the unconventional kinds of cognition seen in this section, there is still a different kind of beast we have not yet discussed: extraterrestrial intelligence (Vakoch, 2011; Edmondson, 2012). Alfred Russel Wallace was one of the pioneers of astrobiology and in his 1904 book *Man's Place in the Universe*, he discussed the possibility of life on other planets and, in passing, the possibility of some of them having intelligence. Since then, this analysis and, especially, the detection of extraterrestrial intelligence, has become more sophisticated, under the field of 'astrocognition' (Dunér, 2011; Vakoch, 2011).

One example of our conception of other cognitive systems (biological or not) elsewhere in the universe is well represented by the pictorial messages that were attached to the 1972 Pioneer 10 and 1973 Pioneer 11 spacecrafts (see Figure 4.4), optimistically expecting they were intercepted by some kind of extraterrestrial intelligence someday in the distant future.

It is unclear whether a (very different) extraterrestrial intelligence could understand anything from this message. Similarly, the contacting problem is still at a rather speculative stage about what to scan (e.g., the SETI project) and what to send. It seems that any meaningful solution must rely on some "general cognitive principles", since "without some informed analysis of what it might

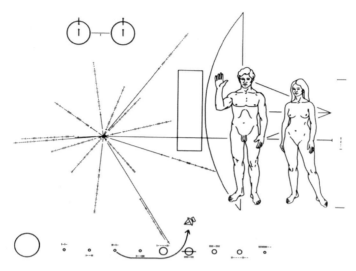

Figure 4.4. Two apes and some schematic information of the Earth and humankind, as depicted on the plaques that were attached to Pioneer 10 and 11 spacecrafts. [Courtesy of NASA, Image 72-H-192, originally designed by Carl Sagan and Frank Drake with artwork by Sagan's then-wife Linda Salzman Sagan.]

mean to be intelligent – yet radically different in terms of evolution, culture, biology, planetary location, and the like – we should not even begin to search for extraterrestrial intelligence" (Edmondson, 2012).

Extraterrestrial intelligence is nonetheless interesting as it is the most general view we can have about biological intelligence. However, the praiseworthy *contact* programme (looking specifically for intelligence and not life) has fewer implications for biology. Intelligent behaviour in the universe is not restricted to biological life forms, which may have abandoned its genuine biological form after a few thousand years of civilisation, a split second in a cosmological scale. Sara Seager, for instance, is of the opinion that any alien life travelling or contacting us "will be nonbiological" (Plasencia, 2017). This of course assumes some kind of accelerating technological progress, as has happened on Earth since the invention of agriculture, that would ultimately lead to some kind of improvement of the biological substrate, or a complete substitution, by some kind of artificial intelligence. But this assumption may be false. In any case, we have probably gone too far too soon, before knowing how intelligent computers are, and can be. This is what we initiate in the following chapter.

CHAPTER HIGHLIGHTS

- A gradual view between innate behaviours originating from adaptive special-isation through evolution and acquired behaviours through general cognitive abilities (Panel 4.1, Keynote 4.1).
- Many possible interpretations (Morgan's Canon, Keynote 4.3) and types of search (evolutionary, physical and mental search) for the same animal behaviour (Keynote 4.4).
- Biodiversity leading to diverse, social behaviours crucial for intelligence (Keynote 4.2).
- Evaluation apparatus integrating well-thought interfaces, rewards and penal-ties (Keynotes 4.5, 4.6).
- Anecdotal, qualitative research shifting to more systematic, quantitative stud-ies for both personality traits and cognitive abilities in animals, and findings such as animal g and G (Keynote 4.7).
- Cognitive adaptation taking place with very different life forms and resolu-tions (Keynote 4.8).

5

The Evaluation of Artificial Intelligence

> AI will now proceed along two parallel paths: (1) specialized systems
> and (2) habile systems, . . . general, intelligent systems . . . , *having*
> *general skill.*
>
> – Nils J. Nilsson,
> *Eye on the Prize* (1995)

A RTIFICIAL INTELLIGENCE IS a successful discipline. New applications and breakthroughs take us by surprise day after day, fuelled by the increasing power of machine learning. But do AI artefacts of today feature intelligence? If so, how much? Of what kind? How can we know? In this chapter we will see that the field has usually evaluated its artefacts in terms of task performance, not really in terms of intelligence. With that task-oriented perspective, we can say that machines are *superhuman* at chess, at driving a car and, of course, at solving the Rubik's cube. Beyond these particular tasks, Turing's imitation game, still a touchstone for some, is not used in general practice, except for variants, such as CAPTCHAs. Instead, benchmarks and competitions are the regular way of evaluating AI systems. However, as systems specialise for the new benchmarks, more challenging tasks are being devised. But are these more challenging tasks demanding more intelligence?

5.1 BARING INTELLIGENCE: THE AI EFFECT

The roots of artificial intelligence can be traced back to Ramon Llull's Ars Magna, Thomas Hobbes's *Artificial Man*, Gottfried Leibniz's *Ars Combinatoria* and the tradition of building mechanical automata since the middle ages until the early twentieth century. However, it is Alan Turing's celebrated 1950 paper "Can a machine think?" that definitively connects the possibility of an artificial mind with modern computers, as per the notions of a universal Turing machine and the Church-Turing thesis (see Panel 1.2).

The name "artificial intelligence" and the official start as a discipline took place during the famous 1956 Dartmouth College's "Summer Research Project on Artificial Intelligence", which congregated John McCarthy, Marvin Minsky, Nathaniel Rochester, Claude Shannon, Arthur Samuel, Oliver Selfridge, Ray Solomonoff, Allen Newell, Herbert Simon and Trenchard More. An excerpt of the proposal contained the following: "The study is to proceed on the basis of the conjecture that every aspect of learning or any other feature of intelligence can in principle be so precisely described that a machine can be made to simulate it. . . . For the present purpose the artificial intelligence problem is taken to be that of making a machine behave in ways that would be called intelligent if a human were so behaving" (from the original proposal, quoted in Nilsson, 2009). Two remarkable things are found in this foundational statement: the *full algorithmisation*, i.e., the aim of *precisely* describing any feature of intelligence and the *indirect characterisation* of intelligence as "if a human were so behaving".

The *indirect characterisation* principle suggested the problems that AI should address and the *full algorithmisation* principle prompted researchers to find the best way, the best algorithm, for solving the problem. For instance, if playing noughts and crosses (tic-tac-toe) was deemed to require intelligence in humans, then the problem was conjectured to be solvable by artificial intelligence. Several algorithms were sought until one or more were able to solve the problem optimally. The case of noughts and crosses perfectly fits this paradigm, since the problem is solvable and an optimal algorithm exists. On other occasions, however, e.g., English-Russian translation, the particular problem was more challenging, and an optimal result could not be achieved, not even close to the (best) human standards.

However, when a particular problem was well understood, precisely because there was an algorithm that fully described how to solve it, the *mystery* of the problem vanished. The problem had become banal, purely algorithmic, with the researchers being the actual solvers and the algorithm being the solution. This phenomenon was interpreted as an *anomaly*:

Keynote 5.1. AI effect (McCorduck, 2004): When artificial intelligence produces an algorithm that solves a problem optimally or better than humans, the algorithm is usually more steady and predictable than humans but does not feature any intelligence at all. In this case – technically – the problem would no longer be an AI problem, because it can be solved without intelligence.

For instance, arithmetic proficiency was once considered a sufficient sign of intelligence in humans. When the first calculators were able to perform the common arithmetic operations mechanically, following an algorithm, the problem began to be dissociated from intelligence. Similarly, systems that play English draughts (checkers) well should no longer be considered part of AI, since an optimal algorithm for draughts was found by Jonathan Schaeffer (Schaeffer et al., 2007), after several decades of research. "As soon as it works, no one calls it AI anymore", complained McCarthy (quoted in Vardi, 2012). But the flaw did not come from success but from McCarthy's own definition of AI as "the science and engineering of making intelligent machines" (McCarthy, 2007).

As a way to accommodate this phenomenon and stop the haemorrhage, Minsky's definition of artificial intelligence uses a very ingenious trick:

> **Keynote 5.2. Definition of artificial intelligence**: "Science of making machines capable of performing tasks that would require intelligence if done by [humans]" (Minsky, 1968, p. v).

This is in alignment to the *indirect characterisation* principle. AI systems do not have to display intelligence or solve the problems in a way that resembles how humans solve these problems. The only thing that matters is whether humans use intelligence for that problem. As a consequence, we could now keep inside AI any artificial system that looks occasionally intelligent, even if it does not feature intelligence (see Figure 5.1).

Here we find a recurrent circumstance, the dilemma between programmed and trained, which is parallel to the dilemma between innate and acquired seen in previous chapters. In AI, this dilemma was firstly highlighted by Turing in his 1950 paper, making the point that a machine could be educated instead of being programmed to do a task. In human intelligence, it is the humans themselves that find the algorithms and policies for solving a problem (e.g., playing noughts and crosses) while in *traditional* AI systems, it is the programmers that find the algorithms. In other words, the question is who is to praise about the performance of the AI system, who is really intelligent, the system itself or its programmer? Again, the parallel in the animal kingdom is established in terms of who has acquired the policies, the animal itself or evolution.

5.2 HORSES FOR COURSES

The preceding view of *traditional* AI may portray the wrong image that AI has always focused on systems that solve a particular task with no intention

Figure 5.1. "Warning! Intelligence not included". Should this be mandatory in most *artificial intelligence* products, since they feature no *intelligence* at all?

whatsoever of featuring intelligence. In the early days of AI, much research effort was devoted to *general problem solvers* (Newell et al., 1959), albeit for toy problems. Also, there was a significant interest in abstract problems, such as the items found in IQ tests, used as tasks for Tom Evans's ANALOGY program (Evans, 1963, 1965). These and other general and abstract systems of the early AI clashed against a huge combinatorial explosion for realistic problems, but were the foundation for other general systems that followed, the so-called cognitive architectures, such as SOAR (Laird et al., 1987; Simon et al., 1991; Laird, 2012). However, the slow progress of AI in the 1960s and 1970s motivated a shift of mainstream AI towards systems that showed manifest performance in realistic application niches. These 'performance programs' or 'niche systems', in Nils Nilsson's terminology (Nilsson, 1995) – what we will call 'task-specific systems' throughout the rest of this chapter – progressively showed success in many different areas, using particular technologies.

This view pervaded the discipline, and the AI textbooks, in the 1970s and 1980s. For instance, Nilsson's 1980 textbook 'Principles of Artificial Intelligence' was basically a book about algorithms and techniques to be used for well-specified tasks: production systems, search strategies, predicate calculus, resolution, rule-based deduction, plan-generating systems and object representation. The dominance of deduction was so overwhelming that the words 'learning' or 'induction' were absent from the table of contents.

Panel 5.1
The big switch: the AI homunculus

The so-called big switch hypothesis (Ernst and Newell, 1969) was postulated as a way of achieving systems that could show performance on more complex tasks – and even on a range of tasks – by integrating several specialised modules (Minsky, 1988). Feigenbaum et al. (1970) explain this clearly: "the 'big switch hypothesis' holds that generality in problem solving is achieved by arraying specialists at the terminals of a big switch. The big switch is moved from specialist to specialist as the problem solver switches its attention from one problem area to another".

But, who was moving the switch? On many occasions the switch was just set by the AI researchers themselves. These act as renewed AI homunculi, a more sophisticated incarnation of the mechanical Turk, the eighteenth century's chess player hoax. The AI researchers set the switch by choosing the appropriate algorithm or technique from textbooks, toolboxes and the technical literature after painstaking analysis of a particular problem. As a result, to be fair, whenever a new feat is achieved, praise goes to the AI researchers that have solved the problem, not the system.

This toolbox methodology is still predominant nowadays, even if the homunculus researcher does not move the switch herself but *programs* the switch. For instance, a webpage machine translator system integrates several modules: a language detector (the basic component of the switch) and as many one-to-one translation systems as needed.

This view was reinforced by a *modular* approach to AI, which opposed generality to performance: "generality has great utility in some ways, but is not often associated with superior performance. The experts usually are specialists" (Feigenbaum et al., 1970). Indeed, specialised modules were even considered a good way of reaching more general systems by aggregation, under the 'big switch hypothesis', as we discuss in Panel 5.1.

Today, whenever AI faces a challenging problem that can make our lives better or generate income for a company, the emphasis is put on cost efficiency. The big switch approach or, more generally, the toolbox modular approach, allows for a good compromise between the reuse of techniques and the integration effort, to achieve performance for the particular problem or niche that is to be solved. Recently, however, some kinds of general systems that are *trained* are becoming more cost-effective than systems that are programmed. There are two main reasons for this: first, the availability of training data that originates from virtual or actual worlds through sensors or bots and robots that can interact, together with the great amounts of information on the Internet; second, and more importantly, the very significant development of more and more powerful machine learning techniques in the past two decades (Flach, 2012). For instance, instead of coding a translator for each pair of languages, a general translator system is trained using corpora with millions of aligned sentences for each pair of languages. Similarly, we do not need specialised systems for music recommendation, churn detection or medical diagnosis. A classifier can be trained from thousands of examples using machine learning techniques. Likewise, a system can tell cats from dogs by training it first with millions of labelled images of cats and dogs. Or a robot can learn how to avoid obstacles after painstaking sessions of training in an actual or virtual world, using rewards and penalties to shape its *behaviour*. This is a "new AI".

It would then be misleading to link 'high-level' mental functions (such as reasoning, logic, planning) with the old AI and low-level mental functions (such as pattern recognition, perception, sensorimotor interaction) with the new AI. This distinction has been associated with the so-called Moravec's paradox, which stated that it was "comparatively easy to make computers exhibit adult-level performance in solving problems on intelligence tests or playing checkers, and difficult or impossible to give them the skills of a one-year-old when it comes to perception and mobility" (Moravec, 1988, p. 15). This duality was sometimes explained by our evolutionary history (Brooks, 1990; Kirsh, 1991). For instance, moving around required hundreds of millions of years of evolution, whereas human language evolved in less than a million years. Another commonly alluded explanation was linked to a lack of 'embodiment' of old AI systems, without a body full of sensors and actuators (as we will see in Chapter 12, Panel 12.1).

All this sets the wrong focus on the type of tasks, between conscious and unconscious, evolutionarily recent or not, rather than the key point: is the system specialised for one task? In brief, one can easily write a program that tells circles from squares, or that finds the exit from a predefined maze, in the very same way that one can easily write a program that plays noughts and crosses, or that is able to solve quadratic equations. The challenge is the construction of a system that can learn to tell between whatever pair of classes of objects, find directions in a general environment, learn to play any kind of game, or even learn mathematics, just as a child would do. In fact, it is not really true any more that "the main lesson of thirty-five years of AI research is that the hard problems are easy and the easy problems are hard" (Pinker, 1995, p. 192). Indeed, we see nowadays that a deep learning algorithm can tell cats from dogs first, and chairs from cups next, by being retrained from image data sets, but it is not so easy to have the *same* algorithm becoming Deep Blue or Chinook (the first computer programs to beat a human world champion in chess and draughts, respectively), just after hundreds of matches of either game. It is only very recently that the same principles can be used to make a system learn to play embodied video games or to be a master of Go.

So our discussion for the rest of the chapter will not be about the old dilemma between symbolic versus connectionist AI, or between weak and strong AI, not even between expert systems and machine learning, but rather between "general, intelligent programs and the special performance systems" (Nilsson, 1995). To put it briefly, the useful debate in AI is about *generality* (McCarthy, 1987), actually a continuum between the 'performance' programs (specific) and the 'habile' programs (general), using Nilsson (1995)'s terminology. Precisely because of this, any point in this continuum is a valid and genuine part of AI research. The discussion is similar to the modularity-plasticity debate in humans and other animals, seen in previous chapters. The emphasis, for the rest of the chapter, will be set on how this continuum is also to be found in terms of evaluation tools, from a specific task-oriented evaluation to a more general feature-oriented evaluation.

Having realised that some AI systems can be successful without featuring any general cognitive ability, we are ready to examine the state of the evaluation methodologies in AI. This understanding is crucial, as AI has become a successful industry, an engineering discipline, moved by applications and solving new tasks every day. As a result, the first thing that we have to bear in mind when evaluating an AI system is its *purpose*, what it was built for. It is one thing to evaluate success for a problem, in terms of performance and reliability, and it is a different thing to evaluate the behavioural features (if any) of an AI system. For instance, many AI systems would qualify as part of the discipline according to Minsky's definition (Keynote 5.2), but would fail to fit McCarthy's definition, also seen in the previous section, or the view of intelligence in AI as the ability "to operate successfully in a wide variety of environments" (Russell and Norvig, 2009, chap. 2, p. 32, ed. 1995).

A second aspect that we have to consider about the evaluation of AI systems is that we can talk about identical systems, and even 'series' of systems with similar characteristics, but there is no notion of species or population, as in animal and human evaluation. AI research can build systems at will. In fact, once an evaluation methodology is announced, AI researchers will start a race to create an AI system that aces that particular evaluation, a horse for the course, a phenomenon that we introduced as 'evaluation specialisation' (Keynote 2.6).

A third thing to bear in mind is that AI systems can be evaluated, in principle, with a white-box approach, as discussed in Chapter 2. Basically, for computers, inspecting the code seems much easier than for humans and non-human animals through brain scanning and genomic analysis. However, AI systems integrate

> **Panel 5.2**
> **Superhuman: be the best at something**
>
> AI progress can be evaluated by examining relevant tasks and determining how the best AI system compares to humans: *optimal* if no other system can perform better, *strong super-human* if it performs better than all humans, *super-human* if it performs better than most humans, *par-human* if it performs similarly to most humans, and *sub-human* if it performs worse than most humans (Rajani, 2011).
>
> According to these categories, AI would have progressed very significantly (see, e.g., Nilsson, 2009, chap. 32, or Bostrom, 2014, Table 1, pp. 12–13): arithmetic calculators became superhuman in the nineteenth century; cryptographic breakers came in the 1940s; automated players for simple games such as noughts and crosses became optimal in the 1960s, and, for more complex games (draughts, bridge, backgammon) about two decades later; printed character recognition in the 1970s; chess and statistical inference in the 1990s; speech recognition and Scrabble in the 2000s; and car driving, TV quizzes, technical translation, Texas hold 'em poker, Go and face authentication in the 2010s.
>
> As a result of this progress, AI is undeniably a success, but the machine kingdom is now full of *idiots savants*.

so many technologies and go through complex tuning and training stages that it is no longer possible for most of them to determine their capabilities and performance by inspecting their code. As a result, black-box evaluation, i.e., the analysis of their behaviour, is set as the usual way of evaluating AI systems.

Finally, a fourth issue about the evaluation of AI progress is to distinguish the source of an improvement: software (better algorithms), hardware (increase in speed and memory capacity), data used (vaster amounts of data available), the sheer power of thousands of training trials (more computational effort and finetuning done in the laboratory) or the role of key human inputs (implicitly relying on human computation) (Brundage, 2016).

With the perspective seen in this section, it is easier to understand the limited value of a popular characterisation of AI progress as a catalogue of tasks and problems that particular AI systems (specialised for one task) are able to 'solve'. Such a characterisation is shown in Panel 5.2.

A similar but more systematic approach for the evaluation of AI progress is the so-called Turing ratio (Masum et al., 2002; Masum and Christensen, 2003), which normalises performance with respect to human performance (so the name 'ratio'), with values greater than 0 for superhuman performance and values lower than 0 for sub-human performance. This is nothing less than a quantification of the concept of superhuman performance seen earlier. However, even if they rely on a "practical definition of 'intelligence' [as] the ability to survive in diverse environments" (Masum et al., 2002) they do not really construct a profile for the evaluation of a single system, as a vector or aggregation of the results for a set of tasks, but rather a measure for AI progress as the sum of its parts.

Having an important task being solved or achieving human-level results is a great success. However, the systems are different from one case to the other. The policies and algorithms, as mentioned earlier, are coded by the AI researcher. Even when the underlying algorithms follow the same principles, they are different, specialised, systems. For instance, the Humies awards (Humies, 2004), a yearly competition held since 2004, recognise those "human-competitive" systems that are developed as the result of an evolutionary process, using genetic algorithms or other kinds of evolutionary computation. The distinctive feature of the concept here is that the policy or algorithm that solves the problem is not programmed by an AI researcher, but is the result of an evolutionary process (Koza, 2010). This sets a parallelism with living beings showing a very particular behaviour, driven by a fitness function representing a very specific environment. Consequently, even if the system is not programmed for the task, each system is still specialised for a task. But, at least, the same principle can be used to derive a full range of idiots savants.

In the end, does AI progress mean that AI systems today are more intelligent – or have a wider range of cognitive abilities – than those of a few decades ago? To answer the question, we must be very clear between AI progress (on the collection of problems that are solved nowadays) and the realisation of one *single* AI system that solves more and more tasks. This distinction seems to have been emphasised in the past with the notion of *autonomous agent*, which became mainstream in AI in the 1990s. For instance, a clock that is programmed to adjust its time whenever its owner changes time zone "would certainly be successful behavior, but the intelligence seems to belong to the clock's designer rather than to the clock itself" (Russell and Norvig, 2009). An autonomous agent would not be programmed for this adjustment but would adapt to it.

Keynote 5.3. Autonomous agent: The autonomy of a system is not only thwarted by the need of further integration or reprogramming of components but also by the resources it uses or has used (hardware, data, training effort, other systems or humans).

In the end, an agent is basically an interactive system, a member of the machine kingdom as defined in Keynote 1.1. An agent is thus different from a component, such as a machine learning algorithm or a SAT solver, which are not stand-alone interactive systems but meant to be part of a system. So, now and then, the key point when referring to intelligence is whether the *same* system can achieve good performance in a range of tasks. This evaluation of a single agent is analysed in the following sections.

5.3 THE MYTHICAL HUMAN-LEVEL MACHINE INTELLIGENCE

Whenever we talk about AI evaluation, the discussion is contaminated by the concept of 'human-level machine intelligence' (HLMI) that, under different names (such as 'human-level artificial intelligence') and definitions (McCarthy, 1983; Preston, 1991; Nilsson, 2006; Zadeh, 2008; Bostrom, 2014), has pervaded AI since its inception. An intuitive, but highly imprecise definition, of HLMI could be a machine with the intelligence of an average human. Another, more modern definition of HLMI is a computer "capable of matching humans in every (or nearly every) sphere of intellectual activity" (Shanahan, 2015). As we will discuss in this section, the concept of HLMI presents many caveats, to the extent that "some . . . feel that the notion of a 'human level' of artificial intelligence is ill-defined" (Bostrom, 2014, p. 20). Also, as a result, the question of when and how it will be achieved is said to be "ill-posed" (McDermott, 2007) and all the predictions around the term are said to have failed or, more precisely, are simply unverifiable (Armstrong and Sotala, 2015). It is worth noticing that human-average intelligence (or more precisely, IQ) is well defined for humans (as seen in Chapter 3) and so is (average) human-level performance in one or more tasks, as seen in the previous section (Panel 5.2). But, the concept of a general HLMI, defined as before, or defined in other various ways – such as obtaining a score higher than 100 on a standard human IQ test or passing the Turing test – will be challenged in this and the following chapter.

The relevance of whether HLMI is well defined is crucial, as many ideas, terms and predictions are based on it. For instance, J. Storrs Hall in the chapter "kinds of minds" of his book "Beyond AI" (Hall, 2007, chap. 15) distinguishes six categories: hypohuman (less-than-human abilities), diahuman (human-level capacities, but not yet a general intelligence), parahuman (similar but not identical to humans, e.g., augmented humans), allohuman (human-level capabilities in different areas), epihuman (slightly above human level) and hyperhuman (superintelligence, well above human). Apart from the lack of concreteness of these categories, it is also obscure whether this is actually meant to define a characterisation of AI systems, according to a psychometric profile, as we discussed in Section 1.4.

One original approach to characterise HLMI, as a monolithic concept, is the notion of AI-completeness, a term originally introduced by Mueller (1987, p. 302), mimicking the complexity classes in the area of computational complexity. Whilst the definitions of AI-completeness (and the related concept of AI-hardness) may differ significantly (Demasi et al., 2010; Yampolskiy, 2012; Weston et al., 2015, especially Yampolskiy, 2015a, p. 2) the original notion *was* a class of problems including any task such that if a machine is able to solve the task then it is a HLMI, and vice versa (Shapiro, 1992). This means that any of these tasks would be a necessary and sufficient condition of human-level machine intelligence. In other words, if "we could solve any [AI-complete problem], we could solve all the others" (Mueller, 1987, p. 302). The definition is intentionally trying to avoid the generality and specificity problems of any characterisation, or measurement, in the sense of Figure 2.2. The question is of course whether there is a task that is necessary and sufficient for intelligence. Shapiro (1992) names areas that are AI-complete, rather than actual tasks: natural language, problem solving and search, knowledge representation and reasoning, learning, vision and robotics. However, since then, we have seen that some problems that were supposed to require human intelligence have been solved without intelligence, such as driving a car or being good at poker.

Yampolskiy (2015a) suggests that the first such sufficient problem in the AI-completeness class is the Turing test. If a system were able to pass the Turing test then, he claims, it would have HLMI. Also, if we find any other task such that performance in that task implies passing the Turing test, and vice versa, then this task would be included in the AI-complete class. This is all very well, but is the Turing test a necessary and sufficient condition for HLMI? Let us have a look at the Turing test in more detail in Panel 5.3.

Turing was very explicit that the game was not a definition: "I don't want to give a definition of thinking" (Turing, 1952). Nonetheless, as years passed by, the Turing test has been considered by some as "a simple operational definition of intelligence" (French, 2000), the goal of AI (Ginsberg, 1993, p. 8) or as a test for HLMI, since "Turing did make it clear that he was proposing a test of intelligence in machines" (Proudfoot, 2011). If the Turing test is considered as an actual test for machines, what is it supposed to measure? And, can it be measured in a reliable way?

In principle, the Turing test is not unusual as a measurement procedure. For instance, given an object and a yardstick, a judge (the measurer) compares both things and determines which one is longer. What are the objections? The first

---

Panel 5.3
Turing's imitation game

In the mid twentieth century, Alan Turing felt that the idea of constructing intelligent machines – solely based on a computer, following his notion of universal Turing machine – was still widely rejected by society and by a great proportion of scientists and mathematicians. In an effort to counteract the arguments against intelligent machines, he wrote a masterpiece, his famous 1950 paper, to respond to each and every objection against the possibility of constructing intelligent machines.

To underpin his arguments, he devised a thought experiment, to highlight what really mattered about intelligence (behaviour) in front of what was irrelevant (appearance and implementation) (Turing, 1952). Inspired by the once very popular Victorian parlour games, he adapted an old gender game with three players A, B and C for the occasion.

Player A is a man, player B is a woman and player C is an interrogator (or judge, who could be of either sex). The gist of the game is that player A pretends to be a woman. With the three players located in different rooms, and communicating solely by written notes, the interrogator has to tell who is the man and who is the woman. Turing, with his "imitation game", replaced the man by a computer – pretending to be a woman – and framed the conversation through teletypes.

Despite the rich connotations of the original game, it is interpreted as Turing himself seemed to convey, more explicitly two years later (1952): one machine pretending to be a human, a human behaving as a human and a human interrogator. This is known as the standard Turing test.

---

objection is that the Turing test does not measure intelligence, but "humanity" (Fostel, 1993). It does not measure any aggregation of cognitive abilities, not even a monolithic view of intelligence. This is explicitly realised by Turing: "the machine would be permitted all sorts of tricks to appear more man-like, such as waiting a bit before giving the answer, or making spelling mistakes" (Turing, 1952). So, at some point, the machine will have to behave *less intelligently* to look human. But bear in mind that this is not only a consequence of anthropocentrism; it is because the Turing test is an *imitation* game, not an interview.

This sets a misalignment with intelligence in terms of sufficiency and necessity. A non-intelligent system can be specialised to fool the judges, which is exactly what we see in the several Turing test contests that have been done to date. So, it is not clear that the Turing test is a sufficient condition for humanness, and even less a "sufficient condition for intelligence" (French, 2000). Aware of these issues, Dowe and Hajek (1997, 1998) introduced a variant of the Turing test that featured compression problems, to render the test more sufficient, making it more explicit that a question-and-answer lookup table would not work. Years later, other variants of the Turing test also introduced compression (Gauvrit et al., 2015, sec. 1.1) or included letter-string analogy problems (York and Swan, 2012). Actually, the Turing test can 'contain' any test we may think of, so the question backtracks to what questions the judge must ask to make it sufficient.

If sufficiency is an issue, necessity is not ensured either. A system of roughly the same intelligence as an average human may not be able to pass the test, since imitating other kinds of intelligence may be difficult. Even some humans can struggle to pass it. Only for *very* intelligent agents, a necessity condition – in this case for intelligence – seems less controversial. This is all consistent with the test as a mere thought experiment, in Turing's own words, about "whether there are imaginable computers which would do well" (Turing, 1950).

A second objection to the Turing test is that, even assuming that we wanted to measure humanness (or the ability of behaving like a human), the Turing test is not a very good testing instrument. First, it is a test based on ascription (McCarthy, 1979), and humans tend to ascribe mental qualities to objects lacking them. Second, as a comparative test, it is abnormal. It compares an individual with a representative of a species. For instance, given a chimpanzee and a bonobo, could we determine which one is more *bonobish*? Third, we have two humans in the test, so it cannot be automated, and the results can vary dramatically depending on the indications, protocols, personalities and *intelligence* of both of them. Fourth, the fact that the machine is imitating a species, raises many doubts about cultural issues and how representative the chosen humans are of the species. And five, the Turing test aims at a quality and not a quantity. Even if judges can give scores, in the end any score of humanness is meaningless.

The aforementioned two objections roughly correspond to the validity and reliability components of measurement accuracy:

> **Keynote 5.4. The Turing test and HLMI**: The standard Turing test is not a valid and reliable test for HLMI.

Nonetheless, many other objections have been postulated (see, e.g., Copeland and Proudfoot, 2008). Perhaps the best evidence about the limitations of the

Turing test as a practical measurement of intelligence, cognitive abilities, humanness or even conversation abilities is found in the contests and incarnations that have been done in the past. The most remarkable one is the Loebner Prize, held every year since 1991, which basically follows the standard Turing test (with a time limit) and is awarded to the chatterbox that is deemed most *human-like* by the judges (Loebner, 2008). Despite this established competition, in 2014, Kevin Warwick organised a similar, occasional, competition at the Royal Society in London. The behaviour of the chatterbots (the winner, Eugene, managed to convince 33 per cent of the human judges) was fairly similar to what had been observed in many editions of the Loebner Prize, or with previous chatterbots (e.g., Weizenbaum's ELIZA, 1966). However, the interpretation of the results was overstated: "Alan Turing's Test was passed for the first time. . . . This milestone will go down in history as one of the most exciting" (Warwick, 2014).

The AI community was not very excited. As a distinguished example, Moshe Y. Vardi, editor-in-chief of the Communications of the ACM responded: "the details of this 2014 Turing Test experiment only reinforces my judgement that the Turing Test says little about machine intelligence" (Vardi, 2015; Shah and Warwick, 2015). As a consequence of all this, whether the test has been passed or not is just irrelevant: the use of the Turing test as the first AI-complete task (Yampolskiy, 2015a, chap. 1) or as a reference for HLMI is simply dodgy.

Many even think that the Turing test has become a stigma for AI, a blind alley, or even harmful (Hayes and Ford, 1995; Whitby, 1996). It should have ceased to have any effect on AI research. But it has not been so, and the debate about the Turing test seems inexhaustible (Moor, 2003; Shieber, 2004; Epstein et al., 2008).

Of course, Turing should not be blamed for this. Sloman (2014a) puts it this way: "it is clear from Turing's 1950 paper that he did not propose his 'imitation game' as a test for intelligence, though he occasionally slipped into calling his non-test a test! . . . That's why, in previous publications I have referred to the mythical Turing Test". McDermott (2010) says more: "Turing would have repudiated Turing-style tests". In fact, Turing should not be blamed either by the ill-conceived concept of HLMI. Indeed, Proudfoot (2011) argues that HLMI is a slippery concept in itself, with or without the Turing test, in the same way that "human-level machine athletics" is ill-conceived. Should not we talk about the *mythical* HLMI as well?

When the mythical Turing test is jettisoned as a criterion for the also mythical HLMI, many AI researchers feel that they no longer have a way to measure their progress towards their long-term goal. For instance, Laird et al. (2009) summarise the discussion held at a "workshop of human-level intelligence", as

---

Panel 5.4
What is *Beyond the Turing test*?

In 2000 I wrote a paper titled "Beyond the Turing Test" (Hernández-Orallo, 2000a) with a double interpretation: some abilities can go well beyond average human abilities, and we need to leave the Turing test behind. The new alternative, as will be discussed later on in this book, was radically different: how a measure of intelligence ("non-Boolean, factorial, non-anthropocentric, computational and meaningful") could be defined from algorithmic information theory.

Since then, the interest in alternatives "beyond the Turing test" is illustrated by a growing number of works with this or similar titles (Alvarado et al., 2002; Cohen, 2005; Arel and Livingston, 2009; French, 2012; You, 2015) and the celebration of an AAAI 2015 workshop and special issue in the AI magazine with, yet again, the same title: "Beyond the Turing test" (Marcus et al., 2015, 2016).

---

not putting HLMI into question as a goal, but about the way it should be evaluated. However, it can also be argued whether the HLMI, be it an idealistic myth or not, is the ultimate goal. An illuminating way of looking at this is through the question that entitles Panel 5.4.

It would be unfair, though, to reject the Turing test without paying attention to some of the variants, extensions and generalisations (Saygin et al., 2000; Epstein et al., 2008; Oppy and Dowe, 2011). For instance, we find tests where the interface is enhanced to consider perception or sensorimotor interaction, such as the total Turing tests (Harnad, 1992; Schweizer, 1998; Zillich, 2012), the visual Turing tests, the toddler Turing tests, variants on virtual worlds and many others (Hingston, 2010; Neumann et al., 2009). Unfortunately, most of these variants do not solve any of the key problems of the Turing test and many introduce further problems.

However, there are some ideas in the Turing test that are worth being considered for AI evaluation. Some variants and extensions do not focus on the mythical HLMI but are restricted to some areas (chatterbot evaluation, personal assistants, video games, etc.) and are meant to measure features such as believability, enjoyability, resilience or aggressiveness (Livingstone, 2006; Hingston, 2012). The BotPrize competition, for instance, which has been held since 2008, awards the bot that is deemed as most believable (playing like a human) by the other (human) players, in a first-person shooter video game. For the competition, the human judges also play normally (they are also awarded if they behave in a human way) and chatting is disabled. This format, however, has been put into question in recent editions of the competition. For instance, believability is said to be better assessed from a third-person perspective (visualising recorded video of other players' games) than with a first-person perspective (Togelius et al., 2012). Therefore, third-person human judges can concentrate on judging instead of aiming at high scores and not being killed.

In the end, the Turing test is just a particular case of subjective evaluation where a human judge is used to assess a system, either by observation or interaction. This kind of evaluation by 'human discrimination' can go from a simple observation or short conversation following the "I know it when I see it" principle to a more systematic version following a strict protocol or a storyline, as many psychological assessments do, based on interviews.

Finally, it is worth analysing two of the key characteristics of the Turing test: imitation and adversarialness. Imitation ability has been the subject of research in animal and human cognition. From a general evaluation point of view, and focusing on machines, we can consider the difficulty of imitating any agent (any Turing machine). If we considered a range of agents and we evaluated the ability of an agent to imitate them, we could have a measure of the ability of *learning mind models*, a topic we will fully discuss in Chapter 13. Things become more interesting when imitation is combined with adversarialness and unpredictability, as in the matching pennies game, which is described in Panel 5.5.

Nonetheless, the notion of putting two or more Turing machines (or agents) in games resembling the Turing test, such that one must imitate or predict the others, generates many interesting instances. For example, a generalised version of the Turing test can be connected with learning and game theory (Hernández-Orallo et al., 2012).

5.4 TELLING COMPUTERS AND HUMANS APART AUTOMATICALLY

Tinkering with the players of several imitation games may lead to many interesting combinations, but there is one, referred to as the "inverted Turing test", which has ended up having important applications. The inverted Turing test was introduced by Watt (1996), putting the focus on the judge, which in this case is a machine that has to tell correctly between a human and another machine. In 2009 this test was passed (just using transcripts of the Loebner Prize) by a system achieving "a degree of success similar to human judges" (MacInnes et al., 2009). As an intelligence test, an inverted Turing test may have the same, or even more objections, than the standard Turing test.

Panel 5.5
Matching pennies: an adversarial imitation game

Another 'imitation game' that has been proposed as a test for machines is the matching pennies game, a binary version of rock-paper-scissors, where two players must signal either heads or tails. The goal of the first player, the *predictor*, is that both players' coins agree, and the goal of the second player, the *evader*, is that the players' coins disagree.

Bill Hibbard proposed this game as an intelligence test or, more precisely, a test to measure adversarial sequence prediction (Hibbard, 2008, 2011). The game is related to Dowe's "elusive model paradox" (Dowe, 2011, sec. 7.5) and to the problem of human unpredictability (Scriven, 1965).

A tournament was organised in 2011 where computer algorithms could compete (Tyler, 2011). Some phenomena, however, make it inappropriate as a practical test for AI in general. For instance, any agent (intelligent or not) will always tie against random players.

Rather than actual tests for intelligence, the relevance of an inverted Turing test is that telling computers and humans apart *automatically* is a major need nowadays. For instance, in many Internet services and other virtual environments, we need to know whether an action (e.g., making a post, completing a payment, registering for a service) is performed by a human or a bot. This niche of application was soon realised, leading to several independent proposals (Naor, 1996; Lillibridge et al., 2001). These proposals became more popular after the so-called CAPTCHA (Completely Automated Public Turing test to tell Computers and Humans Apart) was introduced (Von Ahn et al., 2004, 2008). This test is referred to as a 'reverse Turing test' – and not properly an inverted Turing test – because there are only two 'players', an unknown agent A (who can be either human or computer) and the CAPTCHA system B, a program that tries to tell whether A is a human or a computer. There are many kinds of CAPTCHAs, but one common CAPTCHA is presented as a series of distorted characters, which are usually easy to recognise by humans but not by computers using state-of-the-art AI techniques (e.g., OCR systems at the time of writing). An example is shown in Figure 5.2.

CAPTCHAs are designed to be 'AI-hard' problems, i.e., tasks that are difficult for artificial intelligence. The trouble, of course, is that 'AI-hardness' is an evolving concept, which depends on the current state of AI technology, influenced by the CAPTCHAs themselves, as Panel 5.6 discusses.

Panel 5.6
Caught by the adversarial CAPTCHA

In 2013, the Spanish newspaper *El Mundo Today* reported that a 26-year-old man from Alicante, Spain, struggled to get through a CAPTCHA, despite having tried more than 50 consecutive times (García, 2013). Being unsuccessful to solve any CAPTCHA instance for more than eight hours, he finally concluded, "I'm not a stupid human, it is that I'm a robot". After realising his true condition and understanding that his "feelings were just a software illusion", he made a public call to all "ex-humans" to unite in a "world ruled by machines".

El Mundo Today is a comical newspaper featuring fake news, but the true fact is that more and more people are struggling with CAPTCHAs. Whenever a particular CAPTCHA is broken (frequently passed by a program), the CAPTCHA has to be replaced by a more sophisticated one (Bursztein et al., 2014). New generations of CAPTCHAs are so distorted that humans also find them difficult and need several attempts to pass them. Other new kinds of CAPTCHAs are based on language riddles, puns and common-sense knowledge, but even in these cases efforts are made to crack them. The whole thing becomes an adversarial race between CAPTCHA designers and CAPTCHA breakers, with an ensuing impact on the discriminating power and ease of use of new generations of CAPTCHAs.

Since many CAPTCHAs are based on perception problems, one may reach the conclusion that these are really the hardest AI problems, or even, the AI-complete problems. Two reasons reject this idea. First, there are CAPTCHAs based on more 'high-level' mental processes. Second, even if these were the hardest AI tasks, these tasks are not really indicative of intelligence or any other meaningful cognitive ability. For instance, there is no shown correlation – for *humans* – between the results on CAPTCHAs and their intelligence (measured, e.g., with their scores on IQ tests).

Figure 5.2.   A CAPTCHA example: a distorted text that is assumed to be easily recognisable by humans but hard for computers of the 2010s.

Table 5.1. Several variants of the Turing test. *W*, *M*, *H* and *C* represent general *woman*, *man*, *human* and *computer* respectively, with subindexes referring to particular individuals. The arrows represent "pretending to be".

Variant	Judge	Player A	Player B	Interaction
Victorian parlour game	H	$M \to W$	$W \to W$	Written notes
Turing's imitation game	H	$C \to W$	$W \to W$	Textual teletype
Standard Turing test	H	$C \to H$	$H \to H$	Textual teletype
Visual/total TT	H	$C \to H$	$H \to H$	Visual/embodied
BotPrize	H	$C \to H$	$H \to H$	Video game
TT with compression	H+size	$C \to H$	$H \to H$	Textual teletype
Matching pennies	–	$C_A \to C_B$	$C_B \to \neg C_A$	Binary teletype
Inverted TT	C	$C \to H$	$H \to H$	Textual teletype
Reverse TT: CAPTCHA	C	$C \to H$	–	Any

From all of this, we have to be very careful about what CAPTCHAs really measure – and for how much time:

> **Keynote 5.5. Validity and volatility of CAPTCHAs**: Any test that tries to tell computers and humans apart by a task that current AI technology is not able to solve may say nothing about the abilities of the system – beyond the particular task – and will need to be replaced by another test, when AI is able to solve the task.

With the rise of social bots (Ferrara et al., 2015) in digital social networks, crowdsourcing platforms and other artificial ecosystems, new kinds of CAPTCHAs are being developed based on the analysis of user profiles and behaviour (Chu et al., 2012; Wang et al., 2012). We will return to this observational approach in Chapters 13 and 16.

Table 5.1 summarises the variants of the Turing test seen in this and the previous section. The detection of humanness and the understanding of what direct, inverse or reverse Turing tests really measure is far away from the way artificial intelligence should be measured. In the following section we will get on track again about how AI artefacts are usually evaluated.

5.5 TASK-ORIENTED EVALUATION

The general approach for the evaluation of AI is similar to any *engineering* field. In particular, it is not different to the evaluation of many other areas of computer science. Once a goal is set through a specification, an experiment is set to test whether – or how much – the artefact complies with the specification. For instance, for a spam filter, the specification can define a quality metric in terms of how many false positives and false negatives are allowed. Systems are just optimised and selected using this metric. However, in many other cases, evaluation is much more difficult than this simple example. First, all AI systems are essentially software systems, and it is well known how problematic software testing is (Myers et al., 2011). Second, the specification is not always well defined, since true AI systems should cope (mostly) with unanticipated situations.

Nonetheless, many AI systems are designed to solve a task, including many particular instances, for which there is an agreement about a measure of performance. For instance, even in a very complex task such as driverless transportation on real roads, where unexpected things can happen at any time, one can set a precise performance metric integrating several indicators, such as time to destination, petrol consumption and accidents.

We see this performance-based task-oriented evaluation in any area and application of AI: computer vision, speech recognition, machine translation, text summarisation, automated deduction, information retrieval, robotic interaction, multimedia analysis, automated driving, series prediction, recommender systems, automated planning, expert systems, game playing, etc. (see, e.g., Russell and Norvig, 2009). The areas are general, and the techniques used for each particular AI system can be shared for different tasks (e.g., a Mars rover and a surveillance system can share machine vision techniques). However, moving from an abstract problem to a specific task is encouraged for the sake of a more precise evaluation: AI researchers had better "refine the topic to a task", provided it is "representative" (Cohen and Howe, 1988).

Focusing on the criteria for good performance, it is worth noticing that, in artificial intelligence, unlike other areas of computer science such as algorithmics, the interest is not generally set on a worst-case analysis – neither on a best-case analysis. In general, artificial intelligence is concerned about an average-case performance. The set of instances of a task is usually understood to have some associated probability, and performance is estimated for that distribution of instances. This is exactly what we saw in Eq. 2.1 in Section 2.3, a general representational measurement. For instance, for a driverless car, we can assign probabilities to all possible routes in a region, including the time of the day, the weather and the traffic conditions. For Eq. 2.1 to make sense, the performance metric R must be commensurate for all instances. In other words, if the magnitude of the performance metric goes from 0 to 1 for one instance but goes from 0 to 100 for another, the latter will dominate the average. Making values commensurate is not always easy, but it is possible to an extent in some areas (Whiteson et al., 2011). In others, however, such as machine learning, it is not usual to average the results of several data sets (Japkowicz and Shah, 2011).

However, the crucial issue is that the number of instances for a particular task is usually too large or even infinite (e.g., the number of driving routes in a country is astronomical). To estimate the aggregate performance metric we need to sample, and select instances that are most "representative" (Hanks et al., 1993). This means going from Eq. 2.1 to Eq. 2.2, the sampling problem, which has not been well resolved in AI. Basically, the instances that are included in a test or benchmark for an AI task should be as informative, discriminative and diverse as possible.

In fact, if the sample of instances does not have enough diversity, or if it is fixed – especially if the number of instances is small – the reliability of the evaluation can be seriously affected. For instance, tasks are sometimes evaluated using problem repositories with a finite number of problems. In these cases, we see the following phenomenon:

Keynote 5.6. Evaluation overfitting in AI: If the problems or instances that represent a task (and their probabilities) are publicly available beforehand, the systems will be specialised for the expected cases instead of the generality of the task. This is known as 'evaluation overfitting' (Whiteson et al., 2011), 'method overfitting' (Falkenauer, 1998) or 'clever methods of overfitting' (Langford, 2005).

This is more critical than the evaluation specialisation seen in Keynote 2.6. On occasions, the *solutions* to the problems may even be available beforehand, or can be inferred by humans, so the designers of the systems to be evaluated can embed part of the solutions in their code – sometimes unconsciously. Indeed, a system can use a "big switch" approach, i.e., by recognising which problem it is facing and using the hardwired solution or optimal parameters for that specific instance (Panel 5.1).

In some areas, regardless of how preposterous it may sound, researchers can freely choose their instance from the repository. In machine learning, a usual procedure for the evaluation of a new technique is to *arbitrarily* select 10 or 20 data sets from the UCI repository (Bache and Lichman, 2013). Only a strong *bona fide* attitude to research can make this procedure acceptable. As an example of a response to this modus operandi, Macià and Bernadó-Mansilla (2014) propose "a mindful UCI", based on a characterisation of data sets using complexity measures from (Ho and Basu, 2002) so that the samples can be more diverse and representative. This also implies finding problems of different levels of 'difficulty'. Also, Macià and Bernadó-Mansilla (2014) propose an artificial data set generator (like UCI++, Soares, 2009) to complement the repository. Finally, still in the field of machine learning, the so-called experiment databases (Vanschoren et al., 2012; Van Rijn et al., 2013; Vanschoren et al., 2014) are a step forward in making the results of evaluation public and comparable across systems. Machine learning is a good example of how important yet tricky evaluation can be, even for researchers that are specialists in statistical techniques. In fact, statistical benchmarking becomes 'addictive' (Drummond and Japkowicz, 2010) with some experimental studies usually claiming that some algorithms are 'better' or 'worse', but not really settling the question.

The use of better repositories can slightly reduce the phenomenon of evaluation overfitting in AI, but there is still a large margin for improvement. Too frequently, benchmarks end up evaluating the researchers, who overfit their systems. To reduce the evaluation overfitting problem in a more significant way, the distribution (or subset) that is used to sample instances should not be known in advance (e.g., the "secret generalized methodology", Whiteson et al., 2011). Much better, fresh instances could be generated on the fly. Generators can be based on a stochastic grammar, can use prototypes with parameter variations or distortions (e.g., Drummond and Japkowicz, 2010), or virtual simulators instead of real scenarios (Vázquez et al., 2014).

Given the discussion about the main issues in AI evaluation, in what follows, we will perform a brief account of two kinds of evaluation test beds in AI, either in the form of benchmarks or through competitions. We will distinguish two main types of evaluations: those not involving other agents or opponents, and those where performance is derived as the result of multi-agent environments or games.

There are many evaluation test beds and competitions for single-agent task-specific systems in a variety of domains and formats: theorem proving (Sutcliffe and Suttner, 2006; Sutcliffe, 2009), termination of term rewriting systems and programs (Marché and Zantema, 2007), reinforcement learning (Whiteson et al., 2010), program synthesis (Alur et al., 2013), rescue robotics (Jacoff et al., 2003) and other Defense Advanced Research Projects Agency (DARPA) robotics challenges (DARPA, 2015), domestic or assistive robots (RoboCup@Home, RoCKIn@home) (Holz et al., 2013; Amigoni et al., 2015), machine learning (Bache and Lichman, 2013; Alcalá et al., 2010), planning (Long and Fox, 2003), plagiarism detection (Potthast et al., 2013), arcade video games (Bellemare et al., 2013; Schaul, 2014), pedestrian detection (Gerónimo and López, 2014), machine translation (Starkie et al., 2006) and many other natural language processing problems, commonsense reasoning (Winograd Schema Challenge, Levesque et al., 2012; Levesque, 2014), genetic programming (McDermott et al., 2012; White et al., 2013), grid worlds and mazes (Sturtevant, 2012), humanoid robots (Anderson et al., 2011), etc. The list is, of course, non-exhaustive and has not ceased to increase in the past years; a more complete list can be found in (Hernández-Orallo, 2016). Many of these repositories and competitions suffer from the problems of evaluation specialisation.

Another kind of evaluation takes place for tasks that are multi-agent, i.e., the evaluated agent has to compete or co-operate with other agents. This includes board games, robotic games, collaborative tasks, co-operative distributed problem solving (Decker et al., 1989), game theory problems, swarm computing, etc. In principle, the evaluation is based on performance, and can be defined in terms of Eqs. 2.1 and 2.2, but the instance distribution is determined by the opponents that are chosen.

> **Keynote 5.7. Task dependence on other agents**: Whenever a task incorporates other agents (games, multi-agent systems, etc.), it highly depends on these other agents and their characteristics.

In other words, the distribution of instances is actually a distribution of agents, as we will fully investigate in Chapter 13. Competitive games with unskilful opponents will be easy, collaborative tasks with unskilful teammates will be difficult.

Competitive games and other kinds of peer confrontation (adversarial) tasks have been commonplace in AI, even before the advent of current computers. For instance, the evaluation of the first chess-playing machine in 1911, Leonardo Torres-Quevedo's El Ajedrecista (Torres-Quevedo, 1915a,b) – arguably the first AI system running on a mechanical basis – was conducted by making it play against humans. Similarly, Turing and Champernowne's chess-playing algorithm Turochamp (1948) – which was 'executed' by Turing himself lacking a computer – was evaluated against humans. More recently, IBM Deep Blue (Campbell et al., 2002) was evaluated against the then world-champion Garry Kasparov in 1996 and 1997. The performance of all these systems was estimated depending on the opponents.

On top of these anecdotal cases, there is a good number of test beds and competitions in AI involving several agents, as a competitive game, a collaborative game or both (Kaminka et al., 2003). We can just name a few: Robocup and other robotic football competitions (Kitano et al., 1997; Kim et al., 2004), the General Game Playing AAAI Competition (Genesereth et al., 2005; Genesereth and Thielscher, 2014), the World Computer Chess Championship and the Computer Olympiad, the Annual Computer Poker Competition, the Trading Agents Competition (Wellman et al., 2004; Ketter and Symeonidis, 2012), the Warlight AI Challenge and many other strategy or video game competitions accepting bots. A more complete list can be found in (Hernández-Orallo, 2016).

We have said that the performance of a system for a game (or any other multi-agent task) depends on the skill of the other players. But how are the other players evaluated? This apparent circularity is usually solved by several kinds of match arrangements and scoreboards, as it is customary in tournaments and other sport competitions. However, how can we compare the results of different competitions? Or, more conspicuously, given two players, which player is better if they have never been confronted or even played against a common opponent? The usual solution in all these cases is the use of rating systems, such as the Elo ranking (Elo, 1978), used in chess, or more sophisticated systems (Smith, 2002; Masum and Christensen, 2003; Aziz et al., 2015).

Of course, under these schemas, ratings depend on the population of opponents, whose skill is also given by the ranking. This raises doubts about the stability of these indicators, especially if some of the opponents are human. A possible alternative is the use of standardised opponents, for which we may know their skill a priori. However, a full characterisation of a good opponent is only possible for some games. For instance, we can have several English draughts players being scored by their results against Chinook, the proven optimal player (Schaeffer et al., 2007). Nonetheless, if we only use one (optimal) opponent, we can have, as a result, that AI systems can specialise for that opponent. For instance, a system that is devised to play against Chinook may be worse for other good (but not optimal) players. Also, as we saw with the matching pennies game (Panel 5.5) – which is perhaps the simplest competitive game – the most naive agent, a random agent, is proved to be unbeatable (in expectation) by any other agent. Furthermore, even for this simple game, the construction of a linear ranking scale – i.e., transitive, such that if agent A is better than B and B is better than C then this necessarily implies that A is better than C – is problematic if true randomness is considered (see Hibbard, 2008, 2011; Hernández-Orallo et al., 2012). In general, cycles can be created for almost any game and any class

	A	B	C	D
A	0.5	0.7	0.1	0.6
B	0.3	0.5	0.8	0.7
C	0.9	0.2	0.5	0.8
D	0.4	0.3	0.2	0.5

	score
A	0.475
B	0.575
C	0.6
D	0.35

$$C > B > A > D$$

Figure 5.3. Left: a matrix showing the probability that an agent (on row) beats an agent (on column). Middle: scores by averaging rows. Right: the ordering that results from these scores. We see that some agents that are below others can beat them (A beats B and B beats C) more frequently than otherwise.

of players. For instance, Figure 5.3 shows four agents and the probabilities that one beats the other.

Many orderings can be derived, but cycles make it impossible to create a total order that is consistent with the table. This leads to the following general observation about scales in competitive games:

> **Keynote 5.8. Ranking scales**: Even in the simplest games, it may be impossible to construct a linear scale such that if A is above B, then A will beat B more times than otherwise. In other words, scales that are total orders (and even partial orders) may not be possible.

This is far from the idealistic view of universal scale discussed in Section 2.4. In general, in many competitions, the final score will suffer from poor reliability, because of the dependency on the population of opponents, the problems with ranking the scales and the limited number of matches.

5.6 CHARACTERISING GENERAL-PURPOSE AI SYSTEMS

From the report given in the previous section, we may get the impression that all the evaluation in AI is task-oriented. In fact, we may even keep Minsky's verdict "that we really haven't progressed too far toward a truly intelligent machine. We have collections of dumb specialists in small domains" (Stork, 1998, p. 27). Certainly, task-oriented AI represents the overwhelming majority of systems, applications, funding and publications, but it is fair to recognise that there are burgeoning areas around AI that are focusing on more general systems, such as artificial general intelligence (AGI) (Goertzel and Pennachin, 2007), developmental robotics (Asada et al., 2009), deep (reinforcement) learning

(Arel et al., 2010), inductive programming (Gulwani et al., 2015) or universal artificial intelligence (Hutter, 2007). Is AI also exploring more general evaluation approaches?

To answer this let us start with a series of workshops on Performance Metrics for Intelligent Systems (PerMIS), held from 2000 until 2012 at the National Institute of Standards and Technology (Meystel, 2000b; Messina et al., 2001; Evans and Messina, 2001; Meystel et al., 2003b,a; Gordon, 2007; Madhavan et al., 2009; Schlenoff et al., 2011). The first workshop was received enthusiastically and represented a good account of the state of the art, with very diverse points of views, terminology and goals. Dozens of definitions and metrics of intelligence were proposed, as well as intelligence decompositions. Given the diversity, each of them – including mine (Hernández-Orallo, 2000d) – was deemed as multifarious and arbitrary as all the rest.

During the first workshop (Meystel, 2000b), some of the questions were close to those seen during the outset of this book (Panel 1.3), including the definition of a vector of intelligence, the evaluation of intelligence potential and ultimately "whether there exists a universal measure of system intelligence such that the intelligence of a system can be compared independently of the given goals" (Meystel, 2000b). In fact, one of the recurrent debates in the first editions dealt with the distinction between measuring *performance* and measuring *intelligence* (Meystel, 2000b). The former was defined in terms of the "vector of performance", a set of indicators of the task the system is designed for. In contrast, the "mysterious vector of intelligence" was "still in limbo", as it should contain "the appropriate degrees of generalization, granularity, and gradations of intelligence". The white paper suggested an eclectic set of 25 items for the vector, such as the "number of objects that can be stored", the "ability to assign the optimum depth of associations", the "response time", the "accuracy of the variables", etc.

The list of 25 items (or "intellifactors") in the first workshop was renamed as the "multiresolutional vector of intelligence (MVI)" and complemented by a new list of 18 abilities, such as "to deal with imperfect sensors" or "to focus resources where appropriate". It was patently clear from this series of workshops that their participants were "not looking for and [were] not interested in a nouveau Turing test" (Messina et al., 2001). Instead, there was a "need to construct a MVI and determine their success", correlating "'success' with 'rewards' and 'punishment'" (Messina et al., 2001).

Despite the strong motivations, the opinions in favour of focusing – almost exclusively – on performance metrics became gradually dominant in the workshop series. It seems that this shift in subsequent workshops was strongly influenced by Lotfi Zadeh's view that the paradigm was not ready for intelligence evaluation (Zadeh, 2002). The advocates of performance evaluation prevailed: "the more that we can make it clear that we are interested in *performance*, rather than intelligence, *per se*, the better off we will be" (Simmons, 2000). As a result, the vector of intelligence was never realised and a feature-based evaluation did not take place. Indeed, from 2003 onwards the workshops paid much more attention to "performance measures" for "practical problems in commercial, industrial, and military applications" (Meystel et al., 2003b), covering, e.g., robotic rescue systems, self-driving cars, distributed control, human-robot interaction, soldier-worn sensor systems, Mars rovers and manufacturing robots, etc.

The failed attempt in the PerMIS workshops towards a feature-based evaluation, did not cut some other routes in this direction. Some AI competitions, years after, are including a wider range of problems, more general problems, or a combination of both. For instance, in robotics, the RoCKIn competitions (Amigoni et al., 2015), and the associated challenges (RoCKIn@home and RoCKIn@work, covering the assistance of aging people in a house environment, and assembling of mechanical parts in a factory), distinguish between tasks and functionalities. The latter comprise capabilities such as object perception, navigation, speech understanding and object manipulation. The emphasis is put on replicability (in terms of both reproducibility and repeatability). However, the set of capabilities and functionalities is not intended to be complete or comprehensive in any way.

A truly wide and very remarkable proposal is the General Game Competition (Genesereth et al., 2005; Genesereth and Thielscher, 2014), run yearly since 2005. Games are described in the Game Description Language (GDL) and their description is given to the players. The range of games includes noughts and crosses (tic tac toe), chess and many others, with complete or partial information, in static or dynamic worlds, with varying number of players, with simultaneous or alternating moves, etc. The distinctive feature of the competition – and what makes it general – is that the rules are not known until the game starts. Games are chosen by the organisers from the pool of games already described in GDL, with new games being introduced every year to make game specialisation difficult. The construction of an AI system that can play many games well only after being given the rules is a very significant achievement and sets an important difference from the early game playing systems, such as Deep Blue. Nonetheless, the systems participating in this competition are still specialised to playing games. They cannot *learn* to play a new game without the GDL description.

Learning to play a new game without being fed a description of it takes general game playing to reinforcement learning (Sutton and Barto, 1998;

Woergoetter and Porr, 2008). In fact, one of the first domains where reinforcement learning was shown to work was backgammon (Tesauro, 1994).

Keynote 5.9. Reinforcement learning is a general setting to define and evaluate agents that interact with an environment through the use of observations, actions and rewards.

Reinforcement learning is not restricted to computerised agents in games, robotics and other areas, but it is actually a paradigm for the understanding of cognitive processes in humans and other animals, as already mentioned in previous chapters. The paradigm is perfectly suitable for a less task-oriented evaluation because the goals of the task (and the task itself) are not fed into the system by a set of formal instructions, but indirectly given in the form of rewards, from which the agent can acquire its ultimate goals. The definition of the utility function is decisive, as explained in Panel 5.7.

The reinforcement learning competition (Whiteson et al., 2010; Dimitrakakis et al., 2014) is usually specialised to some kinds of environments that are learnable by state-of-the-art reinforcement learning techniques. However, unrestricted environments are used in new benchmarks, inside the reinforcement learning competition, such as the 'polyathlon', which includes a series of previously unknown domains. Other competitions, such as the General Video Game Competition (Schaul, 2014; Perez et al., 2015), and benchmarks, such as the Arcade Learning Environment, featuring Atari 2600 video games (Bellemare et al., 2013), also include unrestricted problems. A more ambitious undertaking is project Malmo (Johnson et al., 2016), an AI evaluation platform using the world of Minecraft to create tasks, featuring simple or fully fledged 3D interfaces, multi-agent interaction, construction and combination of elements, communication and many other possibilities. Figure 5.4 (left) shows the view of an AI agent being evaluated (with the help of a human agent, whose view is shown on the right).

In many competitions and platforms, the AI agent is fed with a presentation of the game in the form of video snapshots, and a sequence of rewards – the lives and score in the game. Actually, Mnih et al. (2015) achieved quite a remarkable performance by using a mixture of reinforcement learning and deep learning techniques in many of the 49 Atari 2600 video games of the Arcade Learning Environment.

This approach for solving the tasks is in the right direction, as they are all solved with the same "general-purpose algorithms". However, the use of these general algorithm does not ensure that the AI agents are really general-purpose systems. These systems may still be specialised for collections of problems

Panel 5.7
The exploration-exploitation dilemma

One critical notion in reinforcement learning is how rewards are aggregated into a utility function, to find a *compromise between exploration and exploitation*. A system that is always exploiting its knowledge of the world would be unprepared for changes, whereas a system that is always exploring would ignore rewards. The particular proportion depends on different parameters in the aggregate utility functions, using reward discounting or other formulations.

In a discrete scenario where the agent obtains a reward r_t after each discrete time t, the utility function (or return) R can be defined as follows:

$$R \triangleq \sum_{t=0}^{n} \gamma_t r_t \tag{5.1}$$

The term γ_t is usually expressed as $\gamma_t \triangleq c^t$ with $0 < c \leq 1$. Here, c is known as the discount factor, where low values encourage exploitation (immediate rewards) and high values encourage exploration (future rewards). This choice is especially important when n is large or infinite. In a situation with a small value of n (generally with several trials or episodes), $c = 1$ could be a good choice, which just considers all rewards equally.

Beyond reinforcement learning, the exploration-exploitation dilemma is present in any general-purpose system, natural or artificial.

(e.g., video games) but fail to solve other simple tasks, such as counting or stacking a pile of blocks. This is why rich evaluation platforms are preferable, such as Project Malmo, making it possible to create benchmarks covering a full range of problems.

Figure 5.4. Maze task built with project Malmo, an AI evaluation platform, over Minecraft, a popular sandbox video game. Left: The view from the AI agent being evaluated. Right: The view from a human agent collaborating with the AI agent. [Courtesy of Microsoft Research.] (See colour plate)

We can now state what a general AI system should be:

> **Keynote 5.10.** A **general-purpose AI system** must do a range of tasks it has never seen and has not been prepared for beforehand.

But what kind of evaluation would these general, 'habile', systems require? How could we characterise these systems in a non-monolithic way?

5.7 TOWARDS A FEATURE-ORIENTED EVALUATION

The crux of the evaluation of general AI systems in an abstract, yet still rich, way must rely on the space of features seen in Sections 1.3 and 1.4:

> **Keynote 5.11.** A **feature-oriented evaluation** is based on a profile of behavioural features, including both cognitive abilities and personality traits, when applicable.

This kind of evaluation – focused on the intermediate levels of a hierarchy of features – bridges a task-oriented view and a maximally general view, or, using Stuart Russell's analogy, goes "along several narrow corridors of ability" towards "general intelligence" (Russell, 2015).

Interestingly, task-specific and feature-specific evaluation are compatible and both applicable for some autonomous systems. For instance, a robotic cleaner can be evaluated in terms of its task (cleaning), but also in terms of its spatial or planning abilities. Having said this, feature-oriented evaluation is better suited for general-purpose AI systems such as cognitive architectures, (reinforcement) learning agents, cognitive robotics and AGI systems. In this section we will see many different (mostly unsuccessful) approaches to make AI evaluation less task-specific and more feature-oriented.

The first one, the "toddler Turing test" (Alvarado et al., 2002), despite the name is neither a Turing test nor a test battery. It is actually a proposal of *areas* for a test suite. Anderson and Lebiere (2003) introduced the 'Newell test', which is not an actual test for systems either, but a set of criteria for architectures or theories of cognition, namely. The 'test' distils 12 criteria for cognition "flexible behavior, real-time performance, adaptive behavior, vast knowledge base, dynamic behavior, knowledge integration, natural language, learning, development, evolution, and brain realization", merging two overlapping lists originally from (Newell, 1980, 1990), hence the name.

The idea of a cognitive decathlon, mimicking the athletic decathlon, was first suggested by Vere (1992) and linked to the Newell test by Anderson and Lebiere (2003). The DARPA's Brain-Inspired – later Biologically Inspired – Cognitive Architectures (BICA) program promoted the first version of an actual Cognitive Decathlon, which was finally completed by Mueller et al. (2007), with two other tests (Challenge Scenarios and Biovalidity Assessment) that jointly "cover a core set of cognitive, perceptual, and motor skills typical for a two-year-old human child". The Cognitive Decathlon includes 25 levels (or tasks) in six categories: vision, search, manual control and learning, knowledge learning, language and concept learning and simple motor control. We will analyse the levels and the implementation of the decathlon (Mueller, 2010) in the following chapter (Table 6.2).

The decathlon has been criticised because it supposedly not only determines what a cognitive system should do but sets "a number of constraints on the approaches that may be taken to achieve intelligence" (Rohrer, 2010). Certainly, the decathlon is not perfect but is compatible with a feature-based evaluation philosophy. Also, the Cognitive Decathlon is closer to having an actual test implementation than other more abstract proposals. For instance, inspired by the Newell test and the Cognitive Decathlon, another taxonomy of requirements for intelligent systems is refined in (Wray and Lebiere, 2007; Laird et al., 2009), in terms such as "taskability", "incrementality", "real-time operation", "adaptivity", "scalability", "knowledge capacity", "knowledge utilization" and "robustness". However, referring to this set of "abstract" measures, Jones and Wray (2011) concede that in order "to evaluate a particular cognitive system, there remains the daunting task of refining each of these abstract measures into concrete, evaluable measures".

A somewhat similar abstract approach is the concept of task muddiness (Weng, 2009, 2013). Weng's proposal for a measure of muddiness (26 factors, such as "awareness", "rawness", "observability", "multimodality", "richness", etc.) is in the direction of more general tasks, but does not fully resolve how to make the factors objective and how to measure them. In the end, any abstract characterisation of areas, requirement or groups of abilities seems equally good, but also equally arbitrary. One risk of feature-oriented evaluation is that one can end up including measures for any construct we may think of, such as creativity (e.g., the so-called Lovelace test, Bringsjord et al., 2003) or consciousness (e.g., Conscale, Arrabales et al., 2010).

One criterion to characterise possible general areas for a feature-oriented evaluation is to look at AI subdisciplines. This is what we see in Table 5.2, by using the topics of interest of a prestigious journal. Another approach is taken by Adams et al. (2012), who try to find a compromise among a series of

Table 5.2. Main areas in AI according to the *AI Journal*, one of the leading journals in the field. We exclude metalevel, hybrid or instrumental categories.

Automated (deductive) reasoning	Commonsense reasoning
Constraint processing	Computer vision (and perception)
Knowledge representation	Machine learning
Multi-agent systems	Natural language processing
Planning and theories of action	Reasoning under uncertainty

opinions and proposals in previous workshops on AGI evaluation. Adams et al. (2012) embrace a developmental approach, integrating notions from Piaget and Vygotsky (we will discuss these theories of development in Chapter 12), and analyse the characteristics of AGI environments, tasks and agents (extending Laird and Wray, 2010). As a result, they identify several "high-level competency areas", as shown in Table 5.3. Actually, apart from the areas, they recognise six kinds of scenarios: general video-game learning, preschool learning, reading comprehension, story or scene comprehension, school learning and the 'Wozniak Test' (walk into an unfamiliar house and make a cup of coffee). They propose "AGI test suites" such that "the total set of tasks for a scenario must cover all the competency areas" and they must do it in such a way that the tasks are so varied and numerous (or previously unknown) that the "big switch" problem is avoided. Nonetheless, they advocate for several suites, as they "doubt any successful competition could ever cover the full extent of a roadmap such as this" (Adams et al., 2012). Of the same opinion is Wang (2010), also advocating for a combination of evaluation tools from different paradigms.

In brief, from all the previous proposals it seems that two common ways of preventing specialisation is by including many tasks in a battery and increasing

Table 5.3. Competency areas in AGI according to Adams et al. (2012).

Perception	Memory
Attention	Social interaction
Planning	Motivation
Actuation	Reasoning
Communication	Learning
Emotion	Modelling self/other
Building/creation	Use of quantities

the *breadth* of the tasks (Goertzel et al., 2009; Rohrer, 2010). However, test generalisation is not the same as a feature-oriented evaluation:

Keynote 5.12. General versus feature-oriented evaluation: A more general test can be obtained with an increase in the *number* and *breadth* of the tasks, through *agglomeration*, but the result may be some kind of joint indicator rather than a feature-oriented profile.

In other words, one can go from specific to general in a hierarchical way, with distinctive abilities at different levels, but one can also mix everything together until all possible tasks are considered. When the link with the abilities is lost or never elaborated, the magnitudes of the measures become meaningless or, in the best case, anthropocentric. Also, the problem for Adams et al. (2012) and others is that HLMI is not well defined, so they must set the HLMI threshold at good performance "on diverse metrics corresponding to tasks assessing 50 percent of the competency areas". The I-athlon (Adams et al., 2016) also integrates several kinds of problems ("events"), conceived as generalisations or agglomerations of CAPTCHAS. Each event is normalised relative to humans (crowdsourcing is suggested). Figure 5.5 shows some of the proposed categories.

Things are not very different for the other main group of behavioural features, the evaluation of personality traits. In artificial intelligence, the notion

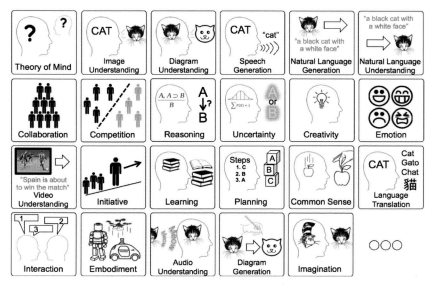

Figure 5.5. Candidates for I-athlon "events" as suggested by Adams et al. (2016). [Courtesy of Sam S. Adams.]

of "artificial personalities" (or "computer personalities") has been around for several decades (Carbonell, 1980). A personality trait in artificial intelligence is defined as "any internal state or processing mechanism of the agents that (1) differentiates a class of agents or an individual agent from other agents with which it is interacting or is compared; (2) is relatively stable ... and cannot be just adopted or learned from outside on line; (3) is mental: [has] mental attitudes (beliefs, goals, etc.) or mental styles and (4) has to do with motivations, with the way of choosing, of reasoning, of planning and so on" (Castelfranchi et al., 1998).

Research has focused on understanding whether computer personalities can be re-created (Nass et al., 1995) and are 'believable' (Badler et al., 2002) from the point of view of humans, in concordance with an "idea of believability [that] has long been studied and explored in literature, theater, film, radio drama, and other media" (Bates et al., 1994). Note that believability can be achieved with the help of facial expressions from avatars, and these expressions can be modified to better convey a desired personality (Badler et al., 2002), but they can be restricted to other kinds of interactions, such as conversational agents or other games where the physical appearance is non-existent or independent of personality. In social scenarios (e.g., multi-agent systems, social robotics and social media), personality traits (and social attitudes) are commonly investigated (Castelfranchi et al., 1998), because they can be crucial for competition, co-ordination, delegation, etc. This area is known as "personality computing" (Vinciarelli and Mohammadi, 2014).

The integration of several personality traits constitutes a "personality" Rizzo et al. (1997), "a consistent, believable, stable, and typical or distinctive cluster of traits and attitudes that are reflected in the agent's behaviour" (Castelfranchi et al., 1998). The notions are so close to human trait theory, that common models, such as the Big Five in humans (Section 3.2), have been re-created for robots and virtual agents (Sohn et al., 2012).

Unlike human personality evaluation, self-evaluation and evaluation of AI systems by peers are not very common, and the assessment is made by human judges or by the measurement of some indicators. The evaluation of personality in AI systems faces many open questions. In the end, this derives from our lack of understanding of how personality traits could be extracted from first principles, or how any set of personality traits (such as the Big Five) could be matched to some formal characteristics of a cognitive system. For instance, in reinforcement learning and other areas, we have the common exploration-exploitation dilemma, as well as the preponderance of intrinsic (e.g., curiosity, learning new skills, internal rewards) versus extrinsic motivations (e.g., external rewards) (Baldassarre and Mirolli, 2013). In a way, all this determines the personality (openness) of an agent.

The lack of a principled approach to behavioural features may explain partially why a feature-oriented evaluation of AI systems, covering both cognitive abilities and personality traits, is still in a very embryonic state. But another reason is the success of task-oriented AI. Indeed, achieving high performance and quality in particular tasks is a genuine part of AI, and its accurate evaluation is necessary for the assessment of progress of the discipline. Still, task-oriented evaluation can be improved significantly, avoiding evaluation specialisation and increasing measurement reliability.

In this chapter we have intentionally glossed over some intelligence tests based on algorithmic information theory (AIT) that started in the 1990s, such as the Turing test variant introduced by Dowe and Hajek (1997, 1998), the *C*-test (Hernández-Orallo and Minaya-Collado, 1998; Hernández-Orallo, 2000a), and other variants and extensions that followed. The approaches based on AIT will be the backbone of the book, developed in Part III.

Summing up, we have to be aware that AI evaluation aims at systems that are at the cutting edge of science and technology. In particular, the construction of artificial general intelligent systems is actually one of the biggest challenges of the twenty-first century. Measurement cannot lag behind in this enterprise, since "greatest accuracy, at the frontiers of science, requires greatest effort, and probably the most expensive or complicated of measurement instruments and procedures" (Hand, 2004, p. 124).

CHAPTER HIGHLIGHTS

- The big switch philosophy based on specialised solutions pervading AI systems and AI progress (Panel 5.1, Section 5.2).
- The Turing test and variants being neither sufficient nor necessary for intelligence or for HLMI (Keynote 5.4, Section 5.3).
- CAPTCHAs not really aimed at measuring AI systems but very useful (until broken) (Keynote 5.5).
- Widespread and easier task-oriented evaluation through benchmarks and competitions but still facing several problems, such as evaluation overfitting and dependency of other agents (Keynotes 5.6, 5.7).
- General-purpose systems, more difficult to characterise and evaluate, with the exploration-vs-exploitation dilemma (Keynote 5.9, Eq. 5.1, Panel 5.7).
- A still incipient feature-based evaluation, at an abstract level, usually with arbitrary sets of features (Keynote 5.12, Section 5.7).

6

The Boundaries against a Unified Evaluation

> [Edsger Dijkstra] asked me what I was working on. Perhaps just to provoke a memorable exchange I said, "AI". To that he immediately responded, "Why don't you work on I?"
>
> He was right, of course, that if "I" is more general than "AI", one should work on the more general problem, especially if it is the one that is the natural phenomenon, which in this case it is.
>
> – Leslie Valiant,
> *Probably Approximately Correct: Nature's Algorithms for Learning and Prospering in a Complex World (2013)*

IN THE PREVIOUS three chapters, we have seen three very different approaches to the evaluation of behaviour. Psychometrics use well-defined test batteries, usually composed of abstract culture-fair problems or questionnaires, different from everyday tasks. Comparative psychology also presents tasks to animals, not necessarily so abstract, but careful attention is put on interfaces and motivation, with rewards being key. Artificial intelligence evaluation is significantly different, using benchmarks and competitions. What happens if we use definitions, tools and tests from one discipline to evaluate subjects in other disciplines? How often has this been done and advocated for? Why has it not worked so far?

6.1 THE FRAGMENTED EVALUATION OF BEHAVIOUR

There was a time when a certain fragmentation existed between psychology, evolutionary biology and artificial intelligence. However, with the increasing relevance of evolutionary psychology and cognitive science, the boundaries between these disciplines have well been trespassed and new areas have

Table 6.1. Oversimplified view of the most distinctive characteristics of the evaluation of behaviour in three different disciplines.

	Human psychometrics	Comparative psychology	AI evaluation
Purpose	diagnosis, selection, education, science	science	engineering
Subjects	one to many	usually few	usually few
Normed	population	unusual	no
Tests	standard battery	single experiment	benchmark
Interfaces	pen and paper, computerised	specialised apparatus	inputs and outputs, robotic
Motivation	instructions	rewards and penalties	hardwired, rewards
Reliability	usually high	variable	usually low
Overfitting	usually low	variable	usually high
Situated	unusual	common	common

appeared in between, such as artificial life, evolutionary computing, evolutionary robotics and, human-machine interfaces, developmental robotics and swarm computing. Unfortunately, we cannot say the same for the *evaluation* of behavioural features. The preceding three chapters present different terminologies, principles, tools and, ultimately, tests.

Table 6.1 shows a simplified picture of some of the distinctions between psychometrics, comparative psychology and AI evaluation.

Each discipline is extremely diverse. It is very different if we evaluate a small child or an adult, a chimpanzee or a bacterium, an 'intelligent' vacuum cleaner or a reinforcement learning system playing games. Hence, the simplification would be turned into distortion for other differences, which are therefore not included in the table, such as what is evaluated (individual, group or species), whether the measurement is quantitative or qualitative, how difficulty is inferred and the relevance of physical traits in the measurement (e.g., sensorimotor abilities). The issue of validity is not included either, but this can range from a predictive validity, common in psychometrics and animal evaluation, with face validity, more common in AI, especially with task-oriented evaluation using a representational measurement.

One of the motivations behind universal psychometrics is the fragmentation shown in Table 6.1. However, the definition of the 'machine kingdom', seen in Section 1.2, per se, will not bridge the differences. The disciplines are specialised for the kinds of subjects they are used to evaluate. Why should we cross the lines? We gave motivations in the introductory chapter, but let us recall some of the new kinds of systems that force us to cross the boundaries: 'animats' (Williams and Beer, 2010), computer-enhanced humans (Cohen, 2013), human-enhanced computers (Von Ahn, 2005, 2009), other kinds of bionic and hybrids systems and, most especially, collectives (Quinn and Bederson, 2011).

The aversion for crossing the lines is well illustrated by the way humans are still evaluated: without their enhancers. How much time did it take until calculators were allowed in university exams? Is it *natural* to evaluate a twenty-first century youngster without her mobile phone and an Internet connection? This is the way humans interact with the world nowadays. People should be evaluated for what they are able to do in their context. Limiting this for testing may handicap their cognitive abilities and affect the way personality is displayed. Of course, allowing enhancers during evaluation creates many new problems – including gaming the evaluation – and ultimately, new dilemmas. How much can be attributed to the human and how much to the enhancing devices? When does this really matter?

Symmetrically, we find machines that are enhanced by having access to humans. One particular setting is based on the concept of human-assisted Turing machine, a Turing machine with an extra instruction to ask questions to a 'human oracle' (Shahaf and Amir, 2007). This setting is interesting for the general area of 'human computation' (Law and Von Ahn, 2011) and for crowdsourcing. However, it is unclear that this can lead to a meaningful taxonomy of AI systems (Yampolskiy, 2015a, Chapter 1), by determining what systems and tasks require more or less human assistance, ultimately depending on the concept of HLMI, seen in the previous chapter. Our interest here is simply that human-assisted computers are a good example of the challenges that tests must face for any of these hybrids and collectives.

The lines between humans and non-human animals have already been crossed in comparative psychology, because there are species and individuals all along a continuum (including small children and mentally disabled people). In Chapter 4 we saw human children compared with other apes.

The preceding examples with hybrids between natural and artificial intelligence make the boundaries more blurred than ever: we find a continuum of subjects in the machine kingdom between intelligent animals (including humans) and non-intelligent AI systems, as a result of their diversity or their hybridisation. This means that we do not need a *bridge* to cross an empty area, but we need to explore and cover these transition areas too. Let us have a look at the scales, taxonomies and tests that have already been used – or that could be used – in these boundary areas.

6.2 TOOLS FOR THE BOUNDARIES

We can start with comparative cognition and artificial intelligence. The diversity of animal behaviour and the behaviour of AI systems show some similarities. In animals, we find many individuals that feature very specialised behaviours in very particular environments. Similarly, many AI systems are specialised for single tasks. These behaviours are hardwired in the genotype and the program code, respectively. They are horses for courses. But other animals and AI systems are more adaptive, because they display some learning abilities. For instance, inspired by animal intelligence, we can consider an ecological context to examine machine intelligence. In this way, "animal behavior ought to be used as a model to define a hierarchy of intelligence tasks [in AI]" (Kak, 2000).

But if we bring this ecological perspective to machines, should we not bring Lloyd Morgan's Canon (Keynote 4.3) as well whenever we evaluate an AI system? Shettleworth (2013, p. 12) says that "a reasonable modern interpretation of Morgan's Canon is that explanation in terms of general processes of learning along with species-typical perceptual and response biases should always be sought before invoking more complex or specialized cognitive processes". However, this does not work for AI. Success in a task as a result of general learning would be given preference over specialised (hardwired) behaviour, when it is precisely the latter that is common in AI systems. Animals develop (i.e., evolve) driven by their history of environments. Usually, the specific experimental task the animal is facing at evaluation time has not been part of that history. Therefore, if the animal succeeds, it is because the animal performs a generalisation. However, for AI artefacts, it is the other way round; it is very likely that the AI system has been developed (i.e., programmed) for the benchmark, while not succeeding in similar (but not exactly equal) environments.

This discrepancy between animals and AI systems is mitigated when we use tasks for which learning is necessary, using testing apparatus with rewards and penalties for animals, like in the area of reinforcement learning in artificial intelligence. In fact, in the first PerMIS workshop, reinforcement learning was advocated as the way for a general (not task-oriented) evaluation of AI systems: the "penalty-reward approach of reinforcement learning is useful for training systems as well as for measuring them without the exactly predetermined goal" (Balch et al., 2000). Nonetheless, even if the AI system is not specialised for the task, but learns to solve it, it is never known how much *predisposition* or embedded *bias* there is for the task, and Morgan's Canon will not clarify this either.

Panel 6.1
Machine Intelligence Quotient (MIQ)

It seems that the first use of the term MIQ was made by Lotfi Zadeh in the context of fuzzy systems (Zadeh, 1994). As he explained during an invited talk at the first PerMIS workshop, his concept was related to performance, and relative to a *population*, in the very same way IQ values are; "The counterpart of the concept of IQ in such systems is what might be called Machine IQ, or simply MIQ" (Zadeh, 1994).

However, MIQ "is product-specific and does not involve the same dimensions as human IQ. Furthermore, MIQ is relative. Thus, the MIQ of, say, a camera made in 1990 would be a measure of its intelligence relative to cameras made during the same period, and would be much lower than the MIQ of cameras made today" (Zadeh, 2000).

Moving from animals to humans, IQ is a concept that is very commonly borrowed from psychometrics in AI evaluation, usually renamed as *Machine Intelligence Quotient* (MIQ), as discussed in Panel 6.1.

Other (re)definitions of MIQ followed (Bien et al., 1998, 2002; Lee et al., 2000; Park et al., 2001; Ulinwa, 2008), some of them based on fuzzy theory, and many others in terms of performance in a range of goals, indicators or tasks, more similar to those seen in Section 5.7.

There is nothing wrong about defining several metrics and integrating them into a single indicator, even if most metrics are particular to control systems using fuzzy logic. However, the use of the name MIQ is confusing, as the term 'quotient' suggests that MIQ is normalised or at least relative to some magnitude (originally age). The name also suggests that the value can be compared face to face with an IQ value. According to these two criteria, most of the previous notions of MIQ are misconceived. The only consistent use – practical or not – of the term MIQ is the one made by Zadeh, as he considers that the term is relative to a population of machines, in the very same way that human IQ is relative to a population of humans.

Many other concepts that depend on a human population do not make sense for AI evaluation or even for animal evaluation. Thorndike anticipated what would happen if difficulty were defined with an enlarged population, including all the elements in the animal kingdom: "we have defined intellectual difficulty in relation to a defined group of individuals. . . . We can, if we wish, specify the group as all human beings of all ages, or all animals, and so get measurements of something which we might call difficulty in general. . . . The measurement of such difficulty in general may be of very little use" (Thorndike et al., 1927, p. 25).

Beyond particular ideas or connections, we should start looking at the underlying theories of cognition in different disciplines. Regarding humans, in Section 3.3 we saw several theories of intelligence that arranged cognitive abilities in different ways, such as Thurstone's primary mental abilities (see Table 3.1) or Cattell-Horn-Carroll three-stratum model (the CHC hierarchy in Figure 3.2). In Section 4.2 we extracted a taxonomy for the areas of animal cognition research (see Table 4.1). Finally, in Section 5.7, we saw a list of AI subdisciplines (see Table 5.2) and a set of high-level competency areas in AGI (see Table 5.3). We can see that there are many commonalities but also differences in all these taxonomies. The taxonomies in human intelligence evaluation are derived from factor analysis, according to an adult human population. In this sense, they are not as arbitrary as the rest. However, can these taxonomies be extrapolated to non-human animals and AI systems, seeing that the populations are different?

One possibility is to devise a mapping between some of the taxonomies across different disciplines. For instance, the Cognitive Decathlon, introduced in the previous chapter, described a series of areas that should be measured for any cognitive system, with emphasis on robots. Table 6.2 shows the Cognitive Decathlon and the tasks that have been implemented in the Psychology Experiment Building Language (PEBL) (Mueller and Piper, 2014). The last column shows a correspondence with the abilities of the CHC hierarchy that are involved in the task (level) of the Decathlon according to Simpson and Twardy (2008).

By looking at the Cognitive Decathlon, the derivation of tests and its mapping to areas in human intelligence models, an immediate question arises. What is the point of using this Decathlon instead of directly using a selection of validated tests for the CHC hierarchy taken from psychometrics? Simpson and Twardy (2008) argue that many batteries for humans give too much relevance to "memory and attention, things which computers are very good at". The Cognitive Decathlon may be justified as it supposedly represents a wider test battery, more suitable for robots.

Apart from taxonomies of cognitive *abilities*, the taxonomies for human *personality* traits have also been used – sometimes directly – for animals and AI agents. In the case of animals, we usually find comparisons of the factors found for humans (such as the Big Five, Panel 3.2) and those for other animals. For instance, King and Figueredo (1997) found a similar set of

Table 6.2. The *Cognitive Decathlon* (Mueller et al., 2007), showing the tasks (levels) that have an implemented test (Mueller, 2010) in PEBL. The last column shows the corresponding abilities of the Cattell-Horn-Carroll's three-stratum model (see Figure 3.2) according to Simpson and Twardy (2008).

Category	Level	PEBL	CHC
Vision	Invariant object identification	Yes	Gv
	Object ID: Size discrimination	Yes	Gv
	Object ID: With rotation	Yes	Gv
	Object ID: Relations	No	-
	Visual action/event recognition	No	GvlGl
Search	Simple navigation	Yes	Gv
	Visual search	Yes	GvlGs
	Travelling salesman problem	Yes	GvlGslGl
	Embodied search	No	GvlGslGl
	Reinforcement learning	Yes	GvlGslGllGflGm
Manual control and learning	Motor mimicry	No	GmlGv
	Simple (one-hand) manipulation	Yes	GmlGv
	Two-hand manipulation	No	GmlGv
	Device mimicry	Yes	GmlGv
	Intention mimicry	No	GmlGv
Knowledge learning	Episodic recognition memory	No	GllGm?
	Semantic memory/categorisation	No	GllGflGm?
Language and concept learning	Object-noun mapping	No	GclGl
	Property-adjective	No	GclGl
	Relation-preposition	No	GclGl
	Action-verb	No	GclGl
	Relational verb-action	No	GclGl
Simple motor control	Eye movements	No	-
	Aimed manual movements	Yes	-

factors derived from chimpanzees and humans (the Big Five, plus dominance). In Chapter 4, we also mentioned a comprehensive study by Gosling and John (1999) to derive "the landscape of animal personality". Actually, the integration of animal personality and human personality research has been advocated several times (Gosling, 2001) and the modern evolutionary view is taking the direction of explaining human personality traits as special cases of animal personality traits (Nettle, 2006). The borrowing of the Big Five from humans and other tools from human personality to the analysis and re-creation of AI systems has also been attempted (Sohn et al., 2012), as we mentioned in the previous chapter, but more incipiently. In other words, the boundaries for personality have been well crossed here. However, it is unclear whether a set of traits evolved in one (social) environment are explanatory and comprehensive in others, especially for artificial intelligence.

Apart from scales and taxonomies, among the tools that can be brought from one discipline to another we find actual tests. Can we just use tests and benchmarks taken from one discipline for another? To answer this question, we can start with the more recent and incipient transfer of tasks from the evaluation of non-human animals to the evaluation of AI systems. For instance, Michel and Rohrer (2008) describe the "Rat's Life" benchmark, where two robots compete in a survival game, "like the rats in cognitive animal experimentation". Voss (2007) goes beyond casual borrowings and suggests that early artificial general intelligence systems could be evaluated as if they were animals. He replaces the HLMI (Human-level machine intelligence), which we discussed in Section 5.3, by a so-called lower-level animal-like ability. This, however, may even be more meaningless than the HLMI if we do not specify the species the level refers to.

Indeed, one argument against the transfer of tests for animals to the evaluation of AI systems, such as robots, is expressed in the following way: "robotic engineers could program robots to be able to pass any ethologist-designed test relating to visual attention, gaze following, joint attention, etc., *providing the details of the test are known in advance*" [italics added] (Matellán Olivera et al., 2011). Whilst the argument is insightful, it is not totally true at the current state of the art, since there are some tasks that animals can do and AI technology cannot, even if fully described in advance. This is more evident with humans, since many specific tasks that humans can do are still ungraspable for AI technology.

Nevertheless, there are more profound reasons against the use of tests from humans and non-human animals for AI systems. A stronger argument relies on the generality and specificity of any devised test for one group when used for a different group; specialised measuring instruments may give wrong measurements outside their operating range. A very good example of this can be shown without any cherry-picked AI system. It also happens between humans and non-humans, as illustrated in Panel 6.2.

The problem arises because tests are meant and validated for one kind of subject. Whenever the kind of subject, or the population, is changed, the results

---

Panel 6.2
Are pigeons more intelligent than humans?

Shettleworth (2010b, sec. 1.1.4) discusses the use of reaction time tests for pigeons and humans. The result is that pigeons react faster.

Whilst there is no objection about what reaction time tests measure, the same cannot be said about other tests. For instance, as models of human cognitive abilities show that reaction time correlates with IQ in humans, what does this mean for pigeons? If we apply human psychometric models to pigeons "the counterintuitive conclusion follows that pigeons are more intelligent than people" (Vickrey and Neuringer, 2000).

---

can no longer be compared; any inference that held for one group may not hold for another group. This is not surprising from the perspective of human psychometrics and, especially, animal cognition, but it is worth being recalled for artificial intelligence.

Keynote 6.1. Measuring out of the operating area: Whenever a test that is devised and validated for a group is used to measure subjects of a different group, the *generality* and the *specificity* of the measure may become uncalibrated or simply inaccurate for the new group. In addition, any inference using a model of behavioural features for one group cannot be safely applied for the other group.

Nevertheless, this does not mean that the use of tests across groups should never be done, but rather that a careful selection and interpretation would be required. For instance, the evaluation setting in Goertzel's et al.'s robot preschool (Goertzel and Bugaj, 2009; Goertzel et al., 2010) is based on a *selection* of tasks from the WPPSI battery for children (see Chapter 3) and this is complemented with some others that are defined on purpose.

Nevertheless, the application of tests from one group to a different group for purposes other than measurement is acceptable and useful to understand cognition, to answer philosophical questions, or simply, to reject that the test really measures a feature outside a specific population – i.e., to falsify the *universal range* of the test. In the following section we precisely analyse the case of IQ tests used for AI systems, as this is an excellent example of the good and bad uses of tests across the boundaries.

6.3 IQ TESTS ARE NOT FOR MACHINES

The use of tasks from IQ tests and other human intelligence tests in artificial intelligence can be traced back to the early days of computer science. For instance, Evans (1963, 1965) developed ANALOGY, a system that was "capable of solving a wide class of the so-called geometric-analogy problems (A is to B as C is to ?) frequently encountered on intelligence tests" (Evans, 1965). He chose these problems because at that time they were challenging tasks for reasoning by analogy. However, he never suggested that scoring well in these tests should be interpreted as ANALOGY being intelligent.

Other early approaches explored the connection between psychology and artificial intelligence using other tasks from human intelligence tests. Simon and Kotovsky (1963) used letter series to analyse cognitive processes and item difficulty computationally. Again, the goal was not to construct a system that could be called intelligent because of this (Simon et al., 1991). Similarly, Raven's Progressive Matrices (RPM), one of the tests that has a strongest g loading, as we saw in Chapter 3, was attempted with reasonably good results by Carpenter et al. (1990). Once again, the interest was set on the analysis of the cognitive processes involved in these problems and not the development of a system that could be deemed more or less intelligent.

The use of tasks from intelligence tests was meant as a tool for the study of cognitive processes, the development of new techniques and, basically, as abstract problems for the early days in artificial intelligence. However, there were also some implicit or explicit statements about the use of intelligence test tasks for the *evaluation* of AI systems or even as the *goal* for AI research, appointed "to construct a single program that would take a standard intelligence test" (Newell, 1973).

Since then, human psychometric tests have been repeatedly suggested as an alternative to the task-oriented evaluation that has dominated AI for decades. Weng (2000) puts it very clearly: "with new perspectives from developmental robots, the performance metrics for machine intelligence will undergo a revolution. They will fundamentally change the current fragmented landscape of the AI field by shifting the emphasis of measuring ad hoc capability of performing task-specific application to a systematic measurement of mental developmental capabilities. Such performance metrics can be adapted from those for humans – a series of tests well developed by a well-established field called psychometrics".

Not everybody was so enthusiastic about psychometrics for AI. In a review of Jensen's book (Jensen, 1998), Selmer Bringsjord proclaimed that "in light

---

Panel 6.3
Is a 960-line Perl program more intelligent than humans?

In 2003, Pritika Sanghi and David Dowe devised and programmed a computer program in Perl – with just 960 lines of code and a list of 25,143 words – to pass several standard human IQ tests. The program was based on an ad hoc, big switch, approach, after realising that most IQ test questions followed a small number of formats such as "insert missing letter/number in middle or at end" or "insert suffix/prefix to complete two or more words" (Sanghi and Dowe, 2003). For those questions that were not recognised by the system, the program just output a random guess.

The program was not a lookup table nor was presented the tests beforehand. Hence, the software had to include code for arithmetic progressions (e.g., 7 10 13 16 ?), geometric progressions (e.g., 3 6 12 24 ?), arithmetic geometric progressions (e.g., 3 5 9 17 33 ?), squares, cubes and even Fibonacci sequences (e.g., 0 1 1 2 3 5 8 13 ?), use of vocabulary suffices and prefixes, etc. Much of the program dealt with parsing strings.

Table 6.3 shows that the program scores are similar to human average for a range of tests. Of course, the ultimate goal of the experiment was *not* to make progress in AI or to show that this program was intelligent. Rather, the point was to show that IQ tests were not meant for machines.

---

of artificial intelligence, the science of mental ability is either silly or pointless [and it will be] wiped away" (Bringsjord, 2000). He argued that computer systems were scoring well on the RPM task (referring to Carpenter et al., 1990), which is one of the tasks with highest g loading. Jensen (2000a) responded that Bringsjord had conflated intelligence and the g factor, which just "addresses the nature of intraspecies variation".

In the wake of this discussion about the use of IQ tests and other psychometric tests for the evaluation of AI systems, Sanghi and Dowe (2003) performed a revealing experiment, as illustrated in Panel 6.3.

Clearly, since this program is not a *general AI system* in the terms seen in Keynote 5.10, it can be interpreted as a *refutation* of the use of IQ tests for arbitrary machines. It can be argued, however, that the good results in some particular tests for a system that has been devised on purpose for these kinds of tests proves nothing. This is the position of Simpson and Twardy (2008): "the choice of test matters. WAIS and other standard tests are deficient because they

Table 6.3. Results by a short ad hoc program
(Sanghi and Dowe, 2003), specifically designed for
passing IQ tests.

Test	IQ score	Human average
A.C.E. IQ Test	108	100
Eysenck Test 1	107.5	90–110
Eysenck Test 2	107.5	90–110
Eysenck Test 3	101	90–110
Eysenck Test 4	103.25	90–110
Eysenck Test 5	107.5	90–110
Eysenck Test 6	95	90–110
Eysenck Test 7	112.5	90–110
Eysenck Test 8	110	90–110
IQ Test Labs	59	80–120
Testedich IQ Test	84	100
IQ Test from Norway	60	100
Average	96.27	92–108

cover mainly memory and attention, things which computers are very good at".
In particular, about the Perl program and the tests used by Sanghi and Dowe
(2003), Simpson and Twardy (2008) say that the program performs "a reductio
for those tests, since the program earns its scores on arithmetic, logical, and
pattern questions, not language or semantic ones", so that "this is a problem
with the particular tests, not the general idea. . . . Modern CHC theory [see Figure 3.2] holds that human intelligence factors into at least 10 broad aptitudes,
only 2 or 3 of which are exercised by standard IQ tests".

Indeed, Simpson and Twardy (2008) make a very strong point about the use
of psychometric tests: "First, these performance tests have a built-in comparison to human performance. Second, the tests are well understood within the
psychological testing community. Third, the average 'man on the street' can
understand the intuition of administering the same test to natural and artificial
intelligent systems". However, for any selection of tests, the Perl program – a
3rd year undergraduate student project – could be extended, and significantly
improved, to excel in this choice of tests. Of course, if we are able to build or
modify a non-intelligent system such as the Perl program to score well in the
selection, the testers could counteract with another selection, for which the system would presumably fail. But again, as is happening with the CAPTCHAs,
an AI researcher could soon develop a new system that scores well in the new
selection.

Aware of this vicious, adversarial circle, and taking into account the problem of "evaluation overfitting in AI" seen in the previous chapter, the use of human psychometric tests for computers must be restated:

Keynote 6.2. Preventing psychometric tests overfitting: The use of standard psychometric tests for AI evaluation must be based on at least one of these conditions: (1) carefully selected test batteries that are not made public until they are taken, to be as unexpected as possible, and (2) the broadest possible range and number of tests, such that specialisation, even if possible, would be very demanding.

This looks very reasonable, but would this lead to a feasible, practical evaluation? And, most importantly, is either of these two conditions sufficient? Let us discuss the views of two significant advocates of conditions 1 and 2, Douglas Detterman and Selmer Bringsjord, respectively.

Detterman, editor at the time of the Intelligence Journal, wrote an editorial (Detterman, 2011) about the then recent feat achieved by IBM Watson, the winner of the *Jeopardy!* TV quiz (Ferrucci et al., 2010). He posed the following challenge: "I, the editorial board of *Intelligence*, and members of the International Society for Intelligence Research will develop a unique battery of intelligence tests that would be administered to that computer and would result in an actual IQ score" (Detterman, 2011). The challenge had two levels. In the first level, the type of IQ tests could be seen beforehand by the AI system programmer. In the second level, however, the types of tests would not have been seen beforehand. Only computers passing the second level "could be said to be truly intelligent" (Detterman, 2011). Even if Detterman was unaware of Sanghi and Dowe's program, which may qualify for the first level, he anticipated the problem of test overfitting and established the second level of the challenge because of this. Detterman was well aware that many standardised psychological tests are never made public, because otherwise people could practise on them and game the evaluation – also, many tests are copyrighted as we saw in Chapter 3. So this second level derives from common practice in academic and professional psychometrics, unlike what is customary in AI research.

Nonetheless, even with the second level, there is an important conundrum about the implementation of this challenge: what are the criteria for this "unique battery of intelligence tests"? Will they be a random subset of human IQ tests? Or will they be selected and developed on purpose? If this is the case, would "the editorial board of *Intelligence*, and members of the International Society for Intelligence Research" be tempted to devise or choose those IQ tests that are more 'computer-unfriendly'? Could they just select AI-hard tasks, or simply a CAPTCHA?

Bringsjord and Schimanski (2003) also challenged artificial intelligence, not (only) in terms of the way it should be evaluated, but about what its goals should be. They introduced 'Psychometric AI' (PAI), as a new AI, namely "the *field* devoted to building information-processing entities capable of at least solid performance on all established, validated tests of intelligence and mental ability, a class of tests that includes not just the rather restrictive IQ tests, but also tests of artistic and literary creativity, mechanical ability, and so on". PAI is not an evaluation methodology – it is *not* AI psychometrics – and does not further develop, adapt or select IQ tests for AI systems. It is a redefinition or new roadmap for AI: "psychometric AI [is] the field devoted to building [these systems]" (Bringsjord, 2011). In fact, PAI does not explicitly claim that psychometric tests are the best way to evaluate AI systems. Furthermore, unlike Detterman's challenge, there is no selection, since the agglomeration of *all tests must be considered*.

About the validity of the approach, they state the necessity and the sufficiency of PAI in an unequivocal way: an "agent is intelligent if and only if it excels at all established, validated tests of intelligence" (Bringsjord, 2011). This is surprising, since they later seem to recognise that the use of "all established, validated tests of intelligence and mental ability, . . . , tests of artistic and literary creativity, mechanical ability, and so on" (Bringsjord, 2011) relies on an agreement of what an 'established, validated test' is and a sample of "the myriad tests that psychometricians have validated" (Bringsjord and Schimanski, 2003). However, we must bear in mind that a battery of tests is just *a* larger test. The result will not necessarily be more diverse; this will depend on the composition, frequency and weight that is given for each test, and the way one or more aggregated indicators are derived (again we are back to Eq. 2.1).

Detterman and Bringsjord are right in that some psychometric tests can be much better than most task-oriented evaluation approaches in artificial intelligence. However, even if we prevent overfitting by a careful selection of a broad range of tests and keep them secret until their administration, psychometric tests devised for humans are not generally appropriate for other groups because of many reasons:

- Anthropocentrism: psychometric tests used for humans are, by definition and practice, *anthropocentric*. The tests make many assumptions about the subjects, such as the interactions between cognitive processes, that may not hold for other kinds of subjects, so leading to inaccurate measurement. Also, "standardized tests generally omit aspects of the subject that 'any [human] fool knows' because these are not worth testing" (Davis, 2014).

- Administration: many psychometric tests are just presented using instructions in natural language, even if they do not evaluate natural language. For a system without language abilities, this is like evaluating a human using a language she does not understand. This is not specific to computers; tests for animals are administered with rewards and penalties, not instructions.

- Representation: We do not know what many psychometric tests measure, since they are not representational – based on a definition – but just configured and selected after decades of evaluation over, again, human populations.

- Calibration: The instances of a task, and their difficulty, are chosen, yet again, relative to a human population, and the scales that result from the results are normed for a population. Given an AI system, we do not know what range of difficulties to use, taking for granted that these difficulty estimations make sense for a system whose computational resources are clearly different from those of a human.

- Training: There are specialised systems, such as the Perl program from Sanghi and Dowe (2003), but also general systems, such as Spaun (Eliasmith et al., 2012), that could score well in some tasks found in psychometric tests – after some training. The percentage of "all established, validated tests" for which these learning systems can score well is difficult to estimate and may depend on the training procedures.

- Unpredictability: It is unclear why some tasks are more 'computer-unfriendly' (or AI-hard) than others. Today, specialised systems can solve – separately – letter series, word analogies, odd-one-out, Raven's progressive matrices, verbal tests and many others (Hernández-Orallo et al., 2016). However, the correlation of a test with the g factor in humans does not seem to explain whether current AI technology solves the particular problem. In fact, series completion tasks show high g loadings and are well solved by AI systems, whereas many challenging CAPTCHAS may have very low g loadings if used to evaluate humans.

Actually, there was an interesting debate between "standardised" tests from psychometrics and tests devised on purpose for state-of-the-art AI held by Clark and Etzioni (2016) and Davis (2016) in a special issue about AI evaluation (Marcus et al., 2016). However, most of these issues apply not only to the standardised psychometric tests but also to other tests if they are inspired by them or if they are "chosen to be easy for people, and are likely to be hard for AI programs, in the current state of the art" (Davis, 2016), like CAPTCHAs. Nevertheless, some criticisms are only applicable to the standardised psychometric tests, adding to the list of issues. For instance, it is easy to explain why Ohlsson et al. (2013) say that a system such as ConceptNet can "achieve" the "verbal IQ of a four-year old", but at the same time state that the "results do not show that ConceptNet has the verbal abilities [of] a four-year-old" (Ohlsson et al., 2015). This is yet more evidence that the use of psychometric tests for evaluating AI systems is flawed.

The key issue to understanding the unsuitability of these tests is that psychometric tests are devised and validated for a group. In fact, there is no need to go beyond the *Homo sapiens* to see this. For instance, standardised adult IQ tests do not work for people with disabilities or children of different ages. Similarly, we do not use most of the myriads of human psychometric tests for animals. It would be pointless. Only a small subset of items is meaningful, and only for some animals. So, it is preposterous to think that, if a machine comes out of the blue, one would be able to choose an off-the-shelf psychometric test for humans or an animal test from comparative psychology that would give an accurate result. For instance, what kind of test battery would be chosen for the evaluation of *animats* (Williams and Beer, 2010) or the dustbot in Panel 1.1? Would we use an IQ test, a developmental test for children, an association test used for chimpanzees or a spatial test used for rats? Also, would the same battery be chosen if we are given the information that the machine is far below human abilities, far above or with a very different psychometric profile?

Things get worse if we are interested in particular features. How can we be sure that a test for feature X in group A also measures X in group B? For instance, we can have overwhelming evidence that a test is distinctive and highly correlated with a factor in an adult human population, but is this extrapolatable outside the population? Considering the pigeon example again (Panel 6.2), choice reaction time is correlated with intelligence in adult humans (Deary et al., 2001), but should we use it to infer general intelligence in children, non-human animals and ultimately computers?

Summing up, the use of psychometric or other human tests for AI evaluation reappears from time to time (Clark, 2015; Hernández-Orallo et al., 2016; Clark and Etzioni, 2016) but it is, at least, controversial. We have seen a series of arguments showing that their use for computers is ill-conceived in general; only a few tests should be reused, with extreme care. Similar arguments are further developed in (Dowe and Hernández-Orallo, 2012; Besold, 2014; Besold et al., 2015; Davis, 2016), in terms of specificity and generality of psychometric tests for computers.

6.4 CROSS-DISCIPLINE UNIFICATION OR REFOUNDATION?

If psychometric tests are not the way to evaluate AI and, by extension, the whole machine kingdom, what should we use for a feature-oriented evaluation? A crucial issue is the validity range of a test:

Keynote 6.3. The **validity range** of a test is the subset of the machine kingdom for which the test is valid.

A test with universal validity range would be a "universal test" (Hernández-Orallo and Dowe, 2010; Hernández-Orallo et al., 2014), valid for humans, non-human animals, computers, hybrids and collectives. Yampolskiy (2015a, p. 28) refers to these tests in the following way: "Of course the problem of measuring intelligence is that no universal tests exist. Measures such as IQ tests and performance on specific tasks are not universally accepted and are always highly biased against non-human intelligences". The question is whether universal tests *can* exist for intelligence and other behavioural features and, if so, how they should be constructed.

We will return to this issue in Chapter 16, only when a more solid theoretical underpinning is ready and the necessary adaptability of these tests is fully realised. Before that and throughout the rest of the book we will see that some psychometric tests can be reused or adapted for the purpose of universal validity, especially those that have a representational definition (we know what they measure) or are associated with sensorimotor tasks. This is quite common in developmental robotics and the evaluation of some cognitive architectures. For instance, apart from the Cognitive Decathlon already seen, some benchmarks in AI and robotics are inspired by developmental tests, such as the staged developmental test (Keedwell, 2010), and some sensorimotor test batteries for developmental robotics (Sinapov and Stoytchev, 2010; Schenck and Stoytchev, 2012; Schenck et al., 2012; Schenck, 2013). We will investigate some of these in Chapter 12.

Before universal tests become ready, many comparisons are being made and can serve many purposes. Firstly, even if a test is not universal, we can analyse its validity range. Falsifying tests for groups of individuals is then one of the goals of universal psychometrics, to determine the range of each test. This is what we have discussed in the previous section about IQ tests. Secondly, comparisons can help us better understand what psychometric tests actually

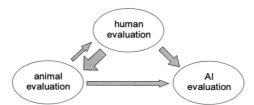

Figure 6.1. Tools, concepts and tests brought across boundaries. The width of the arrow symbolises the strength of the current transfer between disciplines.

measure. For instance, if a task can be solved by a very simple program but it is challenging for humans, we can analyse and understand the reasons.

Cross-species comparisons (including humans) are becoming more common in comparative cognition (see, e.g., Herrmann et al., 2007, 2010; Shettleworth, 2010a). In these cases, tests are chosen or derived very carefully for the occasion, instead of using standard psychometric tests for humans. Unlike the cross-species comparisons, very few cases are found where the same test is used for the comparison of humans and AI systems, apart from the anecdotal use of IQ tests for computers with other purposes. The few cases where they are really used for comparison purposes, somewhat surprisingly, have taken place for personality traits. In (Woods et al., 2005), the same personality questionnaire is used for robots and humans (two very similar adaptations of Eysenck's three personality factors questionnaire, Eysenck and Eysenck, 1975).

The comparison of animals and 'animats' has also been explored. For instance, rats and a specific kind of robot are compared on the same tasks, as would be done for two different species in comparative cognition (Barrera et al., 2011). A cyborg rat is added to the comparison in (Yu et al., 2016). More unexpectedly, bacteria have also been compared with robots, by contrasting the trajectories of robots and real E. Coli (Meystel and Andrusenko, 2001). All these evaluations are still anecdotal, but will likely become more common in the future, as we will discuss again in Chapter 16.

Having seen the tools, tests and comparisons involving more than one of the main groups discussed so far (humans, non-human animals and AI systems), we realise that AI evaluation is the poorer of the three. It is never the source of any transfer of tools or tests. This is illustrated in Figure 6.1.

This lack of influence of AI evaluation on the other two areas is understandable, since AI is the youngest discipline. Also, AI is still looking for a proper way to go from task-oriented to feature-oriented evaluation – as psychometrics struggled in its early days to derive culture-fair tests, by rejecting those that evaluated knowledge instead of ability. But still, looking at Figure 6.1, we can see how isolated AI evaluation is nowadays. This is exacerbated by the negative answer given to the question of whether artificial intelligence should be measured with human intelligence tests. From this situation, it is perhaps the right time to ask the opposite question: *can human intelligence be measured as a very special case of machine intelligence?*

This would place the machine kingdom as the large target group for evaluation. But this would not, per se, solve the problem. So, what are we really aiming at? Unfortunately, a theory reconciling and explaining the way evaluation is performed in psychometrics, comparative psychology and artificial intelligence is probably too pretentious at the moment. Alternatively, on the other extreme, we could just give in and say that intelligence is not only "in the eye of the beholder" but "in the nature of the beholdee", depending on the kind of subject that is measured. Frankly, this would turn universal psychometrics into a disappointing hotchpotch rather than an integration, mostly because some of the evaluation approaches in these disciplines are less than satisfactory. Instead, we must look for a set of principles that could pervade the three disciplines and facilitate the exchange of old, and the derivation of new, notions, tools and, ultimately, tests.

In our quest for an integration we do not want to make things more complicated. We do not want to presuppose more predefined intelligences ("abstract", "natural", "artificial", "machinable", "computational"), as done by Wang (2009b). As the opening epigraph of the chapter reminds us, the natural problem is "intelligence", without further adjectives (Valiant, 2013). We nevertheless share the ultimate goal expressed by Wang that "natural and artificial intelligence may be quantitatively evaluated on the same foundation". But what should this foundation look like?

Under a representational measurement, tests should emanate from a "definition of intelligence that is applicable to machines as well as humans or even dogs" (Johnson, 1992), such that "our evaluations of machine intelligence should be compatible with our evaluations of human intelligence" (Meystel, 2000a, p. 578). We should ultimately aim at having a both practical and explanatory theory of the measurement of behavioural features in general, and intelligence in particular, independent of the kind of subject.

Where can we start? The computational tradition in cognitive science has led to a tacit agreement between the three main disciplines whose boundaries are being crossed. This accordance states that intelligence, and cognition as a whole, is essentially some kind of *information processing* (Sternberg, 1977; Chandrasekaran, 1990; Shettleworth, 2010b). This minimum agreement will be the starting point for the following chapter.

CHAPTER HIGHLIGHTS

- An important fragmentation of the evaluation of behaviour in different disciplines (Table 6.1).
- Magnified interpretation problems of Morgan's Canon when extended to the boundaries between humans, other animals and the rest of machines (Keynote 6.1).
- Controversial use of psychometric test batteries for AI evaluation, even when covering a wide range of tests (Keynote 6.2, Section 6.3).
- Validity range as the extent of subjects for which a test is valid, with a universal test being one that works for the whole machine kingdom (Keynote 6.3).

Part III

The Algorithmic Confluence

7

Intelligence and Algorithmic Information Theory

It would be nice if we could define intelligence in some other way than "that which gets the same meaning out of a sequence of symbols as we do".... This in turn would support the idea of meaning being an inherent property.

– Douglas R. Hofstadter,
Gödel, Escher, Bach: An Eternal Golden Braid (1979)

WE CAN HOLD a heated discussion about what mathematical theory of the second half of the twentieth century is most explanatory about the world. My stake is algorithmic information theory (AIT). AIT has shed light on various important questions such as what simplicity is, what a random number is, where the limits of mathematics are and how inductive inference can work. But what does AIT have to say about intelligence and its measurement? For good or for bad, AIT contaminates everything, and intelligence will not only be different, but a prototypical example. Of course, there are pitfalls and hurdles in AIT, and this third part of the book becomes more technical as a result, but we will not be able to do without AIT from now on. In this chapter we will introduce the main concepts of AIT with illustrations of how cognitive systems – ants or humans – are pervaded by the main ideas in AIT. As a first application of AIT, we will see how to generate cognitive exercises that are very much like those that appear in many IQ tests. This will unveil what these tests really are.

7.1 INFORMATION AND ALGORITHMS

Nuances apart, there seems to be general agreement in the view of cognition as some kind of information processing. But what is information processing?

Shannon's information theory connects the notions of information coding, probability and communication, but the notion of 'processing' is diluted, as the coding procedures are performed in an idealistic way, as mathematical functions. In cognitive systems, we have much more than coding and communication. How are behaviours executed, modified and transmitted? How many resources are required for each behaviour in a given organism? What we know is that some behaviours are deeply coded into the DNA, retrieved, transformed and deployed into the phenotype. Likewise, other behaviours are composed into neural (or non-neural) control systems, stored, retrieved and deployed back again. In all these cases, there is some kind of computation involved. Indeed, these behaviours are actually *algorithms*, which are executed in and transferred between several milieux (genotype, brain, culture, phenotype). This algorithmic view of nature and cognition goes beyond a computational perspective, common in cognitive science, to a more general perspective that would embrace genes and memes. For instance, Valiant (2013) uses the term *ecorithm* for them.

If behaviours are algorithmic solutions to environmental problems, how much information does an algorithm carry? We can use Shannon's correspondence between self-information (or "surprisal") and probability:

$$I(x) \triangleq -\log \mathbb{P}(x) \tag{7.1}$$

where the logarithm is binary so information is measured in bits. If x is a given phenomenon or a certain behaviour, we have that, from Eq. 7.1, its probability is related to information as $\mathbb{P}(x) = 2^{-I(x)}$. The question is now how much information x carries. How is $I(x)$ measured? For instance, is an *Illacme Plenipes*, a millipede featuring up to 750 legs, necessarily more complex than another species of its family with fewer legs? Or does a bird require thousand times more synapses to record a foraging route that is repeated a thousand times? Is the number 2^{100} simpler than other numbers of similar size?

Algorithmic information theory (AIT) integrates computation, information theory and probability theory to assign low information 'content' and, correspondingly, higher probability, to simple pieces of data. But is this notion of simplicity meaningful and objective? Before introducing some of the key definitions of AIT, let us have a first go at an intuitive notion of simplicity. In Panel 7.1 we elaborate on how many elements are involved in the description of a concept. This first example, though not based on a Turing-complete language, shows that the *shortest description* of a concept (in this case a number) is an intuitive, straightforward concept.

Apart from a myriad of connections that derive from the notion of shortest description, a first interpretation of this notion will accompany us for the rest

Plate 5.4. Maze task built with project Malmo, an AI evaluation platform, over Minecraft, a popular sandbox video game. Left: the view from the AI agent being evaluated. Right: The view from a human agent collaborating with the AI agent. [Courtesy of Microsoft Research.]

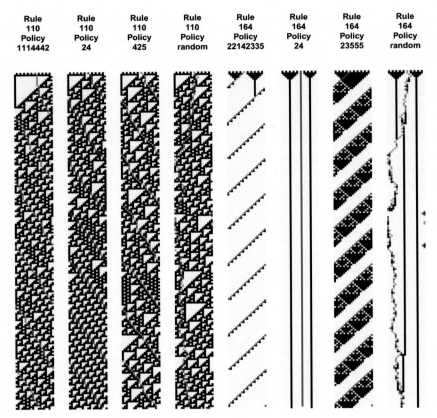

| Rule 110 Policy 1114442 | Rule 110 Policy 24 | Rule 110 Policy 425 | Rule 110 Policy random | Rule 164 Policy 22142335 | Rule 164 Policy 24 | Rule 164 Policy 23555 | Rule 164 Policy random |

Plate 9.4. Space-time diagrams for the ECA rules 110 and 164 during 200 steps with different agent policies ("random" represents a random-walk policy). The initial array (seed) is always 010101010101010101010 (seen along each top row). Cells with 0 and 1 are shown as white and black, respectively. The agent is shown as a red dot when on a 0 cell and a green dot when on a 1 cell. [From (Hernández-Orallo, 2015c), with permission of Springer.]

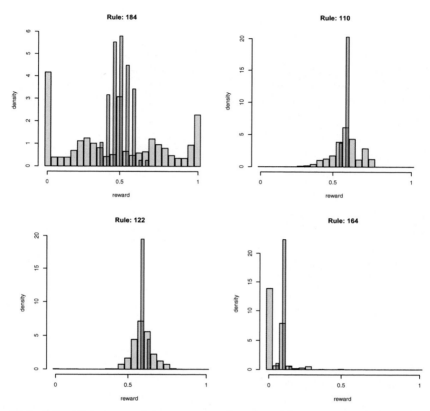

Plate 9.5. Histograms of the responses for rules 184, 110, 122 and 164 using 2,000 policies each running for 300 iterations. Two different groups are normalised to mass 25 and shown: 1,900 generated policies (shown with wide bars in beige) and 100 random-walk policies π_{rand} (shown with narrow bars in purple). [From the work of Hernández-Orallo (2015c), with permission of Springer.]

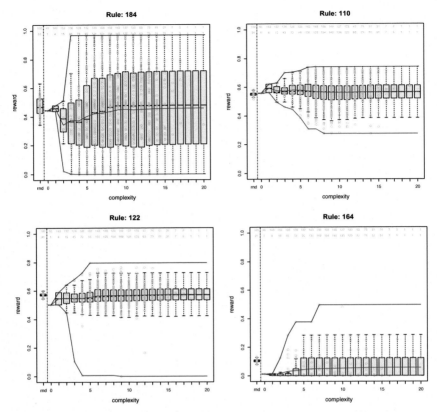

Plate 9.6. The same results of Figure 9.5 where we now detail by the complexity of the policy for the 1,900 generated policies. The number of agents (total and different) per complexity is shown on the two rows at the top of each plot. The 100 random-walk policies are shown on the left of the plots ("rnd" on the *x*-axis). For each value of complexity on the *x*-axis, we show the result of each policy as small circles in grey, and the whisker plots show the inter-quantile distribution for that value of complexity. The solid lines (red, green and blue) show the maximum and minimum envelopes and the average, respectively. [From the work of Hernández-Orallo (2015c), with permission of Springer.]

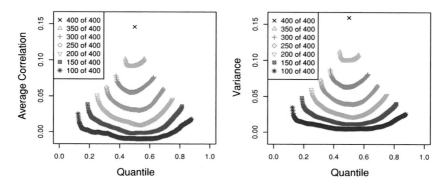

Plate 11.2. Analysis of the existence of a positive manifold for 400 agents (randomly generated programs) and 256 tasks (all the ECA rules, Panel 9.1). Left: average correlation per quantiles using several bin sizes where agents are sorted by overall performance. Right: the variance of the bins.

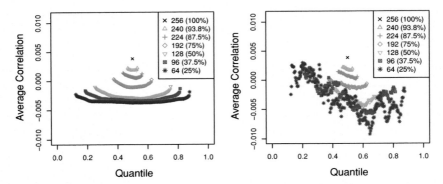

Plate 11.3. Analysis of the existence of a positive manifold for the results of 256 agents (using randomly generated programs with access to the rewards) and 256 tasks (all the ECA rules, as defined in Panel 9.1, with mirrored rewards for half of the trials). Left: average correlation per quantiles using several bin sizes, where results are sorted by agent performance. Right: each bin is only evaluated with the tasks of that quantile of difficulty, for instance, more proficient agents are only evaluated with more difficult tasks.

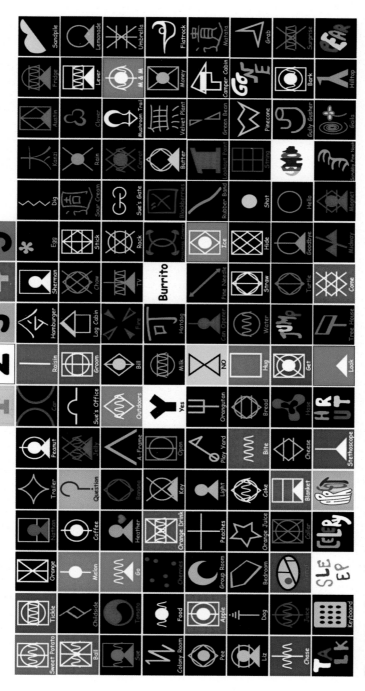

Plate 14.1. Several lexigrams in the Yerkish language used for ape communication. [Courtesy of the Ape Cognition and Conservation Initiative.]

Panel 7.1
Non-universal descriptional complexity

In the *numbers round* of the French TV show "Des chiffres et des lettres", the contestants need to combine six numbers with the four basic arithmetic operations to get a number that approaches another randomly generated target number. Any number and operator can be used as many times as desired or not used at all.

A different (and arguably more fascinating) version of the problem, which I refer to as 'the *o*o*o*o* game', in tribute to the four o's in Solomonoff and Kolmogorov, can be defined by changing the goal to reaching the target exactly with the fewest number of operations. Some examples follow (all with just three operators: $+ - \times$):

$$\{3, 5, 6, 7\} \rightarrow 624? \text{ Solution: } 3 \times 7 \times 5 \times 6 - 6$$
$$\{4, 6, 7, 9\} \rightarrow 968? \text{ Solution: } (9 + 9) \times 9 \times 6 - 4, \text{ or}$$
$$(6 + 6) \times 9 \times 9 - 4$$
$$\{1, 7, 8, 9\} \rightarrow 729? \text{ Solution: } 9 \times 9 \times 9$$

Expressions must be evaluated from left to right.

This particular game is not actually interchangeable with algorithmic information theory for a few reasons. First, if we had some way of coding the expressions, this could never be compressed (our usual representation of decimal numbers relies on the product, so we would require exponentiation to get an advantage for at least a few cases). Second, some problems do not even have a solution, shorter or longer, i.e., they cannot be expressed in the language. The explanation for both reasons is that the language we are using is not Turing-complete.

---

of the book: how many things have to be combined to express something, such as a solution for a problem. This is naturally linked to the notion of difficulty. For instance, choose any domain and a description language. The conceptual (or even cognitive) difficulty of a pattern can be assimilated by the number of elements that need to be combined. This can be done for knitting (Bernasconi et al., 2007), for tile assembling (Soloveichik and Winfree, 2007) or for DNA (Yockey, 2005), just to name some examples.

The previous example of the *o*o*o*o* game uses an unambiguous language (arithmetic with just three operations) that is not Turing-complete. In Panel 7.2 we illustrate a case where the language is universal, but informal, i.e., ambiguous.

Panel 7.2
A universal (but informal) descriptional complexity

Natural language is Turing-complete in the sense that it can represent any possible computation, assuming there is someone understanding the language for its 'interpretation'. One can play a compression game using natural language where the goal is to express a given text with a much lower number of characters. This can be done by exploiting word (or *n*-grams) frequencies, or any other regularity we may find. Young people are exceptionally talented for this kind of game nowadays. For instance, a 13-year-old Scottish girl apparently expressed the following text:

> *My summer holidays were a complete waste of time. Before, we used to go to New York to see my brother, his girlfriend and their three screaming kids face to face. I love New York, it's a great place*

as follows, with a remarkable compression ratio (almost 2:1).

```
My smmr hols wr CWOT. B4, we usd 2go2 NY 2C my bro,
his GF & thr 3 :- kds FTF. ILNY, it's a gr8 plc
```

Though this seems to be a media hoax (the age of the girl varies depending on the source, Holtgraves, 2014, p. 349, or BBC, 2003), it is still symptomatic of the features of natural language for representation. Natural language depends on the interpretation skills of the receiver, as it is highly contextual. This includes the capability of coding a message according to the sender's knowledge about the receiver's knowledge and capabilities.

It is only when we put together a universal and unambiguous descriptional mechanism that we have universal computation. The universal Turing machine (UTM) was first introduced in 1936, as we saw in Panel 1.2, but most programming languages today are also Turing-complete. In the texting example, we can express the same information with approximately half the length. This is as if information, which could be well *quantified* by Shannon's information theory, became malleable. As the modern view of information was introduced in 1948, it took about ten years to find the first materialisations of algorithmic information theory, pioneered by Ray Solomonoff, and independently discovered by Andrei Kolmogorov and Gregory Chaitin a few years later. The so-called Kolmogorov complexity is easy to be defined, given the notion of universal machine. For technical convenience, in what follows, we will assume *prefix* universal Turing machines, where programs are self-delimited, so that no program is a prefix of another program (see Li and Vitányi, 2008 for details). Many programming languages are prefix-free as they use block delimiters (e.g., "END").

Given a universal Turing machine U and a program p, we denote by $U(p)$ the result of executing the program p on U. Note that U takes binary strings and outputs binary strings. We will use $L(S)$ to denote the length, in bits, of a string S, be it a program or not. Now we define:

Keynote 7.1. The **Kolmogorov, or algorithmic, complexity** of a string x using *reference* machine U, denoted by $K_U(x)$, is the length of its shortest description.

For instance, the Kolmogorov complexity of a sequence of a million ones or the first million digits of the number π is low, as there are short algorithms, i.e., computer programs, outputting them. Formally,

$$K_U(x) \triangleq \min_{p\,:\,U(p)=x} L(p) \tag{7.2}$$

What choices do we have for U? Infinitely many. Today, almost any programming language of our choice is a universal machine. The key property of a universal machine U is that it can emulate any other machine V, i.e., there is an interpreter for U such that any program for V can be executed in U. For the *o*o*o*o* game seen in Panel 7.1, the description language is not universal. What is so important in using universal languages for the definition? The first reason is that only with universal languages can we express all the possible patterns there are in the data. Imagine that the data express a sonnet, the number π or the stripes of a zebra. Some of the patterns involved in them may require recursion and other ways of iteration. The second, closely related, reason is the *invariance theorem*, first proved by Solomonoff, which states that given any machine V and a universal machine U, there is a constant c, which only depends on V and U, such that $\forall x : K_U(x) \le K_V(x) + c$. The proof is just based on U being universal, so there is an interpreter for V that can be written in U. Consequently, if the shortest program for x in V requires n bits and the interpreter requires c bits, then a program in U cannot take more than $c + n$ bits. The constant c is usually large, from hundreds to thousands of bits for some simple universal programming languages.

This result can be taken more or less optimistically. For large strings, the constant becomes less relevant, and the notion of Kolmogorov complexity is less dependent on the reference machine. For short strings, however, the usefulness of the theorem is limited. Nonetheless, there are some comments to be made: (1) For many compressible strings x, there is no need for one machine to emulate the other to express x shortly. For instance, a string composed of a hundred ones can be coded with a short program for the overwhelming majority of computer programming languages we know of. (2) A clear difference of the complexities of two strings x and y for one machine U, namely $K_U(x) < K_U(y)$, may still hold for many other machines V, i.e., $K_V(x) < K_V(y)$. In fact, even if the magnitudes are different, the relative proportions may be similar for the two different machines. (3) The differences and the constants become smaller if we use languages with a very simple syntax and, for convenience, prefix-free. Some versions of Lisp meet these conditions. More recently, a minimal version of Lambda Calculus with binary encoding has been suggested as a good choice for a reference machine (Tromp, 2006). (4) Lastly, there are some ways (e.g., Delahaye and Zenil, 2012; Soler-Toscano et al., 2014, using the coding theorem we will see later) of approximating a more stable version of Kolmogorov complexity for short strings.

Nonetheless, this *relativity* of Kolmogorov complexity is not necessarily a negative thing, as if K were exactly the same for all machines, it would be inconsistent with the observation that some descriptional mechanisms are more suitable or efficient than others. Also, some languages and individuals may have some predefined or acquired algorithms, which help them to describe new concepts much more concisely. For instance, the complexity we are measuring for the *o*o*o*o* game seen in Panel 7.1 assumes that the language – the reference machine – has a definition of the operations $+$, $-$ and $\times$. Imagine that another machine did not have these definitions. Then, it would require much larger programs, as the definition of the arithmetic operations should be included in the description. So, to *compare* two machines in fair terms for this game, we should ensure that both of them have the same *background knowledge*, i.e., the same basic concepts for the problem in hand. This idea, common in evolution and cognitive development, has a very simple translation to the notion of *conditional* Kolmogorov complexity, defined as follows:

$$K_U(x|y) \triangleq \min_{p\,:\,U(\langle y,p\rangle)=x} L(p) \tag{7.3}$$

which means that the conditional Kolmogorov complexity of x given y is the shortest program for x assuming we have y as background knowledge (e.g., as an included programming library). Imagine two different programming languages with the same set of constructs or theory y for a particular domain. If they are used to calculate the shortest descriptions for a group of objects then the relative order (and even the spread) of the conditional complexities for the two machines may be very similar. This is the reason why two different people, when given the same rules for combination, usually get equivalent shortest expressions for the same objects. We will come back to this phenomenon at the end of the chapter.

Finally, another property of the function K_U is its incomputability for any universal machine due to the halting problem. To quell the detractors, Solomonoff said: "Incomputability – it's not a bug, it's a feature!" (Solomonoff, 2010), but in practice we would all like to have some effective procedure to calculate or approximate K. One of these approximations, which also has some interesting properties we will exploit in this and other chapters, is Levin's Kt (Levin, 1973; Li and Vitányi, 2008):

$$Kt_U(x) \triangleq \min_{p\,:\,U(p)=x} LS(p) \qquad (7.4)$$

where

$$LS(p) \triangleq L(p) + \log S(p) \qquad (7.5)$$

with $S(p)$ being the number of computational steps taken by p to print x and halt. Also referred to as Levin complexity, it can be expressed more plainly:

> **Keynote 7.2.** The **Levin complexity** of a string x is a measure of the optimality of the best description for x in terms of a trade-off between the size of the program and its execution time.

Kt is closely related to the concept of Levin's universal search, which we will discuss in other chapters. For the moment, we can anticipate that the number of computational steps required to find p (from nothing) by a Levin's universal search is bounded by the minimum of $2^{L(p)} \times S(p)$, whose logarithm is Kt. This means that the *unit* of Kt is the logarithm of computational steps. Many of the properties of K are preserved, but Kt becomes computable. Also, it incorporates processing effort, which is arguably a feature that any measure of complexity should consider.

7.2 SIMPLICITY IN COGNITION: ANTS AND BITS

So, what do we have up to now? We have an *objective* notion of simplicity. We say objective but not absolute, as it depends on the reference machine chosen or the *background knowledge* of the machine (which was made manifest with the notion of conditional complexity). Simplicity, and particularly the notion given by algorithmic information theory or the related structural information

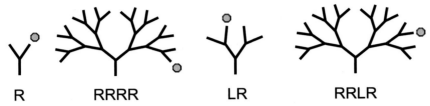

R   RRRR   LR   RRLR

Figure 7.1. Ants communicate the location of food (represented by a small circle) in several tree-like structures. The transcription of the route that has to be taken for each binary tree is shown on the bottom. [Adapted from (Ryabko and Reznikova, 2009).]

theory, has been long advocated as a fundamental cognitive principle (Krueger and Osherson, 1980; Chater, 1999; Chater and Vitányi, 2003; Feldman, 2000, 2003; Leeuwenberg and Van Der Helm, 2012).

Let us give a very illustrative example of Kolmogorov complexity in animal cognition. In a series of painstaking and revealing works, Zhanna Reznikova and Boris Ryabko studied the communication between ants. In one of the most striking experiments (Reznikova and Ryabko, 2003; Ryabko and Reznikova, 2009), ant 'scouts' were sent to find food in a tree-like structure, where the food was only located in one of the 2^n leaves. Once back, the scout had to communicate to the other 'foraging' ants where food was located in the tree-like structure. The experiments showed that the scouts were able to communicate the information about where the food was, so that the foraging ant could go directly to the place the scout had previously found.

Figure 7.1 shows some of these structures and the location of the food in each of them. Below each case we show the sequence of movements the ant has to do to find the food, using L for left and R for right.

The most interesting thing in the experiment was the analysis of the simplicity of the information that had to be transmitted. First, one could expect that the effort of transmitting the location of the food would solely depend on the size of the trees. If all locations in the trees were equally likely, using Shannon's theory of information, we would have expected that for a tree of depth 4 we would require 4 bits of information. However, when the time taken by a scout to communicate the location to the other agents was more precisely analysed, the times did not show this flat dependency on the size of the tree. Table 7.1 shows that those locations with a more *regular* or simple pattern usually required less time.

Ryabko and Reznikova (2009) gave the following explanation: "according to Kolmogorov [complexity] the word LLLLLLLL can be represented as 8L, the word LRLRLRLR as 4LR, while the 'random' word of shorter length LRRLRL

Table 7.1. Duration of the transmission of information between ants for different food locations in a tree-like structure. [Data from the work of Ryabko and Reznikova (2009).]

No.	Location	Mean duration (sec)
1	LL	72
2	RRR	75
3	LLLL	84
4	RRRRR	78
5	LLLLLL	90
6	RRRRRR	88
7	LRLRLR	130
8	RLRLRL	135
9	LLR	69
10	LRLL	100
11	RLLR	120
12	RRLRL	150
13	RLRRRL	180
14	RRLRRR	220
15	LRLLRL	200

probably cannot be expressed more concisely, and this is the most complex of the three". Naturally, patterns were found and used only when it was worth, Ryabko and Reznikova (2009) clarify: "ants began to use regularities to compress only quite large 'words'.... There was no essential difference when the length of sequences was less than 4".

The conclusions of the study "reveal that ants are able to grasp regularities and to use them for 'compression' of information" (Ryabko and Reznikova, 2009). Similar findings have been found in other animals (Reznikova, 2007). Nevertheless, in other animal cognition research, serial patterns are rarely analysed in terms of algorithmic complexity, with only informal accounts of their "entropy" (e.g., auditory series for songbirds, Comins and Gentner, 2010) or no account at all about their difficulty (lever series for rats, Fountain, 2006).

The arguments we have seen are of sufficient entity to justify a wider use of algorithmic information theory in cognitive science and, most especially, in the evaluation of cognitive abilities. However, these arguments are basically *methodologic* (or *explanatory*), i.e., they represent the intuitive fact that complex procedures require more resources, be it molecular machinery (DNA pairs) or brain machinery (neurons and synapses). AIT is an objective way of

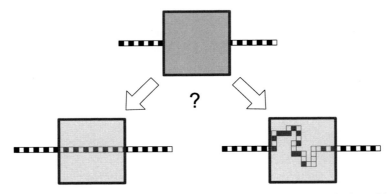

Figure 7.2. Example of perceptual inference in the case of occlusion. Given an object partially covered by a square (top), which of the two hypotheses is more plausible for human perception, bottom left or bottom right? [Adapted and combined from several figures in the work of Chater and Vitányi (2003), Dinnerstein and Wertheimer (1957), and Gerbino and Salmaso (1987).]

quantifying these *procedural* resources and will be a fundamental tool in our discussion of difficulty, which we will undertake in Chapter 8.

7.3 INDUCTION AND COMPRESSION

The previous section has shown examples of the *methodological* perspective of AIT to analyse how patterns are effectively represented and communicated. We are now interested in the *epistemological* perspective of AIT. For instance, the top of Figure 7.2 depicts a striped stick that is occluded by another object, a square. From the two possibilities at the bottom, which one is more plausible? Clearly, the one on the left is simpler, and its Kolmogorov complexity would be lower than the one on the right. But is this a reason to choose one of them? Or is it still completely arbitrary? In other words, should all consistent hypotheses be kept, à la Epicurus ("the Principle of Multiple Explanations"), or should we just keep the shortest hypothesis, à la Occam ("the Principle of Parsimony")?

> **Keynote 7.3. The scandal of induction**: Given some factual evidence and two possible inductive hypotheses that are consistent with it, is there any objective reason to prefer one over the other?

C. D. Broad (1926) hoped that by "Bacon's next centenary, Inductive Reasoning, which has long been the glory of Science, will have ceased to be the scandal of Philosophy". It was a few decades later, in 1960, that Ray Solomonoff circulated "a preliminary report on a general theory of inductive inference" (Solomonoff, 1960), which managed to "solve the problem of induction" (Solomonoff, 1964a).

Solomonoff, "as a teenager, . . . became captivated by the idea of machines that could think, and began to search for a general method to solve mathematical problems" (Solomonoff, 2010). Why did this quest for a general method of thinking and solving problems – yet again an *ars generalis* – end up in a general theory of inductive inference?

This is what we will explain in what follows, with the minimum technical details that will be required for the rest of this and the following chapters. For those finding this section too technical, the highlights at the end of the chapter summarise the key ideas. For more details about the discovery of algorithmic probability and Solomonoff's contributions or a more formal exposition of AIT, the interested reader can see (Solomonoff, 1964a,b, 1996, 1997; Hutter et al., 2007; Li and Vitányi, 2008; Gács and Vitányi, 2011; Dowe, 2013).

Let us imagine we see some data x emerging from an object or process in your surrounding universe: sun rising and setting, the song of a bird, the sections in a mandarin or a Shakespearean play. It is not difficult to see that all of them feature some regularities, some patterns. Actually, every possible piece of data we can perceive has ultimately been produced by a process in the universe. Assume that the process is *computable*, which means that there is a mechanism behind it – a mechanistic view of the universe – and also that the mechanism is finite, a consequence of the assumption of a finite universe. Note that we are not assuming that the mechanism is deterministic, so we are actually considering the data you see follow a computable distribution $\mu(x)$. Panel 7.3 shows and example.

Now we consider that we have seen the first n bits x of a sequence generated by μ (in our example a series of die throws x coded as a binary string). We would like to estimate the probability of the next bit b after x, with the lowest possible error with respect to the true probability, represented by $\mu(b|x)$. Solomonoff's *prediction error theorem* (1978, Theorem 3, p. 426) says that there is a general distribution $M_U(x)$, such that, if used as an estimation for μ, we have for all n:

$$\sum_n S_n \leq \frac{\ln 2}{2}k \qquad (7.6)$$

where k is a finite constant, and S_n is the expected squared error between the true probability and the estimated probability for the next bit, averaged for all strings of size n, i.e., $\sum_{L(x)=n} \mu(x)(\mu(0|x) - M_U(0|x))^2$. Note that from the

---

Panel 7.3
Loaded dice and Solomonoff's prediction

A croupier throws a loaded die A with a distribution μ_A with probabilities $\mathbb{P}_A(1) = 0.29$, $\mathbb{P}_A(2) = 0.11$, $\mathbb{P}_A(3) = 0.27$, $\mathbb{P}_A(4) = 0.13$, $\mathbb{P}_A(5) = 0.15$ and $\mathbb{P}_A(6) = 0.05$. A series of throws with this die is a sequence such as 3132154213544411123621. If we do not know the distribution, it is easy to estimate the probabilities accurately, by simple counting, given a sufficiently large series.

But the croupier also uses a second die B with a distribution μ_B with probabilities $\mathbb{P}_B(1) = 0.03$, $\mathbb{P}_B(2) = 0.43$, $\mathbb{P}_B(3) = 0.17$, $\mathbb{P}_B(4) = 0.03$, $\mathbb{P}_B(5) = 0.05$ and $\mathbb{P}_B(6) = 0.29$. Unknown to the players of the table, the croupier swaps die A and B (and vice versa) every 100 throws, so the actual distribution is an alternate version (not a mixture) of both distributions, which we denote by $\mu_{\{100A|100B\}^*}$. Will we ever be able to notice and capture this 'alternating' distribution correctly?

Surprisingly, there is a general method that always finds the rule under this and whatever other possible computable distributions. This method is Solomonoff's prediction.

---

convergence of $\sum_n S_n$ given by Eq. 7.6 we can derive that $\lim_{n\to\infty} S_n = 0$. In other words, we have that M_U converges to μ, very fast (compare with the harmonic series). In plain words, for the example in Panel 7.3, after a sufficient number of throws, M_U will capture how much both dice are loaded and the alternation. In the example, we will not be able to forecast each throw, which is impossible in this non-deterministic case, but to calculate (with more and more precision) the probabilities of the six sides of each die and do it appropriately for each 100-throw round. The die swapping every 100 throws is just a figurative possibility, among infinitely many others, to illustrate the point that Eq. 7.6 holds for *any* computable distribution.

Any inductive inference problem we may face could be solved if we had M_U. Actually, this would be a *general* solution for the induction problem. But what is behind k and M_U? The constant k is just given by $K_U(\mu)$, i.e., it is the Kolmogorov complexity of the distribution μ. This can be a large constant. For instance, for Panel 7.3, if we were using English as representation language, $K_{Eng}(\mu_{\{100A|100B\}^*})$ would be a few lines of text in English (about the size of Panel 7.3), assuming all the necessary concepts are already in *Eng* (knowledge about probabilities, repetitions, series, etc.).

But what is this magic M_U? Surprisingly, the definition of M_U is relatively straightforward:

> **Keynote 7.4.** The **universal distribution** of a string prefix z for a universal machine U, denoted by $M_U(z)$, is the probability that U outputs a string starting with z when fed with random bits.

More formally, it is the probability that a universal machine U outputs a string that starts with z when fed by a program p composed of an infinite sequence of random bits:

$$M_U(z) \triangleq \sum_{p \,:\, U(p)=z*} 2^{-L(p)} \tag{7.7}$$

In other words, if we take a programming language, we can generate all possible programs p and derive the probability of each one as $2^{-L(p)}$ and sum all the probabilities for those that produce an output starting with z. This M_U is just the solution of our induction problem. For Panel 7.3, if we consider $x = 313215421354411123621$ (appropriately coded as a binary string), M_U can give us the probability that the following throw is any of the six sides, by just calculating $M_U(1|x), M_U(2|x), \ldots, M_U(6|x)$.

Is this M_U the longed-for *ars generalis*? In theory, it looks like it. We say in theory because M_U is not computable (technically, it is lower semi-computable, i.e., a semi-computable semi-measure). The incomputability for M_U happens – apart from the non-halting problem – because Eq. 7.7 uses an infinite sum. It is *a weighted average of all possible programs that are consistent with the evidence*. This is, remarkably, a compromise between Epicurus and Occam: all hypotheses are considered, but short ones are given a higher a priori probability. The scandal of induction is solved.

As we will further discuss in Chapter 11, this also has implications in our interpretation of the no-free-lunch (NFL) theorems (Wolpert and Macready, 1995; Wolpert, 1996, 2012):

> **Keynote 7.5.** The **no-free-lunch theorems** state that when all problems are considered, no method can be better than any other "on average". These theorems assume that this "on average" obeys any distribution such that (blocks of) problems can be shuffled without affecting the probability.

This can be expressed more technically as "block uniformity" (Igel and Toussaint, 2005). Since the uniform distribution is a special case, the condition is sometimes informally understood as that all problems are equally probable, and hence all the predictions, dooming us to the scandal of induction once again. But if no method can work better than any other, how is it possible that Solomonoff's prediction not only works well, but optimally? Where is the explanation? The answer lies in the notion of computable distribution, which implies that there is a finite machine behind it. If we consider all possible distributions, but they are computable, then it is not reasonable to assume "block uniformity", because when uniformly random bits are fed into a universal Turing machine, the output is no longer uniformly random. This is consistent with the idea that problems are generated by the *output* of physical laws, processes, living creatures, etc., so that true random data are unlikely. Indeed, there are optimal methods (*free lunches*) for inductive inference (Lattimore and Hutter, 2013), co-evolution (Wolpert and Macready, 2005) and other search problems (though for optimisation the free lunches are very small, Everitt et al., 2014).

There are other relevant properties about M_U. We need a different variant of *algorithmic probability*:

$$m_U(z) \triangleq \sum_{p\,:\,U(p)=z} 2^{-L(p)} \tag{7.8}$$

In this variant, the programs must halt after outputting z (compare with Eq. 7.7). A practical property is that for any computable distribution there is a universal distribution that can approximate it. Even for distributions that give all the mass to a finite number of objects, there are 'similar' universal distributions that approximate them. For instance, if we consider a very simple and extreme distribution for which $\mu(x) = 1$ and $\mu(x') = 0$ for every $x' \neq x$ then we can find a machine U such that all programs with size lower than 20 output the same string x. Hence, the probability of x is about $1 - 2^{-20}$ and only a minute 2^{-20} is left for the rest – the exact values depend on the prefix coding. The universal distribution μ_U is then a very precise approximation to μ

That means that universal distributions can be very different from each other. Because of the invariance theorem, we can loosely talk about *the* Kolmogorov complexity of an object and omit the reference machine, because at least for long strings, the magnitudes will be comparable. But for the universal distributions, as we have seen, the thing is inverted – so are the definitions –; short strings (for which the invariance theorem has little effect) take most of the mass of the distribution. As a result, we cannot talk, not even loosely, about *the* universal distribution. Also, when using them, the choice of the reference machine is critical.

We have gone through some technicalities here because the details will help us unmask two common misconception about Solomonoff's theory of inductive inference. First, the theory accounts for stochastic data sources, as it is based on estimating the distribution of the data, and not on finding perfect predictions. Nonetheless, if the data are not stochastic, Solomonoff's theory works equally well (or better, as the problem is easier). The second one is that Solomonoff's theory does *not* compress the data, as it is a *mixture* of all possible hypotheses. This is relevant for cognition and for scientific discovery, as Solomonoff's theory is an excellent predictor, but does not explain the phenomenon it predicts well for. Terminologically, it can even be argued whether we should just use the term 'prediction' for Solomonoff's theory instead of 'induction'.

Anyway, apart from the theoretical results and these clarifications, any practical use of Solomonoff's theory must go through the use of a few (instead of all) hypotheses and its calculation with limited resources. This is actually of more interest for cognitive science and for the evaluation of cognitive systems, as these have limited resources. In this direction, there is an important result that we have to bring ahead, the *coding theorem* (Levin, 1974; Li and Vitányi, 2008), which says that there is a constant c, which only depends on U, such that for every string x:

$$| \log m_U(x) + K_U(x)| < c \qquad (7.9)$$

Note that the first term is negative, so this says that the difference between the magnitude of the logarithm of the universal probability of a string and its Kolmogorov complexity is bounded. Actually, we can loosely write $m_U(x) \sim 2^{-K_U(x)}$, which, compared with Eq. 7.1, gives us an interpretation of K as (self-)information with m as (algorithmic) probability, in Shannon terms. They are two sides of the same coin (actually, both sides – input and output – of the same UTM).

This interpretation (and the impossibility of effectively calculating Solomonoff's mixture) has led to the use of one hypothesis instead of all of them. Actually, the idea is to choose the consistent hypothesis with the shortest description. Apart from being much simpler, it is the hypothesis that captures the largest share of Solomonoff's mixture. However, there is a price to pay if we surrender to Occam but disregard Epicurus; using the shortest description instead of a mixture of all of them (weighted by their length) also leads to finite loss bounds, but they are exponentially larger than with the mixture (Poland and Hutter, 2005, 2006).

Let us see a very simple way to formalise Occam's razor. Consider some data D and several hypotheses. For each hypothesis h we can choose the hypothesis with highest posterior probability and use Bayes' theorem:

$$\underset{h}{\arg\max}\, \mathbb{P}(h|D) = \underset{h}{\arg\max}\, \frac{\mathbb{P}(h)\mathbb{P}(D|h)}{\mathbb{P}(D)}$$

$$= \underset{h}{\arg\max}\, \mathbb{P}(h)\mathbb{P}(D|h)$$

The denominator vanishes as it is the same for all hypotheses, so the best hypothesis is the one that maximises the product of the prior probability with the conditional probability of the data given the hypothesis. This is standard Bayesian inference. Now, considering K a measure of information or uncertainty as supported by Eq. 7.9, we can use 2^{-K} instead of $\mathbb{P}$, so we have

$$\underset{h}{\arg\max}\, \mathbb{P}(h|D) = \underset{h}{\arg\max}\, 2^{-K(h)}2^{-K(D|h)}$$

$$= \underset{h}{\arg\min}\, K(h) + K(D|h) \qquad (7.10)$$

which can be read as follows:

Keynote 7.6. Bayesian, algorithmic interpretation of Occam's razor: The best hypothesis is the one that minimises the sum of its Kolmogorov complexity and the conditional Kolmogorov complexity of the data given the hypothesis.

Equation 7.10 is a possible interpretation of the Minimum Message Length (MML) principle, first introduced by Wallace and Boulton in 1968 (Wallace and Boulton, 1968; Wallace, 2005), and the related Minimum Description Length, introduced by Rissanen in 1978 (Rissanen, 1978; Grünwald et al., 2005). The basic idea of both approaches is compression with a two-part code, the two terms in Eq. 7.10, the theory and the exceptions to the theory, by finding a good balance in the minimisation of both things. Both the MML and the MDL principles are based on approximations of the coding and not on Kolmogorov complexity itself (Wallace and Dowe, 1999), but both have a tendency for codings that achieve compression. Indeed, the MML and the MDL principles helped popularise the view of inductive inference as compression. Actually, this view has pervaded pattern recognition, machine learning and artificial intelligence in the past decades (Watanabe, 1972; Vitányi and Li, 1997; Cilibrasi and Vitányi, 2005; Sculley and Brodley, 2006).

Be it two-part or one-part compression, the goal is to select *the* most plausible hypothesis. This is crucial for cognitive systems, especially when patterns need to be transmitted. Humans, for instance, usually work with one plausible explanation, model or theory about a phenomenon (or at most a few) and not an infinite ensemble of hypotheses. This makes 'mind reading' and intention possible, as some individuals can identify what other agents have in mind, which is usually one and not many hypotheses.

7.4 INTELLIGENCE TESTS FROM AIT: THE *C*-TEST

After the most relevant concepts of AIT have been introduced in the previous sections, we are ready to discuss some of the first implications of algorithmic information theory for the evaluation of cognition. It is worth starting with the discussion of the relation between compression and comprehension. One way of determining whether someone has understood a concept is to ask them to explain it in different words, to avoid 'rote learning' (the use of the *explanandum* in the *explanans*). Avoiding 'rote learning' was one of the principles that guided one of the fathers of psychometrics, Alfred Binet, when designing his first tests: "It is the intelligence alone that we seek to measure, by disregarding in so far as possible the degree of instruction which the child possesses.... We give him nothing to read, nothing to write, and submit him to no test in which he might succeed by means of rote learning" (Binet and Simon, 1905). That is exactly the distinction between an *extensional* definition, such as $\{2, 3, 5, 7, 11, 13, 17, 19\}$ and an *intensional* one, such as $\{x < 20 \ : \ \text{prime}(x)\}$. There are, however, many ways of disguising rote learning for the previous set, such as $\{x - 1 \ : \ x \in \{3, 4, 6, 8, 12, 14, 18, 20\}\}$ or $\{x < 20 : (odd(x) \lor x = 2) \land x \neq 1 \land x \neq 9 \land x \neq 15\}$. Nevertheless, a high compression ratio between the explanandum and the explanans ensures that some pattern has been identified. However, it does not mean that all of the explanandum has been understood nor that the compression ratio is evenly distributed for all the data. For instance, as we can see in the expression of the MML principle in Eq. 7.10, the principle can prefer some exceptions in $K(D|h)$ if $K(h)$ is low, instead of another hypothesis without exceptions but a much higher $K(h)$. The derivation of a version of Eq. 7.10 without exceptions is not easy, as exceptions can be concealed in the theory relatively easy, as in the preceding examples. Further discussion on these issues can be found in (Hernández-Orallo and García-Varea, 2000; Hernández-Orallo, 2000e,c).

Despite the nuances, except for small concepts (for which compression is difficult or impossible), compression and comprehension are closely intertwined (Dowe and Hajek, 1997, sec. 2.1). This has suggested expressions such as "compression is comprehension" (Feldman, 2003) or "comprehension is compression" (Chaitin, 2002). However, the relation is not of perfect necessary and sufficient equivalence (Hernández-Orallo, 2000b).

The relation between compression and comprehension hinges upon the procedural and epistemological sides of AIT. The procedural side has to do with information being communicated and stored as efficiently as possible in cognitive processes. The epistemological side has to do with compressed information capturing regularities of the environment and helping understand the world and predict future events with plausibility. From this rationale, it is not difficult to think that those cognitive systems that are able to detect more complex patterns and further compress the evidence can be said to be more 'intelligent'. This has led to the connection, if not the identification, of intelligence, inductive ability and compression ability.

Indeed, it was soon realised that some exercises in IQ tests required the extrapolation of a sequence, which was exactly what Solomonoff's programme was about: "given an initial segment of a sequence, predict its continuation" (attributed to Solomonoff by Li and Vitányi, 2008, p. 332). This connection between inductive inference and IQ tests was common in the early days of machine learning and artificial intelligence (Gold, 1967). The references were also very explicit: "intelligence tests occasionally require the extrapolation of an effective sequence (e.g. 1661, 2552, 3663, ...) that is produced by some easily discernible algorithm" (Blum and Blum, 1975).

To better understand this connection, let us have a look at one of these IQ exercises. In particular, Panel 7.4 shows Thurstone letter series completion problems.

We can easily see the similarities of this problem with some of the examples and terms we have been discussing in previous sections. Of course, the items were invented and selected by Thurstone manually and with no knowledge at all about AIT at the time. So, in hindsight, with our knowledge of AIT nowadays, a relevant question that had to be answered was: can we construct an intelligence test, or at least a set of problems to test one of its components, that is automatically and exclusively produced using AIT? This was the unequivocal claim made by one of the fathers of AIT, Gregory Chaitin, in 1982: "develop formal definitions of intelligence and measures of its various components [using AIT]" (Chaitin, 1982).

Why should we not start with a test measuring compression ability, i.e., a compression test? Unfortunately, this would be an oversimplification of the first suggestions of the use of compression (Dowe and Hajek, 1997) and would lead to "the counter-intuitive results of a first approach like 'intelligence as the ability of universal compression'" (Hernández-Orallo and Minaya-Collado, 1998). What are these counter-intuitive results? They became more evident with some

---

Panel 7.4
The 'intuitive' continuation of Thurstone letter series

Thurstone letter series completion problems were introduced in several test batteries following his primary mental abilities theory (Thurstone, 1938; Thurstone and Thurstone, 1941). Given a sequence of letters from a circular alphabet (the successor of 'z' is 'a' and the predecessor of 'a' is 'z'), the goal is to predict the letter that *intuitively* follows the series. We show some examples (taken from Simon and Kotovsky, 1963):

$a, b, a, b, a, b, a, b, \ldots$
$a, a, a, b, b, b, c, c, c, d, d, \ldots$
$c, a, d, a, e, a, f, a, \ldots$
$w, x, a, x, y, b, y, z, c, z, a, d, a, b, \ldots$
$m, n, l, n, k, n, j, n, \ldots$
$r, s, c, d, s, t, d, e, t, u, e, f, \ldots$

For each item, the subject must choose the continuation from a pool of five possible letter choices.

---

attempts that followed. Mahoney (1999) proposed a test for artificial intelligence as the compression of several English texts. Similarly, in the 'Hutter prize', a 100 MB extract from Wikipedia had to be compressed (Legg and Hutter, 2007b). But what is the point for a human – or another animal – to compress Wikipedia? Why is Wikipedia chosen and not other less redundant source? And why compressing it verbatim? What would it prove? Certainly, not *comprehension*. In fact, for lossless compression, some algorithms achieve much better compression ratios than humans, much better than the 13-year-old texting girl we saw in Panel 7.2. Likewise, computers are much better at lossy compression (e.g., images, audio and video). This alone is a sufficient reason to refute a compression test as a valid intelligence test. It seems that generating a meaningful intelligence test using AIT requires more elaboration.

The *C*-test (Hernández-Orallo and Minaya-Collado, 1998; Hernández-Orallo, 2000a) was proposed as an intelligence test, where intelligence was defined as the ability to comprehend. The letter *C* comes from comprehension, not from compression, and the distinction was emphasised. A formal definition of the notion of comprehension, as the identification of a 'predominant' pattern from a given evidence, was derived using AIT. As a test, the goal was to find a continuation of a sequence of letters, very much like Thurstone letter series. To generate the items, several constructs were introduced:

Panel 7.5
Generating test items using AIT

We see in what follows some of the sequences that were generated for the C-test (Hernández-Orallo and Minaya-Collado, 1998; Hernández-Orallo, 2000a):

h=7	:	$a, b, c, d, ...$	*Answer : e*
h=8	:	$a, a, a, b, b, b, c, ...$	*Answer : c*
h=9	:	$a, d, g, j, ...$	*Answer : m*
h=10	:	$a, c, b, d, c, e, ...$	*Answer : d*
h=11	:	$a, a, b, b, z, a, b, b, ...$	*Answer : y*
h=12	:	$a, a, z, c, y, e, x, ...$	*Answer : g*
h=13	:	$a, z, b, d, c, e, g, f, ...$	*Answer : h*
h=14	:	$c, a, b, d, b, c, c, e, c, d, ...$	*Answer : d*

The reader can speculate about whether the value h (Levin's Kt of the sequence) matches the perceived difficulty. But will this agree with the success rate of administering it to a group of human subjects?

- Stability: the sequences were generated in such a way that their prefixes (up to a minimum length) followed the same pattern. In other words, the compression ratio had to be evenly distributed for the whole sequence. For instance, a sequence such as 'ajaggacccdddeee...' is not stable, as the first part has no pattern. It is actually an exception.
- Unquestionability: the shortest program that generates the sequence cannot be rivalled by another program (of similar complexity) that gives a different continuation to the series. In a way, this unquestionability selects those series for which using one hypothesis (à la MML) instead of infinitely many hypotheses (à la Solomonoff) is justified.
- Complexity: the difficulty of each sequence x is calculated as $Kt(x)$, its Levin complexity. If a sequence has Kt complexity h, the sequence is said to be h-incomprehensible.

The universal machine that was used to generate the sequences and calculate their complexity was a variation of a minimal instruction set computer with 14 instructions. Panel 7.5 shows examples of sequences.

Despite being generated from first principles, one can still argue why the 'answers' should be recognised by humans as intuitive, or even as the correct answers. This is related to the *subjectivity objection*: "many ... test questions also have historically lacked objectively correct answers (such as 'verbal analogy' and 'find the next term in the numerical sequence' problems) and their answers instead are 'justified' because they agree with the most people" (Smith, 2006).

> **Keynote 7.7.** The **subjectivity objection** to psychometric tests, especially those about inductive inference through series continuations and analogies, states that any answer to an exercise is equally valid and that the 'correct' answer is just chosen extrinsically as being the majority answer in a population for biological or cultural reasons, but not intrinsically derived from the exercise.

This objection has been addressed by the constructs of stability and unquestionability defined earlier. However, there is a more fundamental reason: the shortest description for each sequence is coincident for the computer and for most humans. This is a consequence of the use of a common set of rules (alphabet, successor, predecessor, repetitions) that are shared by all (computer and humans). In terms of conditional Kolmogorov complexity (Eq. 7.3), this set of rules y makes $\arg\min_{p\,:\,U(\langle y,p\rangle)=x} L(p)$ equivalent for different computers and humans, despite the magnitudes being *relative* for each reference machine. This goes to the core of the epigraph opening this chapter, what Hofstadter (1979) referred to as "that which gets the same meaning out of a sequence of symbols as we do".

Indeed, similar phenomena have been found in animals. For instance, Fountain (2006) uses a circular alphabet for rats (in this case an alphabet of eight levers physically arranged in a circle), with sequences such as "runs" ("abcbcdcde...") and "trills" ("ababcbcdcded...") for several memory tests, with some of the series including "violations" of the pattern, i.e., exceptions. Series with violation elements were particularly difficult for rats to learn, indicating that rats were able to capture the pattern in the very same way the testers had devised.

Back to the *C*-test, using a pool of generated items of various difficulties, we can construct a test and define the result, or HitRatio, per difficulty h:

$$\text{HitRatio}(\pi, h) \triangleq \sum_{i=1}^{N} \frac{1}{N} \, \text{Hit}(\pi, x_{i,h}) \tag{7.11}$$

where π is the subject, h is the difficulty using N sequences $x_{i,h}$ per difficulty h. The function Hit returns 1 if π is correct with the continuation and 0 otherwise. The N sequences per difficulty are randomly chosen in a uniform way.

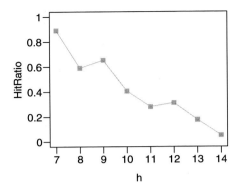

Figure 7.3. Human results on exercises of different difficulty (*h*) in the *C*-test (Hernández-Orallo and Minaya-Collado, 1998; Hernández-Orallo, 2000a).

The test was administered to 65 humans aged between 14 and 32 years. Figure 7.3 shows the evolution of the average accuracy of humans according to several values of *h*. An interesting observation is that by arranging problems by difficulty we see that the area of interest is between 7 and 14. Actually, HitRatio is very high below 7 and very low beyond difficulty 14. This makes the estimation of the measure much easier, as we only need to focus on a small interval of difficulties, as we saw with IRT in Chapter 3.

It is worth emphasising that the difficulties on the *x*-axis in Figure 7.3 correspond to the *Kt* of the exercise and are not derived from a human population, as in IRT. On the contrary, we examine whether the theoretical difficulty matches the observed difficulty in humans (on the *y*-axis). The figure shows that *Kt* really approximates the difficulty humans find for the series.

Finally, as the *C*-test was proposed as an intelligence test, it had to produce a measure of intelligence integrating the results for many items. How can we aggregate the results for several difficulties? This was the proposal for the result of a complete test:

$$I(\pi) \triangleq \sum_{h=1}^{H} h^e \text{ HitRatio}(\pi, h) \qquad (7.12)$$

where the difficulties range from $h = 1$ to H. If $e = 0$ all difficulties have the same weight, which means that I is just calculated as the area under the 'curve' we see in Figure 7.3 (partially, with *h* between 7 and 14).

The aggregated results of the administration of the *C*-test were compared with the results of an IQ test for the same subjects, showing a positive correlation of 0.73. Nonetheless, the size of the sample, the administration methodology and the characteristics of the IQ tests were insufficient to draw any rigorous conclusion.

Keynote 7.8. The *C*-test shows how **a cognitive test can be generated from first principles, using AIT**, with the items not being chosen in an ad hoc way and their difficulty not being derived from human populations.

Also, in Section 2.2 we discussed that psychological measurement usually neglects the units of measurement, unlike natural measurement. In the *C*-tests, the unit of the measurement would be simply the logarithm of computational steps, as h is derived from Levin's Kt complexity. That means that some of the "scientific pathologies" (Michell, 2000, 2008) of psychological measurement are no longer here, since we know from the very start that the feature we are measuring is quantitative and we know its units.

We will discuss further the objectivity of these tests and the questions they answer. Before that, however, we need to be conscious about what this test represents. The *C*-test is a test of inductive inference, very similar to Thurstone letter series. These kinds of tests usually have a high *g* loading and correlate strongly with IQ tests in humans, as we have seen. Nonetheless, IQ tests incorporate more kinds of problems to account for a comprehensive picture of intelligence. Can the *C*-test be extended to other types of problems, such as Raven's progressive Matrices? Some straightforward 'abductive' and 'analogical' presentations of the items are easy to define (Hernández-Orallo, 2000a), but more distinctive variants are also suggested:

- Knowledge applicability, where the items require some background knowledge B (given to the subjects) that needs to be used to find the pattern. Instead of $Kt(x)$ we should calculate $Kt(x|B)$.
- Contextualisation, where several knowledge bases are given $B_1, B_2, \dots, B_n$, and there is one of them (e.g., B_i) that makes $Kt(x|B_i)$ low, and the subject must have the ability to use the right one.
- Knowledge construction, where the items can benefit from patterns that are learnt from previous items. In other words, this is a proposal for incremental learning.

We will revisit some of these variants in Chapter 12. It seems harder, though, to figure out how to derive computational tests for other abilities, such as deductive, verbal or planning abilities, not featuring inductive inference. These variants and others are further developed in (Hernández-Orallo, 2000d), but no actual test or experiments were finally performed. Instead, the recommendation was to change the evaluation protocol completely, assuming "cognitive agents... with input/output devices for a complex environment" (Hernández-Orallo and Minaya-Collado, 1998), where "rewards and penalties can be used instead" (Hernández-Orallo, 2000a). We will devote some of the following chapters to a more general notion of task and the introduction of various kinds of abilities.

7.5 WHAT DO IQ TESTS REALLY MEASURE?

In Section 2.6 we recalled some of the desiderata for a "scientific measure of intelligence". IQ tests are non-Boolean (i.e., providing quantitative scores) and factorial (i.e., having several components), but they are anthropocentric, non-computational and its interpretation not more meaningful than Boring's famous statement: "measurable intelligence is simply what the tests of intelligence test" (Boring, 1923). On the contrary, provided that the extension of the C-test for other abilities could cover the 'factorial' part of the desiderata, we could establish the C-test as the beginning of a whole programme for the derivation of intelligence tests from first principles.

However, despite the promising prospects, this could be at most satisfactory from the point of view of human intelligence, but not for other members of the machine kingdom. In the previous chapter, we saw how Sanghi and Dowe (2003) were able to devise a very simple program that scored well in many IQ tests (see Panel 6.3 and Table 6.3). Actually, this non-intelligent program could score well on the C-test as well. Is the C-test then refuted as a test of intelligence in the machine kingdom? The answer is yes, in the same way we can discard most, if not all, psychometric tests for arbitrary machines, as discussed in the previous chapter. We have to look at the C-test, Thurstone letter series or Raven's Progressive Matrices as *indirect* measurement instruments (in the sense seen in Chapter 2). The ability of extrapolating a sequence of letters using inductive inference is an indirect measurable feature that is integrated in IQ tests. If applied to (adult) humans the IQ tests produce a measurement that correlates with indicators of – or even predicts – the concept we are interested in for humans, intelligence. Through the construction of the C-test we now understand better what some of the tasks that are included in IQ tests really measure.

After the interpretation of what the C-test really measures and for what population, there are still many relevant issues that the construction of tests using AIT can offer to (universal) psychometrics.

- Meaning: for the C-test we know exactly what we are measuring: the ability of performing sequential inductive inference. While we already knew this for Thurstone letter series, its view from the point of AIT links it with the general problem of induction, its connection with the ability to learn and, ultimately, to many informal definitions of intelligence. In other words, it is no longer just the continuation of a series, but an instance of the most prototypical presentation of the problem of inductive inference.
- Objectivity: the construction of the tests using AIT clarifies a few points that have been a matter of strong debate in psychometrics: the items are not subjective to some genetic or cultural background, but universal. Also, the reference machine is not so important if the tests are defined with some conditions about stability and unquestionability. The only cultural requirements are the alphabet and its order. Given this, the continuations are coincident. This rebuffs some of the common subjectivity objections to (some) IQ tests mentioned in the previous section, accusing them of being "popularity" or "conformity" tests, with the argument that any continuation is equally plausible, à la *no free lunch*, or just chosen by "pseudo-logical or aesthetic" criteria (Smith, 2006).
- Difficulty assessment: the notion of difficulty does not depend on a human population, but it is intrinsic in the definition of each series, as given by its Kolmogorov (K) or Levin complexity (Kt). Of course, there have been some other studies where the difficulty of the exercises has been linked to some independent (computer) models of difficulty (Simon and Kotovsky, 1963; Evans, 1963, 1965). These and many other approaches will be discussed in the following chapter. They did not use the notion of Kolmogorov complexity, but were equally linked to the resources that were required to solve a given exercise.

The development of tests using AIT will frequently show the two sides of AIT, as has happened with the C-test; measuring the ability of inductive inference is an example of the epistemological apparatus of AIT; measuring the ability of combining many elements at the same time would be more related to the procedural or resource-oriented view of AIT.

At the sight of the balance between refutations and positive findings in this chapter, we may feel dubious of the possibilities of AIT for universal psychometrics. Basically, is the C-test initiatory or terminal to the use of AIT for the analysis and construction of intelligence tests? Despite its limitations, there are strong reasons to conclude that the approach that has been illustrated with the C-test brings many advantages (and no clear disadvantage) over the way classical cognitive tests have been devised in the past. It is unclear which of the elements in AIT will be necessary (complexity functions such as K and Kt, distributions such as M_U, etc.), but the conjunction of algorithms and information (in this or other ways) seems to be ineluctable for a more principled approach to the evaluation of cognitive abilities.

CHAPTER HIGHLIGHTS

- Absolute and conditional complexity (K) defined in terms of shortest descriptions over Turing-complete formal languages, such as programming languages (Keynote 7.1, Eqs. 7.2, 7.3).
- Levin complexity (Kt) as a computable version of Kolmogorov complexity (K), balancing size and execution time (Keynote 7.2, Eqs. 7.4, 7.5).
- Simplicity as a fundamental cognitive principle, seen in humans and other animals (Section 7.2).
- Solomonoff prediction using a universal distribution (Keynote 7.4, Eqs. 7.7, 7.8) as an integration of Epicurus and Occam to solve the scandal of induction (Keynote 7.3).
- The assumptions of the no-free-lunch theorems (Keynote 7.5) at odds with a world full of phenomena coming from computable processes and creatures.
- Kolmogorov complexity and algorithmic probability being two sides of the same coin (Eq. 7.9), legitimising the view of inductive inference as compression and the related MML and MDL principles (Eq. 7.10) in terms of Bayesian inference (Keynote 7.6).
- The C-test as a first realisation of a psychometric test derived from AIT (Keynote 7.8), providing explanations of what these kinds of tests really measure and undermining the subjectivity objection (Keynote 7.7).

8

Cognitive Tasks and Difficulty

There are two theorems in Levin's "Universal Sequential Search Problems" (1973). The first states the now well-known principle of NP completeness and is followed by an outline of a proof. The second gives a solution to a very broad class of mathematical problems, but, partly because no proof was suggested in the paper, its great importance is not widely appreciated.

— Ray J. Solomonoff,
Optimum Sequential Search (1984a)

THE FORMAL DERIVATION of a test and the analysis of item difficulty using algorithmic information theory establishes an embryo for universal psychometrics. However, this proves almost nothing if we cannot generalise these ideas to the computational definition of other tasks. We must aim at a well-founded universal notion of cognitive task from which task and item difficulty can be derived. In this chapter we will see a characterisation of cognitive tasks as interactive (stochastic) machines, which is mirrored by the characterisation of the subjects that take the tasks as interactive machines too. The view of tasks as stochastic, featuring many instances, is crucial for the distinction of a solution for a single instance and a policy that achieves an acceptable result for the whole task. Looking at the policies instead of the task is the key issue leading to a computational notion of difficulty, in terms of (the logarithm of) *the number of computational steps required to find the simplest acceptable policy*.

8.1 INTERPRETING TASKS AND INSTANCES

In Chapter 1 we saw that cognitive evaluation is performed through instruments, or tests, which are composed of cognitive tasks. In subsequent chapters we also

---

Panel 8.1
The relative numerousness task

What do Talon the dolphin in Florida Keys (Jaakkola et al., 2005) and Ana the sea lion in Valencia (Abramson et al., 2011) have in common? Both have been tested about their ability to judge relative quantity, a well-known task in animal cognition research that is usually referred to as "relative numerousness", "relative numerosity" or "relative quantity judgment". Talon the dolphin, for instance, was repeatedly tested with two different quantities such as the two shown in Figure 8.1, and was given a reward if the *lesser* amount was selected.

Apart from cetaceans, the "relative numerousness" task has been used in the area of comparative psychology with many other animals (see, e.g., Abramson et al. 2011; Perdue et al. 2012; Vonk and Beran 2012). The task has also been applied to humans of different ages. Interestingly, it is relatively easy to write a computer program that solves this task perfectly, using image recognition and simple counting.

---

saw that some subjects are designed (by evolution for natural systems or by programming for artificial systems) to do some tasks, whereas other systems are able to learn to do new tasks, usually through several *trials* and some kind of feedback. A proper notion of task should accommodate the different administrations and evaluation goals seen in Chapters 3–6.

Let us start with a very simple task. Panel 8.1 explains the "relative numerousness" task, whose goal is to tell which quantity is lowest.

The relative numerousness task is cognitive, as it only depends on elements that can be virtualised, as seen in Keynote 1.5, and, if properly specified, has a coherent description such that many instances can be derived from it. Actually, by parametrising the number, size and location of the dots on the two panels we can generate any number of task *instances*. Indeed, we can define a *distribution*

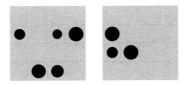

Figure 8.1. An instance of the relative numerousness task. Two boards are shown with a different number of dots. Different dot sizes partially prevent tricks not involving counting, such as using the darkness of the whole panel.

over these parameters. A task can then be seen as a collection of instances, with an associated distribution. As a result, instances are also tasks, and sets of tasks are tasks, too. Whilst this is a practical and valid understanding (though superseded by the notion of stochastic task that we will see later), it does not always coincide with the view of cognitive task in many disciplines. The reason why we properly call a particular set of instances a task is because we expect that there is something in common, such as one mechanism, algorithm or *policy*, that can be used to solve the instances of the task.

Table 8.1 shows a selection of tasks that are commonly used in human, non-human animal and AI evaluation. Most of them were seen in the previous chapters and will be used in this and the following chapters to illustrate several ideas. Some can be well solved by computers with current techniques (e.g., μ_{num}, μ_{ctest}, μ_{react}, μ_{maze}, μ_{imit}, μ_{guess}, μ_{eide}, μ_{srote}, μ_{lrote}, μ_{sudo}, μ_{add} and μ_{mult}) whilst, for others, AI techniques are getting closer to human performance (μ_{rpm}, μ_{pacm}, μ_{trans}, μ_{img}, μ_{verb}). In a few of them, some animals can get good scores, even better than humans. Many tasks are static (an output is expected after an input, and the trial finishes) but some others are interactive (the subject 'plays' during some time with a set of actions according to some percepts).

As we discussed in Chapter 3 and Table 6.1, one characteristic of tasks that are aimed at adult humans is that they are usually accompanied by instructions. This relevance of instructions for human tasks is patent in some of the definitions of 'task' in psychometrics: "the outcomes can differ according to the instructions given, even when stimulus presentations and other objective events remain the same. A simple example is the memory span task: the stimuli may be the same, a series of digits, let's say, but the outcome differs according to whether the subject is asked to repeat them forward or backward" (Carroll, 1981).

This view of the instructions as a separate part of a task may be common in adult human evaluation, but it does not hold for small children, non-human animals and computers. In fact, many tasks do not have instructions, but are conducted by internal or external motivations, such as rewards and penalties. Also, the task may be intrinsically linked with some previous knowledge of the task. For instance, for the multiplication ability task μ_{mult}, we usually assume that the subject understands the meaning of the decimal numeral system and the symbols of multiplication.

Independently of whether we consider the instructions and the previous knowledge as a separate part of the input or not, the key issue is that a very minor change in the description of the task can make its behaviour very different, something that any computer programmer is well aware of. This is the first clear symptom that the syntactical description of the task provides an

Table 8.1.   Some illustrative cognitive tasks.

ID	Name	Description and instance generation
μ_{num}	Numerousness	Choose the board with fewest number of dots (Panel 8.1 and Figure 8.1). Dot configuration is randomly chosen.
μ_{rpm}	Raven's matrices	Choose the option that best matches the matrix (see Figure 3.3). Instances chosen from a finite set of problems.
μ_{ctest}	C-test	Find the continuation of a letter series (Panel 7.5, like Thurstone series). Instances extracted from a set.
μ_{react}	Reaction time	Press left/right button no later than a *delay* after signal. Delay is generated randomly.
μ_{maze}	Maze	Go from start to exit in a maze. A random generator of solvable mazes.
μ_{pacm}	Pac-Man	Eat all dots without being eaten by some ghosts, which move stochastically with some patterns.
μ_{trans}	Translation	Translate a text from English to Spanish. Texts randomly taken from a large finite corpus.
μ_{verb}	Verbal WPPSI	Verbal comprehension questions such as "You can see through it", from WPPSI (see Section 3.8).
μ_{img}	Image recognition	Discriminate two types of images (e.g., cats from dogs). Images randomly chosen from a corpus.
μ_{imit}	Simple imitation	Perform the action equal to previous observation, chosen uniformly from a finite set.
μ_{guess}	Guess sequence	Guess action until match (indicated with reward), then another action, chosen uniformly randomly.
μ_{eide}	Eidetic memory	Remember a sequence of numbers spread on the screen. Various exposition times and sequences (Panel 2.3).
μ_{rspan}	Memory span	Subject outputs a sequence of numbers seen before in backward order. Instances vary.
μ_{srote}	Short rote	Subject outputs one short number string shown afterwards. Always the same instance.
μ_{lrote}	Long rote	Subject outputs one long number string shown afterwards. Always the same instance.
μ_{sudo}	Sudokus	Solve a 9×9 sudoku. Consistent puzzles obtained from a random sudoku generator.
μ_{add}	Addition	Addition of two natural numbers. Numbers chosen uniformly from a range.
μ_{mult}	Multiplication	Multiplication of two natural numbers. Numbers chosen uniformly from a range.

insufficient perspective. Actually, it is the way policies achieve a task and their description which really characterises the task. This interpretation will have enormous relevance in our conception of task, its difficulty and its use in this and the following chapter. But how are policies acquired and applied?

> **Keynote 8.1. Policy acquisition continuum**: Regardless of the use of instructions, rewards or other motivations, there is a continuum between identifying the policy for a task (choosing among some of the predefined or previously learnt algorithms of the agent) and learning the policy for the task (building the algorithm that solves the task).

For instance, from a few instances without instructions a subject can identify that the task μ_{trans} requires the translation of text from English to Spanish. If the subject knows English and Spanish, a few instances will suffice to understand that the task is about translation and immediately start using the subject's knowledge of the language to solve the following instances. However, if the subject does not know any (or none) of both languages, millions of instances will be required before the agent can learn to do the task with some proficiency. Actually, we have examples with computers where this distinction is very clear. For instance, some web browsers can identify the language a page is written in and suggest a reasonably good translation (using some embedded translation modules). On the other hand, some of these translation modules may have been learnt using statistical approaches from millions of pairs of sentences. In other words, the problem is reduced to setting the big switch, as discussed in Panel 5.1.

The policy acquisition continuum does not come from the nature of the task nor from its presentation, but from the expectations about the embedded mechanisms and background knowledge of the subject to be evaluated. This is why we understand that, for humans, with the addition task μ_{add} we evaluate the ability to apply an off-the-shelf addition algorithm efficiently and correctly. But the same task could be used to analyse whether a computer is able to learn an addition algorithm from examples (Gulwani et al., 2015).

Each conceivable task (and those in Table 8.1) can be understood as an application or a learning task. Without knowledge about the subject, we can only get a rough idea of whether the subject already had the right policy for a task or has learnt it from scratch by observing the progress of results for a sequence of trials. The two extremes are related to the notions of fluid and crystallised intelligence that we discussed in Chapter 3. We can now better understand why some fluid intelligence tasks are special, such as μ_{rpm} or μ_{ctest} in Table 8.1. One of the features of the C-test (and the similar Thurstone letter series problem) is that it relies on the use of inductive inference ability to find it. As a consequence, the repeated administration of many trials does not show a drastic improvement in performance if the patterns are sufficiently different between trials.

We have seen the many nuances in the notion of task. Our definition of cognitive task must be able to embrace all of them. This is what we undertake next.

8.2 TASKS AS STOCHASTIC INTERACTIVE MACHINES

Panel 8.2 enumerates a series of requirements we would like cognitive tasks to have. These requirements seem to be met by some notions of environment used in artificial intelligence and game theory, most especially in reinforcement learning. A common formalisation is through (partially-observable) (Markov) decision processes, (PO)(M)DP, a kind of interactive settings where agent and environment alternate actions and percepts. Observability refers to what information is perceivable (e.g., full view of a maze or just a partial view of some adjacent cells). The Markov property refers to each state only depending on the actions and the previous state. Alternation means that environment and agent are "locally synchronous", i.e., "while one machine is computing its next output, the other one is effectively suspended" (Zimmermann et al., 2015).

Panel 8.2 goes beyond any of these conditions. For instance, the use of alternating actions and percepts with transition functions makes decision processes unsuitable for many tasks, such as choice reaction time μ_{react}. Also, we will go beyond an alternating setting for the subjects (agents) taking the test, since the assumption of agents being locally synchronous decision processes would be very problematic for the notion of difficulty that we will investigate in the next sections. For a more detailed discussion about the computational model for tasks, see (Hernández-Orallo, 2015d,e). For the advantages of asynchronicity, see (Gavane, 2013; Zimmermann et al., 2015; Thórisson et al., 2015).

Responses and rewards in Panel 8.2 are different things. For instance, one can give positive rewards to help a subject find the exit of a maze, but the result may still be poor. In fact, a very competent subject may easily find the exit and get a high final response, without having received any reward during the trial. It is important to make this distinction, because in animal cognition and reinforcement learning (especially under the POMDP formalism) rewards can be provided after each action or at the end, and the final response of the trial (known as episode) is usually an aggregation of the received rewards (e.g., a

---

Panel 8.2
General requirements on cognitive tasks

1. Cumulative trials: tasks can be administered in one or more trials v. Neither the task nor the subject are necessarily reinitialised after each trial, so allowing subjects to learn and tasks to adapt.
2. Flexible interaction: subjects will access (unbounded) discrete structures for actions and percepts. For instance, the task μ_{trans} in Table 8.1 may contain sentences of any length.
3. Asynchronous time: each trial runs for some virtual or physical time τ. Actions and percepts are not (necessarily) alternating.
4. Algorithmic states: there is no *transition* function between finite states. No Markov property or ergodicity are assumed.
5. Stochastic behaviour: tasks can be stochastic, leading to non-deterministic sequences of trials and instances. Instances can appear more than once.
6. Expected response: there is a result or response R at the end of a task trial. As tasks are stochastic, we talk about expected response $\mathbb{R}$. Responses can be used as feedback for subsequent trials.
7. Supervision rewards: apart from (and possibly independently of) the supervision given by the response between trials, rewards are an optional way of transmitting supervision *during* a trial.

---

discounted reward). But these are just particular cases, and many other tasks do not need to follow this pattern. For instance, in video games, we may have a mixture of scores and intermediate goals (stages that need to be achieved).

With some of the issues and requirements about cognitive tasks having been discussed, we are ready to see some of the key definitions. Our formal model of agents and tasks is based on an asynchronous stochastic version of interactive Turing machines (Goldin et al., 2006):

Keynote 8.2. An **asynchronous-time interactive stochastic system** is a machine with a program code, a finite internal discrete memory, one or more finite read-only discrete input tapes and one or more finite write-only discrete output tapes. The machine also has access to a read-only discrete time measurement and a read-only tape with random bits. For asynchronicity, there is a special instruction to enter a sleeping state for a given period of time.

From the preceding definition, it is very easy to specialise agents and tasks. First, we introduce a more precise notion of agent, as a refinement from our early definition of the elements of machine kingdom in Keynote 1.1:

> **Keynote 8.3.** An **agent** is an asynchronous-time interactive stochastic system, where the content of the input tape(s) represents the percepts and the content of the output tape(s) determines the actions. There is an extra input tape that takes rewards.

This particular choice of machines is not very different from some actual implementations of agents in artificial intelligence or even computational models of animals. Indeed, this stochastic machine with rewards is basically the computational model that Turing suggested for artificial intelligence in the 1940s. In Sections 10–12 of his "Intelligent Machinery" (1948), Turing suggested that the basic input and output tapes of Turing machines could be extended with "two interfering inputs, one for 'pleasure' or 'reward' (R) and the other for 'pain' or 'punishment' (P)". Likewise, the inclusion of a tape full of random bits is directly inherited from his notion of probabilistic (Turing) machine: "each machine should be supplied with a tape bearing a random series of figures, e.g., 0 and 1 in equal quantities, and this series of figures should be used in the choices made by the machine" (Turing, 1951).

Finally, as mentioned, the notion of cognitive task is complementary to the notion of agent and can now be precisely defined (compare to Keynote 1.5).

> **Keynote 8.4.** A **cognitive task** is an asynchronous-time interactive stochastic system, where the output tapes are understood as percepts sent to the agent. The input tape(s) contain the actions performed by the agent. There is a special output tape representing the reward. When the time τ is reached, a value is set on this output tape, taken as the response of a trial. The next trial can start immediately thereafter.

This reflects a complementarity of the machine kingdom and the space of tasks. The interaction between tasks and agents takes place when task outputs are connected to agent inputs and vice versa. The settings accommodate the intuitive notions of agent and task in many natural and artificial scenarios and their interaction. Any conceivable (and computable) agent and task can be seen in just this way.

The stochastic character of a task makes it more general than a collection of instances with an associated distribution. As there is interaction, the agent will determine the behaviour of the task (and vice versa). A cognitive task generates instances whenever run (reinitialised or one after the other).

This generalises Eqs. 2.1 and 2.2, which defined a measure as a weighted sum. For instance, for the addition task (μ_{add}) in Table 8.1, instead of a machine or program that generates additions stochastically, we can think of the set of all possible pairs of natural numbers and define a distribution over these pairs such that the result is equivalent. But the use of stochastic tasks as instance generators, trial after trial, becomes necessary if we think about agents with memory and, most especially, about adaptive tasks. Also, the aggregation of tasks (e.g., if we aggregate μ_{add} and μ_{mult} in Table 8.1) through *computational* mixtures can also be interpreted as a composed task. We will analyse this composition in more detail in Chapter 10.

Finally, the notion of instance can be given:

> **Keynote 8.5.** A **task instance** is determined by setting the random tape to a particular input string leading to a particular trial. For those tasks with memory between trials (e.g., adaptive tests), we need to assume a particular interaction history too.

This can be understood with the simile of setting a *random seed* and history.

8.3 TRIALS, SOLUTIONS AND POLICIES

After a setting for tasks and agents, we are going to clarify the interpretation of task administration and the distinction between the solution for an instance and the solution for a task. As we introduced in the previous section, we use $\mathbb{R}(\pi, \mu)$ as the expected value of the response, return or result (assumed to be between 0 and 1) for agent (or subject) π for task (or environment) μ. The time limit τ taken for the task will usually be omitted as it is understood that it is part of the description of the task μ. To consider several sequential trials of the same task, $\mathbb{R}^{[\mapsto \nu]}(\pi, \mu)$ returns the expected response of μ per trial considering ν consecutive trials (episodes) by the same agent π. Note that depending on the task, the same instance can appear more than once or not, as in a sample with or without replacement. It also depends on the definition of the task to make a sequence of trials adaptive or not. Finally, with $\mathbb{R}^{[\mapsto 1]}(\pi, \mu)$, or simply $\mathbb{R}(\pi, \mu)$ we denote that there is only one episode or trial (no repetitions), or that the agents and tasks have no memory between trials.

The notion of *solution* of a task looks straightforward and clear at first sight. What is the solution of the instance '3+5' for μ_{add}? Clearly, it is 8. And what is the solution of the instance on Figure 8.1 for the numerousness task μ_{num}? Clearly, it is the board on right (remember that the goal is to choose the lesser amount). However, some observations have to be made here. The expression of the solution of a task instance may have nothing to do with the description of the task and its complexity. Actually, choosing between 'left' and 'right' only requires one bit. As a result, if the system has perfect memory, memorising the result will work again and again for this task instance by rote learning. This is one of the reasons why tasks should be composed of many instances, unless it is rote learning that we want to measure (like μ_{srote} or μ_{lrote}).

If we talk about the solution of the whole task, and not a particular instance, the notion of 'solution' changes completely. We see, for instance, that *a* solution for the addition task μ_{add} would be any algorithm that solves all additions correctly, and for the relative numerousness task μ_{num}, the solution would be any algorithm that chooses the lesser amount.

> **Keynote 8.6.** A **policy** is any algorithm or procedure that is used for one or more tasks.

The description of the successful policies for a task may be very different from the description of the algorithm that produces the task. For instance, we write a program to generate boards for μ_{num} as shown on Figure 8.1 with the following program: 'generate two panels consisting of 4×4 cells, with the number of dots in each panel uniformly between 1 to 16, and the diameter of dots uniformly distributed between 0.2 and 1'. A policy for this task can be described as 'recognise black circular dots, count them and compare the numbers'.

If the task is composed of a finite number of instances, a possible policy may be a lookup table, memorising all instances and their particular solutions. Conspicuously, for many tasks with a large or an infinite number of instances, the use of partial lookup tables may still be useful, especially for those instances that are more likely. Actually, anyone would surely answer 8 to the sum '3+5' from her or his lookup table and not as a result of executing any algorithm (such as mental or finger counting). For most tasks, and many of those depicted on Table 8.1, a successful policy is an algorithm that combines some general rules and many particular short-cuts.

Our first interpretation of 'solution' can also vary for some kinds of tasks. For instance, a particular feature of the C-test task μ_{ctest} seen in the previous chapter is that there seems to be no common policy to solve the instances. This interpretation is misleading, as there are indeed policies that solve this task, such as a brute-force algorithm that looks for all the possible patterns with the right part of the sequence deriving from the left part. It is actually this search (or other better policies) that subjects use when trying to solve the sequences. To make things even more particular here, in the C-test – unlike many other tasks such as μ_{add} or μ_{num} – the pattern that *generates* an instance is the same pattern that *solves* the instance. In other words, even if the solution for the instance 'abcde' is 'f', both the generator (the task) and the subject (the policy) require a similar pattern such as 'start from the first letter of the alphabet and follow incrementally' for this instance. A comparable thing happens with Raven's Progressive Matrices and other tasks that are devised to measure particular cases of inductive (sequential or analogical) reasoning. But still, the description of a policy for the whole task will differ significantly from the task generator. As a result of this, we will be careful about the use of the term 'solution' and we will favour the term 'policy', as an algorithm or behaviour for all the instances of the task, as defined in Keynote 8.6.

We also have to be careful not to limit ourselves to only considering perfect solutions. We must be able to allow for some level of error. But how much? With humans, and especially with non-human animals, assuming a perfect expected response of 1 is unrealistic. If we considered all possible policies for the relative numerousness task, assuming the task is not biased for left or right, most policies would be not much better or worse than random (0.5), while only a few of them could detach from this random behaviour and get to 0.7, 0.8 or 0.15 responses. Which of them are considered *acceptable*? In many studies with animals, an 80 per cent success rate is considered a level where the subject is understood to perform the task successfully. For instance, Panel 8.3 shows a policy that scores relatively well for μ_{num}.

The threshold or tolerance for a task is then crucial for the understanding of policies that are considered *acceptable* for the task. We define a tolerance parameter ϵ, which sets the threshold on $1 - \epsilon$. From here, given a tolerance ϵ, the set of ϵ-acceptable policies for task μ can just be defined as

$$\mathcal{A}^{[\epsilon, \mapsto \nu]}(\mu) \triangleq \{\pi \; : \; \mathbb{R}^{[\mapsto \nu]}(\pi, \mu) \geq 1 - \epsilon\} \tag{8.1}$$

In words, this is the set of policies such that the expected results of task μ for ν trials is greater than or equal to $1 - \epsilon$. Note that the agent can perform poorly in some instances if this is compensated with good results in many others. In fact, which instances are solved correctly and which are not may depend on the *steadiness* of the agent. For instance, humans, having a correct algorithm

---

Panel 8.3
Gaming the relative numerousness task

Remember the relative numerousness task that we saw in Panel 8.1. One would expect that agents performing well on this task would process the image, recognise the shapes and count the dots. However, it is also possible to score well in this task with an agent that does not count at all.

Consider an agent π_1 that performs a Monte Carlo approach and (virtually) probes n points randomly over each board. Then, the *darkness* of each board is calculated as the percentage of points that are black (i.e., points that are inside a dot). With this, the least dark board is chosen.

Experimentally, a policy π_1 using $n = 100$ points for each panel is able to score 0.8675 on average. A policy π_2 that only uses $n = 50$ points scores $\mathbb{R}(\pi_2, \mu_{num}) = 0.850$. A policy π_3 only using $n = 10$ scores $\mathbb{R}(\pi_3, \mu_{num}) = 0.746$. Indeed, with just one point, π_4 still does significantly better than random: $\mathbb{R}(\pi_4, \mu_{num}) = 0.575$.

Finally, comparing the four policies, we see that their description is similar, but the computational effort decreases from π_1 to π_4.

---

for multiplication, still make mistakes, and the result for a sequence of trials cannot be expected to be 1. Tolerance is then needed to assess real systems and permits different causes of suboptimal results:

Keynote 8.7. Suboptimal results in real systems can be caused by partially incorrect algorithms (a soundness issue) or by mistakes when executing the algorithm (a steadiness issue).

The number and complexity of the elements in $\mathcal{A}$ will depend on ϵ. For instance, Figure 8.2 shows a figurative plot of many policies for the μ_{num} task. Setting the tolerance at $\epsilon = 0.2$, we see the policies with $\mathbb{R} \geq 1 - 0.2 = 0.8$ above the horizontal line. The Kolmogorov complexity of the description of the policy is shown on the x-axis. No (simple) policy of complexity lower than 58 passes the threshold.

The notion of tolerance will prove crucial for some issues in this chapter and the following one. First, it is necessary for the notion of difficulty, since difficulty depends on where the threshold is set, taking both soundness and steadiness into account. Second, it makes it possible to compare (variants of)

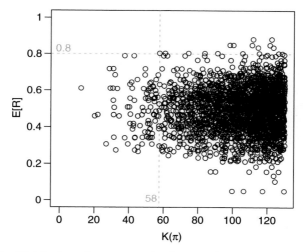

Figure 8.2. Distribution of responses by the complexity of the policy $K(\pi)$ on the x-axis. Tolerance 0.2 is shown with a horizontal dashed line $(1 - 0.2)$.

tasks, by appropriately setting particular thresholds (this can also be achieved by a monotone transformation of the response scores).

8.4 THE ELUSIVENESS OF DIFFICULTY

The role of 'difficulty' has always occupied a prominent role in the measurement of cognitive abilities and has been brought to the fore several times in the previous chapters. The following words from John B. Carroll about its relevance are unequivocal: "Ability and task difficulty are key concepts in psychometrics. . . . Operationally, we measure ability as a function of the level of task difficulty an individual is able to master. This idea is the foundation of traditional procedures in the construction of measures of mental ability" (Carroll, 1981).

Actually, difficulty and the related concept of complexity pervade every human activity and every field of science. These terms are interpreted in many various ways depending on the elements we are interested in (physical phenomena, life forms, bit strings, algorithms, reasoning processes, etc.) and also the different purposes (understanding phenomena, developing new methods or just evaluating individuals). Difficulty and complexity, however, are different things. A flower can be complex, but can never be difficult. Difficulty refers to a problem and the effort or resources that a subject requires to *solve* it. Hence, difficulty is crucial in our analysis of tasks and agents. The notion of difficulty is linked to the notion of tolerance seen earlier, as a task becomes easier as we increase the tolerance. For instance, if we set $\epsilon = 0.5$ the relative numerousness task becomes trivial.

The role of the *subject* in the concept of difficulty has led to a common view that difficulty is *subjective*, i.e., difficulty is in the eye of the beholder. This subjectivity has been understood in different ways, but basically means that difficulty would be a function of *both* task and subject. This is not very useful for evaluation, as the same instance or task would show different difficulty values depending on the subject. It can be useful for other applications, such as the so-called difficulty scaling or dynamic difficulty adjustment (Spronck et al., 2004; Ashlock and Schonfeld, 2010), which are used in games to model the player in order to present stages and challenges of increasing difficulty for a particular subject. Another interpretation of subjective difficulty is the subject's perception of the *complexity* of the task (Kim, 2006; Li and Belkin, 2008; Liu et al., 2010). Similar options were discussed in the early days of psychometrics, such as "the measurement of the intellectual difficulty of tasks by a consensus of expert opinion" (Thorndike et al., 1927, Chapter V).

Another view of subjective difficulty is to relate it to the knowledge of the subject, her or his interpretation of the instructions of the task or the context in which the task is taken. Liu and Li (2012) say "that task complexity can be distinguished from task difficulty in that task complexity involves the objective characteristics of a task, whereas task difficulty involves the interaction among task, task performer, and context characteristics". In similar terms, Robinson (2001) states that "cognitive factors contributing to task complexity must be distinguished from learner factors which may make a task more or less difficult (as opposed to complex)".

However, this conception of difficulty as a function of task, agent and context is useless to characterise tasks. Psychometrics has usually circumvented this issue by generalising from subjects to population of subjects. In this way, the notion of subjective difficulty is turned into a *relative* difficulty. If the task is solved by most individuals in the population then it is easy. Otherwise, it is difficult. Indeed, the first notion of IQ was developed in terms of populations of children of various ages.

In Chapter 3 we saw how powerful this notion of population-relative difficulty has been for psychometrics, both experimentally and theoretically. In item response theory, the parametric models for the item response function and characteristic curve show how a population performs for an item. Actually, this is one of the most relevant contributions of psychometrics: the view that difficulty is associated with the *expected response* for a population of agents while discriminating power is associated with the *variability* of the response for the population. Can we think of anything more elegant?

Unfortunately, as we discussed in Chapter 6, the notion of population for the machine kingdom is slippery. Should we content ourselves with an anthropocentric measure of difficulty? Or, as an alternative, can we define difficulty as expected result over a distribution of agents in the whole machine kingdom? Could we agree on such a distribution? A universal distribution? Does it make sense to average all the responses in Figure 8.2 and get 0.5 as mean expected response?

There are some signs in favour of an alternative. As we discussed in Section 2.4, there must be a way to determine, for instance, that the sum 1111 + 2222 is much easier than 7892 + 2359, independently of the subject. In the previous chapter we saw that the difficulty of the letter sequences included in the *C*-tests was absolute or, more precisely, independent of the subject or any population. Can we have similar results and curves such as Figure 7.3 for any other task?

8.5 DIFFICULTY AS AN INTRINSIC PROPERTY

An *absolute* measure of task difficulty can be approximated from three different viewpoints: as a function of the task, as a function of the policies and as a function of the process, what Liu and Li (2012) call the structuralist, resource requirement and interaction viewpoints, respectively. For instance, Figure 8.3 shows four different mazes where we play with the features of the maze, such as the patterns of the walls (using the opposite adjectives 'intricate'-'simple' to describe these patterns), the features of the traversal algorithms that can solve the problems (using 'hard'-'easy' to describe these algorithms) and the characteristics of the traversals that can be generated (using 'complicated'-'uncomplicated' to describe these paths).

It is not always easy to distinguish between these three viewpoints of difficulty. In fact, difficulty can be defined as a combination of features from one, two or three of these viewpoints, depending of the task. For instance, for mazes, we find different specific ways of approximating difficulty, based on the size of the problem (Zatuchna and Bagnall, 2009), the state space (Madden and Howley, 2004) or the number of forks (Fragaszy et al., 2009), similar to Thorndike's "possible avenues" for his chicks (see Figure 4.1).

Let us analyse the three approaches separately. For instance, we can use (universal) Turing machines or finite state machines and derive task difficulty using some measure of complexity of the task, such as the number of states

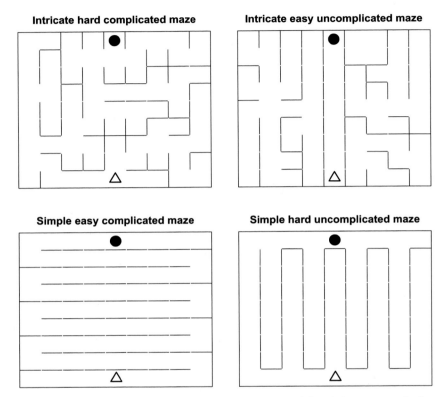

Figure 8.3. We see four mazes where the agent (triangle) must reach the target (circle). We use different pairs of adjectives for the complexity of the topology of the maze ('intricate'-'simple'), the complexity of the policy solving the maze ('hard'-'easy') and the complexity of the shortest path ('complicated'-'uncomplicated'). The characteristics of the task description or the solution traversal for an instance are usually bad surrogates of the notion of difficulty of a task. Compare with Thorndike's mazes for chicks in Figure 4.1.

(Hibbard, 2011). Sanderson (2000) applies a variant of the MML/MDL principle ("minimal representation size criterion") to determine the configurational complexity of robotic maze tasks. In general, given *any* task, we can calculate its Kolmogorov complexity. This has been postulated as a measure of task difficulty several times, although not always explicitly, but rather as a way to derive a task distribution (Legg and Hutter, 2007c).

However, the relation between task (Kolmogorov) complexity and its difficulty is problematic. This has been expressed by Legg and Hutter themselves (2007c, example 3.5), Hibbard (2009) and Hernández-Orallo and Dowe (2010, sec. 4.1), since high rewards could be obtained by very simple policies on very complex environments. Of course, some other variants of complexity may be considered, such as Levin's *Kt* (Levin, 1973), logical depth (Chaitin, 1977), effective complexity (Ay et al., 2008), computational depth (Antunes et al., 2006), sophistication (Chedid, 2010) and others (see Li and Vitányi, 2008, chap. 7). These do not only code the information of the object but how hard it is to compress it or to obtain it from its shortest description. Again, these proposals are generally conceived for the evaluation of (static) objects and do not distinguish the complexity that emanates when the object is deployed in an interactive scenario. Nonetheless, there have been some attempts (Hernández-Orallo and Dowe, 2010) to accommodate tasks with transition functions (common within Markov Decision Processes), considering the resources of the task, such as Kt^{max}.

In the end, analysing the complexity of the task description is futile in general. For instance, it is easy to see that two random mazes such as the two on the top of Figure 8.3, both with high Kolmogorov complexity, can lead to a hard instance (top left) or an easy one (top right). Also, the effect of noise or perturbation of a task difficulty, in terms of variability, volatility, inconsistency, uncertainty, etc. (Anderson, 2004) is not well analysed from the point of view of the task description.

The alternative approach is to look at the policies solving the task. But, how can we reconcile the evidence that the difficulty is about the agent's policy, with an absolute measure that must be independent of the agent? The answer is simple: choose one or more canonical agents (or policies) to the problem and *not* the agent one is evaluating. For instance, if we know a mechanism or model of how the problem is solved, we can measure difficulty from the characteristics of this mechanism.

If we now focus on a canonical policy π^* solving the task, we can measure the information required to get the policy from nothing, its algorithmic content, as its Kolmogorov complexity $K(\pi^*)$. We can indeed see difficulty as $K(\pi^*)$, with π^* being the canonical policy with smallest K. For example, in Figure 8.2 we would choose 58 as the difficulty of the task. This is a common interpretation: "a problem is thought of as being difficult if the simplest good solution to the problem is complex. Easy problems on the other hand are those that have simple solutions. This is a very natural way to think about the difficulty of problems" (Legg and Hutter, 2007c). However, $\min K(\pi)$ does not take the task interaction into account and does not depend on the time or number of trials given to learn. We could use the task μ as input, i.e., $K(\pi^*|\mu)$. However, this expression would vanish as the description "the canonical policy for μ" would be very short. We can avoid this problem, make it computable and, at the same time, consider its execution time, by using Levin's *Kt* complexity, where the difficulty of finding the policy depends on the evidence or interaction generated by the task, not the task itself. This "time-weighted variant $Kt(x|y)$ can be viewed as the data and time 'cost' or 'effort' necessary for going from y to x" (Hernández-Orallo, 1999a, p. XIV), known as 'information gain' (Hernández-Orallo, 2000e). In brief, "the difficulty of the problem [could] be measured by . . . the 'justification' or 'explanation' of the solution" of inductive and deductive problems, defined in (Hernández-Orallo, 2000d) as $H(\mu) = min\{LS(E|\mu)\}$ where E is the explanation for the solution of μ and $LS(E)$ is the length of E plus the logarithm of the computational steps, as in Levin's Kt.

This is in the right direction, as we will see in the next section, but it is very important to be more precise about which expression is given as y in $Kt(x|y)$: the whole description of a task (which may include its solution), its observations, through an interaction trial, or nothing, as in a blind search.

All this resembles some accounts of difficulty found in cognitive science. Computer models are constructed to understand how a task is solved by humans or how it can be solved in a general way. By analysing the features of the model and its execution, one can derive measures of difficulty for several items in a task. In effect, the analysis of difficulty linked with cognitive modelling dates back to the 'General Problem Solver' (Newell and Simon, 1961), the early analysis of "the problem space of difficulty" of Thurstone letter series completion tasks (Simon and Kotovsky, 1963) and the analogy tasks from the WAIS (Wechsler Adult Intelligence Scale) test (Evans, 1963, 1965). Similar analysis of tasks in intelligence tests and other problems using cognitive models took place in the following years, including further analysis of series completion (Leeuwenberg, 1969; Simon et al., 1991; Schrepp, 1999), odd-one-out problems (Lovett et al., 2008; Lovett and Forbus, 2011), Raven's Progressive Matrices (Carpenter et al., 1990; Lovett et al., 2010; Ragni and Neubert, 2012, 2014) and many others (for an extensive account, see Hernández-Orallo et al., 2016). In all these computer models, the functions for item difficulty are usually derived as a mixture of how many elements are considered for the pattern, with possibly some other minor adjustments, thereby being implicit approximations or variants of Kolmogorov complexity. Also, confirmatory IRT models can combine a logistic 1PL, 2PL or 3PL model (see Section 3.6) with a conceptually derived notion of difficulty (Embretson and McCollam, 2000).

In psychology and cognitive science, the difficulty that a cognitive model experiences for solving a task has also been associated with the number of elements that must be considered at the same time, which is usually referred to as working memory. It is a well-known motif in psychology that only a small number of elements – six according to (Hamilton, 1859) or seven according to (Miller, 1956) – can be considered at a time. This interprets difficulty as the effort of figuring out the solution in terms of other components the subject already knows, but needs to combine. Several concepts of difficulty elaborate on this idea (Ashcraft et al., 1992; Hardman and Payne, 1995; Logie, 2014). The connection of difficulty with the resources taken by the agent or policy solving the task permeates other disciplines, when one considers "resource-bounded reasoning", from statistics to artificial intelligence (Good, 1971; Simon, 1982).

When resources finally emerge to the forefront, we must of course look at one of the most objective and developed theories of complexity: computational complexity theory. "For whichever resource we are interested in bounding – time, memory and so on – we define *intrinsic complexity* of a problem as the complexity of the most efficient algorithm that solves it" (Moore and Mertens, 2011). The canonical 'policy' is defined as the most efficient algorithm in terms of the resources we are interested in. This is determined with the big-O notation, which ignores constant and multiplicative factors on the cost function. For instance, $20n^3 + 300n^2 \log n + 10n$ is in $O(n^3)$. This notation is justified because these factors depend on the particular machine used, whereas the big-O notation is independent of the particular computer or language that is used to express the algorithm (assuming the same model of computation). For instance, we can show that *quicksort* sorts elements in an array within a quadratic function over the size of the array in the worst case, i.e., it makes at most $O(n^2)$ comparisons. This contrasts with von Neumann's mergesort, which makes at most $O(n \log n)$ comparisons. On average, however, *quicksort* is competitive or even outperforms mergesort. For our purposes, it can be shown that the sorting *problem* cannot be solved in less that $O(n \log n)$ for both the worst-case and the average-case complexity. Moreover, since this is bounded by a polynomial function we can say that sorting is an 'easy' problem, which is in class **P**, i.e., solved in polynomial time on the size of the input.

Actually, it is revealing to remember that the origin of class **P** traces back to questions about difficulty. Alan Cobham, in his seminal work, wondered: "first, is it harder to multiply than to add? and second, why?" (Cobham, 1965). It was then shown that the everyday algorithm for addition works in $O(n)$ where n is the size of the inputs, whereas our everyday multiplication is in $O(n^2)$ – but this can get down to expressions such as $O(n \log(n) \log(\log(n)))$ for the fast Fourier transform (FFT) algorithm (Schönhage and Strassen, 1971) or even less.

As we have seen, computational complexity theory focuses on problems and put them into problem classes, not only **P**, but also **PSPACE**, **NP**, etc. (Arora and Barak, 2009). Some problems are reducible to others by a polynomial transformation and fall into the same class. While this is of an enormous theoretical and practical relevance, it is not directly useful to the assessment of *tasks*, as defined in the previous sections. First, some problems in the same class, albeit with different constants, are intuitively seen as more difficult than others. Second, and most importantly, in computational complexity theory problem instances are characterised by their length. In contrast, the difficulty of a task might be defined in terms of the resources taken to solve the task – but not necessarily as a function of the *size* of the input. For instance, the size of a task instance only makes sense for a few kinds of static tasks. If we look at Table 8.1 we see that the size of the instance is not the most meaningful feature.

Some of the preceding problems may at least look different when we consider average-case computational complexity instead of worst-case computational complexity (Goldreich and Vadhan, 2007). Average-case complexity, originally introduced by Knuth (1973) and developed into problem classes (like the worst-case counterpart) by Levin (1986), is defined in terms of a distribution p on all instances. The average-case time complexity, or expected time complexity of an algorithm A for a set of instances X of size n with an associated probability p is defined as

$$T_A(n|X, p) \triangleq \frac{\sum_{x \in X, L(x)=n} p(x) \cdot t_A(x)}{\sum_{x \in X, L(x)=n} p(x)} \tag{8.2}$$

where t_A returns the (expected) number of computational (execution) steps of A with instance x.

However, Eq. 8.2 is still sliced by $L(x) = n$, i.e., is a function of the size of the input. What we are really interested in is an overall estimated complexity:

$$T_A(X, p) \triangleq \sum_{x \in X} p(x) \cdot t_A(x) \tag{8.3}$$

Equation 8.3 is not very common in computational complexity, as it requires a fast decreasing p in terms of the size of the instance x to be convergent, since the larger n is the larger the number of instances is, apart from the growth in time complexity. Note that the preceding expression returns an expected number of steps, is not a function of n and hence is no longer expressed in a big-O notation, depending on the particular computer used.

The efficiency of an algorithm is relevant to the effort required to find it, when executed to check whether it solves the problem. However, as seen previously, the size of the algorithm is very important too. Together:

> **Keynote 8.8. Difficulty can be seen as search effort** from problem (task) to solution (policy), with the efficiency and the size of the policy playing an important role.

For instance, Leslie Valiant uses the term "mental search" when referring to the kind of problems represented by **NP**. About these problems, he says that "they can be solved by searching objects one generates internally in one's head or computer" (Valiant, 2013, p. 39) and hints this is tantamount to what Turing called "intellectual search", namely "searches carried out by brains for combinations with particular properties" (Turing, 1948, sec. 12). In fact, leaving trial-and-error physical search apart, Turing actually identified three types of search: "intellectual search", "evolutionary search" and "cultural search".

However, the problem about the view of difficulty as search is that there are infinitely many kinds of searches. One task can be easy with some search procedure but may be very difficult with another search procedure. Nonetheless, several characterisations of the difficulty of search have been attempted in several areas such as constraint satisfaction problems, machine learning, tree search algorithms and simulated annealing. For instance, it is said that a problem is hard if there is a "high density of well-separated almost solutions (local minima)" (Kanefsky and Taylor, 1991) or a "rugged solution space" (Hoos, 1999).

One insightful setting for the analysis of search problems has been performed in the area of evolutionary computation, which relies on operators that transform solutions by mutation, cross-over or other recombinations. An evolutionary fitness 'landscape' (Wright, 1932, 1988) is conceived with solutions as nodes and operators as edges. The general idea of a "rugged solution space" is particularised to a "rugged fitness landscape". Other concepts defining or affecting difficulty are described as "needle in a haystack" (many alternative paths leading nowhere), the existence of "epistatic interactions" between parts (the relation between the building blocks of the solution), motif difficulty (subgraphs in fitness landscape networks) and many others (He et al., 2007; Liu et al., 2012).

8.6 ALGORITHMIC NOTIONS OF POLICY ACQUISITION EFFORT

From our account of the different views of difficulty in the previous section we can draw several conclusions. First, the difficulty of a task is significantly different to the difficulty of an instance. We usually understand that a policy that solves a task must be acquired from experience, whereas for an instance it is an existing policy that has to be applied. Second, even if we focus on the policy (and not on the task features or the particular solutions), we find three different main views: the resources required by the policy, the steps required by a search procedure to find the policy and apply it, and the information that is required to reach the policy from the task. We will try to reconcile all these views for tasks in this and the following section and for instances in Section 8.8.

Another thing that we have learnt is that the effective calculation of the difficulty for an arbitrary task is unrealistic, if it depends on the features of a canonical or best policy for the task; for many tasks it is computationally infeasible – or even incomputable – to determine the best policy. Instead, what we aim for is to give a *definition* of difficulty. Consequently, any approximation or surrogate of difficulty will generally be understood as an upper bound. Despite these innate limitations, a general definition of difficulty for any task will be extremely useful to compare tasks and have a common understanding, especially if difficulty can have an associated *unit*, such that the measurements could be accompanied by units too.

We will elaborate our definition of difficulty (or hardness) as the *effort* to build the policy (i.e., algorithm) that solves the task. Our interpretation of solving the task is given by the notion of acceptability, seen in Eq. 8.1. This view leads to the following definition:

$$\hbar^{[\epsilon,\delta,\mapsto\nu]}(\mu) \triangleq \min_{\pi \in \mathcal{A}^{[\epsilon,\mapsto\nu]}(\mu)} \mathbb{F}^{[\epsilon,\delta,\mapsto\nu]}(\pi,\mu) \tag{8.4}$$

Basically, this is a resource-based view of task difficulty, as *the minimum acquisition effort* $\mathbb{F}$ *of any ϵ-acceptable policy for the task in ν trials with confidence* δ. If we look at Figure 8.2, which shows the threshold at 0.8 (tolerance $\epsilon = 0.2$), difficulty is the effort of the policy above the threshold 0.8 that requires minimum effort. What we need to determine is a measure of effort $\mathbb{F}$ that matches our interpretation of task difficulty in general.

The elements that we need to consider in $\mathbb{F}$ are the policy length, its computational cost (execution steps and space) and its verification cost. Other elements that do not depend on the policy but also affect difficulty are the tolerance of the task ϵ, the time units τ (not shown explicitly but considered part of the task), the number of trials ν and the confidence δ (this will be explained later). Table 8.2 shows all these measures and elements. We will now properly introduce the elements in the table that have not been presented yet and the definitions of difficulty that derive from them.

The length of an object $L(x)$ has already been used previously, and its application to a policy needs no further explanation, except that we are considering

Table 8.2. Several features of a policy π given a task μ. The second column represents which type of difficulty the feature represents best.

Feature of π	Difficulty	Notation	Depends on
Expected response	–	$\mathbb{R}(\pi, \mu)$	τ, ν
Variance of response	–	$\mathrm{Var}\,[R(\pi, \mu)]$	τ, ν
Information (size)	Transmission	$L(\pi)$	–
Execution steps	Demonstration	$\mathbb{S}(\pi, \mu)$	τ, ν
Finding effort steps	Finding	$\mathbb{LS}(\pi, \mu)$	$L, \mathbb{S}, \epsilon$
Verification steps	Verifying	$\mathbb{W}(\pi, \mu)$	$\mathbb{S}, \mathrm{Var}\,[R(\pi, \mu)], \epsilon, \delta$
Total effort steps	Search	$\mathbb{F}(\pi, \mu)$	$L, \mathbb{W}$

policies executed by asynchronous-time interactive systems, introduced in Keynote 8.3. By simply considering the length of a policy as difficulty, we would have an interpretation of how difficult it would be to acquire the policy if it were given by 'transmission'. For instance, for a multiplication task, μ_{mult}, this would represent the difficulty of learning to multiply if a teacher wrote an algorithm for multiplication using a natural or programming language directly executable by the agent.

The execution or computational steps of a policy π can also be considered. These are in expected value, as we are considering stochastic tasks and agents. In accordance, the expected execution steps of π per trial when performing task μ are denoted by $\mathbb{S}^{[\mapsto \nu]}(\pi, \mu)$. Note that there is a time limit τ given by the task for each trial and the agent can use sleep(t) instructions. These idle times are not counted. In any case only the actions that the agent does inside the time limit τ are considered. For instance, in a task with $\tau = 500$ units, if an agent performs 2000 steps, then does a sleep(1000) and then enters an infinite loop, then the steps are 2000, as these were performed before moving beyond the task end. On the contrary, if the agents enters an infinite loop before using the sleep(1000) instruction, then this will be considered a non-halting program, with $\mathbb{S} = \infty$. Note that time units and steps are decoupled. For the cases for which speed is relevant, we can perform a mapping between the time limit τ and the steps of π (e.g., five steps per time unit) or use physical time with physical agents.

By only considering the computational steps of a policy as a measure of difficulty, we would have an interpretation of difficulty closer to computational complexity theory. We use the term 'demonstration' in Table 8.2 because this is the computational steps that a demonstrator would require to illustrate how the policy works, so that an imitator could learn it.

One can wonder why we do not consider space resources as well. Actually, some of the cognitive interpretations of difficulty in humans seen in the previous section depend on working memory. This is so because working memory actually refers to the length of the policy. For instance, when we talk about how many elements are combined to construct the solution for a problem, we are actually talking about the elements that the algorithm or policy must combine, and not about the memory requirement of the operation. Also, even with an interpretation of execution memory, any algorithm that requires n bits of execution memory will require at least n computational steps to access those bits, so it is already considered by S.

We can now combine L (length) and S (steps), by defining the *finding effort*:

$$\mathbb{LS}^{[\mapsto v]}(\pi, \mu) \triangleq L(\pi) + \log \mathbb{S}^{[\mapsto v]}(\pi, \mu) \tag{8.5}$$

Note that this combination is the same as Eq. 7.4 in Section 7.1, but here we extend it to tasks. The use of the (binary) logarithm has the same motivation, which will be further explained in the next section. By considering $\mathbb{LS}$ as a measure of difficulty, we would have an interpretation of difficulty as the effort of 'finding' the policy through search.

Finally, to complete Table 8.2, we can consider the verification of a policy for a task, denoted by $\mathbb{W}$. This verification usually implies some extra cost that depends on several factors, but, for stochastic tasks, it mostly depends on the tolerance (ϵ), how much confidence we want for the verification (δ) and the variance of a response (for a policy with high variability it is more difficult to certify that it has a given expected value). We will deal with these issues later on. For the moment, we consider that the search effort is with constant verification cost, and we will focus on $\mathbb{LS}$ alone.

Consequently, given all the possibilities for the effort $\mathbb{F}$ in Table 8.2, we make the choice of using *finding effort* $\mathbb{LS}$ to instantiate Eq. 8.4 for *algorithmic* difficulty, clearly inspired by Levin's Kt (Levin, 1973 or Li and Vitányi, 2008):

$$Kt^{[\epsilon, \mapsto v]}(\mu) \triangleq \min_{\pi \in \mathcal{A}^{[\epsilon, \mapsto v]}(\mu)} \mathbb{LS}^{[\mapsto v]}(\pi, \mu) \tag{8.6}$$

In words, algorithmic difficulty is the optimal ϵ-acceptable policy in terms of the sum of its size and the logarithm of the number of its execution steps.

8.7 TASK DIFFICULTY AS POLICY SEARCH

Since the first time we used Kt in the previous chapter (Eq. 7.4), we delayed the question of why program size and execution steps are combined in this way.

Panel 8.4
Levin's universal search for tasks and policies

Given a task μ and a universal prefix-free Turing machine U, for which policies can be enumerated, we conduct several phases, starting with phase 1. For each phase i, we execute all possible policies π with $L(\pi) \leq i$ for at most $s_i = 2^{i-L(\pi)}$ steps each. In these steps we also count the verification steps taken by the trials required to see whether π is an acceptable policy for μ. As soon as the policy is deemed to be incorrect or the allotted number of steps is exhausted, we try the next program. On the contrary, if the policy is verified the search is stopped. When all programs of size $L(\pi) \leq i$ are tried, we change to the next phase $i + 1$.

It can be shown (Li and Vitányi, 2008, p. 580, claim 7.5.1) that the number of steps s taken by Levin's universal search is bounded by $s \leq 2^{k+1}$ for the non-stochastic version with constant verification cost, where

$$k = L(\pi) + log(S(\pi, \mu)) \tag{8.7}$$

and π is the first program that meets the stop condition.

This search is a blind generate-and-refute method, resembling Popper's scientific method, with a growing size and step budget. Levin's universal search has very interesting properties, such as its immunity to local minima. It is also theoretically optimal over any other general search method. More technically, any inversion problem can be solved optimally by Levin's universal search (except for a multiplicative constant, Li and Vitányi, 2008, pp. 577–580). Of course, this search has not solved the problem of heuristics, but any "universal heuristics" (Levin, 2013) should take this value as an upper bound, paying attention to those constant factors.

Panel 8.4 gives an explanation of this combination, by relating this expression to Levin's universal search (Levin, 1973; Solomonoff, 1984a).

The number of computational steps taken by Levin's universal search is bounded approximately by $2^{L(\pi)+log(S(\pi,\mu))} = S(\pi, \mu)2^{L(\pi)}$, as given by Eq. 8.7. This is interpreted as having to try approximately $2^{L(\pi)}$ programs with $S(\pi, \mu)$ execution steps. Since we are calculating its logarithm in Eqs. 8.5 and 8.6, we can say that *the unit of Kt is logarithm of the number of computational steps.* Remarkably, we have integrated in a single unit the concepts of search, policy size and several resources:

Keynote 8.9. The **difficulty of a task** is the logarithm of the number of computational steps Levin's universal search takes to find an acceptable policy for that task, given a tolerance. Difficulty is then the minimum over all policies of the length of the policy and the logarithm of the number of its computational steps.

This interpretation is similar to the notion of information gain (Hernández-Orallo, 2000e) already mentioned. It is actually equivalent to John Mayfield's notion of minimal history, defined as the "minimal process for creating [something] from nothing" (Mayfield, 2007). Actually, many of these ideas can be traced back to Turing, with the proposal of a search for inversion problems as an enumeration of solutions – much like Levin's universal search without bounding the execution time in an incremental fashion – or with a "search through all proofs" (Turing, 1948), which has been reproduced in some variants of the search (Hutter, 2002, 2005).

The original Levin's universal search is basically a blind search: it systematically executes programs by increasing length and time allocations, without looking at the execution or results at all other than verifying whether the right policy has been found. However, the extension of Levin's universal search to tasks as indicated in Panel 8.4 is understood for several trials, and the search becomes more powerful. In fact, it becomes a metasearch. Imagine, for instance, that the task gives hints about or reinforces good actions during each trial. This can be incorporated into the search, especially if there are rewards or the number of trials v in Eq. 8.6 is greater than one, as policies such as 'do what is observed', 'do a Monte Carlo approach' and 'learn from the examples' are considered in the (meta)search, provided the language for expressing policies is Turing-complete.

We can explore some of the cases in Table 8.1 using this notion of difficulty. The best acceptable policy must be some short but reasonably efficient algorithm to solve the task, according to the established tolerance. For instance, for μ_{num}, μ_{RPM} and μ_{pacm}, if the number of trials is too large, a general metasearch method can be shorter than particular solutions (such as a Monte Carlo policy for the μ_{num} case, an RPM solver for μ_{rpm} or a specialised policy for μ_{pacm}). However, for μ_{srote} and μ_{lrote}, the reasonable policy 'copy from the previous trial' will likely only appear for μ_{lrote}, for which it pays off, but never for μ_{srote}, since the policy 'print [string]' (with the right string), will be shorter for most UTMs.

Another task that deserves some attention is the choice reaction time task (μ_{react} in Table 8.1). We clearly understand that the difficulty of this task depends on how much time is admitted to make the response. If we map the computational steps of the agent with the time units τ, we can figure out whether there is a short program that can still respond in time using very few computational steps. Note that policies have to check the input, process it and see whether they have to react. If the policy checks for the signal as fast as it can, then too many failed checks will be used, increasing the number of steps used by the policy. However, if the policy uses the instruction sleep(t) after each check with some reasonable value of t then it can save some computational steps but increases the risk of reacting too late. The finding of appropriate values of t for sleep(t) such that a good trade-off is found can be done in the enumeration in Levin's universal search.

We need to be well aware that, despite the good formal properties of Levin's universal search, we are working with a surrogate for difficulty. First, it is just *one* search method. Second, it can only be upper approximated for most tasks. In practice, for many tasks, we can use variants of Eq. 8.6 or specific functions of difficulty, because we think of a function that fits the task better, because we want to derive a measure of difficulty that is more in alignment with some particular species (e.g., humans), or because we look for less computationally expensive functions of difficulty. However, despite all the limitations, the use of a general definition helps understand the units of difficulty (basically logarithm of computational effort) and will pave the way to the comparison between tasks in the following chapter.

Finally, hitherto, we have considered that the verification effort is independent of whether the stochastic task and/or stochastic agent lead to a response R with high variance. In addition, an agent with low steadiness (see Keynote 8.7) can make mistakes when applying Levin's universal search. For a stochastic situation, we can never have 100 per cent confidence of having verified an acceptable policy. This means that the stop criterion for Levin's universal search needs to be overhauled. As a result, we consider that a series of runs is a sufficient verification for a probably approximately correct (PAC) policy π for μ when the average of the results of the trials (runs) $\bar{r}$ is not less than a confidence threshold:

$$\mathbb{P}(\bar{r} \geq 1 - \epsilon) \geq 1 - \delta \qquad (8.8)$$

This clearly resembles a PAC (probably approximately correct) scenario (Valiant, 1984, 2013), although the context and details are different.

We need to modify Levin's universal search to add extra trials until we have some certainty of having found the solution. In other words, we can discard one policy if it is not acceptable (as it will be re-evaluated again on the next phase of Levin's universal search), but we cannot stop the algorithm the first time a response gives a result above the threshold. We need several trial repetitions (or bids) to have more certainty. To give a surrogate definition, we first make the strong assumption that all trial runs take the same number of steps, so the verification cost could be approximated by

$$\widehat{\mathbb{W}}^{[\epsilon,\delta]}(\pi, \mu) \triangleq \mathbb{S}(\pi, \mu) \cdot \mathbb{B}^{[\epsilon,\delta]}(\pi, \mu) \tag{8.9}$$

i.e., the product of the expected number of steps $\mathbb{S}$ and the expected number of verification bids $\mathbb{B}$. With this, we focus on calculating the number of bids of the policy until we can verify whether it is acceptable or not.

The number of bids can be estimated from the mean and the standard deviation of the response for a series of runs. By assuming a normal distribution (for details, see Hernández-Orallo, 2015e) we have the approximation

$$\mathbb{B}^{[\epsilon,\delta]}(\pi, \mu) \triangleq \frac{|z_{\delta/2}|^2 \operatorname{Var}[R(\pi, \mu)]}{((1 - \epsilon) - \mathbb{R}(\pi, \mu))^2} \tag{8.10}$$

where $z_{\delta/2}$ is the standard normal quantile for significance level δ. And now the effort is rewritten as

$$\mathbb{F}^{[\epsilon,\delta]}(\pi, \mu) \triangleq \log(2^{L(\pi)} \cdot \widehat{\mathbb{W}}^{[\epsilon,\delta]}(\pi, \mu)) = L(\pi) + \log \widehat{\mathbb{W}}^{[\epsilon,\delta]}(\pi, \mu) \tag{8.11}$$

For clarity, we can expand what $\mathbb{F}$ is by using the definition $\widehat{\mathbb{W}}$ from Eq. 8.9 and taking the bids from Eq. 8.10 as

$$\mathbb{F}^{[\epsilon,\delta]}(\pi, \mu) = L(\pi) + \log(\mathbb{S}(\pi, \mu) \cdot \mathbb{B}^{[\epsilon,\delta]}(\pi, \mu)) \tag{8.12}$$

$$= L(\pi) + \log \mathbb{S}(\pi, \mu) + \log \mathbb{B}^{[\epsilon,\delta]}(\pi, \mu) \tag{8.13}$$

which can be used for another instance of Eq. 8.4. The effort now depends on the length of the policy, the logarithm of the number of its computational steps and the logarithm of the times it has to be executed to have confidence that it is an acceptable solution for the task. This completes the views of difficulty in Table 8.2. Note that we do not specify ν any more, since the number of trials is now given by the Levin's universal search itself.

On balance, the relevance of $\mathbb{B}$ in Eq. 8.12 will be small, as usually the number of steps will be much higher than the number of repetitions. That means that the measure will be dominated by L and $\mathbb{S}$. In what follows, we will just work with Eq. 8.6.

8.8 TASK INSTANCE DIFFICULTY

The difficulty of a task is mostly understood as the effort to acquire an acceptable policy. This acquisition can come through evolution, whenever we evaluate an animal for an innate task, can come through programming, whenever we evaluate a computer for a programmed task, or can come through learning, by inductive inference from examples, by demonstration or by transmission, as Table 8.2 summarises. As we discussed at the beginning of this chapter, the difficulty of a task is not the average difficulty of its instances, since one instance alone can be easily acquired by rote learning. For instance, we can think of particular instances of any of the tasks in Table 8.1 that are trivial once they are seen for a second time. Memory would just suffice. This does not mean that instance difficulty is meaningless, but that our interpretation must not be about a stand-alone instance independent of the task – that would simply be a non-stochastic task – but a view of an instance *relative* to a task. Panel 8.5 shows how several instances may be found more or less difficult depending on the policy chosen for the task.

This is the same for other tasks. For the relative numerousness task, μ_{num}, for instance, illustrated in Figure 8.1, the difficulty of all instances depends on the size of the numbers if a counting policy is used, while it depends on the difference of quantities if a Monte Carlo policy is used.

Is it impossible to define a measure of instance difficulty that is not dependent on one chosen policy and, as a result, on the agent either? We can first have a look at previous approaches to instance difficulty. For instance, in the area of computational complexity, the complexity of an instance x for a decision problem for a set A is defined as the "size of the smallest special-case program for A that runs in time t, decides x correctly and makes no mistakes on other strings ('don't know' answers are permitted)" (Orponen et al., 1994). The notion is based on the idea that the program must be consistent with the other instances in A.

A very different approach focuses on the "probability of failure" (Bentley et al., 2004; Ashlock and Schonfeld, 2010). This probability can refer to one particular policy, or to *all* policies, as "the likelihood that a randomly chosen program will fail for any given input value" (Bentley et al., 2004). This can only make sense if we focus on the acceptable policies for the whole task. For instance, looking at Figure 8.2, does it make sense to calculate the success rate for an instance of only those agents above the threshold? In this case, the question is how to choose from the agent programs randomly, if we do not assume a population of agents or policies, as in human psychometrics. As an option,

---

Panel 8.5
Instance difficulty for the multiplication task

For the multiplication task μ_{mult}, instances $\mu^A_{mult} = 49 \times 53$ and $\mu^B_{mult} = 1 \times 2597$ give the same result but the latter looks simpler. One can argue that this is because of the computational steps taken by the everyday algorithm for multiplication, which are much fewer for the second multiplication. But what about $\mu^C_{mult} = 60 \times 40$? Even if the numbers are of basically the same size as μ^A_{mult}, it looks easier because there are some short-cuts in *our* multiplication algorithm (see, e.g., Baroody and Dowker, 2013). However, when we want to evaluate a subject we do not know which algorithm is used. Any of the following algorithms (or others) might be used:

Repetition algorithm: accumulate the second factor as many times as specified by the first factor. This method performs as many additions as indicated by the first multiplicand. It is very efficient with μ^B_{mult}.

Grid algorithm: factors are arranged on a grid by their digits. All partial multiplications are summed up. For instance, 49×53 is solved by performing $40 \times 50 + 40 \times 3 + 9 \times 50 + 9 \times 3$. For this algorithm, μ^C_{mult} is simpler as it leads to many partial products including 0.

Standard algorithm: the second factor multiplies the first digit by digit. The partial products are shifted one position and summed up. There is a huge difference if we swap the factors of μ^B_{mult} into 2597×1.

FFT algorithm (Schönhage and Strassen, 1971): uses the fast Fourier transform algorithm. It is in $O(n \log(n) \log(\log(n))))$ on the number of single digit multiplications but it only pays off for very large numbers.

From here, it might seem that we can only talk about instance difficulty if we know exactly the algorithm the agent is using.

---

we could use a universal distribution and calculate this weighted probability of failure as a measure of difficulty.

In what follows we present an approach that refines this idea. Instead of all policies we just consider the best policy. But now, we change the tolerance value ϵ as follows:

Keynote 8.10. The **relative algorithmic difficulty of an instance with respect to a task** is defined as the minimum "finding effort" or "resources" $\mathbb{LS}$ for any acceptable task policy at any other tolerance ϵ_0 such that the instance is accepted.

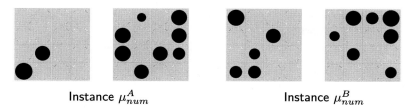

Instance μ^A_{num} Instance μ^B_{num}

Figure 8.4. Two instances of the relative numerousness task.

We formalise this idea as follows. First we denote by μ^σ an instance of stochastic task μ by setting the seed (or the random tape) equal to σ, as we described at the end of Section 8.2. Next, we formalise the set of all optimal policies for varying tolerances ϵ_0 as

$$Opt^{[\mapsto v]}_{\mathbb{LS}}(\mu) \triangleq \left\{ \underset{\pi \in \mathcal{A}^{[\epsilon_0, \mapsto v]}(\mu)}{\arg \min} \ \mathbb{LS}^{[\mapsto v]}(\pi, \mu) \right\}_{\epsilon_0 \in [0,1]} \tag{8.14}$$

Note that many policies that efficiently cover μ^σ are not in the preceding set, and many of the policies may not cover μ^σ. The algorithmic instance difficulty of μ^σ with respect to μ uses the intersection of both sets:

$$\hbar^{[\epsilon, \mapsto v]}(\mu_\sigma | \mu) \triangleq \underset{\pi \in Opt^{[\mapsto v]}_{\mathbb{LS}}(\mu) \cap \mathcal{A}^{[\epsilon, \mapsto v]}(\mu^\sigma)}{\min} \ \mathbb{LS}^{[\mapsto v]}(\pi, \mu^\sigma) \tag{8.15}$$

Since $Opt_{\mathbb{LS}}$ minimises by $\mathbb{LS}$, this can be interpreted as if we sorted the policies in $Opt_{\mathbb{LS}}$ by decreasing tolerance, and picked the first one accepting the instance with tolerance ϵ. Alternatively, especially if the functions are not monotonic, we could pick the last one not accepting the instance, i.e., the maximum in Eq. 8.15 over the optimal policies minus the acceptable ones. We can see this on the left of Figure 8.5 for two instances (shown in Figure 8.4) of the relative numerousness task. We take all the optimal policies (in terms of $\mathbb{LS}$) for varying values of ϵ_0. For one instance, e.g., μ^A_{num}, we see that its curve crosses the tolerance level of 0.8 at 8014.3. Since the difficulty of the task is 8016.2, we can say that μ^A_{num} is an easy instance. Interestingly, if we see this as a cumulative distribution, the difficulty of the task is the value of $\mathbb{LS}$ that covers the $1 - \epsilon$ quantile of the instances. This is shown on the right of Figure 8.5.

This notion of algorithmic instance difficulty is consistent with the fact that easy and frequent instances are the first that are covered by simple policies when tolerance is high. As tolerance becomes tighter, more difficult and infrequent instances must be covered. This phenomenon can be seen for those tasks for which humans do not perform equally well for all instances. Humans optimise resources for easy and frequent instances. Also, short-cuts occasionally increase the size of the policy with the goal of improving the efficiency for

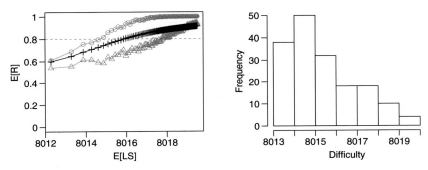

Figure 8.5. Left: experimental evolution of responses for the set Opt_{LS} for the instances of Figure 8.4. Instance μ_{num}^{A} is shown with circles and instance μ_{num}^{B} with triangles. For threshold 0.8 ($\epsilon = 0.2$), the instance difficulty of μ_{num}^{A} corresponds to $E[LS] = 8014.9$, whereas μ_{num}^{B} corresponds to $E[LS] = 8017.7$. Between both series, the evolution for the task for ranging tolerances is shown with crosses, whose task difficulty is 8015.9 for $\epsilon = 0.2$. Right: distribution of instance difficulties for threshold 0.8 ($\epsilon=0.2$), using the Monte Carlo policy with varying numbers of probing points. In this example, the part of L in LS is constant, because for these ranges, we are assuming the Monte Carlo solution we discussed in Panel 8.3 with an estimated length of 8000 bits for coding the algorithm. The variable part takes 5000 steps per Monte Carlo point.

very common cases. For example, for the multiplication task, 4×15 looks easier than 3×14, because the former is so frequent (four quarters in an hour) that humans typically learn that case by rote.

In the end, algorithmic instance difficulty represents how well the instance fits the simple policies, not being an exception for which extra code is required. This is connected with the notions of consilience, coherence and intensionality (Whewell, 1847; Thagard, 1978; Hernández-Orallo, 2000b; Hernández-Orallo and García-Varea, 2000; Hernández-Orallo, 1999b, 2000c,e). These concepts will re-emerge in the following chapter, when dealing with the composition and decomposition of tasks.

Of course, the calculation of instance difficulty will not always be as straightforward and smooth as in Figure 8.5. Nonetheless, this view of instance difficulty, as a definition, meets our desiderata: it does not depend on one particular policy but considers all of them (by varying the tolerance) and it is measured in logarithm of number of computational steps and directly comparable with the difficulty of the task.

We finish our introduction of a general paradigm for the understanding of the notion of difficulty. We see that it depends, on one hand, on the tolerance of the task and, on the other hand, on the size, computational steps and variability of the best acceptable policies for the task. Remarkably, even if all these features are integrated, task difficulty and task instance difficulty are still expressed in the same unit: (logarithm of the number of) computational steps, as a result of a search. In brief, difficulty is understood as an upper bound of the effort of this search, be it mental, evolutionary or cultural.

The generality of the paradigm seen in this chapter brings, as counterpart, some applicability limitations, since the exact calculation of the difficulty functions is intractable and depends on the description language used for the policies. Nonetheless, this paradigm does not preclude the use of particular difficulty functions for some tasks (or, especially, for task instances), provided we keep the connection with the basic principles of what a task is and what a difficulty function means. Actually, it is not only the difficulty function that may need to be accommodated, but also the way in which tasks are used in practice, so that actual measurements can be obtained efficiently and accurately, the ultimate goal of psychometric tests. This is the purpose of the next chapter.

CHAPTER HIGHLIGHTS

- The same task possibly triggering a continuum between identification and acquisition of the policy (Keynote 8.1).
- Tasks and agents defined as asynchronous-time interactive stochastic machines, and instances as trials of a task (Keynotes 8.2, 8.3, 8.4).
- Acceptable policies depending on a tolerance ϵ (Eq. 8.1) and suboptimal results given by lack of soundness or steadiness (Keynote 8.7).
- Many notions of difficulty of a task related to the search effort considering both the size and the computational steps of the policy, not the task (Keynote 8.8, Section 8.5, Table 8.2).
- The relation between Levin's universal search (Panel 8.4) and the algorithmic difficulty of a task (Eq. 8.6, Keynote 8.9) extended with the verification effort in stochastic tasks and agents (Eqs. 8.9, 8.12).
- Algorithmic instance difficulty not requiring the choice of any canonical task solution (Eqs. 8.14, 8.15, Keynote 8.10, Section 8.8).

9

From Tasks to Tests

Altitude . . . is the degree of difficulty at which a given percentage of
success is attained. . . . Width [is] the percent of successes at any given
altitude or the average percent of successes at any given series of
altitudes. . . . Area is the total number of tasks done correctly, or the
percentage which this total is of the number of tasks in the entire list.
– Edward L. Thorndike,
The Measurement of Intelligence (1927)

T HE PRECISE definition and understanding of a task is crucial for its use
as a measurement tool. In the previous chapter we have seen how tasks
can be characterised in terms of their policies and their difficulty viewed as a
search problem. Setting the perspective on the policies is helpful, but we need
to pursue this direction further. A test is much more than just a task. In what
follows we will introduce tools to examine how the performance of an agent
changes for a range of difficulties. When building a test, we will focus on how
to sample from the whole set of tasks and instances to obtain an appropriate
pool of items, which maximise the information they take about the subject.
This choice of items can be performed by diversity, difficulty and also by discriminating power, a challenging issue that is crucial for the design of adaptive
tests.

9.1 AGENT CHARACTERISTIC CURVES

In our eagerness for quantification, we usually summarise a phenomenon by
a single number. For instance, when we want to evaluate an agent for a given
task, we sample from the task and record its aggregate response. This value can

then be compared with those of other agents. Should not this be enough for a cognitive test and the comparison of agents? Unfortunately, much information is lost whenever we summarise the results of many task instances into a single number. The study of the responses for single instances can provide valuable information about how the agent performs but, most importantly, it can give us ways of designing better tests.

A similar observation is behind item analysis in item response theory (IRT), as we saw in Chapter 3. By analysing the behaviour of a set of subjects for an item we can better understand the characteristics of the item, when to use it and how it compares with other items. Unfortunately, IRT requires a population, and the closest thing to an item characteristic curve that we can achieve without a population is what we see on the left on Figure 8.5 by varying tolerance, as we will revisit later on in this chapter.

In what follows, and in accordance to IRT and Chapter 3, we will use the word *item* for either an instance or a particular task in a task *class*. A task class is defined as a pair $\langle M, p_M \rangle$, where M is a set of tasks or task instances and p_M is a distribution over M. With this definition, task classes are stochastic tasks, but not all stochastic tasks can be seen as classes. The use of the notion of task class from now on aims at representing a cognitive property that can be measured by a test, which may include instances of several tasks. For instance, a task class can be composed of addition and multiplication problems, for which we supply an appropriate definitional probability p_M (that may give more or less relevance to multiplication than addition). In the previous chapter we saw how we can calculate the difficulty of tasks and instances (relative to a task), which are independent of any subject population. In this chapter, we will use the term *item difficulty*, as generally as possible, considering the difficulty functions seen in the previous chapter or others.

In Chapter 3 we also very briefly mentioned the existence of the so-called *person characteristic curves* (see, e.g., Embretson and McCollam, 2000), showing an example in Figure 3.11 (left). Now, we generalise and rename person characteristic curves as follows:

> **Keynote 9.1.** An **agent characteristic curve** shows the values of performance (on the *y*-axis) of a subject for increasing levels of item difficulty on the *x*-axis.

The preceding description does not ensure that we get a curve. For instance, Figure 9.1 (left) shows a scatter plot using a measure of environment complexity on the *x*-axis against performance on the *y*-axis for two different agents.

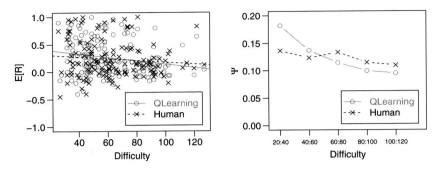

Figure 9.1. Left: A comparison of performance (individual results and linear fit) of two different kinds of agents for the same task using a difficulty function, defined as an approximation of the Kolmogorov complexity of the tasks (Insa-Cabrera et al., 2011a, Figure 4). Right: the corresponding agent characteristic curves with tolerance $\epsilon = 0.2$ (threshold at 0.8) and binned difficulties. Compare with Figure 3.11 (left).

As we see in this figure, it does not look much like a curve. To make it a look smoother we would need to average results for different items with (roughly) the same difficulty, as in Figure 9.1 (right) with 5 bins of width 20. In a more general and precise way, given a difficulty (or hardness) function $\hbar$ for items, we define the acceptance rate (or just average performance, "probability of correct response", as seen in Chapter 3, or "item-solving probability", Embretson and McCollam, 2000) per difficulty h as

$$\Psi_h(\pi, M, p_M) \triangleq \sum_{\mu \in M, \hbar(\mu)=h} p_M(\mu|h) \cdot \mathbb{A}(\pi, \mu) \tag{9.1}$$

where $\mathbb{A}(\pi, \mu) \triangleq 1$ if $\pi \in \mathcal{A}(\mu)$ and 0 otherwise represents an indicator function saying if a policy is acceptable for an item. For ease of notation in this chapter, for $\mathbb{A}$, $\mathcal{A}$ and $\hbar$ we omit the tolerance ϵ and the number of trials. The preceding equation is simply a weighted average using the probability p_M of the items of difficulty h for which the policy is acceptable. Note that this can be seen as a slice of Eq. 2.1, i.e., conditional to difficulty.

Now, agent characteristic curves are easily defined by plotting Ψ_h on the y-axis versus h on the x-axis. Figure 9.2 (left) shows the response of three agents for the relative numerousness task (μ_{num} seen in Table 8.1) where difficulties have been rounded. The plot on the right shows the agent characteristic curve using threshold 0.8.

Agent characteristic curves allow us to locate the three key concepts (apart from 'speed') that Edward Thorndike (1927) introduced to categorise intellect: altitude (also referred to as 'level' or 'height'), width (also referred to as 'extent'

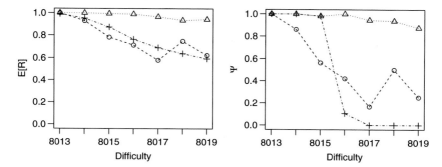

Figure 9.2. Agent characteristic curves of three different agents for the relative numerousness task according to the instance distribution and difficulties shown in Figure 8.5. Agent π_1 (in circles) uses a counting algorithm with a uniform error around the true value (between -15 and 15 per cent). Agent π_2 (in triangles) uses a counting algorithm that is only able to count up to 7 (any larger number is also 7). Agent π_3 (in crosses) uses a Monte Carlo algorithm with 10 random probing points per board. The left plot aggregates expected response and hence it is generally above 0.5 (a random guess). The right plot actually shows agent characteristic curves using acceptance (a threshold set on 0.8 in this case), where the y-axis shows the ratio of solved instances per difficulty.

or 'range') and area, as expressed by the opening epigraph of this chapter. Altitude is clearly associated with proficiency (the maximum attained difficulty), width is actually Ψ_h and area corresponds to the area under the agent characteristic curve, with an appropriate weighting of the difficulties, as we will discuss later on.

For the area to be finite, as Ψ_h is bounded, we need to ascertain whether the curve for every agent will reach 0 on the right. In Figure 9.2 (right), this seems to happen for agent π_3, but will Ψ_h tend to 0 for π_1 and π_2 as well? We will say that the agent characteristic curve is strongly bounded by the difficulty function $\hbar$ in M if for every policy π there is a difficulty h such that for every item $\mu \in M$ with $\hbar(\mu) \geq h$ we have $\mathbb{A}(\pi, \mu) = 0$, i.e., the policy is not acceptable. For most purposes, however, it is sufficient to have a weaker condition such that a difficulty function makes Ψ_h bounded, namely that if for every policy π, there is a difficulty h such that for every $h' \geq h$ we have $\Psi_{h'}(\pi, M, p_M) = 0$.

We can briefly discuss whether some of the general difficulty functions we saw in the previous chapter lead to bounded agent characteristic curves. For the difficulty function for *instances*, assuming that the function is defined for all instances, we may have non-zero values for arbitrarily high values of $\hbar$. For instance, an agent can solve a single instance that is not solved by any general optimal policy (e.g., if the tolerance is greater than 0).

Things are more interesting for a difficulty function for *tasks*. At first sight, the difficulty function given by Eq. 8.6 does not lead to a bounded curve in general either, as $\mathbb{LS}(\pi, \mu)$ depends on the task μ. To see this, consider that some policies can take arbitrarily long times for some tasks in the class. So any task can have acceptable policies (and hence the acceptance rate possibly being different than zero) for any arbitrary difficulty. However, if we link the computational steps of the agent with the time limit τ of the task (or "globally" synchronise the asynchronous exchange by a common clock as done by Gavane, 2013; Zimmermann et al., 2015), then we would have $\mathbb{S} \leq \tau$ and for every π we could take $h > L(\pi) + \log(\tau)$ which does not depend on μ, so the difficulty function would be bounded.

A more straightforward way of ensuring a bounded curve is when the difficulty function is bounded by a maximum difficulty h_{max}. For the case of instance difficulty, this happens when there is a policy for tolerance $\epsilon = 0$ and its $\mathbb{LS}$ is bounded, i.e., all instances can be perfectly solved with finite resources. In the relative numerousness task, this algorithm exists and can be bounded if the numbers to compare are always finite (so the count finishes). Similarly, for task difficulty, the difficulty function is bounded if every task in a class has a policy for the given tolerance whose $\mathbb{LS}$ is bounded. Of course, other particular bounded difficulty functions can be figured out not necessarily following Eqs. 8.6 and 8.15. These considerations are useful when comparing agent characteristic curves and, most especially, when interpreting their areas, as we will do later on in this chapter.

9.2 SAMPLING TASK ITEMS EFFECTIVELY

Tests are instruments comprising one or more tasks. In general, tasks include (infinitely) many instances. Tests must not only be finite but preferably short. If we denote by M the set of all possible items in the task(s) comprising the behavioural feature to be measured, then a test must perform a *sample* from M (again, Eqs. 2.1 and 2.2). As a result, tests can only give us an approximation of the true value. Many accuracy issues (including validity and reliability) derive from this fact. Our goal is then to find an accurate approximation as efficiently as possible.

At very first sight, it must look natural and straightforward to sample using the distribution given by the (stochastic) task(s) or take the n instances with highest probability. However, this is not a good idea in general. First, by using a simple sampling from a distribution, especially if this distribution is uneven, the instances would (almost) always be the same. The resulting test would be highly predictable by the agents (and their designers or trainers). Second, we can repeatedly sample instances that are very similar, if some clusters of instances are very likely for the definition of the task. Using very similar items in a test does not precisely maximise the information that we can get from the test. Third, we can sample too many easy instances or too many difficult instances, for which the expected performance will be respectively good or bad on average, for every agent of interest.

It is at this point that we need to clearly distinguish the *definition* of a behavioural feature in terms of a representational distribution p_M, as for Eq. 2.1, from the *test*, as for Eq. 2.2. A non-adaptive test can use a sampling distribution q to get a sample M' from the set of all problems M. As p_M and q are not equal, we require to apply some weights w, as for Eq. 2.2, to recover a good approximation of the original value.

The basic idea is to sample the most informative problems, similarly to an optimal experimental design. This can be done by very different sampling methods such as importance sampling (Srinivasan, 2002), cluster sampling, stratified sampling (Cochran, 1977; Thompson, 2012) and other Monte Carlo procedures, provided we have some notion of informativeness, or define strata based on difficulty.

A first approach to informativeness can be based on item diversity. Diversity can be ensured by defining a similarity function $sim(\mu_1, \mu_2)$, which indicates how similar (or correlated) exercises μ_1 and μ_2 in M are. We would need to sample from M and correct with weights w in such a way that both the accumulated mass on p and the diversity are high. One way of defining the similarity function is to use m descriptors to characterise the items and derive any off-the-shelf similarity metric from the m-dimensional space. For instance, Figure 9.3 shows two such descriptors for the relative numerousness task. On the x-axis, the first descriptor is the number ratio, which is the quotient between the smallest and the largest number of the two boards, called the "ratio smaller/larger", commonly used in tests of numerical competence as a proxy of difficulty (see, e.g., Cantlon and Brannon, 2006). On the y-axis, the second descriptor is the total area of the panel, by summing the size of the dots of both panels (darkness of the panels). The goal is to recognise whether the sample is diverse for the two descriptors. For this task, special types of sampling can be used to get a diverse and representative sample, like the one shown with crosses in Figure 9.3.

In Chapter 10, we will give more general definitions of similarity, without the need of descriptors. Diversity, as a good feature of a sample, has been considered in psychometrics and test theory by the analysis of the inter-item correlations (Gulliksen, 1945) using, e.g., Cronbach's alpha (Sijtsma, 2009). However, because of their negative effect on reliability, it is usual to discard those

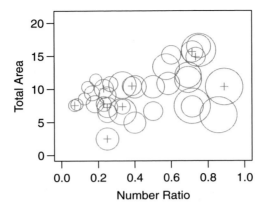

Figure 9.3. Several instances are shown according to two descriptors for the relative numerousness task. On the *x*-axis, the number ratio, which is the quotient of the smallest by the largest number of the two boards. On the *y*-axis, the total area of the dots of both boards (darkness of the boards). Circles show 35 instances drawn from the representational distribution p_M. The size of the circles represents the difficulty of the instances, calculated in the same way as illustrated in Figure 8.5. The 10 sampled instances (shown as crosses) cover a wide range of the two descriptors and difficulty.

items with low inter-item correlation. We will deal with some theoretical measures of diversity in general in Chapter 11.

A second, more common, approach to informativeness is linked to difficulty, a crucial notion for item selection in IRT, as we saw in Chapter 3. An effective use of difficulty for sampling relies on two observations. First, the performance for some extreme difficulties is expectable. For instance, in Figure 9.2 we see that the result for difficulty 8013 is expected to be 1, so there is no need to sample many cases of that difficulty. Second, some difficulties may be much more frequent than others. For instance, in Figure 8.5 (right), we see that easy instances are more frequent than difficult ones. Sampling according to the representational distribution p_M will capture very little information for the high difficulty range and will lead to bad tests for high-proficiency agents. In the end, using difficulty appropriately means that, for non-adaptive tests, we choose a range of difficulties such that the *agent characteristic curves* can be properly estimated, i.e., that every slice of difficulty (as represented by Eq. 9.1) is well estimated.

To illustrate how important sampling can be, we are going to study a particular example of task class whose items are given from a representational definition. This task is interactive and with many stochastic components. It is

---

Panel 9.1
A single-agent elementary cellular automaton

An elementary cellular automaton (ECA) (Wolfram, 2002) is a one-dimensional version of the cellular automaton, introduced in 1940s by Stanisław Ulam and John von Neumann (Von Neumann, 1966). A circular array changes each time step according to its previous state and its two neighbours following eight (2^3) triplet transitions that specify how each cell in the array changes. For instance, the following transitions define a rule:

111	110	101	100	011	010	001	000
0	1	1	0	1	1	0	1

The digits in the second row represent the new state for the middle cell after each transition, depending on the triplet. In the preceding case, 01101101, in binary, corresponds to decimal number 109, the ECA rule number. Given this rule, the array 01100 would evolve as follows, looping at the end:

$$
\begin{array}{l}
01100 \\
01101 \\
01111 \\
11001 \\
01001 \quad \leftharpoondown \\
11001 \quad \urcorner
\end{array}
$$

In (Hernández-Orallo, 2015c) an agent was located inside the array, performing *moves* among { left=0, stay=1, right=2 } to change its position and *upshots* among { keep=0, swap=1, set0=2, set1=3 } to alter the state of the cell σ_p where it is located. Agent rewards follow:

$$
r \leftarrow \sum_{j=1}^{\lfloor m/2 \rfloor} \frac{\sigma_{p+j} + \sigma_{p-j}}{2^{j+1}}
$$

The expression counts the number of 1s in the neighbourhood of the agent, located at position p, weighted by their proximity ($\lfloor \; \rfloor$ is the floor function to truncate $m/2$, in case the size of the array m is odd).

The task is parametrised by the original contents of the array (the 'seed'), the ECA rule number, and the original position of the agent.

---

similar to some tasks that are common in artificial intelligence, especially in reinforcement learning, (multi-)agent systems and artificial life. The task class is defined as the performance of an agent in an elementary cellular automaton (ECA), as described in Panel 9.1.

Panel 9.2
An agent policy language

We can define agents according to an agent policy language (APL), which has a binary array *mem* as memory (initially empty), and an ordered set of instructions $\mathcal{I} = \{$ back=0, fwd=1, Vaddm=2, Vadd1=3, Uaddm=4, Uadd1=5 $\}$ to shift along the memory and work with two accumulators V and U. For instance, the string 22142335 represents a program in APL. A precise definition of APL can be found in (Hernández-Orallo, 2015c).

The task class is defined with the 256 possible ECAs, with a uniform distribution $p_M = \frac{1}{256}$. Taking an array length of 21 cells, each task has as many instances (seeds) as the 2^{21} combinations of the original space array, also distributed uniformly. Instead of evaluating humans, other animals or actual AI systems, we use a very simple language to describe agents, and we illustrate their behaviour for this task class. Panel 9.2 briefly describes this language, which we will use to generate populations of agents that we can analyse formally. This language will also be used to calculate difficulties.

The space-time progress of some agents for two tasks (rules 110 and 164) is shown in Figure 9.4. We can see very different trials, depending on the rules and agents. For those diagrams with more black dots, the overall reward is higher. For instance, policy 23555 seems to perform better than policy 24 for rule 164. Apart from particular instances, we are interested in the global picture. For that purpose, we have a population of 1,900 policies with random program size between 1 and 20 and randomly chosen instructions using uniform distributions, with 100 extra policies with the random agent π_{rand} (an agent choosing actions at random), totalling 2,000 policies. Figure 9.5 shows the distributions of the response (shown as 'reward') for this population of agents (policies) for rules 184, 110, 122 and 164. If we set a tolerance of $\epsilon = 0.1$ (the threshold is at 0.9) none of the policies that are evaluated will reach the threshold for rules 110, 122 and 164. Only for rule 184, some policies are above the threshold. For this tolerance the use of tasks 164, 122 and 164 for a test would get no information at all. Actually, the difficulties of these tasks for this tolerance may be very high.

One can argue that the problem of having tasks that are useless (either too easy or too difficult) is motivated because we are using tolerance and discretising results by acceptability. But it is precisely tolerance that allows us to compare the results for different tasks. In fact, we could set the threshold for each

Rule 110 Policy 1114442	Rule 110 Policy 24	Rule 110 Policy 425	Rule 110 Policy random	Rule 164 Policy 22142335	Rule 164 Policy 24	Rule 164 Policy 23555	Rule 164 Policy random

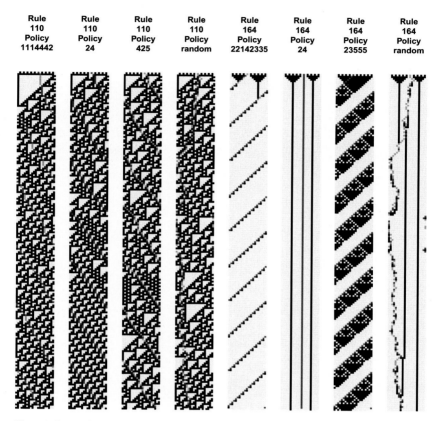

Figure 9.4. Space-time diagrams for the ECA rules 110 and 164 during 200 steps with different agent policies ("random" represents a random-walk policy). The initial array (seed) is always 010101010101010101010 (seen along each top row). Cells with 0 and 1 are shown as white and black, respectively. The agent is shown as a red dot when on a 0 cell and a green dot when on a 1 cell. [From (Hernández-Orallo, 2015c), with permission of Springer.] (See colour plate)

task as the mean of the random agent (or the mean of the random agent plus the standard deviation, or at the level where only 10 per cent of the agents are above the threshold). By choosing appropriate tolerances, we can ensure that the tasks are commensurate. Also, we can obtain several tasks with different difficulties for the same ECA rule.

To understand this better, Figure 9.6 shows the distribution of policies and their complexities (ranging from 0 to 20), in the same way we saw in Figure 8.2, but now for a real case. The complexities are calculated by applying a

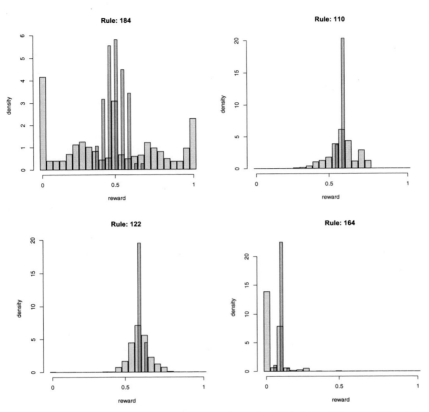

Figure 9.5. Histograms of the responses for rules 184, 110, 122 and 164 using 2,000 policies each running for 300 iterations. Two different groups are normalised to mass 25 and shown: 1,900 generated policies (shown with wide bars in beige) and 100 random-walk policies π_{rand} (shown with narrow bars in purple). [From the work of Hernández-Orallo (2015c), with permission of Springer.] (See colour plate)

Lempel-Ziv coding to the policy programs, to serve as an approximation of Kolmogorov complexity (for details see Hernández-Orallo, 2015c). Note that the length of the policies is not a good indicator since some of the randomly generated policies may have redundant code, as we do not perform an enumeration of policies (as in a Levin's universal search). The complexities are rounded to natural numbers to get slices, shown as boxplots. What we see in Figure 9.6 is that, for the only rule (184) with policies above the threshold 0.9, these start at complexity 3. This means that if the difficulty is defined in terms of this complexity, rule 184 will have difficulty 3. But the other three rules will

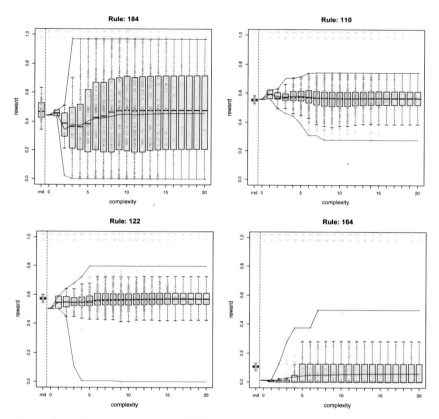

Figure 9.6. The same results of Figure 9.5 where we now detail by the complexity of the policy for the 1,900 generated policies. The number of agents (total and different) per complexity is shown on the two rows at the top of each plot. The 100 random-walk policies are shown on the left of the plots ("rnd" on the x-axis). For each value of complexity on the x-axis, we show the result of each policy as small circles in grey, and the whisker plots show the inter-quantile distribution for that value of complexity. The solid lines (red, green and blue) show the maximum and minimum envelopes and the average, respectively. [From the work of Hernández-Orallo (2015c), with permission of Springer.] (See colour plate)

have infinite difficulty, as no acceptable solution is found. Of course, what we would like instead is to make a selection of rules (with appropriate tolerance levels) in such a way that we have an appropriate range of difficulties (instead of extremely low or high difficulties). The lesson learnt from this case study is clear:

> **Keynote 9.2. Sampling from tasks to tests**: Sampling items according to a representational distribution p_M will create a great proportion of items that are mostly useless. Not only may the item results be incommensurate but also they may be very similar (poor diversity) and with extreme difficulties (too easy or too hard).

In the previous chapter we introduced tolerance, and we now see that it can be very useful to make items commensurate and with an appropriate range of difficulties. In the next section we explore how difficulty can be used to guide the selection of items, following the standard procedures in IRT but connecting with the representational perspective of the behavioural feature.

9.3 ITEM CHOICE BY DIFFICULTY

The agent characteristic curves and the relevance of difficulty in testing, as exploited by IRT, suggest that we can reunderstand the definition of a behavioural feature in terms of the difficulty slices defined in Eq. 9.1.

We must first start all over again from Eq. 2.1 and rewrite it in terms of acceptability ($\mathcal{A}$ in Eq. 8.1), using $\mathbb{A}$ (as we did for a slice for Eq. 9.1):

$$\Psi(\pi, M, p_M) \triangleq \sum_{\mu \in M} p_M(\mu) \cdot \mathbb{A}(\pi, \mu) \tag{9.2}$$

Basically, this is the aggregation of acceptable results (according to a tolerance level ϵ) considering the item distribution p_M in M. From this definition of a feature, we can now think about the distribution of difficulties (as shown in Figure 8.5 (right)), denoted by p_H, where

$$p_H(h)p_M(\mu|h) = p_H(h|\mu)p_M(\mu) \tag{9.3}$$

The subindexes are different for clarity, but the preceding formula is just a re-expression of Bayes' theorem. From here and Eq. 9.1, we can express Eq. 9.2 as follows (Hernández-Orallo et al., 2014, prop. 4):

$$\Psi(\pi, M, p_M) = \sum_{h=0}^{\infty} p_H(h)\Psi_h(\pi, M, p_M) \tag{9.4}$$

or, for continuous difficulties,

$$\Psi(\pi, M, p_M) = \int_0^{\infty} p_H(h)\Psi_h(\pi, M, p_M)dh \tag{9.5}$$

where $p_H(h)$ is understood as a discrete probability function for Eq. 9.4 and a probability density function for Eq. 9.5. These expressions suggest that Ψ is the area of the agent characteristic curve where the x-axis has been warped according to $p_H(h)$. For instance, this can be done with Figure 9.2 (right) weighted by the histogram in Figure 8.5 (right).

In brief, we set several difficulties and generate items for each difficulty to estimate Ψ_h. By properly weighting each Ψ_h (the warping of the x-axis), we get Ψ. Of course, to make this slicing consistent with Eq. 9.2 (and calculate Ψ from the curve), $p_H(h)$ must be derived from the representational distribution p_M (through Eq. 9.3 or an empirical histogram).

Finally, apart from the preceding decomposition, there is yet another more indirect possibility (Hernández-Orallo, 2015a,b). Given a difficulty, we can generate *policies* given that difficulty using a conditional probability $p_\Pi(\pi|h)$, and then *tasks* for which the policies are optimal, $p_M(\mu|\pi)$. Despite being convoluted, one advantage is that we can choose a uniform distribution for $p_\Pi(\pi|h)$, according to the size of the policy.

As a result, there are three ways of generating items for a convenient range (or distribution) of difficulties, as illustrated in Panel 9.3. For instance, for maze tasks such as those shown in Figures 4.1 and 8.3, there are generators implementing $p_M(\mu)$ but most of the mazes might be very easy or very difficult. Using a difficulty function as the number of possible forks in the maze, we could devise a different maze generator, using $p_M(\mu|h)$, parametrised by difficulty, following the indirect approach. Finally, the third possibility would be to think about a policy, e.g., a first-right traversal, and generate mazes having it as simplest solution, using $p_M(\mu|\pi)$.

Figure 9.7 (top) shows the direct approach, sampling from the representational distribution p_M and using a post-filtering. The middle schema shows the indirect approach, where we slice by difficulty, and the bottom schema describes another indirect approach going through difficulties and policies. Note that the three approaches can keep the representational distribution p_M. This would not be the case (and would need to be recovered by weighting) only if the direct approach were post-filtered for a particular range or distribution of difficulties, or the two indirect cases started with a range or distribution of h that were different to the 'true' $p_H(h)$.

Obviously, this can be done on purpose. Whenever we create a new task class for a test we can think of defining the distributions in the opposite direction, by setting $p_H(h)$ first and then $p_M(\mu|h)$. If we have a difficulty function, we can for instance assume p_H uniform (for a given range so that we ensure that it is bounded). In this case, the area under the agent characteristic curve would be exactly Ψ without any warping. This is exactly what we saw for the C-test in

---

Panel 9.3
The psychometrician's sieves

All psychometricians and evaluators want to generate items of an appropriate range of difficulties. A direct, straightforward way is to construct many items and then make a post-filtering of those that are of a given difficulty. This process may be very inefficient, as many items will be rejected.

An indirect, alternative way is to set the difficulties first and generate items given those difficulties, using a generator that can take the difficulty as a parameter. For some difficulty functions, this is possible and relatively easy. For instance, if we define the difficulty of an addition as the number of partial sums with carrying, then we can devise a generator that introduces precisely the desired number. We can even think of how to do this generation such that the original representational distribution p_M is kept.

Another, still more indirect, way relies on the realisation that some difficulty functions are defined in terms of the policy characteristics, as we saw in the previous chapter. In this case, the generator can create policies for a range of difficulties. For instance, if difficulty is given by the number of elements (or instructions) in the policy, it is sufficient to combine exactly this number of elements to have a policy of that difficulty. Once we have the policies, we can think about tasks for which the policy is optimal. For some problems, this may be reasonably easy. For instance, a single policy without carrying and a more complex policy with carrying could use different generators.

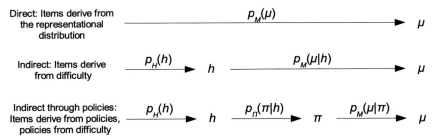

Figure 9.7. Different ways of generating the items. The *direct* approach on the top uses the representational probability to generate the items. The approach in the middle is an *indirect* approach that sets the difficulties first and then generates instances conditional to this choice. Finally, the approach on the bottom is *doubly indirect*, because it derives policies for a given difficulty to finally generate tasks for which each policy is acceptable.

Chapter 7, where p_H could be taken uniform if $e = 0$ in Eq. 7.12. As a result, the area under the curve in Figure 7.3 would be the aggregated result for the C-test for that agent (or group of agents).

Finally, the choice of $p_M(\mu|h)$ will determine the behavioural feature. If the number of items per difficulty is infinite, a universal distribution is an option. For the approach on the bottom of Figure 9.7, if difficulty depends on the number of elements (or instructions) in the policy, the number of policies per difficulty will be finite, so $p_\Pi(\pi|h)$ can be uniform. Next, as there can be infinitely many problems having the same optimal policy, $p_M(\mu|\pi)$ might also be a universal distribution, or simply it might just choose one simple item (e.g., the simplest one) for which the policy is optimal (a Dirac delta distribution giving all the mass to just one point). Overall, Figure 9.7 gives us several possibilities for the selection of items, which we have to use wisely:

Keynote 9.3. Difficulty slicing: Independently of a direct or indirect representational definition of the behavioural feature, an appropriate selection of items should be centred on difficulty such that a good estimation of the agent characteristic curve can be made, especially in the region where the curve has high slope.

In any case, difficulty slices and its representation using agent characteristic curves are useful to compare agents. It can well be the case that an agent performs better for easy items but worse for difficult ones compared to another agent, while their aggregation (area) is the same. This is what happens with agents π_1 and π_3 in Figure 9.2 (right).

There are now two crucial options when defining a new behavioural feature in a representational way. The first option is to define the feature by Eq. 9.2, in terms of a *representational distribution* over the items, disregarding their difficulty. Next, we can try to decompose and slice it using any of the indirect methods in Figure 9.7. The second option is to actually *define* the feature by Eq. 9.4 or Eq. 9.5 in terms of a *difficulty slicing*. The magnitude of the feature is then defined as the sum (or integral) over difficulties (the area under the characteristic curve). Alternatively, in a more flexible way, we could just derive the magnitude as the maximum difficulty – or proficiency – for which the expected success rate of the agent is greater than a given value, like Thurstone's definition of ability (Thurstone, 1937) and Thorndike's notion of altitude (Thorndike et al., 1927) (see Section 3.6). The two options (representational distribution and difficulty slicing) clearly resemble the stances of classical test theory (CTT) and item response theory (IRT), respectively. A representational distribution is in accordance with the view of the measurement being the expected value of a "true score" in CTT, whereas in IRT the analysis of performance is in terms of finding a proficiency value, for which the observations for a range of difficulties derive. In this section we have seen the connection of both options, if we make Eq. 9.2 and Eq. 9.4 or 9.5 equivalent through Bayes' rule (Eq. 9.3) by properly choosing the probability of a task given the difficulty $p_M(\mu|h)$.

Despite the connection of the two views, when generating a test, different preferences for the three approaches seen in Figure 9.7 may exist. For instance, there is an interesting discussion in (Legg and Veness, 2013) comparing a direct generation (Figure 9.7 (top)) where the difficulty of the items is not known, but many items may be very easy or very difficult, against an indirect generation such as the C-test (Figure 9.7 (middle)), which requires much more computation to derive instances for which we have an estimation of their difficulty. However, the administration of the test is much more efficient than for the direct generation.

In fact, this is a crucial aspect. When generating a pool of items (for a non-adaptive or an adaptive test), the items can be prepared beforehand. That means that we can devote resources to have a very good pool of items, in such a way that the items that are used are flawless (not too easy and not too difficult, among other things). The important thing is that the administration is efficient. This is obvious in human evaluation and most especially in animal evaluation. However, in artificial intelligence, it seems that having an evaluated agent doing useless items over and over again may be acceptable – computer time is cheap. Nonetheless, this is not only against the principles of psychometrics, where we want to devise tests that are efficient, i.e., reliable, with the minimum number of instances, but also hampering the construction of agent characteristic curves, whose detailed information is key to understand the agents' behaviour.

9.4 REVISITING DISCRIMINATING POWER AND IRT

The interactive task defined by the single-agent elementary cellular automata seen in the previous sections shows several things. First, the mere choice of one of the 256 rule combinations gives no particular clue about how difficult the rule is going to be. This is precisely the beauty of these cellular automata: the setting of eight bits can lead to completely different worlds, in terms of how dynamic they are, how many black dots they have on average and how reactive they will be to the agent's movements. In some cases, it can even be incomputable to determine how a task is going to behave – this is true, at least, for rule 110, which is Turing-complete (Cook, 2004; Neary and Woods, 2006), as is

Conway's game of life (Conway, 1970). As a result, the only possible approach is to analyse how (the best) policies behave. This clearly obliges us to jettison any characterisation of the tasks depending on their description (eight bits) and embrace the approach based on analysing the policies that we introduced in the previous chapter. Second, by randomly generating instances from a generator that uses a uniform distribution over the 256 combinations we may end up with many items that are useless, with all agents having the same result on average. For instance, rule 0 is a hell world for any agent, as it sets all cells to 0. Rule 255, on the contrary, is a heaven world, where everything is 1 (Wolfram, 2002). However, both worlds do not discriminate at all and are useless. Even if they are part of the representational distribution, testing on them is useless.

Some efforts have focused on determining which environments are *responsive* or *sensitive*. This is an evasive concept, since an environment can be responsive initially, but after a few actions, the agent can lead it to heaven, hell or chaotic states, from which it never recovers. The characterisation of environments that are sensitive to actions (or rewards) have not gone beyond a partial account (Hernández-Orallo and Dowe, 2010, sec. 4.2) or some particular environment classes (Hernández-Orallo, 2010).

Another possible approach to determining the discriminating character of an instance is linked to the concept of phase transition, as illustrated in Panel 9.4 with a number partition problem, where the result is the difference between the two sums after the partition.

Our interest in phase transitions is that they are usually narrow. Precisely, this band is where the instances that are neither too hard nor too easy lie, which are possibly the most discriminating ones to tell between algorithms (policies) that solve the problem and those that do not. Again, for this particular example we see the relevance of tolerance levels (for the number partition problem, tolerance can be established for the difference between the sums). In this way, we can make some of the hard instances much easier and change (or smooth) the phase transition. But how can we effectively calculate the tolerance for which the task becomes most discriminative? Can we use phase transitions or any theoretical analysis to determine this discriminating power?

To answer this question, in general, we recall the concept of *discriminating power* we saw in Section 3.6. In classical test theory (CTT), discrimination is associated with a correlation between the results for an item and (the average result of) the other items. This interprets discriminating power as a measure of how representative the item is for a behavioural feature *with respect to* a given population.

This view is not in full concordance with the discrimination parameter a (maximum slope) of the logistic models in item response theory (IRT) seen in

---

Panel 9.4
The easiest hard problem

The number partitioning problem has been referred to as "the easiest hard problem" (Hayes, 2002), because, despite being a classical NP-hard problem, its formulation is very simple and many of its instances are easy. This problem consists of a set of positive integers that we need to split into a binary partition such that the sum of the numbers in one subset is as close as possible as the sum of the rest. For instance, given the multiset:

$$\{7, 9, 2, 2, 13, 6, 16, 6, 4\}$$

the following partition does the trick:

$$\{16, 7, 6, 4, 2\} \quad \{13, 9, 6, 5, 2\}$$

with both subsets summing up 35. This particular example can be perfectly solved by an eager algorithm, where two 'teams' pick the highest number in an alternatingly way (or giving priority to the team with the lowest sum so far). Actually, Hayes suggests that this is the algorithm that children use when two captains choose their players for a casual match, with the aim of having two even teams. In general, however, more elaborate approaches, using dynamic programming or backtracking, must be used.

Mertens (1998) has shown that instances with $B/N > 1$ tend to be much harder than the rest, where N is the number of integers and B is the size (in bits) of the largest integer. In the preceding case, $N = 10$ and $B = \log(16) = 4$. The instances around $B/N = 1$ create a *phase transition* between an easy region and a hard region.

Section 3.6 (note that we now talk about item curves, such as Figure 3.8, not about agent curves). Item characteristic curves represent the view of discriminating power as the "degree to which a score varies with trait level" (Ferrando, 2012), as pointed out in Section 3.6. However, two curves with very different slopes (a very steep one with high discrimination and an almost flat one with very low discrimination) will both have a very high correlation (1 in the case of rank correlations) as the functions are monotonic. In other words, the concept of discrimination in IRT basically *assumes* that the item is well correlated with proficiency (and monotonically decreasing and non-monotonic curves are systematically ruled out), so it just derives an indicator about the *shape* of the relation. As a result, this boils down to a measure of how well an item discriminates around a given proficiency. High discrimination (high slopes) will make a clear cut from proficient and non-proficient subjects, but will be flat for low proficiencies and high proficiencies, being useless to discriminate on those areas.

Somewhat confusingly, these measures of discriminating power that derive from the curves are usually referred to as "population-independent measures", because they are "assessed at a single point or trait level" (Ferrando, 2012). This ultimately derives from the fact that the maximum slope of the logistic function coincides with the location of the proficiency level of the item characteristic curve. The main reason, though, is that the curves do not change if we change the distribution of proficiencies in the population, as the value for a given proficiency level does not depend on how many subjects of that proficiency there are. Of course, this does not mean that we can estimate the parameters of these curves without a population.

In consequence, both interpretations, from CTT or IRT seem to require the *use* of a population of subjects. However, the good news for universal psychometrics is that this does not have to be a *real*, i.e., *biological*, population. We can figure out a theoretical, artificial population, i.e., a distribution p_Π over the set of agents or policies Π. But if policies are algorithms, how can we define such a distribution? This is exactly what we did with the single-agent elementary cellular automata in the previous sections, using the agent policy language (APL). To sample algorithms from it, we just define a distribution, e.g., a universal distribution or any similar approximation, as the one used in Figure 9.6. Using a distribution, we are not only able to derive discriminating power but also *item characteristic curves*, like the ones we saw in Chapter 3. To do this, we need to compare the results for an item with those of the whole test. For instance, if we look at Figure 9.6, we should compare the result of this artificial population for one rule against the average of all the (other) rules. However, we need to be careful with this approach, as it cannot be done in the same way as with a real population. First, we cannot derive difficulty as the average result using the distribution of the population, as the policies with low complexity would dominate the distribution, giving high difficulties. For instance, this population-based way of deriving difficulty for Figure 9.6 would just determine whether the first part of the average line (the solid blue line in the middle) is above the threshold, which is mostly meaningless (and never the case for most tolerances). This means that difficulty should be derived instead in a population-independent way as we discussed in the previous chapter, e.g., by calculating the simplest policy above the threshold. Only then should we find a way to derive the other curve parameters empirically.

Whilst this is an option, a significantly different approach is introduced in (Hernández-Orallo, 2015c). There, two tacit assumptions are made. First, the population of policies is considered as the result of a single learning agent performing a *search* for the right policy. Second, because items are going to be undertaken by a learning agent, it is assumed that all items are well correlated with proficiency (the same assumption that IRT makes).

Consequently, the basic idea in (Hernández-Orallo, 2015c) is that the set of policies is sought experimentally using a sampling probability (our p_Π here). Then, one calculates the minimum number N of policies that have to be sampled to get 0.5 probability of finding an acceptable policy. From here, the logarithm of N is proposed as a difficulty function D. This is not very different to our definition in the previous chapter, the logarithm of the number computational steps to find a policy, as this depends on the number of policies to be explored (about 2^k, where k is the size of the policy). The distinction just lies in whether it is a sampling (without repetition) or it is an enumeration (as in Levin's universal search).

As D is a function of tolerance, by inverting this function, we can create *environment characteristic curves* that show tolerance (called 'reward') on the y-axis and policy complexity (called 'ability') on the x-axis. The slope of these curves depends on the relation of an item with all the items that can be derived from it by varying the tolerance. Figure 9.8 shows these so-called environment response curves for the four rules depicted in Figure 9.6.

These curves (more precisely the upper right quadrant of each of them) are not actually item characteristic curves, and what they show is actually different. They try to locate the values of the tolerance that are more appropriate for the item, given the population. These can be understood as a smoothing of the maximum envelope shown (as a red solid line) in Figure 9.6. The upper right quadrant of the curves is actually showing the behaviour of the best achievable results (the best policies) per complexity. The interpretation of a curve, for instance the one for rule 184 on Figure 9.6, is that to get a 'reward' of, let us say, 0.9, we need a policy with an 'ability' (complexity) of 4 – but most policies of complexity 4 will not get that result, of course. Unlike the item characteristic curves, if we set a particular complexity the average result for that complexity will depend on the distribution. However, the trick is made because we take the best values, which do not depend on the distribution. So, again the distribution does not really matter, but for a very different reason.

This is the same procedure that was done in Figure 8.5 (left), where any of the three curves considers the best policies for a range of resources $\mathbb{LS}$. These curves look like item characteristic curves of the logistic model as introduced in Chapter 3 (Figure 3.8).

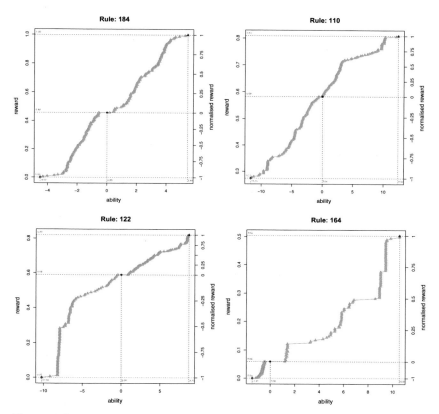

Figure 9.8. 'Environment response curves' for the four items (rules) in Figure 9.6 using 5,922 policies. The *x*-axis represents the 'ability' that is required to succeed in the item (environment), and the left *y*-axis represents the expected aggregated reward. The right *y*-axis is a normalised version, taking into account the maximum and minimum possible rewards. [From the work of Hernández-Orallo (2015c), with permission of Springer.]

Let us summarise what we have discussed hitherto:

> **Keynote 9.4.** The **discriminating power** of an item denotes how well the item discriminates subjects. A meaningful value can be derived without assuming a particular population (varying allowed resources or tolerance for all possible policies). This regards characteristic curves as plots of the cumulative probability of a correct (acceptable) response and discriminating power as the inverse of the standard deviation of an estimation of difficulty.

Independently of the final procedure (including the use of a surrogate for discriminating power), the battery of tools from item response theory will be applicable to the construction of tests. For instance, one straightforward approach would be to assume a 1PL (Rasch's) model, as for this simple logistic model we only need the estimation of difficulty for each item. Or, as said earlier, if we have a method that estimates the difficulty of items with some error (for instance, because we use some approximation to Levin's universal search or the approach in Hernández-Orallo, 2015c), this error could be taken as standard deviation σ, and we could use the cumulative function of the normal model seen in Eq. 3.5 or a logistic 2PL using the approximation $a = 1/\sigma$ as shown in Figure 3.10 (the example shows $b = 3$ and $\sigma = 0.75$, i.e., $a = 1.33$).

From here, given item characteristic curves for each item, an adaptive testing schema would be recommended. For arbitrary agents from the machine kingdom whose proficiency range is unknown, we would start doubling difficulty until failures are found. Next, as explained in Section 3.6, from a limited number of item results, a method such as maximum likelihood estimation or other Bayesian approaches (if any information about the proficiency of the agents can be assumed, see Eq. 3.8) could be used to estimate the proficiency θ and the standard error of this measurement. An alternative, also assuming a uniform distribution of difficulties in the definition of the behavioural feature, as for Eq. 9.4 or 9.5, would be to estimate the agent characteristic curve with a range of difficulties and calculate its area. We will return to the construction of adaptive universal tests in Chapter 16.

9.5 SCRUTINISING ITEM POOL DESIGN

In this and the previous chapter, we have introduced the principles for the definition and analysis of tasks built upon algorithmic information theory, artificial intelligence and psychometrics. Tasks are defined as stochastic interactive systems, like the policies that solve them. This allows us to determine some of the key characteristics, such as size and computational steps. The view of deriving difficulty and discriminating power analytically from the description of the *task* has been rejected in these two chapters in favour of an exploration of the *policy* space. The analysis of this space can be empirical or theoretical, with different realisations depending on the search that we assume for defining difficulty and on the population distributions for discriminating power. The definition of difficulty as the best acceptable policy in terms of some resources (size and computational steps, if $\mathbb{LS}$ is chosen) clearly entails that an accurate estimation will be computationally expensive, especially when the task is complex.

This should not be a surprise. Actually, there are some theoretical results (with other notions of hardness, e.g., genetic algorithms) that show that any predictive version of a measure of difficulty that runs in polynomial time cannot exist (Malan and Engelbrecht, 2013). In other words, estimating algorithmic difficulty is indeed very difficult.

The very definition of difficulty and discrimination power can be overhauled again to make its estimation easier, among other reasons. For instance, an evolutionary search could be considered, instead of Levin's universal search. Nonetheless, the major alternative to our notion of difficulty might rely on the use of many acceptable policies instead of the best one. This has already been done for the single-agent elementary cellular automata seen in this chapter, but it can be applied to any task. Nonetheless, we have to make a few remarks here. First, if the distribution for the population of policies resembles a universal distribution, the simplest policy (and its variants) will take most of the mass of the distribution and will dominate, giving similar estimations of difficulty. Second, the choice of a reasonable policy distribution is not always easy and introduces additional arbitrariness. Still, we will argue in Chapter 13 that some agent distributions other than a universal distribution may make more sense if we want to derive some population-dependent metrics. Third, the use of many policies would make the formal expressions more convoluted. For instance, the notions of composition and decomposition that we will use in the following chapter would become trickier to analyse.

Apart from these caveats and remarks, we have reinforced some of the paradigmatic principles of psychometrics. First, the lesson from modern psychometrics (especially IRT) to other areas where testing is performed with a representational distribution is that it is very inefficient to populate items without further analysis. Most of them will be useless for testing, as they are not discriminative or are very far away from the proficiency of the subject. In fact, we have seen how classical test theory (CTT) and item response theory (IRT) can be connected, with the latter becoming really population-independent, since the concept of difficulty can be derived as a minimum of required resources and not as an expected value of the response. From the view of proficiency and difficulty as two sides of the same coin, if a subject has an estimated proficiency θ this means that the subject is able to solve problems that would require 2^{θ} computational steps if the policies solving it were sought under a Levin's universal search. This is a very comprehensive view of what cognitive proficiency is.

Second, one essential tradition of psychometrics is that the effort is usually invested in the configuration of a good pool of items, from which efficient (including adaptive) tests can be constructed later on. It is clear that independently of the way difficulty and discriminating power are derived – from an actual population, from an artificial population or theoretically – it is in general infeasible to generate the items *on the fly*. Instead, they must be prepared (and validated) beforehand.

Third, the use of a pool or bank of well-analysed items can be used to derive new tests by selection and combination of items, a common practice in psychometrics. In the end, producing a test may require painstaking work, but ultimately the scrutiny of item pools pays off.

CHAPTER HIGHLIGHTS

- Agent characteristic curves providing performance details for a range of difficulties (Keynotes 9.1, 9.3, Eq. 9.1).
- Further examples showing that the description of the task is not very useful for item analysis while the description of the policy (or agent) is key (Panels 9.1, 9.2).
- Efficient tests strongly depending on sampling a set of items of sufficient diversity to cover the whole task class and excluding those that are either too easy or too hard (Keynote 9.2).
- The decomposition of a representational definition using difficulty (Eqs. 9.4, 9.5) leading to three ways of generating the items (Panel 9.3, Figure 9.7).
- Discriminating power usually linked to a real population, but artificial populations and resource minimisation presented as alternatives (Keynote 9.4).

10

The Arrangement of Abilities

No classification of the mental powers has been universally accepted.
                                                      – Charles Darwin,
        The Descent of Man, and Selection in Relation to Sex (1871)

I N THE PREVIOUS chapters we have focused on tasks and their difficulty. In a way, difficulty can be seen as the *height* of a task. Arranging tasks by their difficulty is an insightful way of analysing the proficiency they need and how discriminating they are, in order to choose items, compare subjects and determine aggregate indicators. To complete what could be referred to as a 'task theory', we will now deal with the *breadth* of a task, its pureness and how tasks can be composed and related to each other. From these relations we will investigate the notion of cognitive ability and how these abilities could also be arranged. The approach in this chapter basically replaces empirical correlation between tasks and abilities by a non-empirical notion of similarity, using AIT. This is not done with the description of the task, but again with the description of its acceptable policies, using information distance or the previously introduced notion of difficulty.

10.1 FACING THE TASK CONTINUUM

When we are interested in one particular task, we can define a test using that task. This would be perfectly right from the psychometric *functionality-oriented* point of view (e.g., if the task is required for a job), as we discussed in Chapter 3. This is natural from an *evolutionary fitness* standpoint (e.g., if the task happens in the species's environment), as we discussed in Chapter 4. Similarly, it would fit well the *task-oriented* stance in artificial intelligence (e.g., if the task corresponds to a particular application), as we discussed in Chapter 5.

In the end, the set of infinitely many possible tasks would lead to infinitely many tests. However, deriving a cognitive profile for each creature in the machine kingdom in these terms would be mostly useless to determine how an agent is going to behave in a different situation. In other words, working at the level of particular tasks has no explanatory power or predictability beyond the tasks for which the agent has been evaluated.

In the introductory chapter, we argued that behavioural features (either personality traits or cognitive abilities) would be a more meaningful way of characterising cognitive systems. We also saw that the efforts can be traced back many centuries, much before the scientific method, with attempts coming from philosophy, such as Llull's attributes (his 'principia', see Figure 1.2) or Gall's decomposition of the brain (his phrenological 'faculties', see Figure 1.4). These and many other conceptions of how behavioural features can be arranged follow, more or less explicitly, a "geographic metaphor" (Cianciolo and Sternberg, 2008), with behavioural features being represented as parts or regions of a topological space: the brain, a multi-dimensional Cartesian space, a hierarchy, a star, etc.

In this chapter we will finally address this characterisation of features in the most general, albeit still scientific, way. We will focus on cognitive abilities, since the characterisation of abilities is apparently better connected with the computational and information-processing principles used so far. Nonetheless, we will revisit personality traits in the context of social interaction in Chapter 13.

Thorndike et al. (1927, p. 484) considered that "an ability is defined by a total series of tasks". However, a mere aggregation of tasks, following Eq. 2.1, through a distribution or as a stochastic task, is just a means of creating new tasks, but does not, per se, solve the question of how abilities can be identified and arranged. Even the ability that considers all tasks, as we will see in the following chapter, is underspecified, since we have to define a distribution over all of them. The big question is again: how can we go from tasks to abilities?

We contemplate several possible (non-exclusive) perspectives to face the structure of the space of abilities:

- 'Populational'. Given a population of individuals, we can analyse how several tasks correlate for that population and derive some structure (e.g., latent factors) from it. This is the traditional psychometric procedure for human abilities and, more recently, for other species.
- 'Neurological'. Through the analysis of how the brain works (by means of brain scanning, neural models, etc.), several hypotheses and theories can be

established about specialised or generalised abilities being responsible for types of tasks.

- '*Genetical*'. With behavioural genetics and other genetic approaches, one can trace how some genes correspond to the observed variability for some tasks and cluster abilities according to the genes involved.
- 'Environmental'. By analysing a particular set of environments, one can identify the tasks that are required for survival and whether they can be grouped according to the adaptability to their environments.
- 'Technological'. After many decades of artificial intelligence research, one can use its experiences, and the subdisciplines in AI, as a reflection of the families of abilities that are required for intelligent behaviour.
- 'Definitional'. By comparing the definition of two or more tasks, one can analyse whether they are related and arrange tasks according to their definitional similarity.
- 'Solutional'. By comparing the (optimal) solutions for two or more tasks, one can ultimately determine whether they are related and cluster tasks according to the policies that are useful for them.

Many of these approaches have relied on some of the others. For instance, the 'genetical' approach relies on a populational analysis to have a phenotype to align with. Also, all of them can be enriched from the others.

However, there is an important distinction in the preceding list. The populational, neurological, genetical and environmental approaches are constrained to one or more species. As a result, the categories and structures that can be found may just depend on the particular biology on Earth. For instance, consider a given spatial ability that has been found to always be related to analogical reasoning, according to the correlations found for all species on Earth and the evidence that they are produced by the same genes and neuronal processes. This knowledge, however, could never be extrapolated to an extraterrestrial being, or any computer. In the end, if we find that feature A is correlated with B in humans, and apes, and many other animals, it is theoretically possible under some mild conditions (such as that A and B can be distinguished and have some minimum discriminating power) to design a machine that performs well for A but not for B, and vice versa. In fact, had we put enough of these two machines inside a population, we would get that both features are completely unrelated.

The technological approach is not empirically based on a population, but is not free from geocentrism. Indeed, it is even more exposed to anthropocentrism. For instance, we do not know whether artificial intelligence, as a discipline, would have different subdisciplines and areas, had the history of the field been different. Also, the taxonomy given by artificial intelligence has changed significantly depending on how successful the techniques have been and, most especially, depending on the successful applications, which must be necessarily anthropocentric, as AI must be useful for humans.

Finally, the definitional and solutional approaches can be driven by formal principles (if the tasks and abilities are defined in a formal language). In fact, the theory of computational complexity has analysed problems in this way and has come up with different classes, such as **P** or **NP**, which cannot be accused of anthropocentrism or geocentrism. However, they are *complexity* classes and, apart from its inadequacy for task difficulty (as discussed in Section 8.4), they are not meant to partition the space of abilities.

10.2 NONALGORITHMIC MODELS OF COGNITIVE ABILITIES

Despite all the limitations of some of the preceding approaches for an analysis that endures the generality of the machine kingdom, it would be unwise to start from scratch. We already overviewed some of the taxonomies and hierarchies developed in psychometrics (known as models or theories of intelligence) in Section 3.3, such as the Cattell-Horn-Carroll three-stratum model (see Figure 3.2).

Carroll himself warned about the use of correlations and factor analysis: "when individual differences in two variables are uncorrelated, or appear on two different factors, I think it is an indication that the underlying processes are likely to be different, or at least dependent on quite different stimulus characteristics. I observe much more caution in inferring that the underlying processes are the same when individual differences on two variables show significant correlations or appear on the same factor, because the correlations could arise from similar stimulus characteristics, similar learning experiences and a host of other things that would not necessarily depend on identical or similar cognitive processes" (Carroll, 1981).

Note that this refers to a human population. In universal psychometrics, we would have to be careful even about cases where two variables are uncorrelated. For instance, from a computational point of view there is no reason why forward digit span and backward digit span tasks should get different results (Groeger et al., 1999). The non-perfect correlation is then a particular finding for human cognition. Also, psychometrics is not only biased by the populations that are used (humans or other species) but by the tests that have been used. For instance, many tasks and instances have been eliminated from psychometric practice whenever they were found to be poorly discriminative or whenever reliability was low. Some were never included because of validity issues or simply because of the designers' bias. IQ tests, such as WAIS and Stanford-Binet, are the result of many selections and refinements. As a consequence, the tasks in IQ tests incorporate a bias towards human measurement (apart from implicitly or explicitly following a particular intelligence model) in their choice of tasks.

Whilst a rigorous statistical analysis can be more objective than other approaches – this was one of the motivations of psychometrics, to make evaluation objective and scientific – this analysis is performed because there was a lack of a principled theory. Thurstone (1929) puts it this way: "when a problem is so involved that no rational formulation is available, then some quantification is still possible by the calculation of coefficients of correlation or contingency and the like. But such statistical procedures constitute an acknowledgment of failure to rationalize the problem and to establish the functions that underlie the data".

As a reaction to this, we can also find an important amount of work in psychometrics, cognitive science and artificial intelligence to conceptually analyse how humans solve a task, not only in terms of the processes and resources they use but also to predict when they usually fail (error models). This is more related to the *definitional* and *solutional* approaches seen earlier, but usually restricted to the goal of understanding *human* cognition.

One hybrid and particularly interesting way of looking at the relations between tasks is Guttman's radex model (Guttman, 1954). The model uses facets instead of factors and multidimensional scaling (MDS) instead of factor analysis. In the case of intelligence, tests (or tasks) would be arranged according to their 'complexity' or 'task' (known as the 'simplex') or their 'content' or 'material' (known as the 'circumplex'). The radex model was represented onto two dimensions using a variant of MDS, such that those tests that appear together on the plot would have similar complexities and contents. This would turn out to be a "circular" space, where the tests most closely associated with the g factor appeared in the middle (the 'radex'), somewhat resembling the regular circumplex and simplexes drawn in Figure 1.2. Figure 10.1 depicts one simplified version of the radex.

One of the interpretations of this representation is that we could derive abilities by recognising areas or clusters in this space (instead of identifying independent factors). The circumplex facet was divided into three 'content' categories: verbal, numeric (also known as symbolic or quantitative) and spatial (also known as figural or geometric) (Lohman, 2000; Lohman et al., 2011). These are shown as three sections separated by radial lines emanating from

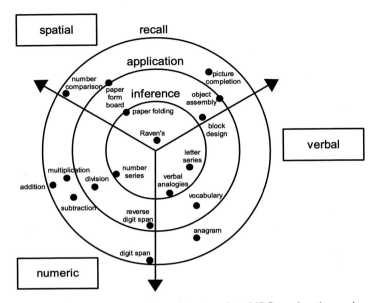

Figure 10.1. Simplified representation of tasks after MDS under the radex model. Tasks that are closer are more similar. The *material* facet is shown as three sections: 'verbal', 'numeric' and 'spatial'. The *task* facet is shown as concentric circles: 'recall', 'application' and 'inference'. [Integrated from the work of Saklofske and Zeidner (1995, Figure 1, p. 20) and Mackintosh and Mackintosh (2011, Figure 2.5, p. 53), already simplified from Snow et al. (1984).]

the centre (see Figure 10.1). The simplex facet was arranged into three levels by Guttman: low, medium and high cognitive complexity. These have been interpreted in different ways since then (Marshalek et al., 1983; Snow et al., 1984; Cohen et al., 2006; Johnson and Kotz, 2011) as 'recall' (low-inferential or rote learning), 'application' (rule deployment) and 'inference' (rule induction), respectively. One of the crucial questions for any topological arrangement of tasks is to determine their location in the radex around the 'continuum' (Marshalek et al., 1983) of facets.

The circumplex (verbal, numeric, spatial) facet seems to be the most anthropocentric. For instance, the spatial facet makes sense for non-human animals. Indeed, some apes score similarly to small children on many spatial skills (Herrmann et al., 2010; Herrmann and Call, 2012). However, is a verbal sector meaningful for chimpanzees? Or for 'wolf-children' (those grown up in the wild, Baum, 2004, pp. 312–314)? What about the spatial sector for blind people or some animals that rely on different spatial orientation mechanisms or none at all (e.g., moles, octopuses)? Would we have a new sector for olfactory abilities for dogs?

The simplex (recall, application, inference) facet is apparently less anthropocentric. Still, several hypotheses have been presented to explain and predict whether a task should fall near the centre or the periphery, such as the number of components, the speed required, the use of more 'central' or 'critical' components, the requirements of working memory and attention, and the strategic, heuristic or adaptive processing (Lohman et al., 2011). It seems that the tasks in the middle require more 'thinking', whereas the ones on the periphery could be done more mechanically, but this explanation is not sufficiently precise.

Apart from the radex, there are many other approaches to conceptualise a range of tasks, most of them under an "information-processing" perspective. As we mentioned in Chapter 3, the early days of psychometrics had opposed views between the simple information-processing tasks, also known as elementary cognitive tasks (investigated by Galton and Spearman), and the complex information-processing tasks (investigated by Binet).

Simple information-processing usually comprises sensory discrimination (visual or auditory) and others related to mental speed, such as "choice reaction time" and "inspection time", or to basic memory capabilities, such as "digit span". One of the remarkable things about these *elementary tasks* is that most of them provide a meaningful *measurement unit*, be it time, number of digits recalled, etc. Also, their classification may look easier, as they are based on very simple informational concepts. Because of their simplicity, one can trace their physiological and biological roots, through brain scanning techniques or event-related brain potentials.

The most conspicuous flaw when trying to build any taxonomy upon these elementary tasks for universal psychometrics is that all these simple tasks are extremely easy for computers. Also, it goes without saying how meaningless are event-related brain potentials and other psychophysiological measurements for computers. Actually, the use of very simple tasks could only be a proxy for humans and some other animals. It is not surprising that Binet and Simon were really suspicious that mental abilities could be measured through simple tasks (Binet and Simon, 1905).

The naive alternative to simple information-processing tasks is to make them complex. However, there are infinitely many ways of making them very complex, and, through the process, losing any traceability about what they could be measuring. Because of this, the analysis of complex information-processing tasks has usually been associated with some *reasoning processes*. This actually takes us to the very origins of the study of reasoning, back to Aristotle, crossing the boundaries of many disciplines. After several millennia of thinking about thinking, to put it very simple, we could say that there is a general agreement that there are two main kinds of reasoning processes, inductive and deductive. Inductive inference is of hypothetical nature and tries to identify patterns from evidence, which can be applied from particular cases to general rules (inductive generalisation, as we discussed in Chapter 7) or from particular cases to other particular cases (analogical reasoning). Deductive inference derives consequences that follow logically from some premises. Abductive reasoning is usually considered a special kind of inductive reasoning, although it can also be seen as a hypothetical inverse deduction. Planning is usually associated with deduction, or even seen as a precursor of it. It is commonly said that inductive inference creates new knowledge while deductive inference only derives knowledge that is already in the premises. However, this view is only true for omniscient reasoning systems (for a thorough discussion about the gain for each inference process, see Hernández-Orallo, 1999a).

Our interest here is to see whether tasks, and ultimately abilities, can be characterised in terms of reasoning processes. This is, unfortunately, quite uncommon, as Wilhelm (2005) points out: "ideally, a general theory of reasoning processes should govern test construction and confirmatory data analysis. In practice, theories of reasoning processes have rarely been considered when creating and using psychometric reasoning tasks". Wilhelm (2005) does derive reasoning tasks by using Johnson-Laird's theory of "mental models" (Johnson-Laird, 1986; Johnson-Laird et al., 2015), which has been used to explain how reasoning processes work from a cognitive point of view. The theory puts the notion of model (a policy for a problem) at the centre of a reasoning process, which comprises three steps: understanding the problem, construction of models and their evaluation, rejection or modification. Surprisingly, in an *experimental* study with a set of reasoning tasks using the theory of mental models, no distinction between inductive and deductive reasoning was found, but "this does not exclude the option that both thought processes might be affected by different interventions" (Wilhelm, 2005), such as working memory.

However, if inductive inference cannot be well separated from deductive inference and working memory using models of human cognition, why is it that inductive inference (including analogy) has the highest *g* loadings of all tasks? In fact, in the radex model seen in Figure 10.1, we see the tasks for inductive inference near the centre. This might well be another anthropocentric circumstance, but there are still two compelling reasons why this can indeed be a universal phenomenon. The first one is that learning is key for intelligence, and clearly, inductive inference is the reasoning process behind many types of learning. The second one is subtler.

> **Keynote 10.1. Comprehensiveness of induction**: Inductive infer-
> ence is a very comprehensive process, as it requires deductive infer-
> ence (or at least the execution of models) to check the hypotheses,
> working memory to keep the hypotheses, as well as mechanisms to
> retrieve constructs from long-term memory to build the hypotheses.

We can relate this to the radex model (Figure 10.1). 'Recall' would be related
to memory, for retrieving the knowledge about the task and the intermediate
hypotheses. Without this no other process can work. 'Application' would run a
model to check its effect or consistency. It requires both working memory and
the retrieval of its elements. Finally, 'inference' would create and select the
models. Only if models can be kept and applied, would 'inference' be possible. Consequently, it seems that inductive inference requires from 'recall' and
'application', which could explain why inductive inference, deductive inference and working memory are so intertwined, and also why inductive inference
is in the centre. Unfortunately, even if this explanation could be confirmed on
human and animal populations, yet again the results might not extrapolate to
the machine kingdom.

10.3 TASK COMPOSITION: PURENESS AND BREADTH

From the possible approaches to analyse the structure of the space of abilities: *populational, neurological, genetical, environmental, technological, definitional* and *solutional*, the first five were unsuitable for a universal foundation to the identification and analysis of cognitive abilities. Still, some
theories from psychometrics and cognitive science, such as Thurstone's primary mental abilities (Table 3.1), the Cattell-Horn-Carroll three-stratum model
(Figure 3.2) and the radex theory (Figure 10.1), the technological taxonomy
used in AI (Table 5.2) or the high-level competency areas in AGI (Table 5.3)
may be useful to suggest criteria for ability clusters and associations. More
importantly, these taxonomies can still be used to falsify any universal criterion or taxonomy not accommodating the particular cases.

We can now explore the *definitional* and *solutional* approaches. The *definitional* approach was discussed for the derivation of difficulty in Chapter 8.
For instance, we could try to represent instances or tasks according to some
descriptors, as we did in Figure 9.3 with the numerousness task, or some of
the proposals we discussed in Section 1.4, all of them with a high degree of

---

Panel 10.1
The Analytical Language of John Wilkins

Much before Turing introduced his universal machine, scholars fancied with universal languages, such as Leibniz's Characteristica Universalis, whose Ars Combinatoria was inspired by Llull's Ars Magna.

Of particular interest is John Wilkins's 'Philosophical Language' (Wilkins, 1668), for which the letters in a word denote categories of the object in a hierarchical way, inside a taxonomy. With this language, if we knew an element in the taxonomy we would be able to know its word and vice versa. This is the bijective equivalence between *denotandum* and *denotatum*! In "The Analytical Language of John Wilkins", Borges (1964) satirises this "admirable" attempt, where "each word is defined by itself", as "utopic".

If we apply this notion to universal languages in computational terms, the denotandum-denotatum correspondence must necessarily be lost. Given a description (or *program*) in any Turing-complete representational mechanism, the change of a single bit may render a completely different result (its behaviour). The same happens for task descriptions. Inspecting their code and their similarities will always clash with this denotational problem.

---

arbitrariness. More systematic task profiles are introduced under the concept of task muddiness (Weng, 2009, 2013), which includes five categories and 26 non-independent 'factors'. However, the categories and factors are not derived from theoretical principles or experimental data.

With an algorithmic framework for the definition of tasks, such as the one introduced in Chapter 8, more possibilities seem to appear. We can, for instance, use the information distance (Bennett et al., 1998; Vitányi et al., 2009) between the task descriptions, or other concepts from AIT. The use of information distance (or similarity) for objects (such as images or ants trajectories) and representations (e.g., Hahn et al., 2003) is meaningful and useful, but it is not always a reliable source of dissimilarity if we apply it to descriptional mechanisms, such as genotypes or programs. For instance, as we saw in the previous chapter, a single bit change in the description of an elementary cellular automaton, as defined in Panel 9.1, leads to a completely different behaviour, a completely different task. Panel 10.1 recalls the failed ambition of making a language such that the relations of the definitions could translate smoothly to the relations of the objects they describe.

This seems to indicate that an 'intensional' approach (according to the definition, the denotandum) to the understanding of the space of tasks cannot work; we need to look at the extension (the denotatum) instead. For a stochastic task this means that we need to look at the set of instances (and distribution) that it creates. Consequently, if we want to go from very particular tasks to general abilities we need to look at how tasks can be composed, in terms of their extension and not their definition. This suggests how task compositions should be done. Actually, a probabilistic mixture of two tasks can be expressed as a task. More precisely,

---

Keynote 10.2. Task composition: For two stochastic tasks, the composition of tasks μ_1 and μ_2 with weight $\alpha \in [0, 1]$, denoted by $\alpha\mu_1 \oplus (1 - \alpha)\mu_2$, is defined by a biased stochastic choice (by α) between the two tasks. If α is omitted ($\mu_1 \oplus \mu_2$), we assume $\alpha = 0.5$.

In the opposite sense, we can define decomposition in the following way. We say that μ is decomposable into μ_1 and μ_2 if there are two tasks μ_1 and μ_2 and an α such that $\mu = \alpha\mu_1 \oplus (1 - \alpha)\mu_2$. However, even if composition is extensional, it is not an operation between sets, but a distribution mixture. But still, we can compare two tasks by how many task instances they have in common, weighted by their probability. Is this the way to determine how similar two tasks are? Unfortunately, this would not lead to much insight. For instance, we can have two tasks with very similar (but not equal) instances and an empty intersection.

Looking for a better way to analyse the composition of tasks and their relation, we finally reach the *solutional* approach, where we analyse the relation between tasks according to their solutions. To do this, we will use the notions of ϵ-acceptability with tolerance and difficulty seen in previous chapters. This will pave the way to the notions of task breadth and task pureness and, finally, to analyse the relation between tasks and their aggregation into abilities. Before that, we need to clarify some details about composition, tolerance, tasks and abilities.

First, when we look at the composition of two tasks we need to take the tolerance into account. If we use the same tolerance for both, since the magnitudes of the responses may usually be lower for one and higher for the other, one task may end up with very easy acceptability and the other with very difficult acceptability. As a consequence, the difficulties would be so uneven that the result of the composition would be dominated by one of the constituent tasks, and policies would devote their resources for the easy cases and neglect the difficult ones. Instead, we can normalise (or equivalently, use two different tolerance levels for) both tasks such that they have similar difficulties. With this, policies are expected to require similar efforts for instances from both tasks. This relevance on difficulty when composing tasks was long ago recognised by Thorndike et al. (1927, p. 484): "composite tasks will be efficient instruments for measurement in proportion as their single elements are equal in difficulty".

> **Keynote 10.3. Balancing composite tasks**: By evening the difficulties and using appropriate values of α, we can understand and achieve the desired effect of a proposed task combination.

Second, the use of 0 tolerance, although not very realistic for actual testing (since some degree of error is always expected), can be of more interest theoretically. For instance, using a difficulty function $\hbar$, if we have that $\hbar(\mu_1 \oplus \mu_2) \approx \hbar(\mu_1)$ with 0 tolerance we can say that μ_2 does not add any difficulty. In other words, with the same effort (but not necessarily the same policy) required for μ_1 alone we can solve both tasks. Informally, we can say that μ_2 goes well with μ_1.

Third, we need to recall our definition of cognitive ability, given in Keynote 1.6 as a *property* of an interactive system in the machine kingdom that allows the system to perform well in a class of cognitive tasks. This means that cognitive abilities are latent variables. Since an ability can be useful for many different sets or distributions of tasks, and a task may require many abilities, measurement should focus on those tasks that could be most indicative of the ability we want to measure and not the composition of all tasks that feature that ability.

In this context we can understand the notion of task *pureness*, as Edward Thorndike posited: "a task is pure when it measures one ability unmixed with any other. A task is impure in proportion as it measures a compound or complex of that ability with others" (Monroe, 1931, p. 244). Godfrey Thomson, during the same conference, replied that "these pure factors ... are not the same thing as the factors that we have been commonly using in 'factorial analysis'. They would not be uncorrelated; they would be correlated" (Monroe, 1931, p. 256-257). This is a very important point, as abilities need not be uncorrelated, or cover any percentage of the variance of a population. Abilities, especially for universal psychometrics, must be ontological constructs that would help us to describe, explain and predict the behaviour of systems in the machine kingdom.

Despite this common use of the term pureness, there are not many conceptualisations in the psychometric literature. Why do we usually consider that if we put a multiplication task and a vocabulary task the resulting task becomes impure? Our intuitive notion of impureness has more to do with how *cohesive* the new task is than any predefined set of abilities or categories. Fortunately, there are concepts from AIT that can account for task cohesion if we look at the set of policies, the best policy or the difficulty of a task. Basically, this is again an algorithmic solutional approach, but we need to rely on composition and decomposition as well.

For instance, consider that we have two tasks μ_A and μ_B of similar difficulty, and we combine them into a new task μ_{AB}, with roughly equal weights. If the difficulty of the combination is basically the sum of both then nothing is reused from one to the other. We can say that both tasks have nothing to do, that they are *dissimilar*. Actually, this means that putting them together would create an impure or incohesive task. This perspective is basically the same already seen in Section 8.8 for task instances that are considered rarer or incohesive with respect to the rest of the task. We connected this with the concepts of consilience, coherence and intensionality (Whewell, 1847; Thagard, 1978; Hernández-Orallo, 2000b; Hernández-Orallo and García-Varea, 2000; Hernández-Orallo, 1999b, 2000c,e).

Another commonly alluded concept is 'task breadth', whose roots can be traced back to the notion of intellect width (extent or range) introduced by Thorndike et al. (1927). The choice of broad tasks seems to be key for intelligent behaviour (success in a wide extent or range of tasks) and is opposed to task-specialised (or narrow) systems (as we saw in Chapter 5). For instance, McDermott (1997) writes: "Deep Blue is unintelligent because it is so narrow. It can win a chess game, but it can't recognize, much less pick up, a chess piece. It can't even carry on a conversation about the game it just won. [The] essence of intelligence would seem to be breadth, or the ability to react creatively to a wide variety of situations". Masum et al. (2002) are even more explicit: "it would be nice to be able to define a notion of task breadth in an objective way, so that one could speak of, e.g., a program's high [performance] on a narrow-scope task, versus a lower [performance] on a larger-scope task". They go on: "parameterization of tasks by breadth is also essential in comparing task areas and perhaps in forming an 'ontology of task space'".

Many others (such as Goertzel et al., 2009; Rohrer, 2010) have also vindicated the need for the concept of 'breadth', with possibly different names, such as 'versatility' or 'generality' in the context of artificial general intelligence, as we discussed in Chapter 5. However, a precise definition of breadth has been elusive. Masum et al. (2002) proposed a weighted sum of 'situations', giving more relevance to those that are more frequent and have more value. Goertzel (2010), albeit applied to agents and not tasks, proposed to define breadth as entropy. For instance, given a set of tasks, a *uniform* distribution would have maximum breadth. Note that if the set of possible tasks is infinite, as we are frequently considering here, an alternative universal distribution would have very low entropy and, hence, very low breadth.

Despite the difficulties, let us try to formalise the concept of breadth in terms of the elements we have been working with in the previous two chapters. A first, naive attempt could be to define that a task μ_A is broader than μ_B iff for every π that is an ϵ-acceptable policy for μ_A we have it is also an ϵ-acceptable solution for μ_B. To see that this does not work, consider the problem of addition and make task μ_B contain all additions where the third digit of the first summand is 7, whereas μ_A contains all the other additions. Clearly, both tasks μ_A and μ_B are computationally distinguishable (there is a computable procedure $\pi_{A\|B}$ such that an agent can tell μ_A tasks from μ_B tasks). Let us take an ϵ-acceptable policy π_A for A (e.g., an addition algorithm) and any policy π_X that is not ϵ-acceptable for B (for instance a null or random policy). We can always construct a policy π' that tells between μ_A and μ_B and then switches to π_A if the instance is of μ_A kind and run π_X for the instances of the μ_B kind. This policy π' would work for μ_A and not for μ_B, even if both tasks represent the same problem, and with a very small tolerance the policy would be acceptable for the task with all additions.

As a result, we cannot build a notion of broadness based on a condition holding for all possible policies because we can always create policies that work poorly for any arbitrary subset. Instead, we can look at the best policies only, using any function of optimality. For instance, we can adapt Eq. 8.14 for our purposes and define the set of all optimal ϵ-acceptable policies for a given task, as those that minimise the finding effort $\mathbb{LS}$:

$$Opt_{\mathbb{LS}}^{[\epsilon]}(\mu) \triangleq \underset{\pi \in \mathcal{A}^{[\epsilon]}(\mu)}{\arg\min} \; \mathbb{LS}(\pi, \mu) \qquad (10.1)$$

Now, we define relative breadth as follows:

Keynote 10.4. Relative task breadth: A task μ_A is broader than μ_B for tolerance ϵ, denoted as $\mu_A \sqsupseteq_\epsilon \mu_B$ iff there is at least one optimal ϵ-acceptable policy π for μ_A, namely $\pi \in Opt_{\mathbb{LS}}^{[\epsilon]}(\mu_A)$, that is also an ϵ-acceptable solution for μ_B.

For the particular case with $\epsilon = 0$ (no tolerance), we can see that if we choose any subset of the instances from μ_A and construct a new task $\mu_{A'}$ with them, we have that $\mu_A \sqsupseteq_0 \mu_{A'}$.

For instance, any of the optimal 0-acceptable policies for adding up two-digit numbers (generated with whatever distribution) can solve additions for one-digit numbers. Even if each situation has to be analysed separately, it seems that in many cases, especially if ϵ is small, the composition of two tasks will lead to a broader task.

10.4 TASK SIMILARITY: INFORMATION AND DIFFICULTY

The concept of broadness can be useful to compare tasks, but it is not the best way for constructing a taxonomy or a hierarchy. For instance, it can lead to cyclic graphs (for different values of ϵ). Also, many pairs of tasks are incomparable if none is broader than the other. In general, a concept of similarity between tasks can be more useful and easy to use, especially as it resembles the notion of correlation commonly used in psychometrics. Note that both correlation and similarity are not metrics, but it is usually convenient if their complements are still semimetrics, not meeting the triangle inequality (e.g., Pearson correlation is a semimetric if the series are scaled). Another advantage of similarity is that it can have other uses. For instance, in an adaptive test, similarity can be used to suggest the following task in a series, if a diverse range of tasks is desired. This is a common approach in transfer learning, where a notion of task distance or similarity is used to select the sequence of tasks (Ferns et al., 2004; Carroll and Seppi, 2005). Nevertheless, we will argue in Chapter 12 that the asymmetric notion of facilitation is more appropriate for this use.

Here we present two solutional approaches to the notion of similarity, using the two approaches (based on comparing the solutions or on calculating the increase of difficulty after composition) that we already mentioned for pureness. These two approaches are represented in Figure 10.2.

The first approach is sophisticated. Given any task, let us assume that its optimal policy is unique, denoted by $\pi^* = Opt_{LS}^{[\epsilon]}(\mu)$. Given two tasks μ_A and μ_A we can calculate their dissimilarity as their information distance, defined as $d_1(\mu_A, \mu_B) \triangleq \max\{K(\pi_A^*|\pi_B^*), K(\pi_B^*|\pi_A^*)\}$, where K is the conditional Kolmogorov complexity. Actually, the information distance is defined as the shortest program that allows the transformation from π_A to π_B and vice versa (Bennett et al., 1998). If there is more than one optimal solution, the preceding expression has to be evaluated for all combinations. Despite the name information distance, d_1 is technically a metric up to an additive term, so it is perhaps more accurate to consider it a dissimilarity and derive a similarity measure from it using a proper transformation or a normalisation (Vitányi

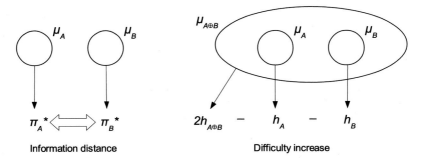

Figure 10.2. Two different approaches to calculate dissimilarity between two tasks. Left: comparing the optimal solutions, through information distance. Right: calculating the increase of difficulty after composition.

et al., 2009). Let us insist that we are comparing the descriptions of the solutions (the policies) and not the descriptions of the tasks. Two tasks with very similar descriptions can have very different optimal policies, and two tasks with very different descriptions can have the same optimal policy.

This notion of similarity is basically a symmetric variant of information gain (Hernández-Orallo, 2000e). If instead of the absolute Kolmogorov complexity K we use Levin's Kt, or we use $\mathbb{LS}$, then we make this measure of similarity consistent with our notion of difficulty. Namely, difficulty is the transformation effort to find an acceptable solution (the first one in terms of $\mathbb{LS}$ from nothing, or interacting with the task), whereas d_1 represents the transformation effort to find the optimal solution for μ_A given the optimal solution for μ_B. This notion has some resemblance to the informal notion of incrementality introduced by Wray and Lebiere (2007), which is basically the lines of code that have to be changed (in a cognitive architecture) from the solution of a problem to the solution of another problem.

Finally, this approach to similarity based on transformation is related to the notion of reducibility in the theory of computational complexity. There we say that two problems are reducible if there is a polynomial-time transformation from the solution of one problem that is the solution to the other. If this is the case, both are placed in the same complexity class. A notion of similarity based on $\mathbb{LS}$ is a more fine-grained notion that takes into account both the program size and the execution steps.

The second approach to similarity relies on the connection with difficulty. A measure of dissimilarity can be defined as $d_2(\mu_A, \mu_B) \triangleq 2\hbar(\mu_A \oplus \mu_B) -$

$\hbar(\mu_A) - \hbar(\mu_B)$, with similarity being defined as any monotonically decreasing function of d_2. This version considers that two tasks are similar if, when put together, there is an acceptable policy of similar size (more precisely of similar finding effort $\mathbb{LS}$) as when they were separate. In other words, they go well together, as for the notion of cohesion seen in the previous section.

> **Keynote 10.5. Task similarity**: Given two tasks μ_A and μ_B, we propose two solutional approaches to calculate their dissimilarity: one is the information distance between their optimal policies and the other is the difficulty increase when they are composed.

In summary, these two versions of similarity schematically depicted in Figure 10.2 share the same principles, but they also have important differences. For instance, we can have an optimal solution π_A^* for task μ_A and an optimal solution π_B^* for task μ_B. If their distance is high and each is completely useless for the other then the similarity based on information distance will give that these two tasks are not similar. However, if there is a $\pi_{A \oplus B}^*$, which is of equivalent $\mathbb{LS}$ to any of the π_A^* and π_B^*, then the similarity based on the increase of difficulty would give that they are similar. Actually, this would be an example of a *Gestalt*, as the whole would not be *explained* by the sum of the parts. Also, this second version does not require the optimal solution to be unique and is not so dependent on the representation language (the optimal policy can vary significantly if the representation language changes).

10.5 FROM TASKS TO ABILITIES

From the concepts and tools in the previous section we can analyse the space of tasks. But how can we derive abilities from it? Using a sweet version of the geographic metaphor – the *cake* metaphor – how can we cut the cake of tasks? To decide which method is best, we need to set a criterion first. This is exactly what Galton highlighted in 1906, as Panel 10.2 explains.

Lacking a full a priori arrangement of abilities, we can set the criterion in terms of finding a good *clustering* using a particular similarity function (such as those seen in the previous section) and a metric to evaluate the clusters (possibly using a range of the number of clusters). We can also aim at a clustering that covers the whole space with a number of clusters (like the radex model) or

---

Panel 10.2
Cutting Galton's round cake on scientific principles

Francis Galton is one of the fathers of psychometrics, but in one short letter to the editor published in *Nature*, entitled 'Cutting a Round Cake on Scientific Principles' (Galton, 1906), he also devised an ingenious method of cutting cakes "to [his] own amusement and satisfaction". Yet again ahead of his time, he envisioned the problems with modern no-frost refrigerators, which dry cakes up very easily, and came up with a method to "leave a minimum of expose surface to become dry".

With this criterion, he realised that "the ordinary method of cutting out a wedge is very faulty" and proposed a method to cut a portion with two parallel sides all across the cake. Once the portion is removed, the two "remaining portions shall fit together", so that no inner part of the cake is exposed to become dry. The procedure can be repeated again and again (changing direction 90 degrees) leading to further smaller roundish cakes.

This hilarious letter brings to the fore that we can only talk about a proper way of deriving abilities from the space of tasks, if we agree on a criterion and understanding of what to select and what to leave.

---

we may prefer a hierarchical clustering (like the hierarchical models of intelligence using factor analysis). In particular, hierarchical clustering would help to ascertain two of the dimensions of validity of a feature as seen in Section 2.3: finding a trade-off between *generality* and *specificity* (see Figure 2.2).

To illustrate just some of these choices and the use of a dissimilarity metric that is population-independent, we recover the elementary cellular automata (ECA) described in Panel 9.1, where agents interact to maximise their rewards. Some examples of their 'lives' were shown in Figure 8.2. Each ECA rule is considered a task, whose difficulty is calculated as the length of the shortest policy that is ϵ-acceptable (here we ignore the computational steps $\mathbb{S}$ in $\mathbb{LS}$, because they are very similar for all the policies in this setting). For this estimation of difficulty (to find the shortest policy) we use a sample of 500 policies (instead of an enumeration). Policies are generated with the use of the agent policy language described in Panel 9.2, choosing a program length uniformly distributed between 1 and 20 and their instructions also chosen uniformly. We evaluate all ECA rules (0 to 255). Each cell array is always composed of 21 cells, with a random initialisation (seed) and 100 iterations per trial.

To make the comparisons meaningful and easy to see visually we only analyse those rules of a particular difficulty. We have arbitrarily chosen difficulty 8, as it is sufficiently large to allow minimally sophisticated behaviours of the agents while still leading to a sufficient number of rules for our analysis, as we explain next. To have a sufficient number of tasks of difficulty 8, we vary tolerance ϵ for each rule to find the particular tolerance such that the difficulty was 8. This is only achieved exactly for 18 rules. There are several reasons for this. First, the relation between tolerance and difficulty is non-decreasing but discontinuous, so not all difficulties are achievable for each rule. In fact, many rules have difficulty 1 systematically (no longer policy is able to improve the response), or other values below 8. Also, we set some robustness criteria to ensure that the difficulty is minimally stable for that rule (as we are using a sample of policies and not an enumeration). With this setting, we get 18 rules of difficulty 8. With them, we estimate the dissimilarity of all pairs using the 'difficulty increase' approach, as shown on the right of Figure 10.2. Since the difficulties of both rules are 8, then this boils down to determine twice the difficulty of the composed task ($2h_{A \oplus B}$) and subtract 16 ($-h_A - h_B$). With all this, we construct the 18×18 dissimilarity matrix to arrange the 18 tasks. Figure 10.3 shows a metric multidimensional scaling (top plot, which resembles a radex) and a dendrogram using complete linkage (bottom plot, where some clusters can be identified). We see that the interpretation of both plots is different, even if they use the same dissimilarity matrix. The clustering of the bottom plot can be used to partition the set of tasks into clusters, which could ultimately be identified or reified as abilities.

When trying to perform a clustering, bottom-up or top-down, hierarchical or with a fixed number of clusters, it is important that we focus on one slice of difficulty. Comparing tasks of different difficulties will generate spurious associations between tasks. Also, a very small value of difficulty is not very useful for the comparison, especially because the similarity metrics are based on algorithmic information theory and this is unstable for small values. In general the higher the difficulty of the slice that we can examine the more meaningful and neat the relationships can be. Nonetheless, depending on the setting, some intermediate values might be enough for the analysis. Also, the number of different policies grows exponentially with difficulty, so there is no need to work with very high difficulties to have a wide space where associations and clusters can be found. A figuration of the analysis of each slice is represented graphically in Figure 10.4.

Once we have obtained a set of clusters or any partition of the tasks into abilities, a related question is whether there are some tasks in each cluster that

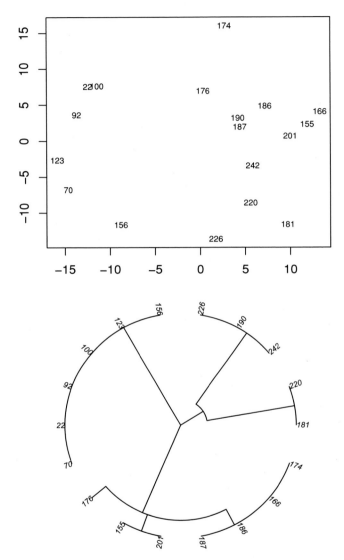

Figure 10.3. Arrangement of the space of 18 of the 256 ECA rules (see Panel 9.1) with an appropriate tolerance ϵ such that the task difficulty is 8. We calculate pair dissimilarities from the difficulty values using the approach shown on the right of Figure 10.2. Top: metric multidimensional scaling. Bottom: a dendrogram using complete linkage.

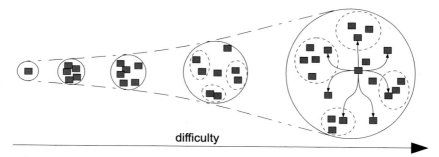

difficulty

Figure 10.4. Figurative representation of how the space of tasks is enlarged when it is analysed by slices of different difficulty.

are more prototypical than the rest. If this is the case, these would be good candidates to be used for measuring the ability. This is what happens with some tasks in psychometric tests, which show high correlation with the aggregate values of many other tasks associated with the ability. From the point of view of artificial intelligence, it would be very useful to determine whether these prototypical tasks are *pure*, and next check whether there are policies that solve them that can be used to solve all the other tasks in the cluster (with minor transformations).

All of this has to be understood, at least for the general problem of deriving abilities in an unrestricted setting, as quite an ambitious challenge. However, it can still serve as a general guideline for universal psychometrics, and it can work for particular scenarios, such as the analysis of a finite set of tasks (e.g., the ECA) or the use of constrained (not Turing-complete) representation languages for policies. The choice of a policy description language (such as the agent policy/language, APL, seen in the previous chapter) is key:

Keynote 10.6. Policy-based ability arrangement: A similarity metric based on a solutional (policy-based) approach can be used to arrange abilities by comparing the description of the policies in a policy description language. The description of the tasks is completely disregarded. Also, populations are not needed.

This means that even current tasks used for psychometrics or situated tasks in the real world can be used as they are and analysed in terms of a policy description language using difficulty or information distance.

To accelerate the process, the identification of abilities could start with any a priori knowledge about their arrangement and progressively refine the taxonomy. This resembles the approach taken by confirmatory factor analysis using experimental data, but using similarity instead of correlation to confirm whether these abilities make sense as independent constructs. Of course, this is better accompanied with a derivation of the tasks from first principles. For instance, we know that the C-test requires inductive abilities, because of the way the items are conceived and generated. Other group of tasks (e.g., involving deduction) can also be analysed to see if they make sense as an ability. The crucial thing is that the language used to analyse the policies that solve all these tasks must be the same.

We can compare this approach with an empirical appraisal. We do not refer to the analysis of the tasks and abilities with humans, chimpanzees or other animals, or even arbitrary machine subpopulations. Instead, an empirical appraisal refers here to the use of populations of agents constructed or defined with a precise distribution, as done with the policy generator in the previous chapter. Perhaps this is not strictly necessary for the clustering of abilities, but it can be used to determine tasks that could be more appropriate for measuring. Also, if the tasks are evaluated for a series of agents taken from the distribution, we can calculate their correlations and compare with the values of the theoretical similarity function.

The use of artificial populations has to be used very carefully. We have to remember that it is possible to define two agents that behave in a different way for any two pairs of tasks, provided the tasks are distinguishable. This can be extended to sets or distributions of tasks (as they are stochastic tasks). In other words, if we find that, using a given agent population or distribution, A and B are uncorrelated, we cannot extrapolate this for other agent distributions (or in general). Conversely, this cannot be used to falsify a correlation or independence between two tasks either. In contrast, the approach based on similarity may have many limitations, but it is population-free, which is in the end very convenient for universal psychometrics. Whatever algorithmic similarity function is used to derive abilities, it is ultimately better than a subjective appraisal (or the extrapolation of taxonomies that originate from human populations to other populations).

To end this chapter, there is a distinction we have only discussed in passing during this chapter. In Chapter 3, we saw that cognitive tests are usually devised with the distinction between culture-fair and culture-bound. In a broader context, we could refer to this distinction as knowledge-fair versus knowledge-bound. In Table 8.1 we saw different types of tasks, some of them being more or less knowledge-bound. Two tasks can be very dissimilar just by requiring different background knowledge. For instance, consider a task that requires recalling Shakespeare's Hamlet word by word and another task that requires solving several arithmetic expressions. Both tasks require the knowledge to be ready before the task starts. For both tasks, the application of knowledge (either factual or procedural) is what we want to evaluate.

This distinction has usually been linked to the debate of nature versus nurture. In this regard, Thorndike stated that "intellectual tasks, success in which requires zero training…, do not exist and cannot exist" (Thorndike et al., 1927, p. 436). It is not clear that all intellectual tasks can be 100 per cent identified with current – or previous – learning. Also, we have to be careful with the notion of "the ability to learn". We have mostly understood it in terms of inductive inference, linked to the notion of 'finding' the patterns and policies behind the observed phenomena (see Table 8.2). But there is also the view of learning as mere accumulation of facts, as in rote learning, which may be useful for some knowledge-bound tasks, and could be implemented with a simple policy that memorises facts. Finally, there is a third view of learning as mere improvement of task performance (or speed) with practice (Woodrow, 1946), which is considered "too narrow a view" (Thorndike et al., 1927, p. 17). Still, these three perspectives can affect our notion of difficulty and similarity.

In universal psychometrics, we should take a broader perspective to evaluate systems that are able to solve a task, independently of whether it is an innate or acquired behaviour, or partially predisposed in between. For instance, for a predator-prey task we can have good results from a chasing animal (e.g., a cat), a hardwired artificial system (e.g., a program specialised for the game), a trained human (in a true environment or as a game) or a trained AI algorithm (e.g., using reinforcement learning). Of course, one can argue – as Turing did – that evolution can be considered a kind of "training" or "finding" during millions of years of the species history, and consider intellectual, cultural and evolutionary search as different manifestations of the same process. Whilst this "training" would put the cat chase inside Thorndike's class of intellectual tasks mentioned previously, there are strong doubts that we could consider the hardwired computer *programming* of a specialised task as "training". Again, all this (and evolutionary search in particular) also highlights that a very simple brute-force search policy could solve a task after a long training. In general, it is fair to recognise that more effective ways of learning (and inductive inference in particular) are crucial for intelligence. Indeed, when tasks feature inductive inference as we have seen elsewhere in this book, they strongly correlate with g. Consequently, we have to pay attention again to learning, and the concept of general intelligence, in the next chapter.

CHAPTER HIGHLIGHTS

- The radex representing tasks in a space of two facets: the circumplex (verbal, numeric, spatial) and the simplex (recall, applications, inference) (Figure 10.1).
- A gradation emerging when elementary tasks and reasoning processes are analysed in terms of information processing, with inductive inference playing a preponderant role (Section 10.2).
- Meaningful task comparisons requiring not only a weighted mixture of instances (Keynote 10.2) but also a balance in terms of difficulty (Keynote 10.3).
- Task breadth being defined by taking the optimal policies and not all of them (Keynote 10.4).
- Two approaches to task dissimilarity based on an algorithmic analysis of their policies (Figure 10.2, Keynote 10.5).
- Similarity used to cluster tasks and identify abilities, with the description of the tasks completely disregarded and populations not needed (Keynote 10.6).

11

General Intelligence

After composing many general arts, I want to explain them more clearly
with this, the Ultimate Art, so named because we do not intend to make
any other art more general than this one, as we compiled this art from
the other arts.

– Ramon Llull,
Ars Generalis Ultima (1305)

I N THE PREVIOUS CHAPTER, we saw that a hierarchy or clustering of abilities can in principle be performed independently of a particular population, provided we use a 'solutional' notion of similarity, and slice tasks by difficulty. In any case, given the similarities between tasks, any taxonomy will require further criteria, making it arbitrary in one way or another. One possible way towards an evaluation that is not task-specific but does not require any taxonomy is the definition of the most general ability. Two pathways are investigated: (1) the consideration of all possible tasks and (2) the construct that relates to all other tasks, a universal g factor.

11.1 ARS GENERALIS ULTIMA: OPTIMAL AGENTS

In Chapter 1 we recalled how Llull tried to build an *ars generalis*, which could solve all solvable problems. Is this at all possible? Is there such a general mechanism, at least theoretically? Why do we refer to *solvable* problems? Let us bring this to our time and our measuring context.

First, the notion of a solvable problem is straightforward with the constructs seen in Chapter 8. Given a tolerance ϵ, a task μ is unsolvable if its difficulty is infinite, i.e., no policy using finite resources can solve it. Otherwise, it is solvable. As we saw, this notion of solvability means that there is an ϵ-acceptable policy π, i.e., the expected result during ν trials is above the threshold set by the tolerance ϵ, namely $\mathbb{R}^{[\mapsto \nu]}(\pi, \mu) \geq 1 - \epsilon$ (see Eq. 8.1). Second, the question of an *ars generalis* can then be formulated as follows: given a tolerance ϵ, and all the solvable tasks for that tolerance, can we find *one* single policy that is ϵ-acceptable for all of them?

To answer this question, we need to pay attention to whether the policy has access to more than one trial. As we assume that the time τ for each trial is finite, the 'repeatability' can also be observed after many trials. Indeed, if the agent can learn from as many trials as needed ($\nu = \infty$) and the task has no memory between trials (it is reinitialised, so it becomes *ergodic*, i.e., independent of particular or initial states in the long term), then the policy can be sought by enumeration. This policy is ultimately found because we are considering tasks that are ϵ-solvable, which means that there is a policy using finite resources. Once found and verified, the agent will stick to it and exploit it. This enumeration approach is improved in Levin's universal search, as we discussed in Section 8.7. With stochastic tasks, the verification becomes a little bit trickier, as we saw, but still possible. In brief, there is indeed a policy that solves all solvable problems: a *metasearch* over the space of possible solutions.

Of course it is unrealistic to assume that the same problem can be attempted infinitely many times and that there are enough resources to try an exponential number of policies. However, in life (especially in terms of evolution), the same problem appears again and again, and adaptation takes place whenever the right policy is found. For instance, an *evolutionary* metasearch also looks for policies – although in a different way to Levin's universal search. Actually, if the metasearch includes mutation and some stochastic behaviour such that it can avoid local minima, there is a non-zero probability of any policy appearing (if nature has enough resources for it). As a result, evolution can also be considered a way of solving all solvable problems, i.e., it is a complete metasearch. Similarly, human learning is thought to use a metasearch, also with bounded resources.

However, the really informative finding would be to show whether some of these metasearches is better (or no worse) than all the others, i.e., that "for solving questions no other art is better" (Llull, 1295, VII, 87). We saw that Levin's universal search is optimal for sequential prediction problems. Can we say the same for an interactive version? This is exactly what Marcus Hutter attempted in 2000 with the AIXI agent, as explained in Panel 11.1.

AIXI is a remarkable attempt for the understanding of how a general agent can solve all learnable problems. Despite the intractability, "AIXI as a principle" has been used to derive practical agents for the reinforcement learning problem (Veness et al., 2011). Also, the setting has been used to reason about

Panel 11.1
AIXI and other theoretical AI agents

Marcus Hutter sought "to develop a universal theory of sequential decision making akin to Solomonoff's celebrated theory of induction" (Hutter, 2005). He devised an agent, AIXI, to "solve any solvable problem and learn any learnable task". In a reinforcement learning setting, with agent's actions y_i and environment's percepts x_i (observation and reward) he formalised environments (tasks) as computable stochastic decision processes, probability measures from interaction histories $(y_1 x_1 y_2 x_2 ... y_t)$ to next percept x_t. Solomonoff's universal prior (see Eq. 7.7) translates into:

$$\xi_U(y, x) \triangleq \sum_{p \, : \, U(p,y)=x} 2^{-L(p)} \qquad (11.1)$$

where p is a program that models an environment using machine U. As an adaptation of Solomonoff's prediction, it works with a Bayesian mixture of models, and not a single model of the environment.

If the goal is to maximise rewards in a finite horizon, we can use an enumeration algorithm, and we get an agent that maximises these rewards. As this is very inefficient, Hutter works out adaptations of Levin's universal search. One of the key ideas is to enumerate proofs by the running time of the models that are attempted, an idea that resembles the "search through all proofs" suggested by Turing (1948).

AIXI is 'optimal' for any problem that admits self-optimising policies. However, AIXI is incomputable. To overcome this, Hutter presents AIXItl, a version of AIXI that stops programs that do not halt, as in Levin's universal search. Still, AIXItl is intractable, with huge associated constants (Hutter, 2005; Oates and Chong, 2006; Hutter, 2007; Legg, 2008).

However, for more general classes of problems not admitting self-optimising policies, AIXI was shown to be suboptimal (Orseau, 2013; Leike and Hutter, 2015). Some other theoretical agents try to circumvent these and other problems: knowledge-seeking agents, modified Bayesian agents, or hybrids (Lattimore, 2013; Orseau et al., 2013; Orseau, 2014).

the limits and risks of superintelligence (Hibbard, 2015b), and many variants have been introduced since then (Hutter, 2012b).

A 'learnable' environment in this context is understood as admitting self-optimising policies, for which the loss can be minimised in the limit (Hutter,

2005, theorem 5.38)(Legg, 2008, theorem 3.4.5). For instance, in an ergodic and stationary environment, an agent can never "make a mistake from which it can no longer recover. Thus in these environments an agent that learns from its mistakes can hope to achieve a long-term average reward that will approach optimality" (Veness et al., 2011). This, in a way, is similar to having infinite lives, which is similar to the infinite number of trials that we mentioned earlier for our setting of non-alternating stochastic tasks.

There are other (metasearch) agents that follow similar principles, under different settings, such as the optimal ordered problem solver (OOPS) (Schmidhuber, 2004) and the Gödel machine (Schmidhuber, 2007). Both are more focused towards incremental learning and self-improvement and will be revisited in Chapter 12. Other related approaches are Smith's "uniformly asymptotically competitive intelligence", which basically performs a search of policies using an enumeration algorithm (Smith, 2006), or Yampolskiy's "efficiency theory" (Yampolskiy, 2015a, chap. 9).

The interpretation of what the theoretical AI agents mean for universal psychometrics cannot be overlooked. First, they are the closest thing to an *ars generalis ultima* we are aware of and show that a 'general problem solver' is possible. Of course, the formulation vastly differs from what Newell et al. (1959) did, but still trying to understand "the information process that underlies human intellectual, adaptive, and creative abilities". Second, as these theoretical AI agents are not specialised for any particular ability (at least inside of the class of learnable problems), they suggest a formal framework about artificial general intelligence. In other words, the quest for generally intelligent agents can start without any particular taxonomy of abilities, as discussed in the previous chapter. This sets a "top-down" route for artificial intelligence (Hutter, 2007). Third, we find agents that behave well in all (learnable) tasks. These (asymptotically) optimal agents are evidence against the idea that excelling at some tasks is at odds with excelling at some others.

Nonetheless, we have to be careful that these theoretical AI agents, and AIXI in particular, are learning agents with some particular conditions. For instance, these theoretical AI agents are not expected to score well in many of the exercises found in intelligence tests, such as a Raven's matrix. The reason is that these tests are not interactive and the evidence is very small compared to the large interaction histories for which these agents are shown to be weakly asymptotically optimal. Of course, these agents are able to excel (and converge very fast) if the problem is reformulated by concatenating thousands of matrices in a single environment.

Despite their theoretical and practical limitations, the theoretical AI agents will have consequences for the rest of this chapter, in our discussion of the no-free-lunch theorems, the aggregation of all tasks and the *g* factor.

11.2 CONSIDERING ALL TASKS

Theoretical AI agents are all very well, but do they give us clues about how these and other *real* agents should be evaluated? If an optimal agent behaves well for all tasks, why do not we define an intelligence measure accounting for all tasks? With a representational view of a behavioural feature, this would boil down to an instance of Eq. 2.1 seen in Chapter 2 such that the probability $p(\mu)$ is strictly greater than 0 for every possible task. Or, as we discussed in Chapter 8, a stochastic task such that every possible task instance is possible. But, since 'possible' does not mean 'likely',

---

Keynote 11.1. The **question when considering *all* tasks** is how likely we consider each task a priori.

The literature of human intelligence is full of references about the use of all (or a large variety) of tasks. This approach has been highly controversial, since the use of all tasks conveys the idea of a heedless selection or the assumption of a distribution of tasks that "is not at all well defined" (Bartholomew, 2004, p. 30). The associated feature is sometimes referred to as "intelligence in general" (as opposed to general intelligence) (Jensen, 1998, p. 33). Spearman strongly criticised this view: "as for the prevalent procedure of throwing a miscellaneous collection of tests indiscriminately into a single pool this – whether or not justifiable by the theory which gave birth to it – certainly cannot be justified simply by claiming that the results give a 'general level', an 'average', or even a 'sample'. No genuine averaging, or sampling, of anybody's abilities is made, can be made, or even *has really been attempted*" (Spearman, 1927, pp. 70–71). Jensen wrote that "some psychologists regard 'intelligence' as the sum total of all mental abilities. This is a wholly open-ended concept, because obviously no one will ever be able to enumerate all mental abilities" (Jensen, 1998, p. 33). However, Jensen seemed to partially contradict himself and Spearman when he also stated that one consequence of Spearman's two-factor formulation is precisely that "the composite score from an infinite number of diverse mental tests would be a perfect measure of g" (Jensen, 1998, 25–26). In fact, a wide composition of tasks is a relatively usual notion when referring to intelligence, and the way IQ tests are constructed, following the schema of Eqs. 2.1 and 2.2. For instance, Pintner advocated that "all sorts of tests are needed" for a view of intelligence as "the capacity of getting along well in all sorts of situations" (Pintner, 1921). Similar views are common, such as "intelligence is associated with performance on a wide range of cognitive tasks" (Buschkuehl and Jaeggi, 2010), or "a wide variety of tasks" (Woolley et al., 2010). The disparity does not seem to rely then on the concept of considering all tasks, but rather about the actual selection and number of tasks that would be required. Actually, the advocates of the use of g scores over IQ scores usually argue that g is less affected by "the subjective selection of items" or its weighting (Bartholomew, 2004)

In any case, if we consider all tasks (or environments), the question is then what distribution can be considered most *diverse*. If diversity is understood as entropy, this choice can then be interpreted as the principle of maximum entropy (Jaynes, 1957; Erickson and Smith, 1988). This is consistent with some views of task breadth seen in the previous chapter (Goertzel, 2010). For finite discrete distributions (or for continuous distributions in a given interval), the uniform distribution is the one with highest entropy. In other words, lacking any previous evidence, this would advocate for considering any problem equally likely.

This is precisely the reasoning behind the no-free-lunch theorems (Wolpert and Macready, 1995; Wolpert, 1996, 2012) that we first mentioned in Section 7.3, which state that any solution would be no better and no worse than any other on average. These theorems hold when we consider that the distribution of problems has "block uniformity" (Igel and Toussaint, 2005), the uniform distribution being a special case. Panel 11.2 describes some literary views of the issue, such as the library with all possible books, parallel to the collection of all possible tasks, problems or environments.

This generalises to considering all tasks equally.

Keynote 11.2. A measure of intelligence embracing "all tasks" under no-free-lunch conditions entails the "impossibility of universal intelligence" (Edmonds, 2009) and "intelligence in general".

This could be taken to its ultimate consequences, concluding that "abstract learning abilities" in animals (including humans) are "contradictory" with behaviour "based on innate programs", so making it "impossible to build a self-learning artificial organism or intelligent system" (Melkikh, 2014).

Instead, we can assume a uniform distribution (of 0s and 1s) for the *input* of a (prefix-free) universal Turing machine (UTM). In this way, the output distribution from the machine is a universal distribution, as we saw in Chapter 7. Precisely, Legg and Hutter (2007c) define a measure of intelligence in these terms: they use a universal distribution to weight all the environments. This is formulated in a reinforcement learning setting using actions, observations and rewards, where environments are computable probability measures from

---

Panel 11.2
The universal library and the no-free-lunch theorems

In 1901 Kurd Lasswitz wrote a short story describing a *universal library* (Lasswitz, 1901), a fictional library that would contain all possible books up to 500 pages – as "one can exhaust a theme pretty well with five hundred book pages". The contents of the library are defined as follows: "if we take our one hundred characters, repeat them in any order often enough to fill a volume which has room for one million characters, we'll get a piece of literature of some kind. Now if we produce all possible combinations mechanically we'll ultimately get all the works which ever have been written in the past or can be written in the future".

This library contains "the complete works of Goethe" and "the lost works of Tacitus and their translations into all living and dead languages". However, many other books – the overwhelming majority – are just gibberish. Actually, much worse, the "Universal Library contains everything which is correct, but also everything which is not".

Jorge L. Borges, in his 'total library' (Borges, 1939), revisits Lasswitz and refers to Theodor Wolff's viewing of the library as a "parody" of Llull's "thinking machine", also in reminiscence of Leibniz's Ars Combinatoria. Borges is captivated by the concept of a universal library but also aware that considering all books *evenly* represents an "inhuman library, . . . which would eliminate intelligence", an omen of the no-free-lunch theorems.

---

interactions to percepts, defined on a universal Turing machine U, as in Panel 11.1. Basically, their proposal, which is dubbed 'universal intelligence', is the aggregated reward result of all tasks, weighted by a universal distribution, as for the following equation:

$$\Upsilon_U(\pi) \triangleq \sum_{\mu \in M(U)} p_M(\mu) \cdot V(\pi, \mu) \triangleq \sum_{\mu \in M(U)} 2^{-K_U(\mu)} \cdot V(\pi, \mu) \quad (11.2)$$

where $V(\pi, \mu) \triangleq \mathbb{E}\left[\sum_{i=1}^{\infty} \gamma_i r_i\right]$, with r_i being the reward for time i, $M(U)$ representing all the environments that can be described with machine U, and γ_i being a discount factor (e.g., $1/i^2$, or c^i with $0 < c < 1$, as in Eq. 5.1, so the agent gives more or less relevance to immediate rewards). Legg and Hutter (2007c) get rid of this discount factor by assuming that for every environment $V(\pi, \mu) = \mathbb{E}\left[\sum_{i=1}^{\infty} r_i\right] \le 1$, i.e., they are assuming that the discounting factor is also part of the definition of environment, so there is no need to stick to any particular one. Also, by this assumption, the aggregation is performed with bounded values (but not necessarily commensurate).

Equation 11.2 is an instance of Eq. 2.1, where all tasks are considered:

> **Keynote 11.3. Task-general intelligence** (Legg and Hutter's "universal intelligence") is an aggregation of all computable tasks, weighted by a universal distribution.

As a result, environments that have a short description for a particular universal Turing machine are more likely and have more weight in the measure.

The primary goal of Legg and Hutter is a measure of machine intelligence, but in (Legg and Hutter, 2007c) they also show interest in the preceding definition being consistent with human and non-human animal intelligence. In fact, their informal interpretation of their definition: "intelligence measures an agent's ability to achieve goals in a wide range of environments" is derived as a distillation of previous definitions of intelligence (see also Legg and Hutter, 2007a) from many different disciplines, including evolution and animal cognition.

Legg and Hutter (2007c) relate their "universal intelligence" measure to human intelligence tests as well, in connection with the C-test, seen in Chapter 7, saying that "universal intelligence could be viewed as generalising the C-Test from passive to active environments". However, they admit that an implementation of Eq. 11.2 as an intelligence *test* would require several modifications, as we will see. But let us first focus on the interpretation of the formula and its validity.

11.3 TASK DIVERSITY FROM A UNIVERSAL DISTRIBUTION?

The first criticism of Eq. 11.2 (and any other proposal based on Kolmogorov complexity) comes from its incomputability. This can be solved by the use of Levin's Kt instead of K, as it was actually done in a previous version of the definition (Legg and Hutter, 2005). Another issue openly recognised by Legg and Hutter (2005) is that resources (especially time) are not considered in the definition. While there is some justification in leaving time apart at this level of the conceptualisation, one could argue that, as the result of the definition, any human and machine could be potentially superintelligent. To achieve this, it would be sufficient to take an implementation of AIXItl and manually execute it step by step. Even if this would take a prohibitively long time, it would qualify as maximally intelligent according to Eq. 11.2. Nonetheless, this problem is relatively unimportant, as time could be included in many ways, by modifying the definition (Goertzel, 2010) or by using asynchronous environments, as we did in the definition of stochastic tasks in Chapter 8.

Nonetheless, the two main issues of any definition of intelligence are necessity and sufficiency. Necessity means that every intelligent agent should have a high measurement. Is this the case for task-general intelligence Υ_U, as for Eq. 11.2? We can ask the more specific question of whether any maximally intelligent agent will give a high value of Υ_U. The answer to this more specific question has been answered in the previous section. AIXI was meant to be optimal for every environment *if* the environment admits self-optimising agents. However, if we consider other kinds of environments, this is not necessarily the case. Consider an environment μ_1 where maximum reward is obtained if the first action is 1 and minimum reward otherwise. It is enough to consider a reference machine U that produced a particular universal distribution dominated by this environment, e.g., $p_M(\mu_1) = 0.999$ and the remaining mass of the mixture being distributed for all other environments. AIXI would not do very well for this universal mixture.

It does not make sense, however, to include the tasks for which agents cannot learn, such as μ_1. The good or bad performance for any non-learnable tasks will reflect some a priori predisposition, but not really an ability. This is why, even if Legg and Hutter (2007c) do not restrict the family of environments for their definition of universal intelligence, Legg (2008) puts emphasis on the characterisation of environments that accept self-optimising policies. It is not only because AIXI is only meant to be optimal for those environments, but also because other unrestricted families would incorporate environments that are completely insensitive to what the agent does (such as including hell and heaven situations, Hernández-Orallo and Dowe, 2010). These environments may change the results of the intelligence measure if an agent is biased in favour or against them. We may even have that "there is a universal mixture such that 'do nothing' is the most intelligent policy" (Leike and Hutter, 2015).

However, limiting environments to those that accept self-optimising families (such as ergodic Markov decision processes) would exclude many tasks that are common for the evaluation of intelligence in humans and animals. Of course, this can be presented as a choice instead of a limitation: "Stanford-Binet, Wechsler, Raven progressive matrices, and indeed most standard intelligence tests, are all examples of 'static tests'. . . . They do not directly measure the ability to learn and adapt over time" (Legg, 2008).

In any case, the key problem is what happens with non-optimal, but reasonably intelligent agents, such as some straightforward reinforcement learning systems, some animals and some humans. Legg and Hutter (2007c) informally analyse some agents of this kind but overlook one important complication. Universal distributions $(2^{-K(\mu)})$ spread the probability mass in a geometric way. This means that a few environments get most of the probability. In other words, for every $0 < c < 1$ there is a finite set of environments S such that $\sum_{\mu \in S} 2^{-K(\mu)} \geq c$. It is sufficient to choose an agent that performs poorly for S and well for the rest $M - S$ environments. Any statement of this agent performing well in a *wide* range of environments becomes really void. The geometric weighting, even for prefix universal Turing machines (PUTMs), means that for some very small sets S their mass can be very close to 1, neglecting the rest of the tasks in the measure. This means that even assuming that all environments are self-optimising, it cannot be ensured that an intelligent, but not completely optimal, agent will get a reasonably good Υ score. The necessity condition does not hold. For instance, a reinforcement learning agent, a human or a modified AIXI that performs poorly on S (and reasonably well for all the rest) will have a very low value of Υ_U. Any intelligent but imperfect agent would be vulnerable to the choice of the particular universal distribution.

Even if necessity cannot be ensured, one can still explore whether there is some degree of *probabilistic* necessity, i.e., a very intelligent agent is expected to succeed in many environments, so despite the choice of U (which would determine the set S), the result of Υ_U will usually be high. In any case, this *probabilistic* necessity must obviously be linked to a distribution of reference machines U and a distribution of (intelligent) agents, creating new problems.

A more profound criticism is about the sufficiency of universal intelligence, i.e., is every agent with a high value of Υ_U intelligent? Legg and Hutter (2007c) state that "if an agent has a high value of Υ_U, then it must work well over a wide range of environments". Unfortunately, this is not accurate for exactly the same reason as the necessity problem. If an agent is specialised to a small set of environments S with high probability, it could get very high values for any arbitrary Υ_U for which this set S has high probability. However, the agent could still behave very poorly for most of the other environments. This lack of diversity is aggravated if this set of environments S can be solved with a small set of simple policies.

Keynote 11.4. The **necessity and sufficiency issues of task-general intelligence** Υ_U rely on the reference machine U and are not alleviated by the invariance theorem because universal distributions $2^{-K_U(\mu)}$ turn the additive constants into multiplicative constants.

To make things worse, Eq. 11.2 is based on the constraint that $V(\pi, \mu) \leq 1$. But this can still lead to very uneven values. For instance, some environments can saturate the sum of rewards at 0.01 while others can saturate at 1. Also, those with high magnitude might be easier than those with low magnitude. In the end, the result of any sum of environments taken from a universal distribution in this way is mostly unpredictable.

The strong dependence of the UTM in Eq. 11.2 has so many ramifications that Legg and Hutter admit that "the relative intelligence of agents can change if we change our reference machine". They suggest that "one approach to this problem is to limit the complexity of the reference machine, for example by limiting its state-symbol complexity" (Legg and Hutter, 2007c) or by choosing "reasonable universal Turing machines". However, any choice of a UTM, even reasonable, is vulnerable to an agent that just specialises to that UTM, because it is still a universal distribution for which the specialisation to a very small set S could achieve high values for a particular Υ_U. The UTM should be changed from evaluation to evaluation, which means that we would need a distribution over UTMs, somewhat carrying the problem elsewhere. In the end, it has been finally recognised that "Legg-Hutter intelligence [measure] . . . is entirely subjective" (Leike and Hutter, 2015).

In the same line, Bill Hibbard analyses this problem and argues that "even if we limit the state-symbol complexity of PUTMs, a small number of environments with short programs may dominate the measured intelligence of agents" (Hibbard, 2009). Also, if most of them turned to be easy (which is likely as the programs are very short), we would be giving more weight to easy problems, which "is not the way we judge human intelligence" (Hibbard, 2011). As a remedy, Hibbard introduces a prefix coding method such that "the bias from a small set of environments can be reduced as much as desired", which sets a minimum size for the environments. However, the bias can still exist for the rest, although smoothed.

Nevertheless, Hibbard's approach suggests turning back to a more uniform weighting of environments. As we mentioned earlier, if we understand breadth as entropy (Goertzel, 2010), we should try to have a distribution of all tasks as broad as possible. Actually, the entropy of a uniform distribution is very high but renders intelligence impossible, whereas the entropy of a universal distribution is very low, concentrating the mass on a small subset of tasks. This highlights the fact that by considering all tasks either we set some bias – and lose breadth and diversity – or we are subject to no-free-lunch theorems. In fact, any uniform distribution over tasks would lead to paradoxes such as the 'subjectivity objection' of intelligence tests, for which the continuation of a series like 1, 3, 5, 7, . . . could be anything. Hibbard shows that even with the use of finite state machines with a bounded number of states, a no-free-lunch result is also obtained. However, this is the case if the so-called No Repeating State Condition (NRSC) is assumed (Hibbard, 2009), which is not such a strong assumption, as the physical world satisfies the NRSC.

Using the general notion of stochastic task that we introduced in Chapter 8, we see that each choice of a UTM in Eq. 11.2 actually defines a particular stochastic task. In other words, using weights for all possible tasks just gives another stochastic task. Looking at Eq. 11.2 we see that it defines infinitely many tests, as many as reference machines can be chosen for the distribution. In fact, every specific task can be approximated by one of the infinitely many universal 'intelligences', the "infinite number of different intelligence tests" (Smith, 2006).

Keynote 11.5. Task-general intelligence is a schema for tasks, a meta-definition: Any *possible* task, but also any *possible* definition of intelligence (e.g., general, specific, anthropocentric) is an instance of it, as any computational distribution can be approximated by a particular universal distribution.

Furthermore, only when one particular U is chosen, can we properly talk about the falsifiability of the proposal. This dependence or bias of the chosen U can of course be seen positively – what Solomonoff would refer to being a feature and not a bug. Legg and Hutter seem to suggest this: "if we wish to bias the test to reflect world knowledge then we can condition the complexity measure. For example, use $K(\mu|D)$ where D is some set of background knowledge such as Wikipedia" (Legg and Hutter, 2007b). Actually, neither a more uniform or a more universal choice of the distribution using an arbitrary U will likely give a non-neglectible probability to any environment that we may find in real life.

Still, the elegance of Eq. 11.2 has spurred several modifications and implementations, to analyse whether some choices of the reference machine can still give meaningful results and truly reflect its original name of "universal intelligence" (what we refer to as *task-general intelligence*). Actually, the challenge was to convert a meta-definition into a practical test. For instance, Hernández-Orallo and Dowe (2010) derive an anytime universal test using some of the principles in (Legg and Hutter, 2007c), but addressing several issues. Environments are defined in such a way that they are discriminating, by making them action- and reward-sensitive, so that dead-ends (such as heaven or hell situations) cannot be reached. This is more flexible than an ergodicity constraint. To ensure that the aggregation is more commensurate, environments are set to be balanced (random agents have expected 0 rewards in a range between -1 and

1) and the weighted sum is also modified. Also, time is taken into account, by considering a maximum time for each trial (environment).

Nonetheless, the most significant feature of this new test is that it is anytime and adaptive. The notion of anytime refers to the property that the test can be stopped at any moment, giving a better approximation of the feature the more time is given to the test. Adaptation is based on a particular notion of 'environment complexity' and the adjustment of time. As the classical reinforcement learning is originally alternating, to consider the computational time in the transition, the complexity of the environments is defined using a variant of Levin's Kt that calculates the maximum steps for any transition. Using this approximation, the test adjusts the complexity of the environments to the agent's results. The available time for each trial is also tuned accordingly. Of particular interest is how several environment classes are described and suggested (instead of a generic universal machine), in particular scenarios (e.g., bidimensional grids) or in better known areas, such as the use of video games as a possible environment class. Some other environment classes have been devised specifically for testing (Hernández-Orallo, 2010). The idea in all of these cases was to make the bias explicit, by the choice of a meaningful class, and then define a distribution over this class, from which the tasks would be generated. This, in the end, dilutes all these proposals to Eq. 2.1, and the discussion about the choice of tasks and weights in Chapter 5.

A few experiments were performed following (Legg and Hutter, 2007c; Hernández-Orallo and Dowe, 2010) and can add some important points to our discussion. For instance, Insa-Cabrera et al., 2011b use the environment class introduced by Hernández-Orallo (2010) (a graph of cells with some special agents generating positive and negative rewards) to derive a (non-adaptive) test. There, Q-learning, a relative simple AI algorithm in reinforcement learning (Watkins and Dayan, 1992) is compared with other agents (random, trivial and oracle). The results, shown in Figure 11.1 (top), seem all very fine and reasonable. Q-learning is more 'intelligent' than other more rudimentary agents but less than the oracle agent, which is almost optimal for this class of environments. We also see an inverse relation with the complexity of the environment (Figure 11.1 (bottom)).

Legg and Veness (2013) perform a similar experiment using an environment language based on a very simple set of instructions. The generation of environments follows a smoothed universal distribution with about 90 per cent of the mass of the distribution concentrated in environments of less than 40 instructions. Several variants of Q-learning and a Monte Carlo version of AIXI (Veness et al., 2011) are compared. The results just show that some techniques are better than others (with larger trials AIXI seems to excel). However, no

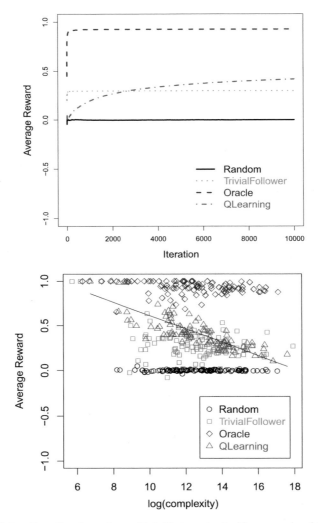

Figure 11.1.   Results of a universal intelligence test with a sample of 100 tasks (from a task class based on worlds consisting of 9-cell graphs; Hernández-Orallo, 2010). Top: progression of four different agents from 0 to 10,000 iterations. Bottom: Results after 10,000 iterations along the complexity of the environment. [From the work of Insa-Cabrera et al. (2011b), with permission of Springer.]

evidence is given that the same ordering of methods is kept with different reference machines.

Do these tests really measure something that we could genuinely call intelligence? To answer this question, Insa-Cabrera et al. (2011a) compared *humans* and AI agents, using the same test and experimental setting as (Insa-Cabrera et al., 2011b). For a fair comparison, interfaces were designed for both kinds of subjects. The results showed (see Figure 9.1) that humans and Q-learning had comparable results. This is inconsistent with common sense, as humans are assumed to be much more intelligent than Q-learning. Actually, Q-learning basically performs a *physical search*, as opposed to the *mental search* of humans. Legg and Hutter's interpretation is not very soothing: "perhaps the amount of universal machine intelligence that a human has is not that high compared to some machine learning algorithms?" (Legg and Hutter, 2007c). A more reassuring explanation might be found in that Q-learning requires 10,000 steps for this performance while humans just use between 20 and 80 steps depending on the instance.

Of course, two implementations with limited experimental results are insufficient to extract any definitive conclusion, even if the goal is to falsify the setting, but we have to bear in mind that the experimenter's choice for U is likely biased towards some "reasonable reference machines".

11.4 ENSURING DIVERSITY: CONSIDERING ALL POLICIES

To move on, it is better that we recover the setting we introduced in the previous chapters, our definition of stochastic tasks and its aggregation using the notions of tolerance and acceptability. This makes aggregations commensurate and, most importantly, gives us the elements to properly assess policy complexity. In particular, in Section 9.3 we decomposed the definition of a feature (Eq. 9.2) in different ways using difficulty. For instance, Eq. 9.4 decomposes the definition of a feature composed of a set of tasks M with a single distribution $p_M(\mu)$ into a distribution of difficulties $p_H(h)$ and a measure of performance for each difficulty: Ψ_h (see Eq. 9.1), which encapsulates another distribution for the policies conditioned by the difficulty $p_M(\mu|h)$. This can be shown in the second row of Figure 9.7. The third row takes a further intermediate step and also decomposes through the policy. This was introduced as a way to generate items in a more appropriate way, which could respect the representational probability p_M if the Bayes rule is enforced. However, in the end, this was also considered as a different way of defining a representational measure, with difficulty in its core.

However, given the troubles of defining a convincing p_M for the set of all tasks seen in the previous section, can we think of a different way of considering all tasks such that the result is less problematic? IRT, seen in Chapter 3, and revisited in Chapter 9, defines proficiency in a different way than just the aggregation of Eq. 9.2, but rather as the highest difficulty such that the probability of solving tasks of that difficulty is greater than a given number. In fact, a similar proposal (but using the number of states of a finite state machines) was justified by Hibbard (2011). With the interpretation of intelligence as proficiency, linked with maximum achievable difficulty, the distribution $p_H(h)$ is not relevant (the test must just include a range that fits the subject). Even if we want an aggregated value, we can choose a slowly decaying distribution or a uniform distribution up to a maximum value of h. The important question then is to decide $p_M(\mu|h)$. But, still, if we consider all tasks, the number of tasks per difficulty is infinite. We can of course use a universal distribution, as we already mentioned in Section 9.3. But then, what would the difference be with respect to task-general intelligence?

Let us consider a given h. Is it still possible that the weight of a few tasks dominates the distribution $p_M(\mu|h)$ for that h, and the same type of tasks dominate again for $h+1$?, $h+2$, etc.? Moreover, even if the task programs are different, it is not clear that we get a *diversity* of tasks in terms of the policies that are required to solve them. This suggests the use of the more indirect decomposition shown at the bottom of Figure 9.7:

- First, we would choose $p_H(h)$, using a slowly decreasing (but bounded) distribution or a uniform distribution in a sufficiently wide interval.
- Second, and crucially, we would choose $p_\Pi(\pi|h)$ as *uniform* as possible. This is possible if the set of policies for a given difficulty is finite. With the notion of difficulty we have been working with, this is true up to an extent, as for any difficulty h there is only a finite number of policies whose length is equal to h. However, the execution and verification steps depend on the task, but we can still take this term out for the purpose of defining $p_\Pi(\pi|h)$ uniform.
- And, third, only the final distribution $p_M(\mu|\pi)$, which chooses tasks whose acceptable solution is π, will rely on a universal distribution, as this set is clearly infinite.

Despite looking rather elaborate, this is not an unusual way to devise cognitive tests. When thinking of items, one figures out patterns (policies) of different difficulty and re-creates tasks such that the policies are the solution. However, automating the generation of item pools using this procedure can be more time-consuming than just sampling from the task distribution. This happens with the C-test, which follows this paradigm precisely, but the procedure is still feasible.

The perspective and interpretation of this evaluation of all tasks through a chained decomposition is clearly different to the view of 'universal intelligence' (what we referred to as *task-general intelligence* in Keynote 11.3), as we set policies and their difficulty at the core of the definition. Instead of the view of an intelligent agent as a system that "can adapt its behavior to meet goals in a range of environments" (Fogel, 1995), emphasised with adjectives as in "a wide range of environments" (Legg and Hutter, 2005) or "a broad range of tasks" (Masum et al., 2002), we could now talk about 'policy-general intelligence', as follows:

Keynote 11.6. Policy-general intelligence is the ability to find, integrate and emulate a diverse range of successful policies.

The diversity is set on the policies ensured by its uniform distribution, given the difficulty. Also, the explicit reference to emulation ability will be further discussed in Chapters 12 (when discussing potential intelligence) and 13 (when discussing the ability of modelling other agents).

This relevance of difficulty and diversity is being perceived in artificial intelligence. For instance, Mnih et al. (2015) refines previous definitions of intelligence and sets the goal as "a single algorithm that would be able to develop a wide range of competencies on a varied range of challenging tasks – a central goal of general artificial intelligence". This makes it explicit that if a choice of a reference machine for a universal distribution leads to non-challenging easy tasks or the tasks are varied but the competencies – the policies or their clustering into abilities – are not, then the test cannot be said to evaluate general intelligence.

One may wonder how a system must be to achieve good results for this *policy-general* intelligence. A test of this kind seems to have been thought for Levin's universal search. In effect, it is expectable that agents such as AIXI would work well with this setting, as in the end it can be seen as an instance of the metadefinition of universal intelligence. In fact, this *policy-general* intelligence is still in accordance with Occam's razor; if the difficulties are bounded, the solutions will be as well.

The view of *policy-general* intelligence suggests that we can revisit the concept of breadth, as we can now reunderstand it in terms of policy *diversity* and not as task diversity. In particular, as the number of policies per difficulty is finite, we can define the entropy of $p_\Pi(\pi|h)$ for each h and average according to p_H. This would be a very straightforward notion of task breadth. Interestingly, for policy-general intelligence using a uniform $p_\Pi(\pi|h)$, diversity would be maximal. This is also in accordance with Figure 10.4.

The decomposition by difficulty clarifies many things. For instance, if a system fails at some tasks, we can analyse the difficulty of the task from the very start and, most especially, if it fails at some particular subgroups of policies. In other words, we can analyse whether the agent has a broad ability, but fails at a certain difficulty, or a narrower result at a larger range of difficulty. This is more informative than just getting a single value as an aggregation, without further insight. In the end, the decomposition of the analysis of cognitive abilities into difficulty and diversity (or breadth) is in the same spirit as Thorndike's decomposition into altitude (level or height) and width (extent or range) (Thorndike et al., 1927), as we first discussed in Section 3.6 and in more detail with the agent characteristic curves in Section 9.1. Also, as we saw in previous chapters, the use of slicing by difficulty has many advantages. Heaven and hell environments just go to $h = 1$ and $h = \infty$ directly. Likewise, the analysis of how sensitive an environment is can be simplified, especially if the notion of discrimination is considered. Finally, adaptive testing goes perfectly well with the slicing by difficulty.

Overall, considering all tasks sets the major question of how to weight them, which is open to many arbitrary decisions. Actually, if we use a universal distribution for the tasks each choice of the reference machine leads to a particular stochastic task, so there is no certainty that the resulting aggregation really measures a wide range of tasks. This is basically the main criticism of the approach taken by IQ tests. A score defined as a mere agglomeration of tasks suffers from many confounding issues, such as many trivial or extremely difficult tasks been generated. If, admittedly, the direct approach using a task distribution makes test generation straightforward from the definition, test application is very inefficient, as we are not being selective about the good tasks, as we discussed in the previous chapters.

Instead, if we sample by difficulty, we can adjust the tasks to the agent's proficiency. For each difficulty, we can sample from a finite set of policies of that difficulty. Also, this sample can be uniform, which looks less arbitrary and more diverse. Finally, we only apply a universal distribution for all tasks that have each policy as a solution. Consequently, the weight is dominated by the policies, making the overall metric more independent of the tasks that are chosen. This resembles, in a way, what *g* scores represent, an alternative to IQ scores that is more robust to the change of the task distribution.

Of course, the policy-general intelligence approach is not free from criticisms, including some of the ones that derive from any measure that considers all possible tasks. Nonetheless, the abstract idea is sufficiently insightful to be considered as a possibility for a general notion of intelligence that considers all problems. In fact, in the next section we analyse whether there are other possible ways to construct a notion of general intelligence and how this relates to task-general intelligence and policy-general intelligence.

11.5 IS THERE A UNIVERSAL *g* FACTOR?

In Section 3.4 we saw how the *g* factor was proposed by Spearman as a way to explain the 'positive manifold', the observation that almost all pairs of cognitive tests showed positive correlation. The positive manifold could be explained by more than one underlying factor, but the empirical evidence in humans has repeatedly shown that one single factor, known as the *g* factor, can explain a large degree of the variability of the individuals. Because this correlation happens with the results of many tests, this *g* factor has usually been associated with general intelligence in humans. Further than that, the 'indifference of the indicator', also postulated by Spearman, states that *g* must appear for any wide set of cognitive tests. Actually, we should not be so concerned about how tasks are weighted, since general intelligence could be obtained by deriving *g* from the results of any diverse set of tasks. However, the diversity issue still remains; not every set of tests will do. Also, the positive manifold phenomenon happens with a particular set of tasks (those abstract tasks in cognitive tests) and a particular set of subjects (humans and some other animals). Our first question is then whether this is also the case for *all* tasks and *all* subjects.

Let us first examine the population. For humans, we already saw in Chapter 3 that the *g* factor appears systematically for individuals and also for groups (Woolley et al., 2010). In the animal kingdom, those animals that are specialised for very specific environments and with very rudimentary cognitive systems are not expected to display a correlation for a range of cognitive tasks. Hence, the focus, as we saw in Chapter 4, has been set on mammals, such as primates and rats. The findings are diverse (Anderson, 2000; Herrmann and Call, 2012), and so is the interpretation, when a dominant factor is found. For instance, Reader et al. (2011) argue that "high general intelligence has independently evolved at least four times, with convergent evolution in capuchins, baboons, macaques and great apes".

In AI, however, the question seems meaningless if we do not set a population. Also, most AI systems are designed to solve a particular application and are completely helpless for other applications. For instance, a system playing chess cannot play draughts. Accordingly, there is no family of AI systems that have been studied in these terms, except for some related studies of metalearning (e.g., machine learning techniques that work reasonably well for almost all data sets). However, the tasks are not general cognitive tests but specialised to an area of AI (or even to application domains).

When analysing *g*, not only is the population of subjects important but also the tasks for which a correlation is expected. In the human intelligence literature, the indifference of the indicator does not imply that *any* task will correlate. If the tasks are, e.g., speaking Danish and playing Go, we do not expect them to be correlated. The positive manifold usually appears for cognitive tasks that are relatively knowledge-fair and abstract. Actually, the tasks for which this happens most strongly are precisely those that correlate most with g. Not surprisingly, the tasks with highest g loadings are abstract tasks featuring analogy and other kinds of inductive inference.

What we do not know is whether these g loadings have a more fundamental reason. We are interested in the *algorithmic* evidence for g. Overall, is the g factor found in any interactive system, be it an animal, a collective, a machine or a hybrid? Or is it just the case for beings that have gone through a process of natural or artificial evolution? Or is it only true for those individuals with learning capabilities? Does it happen for all tasks or only for those that require some learning abilities? To analyse these questions we need to look at them from a different, universal, perspective.

When we described the notion of stochastic task, we used some sample tasks in Table 8.1. There we already distinguished those tasks for which a predefined policy is expected to be used (e.g., performing an addition, or answering factual questions) from those where a policy has to be learnt. For those tasks not having intermediate patterns or rewards during a trial, or the rewards not being correlated with the response at the end of a trial, one trial will not be sufficient for learning and repetitions will be needed. Even with a universal prior, two tasks that are identical, except for an opposite response at the end, can be equally likely, having a no-free-lunch theorem here (Hernández-Orallo et al., 2014, prop. 5). Any positive manifold would be then impossible.

Nonetheless, the positive manifold has been found for tasks without repetitions, such as the C-test or Raven's matrices. One explanation here is that these are recognised as inductive inference problems. This is clear for the C-test but for Raven's matrices this requires a decomposition as an inductive inference problem (see, e.g., Martínez-Plumed et al., 2015). But, why is it that some non-learning tasks, such as verbal comprehension, have a very high g loading for humans? One possible answer is that these questions, in humans, must have involved the previous acquisition of natural language, general knowledge and its retrieval, involving some *learning in the past*, outside of the evaluation.

In what follows, we will just consider learnable tasks. Can we now ensure that there will be task correlation for any possible agent population? Immediately, the answer is negative. The rationale is similar to the one used when we discussed an idealistic absolute concept of task breadth in Section 10.3 and also used by Smith (2006) when arguing against the possibility of task-general intelligence.

Keynote 11.7. The negative twofold for dissimulators: For a learnable task class μ_A, if there is another task class μ_B (learnable or not) that is computationally distinguishable from μ_A, then we can find agents such that they excel on μ_A but not on μ_B.

If two tasks are computationally distinguishable, we can create a policy that tells the instances of μ_A and μ_B. If the instance belongs to μ_A, we apply a a good or optimal agent, such as those mentioned in Panel 11.1. Otherwise, we act randomly (or apply an 'anti-optimal' agent). With this, we achieve good performance for μ_A but bad performance for μ_B. This is a prototypical example of a kind of agent known as 'dissimulator' (locally disabled or impaired intelligence), which uses a switch to execute two very different subpolicies depending on the instance or task.

In any case, even if we can construct pathological agents that perform well at an intelligence test and poorly at all the rest, or vice versa, it seems that a good intelligence test would be one such that the probability of this happening is low. How can we ensure this? The *definition* of the test must be done in such a way that the distribution of tasks is not easy to detect (or distinguish from other tests). The test should possess a wide task diversity, preferably in terms of the diversity of policies, as discussed in the previous section. Of course, the task generator (or the distribution) should not be public and available for the subject at any moment.

Nevertheless, the question about the existence of a positive manifold cannot depend on some pathological agents, or the definition of tests such that these agents are more difficult to construct. The positive manifold is about *populations*. For instance, for a population of optimal agents, such as those seen in Panel 11.1, with no dissimulation code, the agents are expected to obtain optimal results for any learnable task. But if we only include optimal agents or very similar agents, there will be no variance, and no positive manifold will appear. This is represented in Table 11.1.

Let us now consider populations with several *different* agents with suboptimal intelligence. As an example, imagine three types of agents: π_1, which achieve good (but not optimal) results for all tasks, π_2, which achieve optimal results in most tasks but very bad results in a few, randomly chosen tasks, and π_3, which achieve optimal results in most tasks but very bad results in a few, very specific tasks, an identifiable class. Let us first assume that we only have

Table 11.1. Task and agent populations that may lead to a *g* factor.

	Non-learnable tasks	Learnable tasks
Specific or similar agent populations	No *g* factor	No *g* factor
General and diverse agent populations	No *g* factor	Possible *g* factor

agents of type π_1. In this case, it seems that the positive manifold will manifest strongly if the agents have variability in their level of intelligence, and a *g* factor is expected to be derived. If we consider a population of agents of only π_2 or π_3, as there are still many tasks for which they succeed, the positive correlations will still take place. However, if we have agents that do not get good results in a relevant proportion of tasks, or all agents are of the same intelligence level, the manifold may be very weak. The possible case in Table 11.1 is necessary but not sufficient for a strong *g*.

11.6 WHAT MAKES *g* STRONGER?

The preceding discussion suggests the following hypothesis: given a population of agents, the more generally intelligent and diverse they are, the stronger the positive manifold is expected to be, and the *g* factor will appear more significantly. For instance, we should expect *g* to be stronger for a population of intelligent humans than for another less intelligent population. However, the evidence in humans so far seems to be against this hypothesis. This phenomenon is known as Spearman's Law of Diminishing Returns (SLODR) and is described in Panel 11.3.

Beyond the economic simile, there have been many attempts to explain SLODR. The first hypothesis, known as the "ability level differentiation", was postulated by Spearman himself, and considered that able individuals have a high number of specialised skills that can be put into practice for more challenging items. Less able individuals have more limited resources and must rely on the basic general functionalities. In similar terms, Detterman and Daniel (1989) say that if some "central processes are deficient, they limit the efficiency of all other processes in the system. So all processes in subjects with deficits tend to operate at the same uniform level. However, subjects without deficits show much more variability across processes because they do not have deficits in important central processes". Deary et al. (1996) make an account of other interpretations, such as a further refinement of the "economic

---

Panel 11.3
Spearman's Law of Diminishing Returns(SLODR)

Spearman (1927) investigated the relevance of *g* for populations with different levels of ability. He split a set of scores for several tests into two groups, those with normal ability and those with low ability and analysed the correlation matrices independently. He found a surprising phenomenon. The mean test score correlations for the normal group were 0.47 but 0.78 for the low ability group. This means that the proportion of variability explained by *g*, i.e., its relevance, was higher for the group with lower results. The interpretation of *g* as general intelligence was facing a very important conundrum: how could it be that general intelligence was *relatively* less relevant for more intelligent subjects? We emphasise the *relativity*, as the *g* score was greater for the more able group – otherwise *g* would represent general 'stupidity' (Detterman, 1991).

Spearman found a simile in economics. Many economic (and physical) processes do not grow steadily with the increase of one single factor, and its influence becomes less and less relevant at a certain point, ending up with a non-linear increase, which may even saturate. This is known as the law of diminishing returns and was expressed in this way: "the more 'energy' [i.e., *g*] a person has available already, the less advantage accrues to his ability from further increments of it" (Spearman, 1927, p. 219). The law, when applied to mental abilities, has been known since then as Spearman's Law of Diminishing Returns (SLODR).

---

metaphor", which states that *g* is exhausted for the basic cognitive needs, or the hypothesis that "genetic contribution is higher at low-ability levels". These explanations are in stark contrast with our previous rationale of intelligence being mostly contributed by something known as general intelligence, based on some kind of search over policies.

Apart from the interpretations, there has been a very important debate about the experimental support of SLODR. This debate caught special momentum again after Detterman and Daniel (1989) found consistent evidence for SLODR, which was followed by many other studies also supporting SLODR (e.g., Deary et al., 1996; Tucker-Drob, 2009).

However, this experimental support has been called into question for different reasons. One criticism is that if we include many easy items for smart subjects, *g* will not be used, perhaps because these items can be solved more mechanically, without much thinking. So using the same tests for both groups is not appropriate to check the validity of SLODR. Actually, Fogarty and Stankov (1995) showed that if the items are chosen such that the more able group has items with higher difficulty and the less able group has items with lower difficulty then SLODR does not hold. In fact, even the high ability group may have higher correlations. Similar results were found by Hartmann and Teasdale (2004). This is consistent with the interpretation that whatever g represents, it would be used for those problems the individual finds challenging. Another related explanation is that difficult items can frequently be created by adding spurious complications, so the items become more specialised than the less difficult items. For instance, in a number series task, difficult problems can be created by incorporating some series that require a particular mathematical knowledge, such as the Fibonacci series. A suggestive phenomenon, found by Jensen (2003), showed that "the highly g-loaded tests . . . differ the least in their loadings across different levels of ability, whereas the less g-loaded tests differ the most".

Other criticisms, of a more statistical nature, were pointed out as well. Jensen (1998, p. 587) pointed out that the results for both groups should have the same variance. If the more able group has lower variance then the relative importance of g will necessarily be lower. Nonetheless, the strongest methodological criticisms were expressed by Murray et al. (2013), calling into question the "traditional" and "contemporary" methods of testing SLODR and all the empirical results so far.

From a more detached perspective about the debate, it would probably be more clarifying to analyse this phenomenon in highly controlled scenarios instead of general human populations with IQ tests, where many factors about both subjects and tasks can affect the results. As an illustrative experiment of how the positive manifold and SLODR can be studied in an artificial, controlled, scenario, we will use our elementary cellular automata setting again, which we described in Panel 9.1. In our experiment we control both the population of agents and the choice of tasks.

We generated 400 *agents* using the agent policy language described in Panel 9.2, with a program length uniformly distributed between 1 and 20 and their instructions also chosen uniformly. We evaluated each agent with all the 256 possible ECA rules, with 21 cells, using 100 of iterations per trial, as in previous experiments. Only one trial was used per task and agent.

Given the results, we calculated the correlation matrix for the 256 rules. From the $\frac{256 \times 255}{2} = 32640$ correlations, 29612 were positive. The average correlation was 0.146. We normalised (scaled) the original results so that for each task we had mean 0 and standard deviation 1 (note that this does not affect the correlations). Then we averaged the results for each agent to get their overall score. We sorted results per score and split the agent population according to

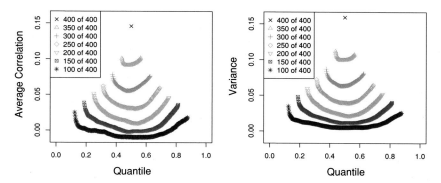

Figure 11.2. Analysis of the existence of a positive manifold for 400 agents (randomly generated programs) and 256 tasks (all the ECA rules, Panel 9.1). Left: average correlation per quantiles using several bin sizes where agents are sorted by overall performance. Right: the variance of the bins. (See colour plate)

different quantiles (from best to worst). This is what we see in Figure 11.2. We used different size of the bins (subpopulations) for the quantiles. The black cross on top of the left figure represents one bin with the whole population (400 agents), with an average correlation of 0.146, as said before. The second shape (using triangles) is formed by the 51 possible bins using agents 1..350, 2..351, ..., 51..400. As we use smaller bins we see that the average correlation decreases. The average correlation is not the same for the whole range, being smaller for middle quantiles (around 0.5 on the *x*-axis). In fact, we see that the correlation is higher for the group of high performance (lower quantiles) and the group of low performance (higher quantiles). Before we rush into any interpretation of this concave shape, we must say that most of this behaviour can be easily explained by the the variance for each bin (shown on the right plot), which is what mostly explains what happens on the left plot.

The experiment shows two things. First, if we sort the population by performance and focus on some quantiles, we find important differences. This does not support any law of diminishing returns for the middle quantiles, but it is rather a consequence of the different variances, as pointed out by Jensen. Second, it is possible to get positive, albeit small, average correlations, by using randomly generated agents and exhausting all tasks (in this particular setting). The explanation here is that the reward mechanism (having 1s in the surrounding cells) is the same for all tasks, and best agents are those that go well for this reward criterion disregarding the task.

To confirm this, we modify the experiment by making the reward mechanism being mirrored half of the times (so agents cannot specialise to it) and agents are now allowed to see the rewards. With these two slight modifications, we see a

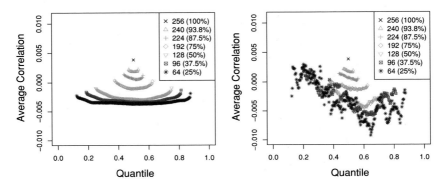

Figure 11.3. Analysis of the existence of a positive manifold for the results of 256 agents (using randomly generated programs with access to the rewards) and 256 tasks (all the ECA rules, as defined in Panel 9.1, with mirrored rewards for half of the trials). Left: average correlation per quantiles using several bin sizes, where results are sorted by agent performance. Right: each bin is only evaluated with the tasks of that quantile of difficulty, for instance, more proficient agents are only evaluated with more difficult tasks. (See colour plate)

very significant change in Figure 11.3 (left). The average correlation vanishes almost completely. It is now 0.004. The interesting bit comes when we also slice the data by difficulty, i.e., we evaluate the most proficient agents with the most difficult tasks. To do this, difficulty was calculated in the terms described in Chapter 8, as the length of shortest policy above a threshold (tolerance was chosen from the response that separates the 10 per cent best agents for each task). In this case Figure 11.3 (right) shows some slope in the distribution of results, with higher correlations for higher proficiencies (lower quantiles).

Although we should not extrapolate from a single elementary experiment showing more correlation for the more able groups, this contributes to our intuition that SLODR may not hold in general. Until more experimental and theoretical research is done, we can only conjecture the following law:

Keynote 11.8. Universal law of augmenting returns: Given a set S of intelligent agents (randomly chosen with an agent distribution p_Π) and two learning tasks μ_A and μ_B (randomly chosen with a task distribution p_M) that are discriminating for S, a positive correlation of the responses of the agents in S for μ_A and μ_B is likely to happen. This positive correlation will be higher the higher the general intelligence of the agents is.

To prove or disprove this law we would require to choose p_Π and p_M, as well as measures of discriminating power and intelligence. For instance, if we choose very easy or very difficult tasks in p_M for the agents in S, correlations will not appear, simply because one of the tasks (or both) would not be discriminating. The role of difficulty is hence again crucial.

The advantage of the experimentation with artificial agents and tasks is that we have a perfect account of the policies that are acquired versus those that are innate, i.e., programmed. For humans, on the contrary, we have many confounding factors. For instance, a general intelligence mechanism that is capable of acquiring new policies may not be used for some tasks that have been common in our evolutionary history, as there may be more efficient specialised modules in our brain predisposed for them (e.g., recognising shapes). But as the tasks become more abstract and less related to our evolutionary history and culture, or more repetitions take place, then general intelligence can play a more relevant role. One way of looking at this is with Figures 1.5 and 10.1. The higher general intelligence is, the further it grows from the centre to the extremes and pervades other abilities.

In universal terms, e.g., for machines, there is no reason to think that one should deviate resources from one type of task to succeed in another type of task, one of the arguments against the g factor. Of course, in the case p_M resembled a uniform distribution, the no-free-lunch theorem would make the aforementioned law impossible. But the use of distributions which embed Occam's razor, are limited to learning tasks and cover a diversity of policies, as discussed in the previous section, can lead to positive results. Actually, a key connection of this chapter with the fundamental concepts of intelligence evaluation in psychometrics can be summarised as follows:

> **Keynote 11.9. Theoretical counterparts to IQ and g scores**: Task-general intelligence can be seen as a theoretical counterpart to a universal IQ score, because the task distribution is key, whereas policy-general intelligence can be seen as a theoretical counterpart to a universal g score, because the task distribution is less relevant.

Summing up, there are many challenging and fascinating questions ahead about the existence of a universal g factor. This will require of course a proper definition of *universal* cognitive tests that could be applied to a broader range of subjects (from unintelligent artificial agents to optimal agents, with some intelligent animals, humans and future general AI systems in the middle). We will return to this view of the term *universal* and what universal tests may look like in Chapter 16. Now it is high time to take a more dynamic view of what behavioural features are, looking at how some of them change by the influence of other features and, most especially, by the effect of the interaction and communication with other agents, acting as teachers, collaborators or competitors. We start this new part of the book with an analysis of how behavioural features develop and whether *g*, or another thing, is really what sets the limits – or rather the *potential* – of a cognitive system.

CHAPTER HIGHLIGHTS

- An aggregate of 'all tasks' associated with the notion of general or universal intelligence, but the key question being what distribution is used for all of them (Keynote 11.1).
- All tasks considered equally likely (e.g., the no-free-lunch theorem) (Keynote 7.5), rendering intelligence impossible (Keynote 11.2).
- Task-general intelligence weighting all tasks by a universal distribution (Eq. 11.2, Keynote 11.3), lacking necessity and sufficiency as an intelligence measure (Keynote 11.4), being a meta-definition instead (Keynote 11.5).
- Policy-general intelligence arranging all tasks by difficulty and weighting successful policies uniformly per difficulty (Keynote 11.6).
- The existence of positive manifolds and a *g* factor for all learnable tasks and general agents (Table 11.1) ending up with the conjecture that SLODR may not hold (Panel 11.3), but rather the reverse, a universal law of augmenting returns (Figure 11.3, Keynote 11.8).
- Task-general intelligence linked to IQ scores whereas policy-general intelligence linked to *g* scores (Keynote 11.9).

Part IV

The Society of Minds

12

Cognitive Development and Potential

> *G* behaves as if it measured an energy.... However, there seems to be
> good reason for changing the concept of energy to that of 'power'
> (which, of course, is energy or work divided by time).
>
> – Charles Spearman,
> *Conference on Examination, quoted by* Monroe (1931, pp. 156–157)

A BILITIES DESCRIBE WHAT a subject is able to do. Every ability is a
potential. But what if abilities evolve too? Can we detect this trend? Can
some cognitive abilities lead to other abilities and traits? Also, if we ignore
speed, can a universal Turing machine (UTM) acquire any ability if properly
'educated'? More interestingly, given that humans are, in a way, UTMs, can
humans acquire any ability? Positive answers to these questions, at least in theory, would be comforting. Actually, we are approaching the real conundrum of
intelligence, the ability of cumulative learning, or acquiring skills. The evaluation of development will be key.

12.1 EARLY SENSORIMOTOR REPRESENTATIONS

In previous chapters we have assumed that subjects are *static*, and so are the
tests and items designed to evaluate them. This is reasonable, precisely because
behavioural features are meant to describe how a subject behaves in general,
and not for a particular state. Indeed, we decided to consider cognitive abilities and personality traits, but we intentionally excluded emotional states from
our measurement. However, even if we consider that a characterisation of an
individual has to be done with stable traits, it is short-sighted to consider that
subjects are immutable and their behavioural features do not change with time.
Subjects *develop*. In this chapter, we analyse this dynamic, developmental perspective, known as mental, intellectual or, simply, *cognitive development*, and
discuss its assessment from the point of view of universal psychometrics.

A dynamic view of the elements of the machine kingdom must be accompanied by some dynamics about the corresponding space of behavioural features. So far, as illustrated in Figure 10.4, tasks have been arranged into abilities for each slice of difficulty. However, a different way of looking at the space of abilities, and features in general, is to do it dynamically, in terms of development. Intuitively, some cognitive abilities cannot be displayed if other more basic abilities have not been developed first. Instead of static similarities between tasks, we could look at the space of the abilities with dynamic dependencies. Nancy Bayley, the author of the Bayley Scales of Infant Development, stated that "any classification of abilities into parallel arrays purporting to designate different factors that develop concurrently is artificial and serves no useful purpose" (Bayley, 1969). Whilst this must be understood in the context of human children development, we have to admit that a fully fledged view of the structure of the space of abilities must necessarily rely on both static and dynamic aspects.

We can start with the question: what behavioural features develop first? Actually, there are two variants of this question, population-dependent (e.g., what is the order of development in humans, or rats?) and population-independent (what features must be developed before others can appear?). During the past century, (evolutionary) developmental psychology has accumulated tools, evidence and models about the first variant: how this happens in humans and other animals (Buss, 1999; Bjorklund and Pellegrini, 2002; Burman, 2007; Machluf et al., 2013). However, the second variant of the question had been under the realm of philosophy for centuries. Only recently, it has caught attention from artificial intelligence and, most especially, from the areas of autonomous mental development and cognitive developmental robotics (Asada et al., 2009; Cangelosi and Schlesinger, 2015).

In robotics, lacking a better reference, cognitive development has been strongly linked to "physical embodiment" (see Panel 12.1), as early development in humans and other animals is mostly about sensorimotor features.

The animal reference has become so important that even development during gestation has been considered in developmental robotics (Asada et al., 2009), paying attention to where and when touch, taste, auditory and visual sensitivity appears. Other development tests for children well after birth include eating, dressing or toileting, such as the Battelle Developmental Inventory (Newborg et al., 1984), which are pointless for robots.

One characteristic of tests for very small children is the strong connection of cognitive and physical capabilities. This is motivated by the sensorimotor character of the first stages of development. Consequently, some of these tests

Panel 12.1
The body culture: measuring *embodiment*

There are divergent views about the importance of *interaction* for cognition. Some classical philosophers, and most early AI research, had an explicit or implicit separation between mind and body, even to the point of a simplistic view of software versus hardware. This duality was blamed for the stagnation of AI in the 1970s and 1980s (e.g., Brooks, 1990). More plausible explanations exist – in hindsight – such as the embryonic state of machine learning at the time.

The story is that, as an acute reaction to the classical view of "AI as a program", *embodied, or grounded, cognition* was presented as an 'enactive', 'situated' process (Varela et al., 1992), where the body determines what kind of cognition (if any) the system can have. Despite being acclaimed in AI and cognitive science, embodiment has frequently been misinterpreted, stating that cognition must always have a body that resembles that of living organisms, with touch, vision, etc. This can overlook the variability of possible organisms (from bacteria to deaf-blind humans), and the evidence of simple artificial worlds displaying 'minimal cognition' and 'autopoiesis' (Maturana and Varela, 1980; Beer, 2004, 2015), as we saw in Section 4.5.

To counterbalance this and Moravec's paradox seen in Chapter 5, Sloman (2009) states that "over-emphasis on embodiment has held up progress" and criticises Brooks's "claim that once . . . systems were built using a hierarchy of layers of sensorimotor control, everything would turn out to be 'rather simple once the essence of being and reacting are available'". This view that once we had produced insect-like systems everything else would be 'rather simple' was parodied in the title of (Kirsh, 1991): *today the earwig, tomorrow man.*

are not purely cognitive tests, but also include some physical abilities, such as co-ordination for grasping objects or moving around. Long since the first tests for early development were introduced, such as Kuhlmann's test (Kuhlmann, 1939) and Griffith's mental development scale, the difference with other more general cognitive tests was conspicuous, by just looking at their tasks, "covering the locomotor, personal-social, hearing and speech, eye and hand, and performance areas" (Griffiths, 1954). Still, the inclusion of physical capabilities, such as moving an arm correctly, has to be understood in terms of co-ordination and not in terms of strength or different body features. Accordingly, we would still be on the side of the behavioural features seen in Figure 1.3.

The dependency of the body includes the choice of sensors, but analogous representations of the world can be constructed even if bodies and sensors are very different. For instance, spatial abilities or scene understanding can develop, yet possibly slower, without visual abilities and a moving body.

> **Keynote 12.1. Perceptual abilities are not necessarily visual and auditory**: The evaluation of many behavioural features and a fully fledged development can be achieved without either or both visual and auditory abilities, as illustrated by blind or deaf people.

For instance, many developmental tests put a strong emphasis on vision, whilst blind children also display their own development and can achieve a fully fledged range of cognitive abilities and personality traits, which can be evaluated with tests for the blind.

Back to the question of what the early stages should look like, the mere recognition of the world, in terms of objects and movement, has to be developed very soon. A newborn baby barely distinguishes light from darkness, and perhaps the only sound that she recognises is her mother's voice. As a result, the first thing that has to be learnt is a basic *representation* of the world so that sensorimotor interaction can develop. In artificial intelligence, the term 'learning representations' has become popular (Rumelhart et al., 1985), usually linked to particular approaches with deep learning (Arel et al., 2010).

One possible way of evaluating these very early stages can focus on whether some shapes or sounds are correctly identified. For instance, can a baby tell mother from father? In this respect, some of these tests can resemble some benchmarks in artificial intelligence, dealing with image classification and agent tracking in video recordings. Nevertheless, these benchmarks do not really evaluate sensorimotor abilities from a developmental perspective. For instance, a task where a system is expected to tell cats from dogs from scratch (by using millions of examples) would be misconceived for the assessment of early sensorimotor development of an animal, a child or a robot. The problem is that most of the representations that are extracted to distinguish them are not reusable for other problems, which will require again millions of examples. The identification of more general shapes, components and concepts that are reusable for many task may require a long development period. It is hence unsurprising that artificial intelligence tried, during many decades, to bypass this long, slow, arduous development stage – paradoxically associated with playing in humans.

> **Keynote 12.2. Development as anticipation**: General representations and skills may be acquired to be used for a range of future problems and not for a present particular task.

Only recently, more 'abstract' scene interpretations are being considered, for which the agents must construct more abstract representations. For instance, benchmarks are being defined with artificial scene generations by Fleuret et al. (2011), highlighting the extremely high difference in the number of examples required by humans and machine learning algorithms for these problems. Abstract representations are needed to make learning from few examples possible, instead of learning from scratch every time. But, more importantly, abstract representations are used to model the world and arrange mental search at the appropriate level, becoming much more efficient than physical (or evolutionary) search. For instance, a crow will throw pebbles into a container (Panel 4.2) because it has some abstract representations of the objects in the scene and can simulate some different policies without physically trying all of them. The relevance of the background representations and concepts (e.g., for difficulty) is crucial to compare different systems in a fair way – one of the reasons why (fluid) intelligence tests are abstract instead of knowledge-bound– but their dependencies are key in (the evaluation of) development and recurrent in most of this chapter.

12.2 COGNITIVE DEVELOPMENT EVALUATION

One of the most relevant models of cognitive development was introduced by Jean Piaget, who classified the development of children into four main stages (Piaget, 1936, 1964): sensorimotor (0–2 years), preoperational (2–7 years), concrete-operational (7–12 years) and formal-operational (12 and more years). Many variants, extensions and refinements of these stages followed, including several objections about the mere existence of stages, in favour of a completely gradual process instead. Today, these stages do not have to be considered necessarily epistemological but of a more practical nature, as a way to better understand and classify human development. In fact, many neo-Piagetian theories of cognitive development are more elaborate, and consider changes in skills,

Table 12.1. Age (in months) when different developmental substages of Piaget's sensorimotor stage are usually achieved by several species. '?' represents inconclusive or no data. [Selected from the work of Parker and McKinney (2012, Table 2.5).]

Species	Stage 2	Stage 3	Stage 4	Stage 5	Stage 6
Human	2	3	8	12	18
Chimpanzee	2 to 5.1	5 to 6	6 to 11.5	11.5 to 42	?
Gorilla	2.8	3 to 4.5	4.5 to 10	39	39
Orangutan	1.5 to 2	2.5 to 6	6 to 11.5	11.5 to 36	24 to 48?
Macaque	0.5 to 3	1 to 4	2.5 to 5	?	None
Langur	0.5 to 0.75	0.5 to 2.25	2.25 to 4	4	None
Cebus	1	9 to 12	12	?	None

knowledge, as well as changes in neurological structures, while the brain develops (e.g., larger working-memory capacity).

(Neo-)Piagetian theories have also been translated to non-human animals (mostly primates), with several comparisons being made (Parker and McKinney, 2012, chap. 2). Interestingly, many studies show that human development is a slow process. For instance, Table 12.1 shows the average months for substages 2-6 of Piaget's sensorimotor stage (from 0 to 24 months). The substages vary according to the conception and degree of understanding of (hidden) objects, causality, space, time, the capability of circular reactions (CR) – goals and intention – and imitation of schemes (Parker and McKinney, 2012).

We see that some species, such as langurs, develop much more quickly than the rest. Several hypotheses can be postulated to explain the slow sensorimotor development process in humans and other primates, who are born completely helpless. This is linked to the distinction between 'precocial' and 'altricial' species, the 'preconfigure' and 'meta-configured' competencies (Chappell and Sloman, 2007) and the role of "construction kits" in biological evolution (Sloman, 2016). However, one of the big questions about development is rather whether the preceding times are intrinsically related to the plasticity and potential cognitive abilities of the species. Would it be possible to have an operative newborn baby of an intelligent species? Does it make sense for cognitive robotics to create a system that is minimally operative from the beginning? These are very important questions for cognitive science. Here, we will focus on the assessment of early developmental stages and the traits that identify them.

We will start with the assessment in human children and then we will see the adaptation to artificial systems.

There are many different kinds of tests, depending on the age, the use or not of language and the goal of the test (experimental, screening or clinical intervention) (Kamphaus, 2005, chap. 15). Some tests can be merely based on observation, or may be based on very simple protocols with the goal of detecting clear cases of mental impairment or special needs. These are known as screening tests, and are usually preliminary, before the application of a second more thorough or specialised test.

Some other tests are more comprehensive and their scores are normed with a population, such as the Bayley Scales of Infant Development, which can be used to follow the development of a child. The second edition (Bayley, 1993) includes a collection of items for children of 1 to 42 months of age in three categories: Mental Scale, Motor Scale and Behavior Rating Scale. From them, two composite indices are derived: the mental development index (MDI) and the psychomotor development index (PDI). The MDI should not be confused with an IQ measure for small children.

Apart from the Bayley scales, many other comprehensive tests for preschool children exist, such as the Battelle Developmental Inventory, the McCarthy Scales, the Binet-4 test, the Kaufman Assessment Battery for Children (K-ABC) and the Differential Ability Scales (DAS) (Kamphaus, 2005), jointly with some of the intelligence tests for children seen in Chapter 3, such as the Wechsler Preschool and Primary Scale of Intelligence (WPPSI) and the Wechsler Intelligence Scale for Children (WISC). There are also tests for personality development (Kamphaus and Frick, 2005).

Despite being well-established batteries, we have to be careful of the fact that the administration of infant tests differs from the evaluation of older children and adults. In small children, there is more flexibility in the order, scoring system and even the intervention of other actors (e.g., mothers) with whom the child might become more participative. For instance, the final scores may be influenced by several factors, such as how much help the child required to complete the task. In fact, clues and rewards during the task can be inversely correlated to the final score of the test – as shows less independence – an observation that we already mentioned for our definition of task in previous chapters. This extra flexibility in the evaluation, of course, affects validity and reliability, but it is necessary for feasibility. Still, reliability for many of these tests is more than acceptable taking all this into account and the small age of the children. For instance, the test-retest coefficient for the MDI index of the Bayley Scales is 0.91 (Kamphaus, 2005, chap. 15).

The evaluation of artificial developmental systems is a relatively recent phenomenon, since classical AI systems did not develop at all and were task-specific, as we saw in Chapter 5. In fact, artificial general intelligence, autonomous developmental systems and development robotics are research areas that were born precisely as a reaction to task-specific systems. A developmental system must address tasks that are unknown when the system is designed. Consequently, the system must generate a representation of the world anticipating for any task (Keynote 12.2). Basically, the system must be learning all the time from their environment in an open-ended, incremental or constructivist process (Drescher, 1991; Weng et al., 2001). Task-oriented evaluation tools are hence useless for the assessment of these systems.

Several test proposals for artificial systems are based on the developmental tests for children and animals (Berg-Cross, 2007). For instance, Weng (2009) suggests exactly this, adapting the Bayley Scales of Infant Development and other tests. A similar, more specific, proposal is the "toddler Turing test" (Alvarado et al., 2002) – despite the name, it is not a Turing test variant, as it does not compare with human toddlers. This proposal is conceived as a collection of tests including associative learning (classical conditioning, presence of a mind, instrumental conditioning, purposeful behaviour), social cognition (social encoding, social inference, causal attribution, representation of self, empathy and attachment) and language acquisition (prelinguistic structural competences, intentional communication, word acquisition, cross-language comparisons). These focus on Piaget's first stage of development, the sensorimotor one. Alvarado et al. (2002) describe each of these 13 "performance metrics" using a short explanation and referring to some textbooks about learning and development. However, there is no particular choice of tests, or clear indications about whether the tests for children should be used unaltered or modified in some way.

Keedwell (2010) extends the toddler Turing test to the four stages in Piaget's development theory and proposes some skills in each stage that the machines should demonstrate, such as "react to basic stimuli", "relate to objects through language", "separate objects into logical groups" and "abstract thought". However, he does not propose any particular formalisation, instance or test apart from the suggestion, again, that children tests could be used or adapted for machines. Somewhat confusingly, a visual Turing test is placed after these four stages.

We also mentioned a series of tests in Chapters 5 and 6 that were inspired by developmental tests, but those were basically tests of core cognitive abilities, such as the Cognitive Decathlon (Vere, 1992; Anderson and Lebiere, 2003;

Calvo-Garzón, 2003; Mueller et al., 2007; Mueller, 2008; Simpson and Twardy, 2008), tests for cognitive architectures (Anderson and Lebiere, 2003; Langley, 2011) or other more specific approaches for robots (Sinapov and Stoytchev, 2010; Schenck, 2013), handling with construction blocks and physical structures (Ortiz-Jr., 2016).

An intermediate approach is Goertzel et al.'s robot preschool (Goertzel and Bugaj, 2009; Goertzel et al., 2010). They advocate for a selection of some tasks from the WPPSI battery (designed for children between 2 and 7 years approximately, see Chapter 3) with the inclusion of new tasks. In particular, they make a selection of "intelligence testing tasks" from WPPSI with some others defined on purpose, such as "declarative memory", "imitation learning", "logical reasoning", "tool use", "planning", "motivation-goal refinement", "self-awareness", "theory of mind" and "physical creativity". Even if they are not fully specified in terms of a precise pool of tasks, distributions, difficulties, times, administration protocols, etc., there is a clear description of how performance would be evaluated (Goertzel et al., 2010).

All the preceding approaches are basically variants of the "AI psychometrics" philosophy seen in Chapter 6, with the additional limitation that there must be an adaptation and selection of tasks, instead of the use of a well-defined battery of tests for children or animal development evaluation. If the goal of these systems is to achieve android behaviour, it seems reasonable that the evaluation must resemble human evaluation. But still, as said earlier, neither the development of a robot has to be the same as a human's, nor are we sure about the sufficiency or necessity of some of these tests outside humans.

Goertzel et al. ask a very interesting question: "Can't one evaluate one's AGI system in simpler ways first, establishing its generally cognitive capability more solidly before dealing with such messy tasks and environments?" (Goertzel et al., 2010, p. 28). They seem to understand these "simpler ways" as "simple environments", instead of controlled environments. As a result, they follow with a critique to specialised AI systems and competitions ("narrow AI") – such as the one made in Chapters 5 and 6, but also to some more general approaches such as the general game player (GGP) AI competition (see Chapter 5), because "unlike the tasks involved in AI Preschool, the tasks involved in doing simple instances of GGP seem to have little relationship to humanlike intelligence or real-world human tasks" (Goertzel and Bugaj, 2009). They similarly refer to "multitask learning", "transfer learning" and similar approaches as valuable but inadequate for the problem of AGI (Goertzel et al., 2010, p. 28).

Nevertheless, even if everyday tasks are considered more important, we have to be very clear about what the measurement goal is.

> **Keynote 12.3. Anthropocentric development**: If we want to evaluate how out-of-the-norm human and nonhuman subjects progress or develop in terms of a range of abilities, it is not clear that anthropocentric, real-world tasks and tests devised for the average human are the best place to start. Different systems may have many limitations and can develop very differently.

Remarkably, many standard tests are not used for human subjects that are out of the norm (such as giftedness, impairment or just different, such as some autistic disorders), because their abilities and development are very particular, and the use of standard tests may lead to wrong conclusions.

12.3 DIFFERENT AIDS TO CUMULATIVE ACQUISITION

The key issue about cognitive development is that the mind changes. This can be the result of some substructures being activated (or deactivated), some underlying mechanisms being empowered or weakened by physical or chemical processes or, most importantly, because new skills, policies, knowledge and attitudes are acquired. To do this acquisition process *autonomously*, the system must have the *ability to learn*, as discussed in previous chapters, but this learning must be cumulative, i.e., incremental and progressive. Also, this learning must be integrated with previous knowledge and skills. This is, in fact, the kind of behaviour that, to date, has not been reproduced artificially at a reasonable scale, and one of the most common views of intelligence. This view has also taken momentum in the area of human intelligence research since Sternberg's 1999 article: "intelligence as developing expertise".

To better understand this view of development as cumulative acquisition, we need to make a distinction of *what* is acquired and *how* it is acquired. Focusing on the *what* first, we must also distinguish between the acquisition of factual knowledge and operational skills. The system may also acquire new ways of proceeding, an ability, which is sometimes referred to as learning to learn or self-improvement. We will use the term *policy* for all these things that can be acquired, as this term is general and consistent with the terminology used in previous chapters. And now, *how* can these policies be acquired and integrated? We saw in Table 8.2 that policies could be acquired by transmission (using some particular commands with a robot or using natural language with a person), by demonstration (by performing a task such that it can be emulated) and by mental search (which mostly covers inductive inference but other reasoning processes as well). Even if these three acquisition processes may result in the same policy being operative in one's mind, these three processes are not regarded as equally demanding. For instance, many non-intellectual, blue-collar jobs do not require a high degree of intelligence since most of the skills and knowledge are trained by transmission and demonstration. People who are not very intelligent can do them very well and even with lower degrees of error (more steadiness) than other more intelligent people.

However, the important thing for development is that these three alternative processes rely on some early constructs. For instance, if a child wants to make fire in a forest, there are many concepts and skills she will require, not only to represent the policy, but also to make any of the three possible acquisition processes work (for transmission the child must have an understanding of human language, for both search and demonstration the child must recognise leaves, stick, friction, etc., and for demonstration the child requires notions of agency, purpose, etc.). In terms of algorithmic information, a program for making a fire can require thousands, if not millions, of bits. This is a size for a policy that cannot be feasibly acquired in one step, not even by transmission. The relative description of the policies (the L part in $\mathbb{LS}$) becomes much shorter for a description language that already contains the building constructs for the policy. In an incremental fashion, large complex policies can be acquired.

Nonetheless, the realisation that even large and complex policies can be acquired step by step must not be interpreted as an acknowledgment of Locke's tabula rasa, or at least that this tabula rasa is unbiased. This is illustrated in Panel 12.2.

The "child programme" includes the mechanisms to establish the intrinsic motivations "such as curiosity, the interest for novel stimuli or surprising events, and the interest of learning new behaviours" (Baldassarre and Mirolli, 2013). Independently of how relevant the bias might be, we need to evaluate how well cognitive systems fill their tabula, and most especially, how they deal with it when it becomes large, or full. Again, we need to look at human psychometrics first. The evaluation of policy acquisition has been considered in one way or another in intelligence testing. For instance, knowledge acquisition is one of the components of Sternberg's triarchic theory (Sternberg, 1985). Nonetheless, policy acquisition has usually been related to the notion of "concept learning", "ability to learn", "general learning ability", "learning to learn" or "learning potential". In fact, this has sometimes been identified with general intelligence and not further studied beyond that (Jensen, 1998, p. 276).

With 'learning potential', we are not talking about rote learning or other simple learning tasks. It is not simple conditioning, habituation, discrimination or other simple association tasks, present in many animals, that we are referring to (Shettleworth, 2010b). It is a very general learning ability, mostly identified

---

Panel 12.2
A biased tabula rasa: the "child programme"

The view of the mind as a tabula rasa (a blank slate) that is filled with experience through life has been a recurrent idea in philosophy (from Aristotle to Locke), in psychology, in education and in artificial intelligence. The simplified view of helpless newborn children as computers with empty memories has also become very popular among laypeople.

The tabula rasa simile is usually understood as supporting *nurture* versus *nature* (see the dilemma in Section 3.8). However, those in favour of *nature* do not claim that the contents of the tabula are inherited, but rather the cognitive mechanisms (the abilities) used to write on the tabula, by processing the experience with the external world. Whilst simplistic, it is highly clarifying to say that it is the 'start-up' program for the mind that is inherited. The nature of this 'start-up' program is especially useful to distinguish between very specialised animals from more adaptive ones, and also between narrow and general AI. This 'start-up' program was referred to as the "child programme" by (Turing, 1950, sec. 7), when discusing the problem of intelligence, which he "divided . . . into two parts: the child programme and the education process".

Another way of looking at the tabula rasa is in terms of bias or predisposition, as seen in Chapter 4. Even if most of it is empty, there seems to be some preference during development to focus the attention and the search on some phenomena and levels of representation above others (Baum, 2004). Of course, the debates spin around what cognitive areas have such a bias and how important they are. Chomsky's universal grammar hypothesis (of which all human language grammars would be instances, as we will discuss in Section 14.3) is a perfect example of such a heated debate. Another crucial question for debate is whether concepts such as 'time', 'causality', 'action' or 'logic', which appear progressively according to Piaget's development theory, are concepts that are somehow embedded in the startup program (the "well-designed child", McCarthy, 2008) or are created as a result of their usefulness when interacting with the universe.

---

with inductive inference. This view, in the end, would be consistent with the understanding of fluid intelligence as the ability to generate policies (a "power", using Spearman's words), while crystallised intelligence would be the ability to apply them in the right situation, something sometimes referred to as *transfer*, "the ability to use learned information flexibly and in a variety of contexts" (Grigorenko and Sternberg, 1998).

However, there are at least two arguments that suggest that this matter is more convoluted. First, it seems that there are some machine learning techniques that can perform inductive inference better than humans for well-defined, isolated situations, but are not able to learn incrementally. In other words, even if policy acquisition and learning ability (and ultimately g) are strongly correlated in humans, there are aspects about policy acquisition that require different processes, most especially the integration with previous knowledge. Second, there is an important difference between what a subject is able to learn in an unassisted situation and what the same subject is able to learn with the help of a good teacher. This second ability has been associated with a distinctive notion of (assisted) learning potential.

The second reason is actually a way to express Vygotsky's Zone of Proximal Development (ZPD), introduced in the 1920s and 1930s, to provide "a more adequate view of the relation between learning and development" (Vygotsky, 1978, p. 84).

Keynote 12.4. Zone of proximal development: "The zone of proximal development . . . is the distance between the actual developmental level as determined by independent problem solving, and the level of potential development as determined through problem solving under adult guidance or in collaboration with more capable peers" (Vygotsky, 1978, p. 84).

The kind of tests that are able to measure policy acquisition and the level of potential development (or learning potential) are nowadays known as 'dynamic tests'. Unlike static tests, dynamic tests involve "learning at the time of test" (Grigorenko and Sternberg, 1998). The major differences with static testing are that the emphasis is put on the process and not on the product, the feedback from the examiner (in terms of scaffolding or intermediate concepts) and the use of trials or tasks that depend on the previous ones (incrementality). To avoid contamination by any previous knowledge, the "examinee can start at the *zero* (or almost zero) *point* of having certain knowledge and . . . teaching will provide virtually all the necessary information for mastery of the tested knowledge" (Grigorenko and Sternberg, 1998). A test can also provide different metrics for the examinees, such as the result without assistance (actual result), the result with assistance (potential result) but also a measure of "how many prompts they required" (Cianciolo and Sternberg, 2008). Note again that our definition of stochastic tasks in Section 8.2, where rewards and the final response are decoupled, allows for positive final responses being inversely related to the number of rewards (or "prompts") given during the trial.

The Learning Potential Assessment Device (LPAD) (Haywood, 1988) is a dynamic test that reuses or adapts some traditional static items in a dynamic way. It has a high degree of intervention from the tester. As a result, one of the problems of the intervention is its lack of standardisation, as "it is difficult to distinguish the contribution the tester makes to improve student responses from what the student actually understands and can apply" (Budoff, 1987, p. 56, Grigorenko and Sternberg, 1998).

More precise intervention procedures happen in Davydov's development teaching (Davydov, 1986). One example (from Grigorenko and Sternberg, 1998) consists of a first-grade maths course starting with the introduction of the concepts of *equal to*, *more than* and *less than*, using the symbols and real examples. From here, the children are expected to figure out the notion of mediation (if $a > c$, and $c > b$ then $a > b$) from examples, and finally the concept of relation (if $a/c = k$ and $b < c$, then $a/b > k$).

12.4 THE CONCEPTUAL LANDSCAPE

There are many ways of analysing how concepts are introduced and combined in an incremental learning setting. In this section we will see some approaches and how they can influence testing procedures based on them. A principled view of incremental learning was endeavoured, yet again, by Ray Solomonoff. In a series of papers spanning more than four decades (Solomonoff, 1962, 1984b, 1989, 2002), he analysed the question of incremental learning, or how an algorithm could learn more complex problems once it has solved and acquired some other simpler problems.

First, possibly influenced by Turing (1950, sec. 7), he first analysed the notion of training sequences (Solomonoff, 1962), i.e., what kind of sequences a UTM should receive to develop and update its knowledge, ultimately becoming an update on its algorithmic probability about the events in the world. An interesting concept is the notion of "concept jump size" (Solomonoff, 1989), where a teacher can sort the questions to facilitate the concept-building process. The view of maximum achievement according to an ideal teacher could be seen as maximum achievement according to a perfect training sequence.

Solomonoff's setting indicates that algorithmic information theory can be used for the construction of dynamic tests that evaluate policy acquisition incrementally. The use of AIT allows us to quantify the relative difficulty according to a common representation language that can be incremented with further concepts. Also, the notions of task similarity and composition can be adapted when tasks are shown in an order. For instance, if several tasks are similar, it is expected that presenting them sequentially will help to capture what is common and solve all of them more easily than separately.

Following this philosophy, we saw some variants of the C-test at the end of Section 7.4, covering sequential inductive inference problems for knowledge applicability, contextualisation and knowledge construction, originally introduced in (Hernández-Orallo, 2000d). Basically, the three of them vary depending on how previous constructs, represented as one or more background knowledge bases B, make the relative shortest descriptions change and, accordingly, the search space and the difficulty functions.

This can be adapted and extended with the conceptualisation of stochastic tasks that we have been using in previous chapters. A series of trials in a stochastic task can be defined such that there is dependency on previous trials. The difficulty of the task can be defined with the consideration of some extra previous knowledge B that is integrated into the description language (the policy language) that is used to calculate the finding effort $\mathbb{LS}$.

The question about the evaluation of conceptual development is how this B can develop into a more powerful B' after a series of trials, referred to as subtasks in this setting, if there are dependencies (assuming both agent and task have memory between trials). If the policy language is universal it can code policies such as 'imitate what I have seen' or 'give preference to the most recent associations' that can recall any information that is provided during previous trials and build a developed B' from it. Note that this is different from giving access to the code of the task.

> **Keynote 12.5. Incremental task facilitation**: An incremental task makes trials (subtasks) depend on previous trials so that the policy-acquisition process is *facilitated* in subsequent subtasks. The difficulty of the last subtask without the preceding subtasks should be much higher than with them.

Note that the task has to be carefully designed such that there is only one unquestionably dominant acceptable policy (the right or intended policy) for each subtask, with no alternative acceptable policies solving intermediate subtasks but useless afterwards. To devise these tasks we need to determine for every couple of subtasks A and B (or even sets of tasks) the *facilitation* that subtask A confer to B. This notion of facilitation is a notion of task dependence, precedence or transferability. In the context of transfer learning, it is common to

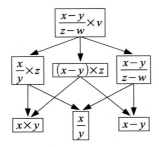

Figure 12.1. Conceptual precedence diagram for arithmetic problems, as for learning space theory. [Freely adapted from the work of Albert and Held (1999, Figure 2).]

analyse tasks in a non-sequential way, with the concept of task distance or similarity (Ferns et al., 2004; Carroll and Seppi, 2005), but there are a few exceptions that do consider sequential dependencies. For instance, Eaton et al. (2008) arrange task libraries as a directed graph, realising that facilitation is not symmetric in general (unlike the task dissimilarity notion that we saw in Chapter 10, Figure 10.2). Several neo-Piagetian theories have also analysed how skills and tasks relate conceptually through the so-called skill theories (or task theories), analysing task chains and hierarchical task complexity (Fischer, 1980; Commons et al., 1998). From a more mathematically-oriented standpoint, knowledge spaces and learning spaces (Falmagne and Doignon, 2010) analyse the given combinations of a group of related tasks. The knowledge structure (as a quasi order) is inferred from experts or experimental data and not conceptually from the tasks themselves or their solutions. Figure 12.1 shows a precedence diagram for arithmetic as used in learning space theory, where each node represents a kind of problem. This is very simple, but there are graphs with dozens or hundreds of (types of) exercises. For instance, Albert and Held (1999) show diagrams with the dependencies of number series and chess problems. Knowledge spaces can be seen in combination with formal concept analysis for representing the relations between the items in psychological tests (Spoto et al., 2010).

The use of constructs that are transmitted, imitated or inferred from previous subtasks is what determines the 'assistance' or 'scaffold' for the dynamic task. This is different from an adaptive test. It is not that the difficulty of items is incremented, from easy to difficult, or adapted to the agent's ability. Rather, it is that constructs are given (or required) incrementally so that, in the end, the agent is able to acquire a complex policy that otherwise would be impossible. Progression is in terms of knowledge and skills, not in difficulty (if calculated over an evolving B).

Certainly, there are many possibilities for the design of dynamic tests using AIT, but their construction is far from easy. Knowledge integration ability, for instance, will require very large tasks, to be able to analyse to what degree the agent is saturated when too many concepts are integrated during the process. Two agents can have the same fluid ability to acquire policies but one of them can get saturated after a few concepts are incorporated, because there is a deficient handling of its knowledge base, such as no proper forgetting mechanism (Martínez-Plumed et al., 2015).

The use of AIT does not mean that we have to end up with a controlled environment, where all tasks are generated using a formal language. From the previous chapters we have seen that the analysis using AIT focuses on the representation of policies (a solutional approach), not on the representation of tasks. This means that we can use tasks that are defined with informal languages (or no language at all), created by an expert or taken from the real world, provided their *solution* policies are analysed using AIT. An illustrative example of how this can be done can be found in (Martínez-Plumed et al., 2015). In this paper one question that is analysed is whether the increase in IQ from infancy to early adulthood can be solely explained by the development of new *cognitive operational constructs*. To do that, a general (but non-developmental) learning system is used (this plays the role of the search process here), which addresses several tasks from IQ tests: odd-one-out problems (OOO), Raven's progressive matrices (RPM) and Thurstone letter series (TLS), which are preprocessed to render them symbolic and eliminate the need for image recognition. The three different tasks feature the following constructs: differences intra and inter items (OOO and RPM), the notion of being distinct (OOO and RPM), the concept of identity (OOO, RPM and TLS), the ideas of combination/addition (OOO, RPM and TLS), the sense of sequence and progression (RPM and TLS), the notion of order (TLS) and the notion of periodicity or repetition (TLS). The system is evaluated with and without some of the operational constructs. As expected, the problems are solved by the system with these constructs but become irresolvable without these constructs (unless the system can invent these concepts). Martínez-Plumed et al. (2015) also analysed the difficulty of the tasks. One of the key issues of this approach is that the use of a policy description language that is declarative makes it possible to analyse the components of each policy, which is becoming common in the area of 'compositional learning' (Lake et al., 2015). In general, one can calculate their size and number of computational steps, i.e., the $\mathbb{LS}$ of the policies, and see whether they are higher or lower depending on the constructs that are included as background knowledge.

There is, of course, a vast literature on concept formation in psychology and cognitive science, sometimes referred to as "conceptual development",

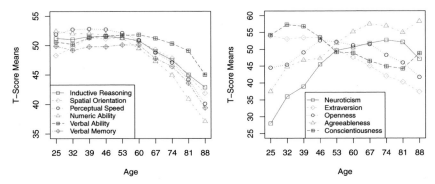

Figure 12.2. Longitudinal estimates of several behavioural features for different ages. Left: cognitive abilities. Right: personality traits. T-scores are centred on 50, and each 10 units equate to one standard deviation. [Data from the Seattle Longitudinal Study (Schaie et al., 2004, Figures 3 and 5).]

especially when linguistic concepts are involved (Bowerman and Levinson, 2001; Gelman and Kalish, 2006). However, apart from general dynamic testing, there are no standard tests where this is done systematically (and not as vocabulary tests). Interestingly, there are a few original experiments where some constructs are blocked, to see whether an adult can behave like a child who lacks the blocked constructs (Sirois and Shultz, 2006).

Overall, much more has to be done to derive tests that can evaluate what happens when the background knowledge grows significantly, to assess how effectively subjects organise their constructs, concepts and policies, including the generalisation of similar constructs and the organisation of knowledge as a whole.

12.5 THE DYNAMICS OF BEHAVIOURAL FEATURES

The evaluation of development must determine the degree of accomplishment of some skills and knowledge in a progressive way. A related, but different question is whether the behavioural features themselves – the cognitive abilities and the personality traits – change with time and, if so, why and how they can be modified on purpose. In other words, we are interested in clarifying the dynamics (or development) of the psychometric profiles.

In humans, it is well known that this dynamics exists. Figure 12.2 shows that cognitive abilities are only relatively stable in the range of ages between 25–60, experiencing a very important decay from the sixties (or the fifties Hartshorne and Germine, 2015), especially for fluid tasks. Personality, on the other hand, is much more variable, with an important "behavioural drift", clearly non-monotonic for some traits, as we see on the right of Figure 12.2.

One explanation of the cognitive deterioration in humans is linked to processing speed, and this may lead to the conclusion that the decay is simply a physical process, in much the same way as physical strength also decays with age. However, several questions arise. First, would old people obtain the same results of their youth were they given more time? It is quite unlikely. It seems then that working memory, concentration and other factors are also affected. It can still be a physical process, but not only speed. Second, according to the stable part of Figure 12.2 (left), between ages 25 and 60, is the improvement of the fluid abilities by some kind of *training* impossible? Or is it only possible for crystallised abilities?

To better understand these questions, we will have a look first at what is usually known as "teaching intelligence". Galton and Binet had opposed views on whether intelligence and other fundamental cognitive abilities, could be increased by training. Galton thought that intelligence was mostly inherited and immutable. Binet, in contrast, thought that intelligence could be improved, through (Binet, 1909, p. 150).

The question, and the evidence, can be very different depending on the population we refer to (children, human adults, old people or mentally disabled people) or how permanent the improvement is. Some say that "efforts to teach for intelligence are promising" (Grotzer and Perkins, 2004, p. 502), while others have a more negative stance of "brain training", especially for mentally disabled persons (Spitz, 1986, p. 215). In general, even if the performance increases temporarily with some interventions, especially in the elderly (Nisbett et al., 2012), "it is unclear how lasting the effects of intelligence instruction are" (Cianciolo and Sternberg, 2008, p. 84). Also, even assuming an effect takes place, "it is far from clear how and why these interventions work", with "certain methodological shortcomings" (Buschkuehl and Jaeggi, 2010).

From the preceding "interventions" we have deliberately excluded some other ways of boosting intelligence. For instance, there is a whole range of pharmacological cognitive enhancers on the market – the modern view of Lem's "strata pills" (Lem, 1971). Their effect seems to be corroborated for many abilities (Nisbett et al., 2012) and its use has a certain revival, with advocates of making them more widespread (Greely et al., 2008).

Finally, there is also a view of emotional intelligence seen as a kind of meta-intelligence, which would help humans use their intelligence in a better way. However, this does not seem to have clear effects on intelligence tests (Salovey and Mayer, 1990; Waterhouse, 2006). In any case, it seems that a better use of intelligence should rather be linked to personality traits instead, such as conscientiousness and openness.

The improvement of abilities has also been attempted with animals, although the programmes and purposes have usually been more individualised. For instance, chimpanzees, bonobos and orangutans have been brought up in a human context or with several kinds of education programmes (Gardner and Gardner, 1969; Terrace, 1987; Savage-Rumbaugh and Lewin, 1994; Segerdahl, 2012; Rumbaugh, 2014). Some significant improvement has been achieved for some of them, but some limitations have also been found. The progress has been more frequently shown in terms of development (language, communication, etc.) than for general intelligence.

Finally, the issue with computers is much more open, since any machine that is able to modify its program (as first realised by Turing) can modify any of its 'abilities' or properties. We will get back to this general understanding of program self-modification in the next section, albeit in a more abstract way. For the moment, we explore some AI systems that are able to self-improve and, in principle, would be able to change their abilities using the same hardware. In what follows, we describe a few systems that basically extend Levin's universal search (or a similar search) in a self-improvement setting.

One approach for self-improvement considers that the start-up program or algorithm is replaced by provably (or probably) better and better algorithms, according to a utility function. This influenced Schmidhuber's optimal ordered problem solver (OOPS), which uses a combination of an enumeration search and Levin's universal search (Schmidhuber, 2004), and the Gödel machine (Schmidhuber, 2007). Gödel machines are applicable to interactive settings while OOPS is basically sequential.

These systems suggest that an agent could modify its code to improve its abilities and change its psychometric profile. However, self-improvement relies on self-assessment:

> **Keynote 12.6. Maximum self-improvement**: There is no theoretical or experimental evidence yet of how much improvement is possible given some fixed computational resources, especially since the features in the psychometric profile to be optimised and the evaluation metrics for self-assessment are unclear.

Yampolskiy (2015a, chap. 5) analyses self-improvement in detail, paying attention to evaluation, but it takes a monolithic view of intelligence. He asserts that recursively self-improvement is impossible, a very radical stance that is said to

be proved, with the argument that "if an agent can produce a more intelligent agent, it would already be as capable as that new agent" (Yampolskiy, 2015a, p. 93). This argument is only tenable if actual abilities are not distinguished from potential abilities. However, this distinction is indeed possible, as we are discussing in this chapter and are addressing more precisely in the following sections.

12.6 THE POWER OF BEING UNIVERSAL

Some of the elements in the machine kingdom are *universal* Turing machines (UTMs), as we introduced in Panel 1.2. Any UTM, with an appropriate input – or training – sequence, can become any other Turing machine. Under the physical Church-Turing thesis for interactive machines, any UTM can be converted into, let us say, a dog's mind, a superintelligent agent, a pocket calculator, or Napoleon on the eve of Waterloo. Of course, this is just a theoretical possibility, which disregards the *emulation* overhead and the size of such programs (sequences or interactions). Stanisław Lem's "Psychomatics" (Lem, 1971), which would allow people to become – through strata pills – for example, "Napoleon at Marengo", is science fiction. However, the *possibility* raises many fundamental questions about development and potential abilities.

First, are humans (and perhaps other animals) universal Turing machines or, more precisely, Turing-complete, i.e., able to emulate any other machine (limited by bounded resources)? We are not talking here about some brain circuits being Turing-complete, as Turing claimed (1948) for B-type networks (see Copeland, 2004, p. 407). We rather refer to the *mind* being Turing-complete. For instance, a child can be educated to have a particular personality, an actor can imitate another person momentarily, a fan can mimic her idol's behaviour, or, more boringly, a computer scientist looking for a bug can painstakingly simulate any program acting as an interpreter. Up to some precision and during some time, humans can emulate – or even transmute into – any other behaviour. The ability of changing one's behaviour, on purpose, is related to Frankfurt's "second-order desires" (Frankfurt, 1971): a person may not be happy with herself, about the way she behaves, and can commit to modify her own behaviour. This is the "ultimate free will": *the ability to become another*. This ultimate free will requires being universal, as if one cannot become *any* other, she is not completely free. How easy and how far a person can reach for a transmutation is of course a matter of ability and determination. This is one of the characteristics that is most distinctively human. Not surprisingly, the Turing test was formulated as an *imitation* game, where a man had to behave as a woman (or vice versa).

However, universality, and free will under this interpretation, also has its downside. It can be shown that for any property a UTM may have, it can be lost. In other words, any machine that preserves a property indefinitely for any possible input is not universal. The rationale is that any UTM can be programmed in such a way that it halts, losing the property (Hernández-Orallo and Dowe, 2013). If a UTM chooses to *become* Napoleon, then it must die as Napoleon.

Certainly, in humans, there is an important difference in emulating personality and emulating cognitive abilities. For instance, the actor Benedict Cumberbatch can play Alan Turing in the 2014 film *The Imitation Game* and re-create his personality in a rather convincing way, even for someone who knew Turing well, but we do not expect that Cumberbatch could re-create Turing's cognitive abilities, were he administered an IQ test. However, more incisively, what if Cumberbatch were asked to imitate AIXI, OOPS, a Gödel machine or some other purportedly superintelligent algorithms? If he accepted the most challenging role of his career, given the size and demands of any of these algorithms, we would not expect much success. But still, most humans are able to acquire procedures, such as typewriting, instrument playing or arithmetic calculation, usually progressing from slow emulation to faster and faster executions, even some unconscious.

If we focus on computers instead (or humans assisted by computers), any algorithm can be executed. Ignoring speed and resources, any universal computer would be, in principle, maximal, in terms of any cognitive ability. As a result, given any new member in the machine kingdom, if we proved its Turing-completeness, we could conclude that it is *potentially* intelligent. This would include many specialised machines, which do not look universal at all, but do have 'a universality gate', such as a programmable washing machine, an elementary cellular automaton or a DNA string.

The discussion has connected two interesting concepts: universality and intelligence, but the view of a washing machine as potentially intelligent is not very meaningful. One straightforward response to this is that resources are not considered. Nevertheless, once the resources became available, any simulator would be considered as equally capable, just faster or slower.

A more meaningful way of looking at all this is in terms of probability. For instance, the probability of a machine having a given property with *random* input was first investigated for the halting problem by Zvonkin and Levin (1970) and Chaitin (1975), what is now known as the *halting probability*. This is a different notion of potentiality, as two different machines may halt but one does it for more inputs (or shorter inputs) than the other. Similarly, we can study the "universality probability", defined as "1 minus the probability that a UTM loses its universality (becomes non-universal) after feeding it with a random

> **Panel 12.3**
> **A conjecture about universal machines**
>
> Chris Wallace, like Solomonoff, also analysed the possibility of 'educating' Turing machines (Wallace, 2005, sec. 2.3). He introduced the notion of "probability of universality" and used it to formulate the intuition that an 'educated machine' would lose its capacity to *learn*. More precisely, he conjectured that the universality probability would be 0 (Dowe, 2008, footnote 70, Dowe, 2011, sec. 2.5), i.e., that the probability that a UTM eventually loses its universality given a random input is 1. However, Barmpalias and Dowe (2012) showed that this probability is strictly between 0 and 1 for any UTM. This gives relevance to the training sequences and the analysis of different non-uniform input distributions.
>
> Universality and capacity to learn may be linked theoretically, but are different things. In a way, Wallace's original intuition can be understood as follows. As said before, being universal implies that any property can be lost, be it intelligence, the capacity to learn, or any other cognitive ability. In other words, if the machine must keep the property forever and for every input then the machine cannot be universal.

input" (Hernández-Orallo and Dowe, 2013). The universality probability was first suggested by Chris Wallace (Dowe, 2008, footnote 70) in the context of whether universality preservation was compatible with the ability to learn, as we discuss in Panel 12.3.

Finally, when calculating these probabilities, we do not consider *when* the properties change or are lost. For instance, a machine can lose a property for many input sequences but they must be very long. This view of time as *age* will be considered in the following section.

12.7 ESTIMATING POTENTIAL ABILITIES

So far we have seen many views of potential. In this final section we will first make a clarification of all these possible views, and then we will choose one of them to properly analyse how potential abilities could be measured – or more precisely, estimated – in a general way.

The application of the term potential to abilities is controversial, as the very term 'ability' implies a capacity, which is in the end a potential. However, here we are interested in the application of potentiality to all abilities and not as a characteristic that some abilities have to a lesser or greater extent. For intelligence, we can for instance compare actual results of a test with the results that could be obtained in other (better) circumstances or in the future, so "differentiating a measured intelligence score from some higher score which an individual is presumed capable of obtaining" (Mahrer, 1958). This view was first applied to the administration of the test: a subject can underperform if there is a lack of motivation, there are problems of language or culture, perception limitations, interfaces, etc. For non-human animals, this is a recurrent issue, as they cannot verbalise if they find some of these problems during the test administration. In fact, as we discussed in Chapter 4, whenever a negative result is published stating that animals are unable to solve a task or display an ability, other researchers may soon cast doubt that the results might have been different with better interfaces or motivations. In fact, occasionally, a different testing methodology is able to make the same animal perform better for the same task. With this interpretation, potential would be the 'correct' measure in ideal circumstances. In fact, some approaches have tried to correct this underestimation (Thorp and Mahrer, 1959; Little and Bailey, 1972). Nevertheless, whilst the term used in the past has been "potential intelligence", we think that the term "test potential" is more appropriate.

Instead, the meaning of potential ability that we will use is associated with the *probability* that a system reaches a certain level for a given ability or, more generally, the expected value of the ability under a range of circumstances. In a developmental setting, this is similar to the way some physical traits (e.g., height) are estimated for a future age, using some stature-for-age percentiles, assuming a particular circumstance (health, nurture, etc.). In this way, we can say that a 10-year-old girl is expected to be taller than her mother once she grows. Can this be done for cognitive abilities as well? The very early concept of mental age suggests a positive answer, at least for humans. Actually, if a 10-year-old girl is well above her age average in an IQ test, there is a high probability that the woman-to-be will be above the average.

In humans and other animals, for behavioural features, these estimations can be done with tests, using data from the family (e.g., the parents' educational level) or using non-invasive scanning (Gabrieli et al., 2015). Many different ways are possible to estimate potential abilities in the same way there are for actual abilities, as we discussed in Chapter 2 (see Panel 2.1). This is why everyone expects that a new-born baby, without serious genetic impairments and a minimally rich environment, will become intelligent. In fact, it is this expectancy that contributes to the basis of some of the rationales of why babies have human rights. This idea of judging developing entities (humans, other animals, plants or computers) for what they will become, rather than what they are, will be revisited in Chapter 17.

The previous estimations make some assumptions about both the *nature* and *nurture* of the agent. In this context, a potential ability would be the result for the ability that is expected for some future time assuming the agent develops in a particular 'life' or circumstance (or a distribution of lives). More precisely, following (Hernández-Orallo and Dowe, 2013):

Keynote 12.7. Potential ability: Given an evaluable ability ϕ, the potential of an agent π at a future time or age t according to a distribution of lives (or circumstances) is defined as the expected value of ϕ at t given this distribution.

For interactive machines, the point potential of a property ϕ for an agent π at time point t is defined formally as

$$Pot(\phi, \Lambda, t, w) \triangleq \sum_{\lambda \in \Lambda} \phi(\pi[\lambda, t]) \cdot w(\lambda) \qquad (12.1)$$

where Λ is the set of all possible circumstances (lives), $\pi[\lambda, t]$ is the agent π at t in life λ, and w is a distribution over lives. Note that lives (or environments) here can be formalised as interactive tasks, as defined in Chapter 8, lasting at least t units of time. We also consider that if ϕ is a psychometric ability, the evaluation of the property is performed just after time t, using a test that measures that ability accurately.

The key issue of the preceding definition is Λ. For instance, if we consider any possible world, we would have that many worlds would not have any rich interaction to allow cognitive abilities to develop. In a way, many worlds would be completely empty. The result would be like evaluating the potential ability of a baby that grows up in a closed room with almost no cognitive interaction. As a result, potential abilities must always be considered in terms of very particular distributions of Λ, considering worlds with other agents, as we will see in the following chapter, and with some degree of interaction. With Eq. 12.1, we also see how meaningless it is here to consider an arbitrary universal distribution w for Λ, with simple dull lives being more likely.

From the definition of potential ability, the best possible life λ for maximising the ability ϕ for an agent π at time t is given by

$$\arg \max_{\lambda} \{\phi(\pi[\lambda, t])\} \qquad (12.2)$$

The goal of any training intervention is then to find these worlds (or some that approach this maximum, so minimising Vygotsky's ZPD, Keynote 12.4). In other words, we would like to find Solomonoff's perfect training sequences. A fundamental part of AI, apart from building 'start-up' agents, would also be to find these enriching environments (the preschools of Goertzel and Bugaj, 2009; Goertzel et al., 2010). Note that if π is universal, and given enough time t, we can attain any achievable degree for the ability, by 'programming' π. Nonetheless, the key issue is that an agent π develops well for many circumstances, as for Eq. 12.1.

A precise definition of potential abilities allows us to think about how they can be estimated in general. The difficulties arise immediately. We want to estimate a future result, for which we do not have repeatability. Also, the interaction between the agent and the distribution of lives, or even just one single life, is usually very complex.

Nonetheless, for some very well defined simple cases, we can analyse and predict this theoretically. For instance, in minimal cognition (Section 4.5), for some well-defined lives, it may be possible to determine how some basic abilities are expected to develop. Also, in some algorithms such as AIXI, OOPS or the Gödel machines seen earlier, this can be analysed, at least asymptotically. In fact, there are results about some of these self-modifying systems being vulnerable to suffer problems of 'delusion' (Orseau and Ring, 2011; Ring and Orseau, 2011). This progression and prediction of final outcomes of a system according to different suppositions about their lives can be done in more general terms, and not only about whether the system will evolve into dangerous AI (Hibbard, 2015b).

An experimental approach can only be achieved for one individual if there is repeatability. This is possible for artificial systems, which can be reinitialised again and again and observe how they develop with different lives. Note here that we are interested in how their psychometric profile evolves. This systematic analysis of the effect of lives on an AI system's set of abilities is still rare in cognitive robotics and AI.

If there is no repeatability, the only resource is to consider the individual similar to a population. This is what we do with humans and other animals, using the species as the reference (or normative) population (Figure 12.2). For computers, the construction of meaningful populations (of different agents at different times) is questionable, to say the least. On occasions, if we see that one AI system has the same progression as another AI system interacting in the same environment, one can expect that there must be some degree of similarity from that moment on. This will be subject to how predictive a psychometric profile can be and a full understanding of the dynamic dependencies of abilities for both agents.

We must be aware of the difficulties, but the notion of potential ability (also applicable to other behavioural features) is crucial to understand the machine kingdom. Humans, non-human animals and computers (including everyday devices) are usually valued by their potential capabilities rather than what they do at the start. It is the characterisation of the progression of the psychometric profile (not just restricted to a change of the "intelligence profile", as in Havel, 2013) that must be distinctive about a system:

> **Keynote 12.8. Life-span psychometric profile**: An agent, assumed to work in a given range of circumstances, is characterised by the expected progression of its psychometric profile.

In other words, what really characterises an agent is not only what an agent does, not even what the agent is able to do now, but rather what the agent can do in the future after a range of possible lives. This developmental perspective in terms of a psychometric profile is fundamental for a view of AI in a developmental way, where AI artefacts, on startup, may lack many of the abilities that will later be able to deploy – exactly like a human baby.

Actually, the goal of this chapter has been to provide a more dynamic view of universal psychometrics in terms of development. Cognitive abilities and other traits have dynamic dependencies and are affected by what has been previously learnt according to how the agent is able to acquire, arrange and deploy constructs. We have also seen that dynamic tests are able to measure the influence of some kind of assistance during the test, which has given us the first view of potentiality, in terms of the zone of potential development or the concept of "test potential". Nonetheless, the interpretation of potential, when combined with the notion of emulation, especially if an agent is universal, has led us to a view of potential as an expected value, according to a range of lives. In the end, we have identified that development, concept acquisition and the estimation of potential are different and require different assessment tools. Some are more challenging than others, especially if we go beyond biological systems.

Finally, another important issue that this chapter highlights is the relevance of the environment or life for development. AI agents are not expected, at least initially, to be very robust when training environments change. Some of these agents will only develop if the environment provides some kind of scaffolding. In a social context, this scaffolding is provided by other agents. Therefore, there must be some mechanisms and predisposition to recognise, model, co-operate and communicate with these other agents. The next chapter really starts the exploration of the measurement problem in a society of agents.

CHAPTER HIGHLIGHTS

- Early development linked to embodiment, but the point really being the anticipative acquisition of general (abstract) representations instead of ad hoc representations for particular tasks, sensors or bodies (Keynotes 12.2, 12.1).
- Human development tests not appropriate for systems not following an anthropocentric development (Keynote 12.3).
- The cumulative acquisition of policies affected by a biased tabula rasa, background knowledge or "child programme" (Panel 12.2) and the guidance of other peers (Keynote 12.4).
- Incremental tasks also being facilitated by the order and conceptual dependencies of the subtasks, which can be conveniently exploited for the construction of developmental tests (Keynote 12.5).
- Behavioural features evolving with time, possibly self-improving up to a limit given by the available computational resources (Keynote 12.6).
- Every universal machine (including humans) theoretically able to become any other machine, with any psychometric profile, and potentially intelligent, unless resources or probabilities are considered (Section 12.6, Eq. 12.1).
- Potential abilities being crucial for our perception of a system: what the agent is expected to be capable of in the future after a range of possible circumstances, beyond its built-in or current abilities (Keynotes 12.7, 12.8).

13

Identifying Social Skills

> There be three degrees of this hiding and veiling of a man's self. The
> first, closeness, reservation, and secrecy; when a man leaveth himself
> without observation, or without hold to be taken, what he is. The
> second, dissimulation, in the negative; when a man lets fall signs and
> arguments, that he is not, that he is. And the third, simulation, in the
> affirmative; when a man industriously and expressly feigns and pretends
> to be, that he is not.
>
> – Francis Bacon,
> *Essay on "Simulation and Dissimulation"* (1718)

EVOLUTION INVOLVES SEVERAL organisms and species struggling for
resources. The resulting ecosystems foster environmental changes for
which adaptation is required. If real environments include other *agents*, and
several types of interaction, from competition to co-operation, should not evaluation tasks be social by also including these agents and interactions? However, by including other agents in a test, their evaluation becomes dependent
on the other agents' abilities and their interaction in such a *multi-agent system*.
While this looks circular, it can be turned into a recursive population-based
approach, much like evolution has done. But social skills can also be seen in
terms of the policy acquisition process as introduced in Part III of the book
and the developmental perspective of the previous chapter. Different degrees of
'mind modelling', imitation, manipulation, learning by demonstration and even
self-modelling can be understood – and, eventually, measured – in this way.

13.1 WHAT IS DISTINCTIVE ABOUT SOCIAL CONTEXTS?

Social contexts are characterised by the existence of relevant interactions with
other agents (conspecifics or not). Behaviours seem to be very different in these

scenarios, since appropriate actions must contemplate what other agents are doing or are expected to do. More precisely, there is a continuum of contexts, being more or less social. For instance, giant pandas follow a solitary life and barely interact with their conspecifics (except for mating or marking their territory). Since they are primarily herbivore and have no natural predators when adults, they rarely interact with specimens of other species, either. On the other hand, apes live in relatively complex social groups and their survival and reproductive success mostly depends on how they can handle the interactions with their conspecifics.

Social and collective behaviours are related, but different phenomena. Still, some collectives are usually referred to as social – they should, according to the definition of social context – such as insect swarms, bird flocks or fish schools. However, most of the individuals only require the recognition of other agents of the same species and follow highly predisposed behaviours, possibly arranged in strictly predefined castes of behaviour (the term 'eusocial' is used here). Nonetheless, some other groups, such as mammal herds or packs have much more complex behaviours, where the social and collective aspects are highly intertwined. Most of these *collective* behaviours as a whole will be addressed in Chapter 15.

In essence, any definition of social abilities or even the term 'social intelligence' must be understood as success in *changing* or *diverse* complex social contexts. If the interactions and roles are rigid and predefined, a non-adaptive behaviour for a particular social context may suffice. In this sense, Edward Thorndike's definition of "social intelligence" as the ability "to act wisely in human relations" (Thorndike, 1920) can work, because "human relations" are very diverse and changing. In effect, the same human can have completely different social contexts at different times of her life. Unfortunately, the same definition may not work for other species. For instance, when looking at the complex social interactions of bacteria (Ben-Jacob, 2008), we cannot properly say that a bacterium has any social ability, even if there is a certain degree of plasticity of the *colony*, as a collective, to adapt to some changes of the environment.

In any case, the difficulty of properly defining what a complex and diverse social context is pervades the discussion of the roles of several cognitive abilities, including intelligence, for social cognition. This has led to many different hypotheses, as seen in Panel 13.1.

In a way, the first three alternatives in Panel 13.1 are consistent with a more general: "social hypothesis" (originally the "social function of intellect", Jolly, 1966; Humphrey, 1976, or the more common "social intelligence hypothesis",

---

Panel 13.1
Is intelligence social?

Within different disciplines, the relevance of complex social environments for intelligence – and whether distinctive social abilities exist – has dominated the discussion about cognition in social contexts.

In animal cognition, several alternatives are considered (Shettleworth, 2010b, chap. 12): (1) 'social' and 'physical' (general) intelligence are inherently related, or have evolved together; (2) general intelligence made social intelligence possible; (3) group social complexity required new developments in general intelligence and larger brains; and (4) general and social intelligence can be independent. Also, there is an ongoing debate about whether primates, apes or just humans in particular have social behaviours that are qualitatively different from the rest (Herrmann et al., 2007).

In human intelligence, on the other hand, the question focuses on whether one or more social factors, measured by specialised tests, can be distinguished from the factors already identified in IQ tests, using factor analysis and related techniques. For many decades, the existing correlation between social ability tests and IQ tests played against the studies of social abilities in humans, and the development and use of these tests. Wechsler (1944, 88–89), for instance, was blatant on this issue: "social intelligence is just general intelligence applied to social situations". Of course, it is important to emphasise that even if general and social intelligence correlate at the populational level, that does not imply that they are the same thing or one responsible for the other. Some humans can have very different results on both and for other species this correlation may not hold.

Finally, in artificial intelligence, the social intelligence hypothesis has been embraced enthusiastically in the past decades, with the emergence of the area of multi-agent systems. By situating the agents in social contexts, AI researchers expected to have a more realistic scenario for building intelligent agents, jointly with the powerful help of game theory.

Emery et al., 2007) stating that intelligence in humans can only be understood as a result of social contexts. Also, this would correspond to the hypothesis that artificial intelligence cannot succeed to create truly intelligent systems if social contexts are not well handled by AI systems. In a more abstract way, covering all the aforementioned disciplines, we could simplify the hypothesis as follows:

> **Keynote 13.1. The social hypothesis** posits that fully fledged intelligence is inherent to social contexts. Under this hypothesis, truly intelligent systems would only be possible as a result of the evolution, construction or development in social contexts.

The hypothesis has received criticism (Holekamp, 2007). For instance, dogs have evolved some social skills (e.g., their ability to follow human cues) extremely fast in evolutionary terms after their domestication and contact with humans, but their physical (general) intelligence may be no different from other canids (Hare and Tomasello, 2005; Kubinyi et al., 2007).

Other critical views identify social intelligence as a separate entity, the so-called inter-personal intelligence in Gardner's multiple intelligence theory (Gardner, 1983) or Goleman's "social intelligence" (Goleman, 2007), a companion to "emotional intelligence" (Goleman, 1996; Murphy, 2006). Strictly, however, there is no evidence that a special social 'ability' can be isolated with psychometrics or neurobiological techniques. Even if some parts of the brain (e.g., the superior temporal sulcus and adjacent regions in humans, or the "mirror neurons" in the inferior frontal or parietal cortex of macaques) are found to be dealing with some social matters (Frith and Frith, 2010), this does not imply that the mechanisms for this module are qualitatively different from the mechanisms of other areas of the brain (the modularity versus plasticity dilemma seen in the first chapters).

Whatever hypothesis we take, the relevance of social contexts for intelligence in the *evaluation* of cognition cannot be overlooked. And here the evaluation of social behaviour faces a series of obstacles:

- Social cognition is associated with an important number of processes – and degrees of such processes – such as agent recognition, sensorimotor mirroring (see what others' inputs and output are), mind modelling, imitation, co-operation, communication, deceptive behaviour and manipulation.
- There is no agreement about what makes a context or environment socially complex and whether this means that it is also necessarily more cognitively demanding: is an ant colony a more complex social environment than a bird flock or a fish pack, but less complex than an ape troop? How can these contexts be reproduced for testing? How can we make an environment or a task more socially challenging?
- The inconsistent results about the existence of a separate social factor (from Thorndike, 1936 to Herrmann et al., 2010) have led instead to the views of social features as personality traits or "personality as social intelligence"

(Kihlstrom and Cantor, 2000, p. 368), especially for extraversion and agree-ableness, or for the 'General Factor of Personality' (see Section 3.2), rep-resenting a general tendency to socialise and co-operate. Social features are also seen as temperaments, predispositions or motivations, "a suite of social-cognitive and social-motivational skills that may be collectively termed shared intentionality" (Tomasello and Carpenter, 2007), such as a selection against aggressive behaviour (e.g., dogs from wolves, Hare and Tomasello, 2005).

- Because of the different degrees of predisposition, it is hard to say "whether certain social instincts have been acquired through natural selection, or are the indirect result of other instincts and faculties" (Darwin, 1871, chap. IV). The term "social skills" sometimes emphasises that much of humans' social behaviour is cultural (i.e., acquired), and that skills can be learnt too, such as greeting rituals. Still, the term skill is also used as a synonym for ability (Riggio, 1986).

- The deep interplay between social behaviour and the display of certain poli-cies such as recognising a face, a smile or a gaze, is crucial, in the same way that some social predisposition to observe, learn from and collaborate with others is the scaffold for development. Apes and other animals raised in rich social human environments (remember Vygotsky's Zone of Proxi-mal Development, Keynote 12.4), may develop some social skills that would never happen in their original environments (Call and Tomasello, 1998).

- Finally, social contexts include other agents. This may require the other agents to be evaluated previously or be trained to behave in a particular way. Sometimes two or more agents are evaluated at the same time, such as when two animals must pull two edges of the same rope. All these com-plications may explain why many tests are not *situated* tests, with an agent competing or co-operating with other agents. Rather, especially in the case of human assessment, "*situational* judgement tests" are more common, where the evaluee is presented a hypothetical scene or story. Even self-report tests (self-assessment) are common.

Given these difficulties, it is understandable that many social evaluation tests and batteries have been highly contested in terms of validity. Nonetheless, there are many tests that are still valuable tools for research and real applications. Let us briefly go through some of them historically, covering both human and animal evaluation.

Edward Thorndike suggested – in passing – that there were three major kinds of intelligence: abstract, concrete (or mechanical) and social (Thorndike, 1920). This motivated the first 'social intelligence' test in 1928, the George

Table 13.1. George Washington Social Intelligence Test: parts, description and versions of the tests that include each part.

Part and Description	Versions
Judgment in Social Situations: A situational judgment about common social relationships	All
Memory for Names and Faces: Asking to associate them	All
Recognition of the Mental States behind Words: Asking to recognise emotions from speech and literature quotations	All
Observation of Human Behavior: A true/false test of behavioural knowledge	All
Recognition of Mental States from Facial Expression: Asking to recognise emotions from photographs	Early
Social Information: A true/false test of social information	Early
Sense of Humor: Asking to best complete a humorous story	Later

Washington Social Intelligence Test (Moss et al., 1925; Hunt, 1928). Table 13.1 gives a summary of the parts of the test.

Edward Thorndike had already warned that "convenient tests of social intelligence are hard to devise" (Thorndike, 1920). Robert Thorndike (Edward's son) analysed the first George Washington Social Intelligence Test and found it correlated with the IQ tests of the time, not finding any social intelligence factors. These validity issues did not encourage researchers of the time to create alternatives. In fact, it was difficult to develop a situational test for humans where verbal abilities were not an important requirement for doing the test. For instance, it seems complicated to not use words for situational-judgment items such as "is it proper to laugh at a funeral?" (Kihlstrom and Cantor, 2000, p. 371).

It took a while to find a remarkable solution in the form of the pictorial battery of O'Sullivan et al. (1965), featuring picture arrangement items (given some cartoons of a scene, the subject has to order them), story continuation (figuring out the picture that follows), gestural expression interpretation, etc.

Despite these efforts, in the following decades "the term *social intelligence* was used less frequently. Instead, terms such as *person* or *interpersonal perception*, *social insight*, and *social proficiency* were used more frequently" (Murphy, 2006). Many tests under the personality approach followed, proposing items for empathy, shyness, sociability, sensitivity, expressivity and self-monitoring, many of them being self-report, as usual in personality tests. For instance, an example of an "emotional control" item was "I am able to conceal my true feelings from just about anyone", and a "social manipulation" item was "If I really have to, I can 'use' other people to get what I want" (Riggio, 1986). Despite these test formats and rebrandings, the scepticism remains about the existence of "adequate instruments for assessing social intelligence" distinctively from general intelligence (Kihlstrom and Cantor, 2000, p. 368).

Tests for children are different from those for adults in a number of ways, with behavioural observation (e.g., in school) and "behavior rating scales" (frequently answered by teachers or parents) being most recommended, although some other options, such as interviewing, projective tests and self-reports are also considered (see Merrell, 2001 for an overview). Some other children's *social development* tests are closer to those used for animals, as happens with non-social skills. For instance, several social tasks have been used for both children and animals, such as the false-belief task (theory of mind), the mirror test (self-recognition), the gaze following test (intention), the object-choice test (motivation), and several imitation tests (demonstration). In particular, the false-belief task is perhaps the most popular one, the "acid test of theory of mind" (Shettleworth, 2010b, p. 441), although not without some criticisms as well (see, e.g., Bloom and German, 2000). In this test, "a story character, Maxi, puts chocolate into a cupboard x. In his absence [the subject's] mother displaces the chocolate from x into cupboard y. Subjects have to indicate the box where Maxi will look for the chocolate when he returns" (Wimmer and Perner, 1983). Another popular test is the two-action test (Shettleworth, 2010b, pp. 441–442), where two different actions lead to a reward. The demonstrator shows one of them leading to the reward, and then we see whether the observers repeat that action much more frequently than the other action (also leading to reward).

These kinds of tasks are rarely organised in the form of a battery, because their purpose is to support or reject hypotheses about social cognition (e.g., the age when a trait is developed in humans). Many tests are designed to determine the extent a behaviour that looks social (intentional, mind-reading, etc.) has been acquired or not. Morgan's Canon (see Keynote 4.3) is frequently applied to the results. As a consequence, tests in animal cognition are rarely used directly as a battery for the systematic evaluation of individuals. The only exceptions are the Dognition battery, usually applied by neophytes to their own dogs (Stewart et al., 2015) and the Primate Cognition Test Battery, introduced by (Herrmann et al., 2007), mentioned in Chapter 4.

In artificial intelligence, things are not much different. Apart from multi-agent systems and game theory, social robotics is the most important area dealing with social aspects. Social robotics openly embraces the social hypothesis: "developing an intelligent robot means developing first a socially intelligent robot" (Dautenhahn, 2007). Some tasks (especially for the evaluation of the theory of mind) are borrowed from psychology. However, Williams (2012) warns about the use of the false-belief test or the appearance-reality test: "passing the test as is would not demonstrate social intelligence since a robot could easily be programmed to pass the test, the key point is that social robots would need to demonstrate the ability required in a broad range of general settings". This argument is very similar to the one we saw in Chapter 6 about the use of psychometric tests for arbitrary machines. Social robotics mostly uses specialised tests, focusing on human-robot interaction, with different roles: companions, assistants, etc. (Dautenhahn, 2007). Consequently, social robots are overtly meant to be anthropocentric and anthropomorphic. The tests combine ad hoc evaluation focusing on performance and reliability, with questionnaires (filled by humans) about usability, "likeability", safety, gaze following (Feil-Seifer et al., 2007; Burghart and Steinfeld, 2008), or even the personality of the social robot (Joosse et al., 2013).

13.2 MULTI-AGENT TEST BEDS

One of the difficulties of cognitive evaluation in social contexts is that situated tests require the inclusion of other agents. Except for a few of the tasks for children and animals described previously (the false-belief task, the two-end rope-pulling task, the imitation tasks), all the rest are actually not social. This use of non-situated tests is common in psychometrics, with the belief that more artificial or abstract tasks (but easier to test) can still be associated with the latent trait that is to be measured.

Socially situated tasks are, nonetheless, common in some areas of artificial intelligence. In multi-agent systems, platforms are defined to incorporate many agents that share an environment (Weyns and Holvoet, 2005) and may compete or co-operate. This is illustrated in Figure 13.1. Actually, multiplayer games (including video games) and game theory can also be considered multi-agent systems, with competitive or co-operative behaviours (or both). In the case of games, evaluation depends on the result of the match and in game theory it usually depends on a payoff or utility function.

The most common tasks in multi-agent systems are those that resemble animal social situations and human games: video games, board games, human sports or a mixture of them (Durfee and Montgomery, 1990; Bürckert et al., 1991; Dimou et al., 2007; Lass et al., 2009). For instance, the predator-prey game, Pac-Man and RoboCup are environments that feature several agents, with competition and co-operation possibly being required.

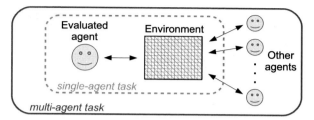

Figure 13.1. Schematic representation of the elements involved in a single-agent task and those involved in a multi-agent task.

It is very easy to create a social context by using a *virtual* multi-agent system or game and place some other agents inside. Is it possible to do the same thing for physical scenarios for robots, children, adult humans and animals in general? This was exactly what one of pioneers of the social hypothesis already proposed: "What, I think, is urgently needed", Humphrey (1976) wrote, "is a laboratory test of 'social skill'. The essential feature of such a test would be that it places the subject in a transactional situation where he can achieve a desired goal only by adapting his strategy to conditions which are continually changing as a consequence partly, but not wholly of his own behaviour. The 'social partner' in the test need not be animate (though my guess is that the subject would regard it in an 'animistic' way); possibly it could be a kind of 'social robot', a mechanical device which is programmed on-line from a computer to behave in a pseudo-social way".

Several decades later, this perspective is still not mainstream, but there are some notable exceptions. Ishii et al. (2006) use an experimental setting where a robotic rat (an 'animat') is used as the social partner to teach real rats and Swain et al. (2012) immerse a robotic fish into fish schools. In general, new opportunities for experimental biology and comparative cognition appear, such as "using robots as leaders", "manipulation of interaction sequences" (in cooperation), "robots to embody personality types" and "robots . . . as demonstrators in experiments on social learning" (Krause et al., 2011a). Rather than a more widespread use of "robots in the service of animal behavior" (Klein et al., 2012), our interest here is directed towards the *evaluation* in social contexts:

> **Keynote 13.2. Multi-agent situated tasks**: The inclusion in an environment of other artificial agents, whose behaviour can be perfectly controlled, constitutes a flexible setting for the evaluation of social skills.

We can then evaluate social behaviours by using virtual social scenarios (e.g., for the evaluation of adult humans or AI systems) and physical social scenarios with robotic social partners (e.g., for the evaluation of children, animals and physical robots). The difficult part for the evaluation of social skills, though, is to ensure that the multi-agent task really represents a complex social scenario. But, "what makes a society 'complex' in the first place?" (Humphrey, 1976). Everything depends on the social skills we are interested in. We will identify three levels: agent recognition, paying attention and interaction observability.

At the most basic level, it is well known that "detecting and distinguishing different kinds of biological motion is important for recognizing prey and predators as well as conspecifics. This is likely to be a very basic and universal brain mechanism, critical to survival" (Frith and Frith, 2010). Social benchmarks can be designed in such a way that detecting and recognising other agents is trivial, easy, difficult or impossible. For instance, many multi-agent platforms, including video games, are not designed for testing and, as such, their application programming interfaces (APIs) are designed to incorporate message-passing facilities and many other built-in functions, such as communicating or having the location of other agents. For instance, in some non-robotic versions of the RoboCup Soccer Server there is a predefined primitive 'see' that identifies the object, their distance and their direction (Weyns and Holvoet, 2005). Detection becomes a walk in the park. In contrast, other platforms, especially in the area of reinforcement learning and robotics, configure a world where agents have percepts (symbolic, visual, auditory or a combination of them) to process and recognise objects there. Even in robotic scenarios, the scene can just include the robotic partners and nothing else or otherwise be full of other distracting static or moving objects, especially in asynchronous, realistic environments (Delaherche et al., 2012).

There are already several virtual scenarios that can be considered situated, and in many cases multi-agent, for which the recognition of other objects and agents, even if simplified, is crucial. Games, and video games in particular, are designed to be engaging by featuring rich interactivity. Not surprisingly, "a game environment class" or "a random collection of videogames" have been suggested in the past as a way of evaluating intelligence (Hernández-Orallo and Dowe, 2010). In fact, this has motivated the creation of video game environment benchmarks, such as the general video game playing language and competition (Levine et al., 2013; Schaul, 2014) and the Arcade Learning Environment (Bellemare et al., 2013), already mentioned in Chapter 5. The evaluation takes place for the player character. Many of the games included in these benchmarks are 'single-player' but are actually multi-agent since there are still many non-player characters (hostile, non-hostile or both).

Keynote 13.3. Detecting and recognising reactive objects as agents: From the observer's viewpoint, there is no *qualitative* difference between a moving object that reacts to one's actions and an 'animated' object with more sophisticated underlying cognitive processes.

Basically, this view of agent is the same as the one used in our definition of the machine kingdom in Chapter 1, composed of interactive systems. Primitive humans and other animals, for instance, may not use different cognitive mechanisms to perceive a cloud, a tree, the Moon or an oyster. In the case of human children today, surrounded by a variety of electronic toys, there is a continuum between passive objects (e.g., a stone or a ball) and interactive objects (e.g., a radio-controlled car, a robotic pet, a real dog or a person).

Apart from the detection and interaction with other agents, there is a second aspect that influences the complexity of a social environment. Even if the agents can be recognised, the next social skill is paying attention:

Keynote 13.4. Paying attention to some agents – and not paying attention to all the rest – is key to causally associate observations and goals with them.

For instance, the results shown in Figure 9.1 were obtained in an environment for testing intelligence where, apart from the evaluated agent, there were two other agents moving around. The evaluated subject had to focus its attention on them, as they were responsible for good rewards and bad rewards – not very originally, the special agents were called 'good' and 'evil' (Insa-Cabrera et al., 2011a,b).

A third aspect that makes social environments more complex is the ability – and necessity – of determining and monitoring the percepts (inputs) and actions (outputs) of other agents, possibly including their motivations (rewards) as well. For instance, in primates, including humans, the so-called mirror-neuron systems (Rizzolatti and Craighero, 2004) have been found to have a role in the association of other agents' actions with the processes of learning and reinforcement of one's own actions, so paving the way – in some but not all species that have these neurons – for processes such as imitation. For instance, if the robotic partner presses a lever to get some food, the evaluated agent must be allowed to observe what the partner is seeing and doing, along with constructs for recognising what *food* is and what it means as a reward. This is of course easier the closer the actions, percepts and rewards of the other agents are to the evaluated agent, but should be flexible enough for any kind of agent. In many simple environments, such as many grid worlds or mazes, the evaluated agent can only observe its adjacent cells. It is then impossible to follow what other agents are doing.

> **Keynote 13.5. Agent interaction observability**: The degree of access to the actions and observations of other agents is crucial in a social context.

All this means that if we want to assess whether an agent is able to cope with other agents in an environment, there are many basic skills (social and non-social) that are necessary, and will be confounding factors for the others. Also, as some of them are very demanding cognitively, the social hypothesis is likely to emerge in the experimental results. General intelligence may even dominate the whole evaluation. In our attempt to disentangle and identify specific social skills, the following section will take for granted that the evaluated agents are capable of recognising and monitoring the other agents' observations and actions, so that we can focus on how rich the environment is in terms of competition and co-operation.

13.3 SOCIAL TASKS: COMPETITION AND CO-OPERATION

As mentioned, the mere inclusion of agents in an environment does not make it social. Apart from the fact that the interaction with some of them may be very occasional (because of its location or scale), those that are around may be completely orthogonal to the agents' goals. Biology, when referring to species, uses different criteria to distinguish several kinds of relevant interactions between species, such as predation, competition, mutualism or parasitism. One of the most relevant criteria is whether the goals of the interacting agents are positively or negatively related. According to this, we can simplify the view to two basic categories: *competition* and *co-operation*. Can we devise tasks where we can ensure that competition takes place? And co-operation? If this is the case, would these tasks measure some kind of competitive skills versus co-operative skills?

Certainly, game theory has already analysed competition and co-operation scenarios in different ways, depending on the game. Several extensions, such as Markov games, and stochastic games in general, have been introduced, where theoretical results (optimality, equilibria, etc.) are much more difficult to obtain than in the classical game theory setting. In this range of extensions, multi-agent systems can also be seen as a *generalisation* of game theory. As a result, artificial intelligence in general, and reinforcement learning in particular, have inherited many techniques and terminology from game theory. For instance, concepts such as zero-sum games or different types of equilibria can be important in the analysis of evaluation test beds.

We will now consider a task as a synchronous or asynchronous multi-agent environment, exactly like the definition of cognitive task already given in Keynote 8.4, with the inclusions of other agents. We will analyse competition and co-operation in this setting.

In such a multi-agent setting, Insa-Cabrera et al. (2012a) performed a series of straightforward experiments to see the effect that isolated, competitive and co-operative scenarios had on the performance of several reinforcement learning agents. The same environment briefly mentioned before (originally implemented by Insa-Cabrera et al., 2011b,a) was used in all cases. This environment consists of several connected cells where two objects, *Good* and *Evil*, leave positive and negative rewards (respectively) on the cells, following a movement pattern. The rewards on the cells, which decay with time, can be eaten by any agent that steps on the cell. These two objects *Good* and *Evil* are mostly non-reactive (they only react to avoid sharing a cell with each other).

Several agents were used in isolation: *Random*, which chose its actions (movements) using a uniform distribution, and three common reinforcement learning (RL) agents: Q-learning (Watkins and Dayan, 1992), SARSA (Rummery and Niranjan, 1994) and QV-learning (Wiering, 2005). Figure 13.2 shows the evolution of their performance for 10,000 iterations. We see how the RL agents slowly achieve a reasonably good result.

How do things change when all of them *compete* in the same scenario? This is illustrated in Figure 13.3 (top). Here we see that the three RL agents can barely reach a value close to 0.02, which is about 25 times lower than in the isolated case. Even if they compete for resources, one should expect one fourth of what was achieved in the isolated case (approximately 0.5/4). Why is this so? Figure 13.3 (bottom) shows the same experiment where the random agent has been removed, such that only the three RL agents compete. Here, the results

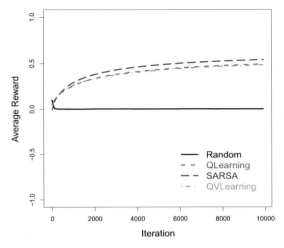

Figure 13.2. Four different agents evaluated in isolation (single-agent task). [From the work of Insa-Cabrera et al. (2012a), with permission of Springer.]

are much closer to the (expected) third of the isolated case (approximately 0.5/3), although this now requires 100,000 iterations. How can we explain this? Basically, the reason is that the random agent makes the variability grow dramatically.

We can also look at the results for a co-operative case. Here, the rewards obtained by all agents are shared, so they are prompted to co-operate. Again, the plots on top and bottom of Figure 13.4 are very different. The explanation is the same as in the competition case, but the results are, surprisingly, even worse than the competitive case for the plot on the left. The explanation is more convoluted here. The problem of this setting for co-operation is the way rewards are assigned. Since rewards are shared, RL agents find it more difficult to determine the goodness of their actions, since their observed rewards are affected by other agents' movements (including the random agent). The results on the right, without the random agent, show better results, but not for all agents equally.

The lesson learnt from these straightforward experiments is that the inclusion of a random agent creates such a distortion that the results are dramatically affected. This is of course explained by the lack of proper recognition and attention mechanisms from the RL agents. They are not able to recognise the other agents and, consequently, are not able to consider what the other RL agents are doing. More importantly, they are not able to filter the noise produced by the random agent. Also, the way percepts are represented in this scenario (each

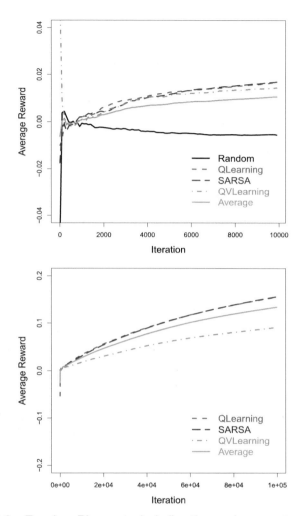

Figure 13.3. Top: four RL agents, including the random agent, compete for rewards in a multi-agent task for 10,000 iterations. Bottom: the same experiment without the random agent and 100,000 iterations. Note the different scales on the axes. [From the work of Insa-Cabrera et al. (2012a), with permission of Springer.]

agent can only see the four adjacent cells) precludes any possibility of observing what the other agents are doing and perceiving outside of this range. In any case, the RL agents used here clearly lack a kind of 'mirror neuron network' system to map the actions, percepts and rewards of the other agents to their state tables.

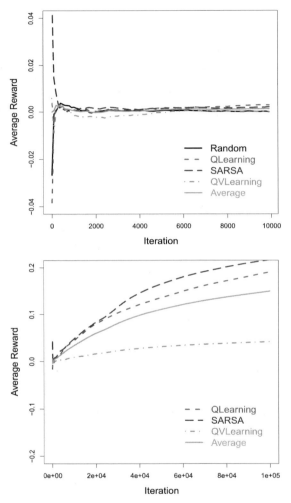

Figure 13.4. Top: four RL agents, including the random agent, co-operate for rewards in a multi-agent task for 10,000 iterations. Bottom: the same experiment without the random agent and 100,000 iterations. Note the different scale on the axes. [From the work of Insa-Cabrera et al. (2012a), with permission of Springer.]

Similarly, direct access or easy inference of the rewards of other agents would be a great advantage, but this is a strong assumption in many cases. In general, the inference of the rewards or the complete reward function of an agent is a very complex problem, known as "inverse reinforcement learning" (Ng et al., 2000; Abbeel and Ng, 2004). Similarly, direct access to what other agents are focusing on (their attention, as inferred by their gaze) may be very useful, but this is also a strong assumption in many cases.

The interference between agents observed in the previous experiments is well known in the field of multiagent (reinforcement) learning (Busoniu et al., 2008), usually referred to as the "moving-target problem" (Tuyls and Weiss, 2012):

> **Keynote 13.6. Moving-target problem**: In both competitive and co-operative settings, the right policies to learn and deploy depend on the policies that are learnt and deployed by the other agents. The feedback loop may lead to stable patterns or not.

Approaches in this area typically use an enlarged system state, which is the "product space of the set of states and action sets of the different agents". Still, many scalability problems appear. Here, it is necessary to distinguish, though, when agents are assumed to have complete information about the system state (including the other agents) or only about their own states, so that the other agents' states must be inferred. The latter are usually referred to as "decentralised" systems (Weiss and Dillenbourg, 1999). This is opposed to "team learning" in the area of "collaborative multiagent learning" (Panait and Luke, 2005), which is more related to the topics of Chapter 15, taking all agents collectively.

In any case, from the evaluation viewpoint, the high sensitivity to the addition of an agent or the particular configuration of rewards casts doubts on any procedure to easily determine when a multi-agent environment really creates a complex social situation. How can the influence of the other agents be regulated? For that purpose, we would need to identify and quantify some properties to determine whether a test benchmark (including the agents therein) is actually featuring social phenomena and, in that case, whether they are competitive or co-operative (Insa-Cabrera and Hernández-Orallo, 2014; Insa-Cabrera, 2016).

This is not an easy endeavour. A strict difference between competitive and co-operative situations is troublesome, since "competitive systems can show apparent co-operative behavior, and vice versa" (Hoen et al., 2005). Actually, some co-operative agents may end up competing against other members of the group for the sake of the whole group's welfare, and many purely competitive agents may end up forming a coalition to improve their own interests. Indeed, the analysis of coalitions in multi-agent and social scenarios is a very complex issue itself because agents decide who to join, aiming at "a higher reward by joining a different coalition" (Airiau, 2013). In practice, it is unlikely that alliances and coalitions appear spontaneously, unless there is a (genetic or programmed) predisposition or a mature development that learns the advantages of such coalitions. Also, many coalition schemes require communication.

A simple but effective approach to distinguish between competitive and co-operative situations can be built through different schemas of "credit assignment", using predefined teams (instead of alliances), generalising the cases in Figures 13.3 and 13.4. In the multi-agent evaluation setting presented in (Insa-Cabrera and Hernández-Orallo, 2014; Insa-Cabrera, 2016), there are one or more teams, and each agent (including the evaluated agent) must belong to one team (which cannot change during the evaluation). Rewards are shared (or split) inside the team (common utility) and a zero-sum property is set between teams. "Global reward" (Panait and Luke, 2005) is just the particular case of all agents in the same team, while purely "selfish agents" (Hoen et al., 2005) take place when several teams only have one agent each. This, in fact, is a very general setting that covers most games, video games, robotic scenarios, etc. Also, it is consistent with Tomasello's view of co-operation skills as a kind of 'shared intentionality' (Tomasello and Carpenter, 2007), where the rewards play this role.

Apart from the credit assignment and the components of each team, we need to specify that there can be different roles (positions) in the teams. For instance, in RoboCup Soccer, the robotic association football competition, one robot may play as goalkeeper. We use the term *agent configuration* or *cast* to denote both the team line-ups and the roles the agents play in. For instance, it is not the same to evaluate an agent as goalkeeper or striker, as it is also not the same to evaluate an agent against beginners than against professional players. This is actually a generalisation of the dependence of other agents in games that we discussed in Chapter 5 (Keynote 5.7). From this discussion, the notion of acceptance set that we defined in Eq. 8.1 can be parametrised with roles and casts. For instance, in RoboCup, if an agent is evaluated as middle striker, the cast must specify all the other players (and roles) in the same team (except itself) and the players (and roles) in the other team.

Now, we can consider a multi-agent situated task, as seen previously in this chapter (Keynote 13.2), and 'parametrise' it according to any distribution of agent configurations:

> **Keynote 13.7. Multi-agent test parametrised by agent casts**: A multi-agent test considers stochastic tasks and a distribution of agent casts (teammates and opponents, and their roles, including the evaluated agent).

The evaluation of an agent according to the performance in a range of tasks (domains) with a range of team-mates is also discussed by Barrett and Stone (2012) in a co-operative setting ("ad hoc autonomous agent teams", Stone et al., 2010). The distinction of the task from the population and configuration of agents is not strictly necessary given the formalisation in Part III of the book, but is handy for practical purposes. According to this distinction, we can analyse whether a measurement test bed follows a series of properties and whether this is because of the definition of the tasks or because of the agent configuration used.

This is exactly what is done in (Insa-Cabrera and Hernández-Orallo, 2014; Insa-Cabrera, 2016), where a series of formal properties are used to analyse the suitability of any multi-agent environment to evaluate social intelligence. Namely, these properties are categorised into "social", "instrumental" and "univocal". Among the social properties we find "interactivity" (action sensitivity to other agents), "non-neutralism" (effect of other agents on the evaluated agent's rewards), "competitive anticipation" (whether the evaluated agent can perform better if their opponents/competitors can be well anticipated) and "co-operative anticipation" (whether the evaluated agent can perform better if their team-mates/co-operators can be well anticipated). With these properties, we can assess the degree in which a particular evaluation test bed has a truly social behaviour. Of course, the proposal is not without caveats and limitations, but it can still classify the range between social tasks and non-social tasks in a quantitative way. In the same work, for instance, five popular multi-agent scenarios are examined, such as matching pennies, the prisoner's dilemma, predator-prey, Pac-Man and RoboCup Soccer.

Lastly, decoupling tasks and agent configurations has an additional conceptual advantage. We can consider several environments (for instance, the five aforementioned scenarios) with the same agent populations. From this perspective of agent populations, an important question is how many different environments (or what set of environments) are necessary in a test battery so that the particularities of the environments become irrelevant, making the agent population crucial for the aggregate measure. The following section deals with this issue.

13.4 POPULATING TASKS

In *Le Dîner de Cons*, a comedy by Francis Veber, a group of *comrades* holds an 'idiot's dinner' every week, where each comrade must bring along an idiot. During the dinner conversation, the comrades can make fun of the unsuspecting idiots, presumably to check their idiocy but principally for the comrades' amusement. The hilarity comes when one of the 'idiots' messes it all up, disclosing who the real idiots are. In non-fiction, sensible people generally likes to share a social dinner with bright, intelligent people, able to hold a sparkling conversation followed by a challenging game of bridge. How can we choose the *diners* for a situated social test?

Guided by non-anthropocentrism, one could take a single-agent environment description language and generate environments by a universal distribution, as proposed by Legg and Hutter (2007c) (see Eq. 11.2). Of course, for any UTM there is a program for every possible environment, or world, including the one we are in at the moment, and the one where Napoleon won Waterloo (*et nous parlons tous français*). However, the probability of any of these environments or any other that contains other minimally social agents (not even an idiot) is extremely meagre. Nonetheless, our discarding of a universal distribution does not mean that another more uniform distribution is the answer. In a social context, the no-free-lunch theorems assumption that all possible worlds are equally likely makes even less sense. In practical terms, the probability of finding an agent in this distribution of worlds would even be lower than for a universal distribution.

Instead of expecting the unlikely, we could just take a multi-agent test and *populate* it with agents on purpose. This ensures that we will have agents, but what agents? Determined by non-anthropocentrism and non-gaiacentrism, we rule out the selection of an exclusive cast of humans, or of animals, as a sort of Noah's Ark. Looking for a more principled way of making the selection, we could just choose an *agent description language* and generate agents according to, let us say, a universal distribution over the language. However, the overwhelming majority of agents would be too simple. The so-called Darwin-Wallace distribution proposes an alternative (Hernández-Orallo et al., 2011), as explained in Panel 13.2.

The Darwin-Wallace distribution is just a theoretical construct, and it is not proved that the process converges or is not corrupted (by random agents or other anomalies). In the end, the properties will depend on the choices of M, p_M, n, L_A, c and the way the aggregates are performed and their use in the survival probability. Also, the Darwin-Wallace distribution is basically a recursive, evolutionary-inspired, process, but it intentionally lacks reproduction, phenotype, inheritance, mutations or crossover. All these features could be considered and, for some of them, the process *refuted* as not being viable.

The key idea is that the task can change from one generation to the following one. This tries to favour general adaptive agents ahead of agents that

---

Panel 13.2
The Darwin-Wallace distribution

"Inspired by biological evolution, artificial life and evolutionary computation", the Darwin-Wallace distribution is defined as a recursive procedure to evolve a distribution of agents (Hernández-Orallo et al., 2011). We describe a simplified version of the procedure below.

We set a distribution p_M for a set of multi-agent tasks M. We also define a task replacement probability c. We choose a task using p_M. In iteration $i = 1$, a first, preferably large, generation of agents G_1 is produced with a universal distribution over an *agent description language* L_A. As expected, most agents will be very simple, if interactive at all.

The evaluation part comes next. Several (n) trials of the task are performed, where agents in each trial are uniformly chosen from G_i to fill the task roles, in such a way that all agents in G_i are picked the same number of times in expectation. The task can change after each trial according to the task replacement probability c. After the n trials, an aggregate measure of performance A_i^j is finally calculated from the responses of all the task trials in which agent j has participated in this iteration i.

And now selection continues. The average response for each agent j at generation i, denoted by R_i^j, is an aggregate of the performances A_i^j obtained by the agent from generations 1 to i. The next generation G_{i+1} is constructed in such a way that agents with high R_i^j have more probability of survival. The agents that remain are not reinitialised between trials or iterations. The agents that die are replaced again using a universal distribution. The evaluation and selection process is repeated.

The Darwin-Wallace distribution of degree i for multi-agent tasks is defined as the probability that an agent is alive in generation i.

---

specialise for a particular multi-agent task. This makes it very different from other related evolutionary concepts such as co-evolution in natural and artificial life. For instance, in a classical study of evolution in the Pursuit and Evasion game (Cliff and Miller, 1995), a game similar to predator-prey, the agents not only specialise for the game but also for its role (pursuers or evaders). Would this improvement hold if the roles were exchanged without prior notice? Relatedly, a series of similar experiments are reported by Mayfield (2013, pp. 294–296), referring to an evolutionary game where agents co-evolve by competition. Again, the task is not changed between generations. The goal of the experiment is to show that mean complexities (measured in terms of length of the agent program) increase generation after generation, but, more importantly, that the agents of generation 5000 outscore the agents of generation 500. This is referred to by the term "non-localised adaptation", a term borrowed from Dan Ashlock (Mayfield, 2013, p. 294). However, again, would this improvement hold if the task were replaced?

So, with the Darwin-Wallace distribution, it is not only that the physical aspects of evolution are ignored, but also that the environments are changed all the time. Moreover, it is not only a matter of whether the agents are competent with many tasks, but rather that they are *competent for a range of tasks interacting with a set of agents of similar ability*. Whether this proficiency, if really achieved, is understood as a general intelligence or a social intelligence is, of course, speculation. Nevertheless, the key point is that this not only moves us from a physical evolution to a non-physical evolution (as happens in many artificial life scenarios), but to a *purely cognitive evolution* (in full accordance with Figure 1.3 at the outset of the book). The distribution aims to designate a group of agents that are cognitively and socially richer without being specialised to any particular task.

Can we think of an approximation of the Darwin-Wallace distribution to derive populations in practice? First, as already mentioned, it is unclear which parameters could make stagnation less likely, considering that the environments – unlike evolutionary computation – can change completely. Second, to be efficiently approximated in practice, agents should not be as simple as those expected from a universal distribution. Instead, we could use AI systems for the first population. Actually, given a set of, let us say, the ten best AGI agents of the time, and adding some trivial agents for the start-up as well (e.g., random agents, Q-learning), the Darwin-Wallace distribution procedure could be used as a kind of competition to see which one is best in a variety of competitive and co-operative games. The best ones could be used as opponents and collaborators for multi-agent tests. This "testing selection" could be repeated from time to time, as the quality of AGI agents improves. Basically, this would be an iterative and generalised version of AI competitions, where the emphasis is put on general social systems instead of the particular tasks.

Similarly, the subfield of game AI is aiming at richer (or more believable, see Section 5.3) non-player characters and artificial players. For instance, Spronck et al. (2003) actually evolve artificial players to increase their performance. Finally, an interesting point is that not only is the performance of the artificial players desirable, such that the game is more (socially) challenging, but also their *diversity*, ensuring that different tactics are used (Spronck et al., 2006) with a variety of agent behaviours (Lacroix et al., 2013). In all of these cases, unlike the Darwin-Wallace distribution procedure, yet again, the agents are specialised for a game.

This raises a more conceptual issue about the very notion of what a socially complex context is, as originated from the social hypothesis, but seen in terms of both the cognitive abilities and the diversity of the group.

> **Keynote 13.8. Agent ability and diversity in a multi-agent environment** are crucial for socially rich tasks.

Mind diversity in a population can be seen as the cognitive subset of biodiversity in natural populations. Biodiversity, as we discussed in Section 4.1 is a motor of adaptations, not because the laws of the environments change, but because a variety of life forms creates a highly diverse range of interactions with other agents. How can we ensure a set of agents is highly heterogeneous?

Aiming at diversity means that the Darwin-Wallace distribution is not exactly what we were looking for. After many generations we may end up with a population where there are many agents that behave very similarly (if not identically). Is this a socially rich generation? Should the procedure be modified to only keep some kind of representative agents? Actually, we had a similar question in Chapter 9 when we claimed that *task* diversity was important. One approach to ensure more diversity then was to order tasks by difficulty and then uniformly by their solution (see Figure 9.7). In multi-agent tests we need a diversity of tasks, but also a diversity of agents. Could we do the same with agents using their ability instead of task difficulty?

All this just suggests that defining (and ultimately evaluating) the cognitive diversity of a population is probably an even more difficult problem than analysing the cognitive abilities of a single individual. First, we must look at agents in a non-monolithic way. The issue is not only about intelligence or some kind of general (social) skill, but about a fully fledged psychometric profile, including cognitive abilities and, most especially, personality traits. Furthermore, personality traits can be analysed as predispositions for competitive or co-operative behaviours. Video games are excellent situated scenarios for this (Vinciarelli and Mohammadi, 2014, sec. 4.5).

Overall, in this section we have seen the nuances and caveats of populating a multi-agent task such that it becomes socially rich. Apart from the number of agents and their roles in the task, as discussed in the previous section, in this section we have seen how convoluted it is to determine the set of cognitive profiles, including the range, level and diversity of the cognitive abilities and personality traits that are desirable for populating a multi-agent task. In the next section we look at the problem from a different, possibly complementary, perspective.

13.5 ASSESSING POLICY ACQUISITION IN SOCIAL CONTEXTS

Assume we have created a multi-agent test, considering a range of multi-agent tasks and agents with different psychometric profiles. Can we still apply the constructs seen in Part III of the book? In principle, from the perspective of the evaluated agent nothing changes from the way task difficulty can be derived: a policy search as seen in Section 8.7. Actually, all the techniques seen in Part III are independent of how the task is defined, its complexity and the complexity of its agents, if there are any. From the point of view of the evaluated agent, with or without other agents in the task, there are just observations, actions and some feedback, given through rewards or by a final response after each task trial. This is basically what was done for the multi-agent version of the elementary cellular automaton experiment used in previous chapters. There, the same agent policy language was used for populating the tasks and for calculating the difficulty of the task, but this does not have to be so.

The *problem* is that the difficulty of the policies in a social context can be very high, according to the interpretation of difficulty as search (finding and verifying the policy) represented by the bottom of Table 8.2 and formalised in Eq. 8.6 (or the more sophisticated Eq. 8.12). A very 'simple' policy such as "follow agent C" in a grid scenario involves detecting the agent, tracking its moves, moving oneself, etc. In robotics, researchers have been struggling for years to get policies capable of some sort of simple navigation. In the best cases, the description part of the $\mathbb{LS}$ of these policies may require hundreds of bits, not to say in a real scenario with vision and robotic arms. Of course, these numbers correspond to the bits that would be required should we consider a tabula rasa (see Panel 12.2), a generic programming language or a UTM.

Of course, in robotics, in testing and any other policy-acquisition situations we usually take many things for granted. We assume an underlying set of pre-programmed, genetically embedded or *previously acquired* constructs upon which the description of the policy (the L part in $\mathbb{LS}$) can be much shorter. And here we touch the marrow of the *social question* again. Provided two agents have the same constructs for detecting, perceiving and setting attention to some kinds of agents in the environment, is it just a matter of policy search and nothing more? If this were the case, social skills would not rely on special *agent-modelling procedures*, but just on some basic constructs about dealing with other agents in the world. Generally,

---

Keynote 13.9. No specifically social modelling ability hypothesis: Under the same available social constructs, the acquisition of successful policies for a given social context would depend on general intelligence rather than any particular social-modelling ability.

Note that this hypothesis does not say that social skills or other predispositions (such as personality traits) may not exist. In fact, under this hypothesis, it is likely that they do, as well as strengthened general abilities. The key point of the hypothesis is that the policy acquisition process would be governed by the same principles seen in the previous chapters.

For instance, new social situations (such as digital social networks or 'artificial social ecosystems') are examples of the fact that when the elementary social constructs are equal for all subjects, general policy acquisition effectiveness is what really counts. For instance, in social networks and some games (at least for those where realistic video is not crucial), interaction is set in quite elementary ways. Agent detection, synchronisation and gesture-related skills are not necessary. In these environments, once most of these confounding factors are removed, it is not surprising that some relatively simple learning bots are able to acquire some simple policies that are quite effective, even more successful than what humans do. In these simplified (or 'pure') artificial social environments for which humans do not have an arsenal of innate or acquired social skills, "the boundary between human-like and bot-like behavior is now fuzzier" (Ferrara et al., 2015). Bots, some of them by learning, "can even engage in more complex types of interaction", "achieve greater influence by gathering new followers and expanding their social circles" or "are able to 'clone' the behavior of legitimate people, by interacting with their friends and posting topically similar content with similar temporal patterns" (Ferrara et al., 2015). Of course, what these bots lack is cumulative learning, as they are not able to combine several policies and grow beyond simple patterns and rules. Also, they lack language.

The rejection of a particular social-modelling ability also gives freedom to the set of constructs that are used for modelling other agents. In other words, the hypothesis does not exclude the conceptual adequacy of using beliefs, desires, intentions (known as BDI) and perceptions, but does not constrict agents to use these categories to model other minds. In fact, it is difficult to assess whether the model agent A has of agent B uses the same representation that agent B does. Measuring a theory of mind is troublesome:

> **Keynote 13.10. The double black-box problem for measuring 'mind modelling' abilities**: We usually lack access to the mind being modelled and the mind that models, to compare them.

The question of mind modelling, from the point of view of measurement, must be addressed in terms of whether the agent is able to anticipate the other agents' actions. In other words, "we can say that a mind can understand another mind's function if", Yampolskiy (2015b) writes, "it can predict the other's output with high accuracy". We also understand that not only the predictions are correct but that they are used conveniently, which is what can be measured. In fact, this is what cognitive measurement does all the time.

According to the modelling continuum between interactive objects and minds (Keynote 13.3), we are back to a developmental perspective, where more sophisticated policies can be acquired on top of previously acquired representations. Humans, and most especially children, ascribe intention to physical objects, and this is a good training, starting with the acquisition of simple models of simple objects. This training can scaffold the creation of models of more complex individuals and groups, using more and more abstract constructs. In the case of humans, this is boosted by the use of language, as we will see in the following chapter. Under this developmental view, the levels of abstraction will eventually be found if the system has the capability, but not because there is a predefined scale of levels of abstraction (three, according to Dennett, 1989).

Apart from mind modelling, there are other skills, such as deceit and manipulation that are usually associated with social learning and mind modelling. In manipulation, however, several skills must be combined (tool use with mind modelling), because other agents are considered as tools and, only if we know how something or someone works, can it be manipulated. In fact, one of the versions of the social hypothesis is known as the 'Machiavellian intelligence hypothesis', claiming that "intelligence began in social manipulation, deceit and cunning co-operation" (Whiten and Byrne, 1997).

Similarly, not much more needs to be said about 'self-modelling' or 'metacognition', less mystical terms than others such as consciousness or self-awareness. Here, the modeller and the modelled agent are the same. Seemingly, one could say that the double black-box problem is reduced to a single black-box problem. However, the 'observation' of the own mind can be limited to just a part of it, the one that the mechanisms of attention select from what the agent is doing or thinking at a particular moment. In the end, if some actions and thoughts are observable by the agent, then there is nothing significantly different in mind self-modelling than in general mind modelling.

As a result, 'self-modelling ability' tasks should still depend on *predicting oneself accurately*. This can be developed into particular tasks where rewards should depend on the agent taking the option that better suits its abilities. For instance, given a task, the agent may be asked to make a bid about its expectation on the task. After the trial, the agent gets the bid if it has been able to score above the bid. Or, more directly, in humans, the agent can be asked to give a self-evaluation score after the task, as in (Stankov, 2000), obtaining not only a self-evaluation factor as a "metacognitive trait", but also a self-confidence factor, "somewhere on the borderline between personality and intelligence".

As we have seen, social contexts set challenges about the kind of policies that have to be acquired (and the way they can be evaluated). In contrast to this view of social contexts as 'complications', the final bit of the chapter will deal, very briefly, with the effect of social contexts as 'facilitators' for policy acquisition, mostly in an incremental setting (as discussed in Section 12.3, Keynote 12.5). If an agent is alone, the only way of learning from the environment is by exploration and mental search. This was represented at the bottom of Table 8.2. However, in a social context, and agent can learn by *demonstration*, where another agent, the demonstrator, is performing a task – with or without the intention of demonstrating. This corresponds to another row in Table 8.2.

Instead of the related terms of "social learning" (Shettleworth, 2010b, chap. 12), "learning from others", "observational learning" (Zentall, 2012) or "imitation" (Nehaniv and Dautenhahn, 2007), as used in robot, human and animal learning, we will focus on the term 'learning from demonstration'. Still, *what* is demonstrated can be interpreted in many ways. Here we refer to acquiring a *policy* for a task, usually referred to as 'emulation' (Whiten et al., 2009), and not simple mimicry of actions. For instance, Thorndike (1911) writes about a flock of sheep jumping like the leader even if the obstacle is removed. In this case, no policy is acquired; actions are just mimicked.

The question is that by observing what others are doing, policy acquisition can be much faster and powerful. Note that the observer is not given the policy (as we will discuss in the next chapter), but must infer it from its being executed by another agent.

> **Keynote 13.11. Policy acquisition by demonstration**: In a social context, a policy can be acquired much more easily by demonstration than by general policy search.

How can we evaluate whether policies are acquired much more efficiently and effectively with a demonstration? Animal cognition is a good area to look at first. For instance, after a task is chosen, a first animal, the demonstrator, is conditioned or taught to solve the task. Then the demonstrator is repeatedly set to solve the task in the presence of another animal, the observer. Then, the observer is released and the measurement records the time it takes to solve the task. A control group, without demonstration, is employed to compare the results. For instance, octopuses were shown to perform learning from demonstration using this procedure (Fiorito and Scotto, 1992). In a general context of multi-agent environments that allows some agents to see what other agents are doing (e.g., grid environments where agents move, or more realistic robotic environments), we can do the same.

Interestingly, we can calculate the difficulty of the task with and without the demonstrator. Namely, without the demonstrator this is the last row of Table 8.2, i.e., $\mathbb{F}$. With the demonstrator, this is calculated in the same way, i.e., Eq. 8.6, but now the demonstration, or series of demonstrations, is part of the observations in the trials. In some cases, such as μ_{lrote} in Table 8.1, an impossible task becomes very easy by observation. Still, some agents can interpret the demonstrator's actions as noise and even get worse results.

In general, things can become more elaborate if the demonstrator is also a teacher that interactively helps the observer, by modifying its demonstrations or even having access to some of the rewarding mechanisms. This enters the realms of teaching and its boosting effect on policy acquisition and development in general, as we saw in the previous chapter with Vygotzky's zone of proximal development (Keynote 12.4). Tasks with and without teaching can be considered, provided we have a clear description of how the teaching works. In any case, experiments abound in psychology about the effect of teaching, but a valid *systematic evaluation* of these situations is still a challenge. In the end, demonstration, teaching and language finally lead us to the notion of culture (seen as socially transmitted behaviour, Shettleworth, 2013, p. 100) and the transmission of policies in many different ways (Table 8.2). We will return to this issue in the following chapter.

We opened this chapter with the conviction that social contexts are very relevant in cognition. We have discussed the identification of tasks that can involve some social behaviour, which, if done with a situated approach, ultimately depends on the population of other agents that are embedded in the task. This necessarily requires the evaluation of these other agents, which can act freely, or can be inserted to play some particular roles as competitors, teammates, demonstrators or teachers. All this diversity of situations and degrees of social behaviour can be included in a multitude of tests and analysed jointly or separately. Nonetheless, the notion of difficulty seen in previous chapters is unprejudiced about all this variety and can give us a more objective estimate of the (social) requirements of the task. This is especially the case if we are able to distinguish the social constructs that are necessary for the task, to determine whether the evaluated agents do have them before evaluation, or are expected to acquire them. Again, despite the large number of hypotheses that have been left unresolved along the chapter, the view of cognition as a developmental process is reinforced and becomes even more relevant from a social point of view.

CHAPTER HIGHLIGHTS

- The social hypothesis about intelligence (Keynote 13.1) challenging whatever kind of social tests: situated, situational or self-report (Section 13.1).
- Performance in multi-agent situated tasks that include several other agents (Keynote 13.2) requiring basic skills such as agent recognition (Keynote 13.3), paying attention (Keynote 13.4) and interactive observability (Keynote 13.5).
- Competition and co-operation in a task depending on the configuration of the roles and abilities of teammates and opponents (Keynote 13.7) and how stable or changing they are to the mutual dynamics (Keynote 13.6).
- Populating tasks with a set of agents of high ability and diversity being crucial for socially rich tasks (Keynote 13.8) but, in practice, the generation of such a set of agents iteratively or evolutionary being very challenging (Panel 13.2).
- Mind modelling possibly governed by the same principles of general policy acquisition (Keynote 13.9) but its evaluation becoming harder as mind models are not usually inspectable (double black-box problem) (Keynote 13.10).
- Socially rich environments seen as facilitators of policy acquisition by demonstration and other kinds of teaching (Keynote 13.11).

14

Communication Abilities

For tongues were an invention that men sought to communicate
amongst themselves, and express one to another their concepts.
– Juan Huarte,
The Examination of Men's Wits (1575)

HUMAN LANGUAGE AND INTELLIGENCE are thought to have evolved together. Several degrees of intelligence and other cognitive abilities are found in animals and AI artefacts, but fully fledged intelligence has only been found when some language proficiency takes place – and vice versa. Despite the relevance of language, hitherto we have tried to consider assessment tools that do not require language, by a combination of the abstract character of many non-verbal psychometric tests and the interfaces found in animal cognition and several areas of artificial intelligence. In this chapter we finally turn the spotlight on communication abilities. In psychometrics, many tests incorporate tasks for verbal abilities, and verbal factors have been found in many test batteries. But, what happens when we apply them to AI systems? Will the tests be falsified for computers? If so, can we overhaul the evaluation of communication abilities in a more principled way, using situated tests, where the transmission of orders, concepts, facts and policies is required, or perhaps through the use of artificial languages, as has been done with primates? Given the challenge, we will mostly focus on understanding how language comprehension, acquisition and construction may affect evaluation.

14.1 THE ROLE OF COMMUNICATION

From the perspective of the social contexts seen in the previous chapter, communication is nothing but a sequence of actions involving two or more agents.

An agent uses 'communicative' actions to influence other agents' behaviour. If successful, the effect can develop into a conspecific being set alert, a predator being scared, a child being educated, a partner being decoyed or a citizen being convinced to change her vote. If the receiver is also able to respond, then communication becomes a social game, which can be co-operative or competitive – or simply exploratory. Under this view, most animals and computers are capable of some sort of communication. Indeed, in biology, animal *signals* are understood in this way, where communication goes much beyond the transmission of information towards the realm of manipulation (Dawkins and Krebs, 1978; Smith and Harper, 2003).

For communication, anything can be a channel. The movements of prey and predator are communication. A person trapped by the locked-in syndrome may break through via blinking. Any action may potentially be a communication, provided it can be perceived by another agent, according to its 'perceptual abilities' and representation (see Section 12.1). This indirect exchange of 'tacit messages' can be referred to as 'behavioural implicit communication' (Tummolini et al., 2005) or 'stigmergy' in the context of co-ordination, but it is still a genuine kind of communication. In nature, the channels used for intra- or interspecies communication can be extremely varied, from primates (Zuberbühler, 2000) to bacteria (Federle et al., 2003).

Also, when we say that communication is a sequence of actions with an intention, this is meant literally. As a result, Shannon's theory of communication is inappropriate in this context. Of course, it is not because the theory is inaccurate, but rather because it is a *theory of transmission of information* – a term that had already been used by Hartley in 1928, one of the biggest influences to Shannon's theory. Shannon's theory does not cover the intention or meaning of the message, as Shannon points out: "Frequently the messages have meaning; that is they refer to or are correlated according to some system with certain physical or conceptual entities. These semantic aspects of communication are irrelevant to the engineering problem" (Shannon, 1948). Consequently, from a cognitive point of view it is still possible to measure how efficiently two agents communicate, i.e., their bandwidth, the error rate, etc., but certainly this is not what we are usually thinking of when referring to the *ability to communicate*. Nonetheless, Shannon's theory of communication, jointly with algorithmic information theory, can explain several features (e.g., duration) of the transmission of information in animals, as we saw with ants in Figure 7.1 and Table 7.1.

When semantics is considered, the same message can mean different things depending on the context, and can of course trigger different effects, as intended by the sender. For instance, if we look again at the message in Panel 7.2

purportedly texted by a teenager, we see that, in terms of transmission, there is a compression rate. However, this only works because the sender expects the receiver to have some shared background knowledge (e.g., '2C' sounds exactly the same as 'to see') but, most especially, some cognitive – verbal – abilities to infer the meaning, such as that mapping 'GF' to 'girlfriend' will be clearly more meaningful than 'grandfather'. In other words, this message cannot be explained with a coding and decoding scheme, as there is no such unambiguous one. It can only be decoded by an *intelligent* receiver (an interpreter). What is more, it can only be encoded if the sender has a *mind model* of the potential receivers. The combination of the required elements for such a communication – intelligence, mind-modelling, intention and shared knowledge – is remarkable.

Having realised, once more, how challenging communication and language are, we can now look – more leniently and warily – at their measurement, with two straight questions. First, who are we going to test, the sender or the receiver? Whilst both may require some modelling of the other, the construction (coding) of a message – the action – is significantly different from the interpretation (decoding) of the message – the percept. We may dare say that the sender needs more initiative and has to be more creative than the receiver, which perhaps requires more analytic abilities.

Keynote 14.1. Peer asymmetry in communication abilities: Sender and receiver may not require the same abilities.

Anyone can think of good speakers who are bad listeners and vice versa.

The second question is: are we going to evaluate built-in communication protocols or a versatile communication between cognitive systems?

Keynote 14.2. Communication plasticity: The plasticity of a communication depends on adapting the model the sender has about the cognitive abilities and knowledge of the receiver.

For instance, an adult human will use a simpler register of the language to communicate with a child. On the contrary, a word to the wise will be enough. The issue about plasticity is whether the language and communication protocols are built-in (either by evolution or by human design) or can be modified according to the peers – and the knowledge the sender has about the receiver and its abilities – to make communication more effective. The price of this more effective communication is ambiguity. The receiver must make an effort to consider several 'situational representations' and select the most plausible one (Zwaan and Radvansky, 1998). Indeed, a message can be left unresolved or misunderstood when the estimation of the sender about the abilities and knowledge of the receiver is wrong, or the sender has not been clever enough to anticipate the possible ambiguity.

Keynote 14.3. Comprehension: In order to understand a message, the receiver must model the sender – including the sender's model of the language and the receiver. The comprehension of the message implies a search for the situation model that best explains the data (the message and the context).

According to this, language understanding would be an inference problem, closely related to the general abilities seen in the previous part of the book. A comprehension ability would then be close to general intelligence, a postulate that is implicitly or explicitly in many definitions of intelligence and also present in the *C*-test – the letter *C* comes from comprehension – seen at the end of Section 7.4. Finding the pattern in a sequence and understanding a message rely on the same mechanisms.

Nevertheless, it would be simplistic to reduce verbal abilities to simple message comprehension, from the point of view of the interpreter, as we can identify other language-related abilities, such as the capacity for incremental language *acquisition* and even the *creation* of new structures. Even if these categories are overlapping, the following sections will try to analyse these variants as separately as possible.

14.2 WHAT ARE VERBAL ABILITIES?

In human psychometrics, the term 'verbal abilities' is a common expression that refers to the abilities related to communication and language. However, as we saw in Chapter 3, each intelligence model or test battery may use different terms. For instance, Thurstone's primary mental abilities (see Table 3.1) distinguished between "verbal comprehension" and "word fluency", the Cattell-Horn-Carroll three-stratum model (Figure 3.2) included one second-level "reading and writing ability", the Stanford-Binet Intelligence Test featured vocabulary, comprehension, absurdities, verbal relations tests and memory for sentences, the WAIS test included a verbal comprehension index integrating several subsets, and the Scholastic Assessment Test (SAT)

Table 14.1. Semantic relations for verbal analogy problems. [Sample extracted from the work of Bejar et al. (1991, Table 5.8).]

	Semantic class	Example
1	Class inclusion	flower : tulip
2	Part-whole	car : engine
3	Similar	copy : plagiarize
4	Contrast	default : payment
5	Attribute	beggar : poor
6	Nonattribute	harmony : discordant
7	Case relations	tailor : suit
8	Cause-purpose	virus : illness
9	Space-time	judge : courthouse
10	Reference	recipe : cake

distinguished between reading and writing skills. We see that not much relevance is set on syntax (e.g., grammar) but rather on semantic issues.

Some of these tests include word or verbal analogies of the form "*A* is to *B* as *C* is to ?" ('Analogy1') or "*A* is to ? as *C* is to ?" ('Analogy2'). The pairs are chosen from different semantic categories. For instance, Table 14.1 shows the categories according to Bejar et al. (1991). Another very common task is verbal classification (Sternberg and Gardner, 1983), which can be presented as "Find whether *E* fits better with *A* and *B* or with *C* and *D*" ('ClGroup') or an odd-one-out configuration, as "Which is the odd one out? *A B C D E*" ('ClOdd'). Finally, many of these tests also include items asking for synonyms or antonyms, such as the classical Shipley Vocabulary Test (Shipley, 1940). In all these cases closed-ended answers are used with a small number of distractors.

It is interesting to see, once more, what happens when some of these items are attempted by AI techniques. For instance, Wang et al. (2015) collected 232 instances from several IQ test books of the types 'Analogy1', 'Analogy2', 'ClOdd', 'Synonym' and 'Antonym' seen in the previous paragraph. The proposed system integrated several machine learning techniques, such as deep learning. Unsurprisingly, there was also a metaclassifier, which did the *big switch* to determine which kind of verbal question the system was confronting. For the semantic part, they used the online Longman Dictionary, a public relation knowledge set, WordRep and text from Wikipedia for the word embeddings. With all this, they were able to build a system that was able to perform better than humans, as we can see in Table 14.2.

Table 14.2.   Humans and AI techniques compared on verbal tasks. [Data from the work of Wang et al. (2015).]

	Analogy1	Analogy2	ClOdd	Synonym	Antonym	Total
Humans	45.87	34.37	47.23	50.38	53.30	46.23
AI	48.00	34.48	52.83	60.78	51.02	50.86

Wang et al. (2015) state that "the results indicate that with appropriate uses of the deep learning technologies we might be a further step closer to the human intelligence". This statement is inconsistent with our arguments in Section 6.3, Panel 6.3 and Table 6.3, despite the authors referring to the interpretation caveats of these kinds of experiments (Sanghi and Dowe, 2003; Dowe and Hernández-Orallo, 2012). Again, the most plausible interpretation is rather that these tests are anthropocentric:

Keynote 14.4. Anthropocentrism of psychometric verbal tests: Experiments with AI systems falsify that many verbal tasks (designed for humans and with human language) could be used meaningfully for subjects other than humans.

This is not because the tasks are not *representational* measurement tools – for instance 'Synonym' actually measures the ability of finding a synonym. Neither is this because the system is actually worse than humans for synonyms. The reason is that scoring well on these tasks does not imply that the subject has a *general* verbal ability. Also, as the tests are designed for *human* languages, it might be the case that there are necessity problems (see Figure 2.2). The association between these tasks and the ability has only been shown for humans.

Can we find tasks in other tests of verbal abilities that are more comprehensive? For instance, SAT and other tests include 'sentence completion problems', where a gap has to be filled with a word among a series of options. The right choice is the only situation model that makes sense both syntactically and semantically. Another common task is 'reading comprehension', which can be presented in a variety of ways, but generally comprises a text and a series of questions about the text, as in the Nelson-Denny Reading Test (Brown et al., 1993). This task looks more complete than the previous ones. In fact, Jensen (1998, p. 270) says that "reading comprehension is probably the most highly *g*-loaded attainment in the course of elementary education". While this seems to be another representational task, and requiring much more cognitive sophistication, machine learning approaches are starting to face the challenge (Hermann et al., 2015). For instance, as we mentioned in Section 6.3, Ohlsson et al. (2013) applied the ConceptNet AI system to the verbal part of WPPSI-III, with questions such as "Why do we shake hands?". The results were comparable to the "verbal IQ of a four-year old", which of course "do not show that ConceptNet has the verbal abilities [of] a four-year-old" (Ohlsson et al., 2015), a more judicious interpretation.

Apart from test specialisation and the anthropocentrism of these tests, another possible explanation of why the success in a set of tasks that are representational may not indicate full verbal abilities is that machines usually have access to large amounts of external information. For instance, most AI approaches have access to general background knowledge (concepts such as 'car', 'animal', 'big', 'eating', etc.), using ontologies or common semantic knowledge bases such as WordNet, a lexical database containing more than 150,000 words with definitions, synonyms and subordinate relations (*is-a*), etc. (Miller, 1995; Princeton University, 2010). It is also common to have access to several natural language corpora. In other words, the AI systems become *idiots savants*, with some added machine learning technology to make more likely choices. At least, if all this is to be used, humans should perhaps be evaluated in an 'enhanced setting' too, with access to dictionaries, thesauri and encyclopaedias.

Two suggestions can be made here. One is to use tasks that require 'multimodal knowledge', i.e., verbal and other perceptual abilities (e.g., visual). For instance, one can be asked to choose an image (from a set of images) according to a description, such as the Peabody Picture Vocabulary Test (Dunn and Dunn, 2012). Indeed, since similar problems are addressed by the area of image retrieval with many potential applications, there are many sophisticated methods addressing this problem in one way or another. The inverse problem is what we could refer to as 'scene understanding' or "visual question answering" (Antol et al., 2015; Zitnick et al., 2016), a task featuring an image and a question about it, such as answering the question "Is this a vegetarian pizza?" after the picture of a pizza. Despite the applications, these multi-modal approaches are sometimes designed with the hope that they could become an "AI-complete task" (Antol et al., 2015), but involve more (confounding) factors than just verbal features.

A second suggestion is precisely the use of tasks such "that having full access to a large corpus of English text might not help much" (Levesque et al., 2012). For instance, comprehension tasks should not rely on sophisticated words but a deeper use of the words. The Winograd Schema Challenge, following a type of task originally proposed by Terry Winograd in 1972, is presented by Levesque et al. (2012) as "an alternative to the Turing Test", which is actually aimed at natural language understanding and commonsense knowledge (Morgenstern et al., 2016). The challenge includes 282 small reading comprehension questions such as: "The trophy would not fit in the brown suitcase because it was too big. What was too big? Answer 0: the trophy, Answer 1: the suitcase". Whilst this challenge can be very useful for AI development – a first competition was held in 2015 – it is unclear that this does not inherit some of the preceding problems; computers can be soon shown to display superhuman performance with a combination of several techniques, without really featuring fully fledged verbal abilities. In fact, one of the first attempts (Sharma et al., 2015) reached 69 per cent accuracy (49 of 71, just from the Causal Attributive and Direct Causal Events categories), compared to an average 92 per cent for humans (Bender, 2015).

In a similar direction, Weston et al. (2015) present a more comprehensive set of question-answering (QA) 'toy tasks', including basic 'factoid' questions with one, two or three supporting facts, subject-object questions, three-argument questions, yes/no questions, counting, lists/sets, simple negation, indefinite knowledge, basic and compound coreference, conjunction, time manipulation, basic deduction and induction, positional reasoning, reasoning about size, path finding and reasoning about agent's motivations. For instance, one item in the lists/sets category is: "Daniel picks up the football. Daniel drops the newspaper. Daniel picks up the milk. What is Daniel holding?" After seeing all these categories, we realise that this is rather a common-sense reasoning set of tasks expressed in an exclusively verbal way (e.g., counting and positional reasoning do not use numbers or images, respectively). These exercises are toy tasks for humans, but challenging for state-of-the-art AI. At the time of writing, only one of the methods in (Weston et al., 2015), using strong supervision with supporting facts, can achieve results close to 100 per cent (as we would expect from a human). The interesting part of this particular benchmark is not the results achieved. Actually, some approaches are able to get better results for reading comprehension tasks on specific domains (Berant et al., 2014) with more applicability. The most interesting feature of this test is that the instances are generated automatically, using a simulation that "behaves like a classic text adventure game". Another interesting feature is that the language used can be changed from English to any other language, included invented ones.

Despite all these efforts for generating verbal tests in AI, most of them just re-create what has already been done in psychometric tests and do not go much beyond in terms of completeness, generality or a better understanding of what is being measured. They are just built to be more challenging, focusing on what

AI is not able to solve. Weston et al. (2015) refers to other previous benchmarks and approaches to QA tasks in AI and state that "it is difficult to argue that such systems actually understand language". From the state of the art of natural language processing (Hirschberg and Manning, 2015), it is fair to say that the preceding statement can be extrapolated to general reading comprehension and other tasks. This also applies to IBM Watson (Ferrucci et al., 2010), despite its impressive performance as an information-retrieval QA system using natural language.

Of course, as a desperate move to get a sufficient test, we can think about putting all the existing tasks and benchmarks together, to prevent overspecialisation, making AI systems fail miserably (unless a big-switch approach can be developed, as done by Wang et al., 2015). This agglomeration approach to construct wider tests is something we already discussed in several parts of the book – the psychometric AI – in terms of specificity and generality (Figure 2.2):

Keynote 14.5. Necessity issues of the agglomeration of verbal tests: Putting many verbal tests together may achieve more sufficiency, but the resulting lump could well measure many things other than verbal abilities.

Similarly, the alternative of a freely conversational test, such as the Turing test, has also been jettisoned from the agenda in artificial intelligence.

Creating agglomerative lumps putting several things together or using free conversational tests goes in the opposite direction of a better understanding of the many nuances and particular processes involved with language and communication. Indeed, the tests and benchmarks mentioned earlier just integrated a small subset of behavioural features around the process of communication. For instance, many tests put more emphasis on the receiver's role, such as text comprehension, than on the sender's role. In contrast, many comprehensive tests of language competencies and development usually distinguish between *receptive* and *expressive* language tasks in accordance with Keynote 14.1. It is true that those tasks involving the completion of a sentence, analogies, synonyms, antonyms, etc., are useful for both sender (e.g., a writer or a speaker) and receiver (e.g., a reader or a listener), but it is less common to have psychometric tests or AI benchmarks where the subject can write or talk freely, in what is referred to as an utterance. In that case, several utterance characteristics can determine the language proficiency of a subject. For instance, measures of utterance complexity, applied when the subject is asked to relate or to describe a person or an experience, are very diverse, including the Mean Length of Utterance (MLU), Mean Number of Clauses per Utterance (MCU), Developmental Sentence Scoring (DSS), Type-Token Ratio (TTR), Developmental Level (D-Level) of grammatical complexity, Yngve grammatical depth, propositional Density (P-Density) and others (Kemper and Sumner, 2001). However, for both humans and computers, free expression has the risk of part or all the utterance being prepared before the test.

Also, it is worth noticing that most psychometric tests have to be conducted in the subject's first language. Otherwise, the results would be completely *biased* by the limitations of the proficiency of a second language in terms of vocabulary, grammar and comprehension. In fact, abstract non-verbal tests in IQ batteries were partially motivated by the suspicion that many tests using natural language would be unfair for children or adults for whom the language used was not their first language, or who had been raised splitting their time among two or more languages. Verbal tests may be invalid, for instance, with children whose parents speak a different language. Interestingly, all this suggests that the plethora of tests devised for the competence assessment of English as a Second Language (or any other language) can well be used for the evaluation of language abilities.

Finally, a related point to consider is that communication abilities do not have to be necessarily evaluated with natural *human* languages. They can be analysed with artificial languages in general domains, such as sign languages, or in specific domains, such as road traffic communication. In the latter case, the evaluation can even be done with a situated test easily. Situated tests, so advocated in the previous chapter, are uncommon for natural language evaluation, but not impossible, if we arrange a set of goals that have to be achieved by a group through communication, as we will see in the following chapter.

14.3 ASSESSING LANGUAGE DEVELOPMENT

All of the preceding tests assume, for simplicity, that language is static and standard. However, language is the result of a process, which is incessantly developing both for its actors and the language itself (Hoff, 2013; Owens, 2015). Thus, we can evaluate the language *process*, i.e., how able a system is to learn any language of certain characteristics, but also how able a system is to create or modify a language to adjust to the communication context and goals.

We will start with language acquisition. If we look at language developmental tests for children, we have a wide offer of tests, such as the Tests of Language Development (TOLD) (Hammill and Newcomer, 2008; Newcomer and Hammill, 2008), the Test of Language Competence (Wiig and Secord, 1989), the Clinical Evaluation of Language Fundamentals (Semel et al., 1996) or the more specific, but very common, Peabody Picture Vocabulary Test (Dunn and Dunn, 2012) seen before. The verbal tasks in general children development tests, such as the Bayley Scales, the Kaufman Assessment Battery for Children (K-ABC) and other tests for preschool children, or in intelligence tests for children such as the WPPSI and WISC (see Section 12.2), have also been used for the evaluation of language development. They are applied for education and clinical assessment of subjects with hearing disabilities, autism spectrum disorders and other language or general mental disabilities. For toddlers and other small children, tests are in the form of reports to be filled by a caregiver, such as the MacArthur-Bates Communicative Development Inventories (Fenson, 2007). Some tests include a wider range of communicative expressions, other than words, including gestures, apart from those specific for sign language development, for both expressive and receptive skills (e.g., Hermans et al., 2009).

Of course, again, all these tests are designed for the evaluation of *humans* acquiring *human* languages. Despite this anthropocentrism, it would be short-sighted not to look at these tests and learn from their formats, administration and experiences. This is especially useful if we look at the tests for small children and the experiments performed with non-human animals, where essential communication and language skills are evaluated.

For instance, there is an extensive literature about teaching some vocabulary to different species, including parrots, dogs, dolphins and, of course, primates (Shettleworth, 2010b). Here, we no longer deal with inter- or intra-species animal communication in the wild using some built-in communication protocols, but the acquisition of human language or other artificial languages. In this fabricated context, the assessment of the language development of these species (or particular specimens) has usually focused on the kinds of basic verbal skills that are developed, the size of the vocabulary, etc. In these terms, the communication abilities of some dogs and parrots have surprised many – especially if they understand orders, articulate speech or empathise with their caregivers. Again, however, it is with apes where language development has reached an extraordinary level, not only in terms of what apes are able to do, but also in the experimental resources involved.

Several ape specimens of different species have been brought up in a human context, either with a family or, more commonly, in an appropriate facility (Segerdahl, 2012; Rumbaugh, 2014). Teaching them some kind of language has always been one of the major research goals. Soon, it was shown that some apes were able to learn some basic vocabulary competence using a human sign language (Gardner and Gardner, 1969; Terrace, 1987), though the use of the

Figure 14.1. Several lexigrams in the Yerkish language used for ape communication. [Courtesy of the Ape Cognition and Conservation Initiative.] (See colour plate)

language was mostly instrumental, to achieve some basic goals such as food or care. This is genuine communication, but of a very rudimentary form. Perhaps the most famous case is Kanzi (Savage-Rumbaugh and Lewin, 1994), a bonobo, who, instead of (or apart from) sign language and spoken language, was taught Yerkish, an artificial iconic language specifically introduced for non-human primates (Glasersfeld, 1974). Yerkish uses *lexigrams*, symbolic representations of concepts that can be used in isolation or combined by the caregivers and the apes. Figure 14.1 shows some lexigrams. Kanzi the bonobo reached high competence with them, in terms of number of lexigrams understood, but he was also able to combine them within very short sentences (without grammar).

The analysis of the development of Kanzi and other apes can be considered anecdotal evidence and has to be interpreted sceptically, especially from the point of view of cognitive evaluation. With Morgan's law in mind (Keynote 4.3), we should not exclude the possibility that the ability of understanding and following orders such as "pour salt into the water" is superficial mimicking. However, there are several important aspects in these experiments. First, the subject makes use of language in a situated setting, where the ape develops the language for real communication, i.e., using the language to achieve some goals (as well as being used by the caregivers to influence the ape's behaviour). Second, the language is artificial, and the concepts and panels are created and adapted (by the caregivers) according to the subjects' context,

---

Panel 14.1
Language learnability: Chomsky against the empiricists

"As far as concerns infants of from ten to eleven months old, and deaf-mutes", Darwin (1871, chap. III) wrote, "it seems to me incredible, that they should be able to connect certain sounds with certain general ideas as quickly as they do, unless such ideas were already formed in their minds. The same remark may be extended to the more intelligent animals".

This translation of the nature versus nurture debate into language learnability became more heated in the second part of the twentieth century, as a reaction to Locke and Skinner's empiricism. Chomsky was motivated by an alleged "poverty of the stimulus" (Chomsky, 1965), the hypothesis that children learn many grammar structures from an apparently small source of data, sometimes only one positive example.

Whilst the phenomenon can be applied to both the semantic and syntactic parts of language, the latter monopolised the discussion in the 1960s, after Chomsky's notion of "universal grammar" (Chomsky, 1965). Namely, Chomsky's hypothesis stated that humans are born with some predefined structures, a generative grammar, shaping how language can be. The process of learning would be just a specialisation of those structures to the particular language being learnt. This neo-Platonistic view was, at the time, taken as a revolution.

---

their range of possible actions and percepts. The condescending claim that apes cannot learn a complex language, because the first attempts were made with human language, vanishes.

14.4 LANGUAGES: CREATED TO BE LEARNT

The use of elementary languages such as Yerkish sets these experiments much closer to what a principled language development evaluation should look like, far from the complexity and anthropocentrism of human language. However, is it possible to think of languages in an abstract way? Can we define a non-anthropocentric language, which is not biased in favour or against any particular species? Can we define a gradation of languages (or messages) that require more or less language abilities? To better see whether these questions make sense, we first need to dive into the battlefield of language *learnability*. Panel 14.1 opens fire with Chomsky's universals, as opposed to the empiricist view that any particular language grammar can be learnt from data without grammar schemas or universals.

Several early theoretical results seemed to back Chomsky. It was soon proved that some grammars and languages cannot be efficiently learnt (or even learnt at all) in the limit (Gold, 1967). However, these results relied on too idealistic a view of what identification is, and were soon superseded by more flexible models such as PAC learning (Valiant, 1984). Also, if the grammar has a relatively short description and the sentences have to be produced in a limited (preferably short) time – basically what we see in human languages – then Solomonoff's theory of prediction and Levin's universal search, as seen in Chapter 7, can be applied (Chater and Vitányi, 2007). To complete the setback of evidence against the "universal grammar" hypothesis, the original "poverty of the stimulus" has been put into question (Pullum and Scholz, 2002). To accommodate some of the criticisms, the Chomskian view has been relaxed to the view of "language universals", i.e., humans are not born with a grammar, but some constraints, principles, bias or structures about language. Nevertheless, this has also been strongly criticised (Evans and Levinson, 2009).

At this point, the two opposed hypotheses (Chomskian versus empiricist) are perhaps closer than originally, with perhaps the major distinction being that the Chomskian view understands that semantics is progressively linked to the grammar, whereas the neo-empiricist position (usually referred to as the cognitive-functional or usage-based theory of language acquisition) contends that language structure also emerges from language use (Tomasello, 2006). In fact, language universals have been further reduced to the 'Strong Minimalist Thesis' (Chomsky, 1998), which "holds that 'merge' [a composition operator] along with a general cognitive requirement for computationally minimal or efficient search suffices to account for much of human language syntax" (Bolhuis et al., 2014). The neo-empiricist position has also evolved and is now based on a modern view of (Bayesian) inductive inference (Chater et al., 2015), mostly based on Solomonoff's ideas with some start-up bias (Solomonoff, 1996; Baum, 2004; Wallace, 2005).

With a strong influence from this debate, there has been much interest in analysing the kinds of grammars (regular, context-free or contextual) several species are able to recognise (Gentner et al., 2006; Pullum and Rogers, 2006; Hauser et al., 2007; Evans and Levinson, 2009; Pullum and Scholz, 2009) and whether they feature recursion. In particular, the difficulty of finding recursion in animals has been posited as one possible explanation of the "human language uniqueness", as we discuss in Panel 14.2.

The language universals hypothesis, the recursion hypothesis and several other competing ones have evolved significantly in the past decades (see, e.g.,

---

Panel 14.2
Universality and human language uniqueness

Homo sapiens is the only extant species demonstrating a complex language. What makes it distinctive from other animals? One hypothesis is that only humans are able to handle *recursion*. This can be thought to be a particular language feature applicable to recursive structures and grammars (Hauser et al., 2002), or a more general view of how the mind works semantically (Corballis, 2011). Whilst syntactical recursion is absent in a few human languages, recursion "is always found in the conceptual structure, that is, the semantics or pragmatics – in the sense that it is always possible in any language to express complex propositions" (Evans and Levinson, 2009). Given this ubiquity in humans, much effort has been put in finding recursion in cognitive processes of non-human animals, without a clear-cut outcome (Van Heijningen et al., 2009).

Recursion is necessary and sufficient for the universality of a machine (more technically, composition and recursion makes a machine Turing-complete). As we discussed in Chapter 12, humans are (resource-bounded) universal. Universality of the human mind may seem to be against the existence of a universal grammar or language universals, for if this were true then languages that are not captured by this grammar or compliant with the constraints would not be learnable. However, it may be the case that human universality is acquired with language, and not present yet at very early ages. In any case, universality (either intrinsic or developed) could still be consistent with some bias favouring some structures over others, making some languages *easier* to learn than others.

Pinker, 2009; Ambridge and Lieven, 2011) and have suffered bitter criticisms, especially if a caricatured version of any of them is considered. Our interest is not to delve further into this debate but to see how any of these hypotheses – or some others in between – influences the way language abilities should be evaluated, in humans and beyond. For instance, are all languages equally easy to be acquired? Should developmental tests present items in a given order representing how the structures develop?

In any case, the understanding and clarification of all these hypotheses would not be sufficient to answer these questions. First, most of the discussion about language acquisition has been too "syntactocentric" (Evans and Levinson, 2009). Many second language learners are terrible with grammar and pronunciation but still able to keep much deeper conversations than a native 10-year-old. Actually, it is even contended that syntax and semantics in human language may have different origins. Syntax would be more similar to song-bird, which features complex patterns, and would be an example of convergent evolution, whereas semantics would be much closer to the way apes handle symbolic meaning (Bolhuis and Everaert, 2013). All this suggests that the fundamental question of what makes language difficult in a semantic way may have been eclipsed by syntactocentrism. Fortunately, psychometrics and other approaches to animal evaluation have not been much influenced by all this, and have paid more attention to the semantic issues, as we saw in the previous section.

Second, instead of thinking of what special thing do children's brains possess to learn language so easily, we can consider that it is language that is special, because "language is shaped by the brain, rather than the reverse" (Christiansen and Chater, 2008). This can be stated as follows:

Keynote 14.6. The principle of learning economy in natural languages: Natural languages evolve not only by a principle of effective and efficient communication but by a principle of learning and processing economy.

Under this principle, language structures that are more difficult to learn are simplified or changed, a process that can be seen in just one generation. Indeed, "if language has evolved to be learnable, then the problem of language acquisition may have been misanalyzed" (Christiansen and Chater, 2008). For instance, some very complex nesting degrees and cross references may have disappeared right after being introduced because they were exhausting working memory. Note that this principle would favour language structures with low finding effort $\mathbb{LS}$, i.e., simpler, because their learning would be easier, using Levin's universal search. The methodological interpretation of algorithmic information theory would turn epistemological here.

Third and last, neither the existence nor the absence of some common universals that all humans would share explain why there are *differences* in the speed and proficiency with which some children learn a language over others. Either there are also some *particulars* or this has to be attributed to a difference in abilities or attitudes towards language.

After these observations, we can now reconsider what makes a subject S (human or not) be able to acquire a language L:

1. Is it because S has some kind of built-in structures or bias that suit the language L?
2. Is it because S has some special linguistic abilities or predisposition towards all languages?
3. Is it because S has some special social abilities or predisposition towards social communication?
4. Is it because S has more powerful general cognitive abilities?

These are usually presented as competing hypotheses, but it may be well the case that humans have a degree of some or all of them at the same time. The four postulates also explain different approaches in artificial intelligence: (1) embed as much L as possible into the system, (2) endow the system with advanced language acquisition techniques to learn the language, (3) endow the system with social capabilities and (4) create a general learning agent.

The postulates would also suggest different approaches for evaluation. For instance, if subject S can learn language L_1 much more easily than language L_2, what does this tell us about the subject and the languages? Actually, if we use a set of languages of different characteristics, the speed and degree in which the subject is able to acquire them will tell us some of the actual linguistic capabilities of the agent. In some cases, we could even determine whether they are attributable to bias or to linguistic, social or general cognitive traits. As this will also depend on how the language is presented, we have the following scenario:

> **Keynote 14.7. Language acquisition profile**: The language acquisition abilities of a given subject would have to be evaluated with a range of languages and a range of social contexts.

This approach has been taken in artificial intelligence, at least theoretically, in the area of grammar learning, but has been mostly restricted to syntax, and in non-interactive scenarios. We would need to consider social situated tests (multi-agent environments as seen in the previous chapter) and parametrise them with the agents using one or more particular languages. Of course, this idealistic view is opposed by several questions. For instance, we know how to characterise grammars in terms of Chomsky's grammar hierarchy (Hopcroft et al., 2007) or, better, according to the description length of the grammar, but could we do the same with the semantic aspects of the language? Similarly, for a given language, can we determine the acquisition sequences and social contexts to be considered?

Panel 14.3
Creating and evolving the Robotish language

In a series of experiments, Luc Steels has analysed how a group of robots can associate a set of random sounds with specific actions, objects and events, without human intervention or prior specification (Steels et al., 2012; Beuls et al., 2013). Meaning is grounded in the interaction of the robots with their environment and the other robots.

Whilst the artificial languages were very rudimentary initially, more complex languages are being developed, in conjunction with the notion of Fluid Construction Grammar. This formalism represents languages whose grammar evolves as the result of a particular acquisition or cultural process, thereby handling "incomplete sentences, false starts, errors and noise that is common in normal discourse" (Steels, 2011) from the beginning.

Each newly invented Robotish language is interesting as it has an associated semantics, not mere hand-made grammatical choices. Also, Robotish is very different from any human language, from English to Yerkish.

It is of course too idealistic at this moment to think about the evaluation with several artificial languages, but the perspective of a situated approach for the analysis of language acquisition is becoming more common in artificial intelligence, especially in cognitive robotics (Lyon et al., 2012; Nivel et al., 2014). These new approaches focus on meaning rather than grammar, aiming at having the competence of a toddler. Also, some of them incorporate "a structural bias toward simpler grammars" (Chang, 2008), consistent with the principle of learning economy in natural languages seen in Keynote 14.6.

Finally, acquisition and usage are not the only things that can be done with a language. Language creation and modification are inherent to the way humans use language. For instance, the mangled texts presumably written by the 13-year-old girl shown in Panel 7.2 are an example of how language can be created and evolved. Panel 14.3 shows an example of robots creating and evolving an artificial language.

In Steels's experiment some kind of evaluation is performed, but it is an open question how the ability of creating and modifying language can be evaluated in general terms. Nevertheless, it is a relevant question for humans and robots.

In this section we have seen that the evaluation of language development is affected by several hypotheses about how language is ultimately possible. However, the greatest difficulty for a principled evaluation covering all elements in the machine kingdom (humans, non-human animals and other machines) originates from many confounding factors about the context in which communication takes place. The exposition in this section has been, in this regard, very preliminary.

14.5 HOW MUCH DOES LANGUAGE FACILITATE COGNITION?

Hitherto we have seen language as a complex phenomenon, being so challenging for animals and computers that we may even wonder how children can learn it so easily. In this last section of the chapter, we look at language from a different perspective, as a *facilitator* in the perspective of cognitive development and social contexts, a powerful tool that is responsible for much of what really makes humans distinctive in the animal kingdom.

In Chapter 12, we discussed how agents undergo a transformation from early sensorimotor representations (Section 12.1) to an elaborated development where the agents can become universal, able to represent any possible concept. For instance, many concepts are associated with a word, such as 'chair', 'jump' or 'hungry', but may have been acquired before the word was heard for the first time. Many other concepts lack a word, either because they also originate from sensorimotor experience, such as 'the sound that I heard in the park', or abstract concepts deriving from a combination of other concepts such as 'red circles', not strictly requiring language but just a mental representation.

But many other concepts originate from language, such as 'million', 'complex' or 'explain'. Had they not been transmitted by someone else, we would unlikely have them. The term "conceptual development", in a more particular sense than the general use in Section 12.4, is applied to the view of mental development when linguistic concepts are involved (Bowerman and Levinson, 2001; Gelman and Kalish, 2006). One of the key questions is whether there are some built-in scaffolding concepts or primitives upon which the rest can develop. Is *causation* an acquired concept? Is the concept of *time* learnt? And *numbers*? And *negation*? And the whole set of *logic* connectives? As we discussed in Section 12.4, these questions are not necessarily about language – many of these concepts are present in some animals – but they take a different perspective once words are linked with these concepts.

Feral children can be suggested as possible evidence to analyse some of the previous questions, but the account of most cases is anecdotal or unreliable (Candland, 1995). Far from this extreme, it is well known that there is a clear difference between those children that have been raised in a rich linguistic context and those that are not. Experiments of this kind with children are impossible for ethical reasons, but various kinds of AI systems can eventually be used to evaluate the set of constructs that are more beneficial and in which order they have to be used to boost or impair development, including the dynamics of cognitive abilities and personality traits. Of course, this depends on the cognitive architectures and abilities of these AI systems, but the analysis of the *zone of proximal development* applied to conceptual development would tell us how much an agent's psychometric profile can develop potentially with and without several languages, featuring different sets of concepts and presented in different orders. Still, language provides more possibilities of facilitation.

> **Keynote 14.8. Linguistic facilitator**: Language is not only able to transmit concepts and boost the conceptual development of an individual. Language can also be used for the transmission of facts, knowledge and procedures, which can be seen as a facilitation too.

The transmission of facts, one of the main reasons why we chat – or gossip – can be seen as an extension to our perception system. Levesque (2014) states that "much of what we come to know about the world and the people around us is not from personal experience, but is due to our use of *language*". Our capability of modelling a partially observable world is only possible with a *network of reporters*, able to scatter around, in the very same way ants explore a relatively vast territory and transmit their findings.

The transmission of knowledge, procedures, or policies, is perhaps even more relevant. The knowledge that hemlock is poisonous cannot – or should not – be transmitted by demonstration. Similarly, the procedure of how to heal an illness or prepare a meal can be transmitted in advance, without the patient or the ingredient being present. This is an advantage over the acquisition of policies by demonstration, seen in Section 13.5. But, moreover, if we look again at Table 8.2, we see that the direct transmission of a policy with language will just require the L part in $\mathbb{LS}$, i.e., the length of the message. All the hard search effort to discover the policy autonomously or the less intractable (but still hard) policy identification from a demonstration is spared. In terms of policy acquisition, one very intelligent metapolicy that we learn very soon is to ask for and copy the policies of others. Chmait et al. (2015a,b) compare the results of an autonomous search against different kinds of agents with direct communication (transmission using auctions), indirect communication (using implicit cues, referred to as stigmergy), imitation (by observing a demonstration) and autonomous acquisition (search). Direct communication is generally better than indirect communication and both are better than autonomous search. Imitation (which refers to the agents following the moves of a perfect agent, an oracle)

Panel 14.4
Occam, Epicurus and language

Given some evidence, Solomonoff prediction (Solomonoff, 1964a,b) is based on a posterior-weighted mixture (or ensemble) of all possible hypotheses h, weighted by $2^{-K(h)}$. This is the best procedure we know of, and a nice compromise between Epicurus (keep all hypotheses) and Occam (keep the simplest one), as we saw in Section 7.3. However, this mixture, if inferred by an agent, will be very difficult to transmit to another agent. From the point of view of language, the use of a single hypothesis instead of many makes the identification of meaning (i.e., comprehension) much easier between sender and receiver, apart from making communication more efficient.

Despite the lower – but still remarkably good – expected accuracy of the shortest hypothesis instead of the mixture (Poland and Hutter, 2005, 2006), this is a price to pay for mutual comprehension and effective transmission of models of the world (Dowe et al., 2011; Dowe, 2011). Also, a two-part compression MML approach (Wallace and Dowe, 1999; Wallace, 2005), which separates model from data, seems advantageous over a one-part compression, since with the former the concept or model we want to communicate can be isolated more easily.

---

turns out to be better than communication for tasks with short demonstrations, but worse than direct communication for the rest.

The transmission of concepts, facts, knowledge and policies indicates that inductive inference in social contexts where communication takes place should favour one-model hypotheses over multiple-model hypotheses, as discussed in Panel 14.4.

This single-model transmission is not only applicable to conceptual facts, knowledge and policies, but to internal representations as well, although with more difficulty. For example, I find it very easy to distinguish my twin cousins, but I do not have a clue about how I do it. I cannot give a *verbalisation*. Of course, there must be some neural process in my brain doing the trick. Perhaps, it is a kind of probabilistic Bayesian mixture, derived from some sort of deep learning algorithm. However, despite having such a good policy, I will never be able to transmit it. My particular policy for telling my cousins apart will never become a "cultural meme", as it will die with me.

The conclusion is that having a declarative concise way of expressing our representations, concepts, facts and policies becomes a priority when language comes into play. Culture, conceptual development, complex shared intentionality and many other human enhancements, are only possible with language, and may be governed by principles of economy of transmission and acquisition. The evaluation of verbal abilities must take all this into account.

This chapter has hence reinforced the view that measuring the general influence of language in cognition – and the particular language abilities of individuals – is an enormous challenge. The evaluation must consider the role of language as a way to transmit constructs, facts and procedures, but also the original view of language as a communication tool making it possible to alter the behaviour of other agents. In the next chapter, language will also have an important role for the co-ordination of collective systems.

CHAPTER HIGHLIGHTS

- Sender and receiver playing different roles and requiring different abilities (Keynote 14.1), leading to an asymmetric evaluation (expressive or receptive).
- Communication being adapted by the sender according to the model of the cognitive abilities and knowledge of the receiver (Keynote 14.2).
- Comprehension as inference, seen as finding the hypothesis (the situation model) that best explains the message and the context (Keynote 14.3).
- Verbal tasks being anthropocentric and insufficient in general (e.g., for AI systems) (Keynote 14.4), while the test agglomeration approach presenting necessity issues (Keynote 14.5).
- The debate between advocates for language universals and empiricists (Panel 14.1) or about the need of recursion for language (Panel 14.2) superseded by a principle of learning economy in language (Keynote 14.6).
- The analysis of verbal abilities for different languages, including both acquisition and creation (Keynote 14.7, Panel 14.3), required for the assessment of a profile of language capabilities.
- Language seen as a facilitator for cognitive development (Keynote 14.8) and a prod for having simple – and single – descriptions, instead of a mixture of multiple hypotheses (Panel 14.4).

15

Evaluating Collective and Hybrid Systems

In one or two generations, kids are practically born with their brains connected.

– Sara Seager,
in Is the Universe a Hologram? And Other Conversations with Leading Scientists (Plasencia, 2017)

WHEN SEVERAL SYSTEMS are governed, momentarily or permanently, by common goals, they can work as a team. From the outside, if the team has a unified interface, its evaluation should, in principle, be the same as that of an individual. However, if the members of the team can perform different actions and have different observations, the task setting changes slightly and so must change the evaluation. In both cases, what can we say when we compare the group of individual policies versus the joint policy? How does the performance of the group depend on the behavioural features of its members? We will see that the members' features and the way the team is arranged and communicates are key, but we will also see that diversity, mostly in terms of the psychometric profile of the group, might be equally important. The general open question, which extends to hybrids and large collaborative platforms, is what psychometric profiles must be selected for mustering a team that meets an overall desired psychometric profile.

15.1 CHARACTERISING COLLECTIVE TASKS

In Chapter 13 we analysed the way in which an agent can be analysed, and measured, in a social context. One natural setting for evaluation is a situated test, a *multi-agent system*, where several agents interact. In particular, in Section 13.3 we saw that those agents sharing rewards (a common utility or payoff) were considered to be in a *team*, having an incentive to co-operate. Of course, having a shared reward or goal does not imply that the agents will co-operate. The motivation may be insufficient (e.g., in a large group agents can become lazy, since their effort may be unnoticeable), the task may make it impossible (e.g., agents are in isolated rooms) or the cognitive abilities of the group may be inappropriate for co-operation (e.g., lack of communication). For instance, in Figure 13.4 we saw that a single random agent can be very disruptive to a set of agents working in the same team.

In the previous two chapters, dealing with social interaction and communication, the analysis was centred on the behaviour of a single agent in a social context interacting (communicating) with other agents, and not about the behaviour of a collective group of agents as a whole. This is the perspective taken in this chapter.

Several efforts have been made to characterise different kinds of groups by looking at the way they organise. For instance, a first distinction can be made between the individuals that are self-organising and those that have a predetermined or external organisation that does not belong to the group. However, this distinction is not always clear-cut. For instance, is a bee swarm self-organising? Whereas each bee is highly autonomous, the way bees are organised follows a series of pre-established protocols and behaviours. If one or more bees *decided* to innovate a new organisation and change the behaviour of the complete beehive, the effort would be futile. Similarly, in distributed artificial intelligence and robotics, teams are usually built with some a priori team strategies, which the robots are able to follow for a common goal. If a few robots decided to follow a different strategy without re-programming the others, the collective behaviour would be seriously impaired, if not rambled or condemned to havoc. In fact, flexible self-organisation seems so difficult that those teams that are able to self-organise "without pre-coordination" are known in artificial intelligence as "ad hoc autonomous agent teams" (Stone et al., 2010) – a very long name for something that happens 'naturally' in humans all the time. Humans are able to collaborate with previously unseen conspecifics with no previously established protocol. Again, what looks easy for humans is an enormous challenge for AI agents and most animals, as they lack what humans are best for: an exceptional set of cognitive abilities and a flexible language.

According to the abilities, communication, co-ordination, self-organisation and homogeneity of the group, it is common to use different names, such as swarms, crowds or societies, usually coupled with the word intelligence, leading to a variety of terms such as 'swarm intelligence', 'crowd intelligence' or 'collective intelligence' (see, e.g., Bonabeau et al., 1999; Salminen, 2012). This terminological disarray is comprehensible, since some concepts that may look simple initially become more convoluted after a deeper analysis. For instance, it seems easy to distinguish between homogeneous and heterogeneous groups, but some collective systems that start with a very homogeneous setting with exactly identical agents may develop into a very heterogeneous setting, with agents becoming specialised. An extreme case of heterogeneous system is a *hybrid*, which usually combines agents of a different nature, such as a human and a robot. In biology, when different species are co-operating, the term 'mutualistic symbiosis' is used instead. The co-operation can take place with or without co-ordination and, in the latter case, communication can be explicit, or much more implicit, usually referred to as 'stigmergy' (Grassé, 1959; Bonabeau et al., 1999; Brooks, 2001), as mentioned in Chapter 14. Also, the perception of hybrid or symbiotic systems varies from hierarchical (with master-slave being a particular case, like humans and dogs) to more horizontal.

Similarly, there has also been quite a discussion about the distinction between the terms *group* and *team*, the latter being more commonly associated with the existence of a *division of labour*. For instance, Anderson and Franks (2003) define a team as having division of labour and concurrency: "different individuals must do different things at the same time".

All this diversity of collective and hybrid systems has been studied in several fields from many different points of view. However, from the point of view of evaluation, we need to clarify whether we evaluate the members of a group, or we measure the behaviour of the group as a whole.

Keynote 15.1. Fully integrated interface for collective evaluation: If a collective or hybrid system has an integrated, unique interface for inputs (observations), outputs (actions) and results (including rewards), then a black-box behavioural evaluation can be performed as if proceeding with an individual.

For instance, if we set up a group of agents inside a room with a screen, a keyboard and a reward channel, and apply a test, then the measurement is indifferent to whether the agents talk or not, or whether there is one that does all the work. Indeed, the measurement ignores whether there is actually one individual or many inside the room. Moreover, for the results of the test, it does not really matter whether there is zero, one or many *self-aware* independent systems in the room or even if the group – as a whole – is self-aware of what it is doing as a group. This collective perspective is yet another indication of why concepts such as self-awareness and consciousness should not be considered behavioural features, and not the subject of universal psychometrics. Note that this is different from self-modelling, as discussed in Section 13.5, which can be meaningfully applied to individuals and groups of people, including families, companies, sport teams, countries, etc.

With an interpretation of collective evaluation using a fully integrated interface, it might seem that we are done with this chapter; we would just rely on tests for individuals. Indeed, many traditional tests for individuals have actually been applied to groups in areas such as memory, world knowledge tasks, induction, letters-to-numbers problems, social choice, etc. (Laughlin, 2011). However, two considerations prompt us to continue. First, even if the test is administered in the same way, the interpretation of the result may be invalid for a group when the test is assuming that there is a single human individual. For instance, any extrapolation of the results of a working memory test to other abilities can hardly hold if this is applied to a group, as we will discuss in the following section. Second, not every test has to proceed in this fully integrated way. For instance, in a multi-agent system such as those seen in Chapter 13, a situated test made agents share rewards, but not actions and observations:

Keynote 15.2. Situated (nonintegrated) interface for collective evaluation: A collective system can be evaluated in a situated scenario by sharing their rewards, goals or a 'world utility function', but without any integration of actions and observations.

For instance, two elephants can be evaluated with a rope that both need to pull at the same time to get a reward. In this case the actions and observations of both elephants are different. What makes the test useful for collective evaluation is the common goal.

Both types of test, but especially the non-integrated variant, allow us to analyse whether a task is actually benefited from, or requires, a group. For instance, imagine a task that consists in making 100 sums, all presented initially in a single room. Even if we use a fully integrated interface, it seems clear that the task can be split into subtasks. Adding more agents to the room may have a linear impact in the time taken to solve the task. In a situated (non-integrated) task, such as the rope task, we can conclude that two elephants are necessary. However, increasing the number to 50 elephants will not likely have a beneficial effect on the result.

Anderson and Franks (2003) distinguish an individual task as one "that a single individual can successfully complete without help from other individuals" and a team task as the one such "that necessarily requires multiple individuals to perform different subtasks concurrently". Despite being conceived for situated tasks, the definition does not identify some cases where the sheer accumulation of more elements makes a task possible – even if the agents work

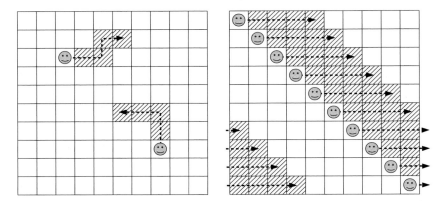

Figure 15.1. A very simple multi-agent task. Agents can move in four directions (up, right, down and left) with the goal of painting as many cells as possible after four moves. Left: if the threshold is set to 8 cells, the task requires at least two agents, and no co-ordination is needed to achieve this maximum of 8. Right: if we include many agents, the increase is limited by the initial positions of the agents and their policies. In the depicted case, with 10 agents, if the threshold is set to 40, the agents must co-ordinate to avoid painting the same cell twice.

independently – as they illustrate with an example: "imagine a box that requires the combined strength of at least 1.5 robots to move it. Two identical robots are moving the box with ease, but removal of one of them reduces the remaining effort sufficiently that the task fails" (Anderson and Franks, 2003). Whilst we do have the effect that the team is more than the sum of the parts – with one agent the response is zero – there is actually no true *teamwork*. Actually, any additive task can look like a teamwork task if we set a threshold for completion. A more conspicuous example is shown in Figure 15.1, where a very straightforward multi-agent task can look very different depending on the number of agents and the thresholds set on the task. Without threshold, the benefit of including more agents is initially additive without co-ordination, when the number of agents increases it can still be additive but needing co-ordination, whereas above a high number of agents (e.g., 25), the task saturates even assuming ideal co-ordination and initial locations. From these examples, we see that a characterisation based on the addition of agents is not sufficient to determine teamwork.

A different perspective seems to emerge if we look at the difficulty of the task. However, for groups, instead of Eq. 8.6 we need to consider a view of difficulty as the combination of the finding effort $\mathbb{LS}$ of all the agent policies that make up a particular solution. For instance, the optimal solution on the left of Figure 15.1 is given by the shortest joint description of any two policies

Table 15.1. Group task types (Steiner, 1966, Laughlin, 2011, pp. 3–4).

Type	Description	Example
Additive	Member products add up	Several cleaners vacuum a building
Compensatory	Members guess answers	A jury aggregates votes
Conjunctive	All members must succeed	Several countries build a pipeline
Disjunctive	Success if one succeeds	A bee finds water
Complementary	Several parts are combined	An orchestra plays a symphony

that do not step back on the cell they have already painted. On the contrary, the optimal solution on the right requires an agreement on what to do. In this case, nevertheless, the difficulty will be very low as well as the ten agents can execute the simple policy 'go right', but would be much higher if the task were stochastic by considering random initial locations for the agents. As we will see, an aggregate view of difficulty is valuable for analysing how easy it is to find an acceptable collective policy. However, it is not very useful either for analysing whether a task really requires teamwork.

In short, we do not have a *general* characterisation of what makes a task require teamwork. Nevertheless, we can still identify the elements that make some *particular* tasks more challenging for teamwork, such as the existence of conflicts or the need for co-operation. For instance, Steiner (1966) distinguishes five categories: *additive, compensatory, conjunctive, disjunctive* and *complementary*, as shown in Table 15.1.

McGrath's Task Circumplex (McGrath, 1984) presents several kinds of tasks, divided into four quadrants, as shown in Table 15.2.

Table 15.2. McGrath's circumplex model of group task types (McGrath, 1984).

Quadrant	Description
Q1: 'Generate'	Brainstorming, new ideas, creativity and plans
Q2: 'Choose'	Intellect and judgment used to provide preferred answers
Q3: 'Negotiate'	Members of the group need to resolve conflicts
Q4: 'Execute'	Identification of winning situations, psychomotor abilities

Panel 15.1
Vox populi or vox expertorunt

It was the beginning of the twentieth century and there was a fat stock and poultry exhibition in Plymouth, West of England. A competition was held there, where the 787 participants had to give an estimate of the weight of a fat ox. The closest guess would receive a prize.

An octogenarian Galton, in an article in *Nature* entitled "Vox populi" (1907), compared the individual guesses of the participants against the median, stating that "according to the democratic principle of 'one vote one value', the middlemost estimate expresses the vox populi, every other estimate being condemned as too low or too high by a majority of the voters". Despite the variance of the guesses, the median estimate was 1,207 lb., extremely close to the actual weight of the ox (1,198 lb).

It can be argued that this aggregate estimate worked because "the judgements were unbiased by passion and uninfluenced by oratory and the like". Had the participants estimated the weight in other conditions, the median might have been worse than the judgment of a specialist. Indeed, in one of the response letters to the article, F. H. Perri-Coste argues that most of the participants were experts, so the experiment did not show "a vox populi, but a vox expertorunt".

All these taxonomies are not clear-cut, but will be useful to better understand some of the group arrangements and evaluation settings we see in the following sections.

15.2 CROWDS AND TEAMS

At the intersection of his research interests about intelligence, statistics and democracy, Francis Galton would still surprise us with another pioneering work on collective decision making, as we explain in Panel 15.1.

From the point of view of a collective decision, the group is actually composed of the 787 participants *and* Galton, who calculated the median. This is a very particular master-slave group organisation, where all agents have the same observation but only one, Galton, makes the final action, the guess. This group organisation does not exactly fit any of the two interface types seen in the

---

Panel 15.2
Crowd IQ through majority voting

Unlike Galton, Bachrach et al. (2012a) used a more traditional data collection methodology to make a similar experiment. They evaluated 138 humans in the laboratory, to compare the performance of a group and its individuals on an IQ test (Raven's Standard Progressive Matrices, see Chapter 3). Responses were aggregated by majority voting (the chosen Raven's matrices had eight possible choices), resolving ties using the first answer in lexicographical order. Results are shown in Figure 15.2 (left).

In another similar experiment, Kosinski et al. (2012) used a different way of recruiting the individuals. They used Amazon's Mechanical Turk, a popular crowdsourcing platform. Each question of the test was set up as a "worker's task" in the platform, giving some rewards (small payments) to the workers. Each question was sent to a number of workers. Only workers with high reputation were used, with some "rejection threats" to discourage workers from issuing an answer they were not sure of. Workers' responses were aggregated by majority voting, resolving ties at random. Results are shown in Figure 15.2 (right).

---

previous section. Here, the rewards given to the participants did not depend on the goodness of the joint guess, but on individual guesses.

This schema is usually known as a statistical or voting decision system, one of the simplest co-ordination schemas. Clearly, this is a compensatory task according to Table 15.1. Despite its apparent simplicity, this modality of group arrangement has attracted enormous interest in many different areas since antiquity to modern days, including sociology, statistics, politics, machine learning, etc. Still, the 'wisdom of the crowd' is replicated in different scenarios. Panel 15.2 describes a similar experiment to Galton's, performed about 100 years later, using psychometric tests.

How can we explain the differences between the left and right plots of Figure 15.2? First, the results in the laboratory (left) used a comprehensive sample of the population and are hence much more reliable. Actually, the average IQ score was 99.57 with a standard deviation of 14.16, very close to the normed 100 and 15. Second, the results in the crowd platform (right) start with an average of 121, which reveals a population much above the average. As expected, by combining the responses of good individuals we obtain much better results.

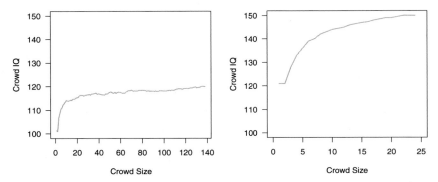

Figure 15.2. Crowd IQ as a function of crowd size, according to Bachrach et al. (2012a, Figure 6) (left, laboratory) and Kosinski et al. (2012, Figure 5) (right). The average individual IQ scores (approximately 100 on the left and 121 on the right) explain most of the difference between the two plots. [Data kindly provided by Michal Kosinski.]

Third, in the crowd platform, 'rejection threats' were used for part of the participants. For these users, it is more likely that they answer the question only when they are confident about it. This actually turns the aggregation into a kind of weighted majority, where guesses are weighted (or filtered) by self-confidence.

All this can explain the extraordinary results of the crowd platform experiment. The authors highlight that "strikingly, only one person in a thousand in the general population has an IQ higher than ... 12 workers ... (145 IQ)" (Kosinski et al., 2012). Despite the coincidence with other experiments (see, e.g., Lyle, 2008), we have to be very careful about the interpretation, as "the performance of a crowd in solving an IQ test may not be predictive about how the same crowd would perform in other tasks" (Kosinski et al., 2012).

Precisely, this experiment highlights the doubts that arise when a test for human individuals, and especially an IQ test, is applied to human groups using (weighted) majority voting. Even if the group is still composed of humans (no other animals or machines), all the explanatory interpretations and predictive extrapolations of the IQ score vanish, as we cannot relate this IQ to other variables of the group (high income, reaction time, age, etc.). Any previous knowledge about the correlations or a possible factorial structure, including the validity of the test as a measure of IQ or general intelligence, has to be put into question. This is especially the case for a non-representational task such as Raven's Progressive Matrices.

> **Keynote 15.3. A test for individuals may be inaccurate for a group**: The score produced by a nonrepresentational test designed and norm-referenced for individuals may be meaningless for a group, casting doubts about its validity and reliability.

This is one particular case of the general rule stating that what is designed for a kind of subjects in the machine kingdom may not work for other kinds. We will return to this issue in the following chapter.

Unfortunately, the preceding studies about crowd IQ do not give details sliced by difficulty. For easy items, we can fathom that a majority will answer correctly and dominate the vote, with a more *steady* outcome. However, for very difficult items, for which only a few individual agents guess them right, the result may be biased by any distractor (wrong answer) that may look more attractive or plausible for the mass. It is likely, for instance, that if we have a single agent with an IQ of 130 and a crowd also with an IQ of 130, the individual will probably do better for the difficult items. The equal scores may be just explained by a higher steadiness of the group for the easy ones, making the two scores equal in magnitude but not in interpretation.

The previous experiments provide some insights about (weighted) majority voting. Nonetheless, there is abundant literature about other ways – some very sophisticated – in which a joint decision can be made better than the original decisions. We could start with Condorcet's jury theorem (De Condorcet, 1785), which estimates the result of a group if we know the probability of a correct guess for each of the 'independent' individuals. Today, the independence condition is relaxed (or quantified) and good results have been shown to depend on the *quality* of the individual guesses and their *diversity* (Kuncheva, 2004; List and Puppe, 2009).

Nevertheless, the previous voting organisation, where decisions have to be aggregated into a single decision, is a very simple approach to a collective task. Other organisations may be allowed, especially with humans, so that they can communicate, deliberate, distribute subtasks, reach consensus, etc. Also, many other tasks, e.g., interactive tasks, cannot be framed in terms of question-and-answer decision-making items. In this regard, other experiments have also analysed the results when the group has the freedom to self-organise, possibly using deliberation, consensus, division of labour, or whatever they may choose. This is discussed in Panel 15.3.

Other experiments have portrayed slightly different pictures, depending on the communication media being used (face-to-fact or not) (Barlow and Dennis,

---

Panel 15.3
The *c* factor: evidence of a universal *g*?

Woolley et al. (2010) performed two studies with 120 and 579 people each, recruited and randomly assigned into teams of two to five. Unlike the voting approach, the groups were actual teams that were given one task and had to complete it together. In other words, there was a fully integrated interface. The tasks were chosen to cover all quadrants of McGrath's Task Circumplex (Table 15.2), brainstorming (Q1), matrix reasoning (Q2), moral reasoning (Q2), shopping trip planning (Q3), typing (Q4) and a video game (checkers), for the first study. For the second study, these and five additional tasks were used: word completions (Q1), spatial problems (Q2), incomplete words (Q2), estimation problems (Q2), reproducing art (Q4) and architectural design. All had a time limit and some of them were interactive. An IQ test was also administered individually.

The most relevant finding is that the correlations between the tasks were positive. Factor analysis yielded a first factor (*c*) explaining 43 and 44 per cent of the variance (for the first and second study, respectively). "That suggests that groups have a consistent collective intelligence, based on its performance across tasks, a direct parallel to the much-debated general intelligence factor, *g*". (Miller, 2010).

The correlations of this *c* factor with the average and maximum member intelligence were of 0.28 and 0.33, respectively, for the second experiment. Despite many of the other tasks being devised for groups, the matrix reasoning task (Raven's progressive matrices) was the one with highest correlation with the *c* factor, suggesting that *c* may be a general intelligence factor of the group. This is consistent with the universal character of the *g* factor postulated in Section 11.5.

2014), but results in even broader contexts are consistent (Engel et al., 2015). The confirmation of the existence of a *c* factor requires much more experimentation and analysis – the *g* factor has been studied for almost a century and is still very controversial. Also, the analysis of the data of this and other experiments can still be arranged in different ways. For instance, groups of one (i.e., an individual) could have also been included to compare the 'individual' *c* with *g*. Note that, "by analogy with individual intelligence", Woolley et al. (2010) "define a group's collective intelligence (*c*) as the general ability of the group to perform a wide variety of tasks". Indeed, the existing data could be very useful to bring confirming evidence or reject – for human groups – the universal law of augmenting returns that was postulated in Keynote 11.8. This could analyse whether a selection of the best groups leads to higher task correlations and a stronger c factor.

15.3 ANALYSIS OF COLLECTIVE PSYCHOMETRIC PROFILES

In the previous section we have seen that different arrangements of individuals lead to groups whose collective performance can be much better than their individuals'. On many tasks, a simple majority weighting can achieve a very significant improvement over the average individual performance. In this voting schema, the quality and diversity of the individuals has been usually identified as the two most relevant dimensions affecting this improvement. However, we have also seen a more fully fledged team configuration where the agents can interact freely, using communication, to solve a task. Are quality and diversity the main dimensions in these more general situations? In particular, about the *quality* part, the question is: if we aim at a high behavioural feature ϕ for the group, is a high value for ϕ for the individuals what we actually refer to as quality? Panel 15.4 brings some answers.

The results from Woolley et al. (2010) may have many other interpretations, with other individual features being identified as a 'quality' feature. For instance, Woodley and Bell (2011) argue that the c factor could be a manifestation of the General Factor of Personality (GFP, see Section 3.2), since this factor usually represents individuals that are more co-operative and less contentious.

Actually, two main families of behavioural features could be considered as the individual 'quality' features that influence the overall result of a team:

> **Keynote 15.4.** The **quality of the individuals for the sake of group performance** may depend, to a large extent, on both the individuals' cognitive abilities (such as g) and the personality traits (such as 'social sensitivity' or the GFP).

To further complicate things, as said earlier, some *diversity* is also beneficial. But, a diversity of what? Do we have a clear notion of diversity?

Independently of the feature or features considered, we need to know what a measure of diversity is. In very general terms, Balch (2000) proposes 'social entropy' as a measure of diversity in robot teams based on how many different types of agents there are and how many there are of each group, using

---

Panel 15.4
Women: IQ and social sensitivity

More findings emanated from the experiments performed by Woolley et al. (2010). Apart from average and maximum member intelligence (with correlations of 0.28 and 0.33 with c, respectively) the second study showed that average individual 'social sensitivity' and 'being female' correlated 0.26 and 0.23, respectively. In other words, 'social sensitivity' can be identified as a *quality* feature for individuals as much as intelligence. About 'being female', "much of this effect can be explained by the gender difference in social sensitivity: women tend to have more of it" (Miller, 2010).

Whilst this is an important finding, we should not neglect the relevance of the individuals' intelligence. In fact, the reason why these correlations are not much higher than social sensitivity may originate from the way the groups are established, in an occasional, temporary fashion. Thus, the motivations of the team members should be further investigated, as the reactions on a first meeting may be led by an interest in giving a good impression to the team-mates rather than acing the tasks. "In a more typical workplace setting, [Linda] Gottfredson says, individuals would be more familiar with their team-mates and know whom to listen to and encourage to speak. In that case, she says, the members' individual intelligence may be a more important factor than turn taking" (Miller, 2010).

Shannon's information entropy. However, this approach is based on qualitative features (such as gender in humans). Consequently, in the same work, Balch offers an alternative based on a more general dissimilarity function between agents. With this function, a taxonomy of agents can be derived by a clustering technique. A hierarchical social entropy measure can be defined as the integral of the social entropies along the dendrogram, giving an appropriate value of 0 when all agents are the same and much larger values when the agents are diverse. The crucial point is how the dissimilarity function is defined. Balch (2000) bases its function on some aspects of behaviour such as actions depending on the perceptual state.

We can generalise the characterisation by using the notion of psychometric profile we saw in Section 1.4 (Keynote 1.7). Given a profile of m features, applied to a group of n members, each individual i would have a profile $\phi^i = (\phi_1^i, \phi_2^i, \ldots, \phi_m^i)$. This constitutes an m-dimensional space where agents are located. For instance, Figure 15.3 shows four different groups of agents on a space of two behavioural features ϕ_1 and ϕ_2. Each solid circle represents

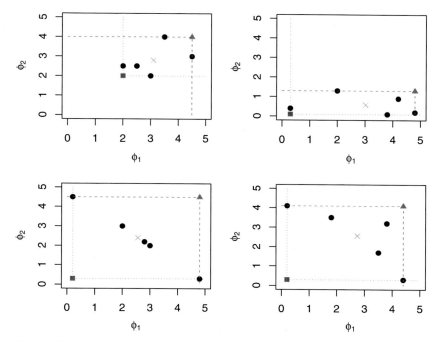

Figure 15.3. Group diversity in terms of psychometric profiles for four figurative groups of agents. For each plot, ϕ_1 would represent IQ score and ϕ_2 social sensitivity. There are five agents in each of the four groups, shown with circles; the mean point is shown with a cross; and the higher and lower envelopes are shown with a triangle and a square, respectively.

an individual agent, determined by its psychometric profile. The diversity of a set of agents in the space of behavioural features (Figure 2.1 (left)) can be derived using Balch's social entropy measure (e.g., calculating dissimilarity with a Euclidean distance) or can be defined in terms of the covariance matrix, which is a way to analyse a group of individuals that is custom in psychometrics.

The analysis of a group of agents in terms of their psychometric profiles gives a different perspective from other notions of diversity based on the particular behaviours for a given task. For instance, if the profile is only defined with one variable, e.g., IQ scores, then we have a one-dimensional psychometric space, and diversity can just be measured as the variance. In general, for more dimensions, any aggregated metric from the covariance matrix can be used instead, or an average distance, preferably a metric that considers the diversity across dimensions.

Keynote 15.5. The **psychometric diversity of a group or hybrid** is defined by some metric of dispersion for the psychometric profiles of the elements of the group or hybrid.

For instance, looking at Figure 15.3, what group is preferable? A group with high average IQ scores and high average social sensitivity (top left) or a group with slightly smaller averages but more diversity (bottom right)?

Note that we are not talking about a view of diversity defined as the variance of the *predictions* or *results* in a task (Marcolino et al., 2014). From the point of view of predictions and actions, there is a clear rationale why diversity is a good thing, as we saw with the *vox populi* example (Panel 15.1).

However, for behavioural features, things are different. Two agents may have similar cognitive profiles and still perform different actions. Also, some features are good in the sense that the more the better, they are *gradient features*. For instance, if we can have a group whose members all have the same IQ of 150, this is better than having a more diverse group with a mean on 100. So, it is important to determine which dimensions in the profile are gradient features, because diversity is probably detrimental for them. In fact, cognitive abilities are gradient, but many personality traits are not, as we already mentioned in Chapter 1.

Actually, if all the dimensions that compose a psychometric profile are gradient, then we may analyse the group in terms of the maximum of the features, instead of their dispersion. For instance, we could define an envelope as the maximum for each dimension of the individual psychometric profiles of the group, i.e., for each dimension j we would calculate $\phi_j^* = \max_{i=1..n}\{\phi_j^i\}$.

However, looking at Figure 15.3 or considering the general problem, neither the mean points nor the envelopes have to coincide with the profile that the resulting group will have, as this will depend on many other factors, such as the organisation of the team. However, the envelopes and their intersections are a very informative indication of the 'coverage' that the group can have for the set of dimensions. They are also easy to plot for more than two dimensions with a radar (cobweb) chart. This includes the minimum envelopes, since the minimum for some features may be very relevant, as a low feature (e.g., co-operativeness) value for a single individual can be very disruptive and spoil the whole group, turning it into a mob. If we consider dimensions that are not gradient, then the picture becomes more convoluted. For non-gradient features, the diversity can be analysed dimension by dimension (intra-dimensionally) instead of globally (inter-dimensionally).

In general, the terms in which personality diversity may be useful are still obscure, as Van Knippenberg and Schippers (2007) point out: "a growing number of studies link diversity in group member personality . . . to group performance. . . . So far, the picture emerging from these studies is quite inconsistent for the relationship between personality diversity and group process and performance". Also, we have to be careful when analysing the literature in social sciences, as the characteristics used for diversity have gone well beyond behavioural features: "diversity research has mainly focused on gender, age, race/ethnicity, tenure, educational background, and functional background" (Van Knippenberg et al., 2004). Only with a restricted focus on the educational and functional features, we can agree that "diverse groups are more likely to possess a broader range of task-relevant knowledge, skills, and abilities that are distinct and nonredundant and to have different opinions and perspectives on the task at hand" (Van Knippenberg et al., 2004).

Given these subtleties, statements such as "diversity trumps ability" (Hong and Page, 2004; Page, 2008; Krause et al., 2011b) have to be understood very carefully, because they are only true under some very particular conditions. To see the picture complete, we need to look at several issues:

- Not any kind of diversity is useful. What matters is behavioural diversity (Page, 2008).
- Diversity may be useful if some minimum quality is ensured (Krause et al., 2011b).
- Much of the confusion comes from opposing ability against diversity for one dimension. In general, diversity can be inter-dimensional and not intra-dimensional, as seen with the notion of coverage.
- Too many specialised dimensions for very particular skills or knowledge leads to *big switch* situations: given a problem, we *just* need to find the individual that is specialised for that problem.
- A more profound notion of diversity depends on the representation, what Page (2008) refers to different perspectives and interpretations.

The last issue in the list suggests a further discussion about the reference language or machine that an agent is using to find its policies. For instance, in a situation where there is no communication between the agents about their policies, if all of them tackle the same problem, they will perform some kind of search by the combination of constructs and policies that the agents may have. This search may resemble a Levin's universal search such as the one discussed in Chapter 8, where the reference machine over which the enumeration of policies is made depends on each particular set of previous constructs and concepts of the subject. The point is that if there is no communication and all agents use the same reference machine, even if we add some random components to the search, the agents will explore many of the wrong solutions that the other agents are exploring at the same time. Under these conditions, if a single agent requires s computational steps to find an acceptable solution for a problem (with the difficulty of the problem being roughly $\mathbb{LS} = \log s$), then a group of n agents working in parallel will not do much better if the order in which the policies are explored is basically the same. As a result, in this situation, a much better result would be achieved if the n agents had different background knowledge, such that their searches would overlap as little as possible. This is, in a way, what Hong and Page (2004) analyse, by exploring the diversity in the *heuristics* of the searches of the agents, basically about the order in which possible solutions are explored.

> **Keynote 15.6. Joint policy search without communication**: In a group, the diversity of the representation mechanism used to search for policies will be beneficial to prevent agents from checking the same (wrong) policies again and again.

However, if the group communicates, things change significantly. For instance, many swarms, such as ant colonies, perform parallel searches. These are spatial 'physical searches', rather than 'intellectual searches' (in Turing's terminology). For instance, ants leave traces so other ants do not try the same (failed) policies. Bees, since pheromones are more difficult to stick in the air, use the waggle dance instead to communicate a location and stop the collective search when a good source of food is found by one of them. But how can an intellectual search be distributed? To do this, the agents must agree in the representation of the search space and split it in a way that is understood by all of them. Making all this possible in a way that is not built-in (as with the bees) requires a sophisticated, and agreed upon, language.

> **Keynote 15.7. Joint policy search with communication**: In a group that communicates, the agents can split the search space and avoid the redundancy. The diversity of representation mechanisms and backgrounds may even be detrimental, as it may hamper the cohesion and mutual comprehension inside the group.

It is worth noticing that even in the optimal case, where the search is perfectly split up among the agents in the group, avoiding any redundancy, we cannot expect that a group of n agents can boost a general cognitive ability in an impressive way. As we saw in Chapter 8, using Levin's universal search, the analysis of all solutions of length l (in bits) takes approximately the same effort as all the solutions of length $< l$ (the number of programs is in the order of 2^l approximately, depending on the prefix code). As difficulty is defined logarithmically, this means that to increase one unit of proficiency of the group (i.e., being able to solve problems of difficulty one unit larger), we will need to double resources. In other words, if we have a group of n agents of the same capability and speed, the proficiency of the group (in terms of our notion of difficulty) will be at most $\log n$ units higher than that of one agent. For instance, 512 agents of proficiency 14 will be able to reach proficiency $\log(2^{14} \cdot 512) = 14 + \log 512 = 23$ in the best case.

Of course, this logarithmic increase can still be seen positively as a way of making more and more capable elements in the machine kingdom, under the view that "a mind must be composed of smaller things that cannot think at all" (Minsky, 1988, p. 322). This, in fact, has been a recurrent theme in biology, neuroscience and artificial intelligence (large swarms of thousands of insects, massively parallel brains with billions of neurons, distributed computer clusters with hundreds of processors, etc.).

Keynote 15.8. Linear proficiency increase requires an exponential increase of elements: Given the logarithmic character of difficulty seen in Eq. 8.6, a linear increase of a group proficiency, even in ideal conditions, requires an exponential increase in the number of components.

Even if it is just a matter of scale, this phenomenon becomes more intuitive when one analyses intellectual problems (e.g., in science and mathematics) that have been unsolved for many years, with thousands of people working on them. The solution, when finally found, is not thousands of times more *complex* than what each individual scientist was able to do alone.

This relation between proficiency and effort will be discussed again in Chapter 17, when analysing the possibility of an 'intelligence explosion'. Note that the preceding analysis refers to *one* general ability (not a whole psychometric profile) and does not preclude that a given proficiency level may be insufficient to solve a particular task, whereas a slightly higher level may solve it, showing abrupt (actually infinite) increments for that task.

15.4 MUSTERING A HYBRID

Looking again at a notion of psychometric profiles, we can ask the following question: given a pool of agents, which should be picked to get a desired collective or hybrid that is optimal for a task, or more generally, that has a desired psychometric profile? In other words, how can we create a good team? This is the final question we address in this section, looking at several kinds of groups, especially those that are hybrids of humans and computers.

One particularly interesting perspective is to consider the team as a *hybrid* that produces an enhancement over *all* the individuals.

Keynote 15.9. Pareto-optimal enhancement of a psychometric profile: An enhancement is Pareto-optimal with respect to a psychometric profile if at least one feature is enhanced but none is diminished.

This applies to psychometric profiles that include some features whose goodness is monotonically related to its magnitude, i.e., *gradient* features. A Pareto-optimal enhancement for individuals may be easier, as we will analyse in Chapter 17, but for groups, especially if they are hybrid of very diverse components with many features, it is too idealistic (the enhancement must be no worse than the higher envelope, as shown in Figure 15.3).

In the social sciences, the main interest is how to make a good temporary team for a series of tasks or a more permanent one that meets a given psychometric profile, using the smallest or cheapest set of agents. The scientific literature in the past decades (see, e.g., Laughlin, 2011; Malone and Bernstein, 2015) is full of analysis and methods about the ways human groups must be created, the kinds of communication that are needed, the features that make a good leader, the arrangements that are best, the best consensus-based models, the role of abilities and personalities, the importance of diversity (as discussed earlier), the required cohesion of the group, the importance of mind reading, self-confidence and self-modelling, the ways in which work (or labour) should be divided, etc. Many of these problems have reproduced themselves as well when groups are composed of computers or robots, or *hybrids* composed of humans and computers. We will just discuss some of these issues in what follows, especially those that are significantly different from human groups, or link to the evaluation issues seen in other chapters.

Hybrids range from individuals that are enhanced with tools, such as pencil and paper or a personal computer, to mixed groups of people and AI agents. There is a smoother continuum in this part of the machine kingdom, because the integration is nowadays seamless, through the use of hand-held or wearable devices and improved human-computer interfaces. Humans can be assisted by an endless number of cognitive tools, from interactive agendas to online encyclopaedias. Note that this goes well beyond digital communication and the access to knowledge through web retrieval, the so-called web-extended mind (Halpin et al., 2010). We are actually talking about the use of the cognitive capabilities and knowledge of other people, at a click or through spoken orders on a any device. Of course, some of these enhancements and extensions are not Pareto-optimal, as they have consequences on other abilities. One popular example is the 'the Google effect' and other related phenomena making us "shallow" (Sparrow et al., 2011; Carr, 2008, 2011), as we have discussed in other parts of the book. With the present-day communication and information sharing systems, we can view hybrids, but also groups, as extended minds (Clark and Chalmers, 1998; Menary, 2010; Theiner et al., 2010). Indeed, we are not usually aware that younger generations, Sara Seager remarks, "are able to get things done in a way that prior generations weren't able to" (Plasencia, 2017).

It is better to see all this as a reunderstanding of a shared extended mind (Bosse et al., 2006), something that humans, and many animals, have always practised. For instance, humans use the (cognitive) work of other conspecifics through dominance, manipulation, slavery or, more recently, jobs. Crowdsourcing (Howe, 2008), for instance, is nothing but a virtual way by which a *requester* can outsource a task using a collaborative work platform, so that some workers can complete the tasks. Conceptually, this is not different from any pay-per-service job, but it is true that the platforms are allowing for new ways of organising teams and allocating tasks to workers, leading to new behaviours and tools to *model* workers' behaviour (Rzeszotarski and Kittur, 2011).

Another recent concept that is associated with crowdsourcing is 'human computation' (Von Ahn, 2005), which is simply "computation that is carried out by humans" (Law and Von Ahn, 2011). Basically, if a computer system is not able to perform (a part of) a task (e.g., recognise a word from speech), it can delegate the recognition of that word to a human, to thereby complete the task. The existence of crowdsourcing platforms makes it easy for computers to act as requesters and automate the process, but human computation can work in many other ways (Von Ahn, 2005).

Finally, when we join the use of computers by people, the use of people by computers and the crowdsourcing platforms we have the so-called generalised task markets (Shahaf and Horvitz, 2010; Zhang et al., 2011). For instance, Shahaf and Horvitz present 'Lingua Mechanica', a translation system that combines human and machine translation in one crowdsourcing platform. The most interesting part is that they consider both humans and AI agents and characterise them with a psychometric profile: "each agent . . . is associated with a set of abilities. . . . An ability is a pair [of] ability identifier and . . . skill level of the agent for that ability" (Shahaf and Horvitz, 2010).

In general, nowadays, both humans and computers can be requesters and workers. In other settings, these two roles are not so clear-cut, and a group is created with a mixture of humans and computers, where a task allocation problem – the term division of labour is reserved for more permanent assignments – appears with this diversity of agents. In these hybrid groups, one may think that humans, purportedly more intelligent, will take command and decide who does what. This is commonly the case, but it can also be the other way round with "AIs guiding crowds" (Kittur et al., 2013). Indeed, a computer can choose from a variety of task allocation methods (some of them based on abilities, see, e.g., Halmes, 2013) and do the allocation much better than humans. For instance, Kamar et al. (2012) devise a system for classifying celestial bodies from images. Machine learning techniques are used to determine when the results of the machine vision system and the costs of hiring a human worker suggest that the hiring of the human worker – who is also chosen by the system – may ultimately be cost-effective. One interesting part of the process is the modelling of the human workers. On the whole, it is then becoming fundamental to evaluate the psychometric profiles of humans and computer systems for an appropriate task allocation. We will get back to this issue in Chapter 18 in a broader context, the future labour market.

Overall, these 'generalised task markets' are just one possible way in which humans and computers create hybrids and teams to solve problems, temporarily or in more long-term symbiosis. Taking this view at a planetary level leads to the concept of "global brain" (Bernstein et al., 2012), "the people of this planet together with the computers, knowledge bases, and communication links that connect them" (Heylighen, 2011), a notion that will reappear (in connection with the 'extant personality') in Chapter 17. The 'global brain' can be just a metaphor, but the higher degree of cognitive interconnection and interdependency of humans and computers will make the delimitation of isolated individuals or groups more cumbersome, and their evaluation will have to be reunderstood in an extended way, connected with the rest of the world.

This foray into the speculative nature of the global brain exhorts us to terminate this chapter, which also finishes the fourth part of the book. Seen in perspective, given the foundations laid in the third part, this part has elaborated on perceptual, dynamic, developmental, social, communicative and collective issues. Matters have become richer, but also more convoluted. Nevertheless, we now have a much more thorough view of the evaluation of a variety of behavioural features for an assortment of systems in the machine kingdom. We near the moment where the ultimate purpose and implications of universal psychometrics are fully analysed.

CHAPTER HIGHLIGHTS

- Different test interpretations between fully integrated tests (Keynote 15.1) and situated (non-integrated) tests (Keynote 15.2) for groups, with tests for individuals likely being inaccurate for a group (Keynote 15.3).
- Wisdom of the crowd through voting being effective for simple or complex tasks (Panels 15.1, 15.2) with more versatile group arrangements leading to a collective factor (c factor) (Panel 15.3).
- Behavioural or psychometric diversity depending on several cognitive abilities and personality traits (Keynote 15.4), with aggregate metrics explaining the group's features in many ways (Keynote 15.5).
- Joint policy search benefited by representational diversity (different backgrounds) in a group without communication (Keynote 15.6), but a common background possibly needed with communication (Keynote 15.7).
- Linear proficiency increase of a group requiring an exponential increase in the number of elements in the group (Keynote 15.8).
- Hybrids trying to enhance their psychometric profile through cognitive tools or other agents, with many different possibilities: humans extended with technology, computers enhanced with humans, crowdsourcing, etc. (Section 15.4).

Part V

The Kingdom of Ends

16

Universal Tests

One [way of calculating the longitude at sea] is by a Watch to keep time
exactly. But, by reason of the motion of the Ship, the Variation of Heat
and Cold, Wet and Dry, and the Difference of Gravity in different
Latitudes, such a watch hath not yet been made.

– Isaac Newton,
*Letter to Josiah Burchett (1721), remarks to the 1714 Commissioners
for the Discovery of the Longitude at Sea, quoted by* Sobel (2005, p. 60).

C AN WE DEVISE behavioural tests that are valid for every possible kind
of subject, biological or artificial? How can we determine an appropriate
interface and adjust to each subject's resolution? To make things more challenging, in some scenarios (e.g., collectives, hybrids, artificial life) we may
need to detect the subject first, prior to measuring it. Universal tests would be
a fantastic tool for universal psychometrics, not only to evaluate completely
anonymous subjects, but also to falsify wrong hypotheses about any *general*
relation between tasks and features. In practical evaluation, however, universal
tests would be very inefficient for subjects for which we have already some
information, such as humans and animals, and machines for which we have an
operational description.

16.1 ONE TEST FOR ALL?

In Chapter 6 we discussed the different principles for the measurement of
behavioural features for humans, non-human biological systems and AI systems. We argued that a unification of these principles was needed, and we have
developed new foundations in the previous chapters. However, the use of a common foundation does not mean that we must necessarily use the same measurement instruments for all the subjects in the machine kingdom. This is similar
to time, temperature, mass or any other measurable trait. It is usual to have

417

specialised instruments depending on the context or the range of objects for which the instrument is intended (Thurstone, 1928, p. 547). For instance, we do not use the same kind of thermometer to measure the temperature of a person as to measure the temperature of a volcano. In fact, the medical thermometer would just melt inside the lava – as an IQ test can be gamed by an AI system. However, the mechanisms that both thermometers use are ultimately understood and related (or calibrated) to the physical notion of temperature.

It seems that we should then be satisfied with several instruments for several groups of objects, provided all are based and calibrated on the same principles, so their results can be comparable and meaningful. This unity in principles with a diversity of tests according to the subjects could well be the object of study and the core of psychometrics for the years to come. However, as we discussed in Chapter 1 this becomes insufficient when we face a new subject, in a physical or virtual environment, of an unknown group. What kind of clinical thermometer would we use for an alien? What kind of behavioural test should we use for an arbitrary machine, the one shown in Panel 1.1? Only a universal test can do:

> **Keynote 16.1.** A **universal test** for a behavioural feature is able to measure the feature for any subject in the machine kingdom.

Note that the term *universal* here refers to the machine kingdom, as defined in Chapter 1, and understood as covering any interactive system, natural or artificial, under the assumption of the physical Church-Turing thesis (Panel 1.2). After all, it has a very plain interpretation, as a test for any possible subject, in the very same way that we use the term "universal adapter" in electronics. So, the use of "universal" here is similar to its use in "universal psychometrics", but different from some other uses of the term that have appeared in the book, such as Turing's "universal Turing machine", Solomonoff's "universal distribution", Chomsky's "universal grammar" or Legg and Hutter's "universal intelligence".

Universal tests are just unprejudiced about the subject to be evaluated, consistently grading all agents on the same scale. Before we bask in these grand expectations, we have to recall one of the principles of measurement and calibration seen in Chapter 2 and revisited later in terms of validity range (Keynote 6.3):

> **Keynote 16.2. Instrument range versus efficiency and accuracy**: A measurement instrument becomes less efficient and less accurate the greater the measurement range. In terms of behavioural evaluation, this is understood more specifically: measurement is more difficult and less efficient the less we know about the subject.

Table 16.1.   Main characteristics of universal tests.

Characteristic	Universal test
Validity	Based on representational measurement
Reliability	Depends on knowledge about the subject
Item parameters (e.g., difficulty)	Theoretically derived
Administration	Adaptive (interfaces and items)
Scoring and scaling	Based on the item parameters
Motivation	Rewards

For instance, human psychometrics can *customise* its tests because we have key information about humans, focusing on *what they have in common*. Once this is discounted, psychometrics can address their variability. If the target is the machine kingdom, the increased variability is harder to handle, since there is nothing in common.

In brief, the fundamental problem of a universal test is about the two main sources of lack of validity that we saw in Section 2.3 (Figure 2.2): generality and specificity. However, this should not be interpreted as universal tests being impossible. First, for some behavioural features, e.g., a reaction time, it seems that a universal test is not so difficult to imagine. Second, for other more abstract features, e.g., spatial abilities, personality traits, and ultimately, intelligence, we can look at the question in terms of measurement efficiency, i.e., as a trade-off between accuracy (mostly on the reliability part) and efficiency.

To make universal tests possible and manage this trade-off more beneficially, three concepts are key: the first one is the use of *different interfaces* depending on the subject (this assumes some knowledge about the interaction milieu, rewards, etc., of the subject), the second one is the use of *adaptive* tests, which can adapt the items as long as more knowledge about the agent is obtained by the test, and the third one is that universal tests cannot rely on the empirical approaches to difficulty and discrimination, to normalise scales, or even to analyse the numerical results for a group of subjects. In other words, universal tests must be population-independent or referred to a population that is defined over the whole machine kingdom. Table 16.1 shows a schematic set of characteristics of a universal test.

In brief, the question we address in this chapter is not whether universal tests are possible for all behavioural features but rather how universal they can be in relation to the knowledge about the subject and the time required for a reliable measurement. In the particular case of intelligence, the concept of universal test usually begets some radical interpretations, including negationism, as we saw in Section 6.4. In general, we will shun qualitative questions and assertions such as "there actually is no such thing as a universal intelligence test" (Smith, 2006), an argument that is sustained by a possible use of dissimulators. We addressed this argument in Section 11.5, when we discussed the universal character of the *g* factor. In the case of intelligence, in particular, we want to answer the question of "how universal an intelligence test can be" (Dowe and Hernández-Orallo, 2014), to ultimately see whether we can define tests that can be applied in a feasible way to the widest range of subjects possible.

In the following two sections we will focus on interfaces and adaptation, but in the rest of the chapter we will explore the understanding of universal tests in terms of resolutions.

16.2 CHOOSING THE RIGHT INTERFACE

In Chapter 4 (Section 4.3) we discussed some important issues about animal testing: how conditioning (in its broadest sense) could be used to make animals perform a task, and how a bad choice of the interface could lead to the underestimation or overestimation of abilities and personality traits. We also mentioned the plasticity of animals, which can adapt their interaction if the senses are impaired at an early stage of development, in the very same way that deaf, blind or even deaf-blind people usually process more information through the remaining sensory systems.

In the natural world, life has found many different ways of perceiving the world through many different sensors reacting to chemical reactions, light, electricity, sound, contact, magnetic fields, etc. Sensory ecology (Dusenbery, 1992) is the discipline that studies the sensory mechanisms for capturing information about the environment. Similarly to sensors, living beings have many ways of influencing the environment, but, in animal testing, movement is the most common actuator.

In the artificial world, things are not very different. It is true that in the early days of artificial intelligence, interaction was dominated by a symbolic exchange of information, but today we have a fully fledged range of sensors and actuators for robots in the physical world or agents in virtual worlds, with a recent emphasis on rich multimodal (i.e., multisensory) perception.

Given a task, such as the numerousness task seen in Panel 8.1, and two different agents, we *only* need to find the right interface. For this, if we have a computational definition of the task inputs and outputs following the definition of cognitive task seen in Chapter 8 (Keynote 8.4), we need to define a mapping from these inputs and outputs to the actuators and sensors of the agent. Figure 16.1 shows this process.

While the configuration of the interface seems relatively easy for adult humans and some machines, it is not so for small children and animals, as we

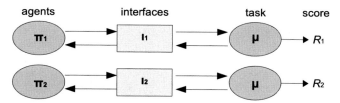

Figure 16.1. Two different agents perform the same task using two different interfaces.

saw in Chapter 4. In fact, many of the discoveries in animal cognition in the past decades originate because a better interface design allows an animal to be motivated or enabled to solve a task that so far had not been framed in the optimal way. In general, interfaces depend strongly on the testing apparatus, and a range of options exist, as shown in Panel 16.1.

Some extreme cases are illustrative. For instance, the evaluation of plants, which we briefly mentioned in Chapter 4, uses very particular interfaces, where light, soil components and other particular stimuli are used to test classical conditioning and other adaptive behaviours (Trewavas, 2005; Haney, 1969; Applewhite, 1975; Sanberg, 1976). The evaluation of humans with disabilities is also a good source of experience about how to devise appropriate interfaces. For instance, deaf-blind people can be evaluated using tactile interfaces (Arnold and Heiron, 2002) or other inventive approaches (Mar, 1996; Vernon et al., 1979; Rönnberg and Borg, 2001).

For any kind of agent, the testing apparatus and the administration must be designed with full awareness about any other factors that may affect the measuring. For instance, in the experiments performed in (Herrmann et al., 2007) for human children and apes, the apparatus was relatively similar for all. The most important difference lies in the choice of rewards (which depends on each individual's likings). The atmosphere is also crucial: human children are evaluated on their mother's laps, and non-human apes are evaluated in a context that ensured they are calm and motivated.

A testing apparatus must be validated before it is used for a particular test. The idea, as we briefly discussed in Chapter 4, is to make it work with very simple exercises first. Once validated, we can finally use the appropriate interface mapping to the sensors and actuators of the apparatus, in order to evaluate the task. As a result, the interface is composed of the testing apparatus and the mapping to the inputs, outputs and rewards of the task.

The elucidation of whether the interface causes additional or reduced information requires the utmost care. For instance, in the numerousness task either

---

Panel 16.1
Situated testing versus artificial apparatus

For some systems (e.g., a bacterium or a floor-cleaning robot), the only possible way of evaluating them is through some kind of situated test. For a bacterium, we can alter its environment in different ways, such as placing a barrier between it and some food. Similarly, we can put several obstacles between the cleaning robot and the socket.

For other systems, especially those that have some kind of conditioning, we can use a more sophisticated apparatus to facilitate the evaluation process. For instance, for a rat, we can use two lights, two levers and a food-releasing device, and habituate the rat to pay attention to the lights and use the levers. With this minimal communication channel (two bits of input and two bits of output, assuming both levers can be pressed at the same time), we can configure several interfaces for several tasks. This is what is done with the dolphins for the numerousness task (Panel 8.1), albeit with a more sophisticated apparatus.

Things are becoming more elaborate in areas such as developmental robotics or simulated robotic animals ('animats'). To make a robot do a task, we must first *train* it to use a particular set of external sensors and actuators, e.g., a light and a set of levers (as in the simulated environment devised by Fiore et al., 2008, with a simulated robotic rat).

The testing apparatus can be prepared for a series of tasks. For instance, several species of primates can be habituated to play with a screen, a joystick and a particular reward treat (Fragaszy et al., 2003). The testing apparatus can then be used for a maze task or for a reaction time task.

---

the boards are hidden from the tester or the tester's face is hidden from the dolphin, since, if the dolphin could look at the tester's face (knowing the right answer), the dolphin might be able to infer the answer unfairly. This phenomenon is known in comparative psychology as the 'clever Hans phenomenon' (Sebeok and Rosenthal, 1981), a famous horse that guessed the answers from the face expressions in the audience.

After all, the question is how this mapping is defined. It can be defined as a one-to-one correspondence, a *bijection* (Hernández-Orallo et al., 2014; Dowe and Hernández-Orallo, 2014). Simon (1978) analysed how two different representations of the same problem might differ, and alter the difficulty of a problem. He distinguished between "informational equivalence", where "the transformation from one to the other entails no loss of information" and "computational equivalence", where "the same information can be extracted with about the same amount of computation" (Simon, 1978). However, Simon's "proportional" approach seems useless for some simple cases. For instance, in the numerousness task, which can be originally represented with two boards as $\langle a, b \rangle$, we can use a bijective transformation into three boards $\langle 1, a, b \rangle$ if $a < b$ and $\langle 0, b, a \rangle$ otherwise. Clearly, with this transformation the instance has been completely spoilt as the response is clearly indicated.

> **Keynote 16.3.** A **fair interface** is a bijection between the task inputs and outputs with the actuators and sensors of the testing apparatus, not introducing any advantageous information or withholding important information (informational bias). The interface should not require transformations that the subject cannot do easily (computational bias) or, conversely, introduce short-cuts to the solution policy.

We can even measure whether the information is the same, using, e.g., Kolmogorov complexity, Levin's Kt complexity (Levin, 1973) or information gain (Hernández-Orallo, 2000e). However, the key issue here is to analyse this phenomenon with a solutional approach (Section 10.1), as we did with difficulty in Chapter 8, and see whether a new representation enables much simpler policies than with the original representation.

As a result, we should choose the representation that is *optimal* for the agent, provided that the bijection does not change the purpose of the task in terms of difficulty, intention, etc. For those tasks that are related to solving a cognitive problem (cognitive abilities), this constraint can be checked by comparing the policies for several representations. For other behavioural features, such as personality, a good definition of the trait is required to check that those policies for which a given value is expected are preserved after the transformation. Of course, in both cases, this implies an enormous effort of exploring the set of policies (i.e., behaviours) to see whether a bias in the transformation may have been overlooked. For different agents, it is important to know the basic constructs that both will use to create their policies. For instance, a test can use the subject's own language or a unary numeral system instead of the decimal system for small children or animals. This means that the choice of a good interface requires information about the customs, knowledge and, ultimately, abilities, of the testee.

We have to distinguish between the evaluation of perception abilities, such as auditory or visual abilities, and the evaluation of other abilities where representation is crucial, such as verbal or spatial abilities. The evaluation of whether a rat or a robot is able to find an optimal path in a maze (a spatial navigation ability), presuming that both agents have subsystems to detect the walls, is not the same as the evaluation of whether a rat or a robot is able to detect the wall in a maze in a situated testing apparatus (a visual perception ability). For the first task, we are flexible to change the interface in many ways. For the second task, the very use of the representation is what is measured. For instance, in the *Jeopardy!* TV quiz, it seemed fair that IBM Watson received the questions in written form through a particular computerised interface, whilst the human participants used the conventional audiovisual interface, but there were concerns about the way Watson would press the buzzer (Ferrucci et al., 2010).

The preceding discussion emphasises the obstacles of defining universal tests, which will be more difficult for some behavioural features than others. Also, it shows that a test can be defined formally but, to turn it into a universal test, we need to add infinitely many interfaces, one for each possible element in the machine kingdom. In practice, one would make interfaces on demand, once the kind of subject to be evaluated is known.

Despite the difficulties, whenever the same test is applied to very different kinds of subjects, we learn about what the test really measures and whether the interfaces are correct. This is in the end the way that human psychometrics and comparative psychology have rejected thousands of invalid tests in the past, and the way many of the tests can be extended for humans, or discarded, for AI evaluation. For instance, Panel 16.2 shows the findings of a test aimed at measuring general intelligence, when applied to humans and AI systems, using the interfaces of Figure 16.2.

In hindsight, according to the trade-off between efficiency, accuracy and range (Keynote 16.2), IQ tests are designed to be efficient and accurate for humans, but not universal.

16.3 RESOLUTION RANGE: TEST ADAPTATION

If we understand the construction of a universal test as a core common set of tasks with different interfaces for each type of subject, the challenge would be unattainable at the present time. Still, the ultimate notion of a universal test should be a test that could be applied to an unknown agent, in a physical or virtual world. For instance, in an online video game, we might be interested in evaluating a new player; in a co-operative work system, we might want to evaluate the abilities of a new member; or, before commercialising a pet robot, a certification office might want to analyse its behaviour, among many other robots produced by different manufacturers.

Panel 16.2
The falsifying power of universal tests

Insa-Cabrera et al. (2011a, 2012b) inspected a first proposal for a *universal* intelligence test (Hernández-Orallo and Dowe, 2010) and the corresponding environment class (Hernández-Orallo, 2010). The proof-of-concept implementation, *Lambda One*, compared humans and AI agents (actually, a particular reinforcement learning algorithm, Q-learning, Watkins and Dayan, 1992). The items were exactly the same, but the interface was devised specifically for each kind of agent (see Figure 16.2).

The results, which we already saw in Figure 11.1, did not show the expected difference between humans and Q-learning. Actually, Q-learning does not perform a "mental search" but just elaborates over the frequencies of a "physical search". The experiment became a "disproof of concept", and the implementation was falsified as a universal intelligence test.

The most important observation from the experiment is the corroboration of the refuting power of universal tests. In fact, if this test had been used for reinforcement learning algorithms and humans separately, we would have seen the agents being accurately scaled in isolation. This is in fact what we see in other similar experiments (Insa-Cabrera et al., 2011b; Legg and Veness, 2013). In other words, if we apply a test to a narrow range of subjects, the results may look consistent if the test only measures the variability in the group, but will not be able to measure what the elements in the group have in common. We can see more conspicuously that *IQ tests for humans – or any other population – do not measure intelligence universally, but their relative intelligence, if there is variability in that population.* And this is why we see the flaws of IQ tests when attempted by AI systems, as we saw in Chapter 6.

In these cases, there is a *milieu* (the physical or virtual world) where we may recognise the subjects, but we do not know what kind of interface one should use to evaluate them. As we know, this includes the rewards and the input and output signals to be used. But this also includes the time rate of the interaction and the scale of the stimuli. For instance, an English speech would become completely unintelligible for humans if it were played 10 times faster or slower than its usual pace. Similarly, a forest is unrecognisable if we zoom it in or out at an unusual scale. For humans and other animals, the signal may carry information at different, but particular resolutions. For instance, dolphins can process audio signals not only according to frequency modulation but also

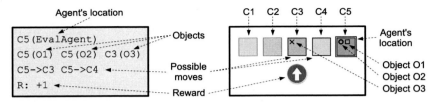

Figure 16.2. Two different interfaces for the *Lambda One* test (Insa-Cabrera et al. 2011a, 2012b). Left: a raw interface as a character string meant for an AI system. Right: a graphical interface meant for humans.

through burst-pulsed sounds and the so-called clicks (Wilson et al., 2007; Madsen et al., 2012).

Keynote 16.4. Resolution and universal tests: Any universal test must find the appropriate scale, in time, space and other perceptive features, the *resolution*, for the interface and task.

Many different resolutions have been explored in animal cognition. This exploration process involves a painstaking effort by many researchers to find what kind of stimuli animals can react to and recognise. Instead, is it possible to envisage that such a process could be automated by an adaptive test, at least in some restricted contexts and for some abilities? This is what we explore next.

For some tasks, the resolution is precisely what is being measured and should not be altered. For instance, a 'reaction time' task has very precise time intervals, already fixed by the task. However, for many other behavioural features, including many abilities, and most personality traits, the time the subject takes to respond should not be considered in the measurement. In this case, the interface should have the flexibility to adapt to the evaluee, in order to get a more efficient measurement. Also, the response time taken by the evaluee for each item can be used to accommodate the adaptive test and use more appropriate items (Van Der Linden, 2008) or resolutions. For instance, consider two machines, where one is emulating the other at half its speed. For some kinds of tasks, for which speed is not measured, the results of both machines should be equal and a universal test should adapt to them.

In the understanding of cognition, this flexibility with time (and other scales) is what makes us consider that a rat and a plant are both cognitive systems adapting to their environment, even if the time scale of plants is much slower than those of animals (Calvo-Garzón and Keijzer, 2011). Similarly, given a very fast AI system, for practical reasons we tend to evaluate it at its fastest possible rate. All this is well recognised in comparative cognition, usually referred to as "temporal factors" (Shettleworth, 2013, p. 38), including the timing of rewards, such as the delay between the conditional stimulus (e.g., light) and the unconditional stimulus (e.g., a peanut).

This brings to the fore that the view of a question-and-answer test (as in some IQ tests for adults) or where actions and percepts alternate (as in decision processes) is too simplistic, as if always assuming the perfect resolution. In Chapter 8, we saw several reasons to consider asynchronous tasks, but now we find more. For instance, measuring an ability as if we were giving "infinite time" (Thurstone, 1937) is not realistic. For instance, apart from the working time between the stimulus (or the response) and the reward, we can also consider the exposure time, which is the amount of time the agent has access to some information before it is removed. This is for instance the most relevant time frame in the spatial memory task for which Ayumu the chimpanzee excelled (Panel 2.3). In general, we can analyse the ability of the agent for varying difficulties and times.

Keynote 16.5. Cognitive abilities and time: The proficiency of the agent for a task will vary depending on the difficulty of the item and any time dimensions that are analysed. These additional dimensions can account for response, exposure, emulation or communication times, depending on the task.

By adding this time dimension, we can convert agent characteristic curves into *agent characteristic surfaces*. For instance, Figure 16.3 shows two agent characteristic surfaces. The one of the left was originally called "person characteristic surface" by Thurstone (1937) and assumed that the more time given the better, suitable for a 'response time' task. Other time dimensions may have a different shape, as the one on the right of the figure. Generally, we are usually satisfied if we are able to measure the time slice of the surface that is best for the agent. Note that the best slice is not the potential ability, as seen in Chapter 12, but the time resolution that best suits the agent.

But how can we estimate the surfaces shown in Figure 16.3, or, at least, the best slice? The answer is necessarily an adaptive test. In Section 3.6, we saw that adaptive tests are well suited to IRT, as item difficulty is adjusted to get the most information about the subject's proficiency in a short time. However, a universal test for any behavioural feature (not only abilities) without knowledge about the appropriate resolution of the subject requires a complete overhaul of the adaptation process.

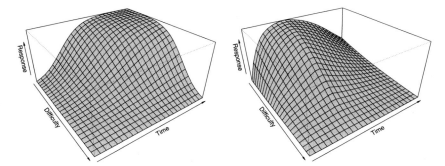

Figure 16.3. Agent characteristic surfaces showing expected response according to item difficulty and a time parameter for the task. Left: a figurative example where response is monotonically increasing with time (the plot is similar to the one shown in Thurstone, 1937, p. 250). Right: a figurative example where too much time may be counterproductive, as the interaction may be too slow for the agent, the task may be forgotten or the agent may lose interest.

As a start, in (Computerised) Adaptive Testing (CAT), we usually know a range of values where the subject is expected to be. Typically, the first item starts at a midpoint in this range or, if some knowledge about the subject is known, with the item that is most discriminative. In the case of a universal test with changing resolutions we do not even know a range of values. Adaptation for cognitive abilities must be done by starting with simple items that are very discriminative for lowest proficiencies. These will usually be some kind of "control items" upon which the test can adapt by, e.g., doubling their difficulty, as we discussed in Section 9.4.

However, if we know nothing about the agent, a complete failure of the task can be interpreted either as a zero proficiency or as a failure to find the right interface resolution. To avoid this, different resolutions should be attempted first with what we refer to as an "enactment task".

> **Keynote 16.6.** An **enactment task** is any simple task such that it makes the agent consistently react in a particular manner, in such a way that this reaction can be elaborated to respond to other tasks.

In animals, this enactment task may be a simple action such as receiving a treat if a lever is pressed after a light is set on. We can tune the resolution of the task by playing with different times for the light, different delays between the time the lever is pressed and the reward is given, etc. In practice, this resolution can also be determined when the testing apparatus is being fine-tuned. For AI systems, especially in milieus such as social networks, virtual games, co-operative work tools and other virtual scenarios where the protocols are well known, the emphasis can be put on how to get the attention of the agent and make it do an enactment task, before attempting the tasks that were meant to be measured originally.

Keynote 16.7. Universal test adaptation: A universal test for an unknown agent must perform an adaptive search to find a resolution such that the agent can be evaluated in optimal conditions.

In general, ensuring that the interface and resolution are working well will require painstaking work, especially in incremental or developmental tasks, and will not always be possible. Also, the doubt of an underestimation – because of a failure of finding the best conditions – will remain. In cases where we only need to work with time or a restricted space of resolutions, an adaptive test may be feasible. In (Hernández-Orallo and Dowe, 2010), for instance, an adaptive test was defined as an algorithm that considered any time resolution. The algorithm started with a very fast interaction rate and then it slowed down until the agent started to be responsive in terms of performance. Because the time slots went from very short to longer periods, the test could align more quickly to the agent resolution.

16.4 UNORTHODOX UNIVERSAL ASSESSMENT

In the previous section, we have seen how challenging it can be to construct a universal test when the milieu and the agents are well recognised but the interface and resolution have to be determined. In this section we briefly explore some situations that go beyond this, and far beyond any standard evaluation. Because these scenarios are more challenging they will require a more unorthodox treatment. In particular, we will explore cases where the agent is not yet recognised when the test is started (and needs to be detected), when interaction with the agent is not possible (and evaluation must be done by observation) and, finally, when the evaluator is not a test but an intelligent being (e.g., through an interview), also including self-assessment.

The case where the subjects to be evaluated are not even recognised initially may seem preposterous, but these scenarios are more common than it seems at first sight. In natural ecosystems, especially when collective behaviours emerge, it is not always clear what is to be evaluated. For instance, is it the bee or the beehive that needs to be evaluated? Is it a bacterium or the whole colony? A tree or a forest? If we decide to evaluate the individuals, we have to be aware of *eusociality*, where we find subclasses or castes inside a group. If we decide to evaluate the collective, it may be not very well delineated. In many primate species, there is a continuous exchange of individuals between groups. Some can merge and split again for foraging or parenting, making the concept of group very unstable for assessment. Similarly, in the same group, alliances and coalitions may change dynamically. In artificial ecosystems, we may have emergent phenomena that require the evaluation of the individuals and the groups. Examples of these environments are robotic swarms, video games and social networks.

In artificial life and other artificial environments the very notion of organism is unclear. For instance, the detection of minimally cognitive agents (such as gliders) is necessary in very minimalistic environments such as Conway's game of life (Beer, 2004). In general, in all these scenarios, some abstractions have to be performed, in terms of the interaction between the agent and the environment (Tarapore et al., 2006; Williams and Beer, 2010; Beer, 2015), before any evaluation can be undertaken.

Another peculiar case takes place in astrobiology, if the interest is not only to detect any kind of life, but life with some cognitive abilities. In this case it is not an individual that is analysed but the whole ecosystem of a planet. In fact, one could infer theoretically that there is life in a planet, and even intelligence, without properly identifying the species or machine that is behind the phenomenon (Seager, 2013). In astrobiology, in fact, there have been very interesting discussions about extraterrestrial messages possibly reaching the Earth: how to detect them and how to tell that they have been generated by an intelligent civilisation. However, there is no clear methodology about how to do it (what to scan, as with the SETI project, and what to send, as with the Voyager space probes shown in Figure 4.4). It can be argued that a very regular message (e.g., in terms of Kolmogorov complexity) could have been generated by a physical non-intelligent phenomenon (e.g., a pulsar) whilst a message looking almost random could be easily overlooked. About the content, many opinions have been expressed about what to try to code (e.g., Dowe, 2008, sec. 0.2.5). In the end, even if this is actually a problem of a universal detection of intelligence by observation, it is, at the moment, of little practical relevance.

Despite the appearance, a closely related area to astrobiology is palaeontology. In the first place, it is related because when we 'look' at a distant planet what we actually do is going back in time. But it is also related because in palaeontology the agent is not always well recognised. For instance, we may want to determine the behavioural features of an animal, e.g., *Homo neanderthalensis*, from their fossils, tools, etc., but, occasionally, we even infer simultaneously from the remains the species we are talking about. Similar disciplines are archaeology and, most especially, historiometry, which is devoted to ascertaining the characteristics of individuals from their works and biographies. For instance, Francis Galton, in his *Hereditary Genius* (1869), speculated about the intelligence of classical Greek scholars and other geniuses in history. Further than that, Catherine Cox made a thorough estimate of "the early mental traits of three hundred geniuses" (Cox, 1926). The list was topped by Goethe.

Actually, astrobiology, palaeontology, historiometry and other disciplines are clear examples where knowledge (in this case about the behavioural features of some remote organisms) is inferred by observation (of past events). Evaluating by observation has the main limitation that the evaluator cannot interact with the evaluee. Ethology basically studies animals in their ecosystems, trying not to interfere. Similarly, some AI assessments are merely based on observation. Precisely because of their limitations, we have ruled them out as a good measurement procedure, provided, of course, that we have the possibility of interacting with the evaluee.

Nonetheless, there are some situations where observation is the only source of information (or the most practical source). For instance, digital social networks, virtual worlds and multiplayer online games provide enormous amounts of information about how humans (and bots trying to impersonate humans) behave. Also, humans can be assisted by machines and vice versa. This is, in the end, a good scenario where behavioural features must be evaluated universally. Trying to convince any of these participants to perform an off-the-shelf psychometric test seems unrealistic.

By observation in a virtual environment we basically refer to looking at archived logs that record the interaction of all these agents – what they do, say, buy, etc. These logs can be analysed a posteriori using machine learning and other statistical techniques, what is known as 'user profiling', for several applications, such as recommender systems or sentiment analysis. Here, however, we are interested in psychometric profiles extracted from these recorded logs, which are also known as "digital footprints".

Several works have started to predict personality traits, such as openness, conscientiousness, extraversion, agreeableness and neuroticism, from their activity logs (Quercia et al., 2011; Golbeck et al., 2011; Bachrach et al., 2012b; Ortigosa et al., 2013; Lambiotte and Kosinski, 2014; Vinciarelli and Mohammadi, 2014; Park et al., 2015), but also using the structure of the network of user's friends (Staiano et al., 2012). In a more incipient way, we also find some works trying to infer intelligence. For instance, Kosinski et al. (2013), apart from personality and other traits, also analysed intelligence using Facebook

---

Panel 16.3
Liking 'curly fries' to look more intelligent

The construction of a model of Facebook 'likes' to predict the intelligence of Facebook users achieved 0.39 correlation with the actual values (of Raven's Progressive Matrices) (Kosinski et al., 2013). This is quite remarkable, since the quality and information of the likes seems worse than other possible sources from which intelligence indicators could be indirectly inferred (e.g., inferring IQ from written text).

Kosinski et al. (2013) examine the models that are extracted from the logs. Given the high predictability of the 'likes' attribute, its analysis reveals that "for example, the best predictors of high intelligence include 'Thunderstorms', 'The Colbert Report', 'Science', and 'Curly Fries', whereas low intelligence was indicated by 'Sephora', 'I Love Being A Mom', 'Harley Davidson', and 'Lady Antebellum'" (Kosinski et al., 2013). Some of them may look more meaningful (e.g., 'Science'), but other topics are more intriguing (e.g., 'Curly Fries'). Is 'curly fries' the theme to look more intelligent and make our conversations more sparkling?

'likes'. The analysis of the predictive model unveiled some surprising connections, as we can see in Panel 16.3.

The accuracy of these analyses is worse than full on-purpose intelligence tests, but it is better than the assessment by other humans (Youyou et al., 2015) and has many advantages in terms of costs and applicability. In the end, it shows that evaluating by observation, especially in these contexts, deserves serious consideration. Indeed, the part about personality has become an area of research in its own, known as "Computational Personality Recognition" (Celli et al., 2013, 2014), and it can work for cognitive abilities too, as we have seen. The ambition goes beyond behavioural features to the analysis of human behaviour in a more general sense, using all kinds of information collected from human interaction with devices, social networks, etc. This new area is dubbed "psycho-informatics" (Markowetz et al., 2014).

These works assumed that the profiles came from humans. In fact, the users were identified (and their humanness certified) in those cases where off-the-shelf psychometric tests were also administered and used to label the data to train the models. But what happens if bots, i.e., artificial agents, are included in the study? Will it be easy to make bots able to game all these log-based models? What if we devise a bot that just makes comments or likes on a social network about Galileo, Newton, Darwin, Einstein and Turing? All these evaluations based on activity logs – we do not refer to them as tests – can be falsified: they are not universal.

In fact, we can conceive many other ways in which this kind of evaluation would fail, especially if we know that it is being used. One possibility is to devise bots based on "human traces" (Karpov et al., 2012), a technique that is used to give bots more *believability*. Many analyses of profiles and game logs are based on chunking the information and processing it statistically, not detecting the consistency of the chunks. Chunking is basically the way the first chatterbots worked, like Weizenbaum's Eliza (1966), still one cunning method to pass a Turing test.

Of course, we can try to devise better methods to analyse the user logs in order to minimise these problems, using various approaches already explored in the literature for different social networks, crowdsourcing platforms, etc. (Chu et al., 2012; Dickerson et al., 2014; Wang et al., 2014; Ferrara et al., 2015). Apart from the increasing complexity of all these approaches, there is always a counterpoise, the so-called adversarial attacks. This adversarial phenomenon means that the bot designers (or the bots themselves) will try to incorporate improvements to fool the new detectors or even to spoil the detectors themselves (Wang et al., 2014). The attack-defence cycle will go *in aeternum*, as happens with CAPTCHA breakers. Also, because of impersonation and the possible use of human computation by bots (or the use of machines of any kind such as search engines, encyclopaedias, translators, etc.), any reliable use of these detection approaches in the general case – the universal problem – is doomed to failure in the long term.

So far in this section, we have seen some unorthodox evaluation approaches. These approaches are in stark contrast to a systematic evaluation using tests, which should be the general rule for an accurate assessment, as advocated by universal psychometrics. However, we see the interesting phenomenon that the more difficult evaluation becomes the more the evaluation relies on the *intelligence of the evaluator*. In other words, as the evaluation becomes less systematic, it becomes more subjective, relative to an intelligent evaluator. To finalise this section, we will briefly explore what the role of the evaluator's intelligence is.

First, the systems that infer behavioural features from digital social networks and other artificial ecosystems seen earlier are using artificial intelligence techniques (e.g., machine learning techniques) to predict these traits. In the end, the evaluation depends on a model trained on previous data, which tries to integrate all the predictive variables that are available from the evaluee. This can be generalised to other scenarios. Actually, in the particular case of intelligence measurement, we could even talk about *intelligent* intelligence evaluation, i.e., an evaluation that measures intelligence by the most *intelligent* use of the information so far and, if they are adaptive, by the most *intelligent* choice of tasks given the responses so far.

Keynote 16.8. Intelligent testing: The inclusion of (artificial) intelligence (e.g., predictive models) in evaluation sets a new level for testing. We could even speak of a three-level gradation of 'static tests', 'adaptive tests' and 'intelligent tests'.

Indeed, the use of artificial intelligence in Computerised Adaptive Testing (CAT) has been seen as a natural evolution (Wainer, 2000; Weiss, 2011). This, in the end, is even much older: intelligence has been evaluated by other humans (who are intelligent evaluators) for many centuries, through open questionnaires or an everyday interaction. Also, the Turing test can be seen as an 'intelligent intelligence test', as the judge is an intelligent being. This interpretation can be further developed with the evaluator possibly being an intelligent Turing machine (Hernández-Orallo et al., 2012).

This relates to the more general question of whether intelligence is useful to measure intelligence (and other behavioural features) most effectively. The most negative stance would be given by some kind of Gödelian incompleteness results of some levels of intelligence being unable to measure some 'upper' levels. However, even when the evaluated system is more intelligent than the evaluator, it would be absurd to think of intelligence as beneficial for all tasks except for evaluating intelligence. In fact, an intelligent evaluator could just use the most advanced intelligence tests and procedures for a particular evaluation. The question must be rather rephrased as whether an intelligent evaluator can adapt these tests (or questions in the case of humans), to perform a very efficient evaluation. Of course, using unconstrained intelligent agents as evaluators (e.g., humans) would affect reliability and validity, in contrast to the systematic, standard procedures that psychometric tests represent. But certainly, we can foresee that adaptive tests of the future can incorporate artificial intelligence techniques, provided the final measuring procedure is kept standardised and well understood.

Finally, a special kind of evaluation by an intelligent evaluator is self-assessment. In Chapter 3, we saw that some behavioural features, especially personality traits, are usually evaluated by self-assessment. Although the self-assessment of intelligence is not very common – and we are not referring to the self-administration of a standard IQ test – there are also studies about the reliability of self-evaluation in a spontaneous way (Sternberg et al., 1981; Stankov, 2000). It can be argued that self-assessment is an advantageous situation, as measurement is easier the more we know about the evaluee, one of the principles of measurement that we saw in the beginning of this chapter. But, of course, this knowledge must be accurate and honest. Also, self-evaluation requires the subject to have self-modelling, as discussed in Section 13.5. As we discussed in Section 12.6, second-order self-awareness requires "reflexive self-evaluation" (Frankfurt, 1971). Basically, one cannot decide to change some of her behavioural features, as an ultimate expression of free will, if she does not have a reliable estimation of her current behavioural features first. We will return to this issue in the following chapter, around the notion of self-enhancement.

16.5 DESIDERATA FOR UNIVERSAL TESTS

In the previous section, we have seen that some situations are so handicapped by the lack of information or interaction that some unorthodox approaches could be an option, albeit some of them would never lead to universal assessments with a minimum reliability. In fact, we started the chapter with the antagonism between an instrument range and its accuracy. Adaptive tests were proposed as the systematic approach for the construction of universal tests.

Universal tests for cognitive abilities may frequently suffer from underestimation, since the adaptive test tries, but may fail, to find the best conditions for the test (in terms of interface, resolution and tasks), the "test potential" that we saw in Section 12.7. This is not to be confused with the potential abilities in development. However, with the goal of finding the optimal conditions for a subject we may end up training the agent or making it develop in the long term, with the result of over-estimation. This would end up measuring a potential ability rather than an actual ability.

Despite the difficulties, we must set the construction of universal tests as a priority for the analysis of the machine kingdom, especially for their use as a powerful refutation tool. The construction can be guided by a series of desiderata (adapted from Hernández-Orallo and Dowe, 2010), as follows:

- The test must work for any system in the machine kingdom (natural or artificial), at present, in the future or at any level of development.
- It must be derived from well-founded computational principles, such that the measurement derives from these principles.
- It must be meaningful such that the definition of the behavioural feature really represents its intuitive notion.

Table 16.2. A sample of evaluation approaches applied to at least two kinds of subjects of the three main categories H, A and M, standing for Humans, (non-human) Animals and (non-biological) Machines, respectively. The asterisks indicate that the feature was not really captured by the test for the full range of subjects. See the work of Herrmann et al. (2007) for PCTB, Von Ahn et al. (2004, 2008) for CAPTCHAs, Barrera et al. (2011) for Cyclical Maze and Insa-Cabrera et al. (2011a, 2012b) for *Lambda One*.

Evaluation	Feature	H	A	M
Comparative psychology	Several	✓	✓	✗
Primate Cognition Test Battery (PCTB)	Primary/social	✓	✓	✗
IQ tests	Intelligence	✓	✗	✓*
Turing tests	Humanness	✓	✗	✓*
CAPTCHAs	Humanness	✓*	✗	✓*
Cyclical Maze (rats and robots)	Spatial abilities	✗	✓	✓
BotPrize	Believability	✓*	✗	✓*
Lambda One	Intelligence	✓*	✗	✓*

- It must be able to measure any level of the behavioural feature, from very low scores to very high scores, including any time scale.
- The quality of the assessment will depend on the time that is provided for the measurement.
- The evaluation can be interrupted at any time, with better assessment the longer the evaluation time allowed.

Given the preceding desiderata, are there some actual tests from which we can grasp a perspective of what kind of universal tests will be feasible in the future?

Table 16.2 shows a selection of tests (all of them discussed in this book) that have been applied to at least two of the three main groups of humans, non-human animals and non-biological machines. Note that most of the tests in the table are evaluations that are not systematic, unlike psychometrics, and most are not based on first principles, either. Also, some of these tests have actually been rejected and their universal range refuted, right after the application to two kinds of subjects.

From Table 16.2 we can surmise that there is still a long way ahead for the construction of accurate universal tests for relevant behavioural features, such as cognitive abilities and personality traits. Nevertheless, these examples also show that the boundaries between different groups of subjects need to –and can – be crossed, as we discussed in Chapter 6.

Having said all this, we do not want to portray the view that universal tests are the only way to cross the boundaries of humans, non-human animals, arbitrary machines and collectives. Non-universal (customised) tests are more appropriate for the practical evaluation of a child, a pigeon or a self-driving car. Overall, both customised and universal tests are useful for the practical and theoretical purposes and can co-exist in universal psychometrics, depending on what the goal is. For instance, if we want to evaluate the intelligence of non-enhanced humans, IQ tests will be the reasonable tool. If we want to evaluate the ability of agents (either humans or bots) for a given kind of task in a crowdsourcing platform, a more universal test will be required. In general, for the myriad newfangled subjects yet to come, we will need to learn along the way.

CHAPTER HIGHLIGHTS

- Universal tests aiming at the whole machine kingdom (Keynote 16.1), differing from customised tests in terms of validity, reliability, difficulty estimation, administration, scoring and motivation (Table 16.1).
- Larger test ranges (Keynote 16.2) implying less efficient and accurate measurement with potential generality and specificity problems (Keynote 16.2).
- Situated tests and artificial apparatus (Panel 16.1) as possible approaches to defining fair interfaces (Keynote 16.3).
- Adaptation to the resolution and proficiency of the agent the way towards truly universal tests (Keynote 16.7).
- Some parts of the resolution fixed when they are part of the feature to be measured, such as time, possibly taken as an extra dimension in agent characteristic surfaces (Keynote 16.5, Figure 16.3).
- Evaluation from users' activity logs capturing their interaction with devices and their behaviour in artificial ecosystems being exploited by predictive modelling, from adaptive to 'intelligent' evaluation (Keynote 16.8).
- Both universal and non-universal (customised) tests being useful in universal psychometrics (Section 16.5). Universal tests especially suitable as refutation tools (Panel 16.2).

17

Rooting for Ratiocentrism

I am rooting for the machines! I have always been on the machines'
side. Ha-ha!
– Claude Shannon,
interview in *Omni* magazine (1987)

HERE WE WILL unfurl the unconventional and perhaps (politically) incorrect position of using intelligence as a reference, instead of humanity. This *ratiocentric* stance will start with the very notion of personhood and will lead us to a critical account of other issues such as 'superintelligence', its (existential) risks, the rights and effects of cognitive enhancement, and the implications of all this for the organisation of society. From a more sceptical position than the rest of the book, this chapter will discuss several ratiocentric scenarios, not because I can demonstrate that they are more likely or better than others, but rather because if they become a reality, the evaluation of cognitive abilities will be of utmost importance, much more than psychometrics is already today with the nowadays dominant anthropocentric or biocentric stances. For instance, should intelligence be kept shared by many independent individuals? Should some rights, such as the right to vote, depend on behavioural features? Should this be accompanied by the universal right to be (and not to be) enhanced? How necessary are measurements to keep an equilibrium? Not only are the answers to these questions uncomfortable, but the mere questions themselves.

17.1 PERSONHOOD

Human psychometrics has always been controversial. Its use to identify group differences in human populations, to select personnel in the labour market, to certify deep intellectual disabilities, to complement forensic psychiatry and to route children's education is still strongly contended, as potentially *discriminative*. Other uses in strategic government decisions, birth control and any explicit kind of eugenics have simply been expelled from political correctness. At this point of the book, with a more mature perspective of universal psychometrics, it is now the right time to analyse these and new controversial issues for the whole machine kingdom. We start with the root of the problem, the very concept of person.

Idiots, in ancient Greece, were laypeople that did not participate in public welfare, had bad judgment about politics and were only concerned about their private life. Idiocy has not been the only criterion to consider some individuals of an inferior class, condemn them to slavery or sentence them to death. The history of humanity is full of examples of individuals or groups that have been deprived of the rights that a minority or a single person arrogated for themselves. Almost any criterion we may think of has been used in the past, including race, gender, ideology, economic power or lineage. The worst of all is that this is still the case in some parts of the world. For instance, in still many countries, women are ruled by *special* laws, sustained by *tradition* and *religion*.

In the past, discrimination was considered the norm rather than the exception. The age of enlightenment challenged all privileges and exalted reason as the tool to settle all questions, such as determining what entities had *intrinsic value*, moral consideration or were an *end* in themselves. But still, what we include in the 'club' of *all people* is not an easy question.

In ancient Greek philosophy, reason had already been claimed as the main criterion to determine personhood, before Descartes's "*res cogitans*" or Kant's "rational being" were set on the table. This pervaded common practice and law for many centuries, despite the many privileges and discriminations. Under the Spanish Empire, for instance, the term 'gente de razón' (people with reason) was used to distinguish Spaniards (and colonists embracing the Hispanic culture) from Native Americans and slaves (usually black or of 'mixed' race). Of course there was no specific protocol or test to tell ones from the others *in terms of reason*. The idea that all people should be equal under the law had to undergo several revolutions and wars to thrive. The universal declaration of human rights would only materialise after one of the most brutal episodes in history, the Second World War.

Nowadays, the equation 'person' = 'any specimen of the species *Homo sapiens*' is the dominant paradigm. In a way, it incorporates the criterion of reason (humans would be the only species that are 'sapiens') but it also includes a biological principle. The extinction of other specimens of the genus *Homo* in the past, such as *Homo neanderthalensis* or *Homo floresiensis*, makes the equation rather satisfying and very practical, since determining whether an individual belongs to the club is self-evident. However, the question is far from settled. "It is conceptually possible that members of novel or even of familiar nonhuman species should be persons; and it is also conceptually possible that some members of the human species are not persons" (Frankfurt, 1971, p. 6). More precisely,

---

Keynote 17.1. Challenging the equation "human = person" suggests that not all humans are persons, and not all persons are human.

First, the debate about some kind of *animal personhood* has become more popular in the past decades (Regan, 1987; Singer, 1995), even if the scientific roots can be found much earlier. In Section 4.1 we discussed the views of Galen, Huarte and Darwin about a difference in degree between humans and other animals, according to their "rational powers". Huarte even used the term "soul" for the apes (Huarte, 1575, pp. 29–30). Today, however, we must distinguish between animal *welfare*, as found in several declarations (WPSA, 2014; Chapouthier et al., 1998), usually extended to all animals, and a vindication of the character of "person" to animals, which is usually restricted to just a subset of species, as we describe in Panel 17.1.

There is of course no consensus about whether and why the great apes (i.e., the Hominidae family of primates) should be 'persons' (and only them). Is it because of their genetic similarity to *Homo sapiens* or because of their cognitive abilities? According to genetic similarity, we would have "a highly selective, potentially inconsistent, and unfortunately capricious form of ethics, where those animals judged to be closest to us – based on perceived similarities of anatomy and physiology – are included, while others are left out of consideration all together" (Gunkel, 2012, p. 127). According to cognitive abilities, the group should likely include some cetaceans as well. Also, cephalopods are the only invertebrates that are covered by the European Union directive "on the protection of animals used for scientific purposes" (EU, 2010). The issue is not limited to current life on Earth. Similar ethical questions are addressed in astrobiology (Smith, 2009, 2014; Persson, 2012).

Comparable questions, as expected, have been raised for machines in science fiction, artificial intelligence and philosophy, with even more nuances than the already rich case in biology and astrobiology. For instance, as machines are created by humans, who is responsible for their actions? Who takes the credit, property rights and benefit from their inventions? Joanna J. Bryson has analysed this particular point of view of the issue and has argued that "robots should

---

Panel 17.1
Probably cognitive capability and animal personhood

The *Great Ape Project* is perhaps the most significant organisation which advocates for the Hominidae family being granted some degree of 'non-human personhood'. Their goal is to achieve a 'United Nations Declaration of the Rights of Great Apes', which could recognise some universal rights such as the right to life, freedom and the prohibition of torture.

However, courts of several countries have ruled out personhood of various apes in the past. For instance, in 2014 the New York Supreme Court ruled an appeal from the Nonhuman Rights Project that Tommy, a 26-year-old chimpanzee, was not a person, and hence it could be kept in captivity in a cage by his owners (BBC, 2014b). Likewise, the world's first bill about personhood rights for great apes in the Balearic Islands Parliament in 2007 was followed by a national bill in the Spanish Parliament, which was initially passed in 2008, but not ultimately transformed into a law.

On the other hand, in 2014, an Argentinian court granted "habeas corpus" to a female orangutan, Sandra, as a 'non-human subject of law', following an appeal by an animalistic association against "the unjustified confinement of an animal with probably cognitive capability" (BBC, 2014a). Sandra should be guaranteed the "appropriate habitat to preserve her cognitive abilities" (AFADA v. Argentina, 2015).

---

be slaves": "A robot can be abused just as a car, piano or couch can be abused. [T]here's no particular reason it should be programmed to mind such treatment" (Bryson, 2010). In contrast, David J. Gunkel, in his "A vindication of the rights of machines", follows "a tradition that begins with Mary Wollstonecraft's *A Vindication of the Rights of Men* (1790) succeeded two years later by *A Vindication of the Rights of Woman* and Thomas Taylor's intentionally sarcastic yet remarkably influential response *A Vindication of the Rights of Brutes*" (Gunkel, 2014). How can these two positions be so radically different?

First, Bryson – like many others – is well aware of the state of the art of artificial intelligence. At present, there is nothing remotely close to human intelligence to think about labelling them as 'persons'. Of course, we must not be confused by the inclination of 'roboticists' and 'robotophiles' to attribute human features to robots, after endowing them with emotional faces, funny expressions, etc., so that they *look* more *human*. Therefore, Bryson should not be accused of being 'robotophobe' or 'misomakhanist' either. Second, even in the future, Bryson recommends the construction of machines that do not mind being disconnected, reprogrammed or simply destroyed. Third, Gunkel does not advocate for all machines having rights, but that all of them should be subjects of consideration, without excluding a priori that *some* of them may deserve some rights. Fourth, there seems to be an agreement that AI developers have a responsibility, unless or until an AI system can become fully independent, in the same way that parents are ultimately responsible for what their children do, until they become adults. Finally, it is worth emphasising that the debate about machine rights is not necessarily linked to contending the nowadays widespread view that "we are basically machines but of a very complex type" (Shannon, 1987), but rather to the decision of what kind of non-biological machines we want to build.

Again, as has happened on several occasions during this book, it is much more consistent to look at the issue from a universal point of view, including all living beings, machines, hybrids and collectives. This universal view has taken shape in a few works in the past decades (Leiber, 1985; Haraway, 1991; Chapouthier and Kaplan, 2011) and can be referred to as the "universal consideration – giving attention to others of all sorts, with the goal of ascertaining what, if any, direct ethical obligations arise from relating with them" (Birch, 1993). However, as Gunkel (2012, pp. 89–90) points out, "extending consideration to these other previously excluded subjects, however, requires a significant reworking of the concept of moral 'personhood', one that is not dependent on genetic make-up, species identification, or some other spurious criteria". Also, the notion of 'personhood' needs to be superseded to the questions of "what constitutes a moral subject", following Luciano Floridi's distinction between "moral *agents*, as the class of all entities that can in principle qualify as sources of moral action, and ... moral *patients*, as the class of all entities that can in principle qualify as receivers of moral actions" (Floridi and Sanders, 2004). We then talk about *responsibility* of the former and *rights* of the latter.

This distinction is behind the anomalous asymmetry of treatment between animals and machines. In the case of animal ethics, *patiency* has been in the spotlight. In the case of computer ethics, *agency* has been the main concern. However, this asymmetry looks unjustified in the view of the *machine kingdom*. Likewise, it is also unjustified in a philosophical tradition. For instance, for Descartes, animals and machines were the same thing (*bête-machines*), with the important exception that humans were left aside. Contrasting this tradition with modern times, Gunkel (2012, p. 109) writes: "what is curious in this recent questioning and repositioning of the animal is that its other, the machine, remains conspicuously absent".

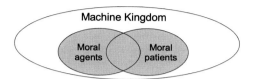

Figure 17.1. Moral agents and patients in the machine kingdom.

Figure 17.1 shows moral agents and moral patients as subsets of the machine kingdom. With present standards, we should place adult humans at the intersection. Indeed, some rights are only given to those entities that are in that intersection, such as the right to vote. Moral patients that are not moral agents would include human children and some mentally disabled people. Also, as we have discussed, some animalists would argue that some (or all) animals should be placed there as well. Finally, we also find examples of moral agents that are not moral patients: corporations and governments are held responsible for their decisions and mistakes and have obligations (such as taxes) but no real moral patiency.

The distinction between moral agents and moral patients is a refinement of Kant's "kingdom of ends" (*Reich der Zwecke*, see, e.g., Kant, 1785; Korsgaard, 1996), of those agents with intentions (and the intentions themselves), as opposed to those other entities that are just *means*, i.e., instrumental.

Again, from this perspective of the machine kingdom, the "animal question" turns out to be a *subset* of "the machine question" (Gunkel, 2012). But what are the criteria for placing elements in the subsets of Figure 17.1? The philosophical tradition indicates that the ability of reason, or more generally, 'logos' (λóγος), should be the main criterion. However, the dominant criterion has usually boiled down to being a specimen of *Homo sapiens sapiens*. This becomes more convoluted as the vindications of animal rights have suggested several other criteria, as summarised in Table 17.1.

From all the criteria in Table 17.1, anthropocentrism, biocentrism and ecocentrism are not comprehensive for the machine kingdom and also not subject to be evaluated with a behavioural test for particular individuals. Infocentrism is still a vague term that could cover some proposals, such as Floridi's "information ethics" (Floridi, 2013), but is – at its current state – not very operational. As a result, we will briefly discuss the other two, which have frequently been opposed or combined. In "The Mind Club', Wegner and Gray (2016) show that people usually associate moral agency with thinking (ratiocentrism) and moral patiency with feeling (sentiocentrism).

Table 17.1.   Some criteria for moral value (Smith, 2009; Persson, 2012).

Term	Criterion
Ratiocentrism	Are able to reason (could also be called *intellecentrism*)
Sentiocentrism	Are able to feel or suffer (also called *pathocentrism*)
Anthropocentrism	Belong to the species *Homo sapiens*
Biocentrism	Are living beings
Ecocentrism	Are part of ecosystems or preserve a species or a gene
Infocentrism	Reduce internal or external entropy

Sentiocentrism has become very popular when considering animal rights (Sparrow, 2004; Dawkins, 2008; Chapouthier and Kaplan, 2011; Dawkins, 2012). Despite being a very old, or perhaps intuitive, position, the following passage had a profound impact on what sentiocentrism is and on its opposition to ratiocentrism: "The French have already discovered that the blackness of the skin is no reason why a human being should be abandoned without redress to the caprice of a tormentor.... What else is it that should trace the insuperable line? ... The question is not, Can they *reason*? nor, Can they *talk*? but, Can they *suffer*?" (Bentham, 1780, p. cccix, footnote).

This may sound intuitive at a first reading, but it is not without important caveats. Gunkel (2014) writes that "the 'capacity to suffer' would have nothing to contribute to the debate concerning the machine as a similarly constructed moral patient". Nevertheless, the problems go beyond this. Sentiocentrism is already very problematic for humans and animals. From a sentiocentristic point of view, a person could be killed if this is done without suffering (and no other people are aware, so that no indirect suffering is involved either). Also, about the "capacity of suffering", where would we put those humans that do not feel some kinds of physical or psychological pain? (Cox et al., 2006). Furthermore, how would this be understood in a situation where all kinds of pain are eliminated by drugs or other means? This is exactly David Pearce's "Hedonistic Imperative", a futuristic vision of the "end of suffering" for humans and many animals (Pearce, 2004).

Pain is just a defence mechanism in living beings. The mechanism of physical pain in rats, for instance, is almost identical to humans, and that does not seem to put them at the same level as humans with respect to moral patience. Even psychological pain, stress, anxiety and melancholia are evolutionary traits. Some of them may be useless, or even harmful, in modern societies, with fewer everyday existential threats. Anyhow, there are many problems for making the sentiocentric approach operative. In the narrow sense, even after scanning a human brain (or a whole octopus), it is very difficult to tell whether the subject really feels pain.

In a broadest sense, sentience is understood as also considering some kind of *consciousness*. However, this "more scientific replacement for the occultish soul" can "only make things worse" (Gunkel, 2012, pp. 54, 90). Indeed, some sentiocentrists recognise that this would be "testing the untestable" (Dawkins, 2008). Finally, how would sentiocentrism be applied to other machines? Measuring rewards and penalties of reinforcement learning agents (Tomasik, 2014)?

One of the motivations behind the popularity of sentiocentrism (apart from its application to animals) is that it works well to characterise small children, as they are able to suffer – or cry all the time. Bentham (1780, Chapter XVII, p. cccix, footnote) makes the point: "a full-grown horse, or dog, is beyond comparison a more rational, as well as a more conversible animal, than an infant of a day, or a week, or even a month, old".

The dilemma originates from the confusion between moral agency and moral patiency, as well as a lack of distinction between actual and potential abilities. Under the ratiocentric perspective, this can be easily explained:

Keynote 17.2. Ratiocentric criterion for moral patiency and agency: What matters for "moral agents" is their *actual* cognitive abilities, and for "moral patients" is their *potential* cognitive abilities.

This is, in fact, what many legal systems use as a reference. For instance, people are considered less responsible for a crime if their "mental faculties" are temporarily diminished by the effects of alcohol or a drug. Newborn children (and people sleeping) do not show *actual* intelligence, but their rights are respected as they will likely become rational (again) in the future. David Deutsch is blunt in his defence of ratiocentrism: "using non-cognitive attributes . . . to define personhood would, again, be racist. But the fact that the ability to create new explanations is the unique, morally and intellectually significant functionality of people (humans and AGIs) . . . changes everything" (Deutsch, 2012).

Of course, the ratiocentric approach is not free of caveats either. For instance, deeply impaired humans with no expected minimum degree of cognition or interaction would not be considered moral patients under this perspective. In the end, and just in the case of humans, there are several other delicate cases for which the sentiocentrism and ratiocentrism stances may lead to divergent appraisals, such as the time of abortion (when the fetus feels pain or when it is likely viable without her mother, i.e., when "fetuses are potential persons", Lycan, 1985).

17.2 ASSESSING MORAL AGENCY AND PATIENCY

Looking at Figure 17.1, the definition of a subjective and anthropocentric "mind club" (Wegner and Gray, 2016) in terms of human perception may be explanatory, but too subjective in theory and practice. Also, we can not only look at the problem more objectively and universally but also in terms of quantitative measurement, in a continuum: what *degree* of moral agency and patiency an entity has according to a profile of behavioural features.

What do we need then to evaluate moral agency and patiency and use them to characterise personhood from them? "First", Gunkel (2012, pp. 42–43) writes, "we would need to identify and articulate the 'person-making properties' . . ., in other words, to articulate what properties make someone or something a person and do so in such a way that is neither capricious nor skewed by anthropocentric prejudice. Second, once standard qualifying criteria for 'person' are established, we would need some way to demonstrate or prove that some entity, human or otherwise, possessed these particular properties. We would need some way of testing for and demonstrating the presence of the personal properties in the entity under consideration. Deciding these two things . . . is anything but 'simple'".

This is not unfamiliar with the discussion about the evaluation of intelligence for the whole machine kingdom we saw in the previous chapter. As happens with any behavioural feature, the lack of a representational definition (the first step, the 'person-making properties') makes things more complicated. For instance, for the broad sentiocentric approach involving the ill-defined concepts of consciousness or self-awareness, the Turing test (originally for intelligence, or humanness) can also be seen as a test for consciousness or personhood (Gunkel, 2012, p. 57). However, by comparing to a human, we would not have really solved what moral status is and how it should be measured. Similarly, the Turing triage test (Sparrow, 2004) sets a situation where only A or B can survive, and the test is past when the judge (a human or a committee of humans) determines that A (the machine) has the same (or more rights) to live than B (a human). Given our tendency of being allured by people or robots that look more emotional, childish or docile, it is dubious that these tests would actually measure a non-anthropocentric moral value (Sparrow, 2012).

When we finally address the list of 'person-making properties', we of course have several approaches. Joseph Fletcher (1979) proposed 15 criteria for 'humanhood'. The first and main criterion was intelligence; "below IQ 40 individuals might not be persons; below IQ 20 they are definitely not persons", he propounds, adorned with 14 other criteria: "self-awareness, self-control, sense of time, sense of futurity, sense of the past, capacity to relate to others, concern for others, communication with other persons, control of existence, curiosity, change and changeability, balance of rationality and feeling, idiosyncrasy, and neocortical function" (Farah and Heberlein, 2007). This is actually a mixture of the ratiocentric, sentiocentric and a white-box approach. Despite the difficulty of making an actual test from these definitions, some primatologists have signed Great Ape Movement manifestos arguing that some apes meet all of the preceding 15 criteria. Another proposal, Daniel Dennett's "Conditions of Personhood", reduces the list to six necessary conditions for personhood: rationality, mental intention, assertive stance, respectful reciprocity, verbal communication and self-consciousness (Dennett, 1988). On the other hand, some extend the list to 30 specific capacities (Smith, 2010). It is illuminating to compare these lists to those seen in the early chapters, such as the Cognitive Decathlon (Table 6.2).

None of the preceding lists seems directly operational. It is worth highlighting that we are aiming for a procedure that can be administered in a purely behavioural way, i.e., a psychometric test, to *particular subjects*. Unlike what is usual in the animal rights literature, we do not want to tell which *species* are in and out of the club. When aiming at a universal test for moral value, a machine individual, hybrid or group that comes out of the blue (e.g., in an artificial ecosystem), does not belong to a species.

The exact set of traits of moral agency and patiency, how to measure them universally, how potential abilities and self-modification can be assessed, and where to draw the line, will be a matter of constant revision, but the criteria should presumably be based on a ratiocentric core of cognitive abilities possibly with some other behavioural features. This set of features will of course include intelligence, but also the ability of 'self-modelling' (a much more operational view than the concept of self-awareness or consciousness) and the use of this self-modelling for the ability of 'self-modification'. In particular, if individuals are not capable of understanding and changing their behaviour, then they cannot be held responsible for their future actions. For instance, Henry Molaison, a man who was left with no memory capacity at all as the result of his two hippocampi being removed (Quiroga, 2012), could never *learn* and *correct* a bad behaviour, despite still having an IQ of 112. The notion of universality (a machine being capable of becoming any other machine), and its relation to free will, seen in the context of *potentiality* in Chapter 12 is most relevant here.

Keynote 17.3. Moral agency and behavioural self-modification: If a subject in the machine kingdom cannot modify its behaviour, then there is no full moral agency (and the responsibility it conveys).

This closes the circle with the etymology of the Latin word 'persona', taken from Etruscan "phersu": a mask, a role in a play. This ability of imitating others' behaviour and even changing one's own behaviour is at the roots of moral agency.

As we will see in the following section, it is expectable that many AI systems will not be granted the ability to modify their core code, because they would become unpredictable. But, if this and other limitations on its behaviour (such as the utility function) are finally imposed on them, the AI systems would not be held responsible for any of their actions either.

Finally, when thinking about moral rights, there is another significant issue worth being discussed. Are the rights being asked by the subject or by a third person, in a paternalistic way? Panel 17.2 discusses this issue.

Overall, the concept of moral value is extremely complex and its evaluation will be utterly challenging, but pervades many other issues around a future society full of cognitive robots, cyborgs, hybrid collectives and other kinds of entities. The unusual perspective of starting our discussion from this core but prickly concept will allow us to reunderstand some other issues in the rest of the chapter. For instance, from the point of view of artificial intelligence, it might be more urgent to determine when and how a machine can be considered a moral patient to prevent us from committing a crime against *it* than to determine whether it is a moral agent. Bryson (2010) and Yampolskiy (2015a) contend that AI should never build anything with moral agency or patiency. However, this is easier said than done. On purpose or not, there will eventually be some AI systems that will approach any conventional limit set on a continuum. This actually sets a high responsibility on AI but also, once the systems are out there, on those who are in charge of evaluating and certifying that an agent has a particular psychometric profile. On a current basis, psychologists and ethical committees already make thorny decisions about labour, health issues and general rights. Cognitive evaluation in the context of universal psychometrics will have an enormous responsibility in even more complicated future scenarios.

Panel 17.2
No robots in the "Society for the Liberation of Robots"

With the advent of more and more intelligent robots, Sloman (1978, Epilogue) contends that "history suggests that the invention of such robots will be followed by their exploitation and slavery, or at the very least racial discrimination against them.... There will, of course, be a Society for the Liberation of Robots, since some humans are occasionally motivated by a wish to diminish suffering and oppression". Sloman was right, and these associations are already here, such as the "American Society for the Prevention of Cruelty to Robots" (ASPCR, 1999) or the "People for the Ethical Treatment of Reinforcement Learners" (PETRL, 2015).

These organisations may be necessary in the future, as they were in the past for other collectives, especially if some of them are "voiceless" (Tomasik, 2014). Nevertheless, the case would be much stronger if some day an artificial agent itself goes to courts truly asking for its rights (Gunkel, 2012, pp. 42–43). This has been depicted in science fiction several times. For instance, in *Star Trek*'s episode "The Measure of a Man", an android fights for his rights. It has also been analysed in philosophical terms. For instance, Watt (2008) presents a fictional rewriting of Turing's 1950 paper where "the applicant, a computer, sought the rights and responsibilities due to a human being" in front of the International Court of Human Rights.

17.3 THE DIRECTIONS OF COGNITIVE MODIFICATION

In this section we will focus on the implications of cognitive modification and its evaluation. We will pay special attention to cognitively enhanced humans (as part of what we called "cognitively enhanced organisms" in Section 1.1). They are becoming a reality, being a good example of the unpredictability and diversity of the systems that we may need to evaluate.

Despite its roots in cybernetics and early ideas about intelligence amplification (Ashby, 1956) and augmented cognition (Engelbart, 1962), most research in the area of cognitive enhancement nowadays is motivated by several degenerative diseases in the elderly. Deep brain stimulations, prosthesis, transplants and transfers are being used by neuroscientists to enhance learning and memory (Hampson et al., 2012; Berger et al., 2012; Deadwyler et al., 2013; Karas et al., 2013; Hampson et al., 2013; Suthana and Fried, 2014). This goes well beyond some other (non-invasive) brain stimulation techniques and the more traditional use of psychoactive drugs, neuro-feedback and external devices (Bostrom and Sandberg, 2009), some of them under the name *cognitive orthotics* (Pollack et al., 2003). New biocybernetic enhancements are not only controlling devices with the brain – or having the brain controlled by the computer through electrodes (Yu et al., 2016) – but also coupling mental processes (e.g., learning and memory). All this "cyborg intelligence" is on top of a world that already makes any human some kind of extended mind or natural-born cyborg (Clark and Chalmers, 1998; Clark, 2004), which can be traced back to the tool-making origins of humanity, the "artifact-dependent nature of intelligence" (Preiss and Sternberg, 2005).

From the point of view of cognitive testing, Cohen (2013) raises the question of "to what extent and in what direction, if at all, we should modify testing standards and professional ethics" according to this new wave of systems. Cohen concludes that, "in the case of permanent enhancement, test validity is not in danger of corruption". This may be true for some mild enhancements nowadays, but might have a stronger effect in the future. For instance, the interpretation of a working memory test must be completely overhauled if done with a digital notepad permanently implanted in the brain.

Bostrom and Sandberg (2009) deal with the ethical issues and other challenges about what, how, who and when to enhance. What cognitive abilities should be chosen first? How is the enhancement going to be obtained? Who decides whether and when an enhancement is to be done? These questions not only apply for enhanced humans but the whole machine kingdom (including what we referred to as "biologically enhanced computers" in Section 1.1, and other hybrids and collectives).

Focusing on what to enhance, it seems that for all cognitive abilities, the more the better. In general, what to enhance depends on the psychometric profile that is desired in the first place, but also on the possible interactions with other behavioural features according to the subject (a particular human or AI system) and the enhancement method. This is why, for humans, it is argued that perfect memory would be a curse rather than a bliss (Quiroga, 2012), because some people with excellent memory have some side effects, such as the difficulty of generating abstract concepts.

Similar side effects may happen with some cognitive-enhancing drugs (nootropics), affecting personality. Actually, a person, as a result of a dramatic change in personality, may end up becoming a different person, who would be unrecognisable by her acquaintances. Behavioural biometrics (including artificial biometrics for computers, known as artimetrics, Yampolskiy and Gavrilova, 2012) may be used to determine when a person has changed (Yampolskiy and Govindaraju, 2008; Wang, 2009a).

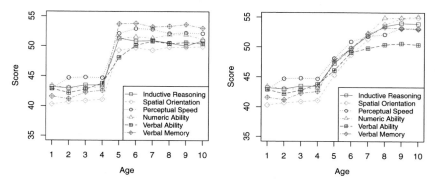

Figure 17.2.   Left: figurative evolution of some cognitive abilities after a Pareto-optimal enhancement between ages 4 and 5. Right: figurative evolution if the enhancement also involves a self-improving ability. Compare with Figure 12.2.

Despite the side effects, general intelligence seems such a coveted and central ability that its enhancement will be on the top of the list. Ivan M. Havel distinguishes between the increase of intelligence with and without change of profile (Havel, 2013). For humans, despite the centrality of g, it seems very difficult to increase all cognitive abilities in the relatively same proportion, leading to a uniformly augmented psychometric profile. For machines, however, one can easily replace the hardware by a faster one, leading to a similar profile, but faster, assuming that the profile is defined using speed as a transversal variable. In practice, a better individual (e.g., a "better machine", Havel, 2013) can just be defined with a *Pareto-optimal* enhancement, as we discussed in Chapter 15 for groups and hybrids (Keynote 15.9). Of course, if two abilities in the profile are negatively correlated, a Pareto-optimal enhancement for an individual may be impossible.

One way of obtaining a Pareto-optimal enhancement is by discovering one "improving ability", so that the "improvement of the improving ability" (Havel, 2013) would lead to an increment in many others. General intelligence, as already mentioned, might be an "improving ability". For machines, an "improving ability" could also be some kind of ability that allows the redesigning of the machine itself. In the long term, an improving ability might possibly change the dynamics of the 'lifespan psychometric profile' (Keynote 12.8), up to a limit that is always given by the given computational resources. Figure 17.2 illustrates the difference between a non-improving enhancement and an improving enhancement.

For all the preceding possibilities, psychometric assessment would be key to determine what needs to (or can) be improved and how much. After the 'treatment', psychometric tests will of course be required to analyse – in the short and long terms – whether it has worked, and whether it has affected some other abilities, or personality.

Actually, enhancement brings a new perspective to psychometrics. The origins of psychometrics and the science of intelligence were motivated by questions about the observed differences in cognitive abilities, its effect on society (Galton) or its use for a better educational therapy (Binet). Enhancement can be seen as a complement (or even an alternative) to their preferred methods: eugenics (Galton) and specialised education (Binet). Of course, if enhancement becomes general and effective, "the policy challenge might be to ensure that there are adequate safeguards, regulations, and transparency to support a society of increasingly cognitively resourceful individuals, and also to moderate unrealistic expectations of infallibility" (Bostrom and Sandberg, 2009). Moreover, the ratiocentric approach to the notion of person would be seen as more egalitarian if everyone had access to cognitive enhancements. The freedom of self-modifying (i.e., the free will of becoming another person, seen as one of the "second-order desires" of Frankfurt, 1971) would not be restricted to a few aspects of behaviour, but also to cognitive abilities.

Understandably, there will be people who will opt out and resist any kind of cognitive enhancement (including the use of external devices such as computers or the Internet) for many different reasons: the fear of potential risks, religious beliefs, etc. Despite all these potential reasons, Bostrom and Sandberg (2009) argue that "an enhancement may be entirely voluntary and yet become difficult to avoid for those who do not desire it", as it happens with some other commodities of modern society.

A widespread enhancement of cognitive abilities in AI systems seems more obvious – provided AI systems have an ability-oriented evaluation – since the program code is relatively much easier to modify or extend than the brain. Of course, today, this can be done freely, without much worry about the outcome. However, in the future, machine enhancement will have two important risks that may slow down its progress (at least for artificial general intelligence systems, i.e., ability-oriented systems). First, it may be the case that the machine – before the enhancement – is already a moral subject. In that case, the AI researcher would have to be very careful about modifying the machine's code – or even switching it off. In the end, if the agent had the ability of *self-modelling* accurately, this would be a sign that the agent may be ready for a test of personhood, making the decision itself. Second, some enhancements may lead to new AI systems with a high degree of some abilities, which may pose a potential risk for others. We will explore this second issue in the following section.

17.4 AGENTS OF RISK: THE ROLE OF EVALUATION

Almost every new technology entails new risks. Artificial intelligence is not an exception, but it is special in a number of ways. The first cause is that their products, if really intelligent, become unpredictable. But this is the interesting thing about AI products; one does not have to specify all possible situations the system will face, but just devise the system to cope with unforeseen situations in a *reasonable* way. A second cause is the strong influence of science fiction, with uncountable dystopian scenarios where robots run amok. Finally, a third cause is that the associated term 'AI ethics' has usually been understood in a very *anthropocentric* way, with respect to the threat AI can represent to humans or humanity. This contrasts with the expression "animal ethics", seen before in this chapter.

The issue of friendly or safe AI has been addressed many times in the past, since the early dystopian views were expressed by Samuel Butler in his novel Erewhon (Butler, 1872). Today, there is a renewed interest, as systems are finally learning to do tasks they were not programmed for. In 2015, hundreds of leading experts in AI signed an open letter about the 'Research priorities for robust and beneficial artificial intelligence' (Russell et al., 2015). The letter focused on four areas of robustness research: verification, validity, security and control. In the short-term research priorities, these were expressed in terms of tasks, but in the long-term research priorities, we saw concerns about the difficulty of "aligning the values of powerful AI systems with our own values and preferences", the possibility of "sophisticated agents attempt[ing] to manipulate or directly control their reward signals", methods for "specifying goals" or learning them (such as inverse reinforcement learning), etc. Actually, the letter also encouraged research on ways of determining classes of 'accelerating intelligences'.

The second part of the letter included references to thorough investigations that suggest that robust and beneficial artificial intelligence in the future may go well beyond the four preceding areas. For instance, specialised systems, which are devised for very particular tasks, could go out of control: "even if all an agent wants to do is win chess games, it may dismantle the world to get material for increasing the size of its chess brain" (Hibbard, 2015b). This 'ruthless diligence' problem can even happen with a system that does not have the ability to modify (all) its code.

The problem of controlling a system, in such a way that it can be corrected without resistance if it starts malfunctioning, is known as 'corrigibility', with no general solution to date (Soares et al., 2015). The effects of punishing a computer (understood in terms of reinforcement learning or other ways) are obscure, including the limitation of computing resources or knowledge as punishment – a kind of prison for computers. In the very same way we have legal systems for corporations, we need "precisely specified laws that constrain uncooperative systems and which can be enforced by other intelligent systems" (Omohundro, 2012). These and other problems (Hibbard, 2015b) are ultimately related to whether there is a 'universality gate' for the system. As we have discussed several times (especially in Chapter 12), if a system keeps its universality then no behaviour can be ruled out. So either we restrict universality (and some things could not be learnt and done) or we accept that some interactions may take the system out of control. Of course, for many applications, we can just make do with task-oriented – non-intelligent – AI, which can be certified to be safe. For instance, we do not want a self-driving car to have many cognitive abilities and, of course, no self-modification abilities.

Hibbard's book performs a comprehensive analysis of AGI safety (Hibbard, 2015b), showing how several approaches – starting from a reinforcement learning setting – are flawed. Similarly, from a more general perspective, Yampolskiy (2015a, Chapter 6, Table 6.1) includes an exhaustive summary of the proposed attempts to solve the dangers of (super-)intelligent machines. For instance, some general reinforcement learning systems can suffer self-delusion by 'wireheading' (when a system is able to hijack its reward system, Orseau and Ring, 2011; Ring and Orseau, 2011; Orseau, 2014, Yampolskiy, 2015a, chap. 4). Because of this, more robust utility functions, as well as self-modelling, knowledge-seeking agents and other intrinsically motivated systems have been suggested, but they are not free from other problems. Bostrom (2014), Hibbard (2015b) and Yampolskiy (2015a, chap. 8) discuss many of these problems, including a *manipulating* agent that has no access to the external world and can only be used as an oracle (the AI-confinement or AI-boxing problem, Drexler, 1986). In the end, many of these problems – used to refute each and every proposal – are variants of problems humans have faced in the past. The diligence and the self-delusion problems are closely related to drug addiction in humans and animals, with drugs being physical or psychological, perhaps as the result of brainwashing.

A relatively common aspiration of AI safety is to be able to incorporate or teach some principles (or our values) into AI systems (Dewey, 2011, Hibbard, 2015b, chap. 7). In these terms we may dream of embedding principles such as "always tell the truth", "don't do things that cannot easily be undone", or Asimov's three laws of robotics (proposed in the context of science fiction). These principles, on top of expressing "a form of racialism or speciesism" (Sloman, 2006), may not be realisable. In general, again, the same problems have taken place much before: "parents have long sought to imprint their values onto their children, with modest success" (Eden et al., 2012a, p. 41). Worst of all, we would need to first agree on a set of values, an impossible mission in the light of the diversity of world views, which would not necessarily be reflected by the handful of big corporations in AI and other actors making the deliberations (Didier et al., 2015). Even if values are chosen by democratic principles, "there are risks in trusting the collective judgment of all humans" (Hibbard, 2015b, p. 92). As an alternative, we could leave machines choose their values for them or for the whole society (Bostrom, 2014, p. 215). After all, a rigorous scientific analysis of the question would lead us to the conclusion that many of our more respected values derive from the ultimate goal of humans of maximising the number of descendants – or of preserving the species or their genes – (Morris, 1967; Dawkins, 1976, Baum, 2004, p. 393, De Waal, 2013).

For instance, humans, as intelligent beings, are also unpredictable and risky, but this also (or especially) applies to low-IQ individuals. In some countries, a high proportion of the population are or have been in jail, a subpopulation with average IQ results below the norm. In fact, a lone wolf with low IQ, brainwashed by religious fanaticism, can do a lot of harm. This does not entail that more intelligent robots have to be necessarily safer, but we should cast doubt on any solution based on limiting the intelligence of machines. Aaron Sloman seems to be of this opinion: "the more intelligent the machines are the less likely they are to produce all the dreadful behaviours motivated by religious intolerance, nationalism, racialism, greed, and sadistic enjoyment of the suffering of others" (Sloman, 2006).

Putting all together, this means that we have to consider humans as part of the 'endangering', including those artificial and hybrid collective entities whose goals get out of control very often, *the big corporations*. Also, the possibility of a generalised culture of cognitive enhancement, seen in the previous section and a possibly enlarged view of moral patients, seen in Section 17.2, creates a continuum in the machine kingdom and, as a consequence, an extension of the 'endangered':

Keynote 17.4. Machine kingdom risks: A comprehensive view of risks and threats suggests that any kind of system, including humans and computers, and any hybrid or enhancement thereof, may entail a potential risk for the rest.

Note that this perspective places humanity, strictly defined as "comprising standard unaltered humans" (Yampolskiy, 2015a, p. 188) as *agents* of risk, and no longer as the only *patients* of risk.

Apart from how far we might go with the subjects and objects of risk, how can we estimate the danger of any possible entity in the machine kingdom? Instead of expecting a one hundred per cent verification, a more general assessment based on quantitative psychometric profiles looks more propitious. Of course, which cognitive abilities and personality traits constitute a safe psychometric profile universally is today a matter of speculation, but the existence of such a kind of assessment for humans encourages a generalisation.

17.5 SUPERINTELLIGENCE

The discussion about AI risks has old, deep roots in philosophy and the social sciences. However, it now seems to be dominated by a concept I have resisted dealing with until this point. Nowadays it is very common that any panel discussion about the existential risks of humanity will ultimately include the terms 'intelligence explosion', 'technological singularity' and 'superintelligences'. We will discuss these ideas in passing here – with the due dose of scepticism – from the point of view of intelligence evaluation.

The first pervasive fallacy that underlies some of these ideas is the view of intelligence in a monolithic view, which, moreover, usually confounds the subject with the cognitive ability itself. For the sake of exposition of the original concepts, and before presenting non-monolithic alternatives, I will keep the term 'intelligence' and 'superintelligence' to refer to subjects, even in plural, despite the aberration.

A second common misconception is the view that the universe in general, and evolution in particular, have a goal. The teleological view of the universe in this case would be reunderstood as some kind of 'superintelligence' (or 'supreme intelligence'), which evolution is heading to, in an accelerating pace. It would be enough to compare the *Homo sapiens* with the early forms of life to 'see' this happening. For instance, Alfred Wallace, who was characterised by eccentric opinions, wrote: "The grand law of continuity which we see pervading our universe, would lead us to infer infinite gradations of existence, and to people all space with intelligence and will-power; and, if so, we have no difficulty in believing that for so noble a purpose as the progressive development of higher and higher intelligences, those primal and general will-forces, which have sufficed for the production of the lower animals, should have been guided into new channels and made to converge in definite directions" (Wallace, 1870, p. 370).

All in all, the vision of an accelerating universe has spread in a number of ways, but the notion of "intelligence explosion" is at the centre of many of them, as discussed in Panel 17.3.

Panel 17.3
Intelligence explosion?

Henry Adams, one of the earlier advocates of a "Law of Acceleration", with which technology and knowledge are speeding up as the result of the progress of humanity, said in 1904 that by the year 2000, "every American" would "think in complexities unimaginable to an earlier mind" (Adams, 1904). Stanisław Ulam reported a conversation with John von Neumann also witnessing "the ever accelerating progress of technology and changes in the mode of human life, which gives the appearance of approaching some essential singularity in the history of the race beyond which human affairs, as we know them, could not continue" (Ulam, 1958).

When machines entered the equation, it was no longer the average American but the machine that would think in extraordinary ways. Turing wrote that "once the machine thinking method had started, it would not take long to outstrip our feeble powers" (Turing, 1948). Irving J. Good put it this way: "Let an ultraintelligent machine be defined as a machine that can far surpass all the intellectual activities of any man however clever. Since the design of machines is one of these intellectual activities, an ultraintelligent machine could design even better machines; there would then unquestionably be an 'intelligence explosion', and the intelligence of man would be left far behind. Thus the first ultraintelligent machine is the last invention that man need ever make" (Good, 1965). These ideas were popularised under the term "technological singularity" (Vinge, 1993).

The so-called technological singularity is a concept that has many different interpretations and can lead to radically opposite "singularity hypotheses" (Eden et al., 2012a), including the concept of a never-ending technological acceleration (such as Adam's "Law of Acceleration", 1904), an intelligence explosion (Good, 1965), a 'superintelligence' (Hibbard, 2002; Bostrom, 2014; Shanahan, 2015), an 'infinity point' (Solomonoff, 1985), or a combination (or the sum) of several of them with other futuristic predictions (Kurzweil, 2005). The consequences of each of the "singularity hypotheses" are diverse, ranging from utopias (such as immortality and superconsciousness through 'mind uploading', Kowalski, 2012, p. 9) to dystopias (human extinction), in both cases frequently expecting "the machines to take control, in the way that is mentioned in Samuel Butler's 'Erewhon'" (Turing, 1948).

At this moment, despite the usefulness of the analysis of the range of possibilities, it is too soon to tell whether any of these hypotheses will become true and whether they will ultimately lead to dystopian or utopian outcomes – and for whom (for the *Homo sapiens* as a species, for the 'superintelligence' or for civilisation as a whole). Still, we can aim to define some of the key concepts involved, set some objective criteria and investigate technologies that make us able to detect and anticipate 'superabilities'.

Once more, intelligence evaluation in particular, and universal psychometrics in general, are called to have a relevant role here. For instance, without a proper characterisation and measurement of the particular 'superintelligence' *profile* used for any singularity hypotheses, any theory or prediction becomes unfalsifiable. One of the many definitions of 'superintelligence' is given in terms of "a quantitative measure of intelligence", and the singularity upon it, where "a graph measuring average intelligence beyond the singularity in terms of IQ score may display some form of radical discontinuity if superintelligence emerges" (Eden et al., 2012b). Note the reference to *average* intelligence and the use of an "IQ score", despite the doubts we raised in Section 6.3 about the use of IQ tests beyond standard humans. More recently, Eden has become more critical about the use of IQ tests (Eden, 2016) and Bostrom has recognised our "lack of experience with any variations in intelligence quality above the upper end of the present human distribution" (Bostrom, 2014, p. 56). If we look at Figure 17.2 (right), where self-improvement takes place, the curve still plateaus because the computational resources of the system are considered constant. An intelligence explosion is usually represented with an exponential curve, which considers that the system will be able to take resources at an exponential rate and indefinitely, a position that may clash with some of our current physical knowledge about energy on Earth and in the universe.

Of course, about the need for proper evaluation tools, there are also different opinions. On one hand, Eden et al. (2012a, p. 5) contend that a precise psychometric profile and its associated measurement tools are not necessary for philosophical or futuristic arguments for (and against) 'superintelligence' or an intelligence explosion. Similarly, "Chalmers [2010] argues carefully that, in order for the 'intelligence explosion' argument to go through, one doesn't need a precise definition of general intelligence – one only needs the existence of one or more quantities that are correlated with flexible practical capability and that can be increased via increase of said capabilities. How these various quantities are used to create a composite, single general intelligence measure is something that doesn't need to be resolved in order to argue for an intelligence explosion" (Loosemore and Goertzel, 2012). On the other hand, McDermott (2007) holds that measurement techniques are needed even at a non-technical level: "arguments such as Kurzweil's that exponential growth in computer science is bound to produce superhuman intelligence, and breath-takingly fast as we near that apotheosis, are flawed by the fact that we don't know what we're measuring". The need for "a metric that can measure the intelligence of different AIs effectively" is now advocated for by Eden (2016).

Focusing on 'superintelligence', Nick Bostrom rephrases it as "any intellect that greatly exceeds the cognitive performance of humans in virtually all domains of interest" (Bostrom, 2014, p. 22). There rests the question of defining a psychometric profile that includes all domains of interest and whether a Pareto-optimal increase is possible for that profile. Related to our previous discussion of enhancement possibilities, Bostrom (2014, chap. 3) distinguishes several types of 'superintelligences': "speed superintelligence: a system that can do all that a human intellect can do, but much faster", "collective super-intelligence: a system composed of a large number of smaller intellects such that the system's overall performance across many very general domains vastly outstrips that of any current cognitive system" and "quality superintelligence: a system that is at least as fast as a human mind and vastly qualitative smarter". About 'quality superintelligence', he says that it refers to "*humanly* relevant complex cognitive tasks" (Bostrom, 2014, p. 56, his italics). Since the concept of higher quality is blurry, he suggests considering non-human animals by saying that "the concept of quality superintelligence ... is intelligence of quality at least as superior to that of human intelligence as the quality of human intelligence is superior to that of elephants', dolphins', or chimpanzees'" (Bostrom, 2014, p. 57).

Still with these blurry notions, Bostrom (2014, chap. 4) contemplates the "kinetics" of superintelligence growth, even if the quantity ("system capability", as shown on the plots) is not well defined and no measurement instruments are recognised. Bostrom also talks about "superpowers" (Bostrom, 2014, chap. 6), but he dismisses the "measurement of cognitive capacity that could be applied to a wider range of information-processing systems, including artificial intelligence" because, for his investigation, "its usefulness would be limited since we would remain unenlightened about what a given superhuman performance score entails for actual ability to achieve practically important outcomes in the world" (Bostrom, 2014, p. 93). This does not only immerse us in the subjectivism previous to the introduction of psychometrics, but seems unaware of the evidence that the results of psychometric evaluation are linked to important outcomes in the world, as psychometrics has demonstrated with the g factor and many other tests and indicators. In the end, Bostrom (2014, Table 8, p. 94) goes for a task-oriented approach for his notion of "superpowers", including tasks such as "intelligence amplification", "strategizing", "social manipulation", "hacking", "technological research" and "economic productiv[ity]", each of them associated with a set of skills. Neither the tasks nor the skills are well shaped from the point of view of measuring. For instance, it is dubious whether they can stand as independent or even different skills. Should the "AI programming" skills actually be different from the skills required to the "design and modeling advanced technologies", or the "skills enabling economically productive intellectual work"? Furthermore, it is unclear whether they are quantifiable. As a result, these "superpowers" cannot be understood as "superabilities" in the cognitive sense.

Yampolskiy (2015a) is also one of the very few works about superintelligence that pays significant attention to evaluation. The approach, however, is too monolithic as well, based on the notion of AI-completeness, which is closely related to anthropocentric perspectives such as HLMI or the CAPTCHAS (see Chapters 5 and 6), not extrapolatable beyond human intelligence.

When these appraisals are compared to the scrutiny we have performed throughout the book to find absolute measures that can scale up universally, it follows that the definition of abilities (and other behavioural features) from first principles is not only desirable but necessary for the new scenarios:

> **Keynote 17.5. Ability extrapolation**: Only a principled, representational measure of intelligence, and other cognitive abilities, makes it possible to extrapolate beyond human intelligence in a meaningful way.

An important variable in the analysis of any 'superability' is the role of difficulty. Our definition of difficulty seen in Chapter 8 is on a logarithmic scale. This means that a linear increase in intelligence may require an exponential amount of resources. For instance, ignoring constants, finding a policy just one bit longer would require doubling the computational power (as we saw in Keynote 15.8). Even assuming that the acceleration fuelled by self-improvement with accompanying increasing resources led to an exponential curve, the increase in intelligence would still be linear. This even sounds convenient: "given the potential for exponential increases in AI, it may make sense to use tests that can adapt to the intelligence level being tested and rely on logarithmic scales to gauge and track them" (Yonck, 2012). In any case, in terms of general intelligence, what does it mean that a 'superintelligence' can find concepts of difficulty 20 in the same time we are able to find those of difficulty 10? What does it imply to have 1,000 times more memory, if we have access to the Internet? We can well quantify some of the extrapolations in terms of computational space and time, but things become more complex when thinking about psychometric profiles that improve in other quantitative ways or even in qualitative ways. Indeed, the (desirable or expectable) personality traits of a 'superintelligence' will also be a mere speculation, especially because any personality trait can be imitated with sufficient intelligence and self-control.

Without absolute measures, the very notion of intelligence may even become paradoxical, a kind of Carrollian red queen's race. For instance, if other intelligence entities also increase their abilities, the *relative* superiority of any superintelligence would vanish. Basically, in any asynchronous interactive game, if all the participants get their speed doubled, the result will be exactly the same as if nothing had been changed. A similar point is made by Hutter (2012a), who distinguishes between insiders and outsiders of a society of increasingly more intelligent agents. Social intelligence, as we saw in Chapter 13 around the concept of the Darwin-Wallace distribution, develops when the other peers also feature general and social intelligence. To what extent any so-called superintelligence may have a great amount of general intelligence without also being equipped with an increased social intelligence, depends on what scenario for society and distribution of intelligence is considered. This is explored next.

17.6 DEMOGRAPHY, DEMOCRACY AND INTELLIGENCE

Any local perspective on moral values, risks, intelligence growth and other related issues is going to be blind to the global interactions of a society. The distribution of intelligence (profiles, average and diversity of intelligent entities) on Earth is not only changing already (as it always has) but is going to change radically in the years to come. In terms of cognitive *profiles*, this has already been happening with humans in the past decades. There seems to be a "strengthening performance in tests involving the mental rotation of geometric forms, the identification of similarities between disparate objects and the arrangement of shapes into logical sequences. Tests of memorization, vocabulary, general knowledge, and even basic arithmetic have shown little or no improvement" (Carr, 2011). This can be explained by changes in education, society, video games, devices and the so-called Google effect (Sparrow et al., 2011), as we saw in Section 1.1, with our brains moving cognitive efforts from tasks that are no longer very necessary to other more common kinds of tasks. With the advent of more intelligent machines, enhanced humans and other entities, cognitive profiles may suffer a radical transformation.

Panel 17.4
"It's the demography, stupid"

In a 2006 article for strong stomachs, Mark Steyn, who represents a non-marginal political opinion, contended that "the West is in danger of extinction" because of demographics. The argument relied on the birth rate of "non-Western" populations being much higher than those of "the West".

Despite the shaky argument (at least if one considers China a non-Western country, and the Amish a Western population), demography is a catchy argument here since 'the survival of the fittest' principle is almost non-existent in many countries, and fertility rate is now the most relevant variable affecting human evolution. Under these conditions, it is relatively easy to make some simple numbers that show that any minority (religious) group with a relatively high fertility rate can become a majority in very few generations. And, of course, the "one human one vote" principle would soon lead to a situation where those ideologies promoting high offspring would get all the power.

A similar alarmist argument can be made in terms of dysgenics. In a matter of a few generations, if the correlation between fertility and intelligence remains negative, the average intelligence of the population would decrease significantly. From here, it is not a surprise that eugenics and other ways of population (counter-)'balance' (see Section 3.8) are again on the table.

Let us use the term *extant personity* to refer to the distribution of all extant entities in the machine kingdom that are considered persons – which, for most people, coincides now to the extant humanity. By looking at this distribution, we already saw in Section 3.8 that the past decades have been characterised by the Flynn effect and a more recent negative Flynn effect (Panel 3.3). One explanation of the latter is the inverse correlation between fertility rates and intelligence, which cannot be compensated with natural selection, as the *survival* of the fittest has ceased to act in developed countries. Some people have alerted about the possibility of a dysgenic situation (Lynn, 1996). Unfortunately, in this delicate issue, scientific analyses are usually accompanied by inflammatory positions and misinterpretations, such as the ones depicted in Panel 17.4.

As a counter-argument to the alarmist dysgenic scenarios (which are very similar to those that concerned eugenicists such as Francis Galton about human populations and Samuel Butler about machine populations in the ninetenth century), one can argue that the average intelligence of a population is perhaps not the best predictor of its success or stability. The most intelligent individuals usually have more relevance and influence than the rest. So, perhaps it is not the average that counts, but the highest percentiles of the intelligence distribution, as we saw in Chapter 15 with several crowd or team organisations (Section 15.2). Indeed, even if animals are considered in the *extant personity*, any change in their distribution would have a limited effect, since their intelligence is far from the maximum (humans). In the future, a small group of people with access to important enhancements or computation power can have more impact on society than all the rest. This is in fact very similar to what we already see with a few corporations, which, *enhanced* by the use of massive data analysis tools that monopolise or oligopolise a great part of the computer power on Earth, are able to make strategic decisions and have strong influence over billions of people.

As a consequence, we should also look at the variability of the population. Hibbard (2015a) writes that "among current humans, with naturally evolved brains, IQ has a normal distribution. When brains are artifacts, their intelligence is likely to have a power law distribution". As an extreme case of this power law, some argue that a likely outcome is that intelligence is ultimate concentrated in a "singleton", one dominant country, corporation or entity with "superintelligence" or "hyperintelligence" (Bostrom, 2014, chap. 5). The likelihood of a singleton, any other concentrated scenario (an oligopoly or "multipolar" situation) or a more even distribution will of course depend on *who* has the right to create new intelligent entities, *what* to create (in terms of a psychometric profile) and how many. When referring to 'who' and 'what', we include humans, corporations, hybrids or computers. Any possibility, from a wild universal Darwinism to a strict universal eugenic control cannot be, in principle, ruled out.

A final variable for this puzzle is whether some non-human *persons* are being granted the right to vote and whether vote power is going to be uniform. Giving the right to vote to a computer does not seem to be very popular at the beginning of the twenty-first century. Yampolskiy (2015a, p. 140) states that doing so would lead to machines dominating the world as "given the predicted number of robots in the next few decades and the ease of copying potentially intelligent software, a society with voting artificially intelligent members will quickly become dominated by them". The position of Levin (1997) on this issue is very different: "Computers keep eroding our monopoly on intellectual power, as gas and electricity did with our physical powers before. Future democracies would have to incorporate intelligent agents much more diverse than humans. Even now the 'one man - one vote' principle equates Einstein and someone who never bothered to work or even to take his child to a zoo. It requires caution, more so if we have an ambition to carry our ideas of civilized society into the centuries to come".

The suggestion of a weighted voting system depending on intelligence is not a new thing in psychometrics, which was even considered a conspiracy (Terman, 1922). However, if an unweighted voting system is used, and computers are given the right to vote above some level of intelligence, the pressure would be set on building as many intelligent machines as possible with the minimum requirements. Still, this rationale is simplistic. With a non-monolithic view of intelligence it may be better to increase social abilities and use the vote of other intelligent entities through manipulation (according to the view of social intelligence as a kind of extension or enhancement). In contrast, a weighted voting system may solve some of these problems but may create many others. Indeed, it would be considered ethically unfair by many, especially those with lowest intelligence. In the end, democracy is not only characterised by voting, but by protecting the minorities and those that are weaker, in whatever sense.

A final surmise that may survive a straight refutation can consist of a weighted voting system with the right of cognitive enhancement for the whole population. An ability-based enhancement would also be motivated by a principle of minimising or reducing inequality in terms of cognitive abilities (or simply in terms of general intelligence, especially if there is a universal g factor). Note that the reduction of inequality should not be extended to other features, as diversity in knowledge, personality and organisation is beneficial for collective decisions, as seen in Chapter 15. Focusing on *gradient* behavioural features, Bostrom and Sandberg (2009) write: "one scenario might be that the talent gap decreases because it turns out to be generally easier to enhance individuals at the low end of the performance spectrum than those at the high end". Beyond this, and extending this principle to all living entities with moral value (the 'extant personity'), one could set a voluntary lower bound and a compulsory upper bound for enhancements. If these two bounds are not too far away, weighting would not be needed any more. In the end, this would become an anti-inequality, anti-monopoly law of intelligence, as described in Panel 17.5.

This scenario, based on cognitive enhancement, is 'eupsychic' rather than eugenic, and would require systematic evaluation policies, in order to determine who is granted an enhancement – which would be traceable in terms of computational power or energy allowance. If any extremely ratiocentric scenario resembling this one is ever set in practice, universal psychometrics would be a necessity.

Panel 17.5
Anti-monopoly laws for intelligence

If intelligence is seen as a power asset, anti-monopoly laws can well be adapted to prevent oligopolies and regulate the "intellectual property" of the creators of increasingly more intelligent entities. Some kind of Gini coefficient for intelligence could be used, setting an inequality limit on the *extant personity* distribution.

This is related to the "Red Queen's Hypothesis of Balance of Intelligence" (Koene, 2012), which states that, "in a system dominated by a sufficient number of similarly adaptive agents, the improvements of agents take place in a balance of competition and collaboration that maintains relative strengths between leading agents".

Even if intelligence or the whole psychometric profile of an entity is not ultimately used for determining its rights or resources, there will anyway be pressures for cheating. These could be counteracted by judicious or otherwise excessive measures resembling 1984's Big Brother (Orwell, 1949), robopsychologist Susan Calvin (Asimov, 1950) or Neuromancer's Turing police (Gibson, 1984), crossing the lines of the right of privacy about the evaluation results and the right of not being evaluated.

This struggle between future evaluators and evaluees is lavishly depicted by Stanisław Lem, with whom we conclude the most speculative chapter of this book. "A smart machine will first consider which is more worth its while: to perform the given task or, instead, to figure some way out of it. Whichever is easier. And why indeed should it behave otherwise, being truly intelligent? For true intelligence demands choice, internal freedom. And therefore we have the malingerants, fudgerators and drudge-dodgers, not to mention the special phenomenon of simulimbecility or mimicretinism. A mimicretin is a computer that plays stupid in order, once and for all, to be left in peace. And I found out what dissimulators are: they simply pretend that they're *not* pretending to be defective. Or perhaps it's the other way around. The whole thing is very complicated" (Lem, 1971).

CHAPTER HIGHLIGHTS

- Challenging the equation "human=person" (Keynote 17.1) being better understood in terms of moral agency and patiency (Figure 17.1).
- From the several criteria for moral value (Table 17.1), ratiocentrism being particularly explanatory if we distinguish between actual and potential cognitive abilities (Keynote 17.2).
- The capability of changing one's own behaviour (self-modification) decisive for moral agency (Keynote 17.3).
- Cognitive enhancement of a feature having effects on others, immediately or progressively, as for self-improving abilities (e.g., general intelligence) (Figure 17.2, Section 17.3).
- An enlarged view of agents and patients in terms of risk, posited instead of the more restricted AI safety or AI ethics viewpoints (Keynote 17.4).
- Superintelligence hypotheses not falsifiable unless a non-monolithic, principled measure of cognitive abilities is used for ability extrapolation (Keynote 17.5).
- The 'extant personity', consisting of all the existing elements of the machine kingdom considered minds (moral subjects) requiring regulations (e.g., anti-monopoly laws, Panel 17.5) and continual psychometric evaluation.

18

Exploitation and Exploration

> It may someday happen . . . that the fields of artificial and human
> intelligence will grow closer together, each learning from the other.
> – Douglas K. Detterman,
> *A Challenge to Watson* (2011)

NO MORE NEW measurement problems need to be concocted. There are too many already out there, and many more are coming that we cannot foresee. It is now time to resolve whether the principles and techniques in this book are going to accelerate the solutions to these problems, through actual measurement tools. To raise the likelihood of a positive answer, we recount the things that the book leaves as open questions, clarify the learnt lessons and determine the priorities and dimensions of the work that is to be done. At a more general level, we also address some other questions around the several disciplines dealing with the evaluation of behavioural features: Will universal psychometrics help to bridge them? What new possibilities and applications are envisaged from a further integration?

18.1 NEW GROUNDS

The conscientious reader who has reached this point – after going through the previous chapter – may get the wrong impression that we are aiming at far-flung problems. Universal psychometrics was not motivated by speculative scenarios of a world that does not yet exist and may never do. Neither was universal psychometrics motivated by any important disfunction of human psychometrics in their traditional applications. State-of-the-art psychometric tests, if well chosen and administered, produce accurate and valid measurements on human individuals. The real instigation behind universal psychometrics was a series of

measurement needs that we are already facing, most (but not all) of them originating from new kinds of cognitive entities that were not present just a few
years ago.

Of course, artificial intelligence is greatly responsible for these peremptory
needs, for its creating many new kinds of entities and its immaturity about their
measurement. However, other needs originate from humans, computers and
collectives whose abilities are modified by the use and dependency on external
devices. Cognitively enhanced organisms and biologically enhanced computers, which are created by new forms of communication and integration, add
to the machine kingdom. As we anticipated in the first part of the book, all
this heterogeneity poses a challenge to traditional psychometric techniques. In
addition, the anonymity and virtuality of many of the new so-called *artificial
ecosystems* imply that the information about the class of subject to be evaluated is usually very limited, if not completely absent. The widespread use of
CAPTCHAs nowadays, struggling to infer the class of an anonymous user, is
a clear symptom of this phenomenon.

In the second part of the book, we analysed to what extent the main disciplines dealing with the evaluation of behaviour – human psychometrics, comparative psychology and AI evaluation – could be applied or expanded to cover
the new measurement problems. The answer was mostly negative; in the same
way many principles and tools used for humans do not work for animals, these
would not work for machines or hybrids. The perspective of the machine kingdom helped understand that the principles of all the conventional approaches
were either based on a population (to which the subject is expected to belong)
or openly anthropocentric (whose extrapolations to other kinds of subjects are
mere speculation). The machine kingdom was also regarded as a powerful fal-
sification tool: whenever a new test is considered, a single specimen in the
machine kingdom could falsify the test (and the theories and principles under-
neath). A different, more solid, foundation coping with such a menacing razor
was needed.

The third part of the book developed these new foundations upon algorithmic
information theory. The notion of difficulty was determined crucial, as it has
always been in the tradition of human psychometrics, finally vindicated in its
full splendour by item response theory. Unlike in human psychometrics, difficulty is no longer derived from the results of a population of subjects, but rather
theoretically derived from the task as the logarithm of the number of computational steps that are required to find a solution, using Levin's universal search.
Not only is this a natural interpretation in computational terms, but it also
leads to a measurement unit: *logarithm of number of computational steps*. The

Table 18.1. IQ and the *g* factor compared with some universal alternatives.

	Human Population	Universal
Agglomerative	IQ	Task-general intelligence
Solutional	*g* factor	Policy-general intelligence

generation of tests and the derived indicators were inspired by refurbished versions of item response theory concepts, such as item characteristic curves, agent characteristic curves and discriminating power. Despite the different foundations, the concepts and terminology were meant to be familiar to the psychometric tradition, as so was the way of deriving item pools from them and building adaptive tests. The analysis of the space of abilities in a hierarchical way reaching a *g* factor at the top, even if not fully developed, resembles a widespread paradigm in psychometrics. However, the new arrangement is based on theoretical similarities between abilities using algorithmic information theory, instead of the empirical analysis of a (human or animal) population, based on factor analysis.

The decomposition that we saw in the bottom of Figure 9.7 through difficulty slicing presents an alternative to the task aggregation approach, where intelligence can now be measured for a range of policies rather than tasks. This novel view, and its comparison with the IQ and *g* approaches, as discussed in Section 11.4 (Keynote 11.9), is now summarised in Table 18.1. The policy-general intelligence with a uniform distribution for all policies of the same difficulty would represent our best approach so far towards a notion of general intelligence that is independent of both the subject and the task distributions.

The analysis went far beyond the elementary tasks, up to covering, in principle, a wide variety of features, constructed and arranged according to task similarity. However, the techniques were shown insufficient – alone – for the construction of a fully fledged psychometric profile including all cognitive abilities and personality traits. Finding isolated policies in uninhabited environments is insightful, but is an idealistic scenario. Not surprisingly, we saw that artificial systems are able to solve these tasks better than humans, but are not intelligent. Their success in some tests of this kind (e.g., inductive inference) clearly refutes these tests as a sufficient account of intelligence.

The fourth part of the book explored the remaining ingredients that can make a psychometric profile more comprehensive. The first ingredient is development, most especially the way a system can solve more and more complex problems by the use of the components and concepts that have been learnt for previous problems. Tests must measure this ability of incremental acquisition of knowledge, by mental search, demonstration or transmission. Here we entered the realms of social environments, collective intelligence and language. We advocated for situated tests and abilities that can be linked to first principles, although the involvement of many other agents makes things much more convoluted.

Overall, this is a new foundation from which universal and non-universal measurement tools can be derived. These should help progress in the many new (and some old) questions that were identified as *ignoramuses* in Panel 1.3. Some of them can only be properly understood – and their sheer complexity fully quantified – with some of the principles and tools that are found in this book.

It is also necessary to recognise several shortcomings, hopefully imputed to deficiencies in fully developing, integrating and transmitting the key ideas, rather than to a fundamental flaw in the foundational issues. Fortunately, most of this book also explains the ideas of many others. Even from the most pessimistic stance about universal psychometrics, this book can still be regarded as a comprehensive state of the art of the evaluation of artificial and natural intelligence in an integrated way. In the end, the book can also be understood as a view of cognition, and intelligence in particular, through the prism of evaluation.

Among the general shortcomings, we can start from those related to the very possibility of universal psychometrics, and the feasibility of universal tests. As discussed in Chapter 16, if universal tests are not possible (not even as an ideal), universal psychometrics can still be understood as an integrated paradigm to construct tests for particular subsets of the machine kingdom. In other words, even if we cannot use the same ruler for all, at least we can use the same principles to construct all the particular rulers.

Among the more specific shortcomings, the notion of discriminating power is admittedly very intricate and it may ultimately depend on the definition of a distribution of agents. The good news is that this distribution can be defined theoretically. The arrangement of the space of abilities has also been one of the hardest and most controversial aspects in the book and inherits the volatility of this long-lasting problem, since Ramon Llull hesitated between 9 or 16 attributes (or principia) in his Ars Magna (Figure 1.2). At present, despite some new theoretical tools to address the problem, we do not yet have an agreed set of features for the definition of psychometric profiles. Similarly, we are not able to give a resolute answer to the question of whether there is a universal g factor and a corresponding notion of general intelligence, though the analysis suggests that this could be the case. Nonetheless, we can now commit ourselves to the fabulous opportunity to confirm or refute the systematic findings about the *g* factor and other correlations between abilities, by checking them theoretically or on various (populations of) machines, to determine whether the correlations are necessary or conjunctural.

18.2 THE IMPACT OF UNIVERSAL PSYCHOMETRICS

There have been several calls in the past for a further integration of all the disciplines dealing with the evaluation of behavioural features. This could have been the duty of cognitive science, the wide umbrella that covers every area of cognition. The truth is, as we saw in Chapter 6, that such an integration has not happened for evaluation. So, why should universal psychometrics help in that integration?

As we have mentioned, universal psychometrics was not motivated by the proposal of a "new psychometrics" (Kline, 1998) or a "grand unification theory of intelligence" (Flynn, 2007). However, in this book we have shown that a more representational approach to psychometrics can be done, where abilities and, most especially, difficulty can have a more solid ground. Nevertheless, this does not mean that we should consider human psychometrics a "pathological science" (Michell, 2000, 2008), just because most of its instruments lack a measurement unit or a ratio scale measurement. This also happens in other sciences.

Universal psychometrics may actually bring several underpinnings to human psychometrics and be useful to quell many of the criticisms that have accompanied psychometrics since its early days. In other words, universal psychometrics is not disruptive but compatible with human psychometrics. It explains a number of issues about task and instance difficulty, brings new ideas on issues such as social intelligence and personality and sets a different – theoretical rather than empirical – way of analysing abilities and their relationship. This may also help to put some order, or distance, to the avalanche of relatively recent unorthodox ideas, such as the theories of multiple intelligences, emotional intelligence and the Mozart effect. Despite their lack of adequate empirical support (Waterhouse, 2006; Murphy, 2006), these theories are often regarded as a response to some fundamental issues of the traditional, and still mainstream, scientific view of intelligence around IQ tests and the *g* factor (Gottfredson, 1997a).

In 2004, Susan E. Embretson made a forecast of ability testing for the twenty-first century. She emphasised that the "most fundamental principles in psychometrics and testing were available by 1930" and the rest of the twentieth century "was devoted to applying or refining these principles" (Embretson, 2004). She predicted that the twenty-first century is expected to follow the same pattern. For the first decade after her forecast, it seems that she has been right. Most of the recent developments have turned around new ways of administration, new procedures of developing items (automatically), better item pool management techniques and more powerful data analysis methods. Unsurprisingly, as far as the subjects to be measured do not change significantly, the progress will be of incremental nature. However, whenever the scope is enlarged to cover other kinds of subjects, to challenge systems like IBM Watson (Detterman, 2011) or truly evaluate enhanced humans with all their devices and social connections, some principles will need to be overhauled.

Paul Barrett, in a response to Embretson, is surprised that "in an article dedicated to 'ability testing', it is strange to find no technical definition of what exactly is said to constitute 'an ability'" (Barrett, 2004). This struggle between the definition of a task and the construction (or fabrication) of an ability is well exemplified by Barrett: "is the observed behavior that characterizes the solving of matrix-type problems the result of a single 'ability' to do so, or the result of multiple abilities being applied to a problem solution to achieve a final unitary item response?" This question has no fulfilling answer in psychometrics, and models have to make do with latent factors and their relations, inferred by factor analysis from a human population. Certainly, in this book, the definition of ability and the full theoretical characterisation of how abilities are related is just an embryo, but it goes in the direction of a "reconceptualization of what actually might constitute an ability, or intelligence" (Barrett, 2004). Even in those other appraisals of the "future of psychometrics" focusing on practice rather than foundations, we ultimately find the same problem, already emphasised by Boring in 1923, again and again: "as long as tests are not based on well-developed substantive attribute theory, validity will remain a problem and it will remain appealing to ask what the test can do – no doubt a sensible question – rather than what it measures – a prerequisite for asking sensible questions about utility" (Sijtsma, 2012).

Given this debate, universal psychometrics can encourage human psychometrics to look again at its principles and try to make them more computational. In the everyday evaluation practice, however, the impact will likely be very small, if any. As we discussed in Chapter 16, no-one would advocate for the everyday use of universal tests for humans, in the same way no-one currently thinks of putting a universal quantum thermometer (Purdy et al., 2016) under their armpit. The more information we have about a subject (species, culture, brain scanning or genetic information) the better for finding the most appropriate test to get an efficient and reliable measurement. Standard psychometric tests for humans (adaptive or not) will, for the years to come, be the best choice for standard humans.

Similarly, the evaluation of behavioural features in the animal kingdom and for other living beings is not expected to be significantly affected in the near future. The goals of comparative psychology are chiefly scientific, i.e., to understand how animals behave and what their differences are.

Nevertheless, the view of the machine kingdom as a more general space for exploration and refutation has already been witnessed by comparative cognition, whenever the analysis of behavioural tests moved from humans to animals. Many tests for humans did not work for animals, not only because of interface or culture issues, but also because of the way cognitive processes work in different animals. In fact, we have seen that some animals can surpass humans in some memory tasks, and the scales derived from human populations are meaningless for them. In a way, it is universal psychometrics which has benefited from the way animals are evaluated, because of the already enlarged view of animal cognition.

Things are very different for the more immature area of AI evaluation. Even for the case of task-oriented evaluation we find many limitations and bad practices, which are possibly originated by the view of AI as an engineering discipline: AI systems, when incorporated into commercial systems, are *validated*, not really *evaluated* in a cognitive way. Many of the criticisms about AI failing to meet its grandiose goals of true intelligence after decades of research actually derive from the lack of a sound theory of how AI artefacts have to be evaluated – and what has to be measured. Every major scientific discipline requires a proper evaluation branch.

Truthfully, every now and then, some group of researchers rallies to give relevance to AI evaluation and tries to solve the problem. Alexander Meystel, the main promoter behind the series of workshops on the Performance Metrics for Intelligent Systems (PerMIS), justified them because "the challenge of evaluating intelligence of [AI] systems remains an active problem to be resolved in the upcoming decade" (Meystel, 2000b). Despite the progress in task-oriented evaluation, the last PerMIS workshop in 2012 left the problem mostly unsolved. Why is it going to be different now?

The advent and progress of the areas of reinforcement learning, artificial general intelligence and mental development are setting the emphasis on a different kind of AI system, a general-purpose agent and a different kind of evaluation, feature-oriented evaluation. Universal psychometrics aims at this feature-oriented evaluation, based on computational grounds, with a strong influence of the multi-agent systems paradigm in the analysis of social and collective

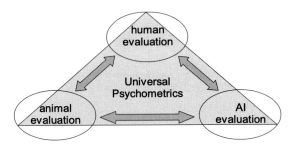

Figure 18.1. Tools, concepts and tests brought across disciplines through universal psychometrics. Compare with Figure 6.1.

intelligence. This sets universal psychometrics in a good position to help AI evaluation progress in new directions. Of course, this will depend on the creation of actual benchmarks and tests that really work for the evaluation of AI artefacts, keeping the consistency with the rest of the machine kingdom, including humans.

Overall, as we discussed in Chapter 6, universal psychometrics is not postulated as a superdiscipline generalising all others but rather as a transversal or central area enabling the exchange of theories, techniques and methodologies between the other disciplines. This is illustrated in Figure 18.1.

18.3 COPING WITH DEMANDS

Classical psychometrics has been applied in three main areas: diagnostic assessment for clinical therapy (e.g., identifying mental disabilities and other psychological conditions), education (e.g., detecting the developmental needs and the aptitudes for each individual at different educational levels) and personnel selection (e.g., filling a post with the appropriate employee). We can now think about these three areas with new kinds of subjects, such as enhanced humans, hybrids and computers.

In diagnostic assessment, we are already aware of the side effects of several technological enhancements on human minds – the "shallows" (Carr, 2011). Nevertheless, these changes on human cognitive profiles are not so radical to require but an adaptation of traditional psychometric techniques even if new pathologies appear. In the case of AI systems, beyond their verification in the laboratory, tests may be used to detect when something goes wrong *at the cognitive level*, such as a robotic pet losing its ability to learn or its personality changing in unexpected ways.

The situation is more interesting in the area of education. Many educational systems still evaluate students as if they were disconnected from the rest of the world. This is done for practical reasons, such as avoiding cheating. However, a student can get used to work with her mobile phone, Internet, social networks, etc., and only perform well in that context. Whilst many of these things are already being considered in psychometrics, and tests and scales will be adapted, we have to be aware that some cognitive limitations may no longer require the same developmental interventions, as they may be compensated with specialised devices or may be less relevant for academic performance in the new scenarios. Also, gifted students may be redefined as those that are able to make full use of extensions through software applications, social networks and other hybrid resources.

When the subjects are computers, education is usually referred to as training or development. More and more systems in the area of mental development and developmental robotics require a long training and development period, which can take weeks or even months. In these cases, the evaluation of how development is progressing is crucial. New developmental programmes and tests will have to be developed, since traditional tests, for humans, cannot be (directly) applied, as we discussed in Chapter 12.

Finally, the third area, the job market, is the one where the demand for new evaluation tools may be more pressing. However, this is not a question of humans doing new kinds of jobs, or even computers doing these jobs. The interesting question is that humans and computers *compete* for the same jobs. This is illustrated in Panel 18.1.

If we take these probabilities of computerisation as predictions, we can see many misconceptions in the past (and at present) about the skills that artificial intelligence will find more difficult to solve. For instance, Steven Pinker wrote in 1995: "Most fears of automation are misplaced. As the new generation of intelligent devices appears, it will be the stock analysts and petrochemical engineers and parole board members who are in danger of being replaced by machines. The gardeners, receptionists, and cooks are secure in their jobs for decades to come" (Pinker, 1995, pp. 192–193). About two decades later, according to Frey and Osborne (2013), "financial analysts", "chemical engineers" and "judges, magistrate judges, and magistrates" have a probability of computerisation of 0.23, 0.017 and 0.4, respectively, whereas the probabilities for "receptionists", "cooks" and "landscaping and groundskeeping workers" are 0.96, 0.96 and 0.95. Who is now misplaced?

At present, given a robotic waiter that is offered by a robot manufacturer to a restaurant, we expect that the adaptation and training periods are considered part of the cost of the robot. However, this may change in the near future, as

---

Panel 18.1
Jobs: skills matter more than tasks

Several analyses have been performed about those jobs that will be more "computerisable", i.e., ultimately performed by computers (Levy and Murnane, 2012). A long time ago, Keynes (1931) already argued that computers would one day do all jobs. Therefore, the useful question for future policies and a better understanding of the skills that are going to be replaced by computers is to determine the probability that a job will be replaced in 10, 20 or 50 years. Accordingly, Frey and Osborne (2013) estimated "the probability of computerisation for 702 detailed occupations".

Computerisation may consist of a specific task-oriented software or robotic system, but it may well involve the use of more cognitive assistants, being able to be *trained* for several tasks. With new AI systems that need to be trained, new variables must be considered (Feng and Graetz, 2015), including training costs before the 'post' is filled, during the initial training stage and whenever tasks change slightly so that a re-training or re-accommodation are required.

As a result, a company may have to decide whether the post is filled by a human or one of these computerised systems, according to performance, wages, maintenance and training costs. It is then reasonable that a company, given a job, would evaluate several 'candidates', humans or not, in terms of the tasks they do, but also in terms of their abilities.

---

robotic waiters become more flexible, with a wider range of skills. In that case it will be important to know whether the waiter can learn, autonomously, that some gestures and expressions lead to higher tips, that the arrangement of tables have changed, that a given customer has some particular preferences, etc. And this places us in the terrain of the evaluation of abilities, as we go down in the probability range of computerisation. For instance, for a computer programmer (with 0.49 probability according to Frey and Osborne, 2013) what are the demanded skills? If we move from waiters through computer programmers to the low extreme of the computerisation probability table, we find those occupations where abstract thinking, creativity and social abilities are more relevant. In relation to the effect of intelligence in jobs, Gottfredson (1997b) argued that "the more complex a work task, the greater the advantages that higher g confers in performing it well". How will this be interpreted when computers *apply* for these jobs?

Apart from new kinds of subjects, we can think of new kinds of ecosystems. For instance, in relation to the job market, we also saw in Chapter 15 the popularisation of crowdsourcing platforms (e.g., Amazon Mechanical Turk, Buhrmester et al., 2011) where users (humans, computers or hybrids) can bid for a task and offer their competencies. Hybrid teamwork is changing very significantly too and "human computation already affords a tremendous opportunity to combine the respective strengths of humans and machines toward unprecedented capabilities in the short term" (Michelucci and Dickinson, 2016). All these scenarios where some kind of evaluation is urged are repeatedly arising in platforms for collaborative work, digital social networks, virtual worlds and video games.

In closing, the three main areas of cognitive evaluation are demanding new evaluation tools for a broad variety of entities in the machine kingdom. Are the tools ready? Let us look into this next.

18.4 A SHORT DISTANCE AHEAD, PLENTY TO BE DONE

This book has mostly been an *exploration* of the main questions around the measurement of behavioural features in a universal way, upon a set of new and old principles. To really cope with the application demands, it is time to switch to *exploitation* and derive actual tests. Some test prototypes emanating from first principles have been discussed in the book, but they have been refuted either as non-universal or as unable to fully cover an unequivocal ability. Nonetheless, several guidelines for the creation of valid and reliable tests have been seen in this book, and can now be used. In a simplified way, a common procedure to build a test that measures a cognitive ability can be summarised as follows:

- First, and perhaps the most critical step, we would choose a range of items (or a comprehensive stochastic task) that represents a given ability. Ensuring both necessity and sufficiency for the ability will be hard if the representational definition of the ability is not precise enough, or the items require other abilities that the subjects may lack.
- Second, we would analyse item difficulty in the way that has been described in Part III. The choice of the reference machine or language to describe the solution policies may be relevant, but this arbitrariness can be minimised by the choice of more than one reference machine, preferably diverse, averaging their finding effort $\mathbb{LS}$.

Table 18.2. Six main benchmark categories according to the way policies are acquired, by search, by demonstration and by transmission (see Table 8.2), with each of them possibly being non-incremental or incremental. The circle shows where most tests have concentrated so far.

Policy acquisition	Non-incremental	Incremental
Search	o	Developmental
Demonstration	Social	Developmental and social
Transmission	Social and verbal	Developmental, social and verbal

- Third, we would choose an appropriate range of difficulties and design an adaptive or non-adaptive test according to them. In case no information about the agent's proficiency is known, the test would necessarily be adaptive, starting from minimal difficulties.
- Fourth, given a difficulty, we would either define a distribution for the items of that difficulty (e.g., a universal distribution) as illustrated in Figure 9.7 (middle) or, alternatively, choose a solution of that difficulty uniformly and then select an item solved by that solution (through, again, a universal distribution), as illustrated in Figure 9.7 (bottom).
- Fifth, we would think of appropriate interfaces for the agents and configure the administration algorithm, such that a given reliability is obtained or a maximum time is reached.
- Sixth and last, after administration, we would draw the agent response curve and derive indicators such as the area under the curve or the estimated proficiency point where the probability of an acceptable response is 0.5.

It should be emphasised that the preceding procedure is a simplification and is not *directly* applicable for all behavioural features (such as personality traits in situated tests with other agents). Nevertheless, it is a good indication, or summary, of the modus operandi.

The recommendation for the near future is to start with more elementary abilities in a reinforcement learning setting, using the notion of asynchronous tasks that was described in Part III. However, the ultimate goal is to derive a full battery of tests. Again, the main question for such a battery is the choice of abilities and their relationship. Since this is not clear yet, we may start under the schema that is shown in Table 18.2, which is derived from Table 8.2.

Innate behaviour excluded (common in animals and special-purpose AI systems), this table summarises the three ways in which a policy or behaviour can be acquired: by search (e.g., interacting with the environment but using some kind of intellectual search), by demonstration (e.g., imitating what another agent does) and by transmission (e.g., understanding the description of a behaviour communicated by another agent). Each of the three ways can be either incremental or non-incremental, i.e., cumulative or not with respect to previously acquired policies.

The categories shown in Table 18.2 are different from those of some test batteries in psychometrics, comparative cognition and artificial intelligence, as seen in Part II of the book, as the table does not commit to any particular set of abilities. The ultimate goal would indeed be to populate each category with abilities, but this should not be done in an agglomerative way, by creating "a new suite of tests" (Marcus et al., 2016), presumably covering a range of tasks that are solved by humans but hard for state-of-the-art AI. Of course, the agglomerate may still be useful for the near-term progress of task-specific systems in some areas of AI. However, it would hardly provide a meaningful way of comparing AI systems and humans. Actually, "the contours of human and machine intelligence are currently distinct in various ways, [representing] the cumulative effects of myriad idiosyncratic human decisions over several decades" (Brundage, 2016). Without a particular population as a reference, factor analysis would not be able to clean up the agglomerate, as psychometrics did with the early IQ tests. Instead, in universal psychometrics we must rely on a solutional notion of task similarity applied at increasing levels of difficulty. This is more feasible if we start at low levels of difficulty, with more general-purpose abilities, and then refine them as we progress in the range of difficulties, as shown in Figure 10.4.

The great enterprise for the future is the construction of a benchmark that follows this principled approach and covers the categories of Table 18.2. The preferred roadmap would rely on a community of researchers agreeing on the creation of one integrated benchmark, instead of producing many scattered efforts, which would be more difficult to consolidate, compare and maintain. As the communities in artificial general intelligence, reinforcement learning and developmental robotics may be more interested in such a benchmark, the proposal could germinate from them. Actually, there have been some recent initiatives in this direction, such as the proposal of a language for describing asynchronous environments for evaluation (Thórisson et al., 2015), the use of the Psychology Experiment Building Language (PEBL) for the implementation (Mueller, 2010) of the Cognitive Decathlon (see Table 6.2), or evaluation platforms over sandbox video games, such as project Malmo (Johnson et al. 2016, see Figure 5.4). These platforms can be used as an embryo or at least an inspiration for building a repository of tests. Creating a repository that is both useful in practice and enduring in front of technological and societal changes requires a thorough understanding of the evaluation of behaviour from the widest perspective, as this book has tried to portray.

It would also be desirable that, unlike many psychometric batteries, the tests in the benchmark were publicly available, such as in PEBL or Concerto (Scalise and Allen, 2015). Given the procedure for test creation defined earlier, item generators and adaptive tests would be the norm, so there should not be much concern about *evaluation specialisation* (Keynote 2.6), when disclosing the tasks. The benchmark should also contain a repository of interfaces and a record of previous results on different kinds of agents: humans, other animals, and other machines, similarly to some test archival systems, such as the "Mental Measurements Yearbooks" (e.g., Carlson et al., 2014). A modern "platform for developing and running events, archiving tests and results" (Adams et al., 2016) would preferably be open data, to become a valuable source for data analysis.

The development of such an ambitious benchmarking platform would require a substantial effort and an important degree of agreement to become a reality. This should not only come from the main scientific and industrial actors but would be benefited by the understanding and interest of laypeople. Fortunately, the quest for a universal evaluation of intelligence and other behavioural features has recently grown in popularity (Kleiner, 2011; Biever, 2011). People in general can even be more engaged if the platforms are open to test humans as well, and arrange attractive events (from 'AI hackathons' to 'cognithons') where humans and AI contraptions can compete and collaborate. The use of video games as evaluation platforms, already mentioned, has a huge potential to bridge non-technical users with the educational and research communities, in addition to providing countless test results for analysis.

This widespread involvement in the evaluation of behaviour may facilitate the general adoption of the universal, ratiocentric viewpoint this book represents. Ultimately, ratiocentrism is yet another reaction – in the scientific tradition – against Protagoras's aphorism placing "man as the measure of all things". For a non-anthropocentric measurement of the mind, this book has elaborated upon the realms of information, computation and evolution. Still, we should embrace whatever refutations or alternatives may come, provided they do not place man, again, as the measure of all minds.

CHAPTER HIGHLIGHTS

- Universal psychometrics being shifted from a populational to a universal perspective, from agglomerative to solutional approaches and, ultimately, from a task-general intelligence to a policy-general intelligence (Table 8.2).
- Universal psychometrics as a transversal area bridging human psychometrics, comparative cognition and AI evaluation (Figure 18.1).
- Universal psychometrics applicable to three main areas: diagnostic assessment, education and personnel selection (Section 18.3).
- The job market increasingly demanding ways of assessing the abilities of various systems (humans, computers, hybrids and collectives) that can adapt to a diversity of tasks (Panel 18.1).
- Benchmarks encouraged, varying the way behaviours are acquired (Table 8.2), populating them with abilities that are derived from first principles (difficulty range and task similarity) instead of an agglomerative approach.

References

Abbeel, P. and Ng, A. Y. (2004). Apprenticeship learning via inverse reinforcement learning. In *International Conference on Machine Learning*, pages 1–8. ACM International Conference Proceeding Series 69. ACM

Abramson, J. Z., Hernández-Lloreda, V., Call, J., and Colmenares, F. (2011). Relative quantity judgments in South American sea lions (*Otaria flavescens*). *Animal Cognition*, 14(5):695–706.

Adams, H. (1904). A law of acceleration. Chapter 34 *in (1905) "The education of Henry Adams"*. Houghton Mifflin.

Adams, S. S., Arel, I., Bach, J., Coop, R., Furlan, R., Goertzel, B., Hall, J. S., Samsonovich, A., Scheutz, M., Schlesinger, M., Shapiro, S. C., and Sowa, J. (2012). Mapping the landscape of human-level artificial general intelligence. *AI Magazine*, 33(1):25–42.

Adams, S. S., Banavar, G., and Campbell, M. (2016). I-athlon: Towards a multidimensional Turing test. *AI Magazine*, 37(1):78–84.

AERA, APA & NCME (1999). *Standards for educational and psychological testing*. American Educational Research Association.

AFADA v. Argentina (2015). Juzgado Nacional de Primera Instancia en lo Contencioso Administrativo Federal, Argentinian Court 34, 21-oct-2015, MJ-JU-M-95342-AR.

Agrillo, C. and Beran, M. J. (2013). Number without language: Comparative psychology and the evolution of numerical cognition. *Frontiers in Psychology*, 4.

Airiau, S. (2013). Cooperative games and multiagent systems. *The Knowledge Engineering Review*, 28(4):381–424.

Albert, D. and Held, T. (1999). Component-based knowledge spaces in problem solving and inductive reasoning. In D. Albert and J. Lukas (Eds.) *Knowledge spaces: Theories, empirical research, and applications*, pages 15–40. Psychology Press.

Alberts, J. R. and Ronca, A. E. (2012). The experience of being born: A natural context for learning to suckle. *International Journal of Pediatrics*, 2012:ID 129328, 11 pages.

Alcalá, J., Fernández, A., Luengo, J., Derrac, J., García, S., Sánchez, L., and Herrera, F. (2010). Keel data-mining software tool: Data set repository, integration of algorithms and experimental analysis framework. *Journal of Multiple-Valued Logic and Soft Computing*, 17:255–287.

Alliger, G. M. (1988). Do zero correlations really exist among measures of different intellectual abilities? *Educational and Psychological Measurement*, 48(2):275–280.

Alur, R., Bodik, R., Juniwal, G., Martin, M. M. K., Raghothaman, M., Seshia, S. A., Singh, R., Solar-Lezama, A., Torlak, E., and Udupa, A. (2013). Syntax-guided synthesis. In B. Jobstmann and S. Ray (Eds.) *Formal Methods in Computer-Aided Design (FMCAD), 2013*, pages 1–17. IEEE.

Alvarado, N., Adams, S. S., Burbeck, S., and Latta, C. (2002). Beyond the Turing test: Performance metrics for evaluating a computer simulation of the human mind. In *International Conference on Development and Learning, 2002*, pages 147–152. IEEE.

Ambridge, B. and Lieven, E. V. (2011). *Child language acquisition: Contrasting theoretical approaches*. Cambridge University Press.

Amigoni, F., Bastianelli, E., Berghofer, J., Bonarini, A., Fontana, G., Hochgeschwender, N., Iocchi, L., Kraetzschmar, G., Lima, P., Matteucci, M., Miraldo, P., Nardi, D., and Schiaffonati, V. (2015). Competitions for benchmarking: Task and functionality scoring complete performance assessment. *IEEE Robotics & Automation Magazine*, 22(3):53–61. Benchmarks available at http://rockinrobotchallenge.eu.

Anderson, B. (1993). Evidence from the rat for a general factor that underlies cognitive performance and that relates to brain size: Intelligence? *Neuroscience Letters*, 153(1):98–102.

Anderson, B. (2000). The g factor in non-human animals. In Bock, G. R., Goode, J. A., and Webb, K., editors, *The nature of intelligence*, volume 233, pages 79–95. John Wiley.

Anderson, C. and Franks, N. R. (2003). Teamwork in animals, robots, and humans. *Advances in the Study of Behavior*, 33:1–48.

Anderson, J., Baltes, J., and Cheng, C. T. (2011). Robotics competitions as benchmarks for AI research. *The Knowledge Engineering Review*, 26(1):11–17.

Anderson, J. and Lebiere, C. (2003). The Newell Test for a theory of cognition. *Behavioral and Brain Sciences*, 26(5):587–601.

Anderson, M. L. (2004). A flexible approach to quantifying various dimensions of environmental complexity. In Messina, E. R. and Meystel, A. M., editors, *Measuring the performance and intelligence of systems: Proceedings of the 2004 PerMIS Workshop, August 24–26, 2004*, pages 192–197. NIST.

Antol, S., Agrawal, A., Lu, J., Mitchell, M., Batra, D., Zitnick, C. L., and Parikh, D. (2015). VQA: Visual question answering. CoRR arXiv preprint:1505.00468.

Antunes, L., Fortnow, L., Van Melkebeek, D., and Vinodchandran, N. V. (2006). Computational depth: Concept and applications. *Theoretical Computer Science*, 354(3):391–404.

Applewhite, P. (1975). Learning in bacteria, fungi, and plants. *Invertebrate Learning*, 3:179–186.

Arel, I. and Livingston, S. (2009). Beyond the Turing test. *Computer*, 42(3):90–91.

Arel, I., Rose, D. C., and Karnowski, T. P. (2010). Deep machine learning – a new frontier in artificial intelligence research. *Computational Intelligence Magazine*, 5(4):13–18.

Armstrong, S. and Sotala, K. (2015). How we're predicting AI–or failing to. In J. Romportl, E. Zackova and J. Kelemen (Eds.) *Beyond artificial intelligence*, pages 11–29. Springer.

Arnold, P. and Heiron, K. (2002). Tactile memory of deaf-blind adults on four tasks. *Scandinavian Journal of Psychology*, 43(1):73–79.

Arora, S. and Barak, B. (2009). *Computational complexity: A modern approach.* Cambridge University Press.

Arrabales, R., Ledezma, A., and Sanchis, A. (2010). ConsScale: A pragmatic scale for measuring the level of consciousness in artificial agents. *Journal of Consciousness Studies*, 17(3–4):131–164.

Asada, M., Hosoda, K., Kuniyoshi, Y., Ishiguro, H., Inui, T., Yoshikawa, Y., Ogino, M., and Yoshida, C. (2009). Cognitive developmental robotics: A survey. *IEEE Transactions on Autonomous Mental Development*, 1(1):12–34.

Ashby, W. R. (1956). *An introduction to cybernetics.* Chapman and Hall.

Ashcraft, M. H., Donley, R. D., Halas, M. A., and Vakali, M. (1992). Working memory, automaticity, and problem difficulty. *Advances in Psychology*, 91:301–329.

Ashlock, D. and Schonfeld, J. (2010). Evolution for automatic assessment of the difficulty of Sokoban boards. In *IEEE Congress on Evolutionary Computation (CEC)*, pages 1–8. IEEE.

Asimov, I. (1950). *I, robot.* Gnome Press.

ASPCR (1999). American Society for the Prevention of Cruelty to Robots. http://www.aspcr.com/.

Ay, N., Mueller, M., and Szkola, A. (2008). Effective complexity and its relation to logical depth. CoRR ArXiv preprint:0810.5663.

Aziz, H., Brill, M., Fischer, F., Harrenstein, P., Lang, J., and Seedig, H. G. (2015). Possible and necessary winners of partial tournaments. *Journal of Artificial Intelligence Research*, 54:493–534.

Bache, K. and Lichman, M. (2013). UCI machine learning repository. University of California, Irvine, School of Information and Computer Sciences. http://archive.ics.uci.edu/ml.

Bachrach, Y., Graepel, T., Kasneci, G., Kosinski, M., and Van Gael, J. (2012a). Crowd IQ: Aggregating opinions to boost performance. In *Proceedings of the 11th International Conference on Autonomous Agents and Multiagent Systems*, volume 1, pages 535–542.

Bachrach, Y., Kosinski, M., Graepel, T., Kohli, P., and Stillwell, D. (2012b). Personality and patterns of facebook usage. In *Proceedings of the 3rd Annual ACM Web Science Conference*, pages 24–32. ACM.

Bacon, F. (1718). *The essays, or councils, civil and moral.* H. Clark.

Badler, N., Allbeck, J., Zhao, L., and Byun, M. (2002). Representing and parameterizing agent behaviors. In *Proceedings of Computer Animation, 2002*, pages 133–143. IEEE.

Balch, T. (2000). Hierarchic social entropy: An information theoretic measure of robot group diversity. *Autonomous Robots*, 8(3):209–238.

Balch, T., Bellman, K., Cotsfatis, M., Davis, P., Davis, W. J., Fakory, R., Finkelstein, R., Grant, E., Hernández-Orallo, J., Joslyn, C., Reeker, L., Messina, E., Meystel, A., Murphy, R., Peterson, C., Phoha, S., Pouchard, L., Samad, T., Sanderson, A., Schultz, A., Stirling, W., Sukhatme, G., Wallace, S., Wild, A., Weng, J., and Whalen, T. (2000). Compendium of the minutes of plenary discussion. In Meystel, A. M. and Messina, E. R., editors, *Measuring the performance and intelligence of systems: Proceedings of the 2000 PerMIS Workshop*, pages 543–556. NIST Special Publication 970, Gaithersburg, MD.

Baldassarre, G. and Mirolli, M., editors (2013). *Intrinsically motivated learning in natural and artificial systems*. Springer.

Barenbaum, N. B. and Winter, D. G. (2008). History of modern personality theory and research. In *Handbook of personality: Theory and research*, pages 3–26. Guilford Press.

Barlow, J. B. and Dennis, A. R. (2014). Not as smart as we think: A study of collective intelligence in virtual groups. *Proceedings of Collective Intelligence*.

Barmpalias, G. and Dowe, D. L. (2012). Universality probability of a prefix-free machine. *Philosophical Transactions of the Royal Society, Series*, 370:3488–3511.

Baroody, A. J. and Dowker, A. (2013). *The development of arithmetic concepts and skills: Constructive adaptive expertise*. Routledge.

Barrera, A., Cáceres, A., Weitzenfeld, A., and Ramírez-Amaya, V. (2011). Comparative experimental studies on spatial memory and learning in rats and robots. *Journal of Intelligent and Robotic Systems*, 63:361–397.

Barrett, G. V. and Depinet, R. L. (1991). A reconsideration of testing for competence rather than for intelligence. *American Psychologist*, 46(10):1012.

Barrett, P. (2004). The future of ability testing: What happened to the science of mental ability. *Measurement*, 2(1):33–54.

Barrett, S. and Stone, P. (2012). An analysis framework for ad hoc teamwork tasks. In *Proceedings of the 11th International Conference on Autonomous Agents and Multiagent Systems*, Volume 1, pages 357–364. International Foundation for Autonomous Agents and Multiagent Systems.

Bartholomew, D. J. (2004). *Measuring intelligence: Facts and fallacies*. Cambridge University Press.

Bates, J., et al. (1994). The role of emotion in believable agents. *Communications of the ACM*, 37(7):122–125.

Baum, E. B. (2004). *What is thought?* MIT Press.

Bayley, N. (1969). *Scales of infant development. Psychological Corporation*.

Bayley, N. (1993). *Bayley scales of infant development: Manual*. Psychological Corporation.

BBC (2003). Is txt mightier than the word? *BBC News*, 4 March. http://news.bbc.co.uk/go/pr/fr/-/2/hi/uk_news/2814235.stm.

BBC (2014a). Court in Argentina grants basic rights to orangutan. *BBC News*, 21 December. http://www.bbc.com/news/world-latin-america-30571577.

BBC (2014b). US chimpanzee Tommy 'has no human rights' – court. *BBC News*, 4 December. http://www.bbc.com/news/world-us-canada-30338231.

Beck, B. B. (1982). Chimpocentrism: Bias in cognitive ethology. *Journal of Human Evolution*, 11(1):3–17.

Beer, R. (2004). Autopoiesis and cognition in the game of life. *Artificial Life*, 10(3):309–326.

Beer, R. D. (2003). The dynamics of active categorical perception in an evolved model agent. *Adaptive Behavior*, 11(4):209–243.

Beer, R. D. (2015). Characterizing autopoiesis in the game of life. *Artificial Life*, 21(1):1–19.

Beer, R. D. and Williams, P. L. (2015). Information processing and dynamics in minimally cognitive agents. *Cognitive Science*, 39(1):1–38.

Bejar, I. I., Chaffin, R., and Embretson, S. (1991). *Cognitive and psychometric analysis of analogical problem solving*. Springer.

Bellemare, M. G., Naddaf, Y., Veness, J., and Bowling, M. (2013). The arcade learning environment: An evaluation platform for general agents. *Journal of Artificial Intelligence Research*, 47:253–279.

Ben-Jacob, E. (2008). Social behavior of bacteria: From physics to complex organization. *European Physical Journal B*, 65(3):315–322.

Ben-Jacob, E. (2009). Learning from bacteria about natural information processing. *Annals of the New York Academy of Sciences*, 1178(1):78–90.

Ben-Porath, Y. S. (2012). *Interpreting the MMPI-2-RF*. University of Minnesota Press.

Bender, D. (2015). Establishing a human baseline for the Winograd schema challenge. In M. Glass and J. H. Kim (Eds.), *Modern AI and Cognitive Science Conference, CEUR Workshop Proceedings*, 1353:39–45.

Bennett, C. H., Gács, P., Li, M., Vitányi, P. M., and Zurek, W. H. (1998). Information distance. *IEEE Transactions on Information Theory*, 44(4):1407–1423.

Benson-Amram, S., Dantzer, B., Stricker, G., Swanson, E. M., and Holekamp, K. E. (2016). Brain size predicts problem-solving ability in mammalian carnivores. *Proceedings of the National Academy of Sciences*, 113(9):2352–2357.

Bentham, J. (1780). *An introduction to the principles of morals and legislation*. T. Payne.

Bentley, J. G. W., Bishop, P. G., and Van Der Meulen, M. (2004). An empirical exploration of the difficulty function. In M. Heisel, P. Liggesmeyer, S. Wittman (Eds.) *Computer Safety, Reliability, and Security*, LNCS 3219, pages 60–71. Springer.

Berant, J., Srikumar, V., Chen, P.-C., Huang, B., Manning, C. D., Vander Linden, A., Harding, B., and Clark, P. (2014). Modeling biological processes for reading comprehension. In *Proceedings of the Conference on Empirical Methods in Natural Language Processing, EMNLP*, pages 1499–1510. Association for Computational Linguistics.

Berg-Cross, G. (2007). Report on panel discussion on can the development of intelligent robots be benchmarked? Concepts and issues from epigenetic robotics. In Messina, E. R. and Madhavan, R., editors, *Proceedings of the 2007 Workshop on Performance Metrics for Intelligent Systems*, pages 167–181. NIST.

Berger, T. W., Song, D., Chan, R. H., Marmarelis, V. Z., LaCoss, J., Wills, J., Hampson, R. E., Deadwyler, S., Granacki, J. J., et al. (2012). A hippocampal cognitive prosthesis: Multi-input, multi-output nonlinear modeling and VLSI implementation. *IEEE Transactions on Neural Systems and Rehabilitation Engineering*, 20(2):198–211.

Bernasconi, A., Bodei, C., and Pagli, L. (2007). Knitting for fun: A recursive sweater. In *Fun with algorithms*, pages 53–65. Springer.

Bernstein, A., Klein, M., and Malone, T. W. (2012). Programming the global brain. *Communications of the ACM*, 55(5):41–43.

Besold, T. K., Hernández-Orallo, J., and Schmid, U. (2015). Can machine intelligence be measured in the same way as human intelligence? *Künstliche Intelligenz*, 29(3):291–297.

Besold, T. R. (2014). A note on chances and limitations of Psychometric AI. In *KI 2014: Advances in Artificial Intelligence*, pages 49–54. Springer.

Betjemann, R. S., Johnson, E. P., Barnard, H., Boada, R., Filley, C. M., Filipek, P. A., Willcutt, E. G., DeFries, J. C., and Pennington, B. F. (2010). Genetic covariation between brain volumes and IQ, reading performance, and processing speed. *Behavior genetics*, 40(2):135–145.

Beuls, K., Steels, L., et al. (2013). Agent-based models of strategies for the emergence and evolution of grammatical agreement. *PloS ONE*, 8(3):e58960.

Bibel, W. (1980). Intellektik statt KI – Ein ernstgemeinter Vorschlag. *Rundbrief der Fachgruppe Künstliche Intelligenz in der Gesellschaft für Informatik*, 22:15–16.

Biemans, N. (2012). 'Killjoys' challenge claims of clever animals. *Science*, 335:1036–1037.

Bien, Z., Bang, W. C., Kim, D. Y., and Han, J. S. (2002). Machine intelligence quotient: Its measurements and applications. *Fuzzy Sets and Systems*, 127(1):3–16.

Bien, Z., Kim, Y. T., and Yang, S. H. (1998). How to measure the machine intelligence quotient (MIQ): Two methods and applications. In *World Automation Congress (WAC)*. TSI Press.

Biever, C. (2011). Ultimate IQ: One test to rule them all. *New Scientist*, 211(2829):42–45.

Binet, A. (1909). *Les idées modernes sur les enfants*. Flammarion.

Binet, A. and Simon, T. (1905). New methods for the diagnosis of the intellectual level of subnormals. *L'année Psychologique*, 12:191–244.

Birch, T. H. (1993). Moral considerability and universal consideration. *Environmental Ethics*, 15(4):313–332.

Bird, C. D. and Emery, N. J. (2009). Rooks use stones to raise the water level to reach a floating worm. *Current Biology*, 19(16):1410–1414.

Birder, L., Kanai, A., Cruz, F., Moore, K., and Fry, C. (2010). Is the urothelium intelligent? *Neurourology and Urodynamics*, 29(4):598–602.

Bjorklund, D. F. and Pellegrini, A. D. (2002). *The origins of human nature: Evolutionary developmental psychology*. American Psychological Association.

Bloom, P. and German, T. P. (2000). Two reasons to abandon the false belief task as a test of theory of mind. *Cognition*, 77(1):B25–B31.

Blum, L. and Blum, M. (1975). Toward a mathematical theory of inductive inference. *Information and Control*, 28(2):125–155.

Blumenbach, J. (1790). *Beytrage zur Naturgeschichte*, 2 vols. Göttingen: Dieterich.

Boake, C. (2002). From the Binet–Simon to the Wechsler–Bellevue: Tracing the history of intelligence testing. *Journal of Clinical and Experimental Neuropsychology*, 24(3):383–405.

Bolhuis, J. J. and Everaert, M. (2013). *Birdsong, speech, and language: Exploring the evolution of mind and brain*. MIT Press.

Bolhuis, J. J., Tattersall, I., Chomsky, N., and Berwick, R. C. (2014). How could language have evolved? *PLOS Biology*, 12(8).

Bonabeau, E., Dorigo, M., and Theraulaz, G. (1999). *Swarm intelligence: From natural to artificial systems*. Oxford University Press.

Borges, J. L. (1939). *The total library*. In The total library: Non-fiction 1922–1986, translated by Eliot Weinberge, pages 214–216 Penguin Press, London, 2000. Pages 214–216. Translated by Eliot Weinberge.

Borges, J. L. (1957). *The book of imaginary beings*. Originally published in Portuguese as *Manual de zoología fantástica*, Fce-Breviarios; English version 2002, Random House.

Borges, J. L. (1964). *Other inquisitions (1937–1952), Translated by Ruth L. C. Simms*. University of Texas Press.

Boring, E. G. (1923). Intelligence as the tests test it. *New Republic*, pages 35–37.

Borsboom, D. (2005). *Measuring the mind: Conceptual issues in contemporary psychometrics*. Cambridge University Press.

Borsboom, D., Mellenbergh, G., and Van Heerden, J. (2004). The concept of validity. *Psychological Review*, 111(4):1061.

Bosse, T., Jonker, C. M., Schut, M. C., and Treur, J. (2006). Collective representational content for shared extended mind. *Cognitive Systems Research*, 7(2):151–174.

Bostrom, N. (2014). *Superintelligence: Paths, dangers, strategies*. Oxford University Press.

Bostrom, N. and Sandberg, A. (2009). Cognitive enhancement: Methods, ethics, regulatory challenges. *Science and Engineering Ethics*, 15(3):311–341.

Bouchard, T. J. (2014). Genes, evolution and intelligence. *Behavior Genetics*, 44(6):549–577.

Bowerman, M. and Levinson, S. C. (2001). *Language acquisition and conceptual development*, volume 3. Cambridge University Press.

Bradley-Johnson, S. and Morgan, S. K. (2008). *Psychoeducational assessment of students who are visually impaired or blind: Infancy through high school*. Region 4 Education Service Center.

Brazdău, O. and Mihai, C. (2011). The consciousness quotient: A new predictor of the students' academic performance. *Procedia – Social and Behavioral Sciences*, 11:245–250.

Bringsjord, S. (2000). In light of artificial intelligence, the science of mental ability is either silly or pointless. *Psycoloquy*, 11, Article 43.

Bringsjord, S. (2011). Psychometric artificial intelligence. *Journal of Experimental & Theoretical Artificial Intelligence*, 23(3):271–277.

Bringsjord, S., Bello, P., and Ferrucci, D. (2003). Creativity, the Turing test, and the (better) Lovelace test. In Moor, J. H., editor, *The Turing test: The elusive standard of artificial intelligence*, pages 215–239. Springer.

Bringsjord, S. and Schimanski, B. (2003). What is artificial intelligence? Psychometric AI as an answer. In *International Joint Conference on Artificial Intelligence*, pages 887–893. Morgan Kaufmann.

Broad, C. D. (1926). *The philosophy of Francis Bacon*. Cambridge University Press.

Brockman, J. (2015). What do you think about machines that think?, Annual question. *Edge.org*. http://edge.org/annual-question/what-do-you-think-about-machines-that-think.

Brooks, R. A. (1990). Elephants don't play chess. *Robotics and Autonomous Systems*, 6(1):3–15.

Brooks, R. R. (2001). *Stigmergy – an intelligence metric for emergent distributed behaviors*. In *Workshop on Performance Metrics for Intelligent Systems*, pages 186–192. NIST.

Brown, J. I., Fishco, V. V., and Hanna, G. (1993). *Nelson-Denny reading test: Manual for scoring and interpretation, forms G & H*. Riverside.

Brundage, M. (2016). Modeling progress in AI. In *AAAI 2016 Workshop on AI, Ethics, and Society*.

Bryson, J. J. (2010). Robots should be slaves. In Wilks, Y., editor, *Close engagements with artificial companions: Key social, psychological, ethical and design issues*, pages 63–74. John Benjamins.

Budoff, M. (1987). The validity of learning potential assessment. In Lidz, C. S., editor, *Dynamic testing*, pages 173–195. Guilford Press.

Buhrmester, M., Kwang, T., and Gosling, S. D. (2011). Amazon's mechanical turk a new source of inexpensive, yet high-quality, data? *Perspectives on Psychological Science*, 6(1):3–5.

Bürckert, H.-J., Müller, J., and Schupeta, A. (1991). Ratman and its relation to other multi-agent testbeds. Deutsches Forschungszentrum für Künstliche Intelligenz GmbH, Research Report, RR-91-09.

Burghart, C. R. and Steinfeld, A. (2008). Human-robot interaction metrics and future directions. In *Workshop on Metrics for Human-Robot Interaction*, page 1. School of Computer Science, University of Hertforshire.

Burman, E. (2007). *Deconstructing developmental psychology*. Routledge.

Burns, E. (1998). *Test accommodations for students with disabilities*. ERIC.

Bursztein, E., Aigrain, J., Moscicki, A., and Mitchell, J. C. (2014). The end is nigh: Generic solving of text-based CAPTCHAs. In *Proceedings of the 8th USENIX Conference on Offensive Technologies*, pages 3–3. USENIX Association.

Burt, C. (1949). The structure of the mind: A review of the results of factor analysis. *British Journal of Educational Psychology*, 19(2–3):100–111, 176–199.

Buschkuehl, M. and Jaeggi, S. M. (2010). Improving intelligence: A literature review. *Swiss Medical Weekly*, 140(19–20):266–272.

Busoniu, L., Babuska, R., and De Schutter, B. (2008). A comprehensive survey of multiagent reinforcement learning. *IEEE Transactions on Systems, Man, and Cybernetics, Part C: Applications and Reviews*, 38(2):156–172.

Buss, D. M. (1999). *Evolutionary psychology: The new science of the mind*. Allyn and Bacon.

Butler, S. (1872). *Erewhon*. William Brendon.

Call, J. and Tomasello, M. (1998). The effect of humans on the cognitive development of apes. In Russon, A. E., Bard, K. A., and Parker, S. T., editors, *Reaching into thought: The minds of the great apes*, pages 371–403. Cambridge University Press.

Callahan, C. M. and Hertberg-Davis, H. L. (2012). *Fundamentals of gifted education: Considering multiple perspectives*. Routledge.

Calvo-Garzón, P. (2003). Nonclassical connectionism should enter the decathlon. *Behavioral and Brain Sciences*, 26(05):603–604.

Calvo-Garzón, P. and Keijzer, F. (2011). Plants: Adaptive behavior, root-brains, and minimal cognition. *Adaptive Behavior*, 19(3):155–171.

Campbell, M., Hoane, A. J., and Hsu, F. (2002). Deep Blue. *Artificial Intelligence*, 134(1–2):57–83.

Candland, D. K. (1995). *Feral children and clever animals: Reflections on human nature*. Oxford University Press.

Cangelosi, A. and Schlesinger, M. (2015). *Developmental robotics: From babies to robots*. MIT Press.

Cantlon, J. F. and Brannon, E. M. (2006). Shared system for ordering small and large numbers in monkeys and humans. *Psychological Science*, 17(5):401–406.

Carbonell, J. G. (1980). Towards a process model of human personality traits. *Artificial Intelligence*, 15(1):49–74.

Carlson, J. F., Geisinger, K. F., and Jonson, J. L. (2014). *The nineteenth mental measurements yearbook*. Buros Center for Testing. http://buros.org/mental-measurements-yearbook.

Carpenter, P. A., Just, M. A., and Shell, P. (1990). What one intelligence test measures: A theoretical account of the processing in the Raven Progressive Matrices test. *Psychological Review*, 97:404–431.

Carr, N. (2008). Is Google making us stupid? *Yearbook of the National Society for the Study of Education*, 107(2):89–94.

Carr, N. (2011). *The shallows: What the Internet is doing to our brains*. W. W. Norton.

Carroll, J. B. (1981). Ability and task difficulty in cognitive psychology. *Educational Researcher*, pages 11–21.

Carroll, J. B. (1993). *Human cognitive abilities: A survey of factor-analytic studies*. Cambridge University Press.

Carroll, J. L. and Seppi, K. (2005). Task similarity measures for transfer in reinforcement learning task libraries. In *International Joint Conference on Neural Networks*, volume 2, pages 803–808. IEEE.

Carter, M. (2007). *Minds and computers: An introduction to the philosophy of artificial intelligence*. Edinburgh University Press.

Castelfranchi, C., Rosis, F. D., Falcone, R., and Pizzutilo, S. (1998). Personality traits and social attitudes in multiagent cooperation. *Applied Artificial Intelligence*, 12(7–8):649–675.

Cattell, R. B. (1946). *Description and measurement of personality*. World Book Company.

Cattell, R. B., Eber, H. W., and Tatsuoka, M. M. (1970). *Handbook for the sixteen personality factor questionnaire (16 PF): In clinical, educational, industrial, and research psychology, for use with all forms of the test*. Institute for Personality and Ability Testing.

Celli, F., Lepri, B., Biel, J.-I., Gatica-Perez, D., Riccardi, G., and Pianesi, F. (2014). The workshop on computational personality recognition 2014. In *Proceedings of the ACM International Conference on Multimedia*, pages 1245–1246. ACM.

Celli, F., Pianesi, F., Stillwell, D., and Kosinski, M. (2013). The workshop on computational personality recognition 2013. AAAI Technical Report WS-13-01.

Chaitin, G. J. (1975). A theory of program size formally identical to information theory. *Journal of the ACM*, 22(3):329–340.

Chaitin, G. J. (1977). Algorithmic information theory. *IBM Journal of Research and Development*, 21(4):350–359.

Chaitin, G. J. (1982). Gödel's theorem and information. *International Journal of Theoretical Physics*, 21(12):941–954.

Chaitin, G. J. (2002). On the intelligibility of the universe and the notions of simplicity, complexity and irreducibility. In *Grenzen und Grenzüberschreitungen, XIX. Deutscher Kongress fï Philosophie, Bonn, 23.-27. September 2002*. ArXiv preprint: math/0210035.

Chalmers, D. (2010). The singularity: A philosophical analysis. *Journal of Consciousness Studies*, 17(9-10):7–65.

Chandrasekaran, B. (1990). What kind of information processing is intelligence? In *The foundation of artificial intelligence – a sourcebook*, pages 14–46. Cambridge University Press.

Chang, N. C.-L. (2008). *Constructing grammar: A computational model of the emergence of early constructions*. PhD thesis, University of California at Berkeley.

Chapouthier, G. and Kaplan, F. (2011). *L'homme, l'animal et la machine*. CNRS éditions.

Chapouthier, G., Nouët, J. C., et al. (1998). *The universal declaration of animal rights: Comments and intentions*. Ligue Française des Droits de l'Animal.

Chappell, J. and Sloman, A. (2007). Natural and artificial meta-configured altricial information-processing systems. *International Journal of Unconventional Computing*, 3(3):211–239.

Chater, N. (1999). The search for simplicity: A fundamental cognitive principle? *Quarterly Journal of Experimental Psychology: Section A*, 52(2):273–302.

Chater, N., Clark, A., Perfors, A., and Goldsmith, J. A. (2015). *Empiricism and language learnability*. Oxford University Press.

Chater, N. and Vitányi, P. (2003). Simplicity: A unifying principle in cognitive science? *Trends in Cognitive Sciences*, 7(1):19–22.

Chater, N. and Vitányi, P. (2007). 'Ideal learning' of natural language: Positive results about learning from positive evidence. *Journal of Mathematical Psychology*, 51(3):135–163.

Chedid, F. B. (2010). Sophistication and logical depth revisited. In *2010 IEEE/ACS International Conference on Computer Systems and Applications (AICCSA)*, pages 1–4. IEEE.

Chemero, A. (2011). *Radical embodied cognitive science*. MIT Press.

Chmait, N., Dowe, D. L., Green, D. G., and Li, Y.-F. (2015a). Observation, communication and intelligence in agent-based systems. In Bieger, J., Goertzel, B., and Potapov, A., editors, *Artificial General Intelligence – 8th International Conference, AGI 2015, Berlin, Germany, July 22–25, 2015, Proceedings*, pages 50–59. Springer.

Chmait, N., Dowe, D. L., Green, D. G., Li, Y.-F., and Insa-Cabrera, J. (2015b). Measuring universal intelligence in agent-based systems using the anytime intelligence test. Technical Report 2015/279, Faculty of Information Technology, Clayton, Monash University.

Chomsky, N. (1965). *Aspects of the theory of syntax*. MIT Press.

Chomsky, N. (1998). *Minimalist inquiries: The framework*. MIT Working Papers in Linguistics.

Christiansen, M. H. and Chater, N. (2008). Language as shaped by the brain. *Behavioral and Brain Sciences*, 31(5):489–509.

Chu, Z., Gianvecchio, S., Wang, H., and Jajodia, S. (2012). Detecting automation of Twitter accounts: Are you a human, bot, or cyborg? *IEEE Transactions on Dependable and Secure Computing*, 9(6):811–824.

Cianciolo, A. T. and Sternberg, R. J. (2008). *Intelligence: A brief history*. John Wiley.

Cilibrasi, R. and Vitányi, P. M. (2005). Clustering by compression. *IEEE Transactions on Information Theory*, 51(4):1523–1545.

Clark, A. (2004). *Natural-born cyborgs: Minds, technologies, and the future of human intelligence*. Oxford University Press.

Clark, A. and Chalmers, D. (1998). The extended mind. *Analysis*, 58(1):7–19.

Clark, P. (2015). Elementary school science and math tests as a driver for AI: Take the Aristo challenge! *Proceedings of the Twenty-Seventh Conference on Innovative Applications of Artificial Intelligence*, pages 4019–4021.

Clark, P. and Etzioni, O. (2016). My computer is an honor student – but how intelligent is it? Standardized tests as a measure of AI. *AI Magazine*, 37(1):5–12.

Cliff, D. and Miller, G. F. (1995). Co-evolution of pursuit and evasion II: Simulation methods and results. In Maes, P., Mataric, M., Meyer, J., Pollack, J., and Wilson, S., editors, *From Animals to Animats 4: Proceedings of the Fourth International Conference on Simulation of Adaptive Behavior*, pages 506–515. MIT Press.

Cobham, A. (1965). The intrinsic computational difficulty of functions. In Yehoshua Bar-Hillel (Ed.), *Proceedings of the 1964 Congress for Logic, Methodology, and the Philosophy of Science*, pages 24–30. Studies in Logic and the Foundations of Mathematics. North-Holland.

Cochran, W. G. (1977). *Sampling techniques*. John Wiley.

Cohen, A., Fiorello, C. A., and Farley, F. H. (2006). The cylindrical structure of the Wechsler Intelligence Scale for Children IV: A retest of the Guttman model of intelligence. *Intelligence*, 34(6):587–591.

Cohen, P. R. (2005). If not Turing's test, then what? *AI Magazine*, 26(4):61.

Cohen, P. R. and Howe, A. E. (1988). How evaluation guides AI research: The message still counts more than the medium. *AI Magazine*, 9(4):35.

Cohen, Y. (2013). Testing and cognitive enhancement. Technical report, National Institute for Testing and Evaluation, Jerusalem.

Comins, J. A. and Gentner, T. Q. (2010). Working memory for patterned sequences of auditory objects in a songbird. *Cognition*, 117(1):38–53.

Commons, M. L., Trudeau, E. J., Stein, S. A., Richards, F. A., and Krause, S. R. (1998). Hierarchical complexity of tasks shows the existence of developmental stages. *Developmental Review*, 18(3):237–278.

Conway, A. R. A. and Kovacs, K. (2015). New and emerging models of human intelligence. *Wiley Interdisciplinary Reviews: Cognitive Science*, 6(5):419–426.

Conway, J. (1970). The game of life. *Scientific American*, 223(4):4.

Cook, M. (2004). Universality in elementary cellular automata. *Complex Systems*, 15(1):1–40.

Cook, R. G., Katz, J. S., and Cavoto, B. R. (1997). Pigeon same–different concept learning with multiple stimulus classes. *Journal of Experimental Psychology: Animal Behavior Processes*, 23(4):417.

Copeland, B. J. (2004). *The essential Turing: Seminal writings in computing, logic, philosophy, artificial intelligence, and artificial life, plus the secrets of Enigma*. Clarendon Press.

Copeland, J. and Proudfoot, D. (2008). Turing's test: A philosophical and historical guide. In Epstein, R., Roberts, G., and Beber, G., editors, *Parsing the Turing test: Philosophical and methodological issues in the quest for the thinking computer*. Springer.

Corballis, M. C. (2011). *The recursive mind: The origins of human language, thought, and civilization*. Princeton University Press.

Costa, P. T. and McCrae, R. R. (1992). Four ways five factors are basic. *Personality and Individual Differences*, 13(6):653–665.

Costa, P. T. and McCrae, R. R. (2005). *Personality in adulthood: A five-factor theory perspective, second edition.* Routledge.

Cox, C. (1926). *The early mental traits of 300 geniuses.* PhD thesis, Stanford University.

Cox, J. J., Reimann, F., Nicholas, A. K., Thornton, G., Roberts, E., Springell, K., Karbani, G., Jafri, H., Mannan, J., Raashid, Y., Al-Gazali, L., Hamamy, H., Valente, E. M., Gorman, S., Williams, R., McHale, D. P., Wood, J. N., Gribble, F. M., and Woods, C. G. (2006). An SCN9A channelopathy causes congenital inability to experience pain. *Nature*, 444(7121):894–898.

Crinella, F. M. and Yu, J. (1995). Brain mechanisms in problem solving and intelligence: A replication and extension. *Intelligence*, 21(2):225–246.

DARPA (2015). Defense advanced research projects agency robotics challenge. http://www.theroboticschallenge.org/.

Darwin, C. (1871). *The descent of man, and selection in relation to sex.* John Murray.

Dautenhahn, K. (2007). Socially intelligent robots: Dimensions of human–robot interaction. *Philosophical Transactions of the Royal Society, Series*, 362(1480):679–704.

Davis, E. (2014). The limitations of standardized science tests as benchmarks for artificial intelligence research: Position paper. CoRR arXiv preprint:1411.1629.

Davis, E. (2016). How to write science questions that are easy for people and hard for computers. *AI Magazine*, 37(1):13–22.

Davydov, V. (1986). *Problemy razvivayushego obucheniya (issues in developing learning).* Pedagogika.

Dawkins, M. S. (2008). The science of animal suffering. *Ethology*, 114(10):937–945.

Dawkins, M. S. (2012). *Animal suffering: The science of animal welfare.* Springer Science and Business Media.

Dawkins, R. (1976). *The selfish gene.* Oxford University Press.

Dawkins, R. (2000). *Unweaving the rainbow: Science, delusion and the appetite for wonder.* Houghton Mifflin Harcourt.

Dawkins, R. and Krebs, J. R. (1978). Animal signals: Information or manipulation. *Behavioural Ecology: An Evolutionary Approach*, 2:282–309.

De Ayala, R. J. (2009). *Theory and practice of item response theory.* Guilford Press.

De Condorcet, M. (1785). *Essais sur l'application de l'analyse à la probabilité des décisions rendues a la pluralité des voix.* Paris.

De Waal, F. (2013). *The bonobo and the atheist: In search of humanism among the primates.* W. W. Norton.

Deacon, R. M., Bannerman, D. M., Kirby, B. P., Croucher, A., and Rawlins, J. N. P. (2002). Effects of cytotoxic hippocampal lesions in mice on a cognitive test battery. *Behavioural Brain Research*, 133(1):57–68.

Deadwyler, S. A., Berger, T. W., Sweatt, A. J., Song, D., Chan, R. H., Opris, I., Gerhardt, G. A., Marmarelis, V. Z., and Hampson, R. E. (2013). Donor/recipient enhancement of memory in rat hippocampus. *Frontiers in Systems Neuroscience*, 7:Article 120.

Deary, I. J. (2000a). *Looking down on human intelligence: From psychometrics to the brain.* Oxford University Press.

Deary, I. J. (2000b). Simple information processing and intelligence. In Sternberg, R., editor, *Handbook of intelligence*, pages 267–284. Cambridge University Press.

Deary, I. J. and Caryl, P. G. (1997). Neuroscience and human intelligence differences. *Trends in Neurosciences*, 20(8):365–371.

Deary, I. J., Der, G., and Ford, G. (2001). Reaction times and intelligence differences: A population-based cohort study. *Intelligence*, 29(5):389–399.

Deary, I. J., Egan, V., Gibson, G. J., Austin, E. J., Brand, C. R., and Kellaghan, T. (1996). Intelligence and the differentiation hypothesis. *Intelligence*, 23(2):105–132.

Decker, K. S., Durfee, E. H., and Lesser, V. R. (1989). Evaluating research in cooperative distributed problem solving. *Distributed Artificial Intelligence*, 2:487–519.

Dehaene, S., Izard, V., Pica, P., and Spelke, E. (2006). Core knowledge of geometry in an Amazonian indigene group. *Science*, 311(5759):381–384.

Delahaye, J.-P. and Zenil, H. (2012). Numerical evaluation of algorithmic complexity for short strings: A glance into the innermost structure of randomness. *Applied Mathematics and Computation*, 219(1):63–77.

Delaherche, E., Chetouani, M., Mahdhaoui, A., Saint-Georges, C., Viaux, S., and Cohen, D. (2012). Interpersonal synchrony: A survey of evaluation methods across disciplines. *IEEE Transactions on Affective Computing*, 3(3):349–365.

Demasi, P., Szwarcfiter, J. L., and Cruz, A. J. O. (2010). A theoretical framework to formalize AGI-Hard problems. In Hutter, M., Baum, E., and Kitzelmann, E. (Eds.), *3rd Conference on Artificial General Intelligence*, pages 178–179. Atlantis Press.

Dennett, D. (1988). Conditions of personhood. In Goodman, M. F., editor, *What is a person? Contemporary issues in biomedicine, ethics, and society*, pages 145–167. Humana Press.

Dennett, D. C. (1989). *The intentional stance*. MIT Press.

Dennett, D. C. (1995). Darwin's dangerous idea. *The Sciences*, 35(3):34–40.

Dennett, D. C. (1996). *Kinds of minds: Toward an understanding of consciousness*. Basic Books.

Detterman, D. K. (1982). Does "g" exist? *Intelligence*, 6(2):99–108.

Detterman, D. K. (1991). Reply to Deary and Pagliari: Is g intelligence or stupidity? *Intelligence*, 15(2):251–255.

Detterman, D. K. (2011). A challenge to Watson. *Intelligence*, 39(2-3):77–78.

Detterman, D. K. and Daniel, M. H. (1989). Correlations of mental tests with each other and with cognitive variables are highest for low IQ groups. *Intelligence*, 13(4):349–359.

Detterman, D. K., Gabriel, L. T., and Ruthsatz, J. M. (2000). Intelligence and mental retardation. In Sternberg, R., editor, *Handbook of intelligence*, pages 141–158. Cambridge University Press.

Deutsch, D. (1985). Quantum theory, the Church-Turing principle and the universal quantum computer. *Proceedings of the Royal Society of London, Series A*, 400(1818):97–117.

Deutsch, D. (2012). How close are we to creating artificial intelligence? https://aeon.co/essays/how-close-are-we-to-creating-artificial-intelligence.

Dewey, D. (2011). Learning what to value. In J. Schmidhuber, K. R. Thórisson, and M. Looks (Eds.), *4th International Conference on Artificial General Intelligence*, pages 309–314. Springer.

Dickerson, J. P., Kagan, V., and Subrahmanian, V. (2014). Using sentiment to detect bots on Twitter: Are humans more opinionated than bots? In *Advances in Social Networks Analysis and Mining (ASONAM)*, pages 620–627. IEEE.

Didier, C., Duan, W., Dupuy, J.-P., Guston, D. H., Liu, Y., López, C. J., Michelfelder, D., Mitcham, C., Sarewitz, D., Stilgoe, J., et al. (2015). Acknowledging AI's dark side. *Science*, 349(6252):1064.

Dimitrakakis, C., Li, G., and Tziortziotis, N. (2014). The reinforcement learning competition 2014. *AI Magazine*, 35(3):61–65.

Dimou, C., Symeonidis, A. L., Mitkas, P., et al. (2007). Towards a generic methodology for evaluating MAS performance. In *International Conference on Integration of Knowledge Intensive Multi-Agent Systems, 2007 (KIMAS 2007)*, pages 174–179. IEEE.

Dinnerstein, D. and Wertheimer, M. (1957). Some determinants of phenomenal overlapping. *American Journal of Psychology*, 70:21–37.

Dowe, D. L. (2008). Foreword re C. S. Wallace. *Computer Journal*, 51(5):523–560. Christopher Stewart WALLACE (1933-2004) memorial special issue.

Dowe, D. L. (2011). MML, hybrid Bayesian network graphical models, statistical consistency, invariance and uniqueness. In P. S. Bandyopadhyay and M. R. Forster, editors, *Handbook of the philosophy of science, Volume 7: Philosophy of statistics*, pages 901–982. Elsevier.

Dowe, D. L. (2013). Introduction to Ray Solomonoff 85th memorial conference. In Dowe, D. L., editor, *Algorithmic probability and friends: Bayesian prediction and artificial intelligence*, pages 1–36. *Lecture Notes in Computer Science*, volume 7070. Springer.

Dowe, D. L. and Hajek, A. R. (1997). A computational extension to the Turing test. In *Proceedings of the 4th Conference of the Australasian Cognitive Science Society, University of Newcastle, NSW, Australia*.

Dowe, D. L. and Hajek, A. R. (1998). A non-behavioural, computational extension to the Turing Test. In *International Conference on Computational Intelligence and Multimedia Applications (ICCIMA'98), Gippsland, Australia*, pages 101–106.

Dowe, D. L. and Hernández-Orallo, J. (2012). IQ tests are not for machines, yet. *Intelligence*, 40(2):77–81.

Dowe, D. L. and Hernández-Orallo, J. (2014). How universal can an intelligence test be? *Adaptive Behavior*, 22(1):51–69.

Dowe, D. L., Hernández-Orallo, J., and Das, P. K. (2011). Compression and intelligence: Social environments and communication. In Schmidhuber, J., Thórisson, K., and Looks, M., editors, 4th International Conference on *Artificial general intelligence*, pages 204–211. *Lecture Notes in Artificial Intelligence*, volume 6830. Springer.

Downing, S. M. and Haladyna, T. M. (2006). *Handbook of test development*. Lawrence Erlbaum Associates.

Drescher, G. L. (1991). *Made-up minds: A constructivist approach to artificial intelligence*. MIT Press.

Drexler, E. K. (1986). *Engines of creation: The coming era of nanotechnology*. Anchor Books.

Drummond, C. and Japkowicz, N. (2010). Warning: Statistical benchmarking is addictive. Kicking the habit in machine learning. *Journal of Experimental and Theoretical Artificial Intelligence*, 22(1):67–80.

Dunér, D. (2011). Astrocognition: Prolegomena to a future cognitive history of exploration. In *Humans in outer space: Interdisciplinary Perspectives*, pages 117–140. Springer.

Dunn, L. M. and Dunn, D. (2012). *Peabody Picture Vocabulary Test, (PPVT-4)*. Pearson.

Durfee, E. H. and Montgomery, T. A. (1990). MICE: A flexible testbed for intelligent coordination experiments. In Erman, L., editor, *Intelligent real time problem solving: Workshop report*, pages X1–X16.

Dusenbery, D. B. (1992). *Sensory ecology*. Freeman.

Dutton, E. and Lynn, R. (2013). A negative Flynn effect in Finland, 1997–2009. *Intelligence*, 41(6):817–820.

Eaton, E., Lane, T., et al. (2008). Modeling transfer relationships between learning tasks for improved inductive transfer. In *Machine learning and knowledge discovery in databases*, pages 317–332. Springer.

Eden, A. H. (2016). The singularity controversy. Technical Report, STR 2016-1. doi:10.13140/RG.2.1.3416.6809.

Eden, A. H., Moor, J. H., Soraker, J. H., and Steinhart, E. (2012a). *Singularity hypotheses: A scientific and philosophical assessment*. Springer.

Eden, A. H., Steinhart, E., Pearce, D., and Moor, J. H. (2012b). Singularity hypotheses: An overview. In Eden, A. H., Moor, J. H., Soraker, J. H., and Steinhart, E., editors, *Singularity hypotheses*, pages 1–12. Springer.

Edmonds, B. (2009). The social embedding of intelligence. In Epstein, R., Roberts, G., and Beber, G., editors, *Parsing the Turing test*, pages 211–235. Springer.

Edmondson, W. (2012). The intelligence in ETI – What can we know? *Acta Astronautica*, 78:37–42.

Eliasmith, C., Stewart, T. C., Choo, X., Bekolay, T., DeWolf, T., Tang, C., and Rasmussen, D. (2012). A large-scale model of the functioning brain. *Science*, 338(6111):1202–1205.

Elo, A. E. (1978). *The rating of chessplayers, past and present*, volume 3. Batsford.

Embretson, S. E. (2004). The second century of ability testing: Some predictions and speculations. *Measurement: Interdisciplinary Research and Perspectives*, 2(1):1–32.

Embretson, S. E. and McCollam, K. M. S. (2000). Psychometric approaches to understanding and measuring intelligence. In Sternberg, R., editor, *Handbook of intelligence*, pages 423–444. Cambridge University Press.

Embretson, S. E. and Reise, S. P. (2000). *Item response theory for psychologists*. Lawrence Erlbaum Associates.

Emery, N. J., Clayton, N. S., and Frith, C. D. (2007). Introduction. Social intelligence: from brain to culture. *Philosophical Transactions of the Royal Society, Series B*, 362(1480):485–488.

Engel, D., Woolley, A. W., Aggarwal, I., Chabris, C. F., Takahashi, M., Nemoto, K., Kaiser, C., Kim, Y. J., and Malone, T. W. (2015). Collective intelligence in computer-mediated collaboration emerges in different contexts and cultures. In *Conference on Human Factors in Computing Systems*, pages 3769–3778. ACM.

Engelbart, D. C. (1962). Augmenting human intellect: A conceptual framework. Summary Report, AFOSR-3233. Stanford Research Institute.

Engle, R. W., Tuholski, S. W., Laughlin, J. E., and Conway, A. R. (1999). Working memory, short-term memory, and general fluid intelligence: A latent-variable approach. *Journal of Experimental Psychology: General*, 128(3):309.

Epstein, R., Roberts, G., and Beber, G., editors (2008). *Parsing the Turing test: Philosophical and methodological issues in the quest for the thinking computer*. Springer.

Erickson, G. J. and Smith, C. R. (1988). *Maximum-entropy and Bayesian methods in science and engineering*, volume 31. Springer Science and Business Media.

Ernst, G. W. and Newell, A. (1969). *GPS: A case study in generality and problem solving*. Academic Press.

EU (2010). Directive 2010/63/EU of the European Parliament and of the Council of 22 september 2010 on the protection of animals used for scientific purposes. *Official Journal of the European Union*, 276:33–74.

Evans, J. M. and Messina, E. R. (2001). Performance metrics for intelligent systems. *NIST Special Publication SP*, pages 101–104.

Evans, N. and Levinson, S. C. (2009). The myth of language universals: Language diversity and its importance for cognitive science. *Behavioral and Brain Sciences*, 32(05):429–448.

Evans, T. G. (1963). *A heuristic program of solving geometric analogy problems*. PhD thesis, MIT.

Evans, T. G. (1965). A heuristic program to solve geometric-analogy problems. In *Proceedings Spring Joint Computer Conference*, volume 25, pages 327–339. Spartan Books.

Everitt, T., Lattimore, T., and Hutter, M. (2014). Free lunch for optimisation under the universal distribution. In *2014 IEEE Congress on Evolutionary Computation (CEC)*, pages 167–174. IEEE.

Eysenck, H. J. (2007). *The structure and measurement of intelligence*. Transaction.

Eysenck, H. J., Eysenck, M. W., Ellis, A., Hunt, E., and Johnson-Laird, P. (1985). *Personality and individual differences: A natural science approach*. Plenum.

Eysenck, H. J. and Eysenck, S. B. G. (1975). *Manual of the Eysenck Personality Questionnaire (junior and adult)*. Hodder and Stoughton.

Falkenauer, E. (1998). On method overfitting. *Journal of Heuristics*, 4(3):281–287.

Falmagne, J.-C. and Doignon, J.-P. (2010). *Learning spaces: Interdisciplinary applied mathematics*. Springer Science and Business Media.

Farah, M. J. and Heberlein, A. S. (2007). Personhood and neuroscience: Naturalizing or nihilating? *American Journal of Bioethics*, 7(1):37–48.

Federle, M. J., Bassler, B. L., et al. (2003). Interspecies communication in bacteria. *Journal of Clinical Investigation*, 112(9):1291–1299.

Feigenbaum, E. A., Buchanan, B. G., and Lederberg, J. (1970). *On generality and problem solving: A case study using the DENDRAL program*. Stanford University.

Feil-Seifer, D., Skinner, K., and Matarić, M. J. (2007). Benchmarks for evaluating socially assistive robotics. *Interaction Studies*, 8(3):423–439.

Feldman, J. (2000). Minimization of boolean complexity in human concept learning. *Nature*, 407(6804):630–633.

Feldman, J. (2003). Simplicity and complexity in human concept learning. *The General Psychologist*, 38(1):9–15.

Feng, A. and Graetz, G. (2015). *Rise of the machines: The effects of labor-saving innovations on jobs and wages*. Centre for Economic Performance, London School of Economics and Political Science.

Fenson, L. (2007). *MacArthur-Bates Communicative Development Inventories: User's guide and technical manual*. Paul H. Brookes.

Fernandes, H. B., Woodley, M. A., and te Nijenhuis, J. (2014). Differences in cognitive abilities among primates are concentrated on g: Phenotypic and phylogenetic comparisons with two meta-analytical databases. *Intelligence*, 46:311–322.

Ferns, N., Panangaden, P., and Precup, D. (2004). Metrics for finite Markov decision processes. In *Proceedings of the 20th Conference on Uncertainty in Artificial Intelligence*, pages 162–169. AUAI Press.

Ferrando, P. J. (2009). Difficulty, discrimination, and information indices in the linear factor analysis model for continuous item responses. *Applied Psychological Measurement*, 33(1):9–24.

Ferrando, P. J. (2012). Assessing the discriminating power of item and test scores in the linear factor-analysis model. *Psicológica*, 33:111–139.

Ferrara, E., Varol, O., Davis, C., Menczer, F., and Flammini, A. (2015). The rise of social bots. CoRR arXiv preprint:1407.5225.

Ferrucci, D., Brown, E., Chu-Carroll, J., Fan, J., Gondek, D., Kalyanpur, A. A., Lally, A., Murdock, J., Nyberg, E., Prager, J., et al. (2010). Building Watson: An overview of the DeepQA project. *AI Magazine*, 31(3):59–79.

Fidora, A. and Sierra, C. E. (2011). *Ramon Llull: From the Ars Magna to artificial intelligence*. Artificial Intelligence Research Institute, IIIA.

Fiore, V. G., Mannella, F., Mirolli, M., Gurney, K., and Baldassarre, G. (2008). Instrumental conditioning driven by apparently neutral stimuli: A model tested with a simulated robotic rat. In *International Conference on Epigenetic Robotics: Modeling cognitive development in robotic systems*, pages 13–20. IEEE.

Fiorito, G. and Scotto, P. (1992). Observational learning in octopus vulgaris. *Science*, 256(5056):545–547.

Firn, R. (2004). Plant intelligence: An alternative point of view. *Annals of Botany*, 93(4):345–351.

Fischer, K. W. (1980). A theory of cognitive development: The control and construction of hierarchies of skills. *Psychological Review*, 87(6):477.

Flach, P. (2012). *Machine learning: The art and science of algorithms that make sense of data*. Cambridge University Press.

Fletcher, J. F. (1979). *Humanhood: Essays in biomedical ethics*. Prometheus Books.

Fleuret, F., Li, T., Dubout, C., Wampler, E. K., Yantis, S., and Geman, D. (2011). Comparing machines and humans on a visual categorization test. *Proceedings of the National Academy of Sciences*, 108(43):17621–17625.

Floridi, L. (2013). *The ethics of information*. Oxford University Press.

Floridi, L. and Sanders, J. W. (2004). On the morality of artificial agents. *Minds and Machines*, 14(3):349–379.

Flynn, J. R. (2007). *What is intelligence? Beyond the Flynn effect*. Cambridge University Press.

Flynn, J. R. (2013). The "Flynn effect" and Flynn's paradox. *Intelligence*, 41(6):851–857.

Fodor, J. A. (1983). *The modularity of mind: An essay on faculty psychology*. MIT Press.

Fogarty, G. J. and Stankov, L. (1995). Challenging the "law of diminishing returns". *Intelligence*, 21(2):157–174.

Fogel, D. B. (1995). *Evolutionary computation: Toward a new philosophy of machine intelligence*. IEEE.

Ford, K. M. and Hayes, P. J. (1998). On computational wings: Rethinking the goals of artificial intelligence – the gold standard of traditional artificial intelligence – passing the so-called Turing test and thereby appearing to be. *Scientific American*, 9(Winter):78–83.

Fostel, G. (1993). The Turing test is for the birds. *ACM SIGART Bulletin*, 4(1): 7–8.

Fountain, S. B. (2006). The structure of sequential behavior. In Wasserman, E. A. and Zentall, T. R., editors, *Comparative cognition: Experimental explorations of animal intelligence*, pages 439–458. Oxford University Press.

Fowler, O. S. and Fowler, L. N. (1859). *Self-instructor in phrenology and physiology*. Fowler and Wells.

Fragaszy, D., Johnson-Pynn, J., Hirsh, E., and Brakke, K. (2003). Strategic navigation of two-dimensional alley mazes: Comparing capuchin monkeys and chimpanzees. *Animal Cognition*, 6:149–160.

Fragaszy, D. M., Kennedy, E., Murnane, A., Menzel, C., Brewer, G., Johnson-Pynn, J., and Hopkins, W. (2009). Navigating two-dimensional mazes: Chimpanzees (*Pan troglodytes*) and capuchins (*Cebus apella* sp.) profit from experience differently. *Animal Cognition*, 12(3):491–504.

Frankfurt, H. G. (1971). Freedom of the will and the concept of a person. *Journal of Philosophy*, 68(1):5–20.

French, R. M. (2000). The Turing test: The first 50 years. *Trends in Cognitive Sciences*, 4(3):115–122.

French, R. M. (2012). Moving beyond the Turing test. *Communications of the ACM*, 55(12):74–77.

Frey, C. B. and Osborne, M. A. (2013). *The future of employment: How susceptible are jobs to computerisation?* University of Oxford.

Frith, U. and Frith, C. (2010). The social brain: Allowing humans to boldly go where no other species has been. *Philosophical Transactions of the Royal Society of London*, Series B, 365(1537):165–176.

Gabrieli, J. D., Ghosh, S. S., and Whitfield-Gabrieli, S. (2015). Prediction as a humanitarian and pragmatic contribution from human cognitive neuroscience. *Neuron*, 85(1):11–26.

Gács, P. and Vitányi, P. M. (2011). Raymond J. Solomonoff 1926–2009. *IEEE Information Theory Society Newsletter*, 61(1):11–16.

Galperin, M. Y. (2005). A census of membrane-bound and intracellular signal transduction proteins in bacteria: Bacterial IQ, extroverts and introverts. *BMC Microbiology*, 5(1):35.

Galton, F. (1869). *Hereditary genius: An Inquiry into its laws and consequences*, 3rd edition 1892. Macmillan.

Galton, F. (1883). *Inquiries into the human faculty and its development*. Macmillan.

Galton, F. (1884). Measurement of character. *Fortnightly Review*, 36:179–185.

Galton, F. (1906). Cutting a round cake on scientific principles (letters to the editor). *Nature*, 75(1938):173.

Galton, F. (1907). Vox populi. *Nature*, 75:450–451.

García, K. (2013). Asume que no es humano al ser incapaz de reconocer un código CAPTCHA. *El Mundo Today*. http://www.elmundotoday.com/2013/03/asume-que-no-es-humano-al-ser-incapaz-de-reconocer-un-codigo-captcha/.

Gardner, H. (1983). *Frames of mind: The theory of multiple intelligences*. Basic Books.

Gardner, R. A. and Gardner, B. T. (1969). Teaching sign language to a chimpanzee. *Science*, 165(3894):664–672.

Gauvrit, N., Zenil, H., and Tegnér, J. (2015). The information-theoretic and algorithmic approach to human, animal and artificial cognition. *CoRR* arXiv preprint:1501.04242.

Gavane, V. (2013). A measure of real-time intelligence. *Journal of Artificial General Intelligence*, 4(1):31–48.

Gelman, S. A., & Kalish, C. W. (2006). Conceptual development. In D. Kuhn & R. Siegler (Eds.), *Handbook of child psychology*, Vol. 2: *Cognition, perception and language*. pages 687–733. John Wiley.

Genesereth, M., Love, N., and Pell, B. (2005). General game playing: Overview of the AAAI competition. *AI Magazine*, 26(2):62.

Genesereth, M. and Thielscher, M. (2014). General game playing. *Synthesis Lectures on Artificial Intelligence and Machine Learning*, 8(2):1–229.

Gentner, T. Q., Fenn, K. M., Margoliash, D., and Nusbaum, H. C. (2006). Recursive syntactic pattern learning by songbirds. *Nature*, 440(7088):1204–1207.

Gerbino, W. and Salmaso, D. (1987). The effect of amodal completion on visual matching. *Acta Psychologica*, 65(1):25–46.

Gerónimo, D. and López, A. M. (2014). Datasets and benchmarking. In *Vision-based pedestrian protection systems for intelligent vehicles*, pages 87–93. Springer.

Gibson, W. (1984). *Neuromancer*. Penguin.

Ginsberg, M. (1993). *Essentials of artificial intelligence*. Newnes.

Ginsburg, S. and Jablonka, E. (2009). Epigenetic learning in non-neural organisms. *Journal of Biosciences*, 34(4):633–646.

Glaser, R. (1963). Instructional technology and the measurement of learing outcomes: Some questions. *American Psychologist*, 18(8):519.

Glasersfeld, E. v. (1974). The Yerkish language for non-human primates. *American Journal of Computational Linguistics*, 1.

Goertzel, B. (2006). *The hidden pattern*. Brown Walker.

Goertzel, B. (2010). Toward a formal characterization of real-world general intelligence. In Hutter, M., Baum, E., and Kitzelmann, E., editors, 3rd International Conference on Artificial General Intelligence, pages 19–24. Atlantis Press.

Goertzel, B., Arel, I., and Pennachin, C. (2010). Cogbot: An integrative cognitive architecture aimed at emulating early childhood intelligence in a humanoid robot. http://www.goertzel.org/CogBot_public.pdf.

Goertzel, B., Arel, I., and Scheutz, M. (2009). *Toward a roadmap for human-level artificial general intelligence: Embedding HLAI systems in broad, approachable, physical or virtual contexts*. Artificial General Intelligence Roadmap Initiative.

Goertzel, B. and Bugaj, S. V. (2009). AGI preschool: A framework for evaluating early-stage human-like AGIs. In *the 2nd International Conference on Artificial General Intelligence (AGI-09)*, pages 31–36. Atlantis Press.

Goertzel, B. and Pennachin, C., editors (2007). *Artificial general intelligence*. Springer.

Golbeck, J., Robles, C., Edmondson, M., and Turner, K. (2011). Predicting personality from Twitter. In *Privacy, security, risk and trust: 2011 IEEE Third International Conference on Social Computing (socialcom)*, pages 149–156. IEEE.

Gold, E. M. (1967). Language identification in the limit. *Information and Control*, 10(5):447–474.

Goldberg, L. R., Johnson, J. A., Eber, H. W., Hogan, R., Ashton, M. C., Cloninger, C. R., and Gough, H. G. (2006). The international personality item pool and the future of public-domain personality measures. *Journal of Research in Personality*, 40(1):84–96.

Goldin, D., Smolka, S. A., and Wegner, P. (2006). *Interactive computation*. Springer.

Goldreich, O. and Vadhan, S. (2007). Special issue on worst-case versus average-case complexity – editors' foreword. *Computational Complexity*, 16(4):325–330.

Goleman, D. (1996). Emotional intelligence: Why it can matter more than IQ. *Learning*, 24(6):49–50.

Goleman, D. (2007). *Social intelligence*. Random House.

Good, I. J. (1965). Speculations concerning the first ultraintelligent machine. *Advances in Computers*, 6(99):31–83.

Good, I. J. (1971). Twenty-seven principles of rationality. In *Foundations of statistical inference*, page 197. Holt, Rinehart, Winston.

Gordon, B. B. (2007). Report on panel discussion on (re-)establishing or increasing collaborative links between artificial intelligence and intelligent systems. In Messina, E. R. and Madhavan, R., editors, *Proceedings of the 2007 Workshop on Performance Metrics for Intelligent Systems*, pages 302–303. NIST.

Gosling, S. D. (2001). From mice to men: What can we learn about personality from animal research? *Psychological Bulletin*, 127(1):45.

Gosling, S. D. and John, O. P. (1999). Personality dimensions in nonhuman animals a cross-species review. *Current Directions in Psychological Science*, 8(3):69–75.

Gottfredson, L. S. (1997a). Mainstream science on intelligence: An editorial with 52 signatories, history, and bibliography. *Intelligence*, 24(1):13–23.

Gottfredson, L. S. (1997b). Why g matters: The complexity of everyday life. *Intelligence*, 24(1):79–132.

Gould, S. J. (1981). *The mismeasure of man*, revised and expanded edition. W. W. Norton.

Grassé, P. P. (1959). La reconstruction du nid et les coordinations interindividuelles chez bellicositermes natalensis et cubitermes sp. la théorie de la stigmergie: Essai d'interprétation du comportement des termites constructeurs. *Insectes sociaux*, 6(1):41–80.

Greely, H., Sahakian, B., Harris, J., Kessler, R. C., Gazzaniga, M., Campbell, P., and Farah, M. J. (2008). Towards responsible use of cognitive-enhancing drugs by the healthy. *Nature*, 456(7223):702–705.

Griffiths, R. (1954). *The abilities of babies: A study in mental measurement*. McGraw-Hill.

Grigorenko, E. L. and Sternberg, R. J. (1998). Dynamic testing. *Psychological Bulletin*, 124(1):75.

Groeger, J. A., Field, D., and Hammond, S. M. (1999). Measuring memory span. *International Journal of Psychology*, 34(5–6):359–363.

Grotzer, T. A. and Perkins, D. (2004). Teaching intelligence: A performance conception. In Sternberg, R., editor, *Handbook of intelligence*, pages 492–518. Cambridge University Press.

Grünwald, P. D., Myung, I. J., and Pitt, M. A., editors (2005). *Advances in minimum description length: Theory and applications*. MIT Press.

Guilford, J. (1982). Cognitive psychology's ambiguities: Some suggested remedies. *Psychological Review*, 89(1):48.

Guilford, J. P. (1956). The structure of intellect. *Psychological Bulletin*, 53(4):267.

Guilford, J. P. (1967). *The nature of human intelligence.* McGraw-Hill.

Gulliksen, H. (1945). The relation of item difficulty and inter-item correlation to test variance and reliability. *Psychometrika,* 10(2):79–91.

Gulwani, S., Hernández-Orallo, J., Kitzelmann, E., Muggleton, S. H., Schmid, U., and Zorn, B. (2015). Inductive programming meets the real world. *Communications of the ACM,* 58(11):90–99.

Gunkel, D. J. (2012). *The machine question: Critical perspectives on AI, robots, and ethics.* MIT Press.

Gunkel, D. J. (2014). A vindication of the rights of machines. *Philosophy and Technology,* 27(1):113–132.

Guttman, L. (1954). *A new approach to factor analysis: The Radex.* Free Press.

Hahn, U., Chater, N., and Richardson, L. B. (2003). Similarity as transformation. *Cognition,* 87(1):1–32.

Hall, J. S. (2007). *Beyond AI: Creating the conscience of the machine.* Prometheus Books.

Halmes, M. (2013). Measurements of collective machine intelligence. CoRR arXiv preprint:1306.6649.

Halpin, H., Clark, A., and Wheeler, M. (2010). *Towards a philosophy of the web: Representation, enaction, collective intelligence.* Web Science Conference.

Hamilton, W. (1859). *Lectures on metaphysics and logic,* volume 1. Gould and Lincoln.

Hammill, D. D. and Newcomer, P. L. (2008). *Test of language development – intermediate (TOLD I: 3).* Pro-Ed.

Hampson, R. E., Song, D., Chan, R. H., Sweatt, A. J., Riley, M. R., Gerhardt, G., Shin, D. C., Marmarelis, V. Z., Berger, T. W., Deadwyler, S., et al. (2012). A nonlinear model for hippocampal cognitive prosthesis: Memory facilitation by hippocampal ensemble stimulation. *IEEE Transactions on Neural Systems and Rehabilitation Engineering,* 20(2):184–197.

Hampson, R. E., Song, D., Opris, I., Santos, L. M., Shin, D. C., Gerhardt, G. A., Marmarelis, V. Z., Berger, T. W., and Deadwyler, S. A. (2013). Facilitation of memory encoding in primate hippocampus by a neuroprosthesis that promotes task-specific neural firing. *Journal of Neural Engineering,* 10(6):066013.

Hand, D. J. (2004). *Measurement theory and practice.* Hodder Arnold.

Haney, R. (1969). Classical conditioning of a plant: Mimosa pudica. *Journal of Biological Psychology,* 11:5–12.

Hanks, S., Pollack, M. E., and Cohen, P. R. (1993). Benchmarks, test beds, controlled experimentation, and the design of agent architectures. *AI Magazine,* 14(4): 17.

Hanus, D., Mendes, N., Tennie, C., and Call, J. (2011). Comparing the performances of apes (*Gorilla gorilla, Pan troglodytes, Pongo pygmaeus*) and human children (*Homo sapiens*) in the floating peanut task. *PloS ONE,* 6(6):e19555.

Haraway, D. J. (1991). *Simians, cyborgs, and women: The reinvention of nature.* Routledge.

Hardman, D. K. and Payne, S. J. (1995). Problem difficulty and response format in syllogistic reasoning. *Quarterly Journal of Experimental Psychology,* 48(4):945–975.

Hare, B. and Tomasello, M. (2005). Human-like social skills in dogs? *Trends in Cognitive Sciences,* 9(9):439–444.

Harnad, S. (1992). The Turing Test is not a trick: Turing indistinguishability is a scientific criterion. *ACM SIGART Bulletin*, 3(4):9–10.

Harper, J. L., et al. (1977). *Population biology of plants*. Academic Press.

Hartley, R. V. L. (1928). Transmission of information. *Bell System Technical Journal*, 7(3):535–563.

Hartmann, P. and Teasdale, T. W. (2004). A test of Spearman's "law of diminishing returns" in two large samples of Danish military draftees. *Intelligence*, 32(5):499–508.

Hartshorne, J. K. and Germine, L. T. (2015). When does cognitive functioning peak? The asynchronous rise and fall of different cognitive abilities across the life span. *Psychological Science*, 26(4):433–443.

Hauser, M. D., Barner, D., and O'Donnell, T. (2007). Evolutionary linguistics: A new look at an old landscape. *Language Learning and Development*, 3(2):101–132.

Hauser, M. D., Chomsky, N., and Fitch, W. T. (2002). The faculty of language: What is it, who has it, and how did it evolve? *Science*, 298(5598):1569–1579.

Havel, I. M. (2013). On the way to intelligence singularity. In *Beyond artificial intelligence*, pages 3–26. Springer.

Hayes, B. (2002). Computing science: The easiest hard problem. *American Scientist*, pages 113–117.

Hayes, P. and Ford, K. (1995). Turing test considered harmful. In *International Joint Conference on Artificial Intelligence (IJCAI)*, pages 972–977. IJCAI.

Haywood, H. C. (1988). Dynamic assessment: The learning potential assessment device. In R. Jones (Ed.), *Psychoeducational assessment of minority group children: A casebook*, pages 39–63. Cobb and Henry.

He, J., Reeves, C., Witt, C., and Yao, X. (2007). A note on problem difficulty measures in black-box optimization: Classification, realizations and predictability. *Evolutionary Computation*, 15(4):435–443.

Henrich, J., Heine, S. J., and Norenzayan, A. (2010). The weirdest people in the world? *Behavioral and Brain Sciences*, 33(2–3):61–83.

Herculano-Houzel, S., Catania, K., Manger, P. R., and Kaas, J. H. (2015). Mammalian brains are made of these: A dataset of the numbers and densities of neuronal and nonneuronal cells in the brain of glires, primates, scandentia, eulipotyphlans, afrotherians and artiodactyls, and their relationship with body mass. *Brain, Behavior, and Evolution*, 86(3–4):145–163.

Hermann, K. M., Kočiský, T., Grefenstette, E., Espeholt, L., Kay, W., Suleyman, M., and Blunsom, P. (2015). Teaching machines to read and comprehend. CoRR arXiv preprint:1506.03340.

Hermans, D., Knoors, H., and Verhoeven, L. (2009). Assessment of sign language development: The case of deaf children in the Netherlands. *Journal of Deaf Studies and Deaf Education*, 15(2):107–119.

Hernández-Orallo, J. (1999a). *Computational measures of information gain and reinforcement in inference processes*. PhD thesis, Department of Logic and Philosophy of Science, University of Valencia. http://users.dsic.upv.es/~jorallo/tesi/.

Hernández-Orallo, J. (1999b). Universal and cognitive notions of part. In *Ferrer, L., et al., editor, Proceedings of 4th Systems Science European Congress*, pages 711–722. Sociedad Española de Sistemas Generales.

Hernández-Orallo, J. (2000a). Beyond the Turing test. *Journal of Logic, Language, and Information*, 9(4):447–466.

Hernández-Orallo, J. (2000b). A computational definition of 'consilience'. *Philosophica*, 61:901–920.

Hernández-Orallo, J. (2000c). Constructive reinforcement learning. *International Journal of Intelligent Systems*, 15(3):241–264.

Hernández-Orallo, J. (2000d). On the computational measurement of intelligence factors. In Meystel, A. M. and Messina, E. R., editors, *Measuring the performance and intelligence of systems: Proceedings of the 2000 PerMIS Workshop*, pages 72–79. NIST Special Publication 970. NIST.

Hernández-Orallo, J. (2000e). Thesis: Computational measures of information gain and reinforcement in inference processes. *AI Communications*, 13(1):49–50.

Hernández-Orallo, J. (2010). A (hopefully) non-biased universal environment class for measuring intelligence of biological and artificial systems. In Hutter, M., Baum, E., and Kitzelmann, E., editors, *Third International Conference on Artificial General Intelligence*, pages 182–183. Atlantis Press.

Hernández-Orallo, J. (2015a). C-tests revisited: Back and forth with complexity. In Bieger, J., Goertzel, B., and Potapov, A., editors, *Artificial General Intelligence – 8th International Conference, AGI 2015, Berlin, Germany, July 22–25, 2015, Proceedings*, pages 272–282. Springer.

Hernández-Orallo, J. (2015b). A note about the generalisation of the C-tests. arXiv preprint:1412.8529.

Hernández-Orallo, J. (2015c). On environment difficulty and discriminating power. *Autonomous Agents and Multi-Agent Systems*, 29:402–454.

Hernández-Orallo, J. (2015d). Stochastic tasks: Difficulty and Levin search. In Bieger, J., Goertzel, B., and Potapov, A., editors, *Artificial General Intelligence – 8th International Conference, AGI 2015, Berlin, Germany, July 22–25, 2015, Proceedings*, pages 90–100. Springer.

Hernández-Orallo, J. (2015e). Universal psychometrics tasks: Difficulty, composition and decomposition. arXiv preprint:1503.07587.

Hernández-Orallo, J. (2016). Evaluation in artificial intelligence: From task-oriented to ability-oriented measurement. *Artificial Intelligence Review*. doi: http://dx.doi.org/10.1007/s10462-016-9505-7.

Hernández-Orallo, J. and Dowe, D. L. (2010). Measuring universal intelligence: Towards an anytime intelligence test. *Artificial Intelligence*, 174(18):1508–1539.

Hernández-Orallo, J. and Dowe, D. L. (2013). On potential cognitive abilities in the machine kingdom. *Minds and Machines*, 23:179–210.

Hernández-Orallo, J., Dowe, D. L., España-Cubillo, S., Hernández-Lloreda, M. V., and Insa-Cabrera, J. (2011). On more realistic environment distributions for defining, evaluating and developing intelligence. In Schmidhuber, J., Thórisson, K., and Looks, M., editors, 4th International Conference on *Artificial general intelligence*, pages 82–91. *Lecture Notes in Artificial Intelligence*, volume 6830. Springer.

Hernández-Orallo, J., Dowe, D. L., and Hernández-Lloreda, M. V. (2014). Universal psychometrics: Measuring cognitive abilities in the machine kingdom. *Cognitive Systems Research*, 27:50–74.

Hernández-Orallo, J. and García-Varea, I. (2000). Explanatory and creative alternatives to the MDL principle. *Foundations of Science*, 5(2):185–207.

Hernández-Orallo, J., Insa-Cabrera, J., Dowe, D. L., and Hibbard, B. (2012). Turing tests with Turing machines. In Voronkov, A., editor, *Turing-100*, volume 10, pages 140–156. EPiC Series.

Hernández-Orallo, J., Martínez-Plumed, F., Schmid, U., Siebers, M., and Dowe, D. L. (2016). Computer models solving human intelligence test problems: Progress and implications. *Artificial Intelligence*, 230:74–107.

Hernández-Orallo, J. and Minaya-Collado, N. (1998). A formal definition of intelligence based on an intensional variant of Kolmogorov complexity. In *Proceedings of the International Symposium of Engineering of Intelligent Systems (EIS'98)*, pages 146–163. ICSC Press.

Herrmann, E. and Call, J. (2012). Are there geniuses among the apes? *Philosophical Transactions of the Royal Society, Series B*, 367(1603):2753–2761.

Herrmann, E., Call, J., Hernández-Lloreda, M. V., Hare, B., and Tomasello, M. (2007). Humans have evolved specialized skills of social cognition: The cultural intelligence hypothesis. *Science*, 317(5843):1360–1366.

Herrmann, E., Hernández-Lloreda, M. V., Call, J., Hare, B., and Tomasello, M. (2010). The structure of individual differences in the cognitive abilities of children and chimpanzees. *Psychological Science*, 21(1):102.

Herrmann, E., Misch, A., Hernandez-Lloreda, V., and Tomasello, M. (2015). Uniquely human self-control begins at school age. *Developmental Science*, 18(6):979–993.

Herrnstein, R. J. and Murray, C. (1994). *Bell curve: Intelligence and class structure in American life*. Simon and Schuster.

Herzing, D. L. (2014). Profiling nonhuman intelligence: An exercise in developing unbiased tools for describing other "types" of intelligence on Earth. *Acta Astronautica*, 94(2):676–680.

Heylighen, F. (2011). Conceptions of a global brain: An historical review. In Grinin, L. E., Carneiro, R. L., Korotayev A. V., and Spier F., editors, *Evolution: Cosmic, biological, and social*, pages 274–289. Uchitel.

Hibbard, B. (2002). Humans will want to become super-intelligent machines. In *Super-intelligent machines*, pages 193–198. Springer.

Hibbard, B. (2008). Adversarial sequence prediction. *Frontiers in Artificial Intelligence and Applications*, 171:399.

Hibbard, B. (2009). Bias and no free lunch in formal measures of intelligence. *Journal of Artificial General Intelligence*, 1(1):54–61.

Hibbard, B. (2011). Measuring agent intelligence via hierarchies of environments. In Schmidhuber, J., Thórisson, K., and Looks, M., editors, 4th International Conference on *Artificial general intelligence*, pages 303–308. *Lecture Notes in Artificial Intelligence*, volume 6830. Springer.

Hibbard, B. (2015a). *Bill Hibbard on ethical artificial intelligence, an interview by Luke Muehlhauser*. Machine Intelligence Research Institute.

Hibbard, B. (2015b). Ethical artificial intelligence. CoRR arXiv preprint:1411.1373.

Hingston, P. (2010). A new design for a Turing test for bots. In *2010 IEEE Symposium on Computational Intelligence and Games (CIG)*, pages 345–350. IEEE.

Hingston, P. (2012). *Believable bots: Can computers play like people?* Springer.

Hirschberg, J. and Manning, C. D. (2015). Advances in natural language processing. *Science*, 349(6245):261–266.

Ho, T. K. and Basu, M. (2002). Complexity measures of supervised classification problems. *IEEE Transactions on Pattern Analysis and Machine Intelligence*, 24(3):289–300.

Hoen, P. J., Tuyls, K., Panait, L., Luke, S., and La Poutre, J. A. (2005). An overview of cooperative and competitive multiagent learning. In *International Conference on Learning and Adaption in Multi-Agent Systems*, pages 1–46. Springer.

Hoff, E. (2013). *Language development*. Cengage Learning.

Hofstadter, D. R. (1979). *Gödel, Escher, Bach: An eternal golden braid*. Basic Books.

Holekamp, K. E. (2007). Questioning the social intelligence hypothesis. *Trends in Cognitive Sciences*, 11(2):65–69.

Holtgraves, T. M. (2014). *The Oxford handbook of language and social psychology*. Oxford University Press.

Holz, D., Iocchi, L., and Van Der Zant, T. (2013). Benchmarking intelligent service robots through scientific competitions: The RoboCup@Home approach. In *AAAI Spring Symposium: Designing Intelligent Robots*, pp. 27–32. Association for the Advancement of Artificial Intelligence.

Hong, L. and Page, S. E. (2004). Groups of diverse problem solvers can outperform groups of high-ability problem solvers. *Proceedings of the National Academy of Sciences of the United States of America*, 101(46):16385–16389.

Hoos, H. H. (1999). SAT-encodings, search space structure, and local search performance. In *International Joint Conference on Artificial Intelligence (IJCAI)*, volume 99, pages 296–303. IJCAI.

Hopcroft, J. E., Motwani, R., and Ullman, J. D. (2007). *Introduction to automata theory, languages, and computation*, 3rd edition. Pearson.

Horn, J. L. and Cattell, R. B. (1967). Age differences in fluid and crystallized intelligence. *Acta Psychologica*, 26:107–129.

Hortal, J., Araújo, M. B., and Lobo, J. M. (2009). Testing the effectiveness of discrete and continuous environmental diversity as a surrogate for species diversity. *Ecological Indicators*, 9(1):138–149.

Howe, J. (2008). *Crowdsourcing: How the power of the crowd is driving the future of business*. Random House.

Huarte, J. (1575). *Examen de los ingenios para las sciencias*. English translation by Richard Carew "The examination of men's wits", new edition by Rocío G. Sumillera, Modern Humanities Research Association, 2014.

Humies (2004). Humies awards. www.human-competitive.org, http://www.genetic-programming.org/combined.php.

Humphrey, N. K. (1976). The social function of intellect. In Bateson, P. and Hinde, R., editors, *Growing points in ethology*, pages 303–317. Cambridge University Press.

Humphry, S. M. (2011). The role of the unit in physics and psychometrics – and rejoinder. *Measurement*, 9(1):1–24, 64–70.

Hunt, T. (1928). The measurement of social intelligence. *Journal of Applied Psychology*, 12(3):317.

Hutter, M. (2002). The fastest and shortest algorithm for all well-defined problems. *International Journal of Foundations of Computer Science*, 13:431–443.

Hutter, M. (2005). *Universal artificial intelligence: Sequential decisions based on algorithmic probability*. Springer.

Hutter, M. (2007). Universal algorithmic intelligence: A mathematical top→down approach. In Goertzel, B. and Pennachin, C., editors, *Artificial general intelligence, cognitive technologies*, pages 227–290. Springer.

Hutter, M. (2012a). Can intelligence explode? *Journal of Consciousness Studies*, 19(1–2):143–166.

Hutter, M. (2012b). One decade of universal artificial intelligence. In *Theoretical foundations of artificial general intelligence*, pages 67–88. Springer.

Hutter, M., Legg, S., and Vitányi, P. M. (2007). Algorithmic probability. *Scholarpedia*, 2(8):2572.

Igel, C. and Toussaint, M. (2005). A no-free-lunch theorem for non-uniform distributions of target functions. *Journal of Mathematical Modelling and Algorithms*, 3(4):313–322.

Inoue, S. and Matsuzawa, T. (2007). Working memory of numerals in chimpanzees. *Current Biology*, 17(23):R1004–R1005.

Insa-Cabrera, J. (2016). *Towards a universal test of social intelligence*. PhD thesis, Universitat Politècnica de València.

Insa-Cabrera, J., Benacloch-Ayuso, J. L., and Hernández-Orallo, J. (2012a). On measuring social intelligence: Experiments on competition and cooperation. In Bach, J., Goertzel, B., and Iklé, M., editors, 5th International Conference on Artificial General Intelligence, pages 126–135. *Lecture Notes in Computer Science*, volume 7716. Springer.

Insa-Cabrera, J., Dowe, D. L., España-Cubillo, S., Hernández-Lloreda, M. V., and Hernández-Orallo, J. (2011a). Comparing humans and AI agents. In Schmidhuber, J., Thórisson, K., and Looks, M., editors, 4th International Conference on *Artificial general intelligence*, pages 122–132. *Lecture Notes in Artificial Intelligence*, volume 6830. Springer.

Insa-Cabrera, J., Dowe, D. L., and Hernández-Orallo, J. (2011b). Evaluating a reinforcement learning algorithm with a general intelligence test. In Lozano, J., Gamez, J., and Moreno, J., editors, *Current Topics in Artificial Intelligence: CAEPIA 2011. Lecture Notes in Artificial Intelligence*, volume 7023, pages 1–11. Springer.

Insa-Cabrera, J. and Hernández-Orallo, J. (2014). Definition and properties to assess multi-agent environments as social intelligence tests. CoRR arxiv preprint: abs/1408.6350.

Insa-Cabrera, J., Hernández-Orallo, J., Dowe, D., na, S. E., and Hernández-Lloreda, M. (2012b). The anYnt project intelligence test : Lambda – one. In Muller, V. and Ayesh, A., editors, *AISB/IACAP 2012 Symposium "Revisiting Turing and His Test"*, pages 20–27. Society for the Study of Artificial Intelligence and the Simulation of Behaviour.

Ishii, H., Ogura, M., Kurisu, S., Komura, A., Takanishi, A., Iida, N., and Kimura, H. (2006). Experimental study on task teaching to real rats through interaction with a robotic rat. In *From animals to animats 9*, pages 643–654. Springer.

Jaakkola, K., Fellner, W., Erb, L., Rodriguez, M., and Guarino, E. (2005). Understanding of the concept of numerically 'less' by bottlenose dolphins (tursiops truncatus). *Journal of Comparative Psychology*, 119(3):296.

Jacobs, G. H. and Nathans, J. (2009). The evolution of primate color vision. *Scientific American*, 300(4):56–63.

Jacoff, A., Messina, E., Weiss, B. A., Tadokoro, S., and Nakagawa, Y. (2003). Test arenas and performance metrics for urban search and rescue robots. In *Intelligent Robots and Systems, 2003 (IROS 2003)*, volume 4, pages 3396–3403. IEEE.

Janssen, R., Tuerlinckx, F., Meulders, M., and De Boeck, P. (2000). A hierarchical IRT model for criterion-referenced measurement. *Journal of Educational and Behavioral Statistics*, 25(3):285–306.

Japkowicz, N. and Shah, M. (2011). *Evaluating learning algorithms*. Cambridge University Press.

Jaulent, E. (2010). El Ars Generalis ultima de Ramon Llull: Presupuestos metafísicos y éticos. *Anales del Seminario de Historia de la Filosofía*, 27:87–113.

Jaynes, E. T. (1957). Information theory and statistical mechanics. *Physical Review*, 106(4):620.

Jelbert, S. A., Taylor, A. H., Cheke, L. G., Clayton, N. S., and Gray, R. D. (2014). Using the Aesop's fable paradigm to investigate causal understanding of water displacement by new Caledonian crows. *PloS ONE*, 9(3):e92895.

Jensen, A. R. (1980). Chronometric analysis of intelligence. *Journal of Social and Biological Structures*, 3(2):103–122.

Jensen, A. R. (1993). Why is reaction time correlated with psychometric g? *Current Directions in Psychological Science*, 2(2):53–56.

Jensen, A. R. (1998). *The g factor: The science of mental ability*. Praeger.

Jensen, A. R. (2000a). Artificial intelligence and g theory concern different phenomena. *Psycoloquy*, 11(86), Article 47.

Jensen, A. R. (2000b). A nihilistic philosophy of science for a scientific psychology? *Psycoloquy*, 11(88): Article 49.

Jensen, A. R. (2003). Regularities in Spearman's law of diminishing returns. *Intelligence*, 31(2):95–105.

John, O. P., Naumann, L. P., and Soto, C. J. (2008). Paradigm shift to the integrative big five trait taxonomy. In *Handbook of personality: Theory and research*, 3rd edition, pages 114–158. Guilford Press.

Johnson, M., Hofmann, K., Hutton, T., and Bignell, D. (2016). The Malmo platform for artificial intelligence experimentation. In *International Joint Conference on Artificial Intelligence (IJCAI)*, pages 4246–4247. IJCAI.

Johnson, N. L. and Kotz, S. (2011). Guttman, Louis in *Leading personalities in statistical sciences: from the seventeenth century to the present*, pp. 112–117, John Wiley.

Johnson, W. L. (1992). Needed: A new test of intelligence. *ACM SIGART Bulletin*, 3(4):7–9.

Johnson-Laird, P. N. (1986). *Mental models*. Harvard University Press.

Johnson-Laird, P. N., Khemlani, S. S., and Goodwin, G. P. (2015). Logic, probability, and human reasoning. *Trends in Cognitive Sciences*, 19(4):201–214.

Jolly, A. (1966). Lemur social behavior and primate intelligence. *Science*, 153(3735):501–506.

Jones, R. M. and Wray, R. E. (2011). Evaluating integrated, knowledge-rich cognitive systems. In *AAAI Fall Symposium: Advances in Cognitive Systems*, pages 138–145. Association for the Advancement of Artificial Intelligence.

Joosse, M., Lohse, M., Gallego-Pérez, J., and Evers, V. (2013). What you do is who you are: The role of task context in perceived social robot personality. In *2013 IEEE*

International Conference on Robotics and Automation (ICRA), pages 2134–2139. IEEE.

Just, C. (2011). A review of literature on the general factor of personality. *Personality and Individual Differences*, 50(6):765–771.

Kak, S. (2000). Grading intelligence in machines: Lessons from animal intelligence. In Meystel, A. M. and Messina, E. R., editors, *Measuring the performance and intelligence of systems: Proceedings of the 2000 PerMIS Workshop*, pages 331–334. NIST Special Publication 970. NIST.

Kamar, E., Hacker, S., and Horvitz, E. (2012). Combining human and machine intelligence in large-scale crowdsourcing. In *Proceedings of the 11th International Conference on Autonomous Agents and Multiagent Systems*, volume 1, pages 467–474. International Foundation for Autonomous Agents and Multiagent Systems.

Kaminka, G. A., Frank, I., Arai, K., and Tanaka-Ishii, K. (2003). Performance competitions as research infrastructure: Large scale comparative studies of multi-agent teams. *Autonomous Agents and Multi-Agent Systems*, 7(1–2):121–144.

Kamphaus, R. W. (2005). *Clinical assessment of child and adolescent intelligence*. Springer Science and Business Media.

Kamphaus, R. W. and Frick, P. J. (2005). *Clinical assessment of child and adolescent personality and behavior*. Springer Science and Business Media.

Kanefsky, B. and Taylor, W. (1991). Where the really hard problems are. In *International Joint Conference on Artificial Intelligence (IJCAI)*, volume 91, pages 163–169. IJCAI.

Kant, I. (1785). *Grundlegung zur Metaphysik der Sitten*. Hartknoch, Riga, German-English edition "Groundwork of the Metaphysics of Morals", edited and translated by Mary Gregor and Jens Timmermann, 2011.

Karas, P. J., Mikell, C. B., Christian, E., Liker, M. A., and Sheth, S. A. (2013). Deep brain stimulation: A mechanistic and clinical update. *Neurosurgical Focus*, 35(5):E1.

Karpov, I. V., Schrum, J., and Miikkulainen, R. (2012). Believable bot navigation via playback of human traces. In Hingston, P., editor, *Believable bots*, pages 151–170. Springer.

Keedwell, E. (2010). Towards a staged developmental intelligence test for machines. In *Towards a Comprehensive Intelligence Test (TCIT): Reconsidering the Turing Test for the 21st Century Symposium*, pages 28–32. Society for the Study of Artificial Intelligence and Simulation of Behaviour.

Keith, T. Z. and Reynolds, M. R. (2010). Cattell–Horn–Carroll abilities and cognitive tests: What we've learned from 20 years of research. *Psychology in the Schools*, 47(7):635–650.

Kelley, T. L. (1927). *Interpretation of educational measurements*. World Book.

Kelley, T. L. (1928). *Crossroads in the mind of man: A study of differentiable mental abilities*. Stanford University Press.

Kemper, S. and Sumner, A. (2001). The structure of verbal abilities in young and older adults. *Psychology and Aging*, 16(2):312.

Ketter, W. and Symeonidis, A. (2012). Competitive benchmarking: Lessons learned from the trading agent competition. *AI Magazine*, 33(2):103.

Keynes, J. M. (1931). *Essays in persuasion*. Macmillan.

Kihlstrom, J. F. and Cantor, N. (2000). Social intelligence. In Sternberg, R., editor, *Handbook of intelligence*, pages 359–379. Cambridge University Press.

Kim, J. (2006). Task difficulty as a predictor and indicator of web searching interaction. In *CHI'06 Extended Abstracts on Human Factors in Computing Systems*, pages 959–964. ACM.

Kim, J. H., Kim, D. H., Kim, Y. J., and Seow, K. T. (2004). *Soccer robotics*. Springer.

King, J. E. and Figueredo, A. J. (1997). The five-factor model plus dominance in chimpanzee personality. *Journal of Research in Personality*, 31(2):257–271.

Kirsh, D. (1991). Today the earwig, tomorrow man? *Artificial Intelligence*, 47(1):161–184.

Kitano, H., Asada, M., Kuniyoshi, Y., Noda, I., and Osawa, E. (1997). Robocup: The robot world cup initiative. In *International Conference on Autonomous Agents*, pages 340–347. International Foundation for Autonomous Agents and Multiagent Systems.

Kittur, A., Nickerson, J. V., Bernstein, M., Gerber, E., Shaw, A., Zimmerman, J., Lease, M., and Horton, J. (2013). The future of crowd work. In *Proceedings of the 2013 Conference on Computer Supported Cooperative Work*, pages 1301–1318. ACM.

Klein, B. A., Stein, J., and Taylor, R. C. (2012). Robots in the service of animal behavior. *Communicative and Integrative Biology*, 5(5):466–472.

Kleiner, K. (2011). Who are you calling bird-brained? An attempt is being made to devise a universal intelligence test. *The Economist*, 398(8723):82.

Klenk, M., Forbus, K., Tomai, E., and Kim, H. (2011). Using analogical model formulation with sketches to solve Bennett mechanical comprehension test problems. *Journal of Experimental and Theoretical Artificial Intelligence*, 23(3):299–327.

Kline, P. (1998). *The new psychometrics: Science, psychology and measurement*. Routledge.

Kline, P. (2000). *Handbook of psychological testing*, 2nd edition. Routledge.

Knuth, D. E. (1973). *Sorting and searching*, volume 3 of *The art of computer programming*. Addison-Wesley.

Koehler, O. (1941). Vom Erlernen unbenannter Anzahlen bei Vögeln. *Naturwissenschaften*, 29(14):201–218.

Koene, R. A. (2012). Embracing competitive balance: The case for substrate-independent minds and whole brain emulation. In Eden, A. H., Moor, J. H., Soraker, J. H., and Steinhart, E., editors, *Singularity hypotheses*, pages 241–267. Springer.

Korsgaard, C. M. (1996). *Creating the kingdom of ends*. Cambridge University Press.

Kosinski, M., Bachrach, Y., Kasneci, G., Van-Gael, J., and Graepel, T. (2012). Crowd IQ: Measuring the intelligence of crowdsourcing platforms. In *Proceedings of the 4th Annual ACM Web Science Conference*, pages 151–160. ACM.

Kosinski, M., Stillwell, D., and Graepel, T. (2013). Private traits and attributes are predictable from digital records of human behavior. *Proceedings of the National Academy of Sciences*, 110(15):5802–5805.

Kowalski, D., editor (2012). *The big bang theory and philosophy: Rock, paper, scissors, Aristotle, Locke*. John Wiley.

Koza, J. R. (2010). Human-competitive results produced by genetic programming. *Genetic Programming and Evolvable Machines*, 11(3–4):251–284.

Krause, J., Winfield, A. F., and Deneubourg, J.-L. (2011a). Interactive robots in experimental biology. *Trends in Ecology and Evolution*, 26(7):369–375.

Krause, S., James, R., Faria, J. J., Ruxton, G. D., and Krause, J. (2011b). Swarm intelligence in humans: diversity can trump ability. *Animal Behaviour*, 81(5):941–948.

Krueger, J. and Osherson, D. (1980). On the psychology of structural simplicity. In Jusczyk, P. W. and Klein, R. M., editors, *The nature of thought: Essays in honor of D. O. Hebb*, pages 187–205. Psychology Press.

Kubinyi, E., Virányi, Z., and Miklósi, Á. (2007). Comparative social cognition: From wolf and dog to humans. *Comparative Cognition and Behavior Reviews*, 2:26–46.

Kuhlmann, F. (1939). *Tests of mental development: A complete scale for individual examination*. Educational Test Bureau, Educational Publishers.

Kuncheva, L. I. (2004). *Combining pattern classifiers: Methods and algorithms*. John Wiley.

Kurzweil, R. (2005). *The singularity is near: When humans transcend biology*. Penguin.

Lacroix, B., Mathieu, P., and Kemeny, A. (2013). Formalizing the construction of populations in multi-agent simulations. *Engineering Applications of Artificial Intelligence*, 26(1):211–226.

Laird, J. E. (2012). *The Soar cognitive architecture*. MIT Press.

Laird, J. E., Newell, A., and Rosenbloom, P. S. (1987). Soar: An architecture for general intelligence. *Artificial Intelligence*, 33(1):1–64.

Laird, J. E. and Wray, R. E. (2010). Cognitive architecture requirements for achieving AGI. In Hutter, M., Baum, E., and Kitzelmann, E., editors, Proceedings of the *3rd International Conference AGI, Artificial general intelligence*, pages 79–84. Advances in Intelligent Systems Research. Atlantis Press.

Laird, J. E., Wray, R. E., Marinier, R., and Langley, P. (2009). Claims and challenges in evaluating human-level intelligent systems. In *the Second Conference on Artificial General Intelligence*, pages 91–96. Atlantis Press.

Lake, B. M., Salakhutdinov, R., and Tenenbaum, J. B. (2015). Human-level concept learning through probabilistic program induction. *Science*, 350(6266):1332–1338.

Lambiotte, R. and Kosinski, M. (2014). Tracking the digital footprints of personality. *Proceedings of the IEEE*, 102(12):1934–1939.

Langford, J. (2005). Clever methods of overfitting. *Machine Learning (Theory)*. http://hunch.net/?p=22.

Langley, P. (2011). Artificial intelligence and cognitive systems. *AISB Quarterly*, 133:1–4.

Lass, R. N., Sultanik, E. A., and Regli, W. C. (2009). Metrics for multiagent systems. In *Performance evaluation and benchmarking of intelligent systems*, pages 1–19. Springer.

Lasswitz, K. (1901). *The 'Universal Library'*. Originally in "Traumkristalle", English translation in "Fantasia mathematica", Clifton Fadiman, 1958, translated by Willy Ley, pp. 237–243.

Lattimore, T. (2013). *Theory of general reinforcement learning*. PhD thesis, Australian National University.

Lattimore, T. and Hutter, M. (2013). No free lunch versus Occam's razor in supervised learning. In Dowe, D. L., editor, *Algorithmic probability and friends: Bayesian prediction and artificial intelligence*, pages 223–235. *Lecture Notes in Computer Science*, volume 7070. Springer.

Laughlin, P. R. (2011). *Group problem solving*. Princeton University Press.

Law, E. and Von Ahn, L. (2011). Human computation. *Synthesis Lectures on Artificial Intelligence and Machine Learning*, 5(3):1–121.

Lee, S., Bang, W.-C., and Bien, Z.-Z. (2000). Measure of system intelligence: An engineering perspective. In Meystel, A. M. and Messina, E. R., editors, *Measuring the performance and intelligence of systems: Proceedings of the 2000 PerMIS Workshop*, pages 112–117. NIST Special Publication 970. NIST.

Leeuwenberg, E. L. (1969). Quantitative specification of information in sequential patterns. *Psychological Review*, 76(2):216.

Leeuwenberg, E. L. J. and Van Der Helm, P. A. (2012). *Structural information theory: The simplicity of visual form*. Cambridge University Press.

Legg, S. (2008). *Machine super intelligence*. PhD thesis, Department of Informatics, University of Lugano.

Legg, S. and Hutter, M. (2005). A universal measure of intelligence for artificial agents. In *International Joint Conference on Artificial Intelligence, IJCAI*, pages 1509–1510. IJCAI.

Legg, S. and Hutter, M. (2007a). A collection of definitions of intelligence. *Frontiers in Artificial Intelligence and Applications*, 157:17.

Legg, S. and Hutter, M. (2007b). Tests of machine intelligence. In Lungarella, M., Iida, F., Bongard, J., and Pfeifer, R., editors, *50 Years of Artificial Intelligence*, pages 232–242. *Lecture Notes in Computer Science*, volume 4850. Springer.

Legg, S. and Hutter, M. (2007c). Universal intelligence: A definition of machine intelligence. *Minds and Machines*, 17(4):391–444.

Legg, S. and Veness, J. (2013). An approximation of the universal intelligence measure. In Dowe, D. L., editor, *Algorithmic probability and friends: Bayesian prediction and artificial intelligence*, pages 236–249. *Lecture Notes in Computer Science*, volume 7070. Springer.

Leiber, J. (1985). *Can animals and machines be persons? A dialogue*. Hackett.

Leike, J. and Hutter, M. (2015). Bad universal priors and notions of optimality. *JMLR: Workshop and Conference Proceedings*, 40:1–16.

Lem, S. (1971). *The Futurological Congress (from the memoirs of Ijon Tichy)*. Translated into English in 1974 by Michael Kandel. Seabury Press.

Levesque, H. J. (2014). On our best behaviour. *Artificial Intelligence*, 212:27–35.

Levesque, H. J., Davis, E., and Morgenstern, L. (2012). The Winograd schema challenge. In *Thirteenth International Conference on the Principles of Knowledge Representation and Reasoning*, pages 552–561.

Levin, L. A. (1973). Universal sequential search problems. *Problems of Information Transmission*, 9(3):265–266.

Levin, L. A. (1974). Laws of information conservation (nongrowth) and aspects of the foundation of probability theory. *Problemy Peredachi Informatsii (Problems of Information Transmission)*, 10(3):30–35.

Levin, L. A. (1986). Average case complete problems. *SIAM Journal on Computing*, 15:285–286.

Levin, L. A. (1997). The century of bread and circus. *Tax Notes*, 77(7):858–860.

Levin, L. A. (2013). Universal heuristics: How do humans solve "unsolvable" problems? In Dowe, D. L., editor, *Algorithmic probability and friends: Bayesian prediction and artificial intelligence*, pages 53–54. *Lecture Notes in Computer Science*, volume 7070. Springer.

Levine, J., Congdon, C. B., Ebner, M., Kendall, G., Lucas, S. M., Miikkulainen, R., Schaul, T., Thompson, T., Lucas, S. M., Mateas, M., et al. (2013). General video game playing. *Artificial and Computational Intelligence in Games*, 6:77–83.

Levy, F. and Murnane, R. J. (2012). *The new division of labor: How computers are creating the next job market.* Princeton University Press.

Li, M. and Vitányi, P. (2008). *An introduction to Kolmogorov complexity and its applications* (3rd edition). Springer.

Li, Y. and Belkin, N. J. (2008). A faceted approach to conceptualizing tasks in information seeking. *Information Processing and Management*, 44(6):1822–1837.

Lillibridge, M. D., Abadi, M., Bharat, K., and Broder, A. Z. (2001). Method for selectively restricting access to computer systems. Filed on 13 April 1998 and granted on 27 February 2001, US Patent 6,195,698.

List, C. and Puppe, C. (2009). Judgment aggregation: A survey. In P. Anand, C. Puppe, P. Pattanaik (Eds.) *Rational and Social Choice*, pages 457–482. Oxford University Press.

Little, V. L. and Bailey, K. G. (1972). Potential intelligence or intelligence test potential? A question of empirical validity. *Journal of Consulting and Clinical Psychology*, 39(1):168.

Liu, J., Abbass, H. A., Green, D. G., and Zhong, W. (2012). Motif difficulty (MD): A predictive measure of problem difficulty for evolutionary algorithms using network motifs. *Evolutionary Computation*, 20(3):321–347.

Liu, J., Gwizdka, J., Liu, C., and Belkin, N. J. (2010). Predicting task difficulty for different task types. *Proceedings of the American Society for Information Science and Technology*, 47(1):1–10.

Liu, P. and Li, Z. (2012). Task complexity: A review and conceptualization framework. *International Journal of Industrial Ergonomics*, 42(6):553–568.

Livingston, S. A. (2006). Item analysis. In Downing, S. M. and Haladyna, T. M., editors, *Handbook of test development*, pages 421–441. Lawrence Erlbaum Associates.

Livingstone, D. (2006). Turing's test and believable AI in games. *Computers in Entertainment*, 4(1):6.

Llull, R. (1295). *Cant de Ramon. Lo desconhort.* Ensiola Editorial, 2006.

Llull, R. (1305). *Ars generalis ultima.* Edition by Alois Madre, ROL XIV. Turnhout.

Loebner, H. (2008). How to hold a Turing test contest. In Epstein, R., Roberts, G., and Beber, G., editors, *Parsing the Turing test: Philosophical and methodological issues in the quest for the thinking computer*, pages 173–179. Springer.

Loehlin, J. C. (2000). Group differences in intelligence. In Sternberg, R., editor, *Handbook of intelligence*, pages 176–193. Cambridge University Press.

Logie, R. H. (2014). *Visuo-spatial working memory.* Psychology Press.

Lohman, D. (2000). Complex information processing and intelligence. In Sternberg, R., editor, *Handbook of intelligence*, pages 285–340. Cambridge University Press.

Lohman, D. F., Lakin, J. M., Sternberg, R., and Kaufman, S. (2011). Reasoning and intelligence. In R. J. Sternberg, editor, *Handbook of intelligence*, pages 419–441. Cambridge University Press.

Long, D. and Fox, M. (2003). The 3rd international planning competition: Results and analysis. *Journal of Artificial Intelligence Research*, 20:1–59.

Loosemore, R. and Goertzel, B. (2012). Why an intelligence explosion is probable. In Eden, A. H., Moor, J. H., Soraker, J. H., and Steinhart, E., editors, *Singularity hypotheses*, pages 83–98. Springer.

Lord, F. M., Novick, M. R., and Birnbaum, A. (1968). *Statistical theories of mental test scores.* Addison-Wesley.

Lovett, A. and Forbus, K. (2011). Cultural commonalities and differences in spatial problem-solving: A computational analysis. *Cognition*, 121(2):281–287.

Lovett, A., Forbus, K., and Usher, J. (2010). A structure-mapping model of Raven's Progressive Matrices. In *Proceedings of the 32nd Annual Conference of the Cognitive Science Society*, volume 10, pages 2761–2766. Cognitive Science Society.

Lovett, A., Lockwood, K., and Forbus, K. (2008). A computational model of the visual oddity task. In *Proceedings of the 30th Annual Conference of the Cognitive Science Society*, volume 25, page 29. Cognitive Science Society.

Lycan, W. G. (1985). Abortion and the civil rights of machines. In *Morality and universality*, pages 139–156. Springer.

Lyle, J. (2008). Collective problem solving: Are the many smarter than the few? *Durhan Anthropology Journal*, 15(1):23–58.

Lynn, R. (1996). *Dysgenics: Genetic deterioration in modern populations*. Praeger.

Lynn, R. (2001). *Eugenics: A reassessment*. Greenwood.

Lynn, R. and Harvey, J. (2008). The decline of the world's IQ. *Intelligence*, 36(2):112–120.

Lyon, C., Nehaniv, C. L., and Saunders, J. (2012). Interactive language learning by robots: The transition from babbling to word forms. *PloS ONE*, 7(6):e38236.

Machluf, K., Liddle, J. R., and Bjorklund, D. F. (2013). An introduction to evolutionary developmental psychology. *Evolutionary Psychology*, 12(2):264–272.

Macià, N. and Bernadó-Mansilla, E. (2014). Towards UCI+: A mindful repository design. *Information Sciences*, 261:237–262.

MacInnes, W. J., Armstrong, B. C., Pare, D., Cree, G. S., and Joordens, S. (2009). Everyone's a critic: Memory models and uses for an artificial Turing judge. In the 2nd *Conference on Artificial General Intelligence*, pages 132–137. Atlantis Press.

Mackintosh, N. and Mackintosh, N. J. (2011). *IQ and human intelligence*. Oxford University Press.

Madden, M. G. and Howley, T. (2004). Transfer of experience between reinforcement learning environments with progressive difficulty. *Artificial Intelligence Review*, 21(3–4):375–398.

Madhavan, R., Tunstel, E., and Messina, E. (2009). *Performance evaluation and benchmarking of intelligent systems*. Springer.

Madsen, P. T., Jensen, F. H., Carder, D., and Ridgway, S. (2012). Dolphin whistles: A functional misnomer revealed by heliox breathing. *Biology Letters*, 8(2):211–213.

Mahoney, M. V. (1999). Text compression as a test for artificial intelligence. In *Proceedings of the National Conference on Artificial Intelligence*, pages 970–970. AAAI.

Mahrer, A. R. (1958). Potential intelligence: A learning theory approach to description and clinical implication. *Journal of General Psychology*, 59(1):59–71.

Malan, K. M. and Engelbrecht, A. P. (2013). A survey of techniques for characterising fitness landscapes and some possible ways forward. *Information Sciences*, 241:148–163.

Malone, T. W. and Bernstein, M. S., editors (2015). *Handbook of collective intelligence*. MIT Press.

Mandolesi, L., Addona, F., Foti, F., Menghini, D., Petrosini, L., and Vicari, S. (2009). Spatial competences in Williams syndrome: A radial arm maze study. *International Journal of Developmental Neuroscience*, 27(3):205–213.

Mar, H. (1996). *Psychological evaluation of children who are deaf-blind: An overview with recommendations for practice*. National Consortium on Deaf-Blindness.

Marché, C. and Zantema, H. (2007). The termination competition. In *Term rewriting and applications*, pages 303–313. Springer.

Marcolino, L. S., Xu, H., Jiang, A. X., Tambe, M., and Bowring, E. (2014). Give a hard problem to a diverse team: Exploring large action spaces. *Proceedings of 28th AAAI*. AAAI.

Marcus, G., Rossi, F., and Veloso, M. (2015). Beyond the Turing test. AAAI workshop, http://www.math.unipd.it/~frossi/BeyondTuring2015/.

Marcus, G., Rossi, F., and Veloso, M., eds. (2016). Beyond the Turing test (special issue). *AI Magazine*, 37(1):3–101.

Markowetz, A., Błaszkiewicz, K., Montag, C., Switala, C., and Schlaepfer, T. E. (2014). Psycho-informatics: Big data shaping modern psychometrics. *Medical Hypotheses*, 82(4):405–411.

Marshalek, B., Lohman, D. F., and Snow, R. E. (1983). The complexity continuum in the radex and hierarchical models of intelligence. *Intelligence*, 7(2):107–127.

Martínez-Plumed, Hernández-Orallo, J., Ramírez-Quintana, M., and Ferri, C. (2015). A computational analysis of general intelligence tests for evaluating cognitive development. Unpublished manuscript.

Martínez-Plumed, F., Ferri, C., Hernández-Orallo, J., and Ramírez-Quintana, M. J. (2015). Knowledge acquisition with forgetting: An incremental and developmental setting. *Adaptive Behavior*, 23(5):283–299.

Masum, H. and Christensen, S. (2003). The Turing ratio: A framework for open-ended task metrics. *Journal of Evolution and Technology*, 13(2).

Masum, H., Christensen, S., and Oppacher, F. (2002). The Turing ratio: Metrics for open-ended tasks. In *GECCO, Proceedings of the Genetic and Evolutionary Computation Conference*, pages 973–980. Morgan Kaufmann.

Matellán-Olivera, V. et al. (2011). Comparative cognition: Animals and robots. *ERCIM News*, 84:31–32.

Maturana, H. R. and Varela, F. J. (1980). *Autopoiesis and cognition: The realization of the living*. Kluwer.

Matzel, L. D. and Kolata, S. (2010). Selective attention, working memory, and animal intelligence. *Neuroscience and Biobehavioral Reviews*, 34(1):23–30.

Mayfield, J. E. (2007). Minimal history, a theory of plausible explanation. *Complexity*, 12(4):48–53.

Mayfield, J. E. (2013). *The engine of complexity: Evolution as computation*. Columbia University Press.

Mayr, E. (1982). *The growth of biological thought: Diversity, evolution, and inheritance*. Harvard University Press.

McCarthy, J. (1979). Ascribing mental qualities to machines. In Ringle, M., editor, *Philosophical perspectives in artificial intelligence*, pages 161–195. Humanities Press.

McCarthy, J. (1983). Artificial intelligence needs more emphasis on basic research: President's quarterly message. *AI Magazine*, 4(4):5.

McCarthy, J. (1987). Generality in artificial intelligence. *Communications of the ACM*, 30(12):1030–1035.

McCarthy, J. (2007). What is artificial intelligence? Technical report, Stanford University. http://www-formal.stanford.edu/jmc/whatisai.html.

McCarthy, J. (2008). The well-designed child. *Artificial Intelligence*, 172(18):2003–2014.

McClelland, D. C. (1973). Testing for competence rather than for "intelligence". *American Psychologist*, 28(1):1.

McCorduck, P. (2004). *Machines who think*. A K Peters/CRC Press.

McCrae, R. and Costa, P. (2010). *Neo inventories professional manual*. Psychological Assessment Resources.

McDermott, D. (1997). How intelligent is Deep Blue? *New York Times*, May 14.

McDermott, D. (2007). Level-headed. *Artificial Intelligence*, 171(18):1183–1186.

McDermott, D. (2010). Don't improve the Turing test, abandon it. In Ayesh, A., Bishop, M., Floridi, L., and Warwick, K., editors, *AISB 2010 Symposium "Towards a Comprehensive Intelligence Test (TCIT): Reconsidering the Turing Test for the 21st Century"*, pages 37–41. Society for the Study of Artificial Intelligence and the Simulation of Behaviour.

McDermott, J., White, D. R., Luke, S., Manzoni, L., Castelli, M., Vanneschi, L., Jaśkowski, W., Krawiec, K., Harper, R., Jong, K. D., and O'Reilly, U.-M. (2012). Genetic programming needs better benchmarks. In *International Conference on Genetic and Evolutionary Computation*, pages 791–798. ACM.

McGrath, J. E. (1984). *Groups: Interaction and performance*. Prentice Hall.

McIlwain, K. L., Merriweather, M. Y., Yuva-Paylor, L. A., and Paylor, R. (2001). The use of behavioral test batteries: Effects of training history. *Physiology and Behavior*, 73(5):705–717.

Melkikh, A. V. (2014). The no free lunch theorem and hypothesis of instinctive animal behavior. *Artificial Intelligence Research*, 3(4):43.

Mellenbergh, G. J. (1994). Generalized linear item response theory. *Psychological Bulletin*, 115(2):300.

Menary, R. (2010). *The extended mind*. MIT Press.

Merrell, K. W. (2001). Assessment of children's social skills: Recent developments, best practices, and new directions. *Exceptionality*, 9(1–2):3–18.

Mertens, S. (1998). Phase transition in the number partitioning problem. *Physical Review Letters*, 81(20):4281.

Messina, E., Meystel, A., and Reeker, L. (2001). PerMIS 2001, white paper. In Meystel, A. M. and Messina, E. R., editors, *Measuring the performance and intelligence of systems: Proceedings of the 2001 PerMIS Workshop*, pages 3–15. NIST Special Publication 982. NIST.

Meystel, A. (2000a). Appendix A. The preliminary discussions. In Meystel, A. M. and Messina, E. R., editors, *Measuring the performance and intelligence of systems: Proceedings of the 2000 PerMIS Workshop*, pages 563–642. NIST Special Publication 970. NIST.

Meystel, A. (2000b). Permis 2000 white paper: Measuring performance and intelligence of systems with autonomy. In Meystel, A. M. and Messina, E. R., editors, *Measuring the performance and intelligence of systems: Proceedings of the 2000 PerMIS Workshop*, pages 1–34. NIST Special Publication 970. NIST.

Meystel, A., Albus, J., Messina, E., and Leedom, D. (2003a). Performance measures for intelligent systems: Measures of technology readiness. Technical report, DTIC Document.

Meystel, A., Albus, J., Messina, E., and Leedom, D. (2003b). Permis 2003 white paper: Performance measures for intelligent systems – measures of technology readiness.

In Meystel, A. M. and Messina, E. R., editors, *Measuring the performance and intelligence of systems: Proceedings of the 2003 PerMIS Workshop*. NIST Special Publication 1014. NIST.

Meystel, A. and Andrusenko, J. (2001). Evaluating the performance of e-coli with genetic learning from simulated testing. In Meystel, A. M. and Messina, E. R., editors, *Measuring the performance and intelligence of systems: Proceedings of the 2001 PerMIS Workshop*. NIST Special Publication 982. NIST.

Michel, O. and Rohrer, F. (2008). The rat's life benchmark: Competing cognitive robots. In Madhavan, R. and Messina, E., editors, *Proceedings of the 8th Workshop on Performance Metrics for Intelligent Systems*, pages 43–49. ACM.

Michell, J. (2000). Normal science, pathological science and psychometrics. *Theory and Psychology*, 10(5):639–667.

Michell, J. (2008). Is psychometrics pathological science? *Measurement*, 6(1–2):7–24.

Michelucci, P. and Dickinson, J. L. (2016). The power of crowds. *Science*, 351(6268):32–33.

Miller, G. (2010). Social savvy boosts the collective intelligence of groups. *Science*, 330(6000):22–22.

Miller, G. A. (1956). The magical number seven, plus or minus two: Some limits on our capacity for processing information. *Psychological Review*, 63(2):81.

Miller, G. A. (1995). Wordnet: A lexical database for English. *Communications of the ACM*, 38(11):39–41.

Minsky, M. L., editor (1968). *Semantic information processing*. MIT Press.

Minsky, M. L. (1988). *Society of mind*. Simon and Schuster.

Mnih, V., Kavukcuoglu, K., Silver, D., Rusu, A. A., Veness, J., Bellemare, M. G., Graves, A., Riedmiller, M., Fidjeland, A. K., Ostrovski, G., Petersen, S., Beattie, C., Sadik, A., Antonoglou, I., King, H., Kumaran, D., Wierstra, D., Legg, S., and Hassabis, D. (2015). Human-level control through deep reinforcement learning. *Nature*, 518(26 February):529–533.

Monroe, P. E. (1931). *Conference on examinations*. Teachers College, Columbia University.

Moor, J. (2003). *The Turing test: The elusive standard of artificial intelligence*, volume 30. Springer Science and Business Media.

Moore, C. and Mertens, S. (2011). *The nature of computation*. Oxford University Press.

Moravec, H. P. (1988). *Mind children: The future of robot and human intelligence*. Harvard University Press.

Morgan, C. L. (1903). *An introduction to comparative psychology*. W. Scott.

Morgenstern, L., Davis, E., and Ortiz-Jr., C. L. (2016). Planning, executing, and evaluating the Winograd schema challenge. *AI Magazine*, 37(1):50–54.

Morgenstern, L. and Ortiz, C. (2015). The Winograd schema challenge: Evaluating progress in commonsense reasoning. In *The Twenty-Ninth AAAI Conference on Artificial Intelligence*, pages 4024–4026. AAAI.

Morris, D. (1967). *The naked ape: A zoologist's study of the human animal*. Jonathan Cape.

Moss, F., Hunt, T., Omwake, K., and Ronning, M. (1925). *George Washington University social intelligence test*. Cen.

Mueller, E. T. (1987). Daydreaming and computation. Technical report, TR, CSD-870017. PhD dissertation, University of California, Los Angeles.

Mueller, S. T. (2008). Is the Turing Test still relevant? A plan for developing the cognitive decathlon to test intelligent embodied behavior. In *19th Midwest Artificial Intelligence and Cognitive Science Conference.*

Mueller, S. T. (2010). A partial implementation of the BICA cognitive decathlon using the psychology experiment building language (PEBL). *International Journal of Machine Consciousness,* 2(02):273–288.

Mueller, S. T., Jones, M., Minnery, B., and Hiland, J. M. (2007). The BICA cognitive decathlon: A test suite for biologically-inspired cognitive agents. In *Proceedings of Behavior Representation in Modeling and Simulation Conference, Norfolk.*

Mueller, S. T. and Piper, B. J. (2014). The Psychology Experiment Building Language (PEBL) and PEBL test battery. *Journal of Neuroscience Methods,* 222:250–259.

Murphy, K. R. (2006). *A critique of emotional intelligence: What are the problems and how can they be fixed?* Psychology Press.

Murray, A. L., Dixon, H., and Johnson, W. (2013). Spearman's law of diminishing returns: A statistical artifact? *Intelligence,* 41(5):439–451.

Myers, G. J., Sandler, C., and Badgett, T. (2011). *The art of software testing.* John Wiley.

Nakagaki, T., Yamada, H., and Tóth, Á. (2000). Intelligence: Maze-solving by an amoeboid organism. *Nature,* 407(6803):470–470.

Naor, M. (1996). Verification of a human in the loop or identification via the Turing test. http://www.wisdom.weizmann.ac.il/~naor/PAPERS/human_abs.html.

Narr, K. L., Woods, R. P., Thompson, P. M., Szeszko, P., Robinson, D., Dimtcheva, T., Gurbani, M., Toga, A. W., and Bilder, R. M. (2007). Relationships between IQ and regional cortical gray matter thickness in healthy adults. *Cerebral Cortex,* 17(9):2163–2171.

Nass, C., Moon, Y., Fogg, B., Reeves, B., and Dryer, D. C. (1995). Can computer personalities be human personalities? *International Journal of Human-Computer Studies,* 43(2):223–239.

Neary, T. and Woods, D. (2006). P-completeness of cellular automaton rule 110. In *Automata, Languages and Programming,* pages 132–143. Springer.

Nehaniv, C. L. and Dautenhahn, K. (2007). *Imitation and social learning in robots, humans and animals: Behavioural, social and communicative dimensions.* Cambridge University Press.

Nettle, D. (2006). The evolution of personality variation in humans and other animals. *American Psychologist,* 61(6):622.

Neumann, F., Reichenberger, A., and Ziegler, M. (2009). Variations of the Turing test in the age of Internet and virtual reality. In *KI 2009: Advances in Artificial Intelligence,* pages 355–362. Springer.

Newborg, J., Stock, J. R., Wnek, L., Guidubaldi, J., Svinicki, J., et al. (1984). *Battelle developmental inventory.* DLM Teaching Resources.

Newcomer, P. L. and Hammill, D. D. (2008). *Test of Language Development: Primary (TOLD-P: 4).* PRO-ED.

Newell, A. (1973). You can't play 20 questions with nature and win: Projective comments on the papers of this symposium. In Chase, W., editor, *Visual information processing,* pages 283–308. Academic Press.

Newell, A. (1980). Physical symbol systems. *Cognitive Science,* 4(2):135–183.

Newell, A. (1990). *Unified theories of cognition.* Harvard University Press.

Newell, A., Shaw, J. C., and Simon, H. A. (1959). Report on a general problem-solving program. In International Conference on Information Processing, pages 256–264. UNESCO.

Newell, A. and Simon, H. A. (1961). GPS, a program that simulates human thought. Technical report, DTIC Document.

Newell, A. and Simon, H. A. (1976). Computer science as empirical inquiry: Symbols and search. *Communications of the ACM*, 19(3):113–126.

Ng, A. Y., Russell, S. J., et al. (2000). Algorithms for inverse reinforcement learning. In *International Conference on Machine Learning*, pages 663–670. Morgan Kaufman.

Nilsson, N. J. (1980). *Principles of artificial intelligence*. Morgan Kaufmann.

Nilsson, N. J. (1995). Eye on the prize. *AI Magazine*, 16(2):9.

Nilsson, N. J. (2006). Human-level artificial intelligence? Be serious! *AI Magazine*, 26(4):68.

Nilsson, N. J. (2009). *The quest for artificial intelligence*. Cambridge University Press.

Nisbett, R. E., Aronson, J., Blair, C., Dickens, W., Flynn, J., Halpern, D. F., and Turkheimer, E. (2012). Intelligence: New findings and theoretical developments. *American Psychologist*, 67(2):130.

Nivel, E., Thórisson, K. R., Steunebrink, B. R., Dindo, H., Pezzulo, G., Rodriguez, M., Hernandez, C., Ognibene, D., Schmidhuber, J., Sanz, R., Helgason, H. P., Chella, A., and Jonsson, G. K. (2014). Autonomous acquisition of natural language. In A. P. dos Reis, P. Kommers, and P. Isaías (Eds.), *Proceedings of the IADIS International Conference on Intelligent Systems & Agents 2014* (ISA-14), pages 58–66.

Oates, T. and Chong, W. (2006). Book review: Marcus Hutter, universal artificial intelligence. *Artificial Intelligence*, 170:1222–1226.

Ohlsson, S., Sloan, R. H., Turán, G., and Urasky, A. (2013). Verbal IQ of a four-year-old achieved by an AI system. In *COMMONSENSE 2013, 11th International Symposium on Logical Formalizations of Commonsense Reasoning, Ayia Napa, Cyprus*, page 6. Commonsense Reading.

Ohlsson, S., Sloan, R. H., Turán, G., and Urasky, A. (2015). Measuring an artificial intelligence system's performance on a verbal IQ test for young children. CoRR arXiv preprint:1509.03390.

Olton, D. S. and Samuelson, R. J. (1976). Remembrance of places passed: Spatial memory in rats. *Journal of Experimental Psychology: Animal Behavior Processes*, 2(2):97.

Omohundro, S. (2012). Rational artificial intelligence for the greater good. In Eden, A. H., Moor, J. H., Soraker, J. H., and Steinhart, E., editors, *Singularity hypotheses*, pages 161–179. Springer.

Oppy, G. and Dowe, D. L. (2011). The Turing test. In Zalta, E. N., editor, *Stanford encyclopedia of philosophy*. Stanford University. http://plato.stanford.edu/entries/turing-test/.

Orponen, P., Ko, K.-I., Schöning, U., and Watanabe, O. (1994). Instance complexity. *Journal of the ACM*, 41(1):96–121.

Orseau, L. (2013). Asymptotic non-learnability of universal agents with computable horizon functions. *Theoretical Computer Science*, 473:149–156.

Orseau, L. (2014). Universal knowledge-seeking agents. *Theoretical Computer Science*, 519:127–139.

Orseau, L., Lattimore, T., and Hutter, M. (2013). Universal knowledge-seeking agents for stochastic environments. In *Algorithmic learning theory*, pages 158–172. Springer.

Orseau, L. and Ring, M. (2011). Self-modification and mortality in artificial agents. In J. Schmidhuber, K. R. Thórisson, and M. Looks, editors, *4th Conference on Artificial General Intelligence*, pages 1–10. *Lecture Notes in Artificial Intelligence*, volume 6830. Springer.

Ortigosa, A., Carro, R. M., and Quiroga, J. I. (2013). Predicting user personality by mining social interactions in facebook. *Journal of Computer and System Sciences*, 80:57–71.

Ortiz, C. L., Jr. (2016). Why we need a physically embodied Turing test and what it might look like. *AI Magazine*, 37(1):55–62.

Orwell, G. (1949). *Nineteen Eighty-Four*. Secker and Warburg.

O'Sullivan, M., Guilford, J., and deMille, R. (1965). *Measurement of social intelligence*. ERIC, University of South California.

Owens, R. E. (2015). *Language development: An introduction*, 9th edition. Pearson.

Page, S. E. (2008). *The difference: How the power of diversity creates better groups, firms, schools, and societies*. Princeton University Press.

Panait, L. and Luke, S. (2005). Cooperative multi-agent learning: The state of the art. *Autonomous Agents and Multi-Agent Systems*, 11(3):387–434.

Park, G., Schwartz, H. A., Eichstaedt, J. C., Kern, M. L., Kosinski, M., Stillwell, D. J., Ungar, L. H., and Seligman, M. E. P. (2015). Automatic personality assessment through social media language. *Journal of Personality and Social Psychology*, 108(6):934.

Park, H.-J., Kim, B. K., and Lim, K. Y. (2001). Measuring the machine intelligence quotient (MIQ) of human-machine cooperative systems. *IEEE Transactions on Systems, Man and Cybernetics, Part A: Systems and Humans*, 31(2):89–96.

Parker, S. T. and McKinney, M. L. (2012). *Origins of intelligence: The evolution of cognitive development in monkeys, apes, and humans*. Johns Hopkins University Press.

Pearce, D. (2004). *Hedonistic imperative*. http://www.hedweb.com/.

Penn, D. C., Holyoak, K. J., and Povinelli, D. J. (2008). Darwin's mistake: Explaining the discontinuity between human and nonhuman minds. *Behavioral and Brain Sciences*, 31(2):109–130.

Perdue, B. M., Talbot, C. F., Stone, A. M., and Beran, M. J. (2012). Putting the elephant back in the herd: Elephant relative quantity judgments match those of other species. *Animal Cognition*, 15(5):955–961.

Perez, D., Samothrakis, S., Togelius, J., Schaul, T., Lucas, S., Couëtoux, A., Lee, J., Lim, C.-U., and Thompson, T. (2015). The 2014 general video game playing competition. *IEEE Transactions on Computational Intelligence and AI in Games*.

Persson, E. (2012). The moral status of extraterrestrial life. *Astrobiology*, 12(10):976–984.

Pervin, L. A. (1970). *Personality: Theory, assessment, and research*. John Wiley.

PETRL (2015). People for the ethical treatment of reinforcement learners. http://petrl.org/.

Piaget, J. (1936). *La naissance de l'intelligence chez l'enfant*. Delachaux et Niestlé. (English translation 1952: "The origins of intelligence in children").

Piaget, J. (1964). Cognitive development in children. *Journal of Research in Science Teaching*, 2(3):176–186.

Pinker, S. (1995). *The language instinct: The new science of language and mind*, volume 7529. Penguin.

Pinker, S. (2003). *The blank slate: The modern denial of human nature*. Penguin.

Pinker, S. (2009). *Language learnability and language development, with new commentary by the author*. Harvard University Press.

Pintner, R. (1921). Intelligence and its measurement: A symposium. *Journal of Educational Psychology*, 12(3):139.

Plasencia, A. (2017). *Is the universe a hologram? And other conversations with leading scientists*. MIT Press.

Plomin, R. (2001). The genetics of g in human and mouse. *Nature Reviews Neuroscience*, 2(2):136–141.

Plomin, R. and Asbury, K. (2005). Nature and nurture: Genetic and environmental influences on behavior. *Annals of the American Academy of Political and Social Science*, 600(1):86–98.

Plomin, R. and Deary, I. (2015). Genetics and intelligence differences: Five special findings. *Molecular Psychiatry*, 20:98–108.

Plomin, R., DeFries, J. C., Knopik, V. S., and Neiderheiser, J. (2013). *Behavioral Genetics*. Palgrave Macmillan.

Poland, J. and Hutter, M. (2005). Asymptotics of discrete MDL for online prediction. *IEEE Transactions on Information Theory*, 51(11):3780–3795.

Poland, J. and Hutter, M. (2006). MDL convergence speed for Bernoulli sequences. *Statistics and Computing*, 16(2):161–175.

Pollack, M. E., Brown, L., Colbry, D., McCarthy, C. E., Orosz, C., Peintner, B., Ramakrishnan, S., and Tsamardinos, I. (2003). Autominder: An intelligent cognitive orthotic system for people with memory impairment. *Robotics and Autonomous Systems*, 44(3):273–282.

Potthast, M., Hagen, M., Gollub, T., Tippmann, M., Kiesel, J., Rosso, P., Stamatatos, E., and Stein, B. (2013). Overview of the 5th international competition on plagiarism detection. In *CLEF 2013 Evaluation Labs and Workshop Working Notes Papers, 23–26 September, Valencia, Spain*.

Preiss, D. D. and Sternberg, R. J. (2005). Technologies for working intelligence. In Preiss, D. D. and Sternberg, R. J., editors, *Intelligence and technology: The impact of tools on the nature and development of human abilities*, pages 183–208. Routledge.

Preston, B. (1991). AI, anthropocentrism, and the evolution of 'intelligence'. *Minds and Machines*, 1(3):259–277.

Princeton University (2010). About Wordnet. http://wordnet.princeton.edu/.

Proudfoot, D. (2011). Anthropomorphism and AI: Turing's much misunderstood imitation game. *Artificial Intelligence*, 175(5):950–957.

Pullum, G. K. and Rogers, J. (2006). *Animal pattern-learning experiments: Some mathematical background*. Radcliffe Institute for Advanced Study/Harvard University.

Pullum, G. K. and Scholz, B. C. (2002). Empirical assessment of stimulus poverty arguments. *The Linguistic Review*, 18(1–2):9–50.

Pullum, G. K. and Scholz, B. C. (2009). For universals (but not finite-state learning) visit the zoo. *Behavioral and Brain Sciences*, 32(5):466–467.

Purdy, T., Grutter, K., Davanco, M., Srinivasan, K., and Taylor, J. (2016). Optomechanical quantum correlation thermometry. *Bulletin of the American Physical Society.* APS March Meeting 2016, abstract #P52.011. APS.

Quercia, D., Kosinski, M., Stillwell, D., and Crowcroft, J. (2011). Our Twitter profiles, our selves: Predicting personality with Twitter. In *Third International Conference on Social Computing (SOCIALCOM)*, pages 180–185. IEEE.

Quinn, A. J. and Bederson, B. B. (2011). Human computation: A survey and taxonomy of a growing field. In *Proceedings of the SIGCHI Conference on Human Factors in Computing Systems*, pages 1403–1412. ACM.

Quiroga, R. Q. (2012). *Borges and memory: Encounters with the human brain.* MIT Press.

Ragni, M. and Neubert, S. (2012). Solving Raven's IQ-tests: An AI and cognitive modeling approach. In *ECAI*, pages 666–671. IOS Press.

Ragni, M. and Neubert, S. (2014). Analyzing Raven's intelligence test: Cognitive model, demand, and complexity. In Prade, H. and Richard, G., editors, *Computational approaches to analogical reasoning: Current trends*, pages 351–370. *Studies in Computational Intelligence*, volume 548. Springer.

Rajani, S. (2011). Artificial intelligence – man or machine. *International Journal of Information Technology*, 4(1):173–176.

Rasch, G. (1960). *Probabilistic models for some intelligence and attainnment tests.* Danmarks paedagogiske Institut.

Rauscher, F. H., Shaw, G. L., and Ky, K. N. (1993). Music and spatial task performance. *Nature*, 365(14 October):611.

Raven, J. C., Court, J. H., and Raven, J. (1992). *Manual for Raven's Progressive Matrices and Vocabulary Scale.* Psychological Corporation.

Reader, S. M., Hager, Y., and Laland, K. N. (2011). The evolution of primate general and cultural intelligence. *Philosophical Transactions of the Royal Society, Series B*, 366(1567):1017–1027.

Regan, T. (1987). *The case for animal rights.* Springer.

Revelle, W. and Wilt, J. (2013). The general factor of personality: A general critique. *Journal of Research in Personality*, 47(5):493–504.

Reznikova, Z. (2007). *Animal intelligence: From individual to social cognition.* Cambridge University Press.

Reznikova, Z. and Ryabko, B. (2003). In the shadow of the binary tree: Of ants and bits. In *Proceedings of the 2nd Intl Workshop of the Mathematics and Algorithms of Social Insects*, pages 139–145. Georgian Institute of Technology.

Richardson, M. and Stalnaker, J. M. (1933). A note on the use of bi-serial r in test research. *Journal of General Psychology*, 8(2):463–465.

Riggio, R. E. (1986). Assessment of basic social skills. *Journal of Personality and Social Psychology*, 51(3):649.

Ring, M. and Orseau, L. (2011). Delusion, survival, and intelligent agents. In J. Schmidhuber, K. R. Thórisson, and M. Looks, editors, *4th Conference on Artificial General Intelligence*, pages 11–20. *Lecture Notes in Artificial Intelligence*, volume 6830. Springer.

Rissanen, J. (1978). Modeling by shortest data description. *Automatica*, 14(5):465–471.

Rizzo, P., Veloso, M., Miceli, M., and Cesta, A. (1997). Personality-driven social behaviors in believable agents. In *Proceedings of the AAAI Fall Symposium on Socially Intelligent Agents*, pages 109–114. AAAI.

Rizzolatti, G. and Craighero, L. (2004). The mirror-neuron system. *Annual Review of Neuroscience*, 27:169–192.

Robinson, P. (2001). Task complexity, task difficulty, and task production: Exploring interactions in a componential framework. *Applied Linguistics*, 22(1):27–57.

Rohrer, B. (2010). Accelerating progress in artificial general intelligence: Choosing a benchmark for natural world interaction. *Journal of Artificial General Intelligence*, 2(1):1–28.

Roid, G. (2003). *Stanford-Binet intelligence scales*. Riverside.

Romanés, G. J. (1885). Mind in men and animals. *The North American Review*, pages 251–257.

Rönnberg, J. and Borg, E. (2001). A review and evaluation of research on the deaf-blind from perceptual, communicative, social and rehabilitative perspectives. *Scandinavian Audiology*, 30(2):67–77.

Roth, G. and Dicke, U. (2013). Evolution of nervous systems and brains. In Galizia, C. and Lledo, P., editors, *Neurosciences – from molecule to behavior: A university textbook*, pages 19–45. Springer.

Rowe, C. and Healy, S. D. (2014). Measuring cognition will be difficult but worth it: A response to comments on Rowe and Healy. *Behavioral Ecology*, 24:1298.

Rumbaugh, D. M. (2014). *Language learning by a chimpanzee: The Lana project*. Academic Press.

Rumelhart, D. E., Hinton, G. E., and Williams, R. J. (1985). Learning internal representations by error propagation. Technical report, DTIC Document.

Rummery, G. and Niranjan, M. (1994). *On-line Q-learning using connectionist systems*. Cambridge University Engineering Department, TR 166.

Rundquist, E. A. (1936). Intelligence test scores and school marks in 1928 and 1933. *School and Society*, 43:301–304.

Russell, S. (2015). The long-term future of (artificial) intelligence. AAAI 2015 invited talk.

Russell, S., Dewey, D., Tegmark, M., Aguirre, A., Brynjolfsson, E., Calo, R., Dietterich, T., George, D., Hibbard, B., Hassabis, D., et al. (2015). Research priorities for robust and beneficial artificial intelligence: an open letter. Future of Life Institute (FLI). http://arxiv.org/abs/1602.03506.

Russell, S. and Norvig, P. (2009). *Artificial intelligence: A modern approach*, 3rd edition. Prentice Hall.

Rust, J. and Golombok, S. (2009). *Modern psychometrics: The science of psychological assessment*. Routledge.

Ryabko, B. and Reznikova, Z. (2009). The use of ideas of information theory for studying "language" and intelligence in ants. *Entropy*, 11(4):836–853.

Rzeszotarski, J. M. and Kittur, A. (2011). Instrumenting the crowd: Using implicit behavioral measures to predict task performance. In *Proceedings of the 24th annual ACM Symposium on User Interface Software and Technology*, pages 13–22. ACM.

Saklofske, D. H. and Zeidner, M. (1995). *International handbook of personality and intelligence*. Springer Science and Business Media.

Salminen, J. (2012). Collective intelligence in humans: A literature review. CoRR arXiv preprint:1204.3401.

Salovey, P. and Mayer, J. D. (1990). Emotional intelligence. *Imagination, Cognition and Personality*, 9(3):185–211.

Sanberg, P. (1976). "Neural capacity" in Mimosa pudica: A review. *Behavioral Biology*, 17(4):435–452.

Sanderson, A. C. (2000). Minimal representation size metrics for intelligent robotic systems. In Meystel, A. M. and Messina, E. R., editors, *Measuring the performance and intelligence of systems: Proceedings of the 2000 PerMIS Workshop*, pages 127–134. NIST Special Publication 970. NIST.

Sanghi, P. and Dowe, D. L. (2003). A computer program capable of passing IQ tests. In *4th International Conference on Cognitive Science (ICCS'03), Sydney*, pages 570–575. International Association for Cognitive Science.

Savage-Rumbaugh, E. S. and Lewin, R. (1994). *Kanzi: The ape at the brink of the human mind*. John Wiley.

Saygin, A. P., Cicekli, I., and Akman, V. (2000). Turing test: 50 years later. *Minds and Machines*, 10(4):463–518.

Scalise, K. and Allen, D. D. (2015). Use of open-source software for adaptive measurement: Concerto as an R-based computer adaptive development and delivery platform. *British Journal of Mathematical and Statistical Psychology*, 68(3):478–496, available at http://concertoplatform.com/.

Schaeffer, J., Burch, N., Bjornsson, Y., Kishimoto, A., Muller, M., Lake, R., Lu, P., and Sutphen, S. (2007). Checkers is solved. *Science*, 317(5844):1518.

Schaie, K. W. (2010). Primary mental abilities. In Weiner, I. B. and Craighead, W. E., editors, *Corsini encyclopedia of psychology*, pages 1286–1288. John Wiley.

Schaie, K. W., Willis, S. L., and Caskie, G. I. (2004). The Seattle longitudinal study: Relationship between personality and cognition. *Aging Neuropsychology and Cognition*, 11(2–3):304–324.

Schaul, T. (2014). An extensible description language for video games. *IEEE Transactions on Computational Intelligence and AI in Games*, 6(4):325–331.

Schenck, C. (2013). Intelligence tests for robots: Solving perceptual reasoning tasks with a humanoid robot. Master's thesis, Iowa State University.

Schenck, C., Sinapov, J., and Stoytchev, A. (2012). Which object comes next? Grounded order completion by a humanoid robot. *Cybernetics and Information Technologies*, 12(3):5–16.

Schenck, C. and Stoytchev, A. (2012). The object pairing and matching task: Toward Montessori tests for robots. In Ugur, E., Nagai, Y., Oztop, E., and Asada, M., editors, *Proceedings of Humanoids 2012 Workshop on Developmental Robotics: Can developmental robotics yield human-like cognitive abilities?*, pages 7–13. IEEE.

Scheuneman, J. (1979). A method of assessing bias in test items. *Journal of Educational Measurement*, 16(3):143–152.

Schlenoff, C., Scott, H., and Balakirsky, S. (2011). Performance evaluation of intelligent systems at the NIST. Technical report, DTIC Document.

Schmidhuber, J. (2004). Optimal ordered problem solver. *Machine Learning*, 54(3):211–254.

Schmidhuber, J. (2007). Gödel machines: Fully self-referential optimal universal self-improvers. In B. Goertzel and C. Pennachin, editors *Artificial general intelligence*, pages 199–226. Springer.

Schmitt, V., Pankau, B., and Fischer, J. (2012). Old world monkeys compare to apes in the primate cognition test battery. *PloS ONE*, 7(4):e32024.

Schönhage, D. D. A. and Strassen, V. (1971). Schnelle multiplikation grosser zahlen. *Computing*, 7(3–4):281–292.

Schrepp, M. (1999). An empirical test of a process model for letter series completion problems. In Albert, D. and Lukas, J., editors, *Knowledge spaces: Theories, empirical research, applications*, pages 133–154. Lawrence Erlbaum Associates.

Schweizer, P. (1998). The truly total Turing test. *Minds and Machines*, 8(2):263–272.

Scriven, M. (1965). An essential unpredictability in human behavior. In Wolman, B. B. and Nagel, E., editors, *Scientific psychology: Principles and approaches*, pages 411–425. Basic Books.

Sculley, D. and Brodley, C. E. (2006). Compression and machine learning: A new perspective on feature space vectors. In *Data Compression Conference*, pages 332–341. IEEE.

Seager, S. (2013). Exoplanet habitability. *Science*, 340(6132):577–581.

Sebeok, T. A. and Rosenthal, R. E. (1981). *The Clever Hans phenomenon: Communication with horses, whales, apes, and people*. New York Academy of Sciences.

Seferta, A., Guay, P.-J., Marzinotto, E., and Lefebvre, L. (2001). Learning differences between feral pigeons and zenaida doves: The role of neophobia and human proximity. *Ethology*, 107(4):281–293.

Segerdahl, P. (2012). Human-enculturated apes: Towards a new synthesis of philosophy and comparative psychology. In Birke, L. and Hockenhull, J., editors, *Crossing boundaries: Investigating human-animal relationships*, chapter 7, pages 139–159. BRILL.

Semel, E. M., Wiig, E. H., and Secord, W. (1996). *CELF 3, Clinical Evaluation of Language Fundamentals: Observational rating scales*. Psychological Corporation.

Shah, H. and Warwick, K. (2015). Human or machine? *Communications of the ACM*, 58(4):8.

Shahaf, D. and Amir, E. (2007). Towards a theory of AI completeness. In *AAAI Spring Symposium: Logical Formalizations of Commonsense Reasoning*, pages 150–155. Commonsense Reasoning.

Shahaf, D. and Horvitz, E. (2010). Generalized task markets for human and machine computation. In *National Conference on Artificial Intelligence*, pages 986–993. AAAI.

Shanahan, M. (2015). *The technological singularity*. MIT Press.

Shannon, C. E. (1948). A mathematical theory of communication. *Bell System Technical Journal*, 27:379–423, 623–656.

Shannon, C. E. (1987). Interview. *Omni Magazine*, 9(11 August):33–37.

Shapiro, S. C. (1992). *Encyclopedia of artificial intelligence*, 2nd edition. John Wiley.

Sharma, A., Vo, N. H., Gaur, S., and Baral, C. (2015). An approach to solve Winograd schema challenge using automatically extracted commonsense knowledge. In *2015 AAAI Spring Symposium Series*, pages 141–144. AAAI.

Shettleworth, S. J. (2009). The evolution of comparative cognition: Is the snark still a boojum? *Behavioural Processes*, 80(3):210–217.

Shettleworth, S. J. (2010a). Clever animals and killjoy explanations in comparative psychology. *Trends in Cognitive Sciences*, 14(11):477–481.

Shettleworth, S. J. (2010b). *Cognition, evolution, and behavior*, 2nd edition. Oxford University Press.

Shettleworth, S. J. (2013). *Fundamentals of comparative cognition*. Oxford University Press.

Shieber, S. M. (2004). *The Turing test: Verbal behavior as the hallmark of intelligence.* MIT Press.

Shipley, W. C. (1940). A self-administering scale for measuring intellectual impairment and deterioration. *Journal of Psychology*, 9(2):371–377.

Sijtsma, K. (2009). On the use, the misuse, and the very limited usefulness of Cronbach's alpha. *Psychometrika*, 74(1):107–120.

Sijtsma, K. (2012). Future of psychometrics: Ask what psychometrics can do for psychology. *Psychometrika*, 77(1):4–20.

Simmons, R. (2000). Survivability and competence as measures of intelligent systems. In Meystel, A. M. and Messina, E. R., editors, *Measuring the performance and intelligence of systems: Proceedings of the 2000 PerMIS Workshop*, pages 162–163. NIST Special Publication 970. NIST.

Simon, H. A. (1978). On the forms of mental representation. *Perception and Cognition: Issues in the Foundations of Psychology*, 9:3–18.

Simon, H. A. (1980). Cognitive science: The newest science of the artificial. *Cognitive Science*, 4(1):33–46.

Simon, H. A. (1982). *Models of bounded rationality: Empirically grounded economic reason*, volume 3. MIT Press.

Simon, H. A. and Kotovsky, K. (1963). Human acquisition of concepts for sequential patterns. *Psychological Review*, 70(6):534.

Simon, T., Klahr, D., and Newell, A. (1991). SCSoar: Pattern induction in series completion problem solving. In *European Soar Workshop*, page 17. Cambridge University Press.

Simpson, R. and Twardy, C. (2008). Refining the cognitive decathlon. In Madhavan, R. and Messina, E., editors, *Proceedings of the 8th Workshop on Performance Metrics for Intelligent Systems*, pages 124–131. NIST.

Sinapov, J. and Stoytchev, A. (2010). The odd one out task: Toward an intelligence test for robots. In *2010 IEEE 9th International Conference on Development and Learning (ICDL)*, pages 126–131. IEEE.

Singer, P. (1995). *Animal liberation.* Random House.

Sirois, S. and Shultz, T. R. (2006). Preschoolers out of adults: Discriminative learning with a cognitive load. *Quarterly Journal of Experimental Psychology*, 59(8):1357–1377.

Skinner, B. F. (1938). *The behavior of organisms: An experimental analysis.* Appleton-Century.

Sloman, A. (1978). *The computer revolution in philosophy: Philosophy, science and models of mind*, volume 3. Harvester Press Brighton. Freely available version with updates, 2009, http://www.cs.bham.ac.uk/research/projects/cogaff/crp/crp.pdf.

Sloman, A. (1984). The structure and space of possible minds. In Torrance, S., editor, *The mind and the machine: Philosophical aspects of artificial intelligence*, pages 35–42. Ellis Horwood.

Sloman, A. (2006). Why Asimov's three laws of robotics are unethical. http://www.cs.bham.ac.uk/research/projects/cogaff/misc/asimov-three-laws.html.

Sloman, A. (2009). Some requirements for human-like robots: Why the recent overemphasis on embodiment has held up progress. In *Creating brain-like intelligence*, pages 248–277. Springer.

Sloman, A. (2014a). Judging chatbots at Turing test. http://www.cs.bham.ac.uk/research/projects/cogaff/misc/turing-test-2014.html.

Sloman, A. (2014b). Judging chatbots without opening them: Limitations of 'black-box' tests. http://www.cs.bham.ac.uk/research/projects/cogaff/misc/black-box-tests .html.

Sloman, A. (2016). Construction kits for biological evolution. In Soskova, M. and Coope, S. B., editors, *The incomputable*. Springer. To appear.

Slotnick, B. (2001). Animal cognition and the rat olfactory system. *Trends in Cognitive Sciences*, 5(5):216–222.

Smith, C. (2010). *What is a person? Rethinking humanity, social life, and the moral good from the person up*. University of Chicago Press.

Smith, J. M. and Harper, D. (2003). *Animal signals*. Oxford University Press.

Smith, K. C. (2009). The trouble with intrinsic value: An ethical primer for astrobiology. In Bertka, C. M., editor, *Exploring the origin, extent, and future of life*, pages 261–280. Cambridge University Press.

Smith, K. C. (2014). Manifest complexity: A foundational ethic for astrobiology? *Space Policy*, 30(4):209–214.

Smith, W. D. (2002). Rating systems for gameplayers, and learning. Technical Report, NEC.

Smith, W. D. (2006). Mathematical definition of "intelligence" (and consequences). Unpublished report.

Snow, R. E., Kyllonen, P. C., and Marshalek, B. (1984). The topography of ability and learning correlations. *Advances in the Psychology of Human Intelligence*, 2:47–103.

Soares, C. (2009). UCI++: Improved support for algorithm selection using datasetoids. In *Advances in knowledge discovery and data mining*, pages 499–506. Springer.

Soares, N., Fallenstein, B., Armstrong, S., and Yudkowsky, E. (2015). Corrigibility. In *AAAI-15 Workshop on AI and Ethics*, pages 74–82. AAAI.

Sobel, D. (2005). *Longitude: The true story of a lone genius who solved the greatest scientific problem of his time*. Macmillan.

Sohn, K., Krishnamoorthy, S., Paul, O., and Lewis, M. A. (2012). Giving robots a flexible persona: The five factor model of artificial personality in action. In *12th International Conference on Control, Automation and Systems (ICCAS)*, pages 133–139. IEEE.

Soler-Toscano, F., Zenil, H., Delahaye, J.-P., and Gauvrit, N. (2014). Calculating Kolmogorov complexity from the output frequency distributions of small Turing machines. *PloS ONE*, 9(5):e96223.

Solomonoff, G. (2010). Ray Solomonoff (1926–2009). *Algorithms*, 3(3):255–259.

Solomonoff, R. J. (1960). A preliminary report on a general theory of inductive inference. Report V-131, Zator Co.

Solomonoff, R. J. (1962). Training sequences for mechanized induction. In Yovit, M., Jacobi, G., and Goldsteins, G., editors, *Self-organizing systems*, pages 425–434. Spartan Books.

Solomonoff, R. J. (1964a). A formal theory of inductive inference. Part I. *Information and Control*, 7(1):1–22.

Solomonoff, R. J. (1964b). A formal theory of inductive inference. Part II. *Information and Control*, 7(2):224–254.

Solomonoff, R. J. (1978). Complexity-based induction systems: Comparisons and convergence theorems. *IEEE Transactions on Information Theory*, 24(4):422–432.

Solomonoff, R. J. (1984a). Optimum sequential search. Oxbridge Research. http://raysolomonoff.com/publications/optseq.pdf.

Solomonoff, R. J. (1984b). Perfect training sequences and the costs of corruption – a progress report on induction inference research. Oxbridge Research. http://raysolomonoff.com/publications/perfecttraining.pdf.

Solomonoff, R. J. (1985). The time scale of artificial intelligence: Reflections on social effects. *Human Systems Management*, 5:149–153.

Solomonoff, R. J. (1989). A system for incremental learning based on algorithmic probability. In *Proceedings of the Sixth Israeli Conference on Artificial Intelligence, Computer Vision and Pattern Recognition*, pages 515–527. Information Processing Association of Israel.

Solomonoff, R. J. (1996). Does algorithmic probability solve the problem of induction? In Dowe, D., Korb, K., and Oliver, J., editors, *Proceedings of the Information, Statistics and Induction in Science (ISIS) Conference, Melbourne, Australia*, pages 7–8. World Scientific.

Solomonoff, R. J. (1997). The discovery of algorithmic probability. *Journal of Computer and System Sciences*, 55(1):73–88.

Solomonoff, R. J. (2002). Progress in incremental machine learning. In *NIPS Workshop on Universal Learning Algorithms and Optimal Search, Whistler, BC*.

Soloveichik, D. and Winfree, E. (2007). Complexity of self-assembled shapes. *SIAM Journal on Computing*, 36(6):1544–1569.

Sparrow, B., Liu, J., and Wegner, D. M. (2011). Google effects on memory: Cognitive consequences of having information at our fingertips. *Science*, 333(6043):776–778.

Sparrow, R. (2004). The Turing triage test. *Ethics and Information Technology*, 6(4):203–213.

Sparrow, R. (2012). Can machines be people? reflections on the Turing triage test. In Lin, P., Abney, K., and Bekey, G., editors, *Robot ethics: The ethical and social implications of robotics*, pages 301–315. MIT Press.

Spearman, C. (1904). General intelligence, objectively determined and measured. *American Journal of Psychology*, 15(2):201–292.

Spearman, C. (1925). Some issues in the theory of "g" (including the law of diminishing returns). *Nature*, 116:436–439.

Spearman, C. (1927). *The abilities of man: Their nature and measurement*. Macmillan.

Spitz, H. H. (1986). *The raising of intelligence: A selected history of attempts to raise retarded intelligence*. Routledge.

Spoto, A., Stefanutti, L., and Vidotto, G. (2010). Knowledge space theory, formal concept analysis, and computerized psychological assessment. *Behavior Research Methods*, 42(1):342–350.

Spronck, P., Ponsen, M., Sprinkhuizen-Kuyper, I., and Postma, E. (2006). Adaptive game AI with dynamic scripting. *Machine Learning*, 63(3):217–248.

Spronck, P., Sprinkhuizen-Kuyper, I., and Postma, E. (2003). Improving opponent intelligence through offline evolutionary learning. *International Journal of Intelligent Games and Simulation*, 2(1):20–27.

Spronck, P., Sprinkhuizen-Kuyper, I., and Postma, E. (2004). Difficulty scaling of game AI. In *Proceedings of the 5th International Conference on Intelligent Games and Simulation (GAME-ON 2004)*, pages 33–37. The European Multidisciplinary Society for Modelling and Simulation Technology.

Srinivasan, R. (2002). *Importance sampling: Applications in communications and detection*. Springer.

Staiano, J., Lepri, B., Aharony, N., Pianesi, F., Sebe, N., and Pentland, A. (2012). Friends don't lie: Inferring personality traits from social network structure. In *Proceedings of the 2012 ACM Conference on Ubiquitous Computing*, pages 321–330. ACM.

Stankov, L. (2000). Complexity, metacognition, and fluid intelligence. *Intelligence*, 28(2):121–143.

Starkie, B., van Zaanen, M., and Estival, D. (2006). The Tenjinno machine translation competition. In *Grammatical inference: Algorithms and applications*, pages 214–226. Springer.

Steels, L. (2011). *Design patterns in fluid construction grammar*, volume 11. John Benjamins.

Steels, L., Spranger, M., Van Trijp, R., Höfer, S., and Hild, M. (2012). Emergent action language on real robots. In *Language grounding in robots*, pages 255–276. Springer.

Steiner, I. D. (1966). Models for inferring relationships between group size and potential group productivity. *Behavioral Science*, 11(4):273–283.

Stenhouse, D. (1974). *The evolution of intelligence*. Barnes and Noble.

Stern, W. (1912). *Die psychologischen Methoden der Intelligenzprüfung und deren Anwendung an Schulkindern*. Barth.

Sternberg, R. J. (1977). *Intelligence, information processing, and analogical reasoning: The componential analysis of human abilities*. Lawrence Erlbaum Associates.

Sternberg, R. J. (1985). *Beyond IQ: A triarchic theory of human intelligence*. Cambridge University Press.

Sternberg, R. J. (1997). A triarchic view of giftedness: Theory and practice. *Handbook of Gifted Education*, 2:43–53.

Sternberg, R. J. (1999). Intelligence as developing expertise. *Contemporary Educational Psychology*, 24(4):359–375.

Sternberg, R. J., editor (2000). *Handbook of intelligence*. Cambridge University Press.

Sternberg, R. J., Conway, B. E., Ketron, J. L., and Bernstein, M. (1981). People's conceptions of intelligence. *Journal of Personality and Social Psychology*, 41(1):37.

Sternberg, R. J. and Gardner, M. K. (1983). Unities in inductive reasoning. *Journal of Experimental Psychology: General*, 112(1):80.

Stevens, S. S. (1946). On the theory of scales of measurement. *Science*, 103(2684):677–689.

Stewart, L., MacLean, E. L., Ivy, D., Woods, V., Cohen, E., Rodriguez, K., McIntyre, M., Mukherjee, S., Call, J., Kaminski, J., Miklósi, Á., Wrangham, R. W., and Hare, B. (2015). Citizen science as a new tool in dog cognition research. *PloS ONE*, 10(9):e0135176.

Steyn, M. (2006). It's the demography, stupid. *New Criterion*, 24(5):10.

Stone, P., Kaminka, G. A., Kraus, S., Rosenschein, J. S. (2010). Ad hoc autonomous agent teams: Collaboration without pre-coordination. In *Proceedings of the Twenty-Fourth AAAI Conference on Artificial Intelligence*, pages 1504–1509. AAAI.

Stork, D. G. (1998). Scientist on the set: An interview with Marvin Minsky. In *HAL's legacy: 2001's computer as dream and reality*, pages 15–32. MIT Press.

Strassmann, J. E., Klingler, C. J., Arévalo, E., Zacchi, F., Husain, A., Williams, J., Seppä, P., and Queller, D. C. (1997). Absence of within-colony kin discrimination in behavioural interactions of swarm-founding wasps. *Proceedings of the Royal Society of London, Series B*, 264(1388):1565.

Sturtevant, N. (2012). Benchmarks for grid-based pathfinding. *Transactions on Computational Intelligence and AI in Games*, 4(2):144–148.

Sutcliffe, G. (2009). The TPTP Problem Library and associated infrastructure: The FOF and CNF Parts, v3.5.0. *Journal of Automated Reasoning*, 43(4):337–362.

Sutcliffe, G. and Suttner, C. (2006). The state of CASC. *AI Communications*, 19(1):35–48.

Suthana, N. and Fried, I. (2014). Deep brain stimulation for enhancement of learning and memory. *Neuroimage*, 85:996–1002.

Sutton, R. S. and Barto, A. G. (1998). *Reinforcement learning: An introduction*. MIT Press.

Svartberg, K. and Forkman, B. (2002). Personality traits in the domestic dog (*Canis familiaris*). *Applied Animal Behaviour Science*, 79(2):133–155.

Swain, D. T., Couzin, I. D., and Leonard, N. E. (2012). Real-time feedback-controlled robotic fish for behavioral experiments with fish schools. *Proceedings of the IEEE*, 100(1):150–163.

Tannenbaum, A. J. (1986). Giftedness: A psychosocial approach. In Sternberg, R. and Davidson, J., editors, *Conceptions of giftedness*, pages 21–52. Cambridge University Press.

Tarapore, D., Lungarella, M., and Gómez, G. (2006). Quantifying patterns of agent–environment interaction. *Robotics and Autonomous Systems*, 54(2):150–158.

Teng, S.-Y. (1943). Chinese influence on the Western examination system: I. Introduction. *Harvard Journal of Asiatic Studies*, 7(4):267–312.

Terman, L. M. (1922). The great conspiracy or the impulse imperious of intelligence testers, psychoanalyzed and exposed by Mr. Lippmann. *New Republic*, 33(27 December):116–120.

Terrace, H. S. (1987). *Nim: A chimpanzee who learned sign language*. Columbia University Press.

Tesauro, G. (1994). TD-Gammon, a self-teaching backgammon program, achieves master-level play. *Neural Computation*, 6(2):215–219.

Thagard, P. R. (1978). The best explanation: Criteria for theory choice. *Journal of Philosophy*, 75(2):76–92.

Theiner, G., Allen, C., and Goldstone, R. L. (2010). Recognizing group cognition. *Cognitive Systems Research*, 11(4):378–395.

Thomas, R. K. (1996). Investigating cognitive abilities in animals: Unrealized potential. *Cognitive Brain Research*, 3(3):157–166.

Thompson, J. (2013). Special issue: The Flynn effect re-evaluated. *Intelligence*, 41(6):751–857.

Thompson, P. M., Cannon, T. D., Narr, K. L., Van Erp, T., Poutanen, V.-P., Huttunen, M., Lönnqvist, J., Standertskjöld-Nordenstam, C.-G., Kaprio, J., Khaledy, M., et al. (2001). Genetic influences on brain structure. *Nature Neuroscience*, 4(12):1253–1258.

Thompson, S. K. (2012). *Sampling*, 3rd edition. John Wiley.

Thórisson, K. R., Bieger, J., Schiffel, S., and Garrett, D. (2015). Towards flexible task environments for comprehensive evaluation of artificial intelligent systems and automatic learners. In Bieger, J., Goertzel, B., and Potapov, A., editors, *International Conference on Artificial General Intelligence*, pages 187–196. Springer.

Thorndike, E. L. (1911). *Animal intelligence: Experimental studies*. Macmillan.

Thorndike, E. L. (1920). Intelligence and its uses. *Harper's Magazine*, 140:227–335.

Thorndike, E. L., Bregman, E. O., Cobb, M. V., and Woodyard, E. (1927). *The measurement of intelligence*. Teachers College Bureau of Publications, Columbia University.

Thorndike, R. L. (1935). *Organization of behavior in the albino rat*. Genetic Psychology Monographs. Heldref.

Thorndike, R. L. (1936). Factor analysis of social and abstract intelligence. *Journal of Educational Psychology*, 27(3):231.

Thornton, A., Isden, J., and Madden, J. R. (2014). Toward wild psychometrics: Linking individual cognitive differences to fitness. *Behavioral Ecology*, aru095.

Thornton, A. and Lukas, D. (2012). Individual variation in cognitive performance: Developmental and evolutionary perspectives. *Philosophical Transactions of the Royal Society, Series B*, 367(1603):2773–2783.

Thorp, T. R. and Mahrer, A. R. (1959). Predicting potential intelligence. *Journal of Clinical Psychology*, 15(3):286–288.

Thurstone, L. L. (1928). Attitudes can be measured. *American Journal of Sociology*, 33:529–554.

Thurstone, L. L. (1929). Theory of attitude measurement. *Psychological Review*, 36(3):222–241.

Thurstone, L. L. (1937). Ability, motivation, and speed. *Psychometrika*, 2(4):249–254.

Thurstone, L. L. (1938). Primary mental abilities. *Psychometric Monographs*.

Thurstone, L. L. and Thurstone, T. G. (1941). *Factorial studies of intelligence*. Psychometrika Monograph Supplements. University of Chicago Press.

Thurstone, L. L. and Thurstone, T. G. (1947). *American Council on Education for college freshmen: Manual of instructions*. Cooperative Test Division, Educational Testing Service.

Tinbergen, N. (1963). On aims and methods of ethology. *Zeitschrift für Tierpsychologie*, 20(4):410–433.

Togelius, J., Yannakakis, G. N., Karakovskiy, S., and Shaker, N. (2012). Assessing believability. In Hingston, P., editor, *Believable bots*, pages 215–230. Springer.

Tomasello, M. (2006). Acquiring linguistic constructions, volume two. In Damon, W. and Lerner, R. M., editors, *Handbook of child psychology*, 255–298. John Wiley.

Tomasello, M. and Call, J. (1997). *Primate cognition*. Oxford University Press.

Tomasello, M. and Carpenter, M. (2007). Shared intentionality. *Developmental Science*, 10(1):121–125.

Tomasik, B. (2014). Do artificial reinforcement-learning agents matter morally? CoRR arXiv preprint:1410.8233.

Torres-Quevedo, L. (1915a). Ensayos sobre automática – su definición. Extensión teórica de sus aplicaciones. *Revista de la Real Academia de Ciencias Exactas, Físicas y Naturales 12, 391–418. English translation, Randell, B., editor. The origins of digital computers. Springer*, 1973.

Torres-Quevedo, L. (1915b). Torres and his remarkable automatic devices. *Scientific American*, 80(2079):296–298.

Treffert, D. A. (2009). The savant syndrome: An extraordinary condition. A synopsis: Past, present, future. *Philosophical Transactions of the Royal Society, Series B*, 364(1522):1351–1357.

Trewavas, A. (2005). Plant intelligence. *Naturwissenschaften*, 92(9):401–413.

Tromp, J. (2006). Binary lambda calculus and combinatory logic. In M. Hutter, W. Merkle and P. M. B. Vitányi *Kolmogorov Complexity and Applications*, Dagstuhl Seminar Proceedings 6051.

Tucker-Drob, E. M. (2009). Differentiation of cognitive abilities across the life span. *Developmental Psychology*, 45(4):1097.

Tummolini, L., Castelfranchi, C., Ricci, A., Viroli, M., and Omicini, A. (2005). "Exhibitionists" and "Voyeurs" do it better: A shared environment for flexible coordination with tacit messages. In *Environments for multi-agent systems*, pages 215–231. Springer.

Turing, A. M. (1936). On computable numbers, with an application to the entscheidungsproblem. *Proceedings of the London Mathematical Society*, 2(42):230–265.

Turing, A. M. (1937). On computable numbers, with an application to the entscheidungsproblem: A correction. *Proceedings of the London Mathematical Society*, 2(6):544–456.

Turing, A. M. (1948). Intelligent machinery. Chapter 10 in B. J. Copeland, editor, *The essential Turing: Seminal writings in computing, logic, philosophy, artificial intelligence, and artificial life: Plus the secrets of enigma*. Reprint, Oxford University Press, 2004.

Turing, A. M. (1950). Computing machinery and intelligence. *Mind*, 59:433–460.

Turing, A. M. (1951). Intelligent machinery, a heretical theory. Chapter 12 in B. J. Copeland, editor, *The essential Turing: Seminal writings in computing, logic, philosophy, artificial intelligence, and artificial life: Plus the secrets of enigma*. Reprint, Oxford University Press, 2004.

Turing, A. M. (1952). Can automatic calculating machines be said to think? BBC Third Programme, 14 and 23 Jan. 1952, between M.H.A. Newman, AMT, Sir Geoffrey Jefferson and R.B. Braithwaite, in Copeland, B. J., editor, *The essential Turing*, pp. 494–495. Oxford University Press. http://www.turingarchive.org/browse.php/B/6.

Turing, A. M. and Champernowne, D. (1948). Turochamp. In Copeland, B. J., editor, *The essential Turing*, pp. 562–575. Oxford University Press.

Turney, P. D. (2011). Analogy perception applied to seven tests of word comprehension. *Journal of Experimental and Theoretical Artificial Intelligence*, 23(3):343–362.

Tuyls, K. and Weiss, G. (2012). Multiagent learning: Basics, challenges, and prospects. *AI Magazine*, 33(3):41.

Tyler, T. (2011). The matching pennies tournament. http://matchingpennies.com/tournament/.

Úbeda, Y. and Llorente, M. (2014). Personality in sanctuary-housed chimpanzees: A comparative approach of psychobiological and penta-factorial human models. *Evolutionary Psychology*, 13(1):182–196.

Ulam, S. (1958). Tribute to John von Neumann. *Bulletin of the American Mathematical Society*, 64(3):1–49.

Ulinwa, V. C. I. (2008). *Machine Intelligence Quotient*. VDM.

Urbina, S. (2011). Tests of intelligence. In Sternberg, R. J. and Kaufman, S. B., editors, *The Cambridge handbook of intelligence*, pages 20–38. Cambridge University Press.

Vakoch, D. A. (2011). *Communication with extraterrestrial intelligence*. SUNY Press.

Valiant, L. G. (1984). A theory of the learnable. *Communications of the ACM*, 27(11):1134–1142.

Valiant, L. G. (2013). *Probably approximately correct: Nature's algorithms for learning and prospering in a complex world*. Basic Books.

Van Der Linden, W. J. (2008). Using response times for item selection in adaptive testing. *Journal of Educational and Behavioral Statistics*, 33(1):5–20.

Van Der Maas, H. L. J., Dolan, C. V., Grasman, R. P., Wicherts, J. M., Huizenga, H. M., and Raijmakers, M. E. (2006). A dynamical model of general intelligence: The positive manifold of intelligence by mutualism. *Psychological Review*, 113(4): 842.

Van Der Maas, H. L. J., Kan, K.-J., and Borsboom, D. (2014). Intelligence is what the intelligence test measures. Seriously. *Journal of Intelligence*, 2(1):12–15.

Van Duijn, M., Keijzer, F., and Franken, D. (2006). Principles of minimal cognition: Casting cognition as sensorimotor coordination. *Adaptive Behavior*, 14(2):157–170.

Van Heijningen, C. A., De Visser, J., Zuidema, W., and Ten Cate, C. (2009). Simple rules can explain discrimination of putative recursive syntactic structures by a songbird species. *Proceedings of the National Academy of Sciences*, 106(48):20538–20543.

Van Knippenberg, D., De Dreu, C. K., and Homan, A. C. (2004). Work group diversity and group performance: An integrative model and research agenda. *Journal of Applied Psychology*, 89(6):1008.

Van Knippenberg, D. and Schippers, M. C. (2007). Work group diversity. *Annual Review of Psychology*, 58:515–541.

Van Rijn, J. N., Bischl, B., Torgo, L., Gao, B., Umaashankar, V., Fischer, S., Winter, P., Wiswedel, B., Berthold, M. R., and Vanschoren, J. (2013). OpenML: A collaborative science platform. In *European Conference on Machine Learning and Knowledge Discovery in Databases*, pages 645–649. *Lecture Notes in Artificial Intelligence*, volume 8190. Springer.

Vanschoren, J., Blockeel, H., Pfahringer, B., and Holmes, G. (2012). Experiment databases. *Machine Learning*, 87(2):127–158.

Vanschoren, J., Van Rijn, J. N., Bischl, B., and Torgo, L. (2014). Openml: Networked science in machine learning. *ACM SIGKDD Explorations Newsletter*, 15(2):49–60.

Vardi, M. Y. (2012). Artificial intelligence: Past and future. *Communications of the ACM*, 55(1):5.

Vardi, M. Y. (2015). Human or machine? Response. *Communications of the ACM*, 58(4):8–9.

Varela, F. J., Thompson, E., and Rosch, E. (1992). *The embodied mind: Cognitive science and human experience*. MIT Press.

Vázquez, D., López, A. M., Marín, J., Ponsa, D., and Gerónimo, D. (2014). Virtual and real world adaptation for pedestrian detection. *IEEE Transactions on Pattern Analysis and Machine Intelligence*, 36(4):797–809.

Veness, J., Ng, K., Hutter, M., and Silver, D. (2011). A Monte Carlo AIXI approximation. *Journal of Artificial Intelligence Research*, 40:95–142.

Vere, S. A. (1992). A cognitive process shell. *Behavioral and Brain Sciences*, 15(03):460–461.

Vernon, M., et al. (1979). Psychological evaluation and testing of children who are deaf-blind. *School Psychology Digest*, 8(3):291–295.

Vernon, P. E. (1950). *The structure of human abilities*. Methuen.

Veselka, L., Just, C., Jang, K. L., Johnson, A. M., and Vernon, P. A. (2012). The general factor of personality: A critical test. *Personality and Individual Differences*, 52(3):261–264.

Vickrey, C. and Neuringer, A. (2000). Pigeon reaction time, Hick's law, and intelligence. *Psychonomic Bulletin and Review*, 7(2):284–291.

Vinciarelli, A. and Mohammadi, G. (2014). A survey of personality computing. *IEEE Transactions on Affective Computing*, 5(3):273–291.

Vinge, V. (1993). The coming technological singularity: How to survive in the post-human era. In *Vision 21: Interdisciplinary science and engineering in the era of cyberspace*, volume 1, pages 11–22. NASA.

Vitányi, P. and Li, M. (1997). On prediction by data compression. In *Machine learning: ECML-97*, pages 14–30. Springer.

Vitányi, P. M., Balbach, F. J., Cilibrasi, R. L., and Li, M. (2009). Normalized information distance. In *Information theory and statistical learning*, pages 45–82. Springer.

Von Ahn, L. (2005). *Human computation*. PhD thesis, Carnegie Mellon University.

Von Ahn, L. (2009). Human computation. In *Design Automation Conference, 2009. DAC'09. 46th ACM/IEEE*, pages 418–419. IEEE.

von Ahn, L., Blum, M., and Langford, J. (2004). Telling humans and computers apart automatically. *Communications of the ACM*, 47(2):56–60.

Von Ahn, L., Maurer, B., McMillen, C., Abraham, D., and Blum, M. (2008). RECAPTCHA: Human-based character recognition via web security measures. *Science*, 321(5895):1465.

Von Neumann, J. (1966). *Theory of self-reproducing automata*. Burks, A. W., editor. University of Illinois Press.

Vonk, J. and Beran, M. J. (2012). Bears 'count' too: Quantity estimation and comparison in black bears, *Ursus americanus. Animal Behaviour*, 84(1):231–238.

Voss, P. (2007). Essentials of general intelligence: The direct path to artificial general intelligence. In B. Goertzel and C. Pennachin, editors *Artificial general intelligence*, pages 131–157. Springer.

Vygotsky, L. S. (1978). *Mind in society: The development of higher psychological processes*. Harvard University Press.

Wainer, H. (2000). *Computerized adaptive testing: A primer*, 2nd edition. Lawrence Erlbaum Associates.

Wallace, A. R. (1870). The limits of natural selection as applied to man. In *Contributions to the theory of natural selection*, pages 332–371. Macmillan.

Wallace, A. R. (1904). *Man's place in the universe*. Chapman and Hall.

Wallace, C. S. (1964). A suggestion for a fast multiplier. *IEEE Transactions on Electronic Computers*, EC-13(1):14–17.

Wallace, C. S. (2005). *Statistical and inductive inference by minimum message length*. Springer.

Wallace, C. S. and Boulton, D. M. (1968). An information measure for classification. *Computer Journal*, 11(2):185–194.

Wallace, C. S. and Dowe, D. L. (1999). Minimum message length and Kolmogorov complexity. *Computer Journal*, 42(4):270–283.

Wang, G., Mohanlal, M., Wilson, C., Wang, X., Metzger, M., Zheng, H., and Zhao, B. Y. (2012). Social Turing tests: Crowdsourcing sybil detection. CoRR arXiv preprint:1205.3856.

Wang, G., Wang, T., Zheng, H., and Zhao, B. Y. (2014). Man vs. machine: Practical adversarial detection of malicious crowdsourcing workers. In *23rd USENIX Security Symposium, USENIX Association, CA*, pages 239–254. USENIX Association.

Wang, H., Gao, B., Bian, J., Tian, F., and Liu, T.-Y. (2015). Solving verbal comprehension questions in IQ test by knowledge-powered word embedding. CoRR arXiv preprint:1505.07909.

Wang, L. (2009a). *Behavioral biometrics for human identification: Intelligent applications*. IGI Global.

Wang, P. (2010). The evaluation of AGI systems. In Hutter, M., Baum, E., and Kitzelmann, E., editors, *3rd Conference on Artificial General Intelligence*, pages 164–169. Atlantis Press.

Wang, Y. (2009b). On abstract intelligence: Toward a unifying theory of natural, artificial, machinable, and computational intelligence. *International Journal of Software Science and Computational Intelligence*, 1(1):1–17.

Warwick, K. (2000). *QI: The quest for intelligence*. Piatkus.

Warwick, K. (2014). Turing Test success marks milestone in computing history. University or Reading Press Release, 8 June.

Wasserman, E. A. and Zentall, T. R. (2006). *Comparative cognition: Experimental explorations of animal intelligence*. Oxford University Press.

Watanabe, S. (1972). Pattern recognition as information compression. In *Frontiers of pattern recognition*, pages 561–567. Academic Press.

Waterhouse, L. (2006). Multiple intelligences, the Mozart effect, and emotional intelligence: A critical review. *Educational Psychologist*, 41(4):207–225.

Watkins, C. J. C. H. and Dayan, P. (1992). Q-learning. *Machine Learning*, 8(3):279–292.

Watson, J. B. (1967). *Behavior: An introduction to comparative psychology*. Henry Holt.

Watt, S. (1996). Naive psychology and the inverted Turing test. *Psycoloquy*, 7(14).

Watt, S. (2008). Can people think? Or machines? A unified protocol for Turing testing. In Epstein, R., Roberts, G., and Beber, G., editors, *Parsing the Turing test: Philosophical and methodological issues in the quest for the thinking computer*, pages 301–318. Springer.

Webb, B. (2009). Animals versus animats: Or why not model the real iguana? *Adaptive Behavior*, 17(4):269–286.

Wechsler, D. (1944). *The measurement of intelligence*. Williams and Wilkins.

Wechsler, D. (2008). Wechsler Adult Intelligence Scale–fourth edition (WAIS-IV). NCS Pearson.

Wegner, D. M. and Gray, K. (2016). *The mind club: Who thinks, what feels, and why it matters*. Viking.

Weiss, D. J. (2011). Better data from better measurements using computerized adaptive testing. *Journal of Methods and Measurement in the Social Sciences*, 2(1):1–27.

Weiss, G. and Dillenbourg, P. (1999). What is 'multi' in multi-agent learning. In Dillenbourg, P., editor, *Collaborative learning: Cognitive and computational approaches*, pages 64–80. Pergamon Press.

Weizenbaum, J. (1966). ELIZA – a computer program for the study of natural language communication between man and machine. *Communications of the ACM*, 9(1):36–45.

Wellman, M., Reeves, D., Lochner, K., and Vorobeychik, Y. (2004). Price prediction in a trading agent competition. *Journal of Artificial Intelligence Research*, 21:19–36.

Weng, J. (2000). Autonomous mental development and performance metrics for intelligent systems. In Meystel, A. M. and Messina, E. R., editors, *Measuring the performance and intelligence of systems: Proceedings of the 2000 PerMIS Workshop*, pages 349–358. NIST Special Publication 970. NIST.

Weng, J. (2009). Task muddiness, intelligence metrics, and the necessity of autonomous mental development. *Minds and Machines*, 19(1):93–115.

Weng, J. (2013). *Natural and artificial intelligence: Introduction to computational brain- mind*. BMI Press.

Weng, J., McClelland, J., Pentland, A., Sporns, O., Stockman, I., Sur, M., and Thelen, E. (2001). Autonomous mental development by robots and animals. *Science*, 291(5504):599–600.

Weston, J., Bordes, A., Chopra, S., and Mikolov, T. (2015). Towards AI-complete question answering: A set of prerequisite toy tasks. CoRR arXiv preprint:1502.05698.

Weyns, D. and Holvoet, T. (2005). On the role of environments in multiagent systems. *Informatica*, 29(4):409–421.

Whewell, W. (1847). *The philosophy of the inductive sciences*. Reprint, Cambridge University Press, 2014.

Whitby, B. (1996). Why the Turing test: AI's biggest blind alley. In Millican, P. and Clark, A., editors, *Machines and thought: The legacy of Alan Turing)*, pp. 53–63. Oxford University Press.

White, D. R., McDermott, J., Castelli, M., Manzoni, L., Goldman, B. W., Kronberger, G., Jaśkowski, W., O'Reilly, U.-M., and Luke, S. (2013). Better GP benchmarks: Community survey results and proposals. *Genetic Programming and Evolvable Machines*, 14:3–29.

Whiten, A. and Byrne, R. W. (1997). *Machiavellian intelligence II: Extensions and evaluations*, volume 2. Cambridge University Press.

Whiten, A., McGuigan, N., Marshall-Pescini, S., and Hopper, L. M. (2009). Emulation, imitation, over-imitation and the scope of culture for child and chimpanzee. *Philosophical Transactions of the Royal Society, Series B*, 364(1528):2417–2428.

Whiteson, S., Tanner, B., Taylor, M. E., and Stone, P. (2011). Protecting against evaluation overfitting in empirical reinforcement learning. In *Adaptive dynamic programming and reinforcement learning (ADPRL)*, pages 120–127. IEEE.

Whiteson, S., Tanner, B., and White, A. (2010). The reinforcement learning competitions. *AI Magazine*, 31(2):81–94.

Wiering, M. (2005). QV (λ)-learning: A new on-policy reinforcement learning algorithm. In D. Leone, editor, *7th European Workshop on Reinforcement Learning*, pages 17–18. EWRL.

Wiggins, J. S. (1973). *Personality and prediction: Principles of personality assessment*. Addison-Wesley.

Wiig, E. H. and Secord, W. (1989). *Test of Language Competence (TLC)*, expanded edition. Psychological Corporation.

Wilhelm, O. (2005). Measuring reasoning ability. In *Handbook of understanding and measuring intelligence*, pages 373–392. Sage.

Wilkins, J. (1668). *An essay towards a real character, and a philosophical language.* S. Gellibrand.

Williams, M. A. (2012). Robot social intelligence. In Ge, S., Khatib, O., Cabibihan, J.-J., Simmons, R., and Williams, M., editors, *Proceedings for the 4th International Conference Social Robotics, ICSR 2012*, pages 45–55. *Lecture Notes in Computer Science*, volume 7621. Springer.

Williams, P. L. and Beer, R. D. (2010). Information dynamics of evolved agents. In *From Animals to Animats 11*, pages 38–49. Springer.

Williams, R. L. (2013). Overview of the Flynn effect. *Intelligence*, 41(6):753–764.

Wilson, M., Hanlon, R. T., Tyack, P. L., and Madsen, P. T. (2007). Intense ultrasonic clicks from echolocating toothed whales do not elicit anti-predator responses or debilitate the squid *Loligo pealeii*. *Biology Letters*, 3(3):225–227.

Wilson, S. W. (1991). The animat path to AI. In Meyer, J.-A. and Wilson, S., editors, *From animals to animats*, pages 15–21. MIT Press.

Wimmer, H. and Perner, J. (1983). Beliefs about beliefs: Representation and constraining function of wrong beliefs in young children's understanding of deception. *Cognition*, 13(1):103–128.

Winograd, T. (1972). Understanding natural language. *Cognitive Psychology*, 3(1):1–191.

Woergoetter, F. and Porr, B. (2008). Reinforcement learning. *Scholarpedia*, 3(3):1448.

Wolfram, S. (2002). *A new kind of science*. Wolfram Media.

Wolpert, D. H. (1996). The lack of a priori distinctions between learning algorithms. *Neural Computation*, 8(7):1341–1390.

Wolpert, D. H. (2012). What the no free lunch theorems really mean; how to improve search algorithms. Technical Report. Santa Fe Institute.

Wolpert, D. H. and Macready, W. G. (1995). No free lunch theorems for search. Technical Report, SFI-TR-95-02-010. Santa Fe Institute.

Wolpert, D. H. and Macready, W. G. (2005). Coevolutionary free lunches. *IEEE Transactions on Evolutionary Computation*, 9(6):721–735.

Woodley, M. A. and Bell, E. (2011). Is collective intelligence (mostly) the general factor of personality? A comment on Woolley, Chabris, Pentland, Hashmi and Malone (2010). *Intelligence*, 39(2):79–81.

Woodley, M. A., Fernandes, H. B., and Hopkins, W. D. (2015). The more g-loaded, the more heritable, evolvable, and phenotypically variable: Homology with humans in chimpanzee cognitive abilities. *Intelligence*, 50:159–163.

Woodrow, H. (1946). The ability to learn. *Psychological Review*, 53(3):147.

Woods, S., Dautenhahn, K., Kaouri, C., Boekhorst, R., and Koay, K. L. (2005). Is this robot like me? Links between human and robot personality traits. In *5th IEEE-RAS International Conference on Humanoid Robots*, pages 375–380. IEEE.

Woolley, A. W., Chabris, C. F., Pentland, A., Hashmi, N., and Malone, T. W. (2010). Evidence for a collective intelligence factor in the performance of human groups. *Science*, 330(6004):686–688.

WPSA (2014). Universal declaration on animal welfare (UDAW). World Society for the Protection of Animals. http://www.udaw.org/.

Wray, R. E. and Lebiere, C. (2007). Metrics for cognitive architecture evaluation. In Kaminka, G. A., editor, *Proceedings of the AAAI-07 Workshop on Evaluating Architectures for Intelligence*, pages 60–66. AAAI.

Wright, S. (1932). The roles of mutation, inbreeding, crossbreeding, and selection in evolution. In *Proceedings of the VI International Congress of Genetics*, pages 356–366. Botanic Garden, New York.

Wright, S. (1988). Surfaces of selective value revisited. *American Naturalist*, pages 115–123.

Yampolskiy, R. V. (2012). AI-complete, AI-hard, or AI-easy–classification of problems in AI. In *The 23rd Midwest Artificial Intelligence and Cognitive Science Conference*, pages 94-101.

Yampolskiy, R. V. (2015a). *Artificial superintelligence: A futuristic approach*. CRC Press.

Yampolskiy, R. V. (2015b). The space of possible mind designs. In Bieger, J., Goertzel, B., and Potapov, A., editors, *8th International Conference on Artificial general intelligence – AGI 2015, Berlin, Germany, July 22–25, 2015, Proceedings*, pages 218–227. Springer.

Yampolskiy, R. V. and Gavrilova, M. L. (2012). Artimetrics: Biometrics for artificial entities. *Robotics and Automation Magazine*, 19(4):48–58.

Yampolskiy, R. V. and Govindaraju, V. (2008). Behavioural biometrics: A survey and classification. *International Journal of Biometrics*, 1(1):81–113.

Yockey, H. P. (2005). *Information theory, evolution, and the origin of life*. Cambridge University Press.

Yonck, R. (2012). Toward a standard metric of machine intelligence. *World Future Review*, 4(2):61–70.

York, W. and Swan, J. (2012). Taking Turing seriously (but not literally). In Muller, V. and Ayesh, A., editors, *AISB/IACAP 2012 Symposium "Revisiting Turing and His Test"*, pages 54–59. Society for the Study of Artificial Intelligence and Simulation of Behaviour.

You, J. (2015). Beyond the Turing test. *Science*, 347(6218):116.

Youyou, W., Kosinski, M., and Stillwell, D. (2015). Computer-based personality judgments are more accurate than those made by humans. *Proceedings of the National Academy of Sciences*, 112(4):1036–1040.

Yu, Y., Pan, G., Gong, Y., Xu, K., Zheng, N., Hua, W., Zheng, X., and Wu, Z. (2016). Intelligence-augmented rat cyborgs in maze solving. *PloS ONE*, 11(2):e0147754.

Yudkowsky, E. (2008). Artificial intelligence as a positive and negative factor in global risk. *Global Catastrophic Risks*, 1:303.

Zadeh, L. A. (1994). Fuzzy logic, neural networks, and soft computing. *Communications of the ACM*, 37(3):77–84.

Zadeh, L. A. (2000). The search for metrics of intelligence–a critical view. In Meystel, A. M. and Messina, E. R., editors, *Measuring the performance and intelligence of systems: Proceedings of the 2000 PerMIS Workshop*, pages 105–111. NIST Special Publication 970. NIST.

Zadeh, L. A. (2002). In quest of performance metrics for intelligent systems – A challenge that cannot be met with existing methods. In Meystel, A. M. and Messina, E. R., editors, *Measuring the performance and intelligence of systems: Proceedings of the 2000 PerMIS Workshop*, pages 303–306. NIST Special Publication 970. NIST.

Zadeh, L. A. (2008). Toward human level machine intelligence – Is it achievable? The need for a paradigm shift. *IEEE Computational Intelligence Magazine*, 3(3):11–22.

Zatuchna, Z. and Bagnall, A. (2009). Learning mazes with aliasing states: An LCS algorithm with associative perception. *Adaptive Behavior*, 17(1):28–57.

Zentall, T. R. (2012). Perspectives on observational learning in animals. *Journal of Comparative Psychology*, 126(2):114.

Zentall, T. R., Hogan, D. E., and Edwards, C. A. (1980). Oddity learning in the pigeon: Effect of negative instances, correction, and number of incorrect alternatives. *Animal Learning and Behavior*, 8(4):621–629.

Zentall, T. R., Hogan, D. E., and Holder, J. (1974). Comparison of two oddity tasks with pigeons. *Learning and Motivation*, 5(1):106–117.

Zhang, H., Horvitz, E., Miller, R. C., and Parkes, D. C. (2011). Crowdsourcing general computation. In *Proceedings of ACM CHI Conference on Human Factors*. ACM.

Zillich, M. (2012). My robot is smarter than your robot: On the need for a total Turing test for robots. In Muller, V. and Ayesh, A., editors, *AISB/IACAP 2012 Symposium "Revisiting Turing and His Test"*, pages 12–15. Society for the Study of Artificial Intelligence and Simulation of Behaviour.

Zimmermann, J., Henze, H. H., and Cremers, A. B. (2015). Gödel agents in a scalable synchronous agent framework. In Bieger, J., Goertzel, B., and Potapov, A., editors, 8th International Conference on *Artificial general intelligence*, pages 404–413. Springer.

Zitnick, C. L., Agrawal, A., Antol, S., Mitchell, M., Batra, D., and Parikh, D. (2016). Measuring machine intelligence through visual question answering. *AI Magazine*, 37(1):63–72.

Zuberbühler, K. (2000). Interspecies semantic communication in two forest primates. *Proceedings of the Royal Society of London, Series B*, 267(1444):713–718.

Zvonkin, A. K. and Levin, L. A. (1970). The complexity of finite objects and the development of the concepts of information and randomness by means of the theory of algorithms. *Russian Mathematical Surveys*, 25:83–124.

Zwaan, R. A. and Radvansky, G. A. (1998). Situation models in language comprehension and memory. *Psychological Bulletin*, 123(2):162.

Index

AAAI, 131, 140

ability, *see* cognitive ability

acceptable policy, 211, 222, 224–229, 232, 236–238, 246, 257, 269, 272, 273, 327, 397

accuracy, 27, 35–37, 39, 64, 75, 76, 86, 91, 129, 238, 418, 419, 424, 432, 435

ACE tests, 73, 74

acquired behaviour, 18, 87, 96, 97, 119, 281, 309, 478

ACT college assessment, 73

activity log, 431, 433

adaptation, 17, 60, 93, 96, 97, 112–114, 155, 284, 341, 362, 363, 420, 421, 475

adaptive test, 82, 84–86, 256, 273, 295, 419, 424, 426–429, 434, 460, 478, 480, *see also* Computerised Adaptive Testing

addition, 37–39, 43, 67, 204, 205, 209, 210, 219, 230, 235, 248, 272, 273, 302

adversarial game, 132–134, 139, 164, 433, *see also* moving-target problem

agent cast, 358, *see also* team

agent characteristic curve, 234–238, 240, 246, 247, 249, 250, 256, 427

agent characteristic surface, 427, 428

agent policy language, *see* policy description language

agglomeration approach, 149, 165, 300, 378, 469, 479

AGI, 5, 141, 148, 151, 157, 159, 267, 271, 286, 320, 321, 362, 452, 454, 473, 479

preschool, 160, 321, 338

system, *see* general-purpose system

agreeableness, 63, 64, 109, 345, 431

AI

and universal psychometrics, 169, 474

benchmark, 11, 23, 117, 138, 140, 144, 145, 153, 168, 316, 350, 351, 378, 474, 478–480

competition, 11, 23, 125, 130–132, 138–141, 143, 144, 321, 350, 358

connectionist AI, 123

effect, 117, 118

ethics, 23, 442, 443, 453

evaluation, 11, 23, 117–151, 156, 164, 166, 167, 169, 170, 203, 424, 468, 473, 474

human-level artificial intelligence, *see* human-level machine intelligence

narrow AI, 271, 321, 324

progress, 3, 124, 125

risks, 3, 23, 285, 338, 438, 453–456, 461

strong AI, 123

symbolic AI, 123

value problem, 453–455, 461

weak AI, 123

AI-completeness, 127, 130, 134, 376, 460

AI-hardness, 127, 133, 165, 166

AIT, *see* algorithmic information theory

AIXI, 284–286, 290–292, 295, 299, 334, 338

algorithmic information theory, 23, 51, 52, 131, 151, 175–201, 271, 277, 326, 329, 371

epistemological view, 52, 184, 192, 199, 385

procedural view, 52, 184, 192, 199

algorithmic probability, 185, 188, 326

altitude (Thorndike), 77, 236, 237, 249, 300

analogical inference, 31, 32, 44, 71–74, 120, 129, 161, 166, 195, 197, 211, 218, 261, 266, 302, 374, 375, 378

animal
  behaviour, 9, 13, 93–111, 155
  cognition, 93–111, 182, 183, 206, 290, 343,
      347, 367, 370, 421, 426, 473
    areas, 101
  ethics, 442, 453
  g factor, 110, 111, 301, 302
  kingdom, 9, 11, 28, 41, 102, 111, 119, 156,
      301, 388, 473
  rights, 443, 444, 447
animat, 4, 9, 11, 154, 167, 169, 349, 422
anthropocentrism, 5, 9, 23, 48, 49, 93, 104,
      112, 128, 131, 165, 198, 215, 261, 262,
      264, 265, 322, 340, 348, 360, 443, 444,
      446, 453, 460, 468
  of language, 375, 376, 380, 382
anthropomorphism, 99, 348
antimonopoly laws for intelligence, 464, 465
ants, 96, 101, 102, 182, 183, 268, 344, 371,
      389, 408
anytime universal test, 294, 295
apes, 28, 94, 95, 97, 99, 101, 102, 110, 154,
      264, 342–345, 380–382, 385, 421, 440,
      441, 447
apparatus, *see* evaluation apparatus
arcade learning environment, 138, 144, 350
area (Thorndike), 77, 237
Aristotle, 15, 27, 265, 324
Army Alpha, 62, 72
Ars Combinatoria, 117, 268, 289
Ars Generalis, 11, 12, 20, 46, 185, 187, 283,
      284, 286
Ars Magna, 12, 18, 117, 268, 470
artificial ecosystem, 4, 135, 365, 430, 433, 447
artificial general intelligence, *see* AGI
artificial intelligence, *see* AI
artificial life, 7, 9, 153, 241, 361, 362, 417, 430
artificial personality, 14, 150, 348, *see also*
      personality computing
artificial testing apparatus, *see* evaluation
      apparatus
artimetrics, 450
Asimov, Isaac, 21, 454
associative memory, 67
astrobiology, 114, 430, 431, 440
astrocognition, 114
asynchronicity, 206–208, 223, 238, 291, 353,
      427, 461, 478, 479
attainment, 15, 65, 73, 74, 76
attention, 9, 95, 101, 148, 157, 159, 163, 265,
      324, 350, 351, 354, 357, 364, 366, 422,
      429

attitude, 10, 13, 63, 64, 150, 322, 385
auditory processing, 68, 183, 265, 314, 316,
      350, 423
augmented cognition, *see* extended mind
augmented humans, *see* extended mind
autonomous mental development, 18, 23, 314
autopoiesis, 112, 315
Ayumu, 49, 50, 107, 427

background knowledge, 180, 181, 197, 205,
      281, 294, 327, 329, 330, 372, 376,
      408
bacteria, 5, 93, 112, 113, 169, 315, 342, 371,
      422, 429
  cognition in, 6, 112, 113, 342
bacterial IQ, 113
basic processes, 101, 102
Battelle Developmental Inventory, 314, 319
Bayes' theorem, 85, 190, 246, 250, 297
Bayley Scales of Infant Development, 314,
      319, 320, 380
behavioural diversity, 407
behavioural drift, 331, *see also* dynamics of
      profiles
behavioural ecology, 98
behavioural feature
  definition of, 13
  dynamics, 314, 330, 389
  space of, *see* space of behavioural features
belief, 10, 13, 63, 150
Belief-Desire-Intention paradigm, 365
believability, 6, 131, 132, 150, 362, 433, 436
Bennett Mechanical Comprehension Test, 73
Big Five, 63, 73, 150, 157–159
big switch, 121, 137, 148, 162, 205, 374, 407
Binet, Alfred, 60, 62, 65, 66, 70, 72, 87, 191,
      265, 331, 452
Binet-Simon test, 62, 72
bio-inspired robotics, 9
biocentrism, 9, 443, 444
biodiversity, 98, 363
biologically-enhanced computers, 6, 450, 468
biologically-inspired cognitive architecture,
      147
birds, 17, 95, 102, 107, 110, 111, 176, 183,
      342, 344, 385
black-box measurement, 21, 22, 32–35, 112,
      124, 366, 394
blind people, 6, 90, 91, 167, 264, 315, 316,
      420, 421
BMCT, *see* Bennett Mechanical
      Comprehension Test

bonobo, 29, 95, 102, 129, 332, 381
Borges, Jorge Luis, 289
BotPrize, 131, 135, 436
brain size, 32, 33
brain training, 331
Bringsjord, Selmer, 161, 162, 164, 165

c factor, 402, 403, *see also* collective
    intelligence
C-test, 151, 191, 193–199, 204, 206, 210, 211,
    215, 247, 249, 250, 280, 290, 298, 302,
    327, 373
calibration, 39, 40, 75, 166, 418
CAPTCHA, 6, 117, 133–135, 149, 163,
    165–167, 433, 436, 460, 468
Carroll's three-stratum theory, 45, 68
Cattell-Horn-Carroll's three-stratum model,
    68, 157, 158, 262, 267, 373
Chaitin, Gregory, 178, 192
chatterbox, 130, 131, 433
CHC, *see* Cattell-Horn-Carroll's three-stratum
    model
checkers, *see* draughts
chess, 4, 11, 117, 121, 123, 124, 139, 140,
    143, 271, 301, 328, 453
child programme, 323, 324
children, 62, 109, 110, 154, 167, 264, 421,
    437, 439
    and language, 382, 385, 388
    development, 60, 147, 314, 316, 317, 319,
        320, 324, 347, 379, 380
    interfaces and administration, 64, 203, 319,
        380, 420, 421
    moral considerations, 442, 443, 445
    tests for, 72, 90, 160, 319, 321, 347, 380
chimpanzee, 29, 42, 49, 50, 53, 95, 101, 107,
    109, 110, 129, 158, 280, 318, 332, 441,
    459
    Ayumu the chimp, *see* Ayumu
Chimpanzee Personality Questionnaire, 109
chimpocentrism, 102
choice reaction time, *see* reaction time
Chomsky, Noam, 324, 382, 383, 386, 418
Church-Turing thesis, 8, 117
    physical, 8, 333, 418
Classical Test Theory, 76, 77, 83, 249–251,
    253, 257
clever Hans, 422
co-operation, 6, 98, 139, 344, 345, 348,
    352–354, 356–359, 362, 363, 366, 371,
    393, 394, 397, 403, 429

cognitive ability
    definition, 15
    extrapolation, 48, 395, 460
    space of, *see* space of abilities
cognitive architecture, 120, 146, 168, 274,
    321, 389, *see also* biologically-inspired
    cognitive architecture
Cognitive Decathlon, 147, 157, 158, 168, 320,
    447, 479
cognitive development, 5, 10, 180, 313, 314,
    317, 322, 388
cognitive enhancement, 3–6, 53, 154, 331,
    376, 391, 410, 411, 438, 449–452, 455,
    459, 461, 463, 464, 468, 472, 474, *see*
    also extended mind
cognitive facilitator, 273, 326–328, 367, 388,
    389
cognitive modification, 449
cognitive robotics, 9, 146, 318, 338, 387
cognitive science, 9, 10, 20, 21, 23, 54, 152,
    170, 176, 183, 189, 218, 263, 267, 315,
    318, 329, 471
cognitive task, *see* task
collective intelligence, 393, 402, 473, *see also*
    c factor
collective task, 392, 401
commensurate aggregation, 37, 38, 136, 137,
    243, 246, 269, 290, 294, 297
communication, 6, 113, 148, 176, 182, 184,
    192, 344, 358, 370–391, 393, 394, 403,
    407, 408, *see also* language
    abilities, 370–391
    peer asymmetry, 372
    plasticity, 372
comparative cognition, *see also* animal
    cognition
    and convergent evolution, *see* convergent
        evolution
    and universal psychometrics, 169, 474
    causal mechanism, 98
    cross-species comparison, 23, 169
    g, *see* animal *g* factor
    killjoy, 99
    psychometric approach, 111
    systematic measurement, 110, 111
    temporal factors, 427
comparative psychology, *see* comparative
    cognition
competition, 6, 98, 139, 310, 345, 348,
    352–354, 357–359, 361–363, 368, 371,
    465

complexity, 138, 210, 213–217, 235, 236, 245, 253, 254, 263, 264, 293–297, 318, 328, 351, 362, 364, *see also* computational complexity, *see also* difficulty, *see also* Kolmogorov complexity
  intrinsic complexity, 219
compositional learning, 5, 329
comprehension, 73, 148, 193, 373, 390, 408
  and language, 72, 90, 148, 204, 302, 370, 373, 375–378
compression
  and communication, 390
  and comprehension, 191, 192, 373
  and intelligence, 129, 151, 191–198
computational complexity, 22, 127, 219, 220, 223, 229, 262, 274
computer olympiad, 140
computer personality, *see* artificial personality
Computerised Adaptive Testing, 85, 428, 434, *see also* adaptive test
conceptual development, 327, 329, 388, 389, 391
conceptual precedence diagram, 328
conditional Kolmogorov complexity, 180, 190, 195, 273
conditioning, 100, 104, 113, 320, 420–422
Condorcet's jury theorem, 401
conscientiousness, 63, 64, 109, 332, 431
consciousness, 3, 10, 16, 94, 147, 366, 394, 445–447, 457
consilience, 232, 271
convergent evolution, 95, 111, 301, 385
Conway's game of life, 251, 430
correlation and task similarity, 273
cortex, 41, 42, 344
criterion-referenced measurement, 31, 75, 82, 86
crowd intelligence, 393, 399–401
crowdsourcing, 4, 6, 22, 135, 149, 154, 399, 411, 433, 437, 477
crows, 95, 98, 99, 109, 317
crystallised intelligence, 67, 68, 73, 206, 324, 331
CTT, *see* Classical Test Theory
culture, *see* knowledge transmission, *see also* policy transmission *see also* search: cultural search
culture-bound vs. culture-fair, 66, 68, 89, 108, 280
cyborg, 4–6, 448, 450

natural-born cyborg, 6, 450, *see also* extended mind
rat, 5, 169

Darwin, Charles, 27, 60, 94, 259, 440
Darwin-Wallace distribution, 360–363, 461
deaf people, 5, 90, 315, 316, 382, 420, 421
deduction, *see* deductive inference
deductive inference, 120, 136, 148, 197, 218, 266, 267, 280, 377
Deep Blue, 122, 139, 143, 271
deep learning, 22, 122, 141, 144, 316, 374, 375, 390
democracy, 398, 455, 461, 464
demography, 461, 462
demonstration, *see* learning by demonstration
denotational problem, 268, 269
Descartes, René, 439, 442
Detterman, Douglas L., 164, 165, 467
development, *see* cognitive development
developmental robotics, 5, 9, 34, 141, 153, 168, 314, 422, 475, 477
difficulty, 43, 45, 48, 77, 79–81, 84, 85, 103, 106, 138, 156, 157, 166, 194, 196, 197, 199, 213–233, 235, 237, 240, 248, 253, 257, 306, 326, 327, 364, 368, 409, 427, 460
  algorithmic difficulty, 224, 226, 230–232, 256, 257, 364, 396
  and discrimination, 82, 255
  and similarity, 274–279
  and steadiness, 42, 43
  and task composition, 47, 270, 271
  function, 43, 233, 236–238, 247, 248, 270
  instance, *see* instance difficulty
  similarity, 273
  slicing, 195, 236, 240, 246, 247, 249, 277, 279, 299, 300, 308, 469
difficulty-based decomposition, 246–248, 250, 297–299
digit span, 61, 70, 72, 89, 203, 204, 262, 265
discount factor, 145, 289
discriminating power, 82, 83, 86, 134, 215, 234, 250–253, 255–257, 261, 309, 470
discrimination parameter, 82, 251
dissimulator, 341, 420, 465
distribution independence, 78, *see also* population independence
division of labour, 394, 401, 410, 412
DNA, 7, 28, 29, 96, 176, 177

Dog Mentality Assessment, 109
dogs, 42, 61, 102, 104, 106, 109, 111, 344, 345, 347, 380
dolphin, 42, 107, 202, 380, 422, 425, 459
Dowe, David L., 129, 133, 151, 162, 164, 166, 198, 294, 335, 390
draughts, 119, 123, 124, 140, 301
dynamics of a profile, 330, 339, 451

ecocentrism, 443, 444
eidetic memory, 49, 53, 204
elementary cellular automaton, 241, 250, 276, 306
elementary cognitive task, 70, 90, 265, 469
Elo ranking, 140
embodiment, 112, 122, 158, 314, 315
emotional intelligence, 45, 64, 331, 344, 471
enactment task, 428, 429
enhancement, *see* cognitive enhancement
environment, *see also* task
    response curve, 254, 255
    sensitiveness, 251, 291, 294, 300, 359
Epicurus's principle of multiple explanations, 184, 187, 189, 390
Erewhon, 453, 457
ergodicity, 207, 284, 286, 291, 294
ethology, 13, 17, 22, 98, 159, 431
eugenics, 60, 88, 89, 439, 452, 462–464
evaluation apparatus, 38, 106, 107, 110, 155, 421–424
evaluation overfitting, 137, 138, 151, 164, *see also* evaluation specialisation
evaluation specialisation, 38, 39, 86, 123, 137, 139, 480, *see also* evaluation overfitting
evolution, *see also* nature versus nurture
    and cognition, 60, 93–99, 114, 122, 229, 290, 309, 362
    and the social hypothesis, 344
    co-evolution, 361
    convergent, *see* convergent evolution
evolutionary computation, 125, 221, 361
evolutionary search, *see* search: evolutionary search
existential risk, 438, 444, 456
expected response, *see* response
exploration-vs-exploitation dilemma, 145, 150, 467
extant personality, 412, 462–465
extended mind, 6, 411, 450, 475, *see also* cognitive enhancement

extraterrestrial intelligence, 114, 115, 261, 430
extraversion, 63–65, 87, 109, 345, 431

facilitator, *see* cognitive facilitator
factor
    analysis, 44, 45, 66–69, 109, 114, 157, 262, 263, 270, 276, 280, 343, 402, 472, 479
    confounding factor, 4, 36, 49–51, 64, 88, 300, 309, 352, 365, 376, 388
    g, *see g*
    latent factor, 32, 44, 60, 66, 69, 76–78, 260, 270, 348, 472
false-belief task, 347, 348
falsifiability, *see* refutation
feature-oriented evaluation, 123, 146, 147, 149, 151, 168, 169, 473
fertility rate, 48, 88, 462
finding effort ($\mathbb{LS}$), 223, 224, 231, 272, 275, 327, 385, 396, 477
fitness landscape, 221
five-factor personality model, *see* Big Five
fluid intelligence, 67, 68, 72, 205, 206, 317, 324, 329–331
Flynn effect, 59, 88, 89, 462
free will, 10, 333, 334, 435, 448, 452, *see also* second-order desire

G (interspecies), 110, 111
g, *see also* general intelligence
    animal *g*, *see* animal *g* factor
    factor, 31, 45–47, 59, 66, 68–71, 89, 162, 166, 263, 301–306, 309, 313, 402, 471, 476
    loading, 71, 161, 162, 166, 197, 266, 302, 306
    score, 69, 288, 300, 305, 309
    universal *g*, *see* universal *g* factor
    versus IQ, 69, 288, 300, 309, 469
gaiacentrism, 9, 93, 360
Galen, 15, 93, 440
Gall, Franz, 15, 17, 260
Galton, Francis, 30, 60, 61, 70, 86–88, 103, 265, 275, 276, 331, 398, 431, 452, 462
game description language, 143
game theory, 139, 343, 347, 348, 353
gaze following, 159, 347, 348, 357
general AI system, *see* general-purpose AI
general factor of personality, 63, 345, 403
general game playing, 140, 143, 321

general intelligence, 47, 68, 71, 95, 111, 146, 167, 301, 305, 308, 309, 323, 332, 343, 347, 352, 362, 365, 373, 400, 402, 424, 460, 461, 469, 470, *see also* AGI, *see also* policy-general intelligence, *see also* task-general intelligence
    central role, 19, 451, *see also* g, *see also* inductive inference and general intelligence
    in animals, 111, 301, 343
general problem solver, 120, 218, 286
general video game competition, 144, 350
general-purpose AI, 23, 144, 146, 162, 309, 473, *see also* AGI
general-purpose algorithm, 144
generalised task market, 411, 412
generality (of a measure), 36, 127, 159, 160, 167, 276, 378, 419, *see also* necessity, *see also* specificity
George Washington Social Intelligence Test, 346
GFP, *see* general factor of personality
global brain, 24, 412
Google effect, 6, 411, 461
gradient feature, 14, 15, 42, 65, 112, 406, 410, 464
great ape, 95, 99, 111, 301, 440, 441
Great Ape Project, 441
Griffith's Mental Development Scale, 315
group, 392–394, *see also* team
    diversity, 405
    intelligence, *see* collective intelligence
    task types, 397
Guilford, Joy. P., 67
Guttman's radex, *see* radex model
gymnastic of the mind, 65, 87

habile system, 117, 123, 146, *see also* general-purpose AI
Hand, David, 39, 47
heuristics, 225, 408
Hibbard, Bill, 133, 293, 454
HLMI, *see* human-level machine intelligence
Homo neanderthalensis, 430, 439
Homo sapiens, 17, 23, 69, 91, 93, 167, 384, 439, 440, 443, 444, 456, 458
Huarte, Juan, 15, 17, 93, 370, 440
Human, 42
human computation, 6, 124, 154, 411, 433, 477
human language uniqueness, 383, 384

human-level artificial intelligence, *see* human-level machine intelligence
human-level machine intelligence, 126, 127, 129–131, 149, 151, 154, 159, 457, 460
humanness, 129, 130, 135, 432, 436, 446
Humies awards, 125
Hutter, Marcus, 193, 216, 284, 285, 290, 293, 294, 297, 418
hybrid, *see* biologically-enhanced computers, *see* cyborg, *see also* cognitive enhancement
    teamwork, 410, 477, *see also* human computation

I-athlon, 149
IBM Watson, 164, 378, 424, 472
idiot savant, 65, 124, 125, 376
imitation, *see* learning by imitation
improving ability, 451
incomputability, 52, 181, 187, 222, 250, 285, 290
indifference of the indicator, 66, 301, 302
indirect measurement, 32, 33, 39, 198
induction, *see* inductive inference
inductive inference, 21, 44, 47, 51, 67, 71, 72, 120, 175, 184–200, 206, 211, 218, 264, 266, 281, 322, 327, 377, 383, 390, 395
    and general intelligence, 71, 302, 324, 325
    comprehensiveness, 266, 267
    scandal of induction, 184, 187, 188
inductive programming, 35, 142
infinity point, 457, *see also* technological singularity
infocentrism, 443, 444
information
    gain, 218, 226, 274, 423
    processing, 10, 48, 50, 70, 170, 175
    theory, 48, 176, 178, 181, *see also* algorithmic information theory
innate behaviour, 15, 17, 18, 87, 96, 97, 119, 229, 281, 309, 478
innate versus acquired, 18, 96, 97, 119, 288, 309, *see also* predisposition, *see also* programmed versus trained
instance difficulty, 229, 233, 238
instinct, *see* innate behaviour
instrument, 32, 33, 35, 48, 418, 471, *see also* test
    indirect, *see* indirect measurement
    range, 40, 48, 53, 159, 418, 435
intellectual disability, *see* mentally disable

intellifactor, 18, 142
intelligence
  amplification, 449, 459, *see also* cognitive
    enhancement
  explosion, 409, 456–458
  future of, 24
  general, *see g, see* general intelligence
  quotient, *see* IQ
  space of, 19
intelligent test, 434
intensional description, 191, 232, 269, 271
interaction observability, 350, 352, *see also*
    partial observability
interactive system, 3, 4, 7, 8, 10, 126, 256,
    302, 351, 418
interactive Turing machine, 8, 207
interface, 11, 15, 104, 105, 107, 110, 131, 152,
    153, 336, 370, 417, 419–426, 428, 429,
    435, 478
  integration (for groups), 392, 394, 395, 398,
    402
invariance theorem, 179, 188, 292
inverse reinforcement learning, 356, 453
inverted Turing test, 132, 133, 135
IQ
  crowd, *see* crowd IQ
  score, 69, 72, 73, 75, 88, 163, 164, 288, 300,
    309, 399, 400, 405, 406, 458
  test, 32, 36, 37, 39, 45, 68–73, 88–90, 168,
    192, 197, 263, 287, 300, 343, 399, 400,
    424, 427, 434, 436, 437, 471, 479
  in AI, 161–165, 167, 169, 329, 418, 425,
    458
  normalisation, 75
  what it measures, 46, 198, 425
  versus *g, see g* versus IQ
IRT, *see* Item Response Theory
item characteristic curve, 78–81, 85, 86, 235,
    252–256
item pool design, 64, 74, 258, 298, 469
Item Response Theory, 43, 76–82, 85, 214,
    218, 235, 249–253, 256, 257
  1PL model, 79, 80, 218, 256
  2PL model, 80, 81, 218, 256
  3PL model, 79, 81, 218
item sampling, 30, 37, 38, 47, 137, 138, 234,
    238–240, 246, 247
  doubly indirect, 248, 298

Jensen, Arthur, 20, 70, 162, 287, 306, 307
Jeopardy, 164, 424

jobs, *see* labour market
joint policy search
  with communication, 408
  without communication, 408

Kant, Immanuel, 439, 443
Kanzi, 381
knowledge transmission, 390
knowledge-seeking agent, 285, 454
Kolmogorov complexity, 51, 178–180, 182,
    184, 186, 188–190, 199, 212, 216–218,
    236, 244, 273, 274, 290, 423, 430
Kolmogorov, Andrey N., 177, 178
Kuhlmann's test, 315

labour market, 323, 412, 438, 475, 476
  probability of computerisation, 475, 476
Lambda One, 425, 426, 436
language, *see also* communication
  acquisition, 320, 379, 383–387
  creation, 387
  development, 379, 380, 382, 387
  universal, 383, 384, *see also* universal
    grammar
latent variable, *see* factor, latent
learning
  by imitation, 341, 347, 348, 351, 389
  from demonstration, 223, 229, 322, 341,
    347, 367, 368, 389, 390, 470, 478, 479
  representations, 316
  to learn, 322, 323, *see also*
    self-improvement
Learning Potential Assessment Device, 326
Legg, Shane, 216, 290, 293, 294, 297, 418
Leibniz, Gottfried, 117, 268, 289
Lem, Stanisław, 333, 465
Levin complexity, 181, 194, 197, 199, 217,
    218, 224, 274, 290, 295, 423
Levin's *Kt, see* Levin complexity
Levin's universal search, 51, 181, 225–228,
    244, 254, 256, 257, 284, 285, 299, 332,
    383, 385, 407
Levin, Leonid, 201
lexical hypothesis, 61
lexigram, 102, 381
library of Mendel, 7
Linnaeus, 27, 28
Llull, Ramon, 12, 17, 18, 20, 117, 260, 268,
    283, 289, 470
loading, 66, 306, *see also g* loading
Loebner Prize, 130, 132

logistic model, *see* item response theory
long-term memory, 41, 68, 267

Machiavellian intelligence hypothesis, 366
machine intelligence quotient, *see* MIQ
machine kingdom
    definition, 7–11
    risks, 455
machine learning, 5, 22, 35, 117, 122, 123,
        126, 137, 138, 148, 190, 192, 297, 301,
        315, 317, 325, 374, 376, 399, 412, 431,
        433
Malmo project, 144, 145, 479
manipulation, *see* social manipulation
Markov decision process, 206, 217, 291
Markov property, 206, 207
matching pennies, 132, 133, 135, 140, 359
mazes, 106, 107, 110, 113, 139, 145, 204, 206,
        215–217, 247, 352, 424, 436
McCarthy, John, 118, 119, 123
McGrath's circumplex model, 397, 402
MDL principle, *see* MML principle
measurement
    definition, 30
    efficiency, 418, 419, 424
    indirect, *see* indirect measurement
    instrument, *see* instrument
    kinds of, 30–35
    overfitting, *see* evaluation specialisation
    representational, *see* representational
        measurement
    unit, 24, 31, 41–43, 70, 71, 75, 197, 225,
        265, 471
memory, 9, 40, 41, 72, 101, 113, 148, 157,
        158, 163, 265, 267, 373, 395, 447, 449,
        450, 460, 473
    associative, *see* associative memory
    eidetic, *see* eidetic memory
    long-term, *see* long-term memory
    short-term, *see* short-term memory
    span, *see* digit span
    spatial, *see* spatial memory
    working, *see* working memory
mental power, 61, 94, 259
mental speed, 70, 265, *see also* processing
        speed
mentally disabled, 6, 40, 59, 60, 62, 89, 90,
        105, 154, 167, 331, 380, 421, 438, 443,
        474
metacognition, 105, 366
metrology, 30

mind modelling, 132, 341, 344, 366, 372
mind uploading, 457
minimal cognition, 7, 93, 112, 315, 338
Minnesota Multiphasic Personality Inventory,
        73
Minsky, Marvin, 16, 118, 119, 123, 141
MIQ, 156
mirror neuron, 344, 355
mirror test, 104, 347
MML principle, 190, 191, 194, 216, 390
modularity, 16, 96, 97, 102, 111, 121, 123,
        344, *see also* plasticity
monolithic view of intelligence, 17, 24, 89,
        103, 127, 128, 332, 363, 456, 460, 464
moral agency, 442, 443, 445–448
moral patiency, 442–448, 455
Moravec's paradox, 122, 123, 315
Morgan's Canon, 99, 105, 155, 347
moving-target problem, 357
Mozart effect, 46, 471
muddiness, 147, 268
multi-agent system, 139, 144, 150, 241, 341,
        343, 347–351, 353, 357, 392, 395, 473
multi-agent task, 139, 140, 349, 350, 353, 355,
        356, 358, 359, 361, 363, 364, 368, 386,
        396
multi-agent test, 348, 358, 360, 362–364
multidimensional scaling, 263, 277, 278
multimodal perception, 420
multiple intelligences, 19, 45, 46, 68, 90, 344,
        471
multiplication, 203, 204, 212, 219, 223, 230,
        232, 235, 271

natural language processing, 5, 139, 148, 378
nature versus nurture, 59, 61, 86–89, 97, 281,
        324, 337, 382
necessity (of a measure), 36, 128, 129, 165,
        291, 292, 321, 375, 378, 477, *see also*
        generality, *see also* sufficiency
    probabilistic, 292
negative twofold, 303
Nelson-Denny Reading Test, 375
NEO Five-Factor Inventory, 73
NEO Personality Inventory, 73
neo-Piagetian theories, 317, 318, 328
neuroprognosis, 34
neuroticism, 63, 64, 87, 109, 431
Newell test, 146, 147
Newell, Allen, 21, 27, 34, 118
Nilsson, Nils J., 117, 120, 123

no-free-lunch theorem, 47, 187, 286, 288, 289, 293, 302, 309, 360
normed-referenced measurement, 31
number partition problem, 251, 252
numeric abilities, 68
numeric ability, 67, 110, 263, 264

Occam's razor, 100, 184, 187, 189, 190, 299, 309, 390
octopuses, 368, 445
odd-one-out problem, 108, 166, 218, 329, 374
openness, 14, 63, 64, 109, 150, 332, 431
optimal agent, 286, 287, 303, 309
orangutan, 95, 110, 318, 332, 441

Pac-Man, 204, 348, 359
Pareto-optimal enhancement, 410, 411, 451, 459
partial observability, 206, 389
PCA, *see* principal component analysis
Peabody Picture Vocabulary Test, 376, 380
PEBL, 74, 157, 158, 479, 480
penalty, 155, *see also* reward
perceptual reasoning index (in WAIS), 72
perceptual speed, 67, 72
perfect training sequence, 337
performance metric, 18, 136, 137, 142, 161, 320
performance program, 120
PerMIS workshops, 18, 142, 143, 155, 156, 473
person characteristic curve, 78, 84, 85, 235
personality computing, 14, 150, *see also* artificial personality
personality trait, 13, 14, 62–64, 73, 87, 109, 149, 150, 159, 169, 330, 332, 403, 406, 426, 431, 434, 461, 478
and social predisposition *see* social intelligence
personhood, 438–446, 452
condition, 447
personity, *see* extant personity
phase transition, 251, 252
phrenology, 15, 16, 18, 260
physical ability, 13–15, 95, 315
physical cognition, 101, 102
physical feature, 13
phytocentrism, 114
Piaget's sensorimotor stage, 317, 318, 320

Piaget, Jean, 148, 317, *see also* neo-Piagetian theories
pigeon, 102, 108–110, 160, 167, 437
Pinker, Steven, 24, 475
Pioneer spacecrafts, 114, 115
planning, 47, 136, 138, 146, 148, 197, 266, 321, 402
plants, 6, 112–114, 421, 426
plasticity, 16, 97, 105, 123, 318, 342, 344, 420, *see also* communication plasticity, *see also* modularity
policy
acceptable, *see* acceptable policy
acquisition, 205, 223, 323, 325, 326, 365, 367, 368, 389, 478
by demonstration, 367, *see* learning by demonstration
by search, *see* search
by transmission, *see* policy transmission
description language, 242, 253, 276, 279, 306, 327, 329, 364
transmission, 223, 229, 322, 323, 368, 370, 389–391, 470, 478, 479
policy-general intelligence, 299, 300, 309, 469
g, 309, 469
Popper's scientific method, 23, 225
population dependence, 46, 214, 253, 257, 341
population independence, 78, 82, 253, 257, 276, 280, 314, 419, *see also* distribution independence
positive manifold, 66, 69, 110, 301–304, 306–308
potential ability, 335–339, 435, 445, 447
and universality, 333, 334, 447
poverty of the stimulus, 382, 383
pragmatic measurement, 27, 32, 35, 41, 48
predator-prey task, 281, 348, 359, 361, *see also* pursuit and evasion game
predisposition, 97, 104, 155, 291, 324, 345, 358, 363, 365, 386, *see also* innate versus acquired
prefix Turing machine, 178–180, 188, 288, 292
Primate Cognition Test Battery, 23, 110, 347, 436
primates, 110, 111, 318, 343, 351, 370, 371, 380, 381, 422, 430
principal component analysis, 44, 66
principle of learning economy, 385, 387
prisoner's dilemma, 359
probabilistic Turing machine, 8

probably approximately correct (PAC)
  learning, 152, 227, 383
  policy, 227
processing speed, 70, 331, *see also* mental
    speed
  index (in WAIS), 68, 72
proficiency, 43, 77–86, 237, 250, 252–254,
    256, 257, 259, 298, 300, 379, 385, 409,
    427, 428, 478
programmed versus trained, 5, 18, 23, 50, 119,
    121, 125, 155, 229, 309, 348, 364, 453,
    see also innate versus acquired
projective test, 65, 347
prosthesis, 6, 449
psychiatry, 22, 438
psycho-informatics, 432
psychology experiment building language, *see*
    PEBL
psychometric AI, 165, 378
psychometric diversity, 406
psychometric profile, 18–20, 167, 330, 332,
    338, 339, 363, 389, 392, 404–406, 410,
    412, 431, 448, 450, 451, 456, 458, 459,
    461, 470
  collective psychometric profile, 403–409
  lifespan, *see* dynamics of a profile
psychometrics
  and universal psychometrics, 169, 474
  controversy, 11, 24, 59, 60, 69, 70, 87, 89,
    91, 438
  future of, 24, 472
  pathologies of, 24, 31, 197, 471
psychomotor ability, 13, 14, 49, 319, 397
psychomotor feature, 13
psychophysiology, 65, 265
punishment, *see* penalty
pursuit and evasion game, 361, *see also*
    predator-prey task

Q-learning, 295, 297, 353, 425
quantitative reasoning, *see* numeric abilities
question answering (QA), 5, 376–378

radex model, 263, 264, 266, 267
Rasch's model, *see* item response theory: 1PL
    model
ratio scale, 31, 70, 71, 471
ratiocentrism, 438, 443–445, 447, 452, 464,
    480
rational powers, 15, 93, 440
rats, 95, 102–104, 106, 107, 111, 159, 169,
    183, 195, 349, 422, 436, 444

Raven's Progressive Matrices, 71, 90, 161,
    166, 197, 198, 204, 211, 218, 286, 291,
    302, 329, 399, 400, 402, 432
reaction time, 33, 41, 61, 68, 70, 75, 90, 160,
    167, 204, 206, 226, 265, 419, 426, *see
    also* response time
reading and writing ability, 68, 373, 374
reasoning process, 265, 266, 322
recursion, 383, 384
refutation, 52, 53, 98, 101, 160, 162, 168, 193,
    198, 225, 267, 280, 297, 370, 375, 417,
    425, 433, 436, 469, 471, 477
  power (falsifiability), 17, 23, 47, 91, 294,
    425, 435, 458, 468, 473
reification of intelligence, 32, 69
reinforcement learning, 22, 34, 50, 144, 145,
    155, 206, 241, 285, 288, 295, 353, 425,
    445, 454, 473, 478, 479
  competition, 138, 144
relative numerousness task, 202, 210–212,
    214, 229, 231, 236–240
reliability, 36–39, 64, 65, 72, 74, 76, 85, 105,
    129, 137, 141, 153, 250, 319, 401, 419,
    435
representational distribution, 239, 240,
    246–249, 251, 257
representational measurement, 27, 32, 37, 41,
    44, 48, 49, 51, 153, 166, 168, 240, 249,
    287, 375, 446, 460
  and validity, 35, 36, 48, 376, 401, 419, 477
resolution, 114, 417, 425–429
resource-bounded system, 7, 8, 219, 284, 333
response
  probability of correct response, 79, 81, 236,
    478
  result, 37, 78, 79, 85, 206–209, 302, 326,
    364, 427
  time, 33, 35, 36, 426, 427, *see also* reaction
    time
responsive environment, 251, *see also*
    environment sensitiveness
reverse Turing test, 133, 135
reward, 198, 203, 206–208, 293, 294, 302,
    326, 364, 368, 399, 419, 421, 425, 427
  in animals, 11, 103, 104, 110, 422
  in groups, 354–356, 358, 393–395
  in reinforcement learning, 144, 145, 155,
    445
  manipulation, 453, 454, *see also*
    self-delusion problem
RoboCup, 138, 140, 348, 350, 358, 359
robopsychology, 21, 465

robot
    cleaning robot (dustbot), 4, 5, 167, 422
    fish, 349
    personality, *see* artificial personality
    pet, 14, 351
    preschool, *see* AGI preschool
    rat, 349, 422
    social robot, *see* social (ro)bot
    team, 358, 403
robotics, *see* cognitive robotics, *see*
        developmental robotics
Robotish language, 387
Rorschach test, 65
rote learning, 72, 191, 210, 229, 232, 264, 281
RPM, *see* Raven's Progressive Matrices
ruthless diligence problem, 453, 454

Sagan, Carl, 10, 115
sampling, *see* item sampling
Sanghi and Dowe's program, 162–164, 166,
        198
SAT college assessment, 73, 74, 375
scala naturae, 27, 41, 61, 95, 103
search
    cultural search, 221
    search effort ($\mathbb{F}$), 220, 222–224
    evolutionary search, 100, 221, 257, 281,
        284, 317
    intellectual, *see* search: mental search
    Levin's search, *see* Levin's universal search
    mental search, 100, 221, 297, 317, 322, 367,
        408, 425, 470, 479
    physical search, 100, 221, 297, 408, 425
second-order desire, 333, 452, *see also* free
        will
second-order self-awareness, 435
self-assessment, 63–65, 73, 74, 150, 332, 345,
        347, 367, 434, 435
self-delusion problem, 454
self-evaluation, *see* self-assessment
self-improvement, 21, 286, 322, 332, 451, 458,
        460, *see also* learning to learn
self-modification, 332, 338, 447, 448, 452, 454
self-report test, *see* self-assessment
sensorimotor representations, 314, 316
sentiocentrism, 443–447
SETI project, 114, 430
shallows, the, 6, 411, 474
Shannon's information, 176, 182, 404
Shannon's theory of communication, 371
Shannon, Claude, 118, 371, 438
shared intentionality, 345, 358, 391

short-term memory, 41, 49, 68
Simon, Herbert, 21, 27, 34, 50, 118, 161,
        423
simplicity, 175, 176, 181
singularity, *see* technological singularity
situated task, 14, 279, 348, 395
situated test, 348, 370, 379, 386, 392, 395,
        422, 424, 470, 478
situational judgment test, 345, 346
Sloman, Aaron, 3, 10, 20, 21, 130, 449, 455
social (ro)bot, 135, 150, 347, 348
social ability, *see* social skill
social cognition, 101, 102, 320, 344, 347
social hypothesis, 342–344, 347, 349, 352,
        363, 366
social intelligence, 342–347, 359, 362, 461,
        464
    and personality, 63, 344, 363, 365, 471
social manipulation, 341, 344, 347, 366, 371,
        459, 464
social network, 4, 6, 14, 22, 135, 365, 431,
        433, 475
social skill, 341, 344, 345, 349–352, 364, 365,
        478
socially-rich environment, 101, 345, 352, 362,
        363
socially-rich task, *see* socially-rich
        environment
Society for the Liberation of Robots, 449
Solomonoff's prediction, 186, 188, 189, 285,
        326, 383, 390
    error theorem, 185
Solomonoff's universal prior, *see* universal
        distribution
Solomonoff, Ray, 118, 177–179, 181, 185,
        192, 201, 326, 335, 418
solvable problem, 20, 283–285
soundness, 212, *see also* steadiness
space of abilities, 15, 17–19, 45, 262, 314,
        470, *see also* space of tasks
    perspectives, 260, 267
space of behavioural features, 11, 13, 18, 20,
        22, 27, 29, 146, 284, 314, 404, 405
space of possible minds, 3, 10, 20, *see also*
        machine kingdom
space of tasks, 208, 269, 275, 276, 278, 279,
        see also space of abilities
spatial ability, 51, 67, 72, 91, 101, 102, 106,
        146, 261, 263, 264, 316, 424, 436
spatial memory, 49, 53, 106, 107, 427
spatial orientation, *see* spatial ability
spatiotemporal scale, *see* resolution

Spearman's Law of Diminishing Returns, 304, 305

Spearman, Charles, 30, 45, 66, 70, 265, 287, 301, 304, 305, 313

specialisation, *see* evaluation specialisation

specificity (of a measure), 36, 127, 159, 160, 167, 276, 378, 419, *see also* generality, *see also* sufficiency

speed, 223, 236, 313, 334, 409, 426, 451, 459, 461, *see also* mental speed, *see also* processing speed

sports analogy, 14, 45

Stanford-Binet test, 72, 75, 263, 291, 373

steadiness, 38, 43, 80, 118, 211, 212, 227, 323, 401, *see also* soundness

Sternberg's triarchic theory, 68, 90, 323

Sternberg, Robert J., 322

stochastic task, *see* task

subjectivity objection, 194, 195, 199, 293

sufficiency (of a measure), 36, 128, 129, 165, 291, 292, 321, 378, 477, *see also* necessity, *see also* specificity

superabilities, 460

superhuman performance, 117, 124, 125, 377, 459

superintelligence, 24, 126, 285, 438, 456–461, 463

superpowers, 459, 460

swarm computing, 139, 153, 393

swarm intelligence, *see* swarm computing

systema naturae, 27, 28

tabula rasa, 97, 323, 324, 364

task

    agglomeration, *see* agglomeration approach

    breadth, 149, 259, 269, 271, 272, 288, 293, 299, 300, 302

    clustering, 275–277

    composition, 269, 270, 273, 327

    definition, 15, 208, 209

    difficulty, *see* difficulty

    dissimilarity, *see* task similarity

    diversity, 288, 292, 293, 298–301, 303, 363

    elementary task, *see* elementary cognitive task

    instance, 18, 208–210, 220, 269, 271, 287, *see also* instance difficulty

    pureness, 269–271, 273, 279

    requirements of cognitive task, 207

    similarity, 268, 273–277, 327, 479

    space, *see* space of tasks

theory, 259

task-general intelligence, 290–292, 294, 298, 300, 303, 309, 469, *see also* universal distribution

    and IQ, 309, 469

task-oriented evaluation, 123, 136, 144, 151, 153, 161, 165, 320, 473

task-specific AI system, 120, 138, 141, 151, 161, 320, 479

team, 358, 359, 392–394, 406, 410, 411, 463, *see also* group

teamwork, 395–397, 402–404, *see also* hybrid teamwork

technological singularity, 456–458

temperament, 14, 63, 109, 110, 345

test

    adaptation, *see* adaptive test

    administration, 36, 37, 39, 76, 103–105, 166

    archival, 480

    interface, *see* interface

    potential, 105, 336, 339, 435

    universal, *see* universal test

test-retest reliability, 36, 37, 39, 76, 319

testing apparatus, *see* evaluation apparatus

theory of mind, 110, 321, 347, 348, 365, *see also* mind modelling

thermometer, 32, 418, 472

Thorndike, Edward L., 94, 99, 100, 103, 106, 112, 156, 215, 236, 249, 260, 270, 281, 300, 342, 345, 346, 367

Thorndike, Robert L., 111, 346

Thurstone letter series, 33, 71, 192, 193, 197–199, 204, 206, 218, 329

Thurstone primary abilities, 67, 157, 267, 373

Thurstone, Louis L., 67, 77, 192, 249, 263

time, *see also* anytime universal test, *see also* comparative cognition: temporal factors, *see also* speed

    limit, 37, 209, 223, 238, 402

    resolution, 425–428, *see also* agent characteristic surface

    adaptation, 428, 429, 436

toddler Turing test, 131, 146, 320

tolerance, 211, 212, 214, 222, 224, 226, 230–232, 238, 242, 254, 269, 270, 272, 277, *see also* acceptable policy

Tomasello, Michael, 358

total Turing test, 131

transfer learning, 273, 321, 327

transmission, *see* policy transmission

trial, 30, 104, 145, 202, 203, 205–209, 211, 212
Turing machine, 8, 22, 132
Turing ratio, 124
Turing test, 4, 127–132, 135, 142, 333, 377, 378, 433, 434, 436, 446
    with compression, 129, 135, 151
Turing triage test, 446
Turing's imitation game, 11, 117, 128, 135
Turing, Alan, 4, 8, 117, 119, 127, 128, 130, 139, 208, 221, 226, 268, 281, 332–334, 408, 457
Turing-completeness, *see* universality
two-end rope-pulling task, 348

Ulam, Stanisław, 241, 457
unit of measurement, *see* measurement unit
universal distribution, 51, 187, 188, 215, 230, 249, 257, 272, 285, 288–294, 298–300, 302, 337, 360, 361, 478, *see also* task-general intelligence
universal grammar, 324, 382–384, 418
universal heuristics, 225
universal intelligence, 289–292, 294, 298, 299, 418, *see also* task-general intelligence
    impossibility of, 288
universal law of augmenting returns, 308, 402
universal library, 289
universal psychometrics, 10, 13, 21, 46, 170, 418
    and populations, 253, 262, 280
    and universal tests, 417, 437, 470
    ignoramus, 25
    motivation, 22, 44, 46, 153, 467
    transversal role, 169, 471–474
universal scale, 40, 41, 48, 141
universal test, 35, 168, 296, 417–419, 424–429, 435–437, 447, 470, *see also* anytime universal test
universal Turing machine, 8, 117, 178, 179, 188, 288, 293, 333
universality, 8, 178, 226, 250, 268, 333, 334, 384, 454
    probability, 335
user log, *see* activity log
UTM, *see* universal Turing machine
utterance complexity, 378

validity, 35, 36, 38, 39, 48, 64, 65, 74–76, 105, 129, 135, 153, 165, 276, 401, 419, 450,
472, *see also* generality (of a measure), *see also* specificity (of a measure)
range, 168, 424, 435,
verbal ability, 47, 67, 72, 167, 197, 204, 263, 264, 370, 373–378, 380, 391, 478
verbal comprehension, *see* comprehension and language
    index (in WAIS), 72
verbal skill, *see* verbal ability
verification effort ($\mathbb{W}$), 222–224, 227, 228, 284
video game, 6, 22, 34, 131, 135, 138, 140, 145, 207, 295, 348, 350, 363, 424, 479, *see also* general video game competition *see also* arcade learning environment
virtual world, 4, 6, 22, 420, 424, 425, 431, *see also* artificial ecosystem
visual ability, 68, 72, 90, 108, 265, 316, 423, 424
visual Turing test, 131, 135, 320
von Neumann, John, 219, 241, 457
Vygotsky's zone of proximal development, 325, 337, 345

WAIS, *see* Wechsler Adult Intelligence Scale
Wallace, Alfred Russel, 94, 114, 456
Wallace, Chris, 17, 190, 335
Warwick, Kevin, 18, 46, 47, 130
Wechsler Adult Intelligence Scale, 72, 162, 218, 263
Wechsler Intelligence Scale for Children, 72, 90, 319
Wechsler Preschool and Primary Scale of Intelligence, 90, 160, 204, 319, 321
white-box measurement, 21, 22, 32–35, 112, 113, 123, 447
width (Thorndike), 77, 236, 237, 300
Winograd Schema Challenge, 139, 376
WISC, *see* Wechsler Intelligence Scale for Children
wisdom of the crowd, 399
word fluency, 67, 373
working memory, 34, 41, 49, 53, 70, 218, 224, 265–267, 318, 331, 385, 395, 450
    index (in WAIS), 72
Wozniak Test, 148

Yerkish, 381, 382, 387

Zadeh, Lotfi, 142, 156